Poverty Law and Advocacy in America

Poverty Law and Advocacy in America

Readings and Materials

Steven M. Virgil
CLINICAL PROFESSOR OF LAW
WAKE FOREST UNIVERSITY SCHOOL OF LAW

Sherri Lawson Clark
ASSISTANT PROFESSOR
DEPARTMENT OF ANTHROPOLOGY
WAKE FOREST UNIVERSITY

CAROLINA ACADEMIC PRESS
Durham, North Carolina

ISBN 978-1-61163-560-7
eISBN 978-1-5310-1161-1
LCCN 2020945384

Carolina Academic Press
700 Kent Street
Durham, North Carolina 27701
Telephone (919) 489-7486
Fax (919) 493-5668
www.cap-press.com

Printed in the United States of America

Contents

Table of Cases

Acknowledgments

This text grew from my Poverty Law class at Wake Forest University School of Law, where it was first used as a loose set of materials for a class that considers poverty as a part of the structure of how we live together in the United States. The final text has greatly benefited from the contributions of students in this class between 2017 and 2019. Holly Ingraham and Zachary Irvine contributed early drafts of the chapters on Environmental Justice and the Criminal Justice system, respectively. Seth Williford, Emily Scotton, France Beard, Jojo Fina, Jessica Cannon, Hannah McGee, Connor Mitchell, Grayson Lowery and Christina Tabora offered revisions to the text and added their own voice to the work. Finally, Hannah Burgin took on the significant task of reviewing the entire text, running down citations, offering edits and suggesting further needed revisions. The finished product would not be where it is without her work. In total, their contributions and insights as law students critically engaged in questioning poverty and the legal system which maintains it were invaluable. Many thanks.

It has been a pleasure working with Dr. Sherri Clark to fulfill this project, which ended up taking longer than either of us expected. She is a great colleague and true friend.

Part One

Poverty Law and Advocacy in America

Introduction

Poverty in America

This book is about poverty in the United States. The reality of poverty in the United States is complex and involves nearly endless factors, usually beginning with income, but moving well beyond money alone. Those who are poor in the United States live in a world of few options; life below the poverty line is stark. There are few material resources that provide the goods and services needed to live with dignity or to counter the forces of the market and government. Social and professional networks rarely lead to economic advancement; and security and prospects for a more prosperous future are limited. It is more difficult for a child born into poverty in 2020 to live in relative economic self-sufficiency later in life than it was for a child born into poverty in 1990. Even when someone lifts himself or herself beyond poverty, they too often find they will return again and again over time as work and the wages it brings fail to provide enough income for economic self-sufficiency. In the end, poverty is no one thing that can be addressed through simple interventions. Instead poverty results from a combination of factors and dynamics that shape the experiences and opportunities for those who are poor—more often than not leaving the poor disadvantaged and alone.

For more than 30 years, the national debate on poverty has focused on the inability of the poor themselves to improve their economic condition. Accordingly, poverty policies have heavily focused on efforts to change individual behavior and compel people into work. It is too simplistic of an idea to believe that poverty can be addressed solely through efforts to increase an individual's ability to earn income. As countless stories from those who have experienced long-term poverty show, poverty is more than a lack of money alone, although access to money and resources undoubtedly have a great deal to do with being poor. Poverty can be seen as a latticework, often times reflecting deeper aspects of how members of a community live together, and of forces that shape the lives of those who are "poor." Those who are poor find themselves living in poverty not only because they lack money but also because they are children, single mothers, members of racial or ethnic minorities, residents in ignored communities, students in neglected public schools and unfortunate in any one of many other ways. Poverty can be seen as a symptom of the challenges that face communities instead of a condition in and of itself.

At times, the poverty latticework can be so complex that it becomes difficult to move beyond. Poverty becomes reflected in every aspect of life and makes life itself seem unmanageable. Without adequate income, a family can easily become overwhelmed with bills. A minor expense, like clothes for a job interview or college visit, may mean that jobs and educational options are lessened. Involvement in the civil or criminal justice system threatens security and brings added costs. Inadequate and irregular nutrition leads to health conditions that limit employment, social mobility, and mental health. For some, the physical space of where they live can make moving forward economically nearly impossible. A child living in poverty on the Pine Ridge Reservation in South Dakota, for example, has few options for employment or educational advancement that do not require significant travel and costs. A child in an urban community can be equally cut off from services or social networks. Telling this child to simply earn more money borders on the irrational.

This book intends to bring readers into a dialogue about poverty that begins with an understanding that the experience of poverty is not just an experience based on a lack of money. This book is intended for readers who are planning to become advocates for the poor as students, teachers, policy makers, community organizers, grassroots activists, urban or rural planners, or in other related capacities. Thus, this book proposes to accomplish three things:

- First, it will help readers understand what poverty is in United States.

- Second, it provides an introductory overview to poverty policy in the United States.

- Third, it explores the role advocates can play in developing anti-poverty strategies at the local, state, and federal levels that provide a life of dignity for the poor.

To get to these points, the consideration of poverty must start with a shared understanding of what this word means.

Defining Poverty

For many people, it is not easy to define exactly what poverty encompasses. Economic definitions, which dominate poverty policy, certainly exist and serve vital roles in efforts to move the poor toward economic self-sufficiency. But poverty is more than an economic state. As Amartya Sen persuasively argues, although economic conditions may be part of poverty, they are not the only part. Poverty has much to do with the ability to live a life that is closely in accord with an individual's potential. In the United States, even in the early part of this Millennium, forces shape the potential of large numbers of people to live their life in accord with their highest capacity. Structural dynamics, including racism, gender bias, and societal intolerance behavior, have shaped the lives of millions of Americans.

The Federal Poverty Line is the objective measure used by policy makers in the United States to determine the number of people with incomes below what is considered necessary to provide for their basic necessities, such as food, housing, and medical care. As measured by the Federal Poverty Measure, poverty remains a significant challenge for millions of Americans.

Poverty in the
United States by the Numbers

The idea that poverty exists in the United States may seem anachronistic to some. Although there are frequent reminders of the need that exists in this country, including the number of homeless individuals and families in U.S. cities or the realities facing American Indian and Alaska Native American communities, there are few places where the poor live in the types of extreme degradation found in developing countries. Despite being the wealthiest country in the history of the world, however, poverty does remain a significant part of the United States experience. Roughly 12.6% of Americans lived below the poverty line in 2017, down from more than 14.8% in 2014, a fall of more than 2% or nearly 7,000,000 people. The millions that fall below the Poverty Line by this measure include: 12.8 million children, 2.4 million families whose members worked more than 30 hours each week, 4.7 million elderly people and 15.9 million married couples.[1]

For families living below the Federal Poverty Line, life is a series of choices some of which are beneficial but most of the time remain difficult. With a limited number of resources, a family living below the poverty line may be forced to decide between a well-balanced diet and a car repair, the latter (i.e., transportation) needed to access work, healthcare, and the world outside of poverty. Although a choice, the illusion of free will is temporary—the family living below the poverty line is ultimately driven by forces outside of themselves.

The Federal Poverty Line is often criticized for being incomplete and inaccurate. Nevertheless, the Federal Poverty Line does provide an objective benchmark that may be applied over time to assess the efficacy of anti-poverty policies. And many policies are proving to ineffective. Significantly, a child born today to a family living below the federal poverty line has less of a chance to live later in life above this line than at any other time in the history of the United States. A 2013 Pew Charitable Trusts report showed that "43 percent of Americans raised at the bottom of the income ladder remain stuck there as adults, and 70 percent never even make it to the middle." Poverty is real in the United States and it affects a huge number of people. More often than not, the effects of poverty tend to run along lines of broader societal bias. While 17 million (8.7%) white Americans lived below the poverty line in 2017, the poverty rate for African Americans was 21.2%, for Latino's 18.3%, and for Native Americans 25.4%.[2]

---

1. JOSEPH DALAKER, CONG. RES. SERV., R45397, POVERTY IN THE UNITED STATES IN 2017: IN BRIEF (2017).

2. Center for American Progress, *Basic Statistics*, TALK POVERTY, https://talkpoverty.org/basics/ (last visited Apr.1, 2019).

The economy seems to provide well for some while so many other people live in or near poverty in the United States. The wealth of the bottom 90% of Americans decreased between 2009 and 2018 to about 22% while the wealth of the top five percent increased by more than 10% holding 65 net worth of all Americans.[3] The United States finds itself facing two powerful forces. One pulls more and more people into poverty each year. The other allows greater and greater wealth to accumulate in the accounts of ever-smaller groups of people. What results is a sense that the United States is not a place of opportunity — at least not for the poor. At the same time, well-established "safety net" welfare programs that work to ensure that all Americans have some measure of economic security continue to face budget decreases.

Welfare Programs in the United States

The scale of anti-poverty programs in the United States is truly impressive. Federal and state governments each year spend at least $350 billion on safety net programs that directly or indirectly serve. More than $23 trillion dollars have been spent on such programs since the start of the War on Poverty in 1965. These programs include: the refundable portions of the Earned Income Tax Credit and Child Tax Credit; programs that provide cash payments to eligible individuals or households, including Supplemental Security Income for the elderly or disabled poor and unemployment insurance; various forms of in-kind assistance for low-income people, including SNAP (food stamps), school meals, low-income housing assistance, child care assistance, and help meeting home energy bills; and various other programs such as those that aid abused and neglected children.[4] Roughly nine percent of the U.S. GDP, this is less than what was spent on Medicare, Medicaid, CHIP, and Marketplace subsidies (26%); Social Security (24%); and Defense and International Security Assistance (15%) in the same year. In any given year, one-third or more of all people living in the United States will qualify for benefits offered through these programs. On average, however, only 21% of Americans participate annually in at least one anti-poverty program.[5]

While efforts to serve the poor have existed in the United States in some form since Colonial times, the robust range of government policies directed at the poor that exists today are the result of 70 years of policy development that began following

---

3. PETER HOOPER ET AL., DEUTSCHE BANK, US INCOME AND WEALTH INEQUALITY (2018).

4. CTR. ON BUDGET AND POL'Y PRIORITIES, POLICY BASICS: WHERE DO OUR FEDERAL TAX DOLLARS Go? https://www.cbpp.org/research/federal-budget/policy-basics-where-do-our-federal-tax-dollars-go (last visited Apr. 5, 2019).

5. Press Release, U.S. Census Bureau, 21.3 Percent of U.S. Population Participates in Government Assistance Programs Each Month (May 28, 2015), https://www.census.gov/newsroom/press-releases/2015/cb15-97.html (last visited Apr. 5, 2019).

the Depression. The scope of anti-poverty efforts cuts across nearly every human need. United States anti-poverty programs reach the need for income (described in previous paragraph above). Little is left out. But for people who seek to access benefits under these welfare programs and others, there is a cost.

All U.S. anti-poverty programs are coupled with policies that intend to shape individual decision making along certain prescribed parameters. TANF, for example, requires beneficiaries to commit to plans that will result in full time employment and allows states to set other requirements, such as refusing to extend benefits for new children born during to a parent receiving TANF funds. Taken together, U.S. anti-poverty programs attempt to direct the behavior and decision making of roughly 30% of U.S. citizens, all of whom have little choice in following along.

Over the course of the last 50 years, state and federal governments have developed policies that address poverty by shaping individual behavior. Government at all levels works to shape the most fundamental of choices for the poor: what to eat, what to feed a family, where to live, how to parent, how to access healthcare, whether a woman must continue in contact with an abusive partner or spouse, family planning, and long-term goal setting. Poverty, defined in terms of income and assets owned by a family, is the only justification for these policies and the role of government in the life of the poor. It is this poverty that empowers government intervention. By depth and breadth, U.S. anti-poverty programs are as intrusive a government intervention into individual and family life as any domestic policy effort. For the poor, no matter whether they are living alone or in families, there is no aspect of life that is not touched by government in an attempt to alter and shape individual autonomy, decision making, and personal liberty—all in the name of moving people above the poverty line. Being poor in the United States ultimately means a loss of personal freedom.

Proponents of U.S. poverty policy and the policy instruments used to shape the behavior of the poor argue that these instruments serve legitimate goals and reflect foundational relationships between individuals and the state. Self-sufficiency should be rewarded above all else and dependency should be avoided no matter the circumstance. Such arguments are dubious at best and, in most cases, reflect an adherence to established social inequality instead of concerns for moving families to economic self-sufficiency. But, even accepting such argument as legitimate, the United States has a five-decade history of following such an approach and this history shows two things: first, the approach is very expensive; and second, it doesn't work.

United States anti-poverty programs (TANF, Section 8, Food stamps, SSI) continue to consume massive amounts of money. Yet, for all of this investment, the poor remain poor, for the most part, and those that move out of poverty remain perilously close to poverty. Social and economic mobility does not occur to any significant degree for nearly all the families that receive benefits. In the end, U.S. anti-poverty programs do not accomplish the goals they are putatively designed to achieve, namely leading families to economic self-sufficiency. But these programs do accomplish other goals.

United States anti-poverty policies promote a vision of the relationship between the individual and government based on economic status and wealth more than any other factor. If you are poor, then you must accept that government may intervene in the most fundamental decisions in your life. The degree of such intervention is determined by your need and the needs of your family. By connecting resources to permissible intervention, U.S. anti-poverty programs promote classism and an economics of exclusion. Government in this instance is not an engine of economic or social advancement. Instead, it is a mechanism for maintaining social divide. Current programs reflect a view of society that is not based on inclusion or even democratic equality. Instead of giving people a chance, the policies are themselves crippling and limiting.

There are alternatives to such policies.

The Alternatives

Policies that effectively address poverty while retaining individual freedoms are possible.

- First, decouple welfare from behavior modification. This will require policy makers to accept that individual families are the source of knowledge about how to allocate their resources.

- Second, create self-support systems that approach poverty as an ecosystem issue. Poverty occurs within a complex system of social and economic dynamics. Therefore, it is proper to respond to poverty in a systemic manner. An environmental response to poverty, instead of an individual management approach as the U.S. currently pursues, will lead to higher numbers of long-term positive outcomes.

- Third, spend more money when doing so will have a positive impact. Instead of providing meager, even miserly, amounts of assistance to families that is parceled out in a steady stream of small payments coupled with attempts to shape and compel behavior, policies should consider making larger, timely investments in the lives of poor people and should do so in strategic ways that target resources to need for maximum impact.

The materials in this book encourage the reader to consider and define such alternatives.

The Structure of This Book

This book is organized into three parts, each reflecting a theme that is explored more thoroughly in related sections. Part One explores what it means to be poor and begins with considering how poverty is defined and measured and includes discussions of the dominant measurement tool in the United States, the Federal Poverty Measure, as well as alternatives that provide more accurate measures of need. Following this, a history of poverty is provided in an effort to place current anti-poverty policies into a historical context. Poverty places individuals into larger dynamics that shape their lives and possible outcomes. Therefore, Part One considers several discrete issues that stem from poverty, including the method of applying constitutional review to laws that impact the poor as well as the unique aspects of poverty related to geography. Finally, Part One concludes by considering poverty in the international context. Although the focus of these materials is poverty in the United States, it is not possible to shield the economic prospects of Americans from the macro forces that shape the world more broadly.

Part Two moves to considering the policies and programs that have been developed to address poverty in the United States. Organized around basic needs, such as income, food, housing, and education, Part Two contains five separate sections each focused on anti-poverty policies specific to a need. Two themes will be found to run through these sections. It will be shown that as poverty policy has developed in the United States, the focus of these policies has shifted to more strongly emphasize the use of anti-poverty programs to shape individual behavior. It will also be shown that a second class of beneficiaries is connected to poverty programs in the United States — the group of intermediaries and private interests that either deliver or benefit from the public money that runs through the welfare programs.

Part Three moves from policy to advocacy with discussions of advocacy efforts in both legal and social justice contexts. A history of legal services shows the movement to enhance access to justice in civil proceedings and the limitations that have been placed on both attorneys and clients. There is a significant history of social action around poverty in the United States and this is explored through the Poor People's Movement of the 1960s and the Living Wage Movement of the 1990s–2000s. Part Three includes a series of capstone exercises through which the reader will reflect on the current state of poverty policy and be asked to articulate models for new policy initiatives.

A Teacher's Manual with Field Exercises supplements these materials to help guide instructors through the readings, along with chapter exercises to facilitate a better understanding of the experiences of poverty, programs established to lessen poverty in the U.S., and the role advocates can play in adapting anti-poverty policies with greater efficacy.

Chapter One

What Is Poverty?

A. Poverty by the Numbers in the United States

The U.S. Census Bureau and the Department of Labor measure poverty in the United States using two metrics: the Federal Poverty Measure and the Federal Poverty Line. These metrics are based upon a family's income and are used to measure how many people live in poverty in any given year.

In January of each year, the U.S. Census Bureau releases an annual report on income and population data in the United States during the previous year. The report is based on data gathered through the Current Population Survey Annual Social and Economic Supplement (the CPS ASEC). The Annual Social and Economic Supplement (ASEC) contains information on income and work experience in America drawn from data gathered with the Current Population Survey (CPS). Dating in its original form from the 1930s and conducted by the Census Bureau since 1948, the CPS is a monthly survey sent to between 60,000 and 100,000 employment-age workers and is jointly administered by U.S. Census Bureau and Department of Labor. Monthly data is used to report on unemployment levels and includes employment and income information, as well as demographic data. In any given year, the CPS ASEC is the most current assessment of poverty in the United States.

The CPS ASEC runs nearly 90 pages each year and begins with a series of "highlights" that focus the public reader's attention on significant changes during the prior year. The most recent survey, including highlights that draw the reader's attention to the reports most salient points, may be found on the U.S. Census Bureau's Income and Poverty website (www.census.gov/topics/income-poverty.html). The "highlights" report on the same poverty measures each year and include, *inter alia*, the official poverty rate, the change in the number of people living below the poverty line, the change in the poverty rate, demographic differences in poverty rates and numbers, and changes in the poverty rate among children. The highlights provide a shorthand overview of the most crucial aspects of poverty in the United States.

In addition to these highlights, the annual CPS report contains a series of tables and graphs, presenting longitudinal views of income and poverty in the United States. These annual graphs reveal a great deal about poverty in the United States. For example, the graph shows stark differences between poverty rates among racial and ethnic groups, as well as changes that recession and economic downturns may have on poverty rates over time. The CPS reveals an overall presence of poverty in the United States that seems at once stable and perhaps benign. But the relative differences across race and ethnicity warrant some pause. If poverty is purely an economic matter, one would assume the burden of being poor would spread evenly across all populations. But it does not.

The CPS provides reliable information on the overall distribution of economic characteristics among the population, but it does not provide information on how those characteristics change for any given person or family across time. Specific information on individual outcomes is not available through this survey, which allows only a broad snapshot of how well families in the United States are doing overall. Several other reports on poverty are regularly produced by nonprofit and faith-based organizations, such as Feeding America and the Catholic Church's Committee for Social Justice.

According to the federal government's method for measuring poverty, the number of people living in poverty in the United States remained fairly constant during the first decade and a half of the twenty-first century. Although distinct differences among poverty rates across race, gender, and locality have persisted, the percentage of people living in poverty within the United States has remained between 12% and 15%. This percentage has seen significant change over longer periods, reaching 20% in 1964 and dropping to 11% 10 years later. The absolute numbers of people living in poverty has similarly varied, with roughly 36 million Americans living below the poverty line in the early 1960s and nearly 50 million in poverty by the beginning of the 2000s.

B. Defining Poverty

In Charles Dickens's novel *David Copperfield*, the character of Mr. Micawber has his own take on the poverty line. He observes, 'Annual income twenty pounds, expenses nineteen pounds and sixpence — result happiness. Annual income twenty pounds, expenses twenty pounds and sixpence — result, misery.' One reason that this quote is so memorable is that it is so silly. Why should so much depend on such a tiny difference? And why is someone who is just below the poverty line classified as poor, and worthy of special assistance or the attention of the World Bank, while someone just above the line needs no help and can be left to his or her own devices? When we don't have much idea what the poverty line should be and have greater difficulty in measuring income, making such Micawberish judgments is doubly absurd. It makes sense to worry more about people the poorer they are, but not to make sharp distinctions at any critical cut-off.

—*Angus Deaton*[1]

---

1. Angus Deaton, The Great Escape: Health, Wealth, and the Origins of Inequality 255–56 (Princeton University Press, 2013) (Deaton was a recipient of the 2015 Nobel Prize in Economics).

1. Introduction

Concerns with poverty move from intent to policy by first adopting a set of clear definitions about poverty and who is poor. A definition allows policy makers to frame a response, usually through supports such as income assistance, housing or food assistance, as well as a goal to aim toward and measure for impact. In practice, the defining line of poverty becomes the threshold for when wider society decides a person deserves or requires society's intervention. Once defined, "poverty" can then be addressed through policies, which inevitably connects the definition of poverty to the response.

The process of definition is, by its very nature, a process of exclusion, where one thing is defined as separate from others—the "poor" and the "nonpoor," in this case. Accordingly, the process of defining poverty involves a series of political and social distinctions that ultimately reflect values concerning what is an acceptable standard of living as well as what is expected of all members of a community. In the United States, the notion of poverty is often defined in ways that exclude individuals who act in ways that are not widely accepted in society, or the dividing line is so low that large numbers of people who are not poor by definition nevertheless face severe economic and social hardships. *poverty as a result of fault v. no fault*

In a world of finite resources, it is necessary to draw meaningful distinctions when allocating resources toward a desired policy goal. Developing working definitions of poverty allows this to happen. For centuries, the "poor" have been limited to those who lack material resources through no fault of their own. These individuals deserved assistance. Those individuals who lacked material resources due to their own actions, such as substance abuse or criminal behavior, were something else. The process of defining poverty and who is poor, as will be shown later, reflects underlying assumptions about individual decision making, the responsibility for individual behavior, what is expected of the poor, and what can be expected from the broader society when addressing poverty.

Defining poverty may seem a direct and straightforward process, but it is not. Significant debate exists regarding how narrowly focused on material goods the definition should be and whether subjective or comparative concerns should be included as well. A definition that looks only at an individual's ability to purchase material goods is very narrow. In fact, a person may have adequate means to purchase material goods needed for a comfortable life, but if they are denied the ability to make the purchases, for example, by class or race bias, it would seem hollow to say that they are nonpoor. A definition of poverty that ignores a person's ability to participate in broader society, therefore, seems inadequate. Conversely, if we include in a definition of poverty nonmaterial considerations, such as the ability to participate fully in the social or cultural life of a community, then the definition risks losing a bit of integrity. For example, in apartheid South Africa the ability of an individual to participate in the social and cultural life of the country largely depended on race.[2] In this context, a definition of

---

2. *See* F. Michael Higginbotham, *The Price of Apartheid*, 38 How. L.J. 371 (1995) (discussing information regarding the history of apartheid in South Africa and the election of Nelson Mandela).

poverty that includes nonmaterial considerations such as the ability to participate in decision making or to be safe from violence, risks confusing factors of racism and colonialism with the unique qualities of poverty.

The factors that define an approach and the decision to use one approach over another when setting policy, whether as an income measure or a measure of social or political participation, reflect underlying assumptions about how the world works, how individuals act within it and the role of policy in addressing poverty. Consider the example of how poverty is first defined and then made relevant to policy by the World Bank. According to the World Bank's 1990 World Development Report, a poverty line can be thought of as comprising two elements: the expenditure necessary to buy a minimum level of nutrition and other basic necessities and a further amount that varies country to country, [that] reflect[s] the cost of participating in everyday life of the society.[3]

Based on this two-part definition, the World Bank lends money along with technical support to fund projects that increase income and enhance quality of life. In 2013, the World Bank announced two official goals: (1) to end extreme poverty globally,[4] and (2) to promote shared prosperity in every country in a sustainable manner.[5] In order to operate effectively with the World Bank rubric, member countries of the World Bank make definitive statements about what constitutes *nutrition, basic necessities*, and *cost of living* for those countries in need of assistance. These statements are then the basis for policies that impact the lives of the poor.

As the United States formally developed its own anti-poverty programs during the early twentieth century, it, too, had to develop a system to determine what constitutes poverty, who is eligible for assistance, and what kind of and how much assistance should be provided, as well as how to pay for the programs.[6] As discussed later, poverty is defined in the United States almost completely through use of income and material considerations.[7] The latter suggests support, both moral and taxpaying, from the majority of American citizens, as well as a statement of what is expected from fellow citizens that, as such, insinuates the government into the lives of the poor.

---

3. The World Bank, World Development Report 1990, at 26 (1990).

4. *See* United Nations Dev. Programme, No Poverty, http://www.undp.org/content/undp/en/home/sustainable-development-goals/goal-1-no-poverty.html (last visited Apr. 1, 2018) (explaining that two years later, the United Nations adopted the same goal when the United Nations General Assembly declared that its first Sustainable Development Goal was to eradicate extreme poverty across the globe by 2030).

5. The World Bank Group, Poverty and Shared Prosperity 2016, at 23 (2016).

6. *See* U.S. Census Bureau, *Measuring America: Poverty: The History of a Measure*, https://www.census.gov/library/visualizations/2014/demo/poverty_measure-history.html (last visited Apr. 1, 2018). A history of poverty in the United States will be addressed in Chapter Three.

7. *See* U.S. Census Bureau, *How the Census Bureau Measures Poverty* (2017), https://www.census.gov/topics/income-poverty/poverty/guidance/poverty-measures.html (last visited Apr. 1, 2018).

The Great Depression (1929–1940) laid a firm foundation for the federal government's proprietorship of the poor.[8] At no time in the history of the United States had so many individuals and families been left completely destitute as after the complete collapse of the stock market in 1929 and the years that followed. The unemployment rate in the United States exceeded 15% in 1931.[9] Millions were out of work with no savings or government safety nets in place to help feed, house, or clothe them. In 1931, newly elected president, Franklin D. Roosevelt, rapidly unveiled his New Deal—first lifting the banking industry from despair, then moving with forward with getting Americans back to work.[10] It was not until his Second New Deal, under duress and opposition, that he moved to actively helping the poor.[11] In 1935, Roosevelt signed into law the Social Security Act stating, "We can never insure one hundred percent of the population against one hundred percent of the hazards and vicissitudes of life, but we have tried to frame a law which will give some measure of protection to the average citizen and to his family against the loss of a job and against poverty-ridden old age."[12]

Roosevelt framed policy responses between two limits. On one side government was limited and would not insure against every loss or guaranty a certain quality of life. On the other, government could provide limited support to a defined group of people—the average citizen who had lost his job. The process of defining poverty mandates policy action, but with that action comes decisions about who deserves assistance and the terms of citizenship that will be placed upon them.

2. The Need to Define Poverty

Establishing a clear definition of poverty serves several goals. First, given a clear definition of poverty, policy makers at every level in the public and private sectors are able to more efficiently allocate resources. Having a set line that defines who is poor allows policy makers to set priorities and allocate resources in ways that target interventions to those most in need. Second, a clear definition provides administrative ease. Administrators can simply and quickly determine who is entitled to assistance and can further draw distinctions on levels and types of assistance. This means that policies can be implemented that offer "stages" of support to beneficiaries as they

---

8. For more information regarding the Great Depression and the increased role of the federal government, *see* Gene Smiley, *Great Depression,* THE CONCISE ENCYCLOPEDIA OF ECON., http://www.econlib.org/library/Enc/GreatDepression.html (last visited Apr. 4, 2018).

9. *See* LINDA LEVINE, CONG. RES. SERV., THE LABOR MARKET DURING THE GREAT DEPRESSION AND THE CURRENT RECESSION 19 (Jun. 19, 2009).

10. For more information regarding the "First New Deal" and the "Second New Deal," *see* WILLIAM E. LEUCHTENBURG, UVA MILLER CENTER, FRANKLIN D. ROOSEVELT: DOMESTIC AFFAIRS (2017), https://millercenter.org/president/fdroosevelt/domestic-affairs (last visited Apr. 1, 2018).

11. *Id.*

12. John Hardman, *The Great Depression and the New Deal, in* ETHICS OF DEV. IN A GLOB. ENV'T (1999), https://web.stanford.edu/class/e297c/poverty_prejudice/soc_sec/hgreat.htm (last visited Apr. 1, 2018).

leave poverty and move into the workforce or some other path to self-sufficiency. Finally, clear definitions of poverty serve the interest of the nonpoor. As indicated above, poverty definitions reflect societal norms, particularly those involving the level of work participation by the poor. Having set a definition for poverty, societal expectations about the standard of living and the social safety net are reinforced for the poor and nonpoor alike.

a. Categories of Definitions *four definitions of poverty*

These materials introduce definitions of poverty that fall into four categories: a monetary approach; a comparative approach; a capability approach; and a participatory approach. A final note is included regarding a subjective approach. This list is not comprehensive. There may be other ways to define poverty, but the list presents the range of definitions, from the narrowest to the broadest—each of which contains elements that can be easily recognized.

i. The Monetary Approach → *United States uses this approach*

The monetary approach—also described as the income or the income/consumption approach—to defining poverty is the most direct. This "physiological deprivation model" concentrates on whether an individual is able to "acquire enough commodities to meet basic material needs adequately."[13] Under this approach, poverty is defined as a person's ability to purchase the things they need to achieve a certain standard of living. That standard is set against the anticipated costs for the basket of goods and services that are needed to support an individual or a family. The approach then defines a threshold for poverty based on personal income compared to the cost of the bundle of goods and services that are needed to meet the person's basic needs. If the total cost to an individual for the bundle of goods and services is more than his family's income, then the person is considered to be in poverty.[14]

The validity of the monetary/income approach relies on two key factors. First, to be valid, the individual's inability to participate in the market at a minimum level must be seen as an appropriate measure of individual well-being and assumes that the individual's ability to maximize utility is an adequate measure of well-being. This may not necessarily be the case. Second, the underlying assumptions about the cost of the goods and services must be accurate; both as to costs of individual goods or services, and as to the composition of the basket of goods and services.[15] It is very

---

13. Michael Lipton, *Defining and Measuring Poverty: Conceptual Issues, in* UNDP, Human Development Papers 1997, at 127 (UNDP/HDRO. New York).

14. For more information regarding the monetary/income approach, *see* Paul Shaffer, United Nations Dep't for Econ. & Soc. Affairs, New Thinking on Poverty: Implications for Poverty Reduction Strategies 4–5 (2001).

15. In the United States, the basket of goods and services consists of three times the cost of a minimum food diet in 1963, and the change in cost and inflation is accounted for through use of the Consumer Price Index. *See* U.S. Census Bureau, *How the Census Bureau Measures Poverty* (2017), https://www.census.gov/topics/income-poverty/poverty/guidance/poverty-measures.html (last visited Apr. 1, 2018); *see also* U.S. Census Bureau, *Measuring America: How the U.S. Census Bureau Measures*

easy for monetary definitions to make invalid assumptions regarding the true costs a family must pay to sustain itself. For example, the costs of public services are often not included in the calculation, nor are in-kind supports, such as access to food through food pantries.[16] Even when the underlying assumptions are validated, the monetary/income approach can still be subject to criticisms. It has been argued that the monetary approach to defining poverty:

(a) Lacks spatial difference—the measure is only valid if it takes into account variations on the cost of living in different spaces. For example, the costs of living in an urban versus rural area.

(b) Focuses on individual needs and achievement; and fails to consider social interactions or supports.

(c) Lacks objectivity. Intrinsic in measuring the costs of the goods and services are value judgments on what should be included. For example, should the cost of prepared food or entertainment be allowed?[17]

The United States uses an objective monetary approach to define poverty. This approach can be clearly seen through their use of a clear set of income benchmarks to determine who is poor, who should receive public support, and the level of entitlement that is to be received.[18] For example, in 2019, a family of four living in the 48 contiguous states is considered to be poor if their income is at or below $25,750.[19] While such an approach provides administrative ease, it also contains significant limitations in addition to those described above. Alternatives to economic measures, including Amartya Sen's capability approach, are said to provide a more nuanced view of what it means to be "poor," but these alternatives then require more multifaceted responses to poverty.[20]

ii. The Comparative Approach

Another way of looking at poverty is not by asking how many material goods a person can procure, but instead asking how a person's ability to secure materials goods and to also participate in society compares with that of other members of the same community. In many European countries, including Austria and Italy, poverty

---

Poverty (2017), https://www.census.gov/library/visualizations/2017/demo/poverty_measure-how.html (last visited Apr. 1, 2018).

16. The U.S. Census Bureau also fails to include the effect that geographic differences have on the cost of living, the impact of modern expenses and resources, and several other changes that have occurred since the 1960s. *See* Inst. Res. on Poverty, How Is Poverty Measured? (2016), https://www.irp.wisc.edu/resources/how-is-poverty-measured/ (last visited Oct. 29, 2019).

17. Frances Stewart, Ruhi Saith & Barbara Harris-White, Defining Poverty in the Developing World 9–14 (2007).

18. For more information regarding how the U.S. Census Bureau measures poverty, *see* U.S. Census Bureau, *How the Census Bureau Measures Poverty* (2017), https://www.census.gov/topics/income-poverty/poverty/guidance/poverty-measures.html (last visited Apr. 1, 2018).

19. *Id.*

20. Amartya Sen's capability approach focuses on an individual's functioning and capabilities. For a more detailed exploration of this approach, see Wiebke Kuklys & Ingrid Robeyns, Sen's Capability Approach 9–30 (2005).

is defined as a percent of income and assets of the median income and assets in the community.[21] A resident of Austria, for example, is considered to be in poverty if they have an income below 50% of the median income among residents in the country.[22] While still heavily focused on material consumption, this approach to defining poverty allows policy makers to also consider nonmaterial factors and relative economic equality.

iii. The Capability Approach

Amartya Sen redefined how poverty may be considered.[23] According to Sen, poverty should be seen as a deprivation of the capacity for human development, not the maximization of utility through income. For Sen, income is not the proper measure of poverty or well-being, and even those with income sufficient to meet their minimum needs may live in poverty. The determinant is whether the individual has the freedom to achieve certain minimum or basic capabilities, defined to include the ability to function at certain minimally adequate levels.[24] Sen advocates for a capability approach over the current income approach:

> ... while low income "is a strong predisposing condition for an impoverished life," poverty *cannot* be simply reduced to a narrow composite of welfare measures and threshold poverty lines. Instead, a capability perspective — one that shifts the focus away from *means* (income) and toward the *ends* "that people have reason to pursue," as well as "the *freedoms* ... able to satisfy these ends" — allows for a much "more illuminating picture" of the factors that enrich and constrain local life.[25]

Sen's approach is compelling. Who would not wish to see a world where all people could live to achieve at least the minimum of what they could become? But it raises significant challenges. How would policy makers enable such a definition to poverty? It is less than clear what goods and services should be included as necessary to achieve capacity actualization. In contrast to the monetary approach, which is based on a list of identified items, Sen's approach requires broad categories of functioning without clear guidance on the inputs required for such functionality. In contrast to income measures, however, the impact of the capability approach is difficult to measure and does not provide a clear line that differentiates the poor from nonpoor. Finally, if

---

21. *See Poverty Rate*, OECD Data (2018), https://data.oecd.org/inequality/poverty-rate.htm (last visited Apr. 1, 2018).

22. *Id.*

23. Amartya Sen received the Nobel Prize in Economics for his works in welfare economics and social choice theory, *see* Amartya Sen, Harvard University, https://scholar.harvard.edu/sen/biocv (last visited Apr. 1, 2018).

24. *See* Amartya Sen, Development as Freedom 87–111 (1999).

25. *Id.* at 87–99 (quoting from *Module 1: How Poverty Should Be Perceived*, Unite for Sight, http://www.uniteforsight.org/community-development/course2/module1) (last visited Apr. 1, 2018).

poverty is seen as a deprivation of capacity, then what are the legitimate ways of defining the capacities that are diminished?

iv. The Participatory Approach

In addition to lacking financial resources and income, the poor face a complex web of social, cultural, and political challenges that shape numerous aspects of life. Researchers have recognized a need to incorporate the political, cultural, and social limitations that accompany poverty into the definition of who is poor. This multidimensional approach, called here the "participatory approach," defines poverty in a way that describes the process of social marginalization that faces the poor, particularly in affluent societies. It also accounts for the notion that the poor may have a unique understanding of their own situation and should be empowered to play a role in, and have a voice about, the policies addressing poverty.[26] As Robert Chambers describes it, the participatory approach "describes a growing family of approaches and methods to enable local people to share, enhance, and analyze their knowledge of life and conditions, to plan and to act."[27]

The World Bank published the first large-scale research report that used the participatory approach and its methods to concentrate on the voices of the poor.[28] The report focuses on common themes expressed by impoverished individuals in more than 40 countries, including the idea that poverty is multidimensional, the state is seen as ineffective, access to NGOs is limited, and the experience of poverty is dominated by pain.[29] The report remarks on the vitality of the participatory approach as it is able to provide "some idea about poor people's realities," which is crucial since poverty "is experienced at the local level, in a specific context, in a specific places, in a specific interaction."[30] Considering the fact that agencies and individuals who work to reduce poverty are often located far from these impoverished communities, the participatory approach aims to communicate the voices of the impoverished to those possessing the power to reduce their pain.[31]

The participatory approach attempts to account for the notion that people living with minimal incomes have reduced choice options for the basic needs of life, including housing, food, education, and healthcare. Any poverty line is inherently a subjective judgment about what is an acceptable minimum standard of living in a particular society. While it is possible to set an income-defined poverty line in a par-

---

26. For more background information regarding the participatory approach, see ANDY NORTON ET AL., A ROUGH GUIDE TO PPAs: PARTICIPATORY POVERTY ASSESSMENT: AN INTRODUCTION TO THEORY AND PRACTICE (2001).

27. Robert Chambers, *The Origins and Practice of Participatory Rural Appraisal*, 22 WORLD DEV. 953, 953 (1994).

28. DEEPA NARAYA ET AL., VOICES OF THE POOR: CAN ANYONE HEAR US? (2000).

29. *Id.* at 6–9.

30. *Id.* at 230.

31. *Id.*

ticipatory way by asking survey respondents what they consider to be the minimal income level necessary to make ends meet and averaging the results, the requirement to judge each person using the same standard means that their individual definition of their own needs is subordinated. The "poor" are labeled as poor by outsiders, not according to their own criteria.

v. The Subjective Approach

Subjective measures of poverty could provide a meaningful alternative to set income guidelines. Under such a subjective approach, poverty is determined by asking people something like: "What income level do you personally consider to be absolutely minimal? That is to say that with less you could not make ends meet." Similar to these questions, other surveys attempting the subjective approach have asked respondents to "rate [their] 'economic welfare' or a broader concept such as 'satisfaction with life' or 'happiness,' on an ordinal scale.... Or the respondent provides money metrics of points of qualitative welfare scales, such as the minimum income needed to 'makes ends meet.'"[32] Accordingly, individuals are considered poor when they don't earn this amount.

There are concerns with such a subjective approach and, consequently, it has remained one of the least used approaches.[33] In particular, the measure lacks consistency across a group or community.[34] One person may feel very well off with a particular income while another may feel they are unable to make ends meet. This may be because a subjective measure depends largely on the individual's consumption patterns, which will vary widely and are likely to increase as the individual has more income. It is difficult to imagine subjective qualitative measures providing meaningful information that can be used to set policy, although the subjective experiences of individuals and families do provide insights into economic challenges facing people in the United States.[35]

b. Measuring Poverty in the United States:
The Federal Poverty Measure and Federal Poverty Line

> "To say who is poor is to use all sorts of value judgments ... there is no particular reason to count the poor unless you are going to do something about them."

> —*Mollie Orshansky, Research Analyst for the*
> *Social Security Administration*[36]

---

32. Andrew E. Clark & Claudia Senik, Happiness & Economic Growth: Lessons from Developing Countries 142 (2014).

33. *Id.* at 152–153.

34. *Id.*

35. For an example of how this approach works, *see* Ibrahima Sy, *The Subjective Approach as a Tool for Understanding Poverty: The Case of Senegal*, 5 Procedia Econ. & Fin. 336 (2013).

36. Mollie Orshansky, *How Poverty Is Measured*, 92 Monthly Lab. Rev. 37, 37 (1969).

As public awareness of civil liberties grew in the United States during the 1950s and 1960s, calls for broader responses from federal and state government agencies emerged; and over the course of several years during the early 1960s, a federal poverty policy developed with the stated goal of ending poverty in the United States.[37] Federal poverty policy, discussed in greater detail in the next chapter, worked in concert with state policy and administrative agencies to reach people living in poverty. As this should readily imply, poverty policy at the federal level necessitated a process for defining who would be considered poor. The United States elected to use a dual component monetary/income approach to define poverty, called the Federal Poverty Measure and the Federal Poverty Line.[38] These two devices define who will be considered as being in poverty and, based on that distinction, who will be eligible to access benefits through federal and state anti-poverty programs. While a seemingly direct process, the development and use of the Federal Poverty Measure raises many questions and criticisms.

i. The Federal Poverty Threshold and Federal Poverty Guidelines

It is important to recognize that the federal government uses two slightly different measurement devices related to poverty. They are the "poverty threshold" and the "poverty guideline."[39] The poverty threshold is a detailed analysis used by the federal government for statistical purposes.[40] The thresholds are the federal government's original version of a federal measure of poverty. Unlike the poverty thresholds, which are released annually by the Census Bureau,[41] the poverty guidelines are released annually by the Department of Health and Human Services.[42] The poverty guidelines are a more simplified device that is primarily used for administrative purposes, such as to determine eligibility for federal or state benefits.

In the fall of each year, usually in late September, the U.S. Census Bureau publishes a report on the number of people living in poverty in the United States titled *Income, Poverty and Health Insurance Coverage in the United States.* The Poverty Report reflects

---

37. For more information regarding the development of a federal poverty policy in the United States, *see* U.S. Census Bureau, *Measuring America: Poverty: The History of a Measure* (2016), https://www.census.gov/library/visualizations/2014/demo/poverty_measure-history.html (last visited Apr. 1, 2018).

38. *See* U.S. Census Bureau, *How the Census Bureau Measures Poverty* (2017), https://www.census.gov/topics/income-poverty/poverty/guidance/poverty-measures.html (last visited Apr. 1, 2018).

39. *See* Inst. for Res. on Poverty, What Are Poverty Thresholds and Poverty Guidelines? https://www.irp.wisc.edu/resources/what-are-poverty-thresholds-and-poverty-guidelines/ (last visited Apr. 3, 2018); U.S. Dep't of Health and Hum. Serv., *U.S. Federal Poverty Guidelines Used to Determine Financial Eligibility for Certain Federal Programs*, https://aspe.hhs.gov/2017-poverty-guidelines (last visited Apr. 3, 2018).

40. *Id.*

41. *See* U.S. Census Bureau, *Poverty Thresholds*, https://www.census.gov/data/tables/time-series/demo/income-poverty/historical-poverty-thresholds.html (last visited Apr. 3, 2018).

42. Annual Update of the HHS Poverty Guidelines, 82 C.F.R. §8831 (2017).

the most recent data collected in the Current Population Survey Annual Social and Economic Supplements (CPS ASEC) conducted by the U.S. Census Bureau.[43] The Poverty Report garners significant media attention and provides a snapshot of the presence and extent of poverty in the United States.[44] Understanding the CPS data begins with appreciating the underlying assumptions about poverty that it reflects, which are first found in the poverty thresholds.

The Poverty Thresholds were developed in 1963 by Mollie Orshansky, an economist with the Social Security Administration.[45] Orshansky's poverty thresholds were adopted as the federal government's official statistical definition of poverty in August 1969.[46] There were a number of unofficial poverty lines in the United States before 1965, with the earliest explicit poverty line developed by Robert Hunter dating back to 1904.[47] Orshansky published her research in order to develop a new measurement that could be used to assess the relative risks of low income across different demographic groups and families.[48] Orshansky's method was based on how much a family budgets for food and a simple calculation.[49] First, Orshansky collected two generally accepted standards for nutrition published by the U.S. Dept. of Agriculture; the "low-cost food plan" and the "economy food plan."[50] These plans represented how much food a family would need under separate assumptions and then calculated the cost of buying this food.[51] Food costs were estimated based on actual market research for each plan.[52] Second, Orshansky assumed that any given family spent roughly 30% of their income on food.[53] Using the U.S. Dept. of Agriculture budget for the economy food plan, which was roughly 70% the costs of the low-cost food plan, Orshansky multiplied by slightly more than three and arrived at a poverty threshold.[54] Those families with incomes below 300% of the cost of the economy food plan were below the Poverty Threshold, or poor.[55]

Orshansky's work provided a tool for two goals within this broader effort; determining who was poor and in need of assistance and then measuring whether interventions were proving to be successful.[56] By 1969, the Johnson Administration ultimately adopted Orshansky's poverty threshold of $3,000 for a family.[57] The

43. U.S. Census Bureau, *Income, Poverty, and Health Insurance Coverage in the United States: 2016*, https://www.census.gov/newsroom/press-releases/2017/income-povery.html (last visited Apr. 4, 2018).

44. *See* U.S. Census Bureau, P60-259, *Incomes and Poverty in the United States: 2016* (2017).

45. Gordon M. Fisher, *The Development and History of the Poverty Thresholds*, 55 Soc. Sec. Bull. 3, 3–4 (1992).

46. *Id.*

47. *Id.*

48. *Id.*

49. *Id.*

50. *Id.*

51. *Id.*

52. *Id.*

53. *Id.*

54. *Id.*

55. *Id.*

56. *Id.*

57. *Id.*

implications of this decision were and remain significant. Once poverty had been defined using Orshansky's Poverty Threshold, Orshansky's methodology and assumptions were incorporated into poverty policy across all levels.[58] If Orshansky made assumptions about family income or expenses that were not aligned with actual levels of need, these became part of policy through adoption.[59] The economy food plan, however, was intended to measure food needs in times of crisis, for "temporary or emergency use when funds are low."[60] The food plan as such includes no additional allowance for meals eaten out or other food eaten away from home. Accordingly, the measure of poverty defined by Orshansky is based upon a heightened state of need and emergency.

Once the federal government declares that there are individuals under its sovereignty who do not have the economic resources to meet basic needs and deserve support, it must establish a regulatory process to identify those individuals.[61] Several questions rise to the forefront when beginning this process—what are *basic needs*? Where does one get their basic needs? How much does it cost to secure these basic needs? Do these basic needs change over time? If so, how often should regulators revisit and revise the list of basic needs? How much and what forms of assistance should the government provide to families in need? For how long? How will the government pay for the assistance provided to families in need? What mechanisms are in place to assure the people that providing for the needy is beneficial to the state?

Surely, there is no one answer to any one of these questions which is a major reason identifying the poor remains one of the largest and, perhaps, the most important challenge to U.S. policymakers. So much of what the state does for the poor is based on this single measure—from who is eligible for cash assistance (TANF) to public housing subsidies to food stamps and health insurance.[62] While Mollie Orshansky is credited with developing the 1963 poverty thresholds, she "later indicated, her original purpose was not to introduce a new general measure of poverty, but to develop a measure to assess the relative risks of low economic status ... among different demographic groups of families with children."[63] Later, reflecting on the efforts underway to measure poverty, Orshansky concluded the following:

> Counting the poor is an exercise in the art of the possible. For deciding who is poor, prayers are more relevant than calculation because poverty, like beauty, likes in the eyes of the beholder. Poverty is a value judgment; it is not something one can verify or demonstrate, except by inference and sug-

---

58. *Id.*

59. *Id.*

60. *Id.*

61. Ann I. Park, *Human Rights and Basic Needs: Using International Human Rights Norms to Inform Constitutional Interpretation*, 34 UCLA L. Rev. 1195, 1198–99 (1987).

62. *See* U.S. Dep't of Health and Hum. Serv., *U.S. Federal Poverty Guidelines Used to Determine Financial Eligibility for Certain Federal Programs*, https://aspe.hhs.gov/poverty-guidelines (last visited Apr. 4, 2018).

63. Fisher, *supra* note 45, at 3.

gestion, even with a measure of error. To say who is poor is to use all sorts of value judgments. The concept has to be limited by the purpose which is to be served by the definition. There is no reason to count the poor unless you are going to do something about them. Whatever the possibilities for socioeconomic research in general, when it comes to defining poverty, you can only be more subjective or less so. You cannot be nonsubjective.[64]

Overcoming Orshansky's apprehension that poverty consists of a series of value judgments and, instead, developing a consistent and comprehensive way to "quantify" or "objectify" poverty has proven an ongoing challenge.

In 1964, the Council of Economic Advisers (CEA) first adopted a poverty measure for government use (two or more people in a family with an annual income less than $3,000 or less than $1,500 annual income for a single person living alone).[65] The measure was used primarily for anti-poverty policy programming, but not for anti-poverty policy eligibility.[66] The CEA measure did not take into consideration family size or composition because these data were not available to them.[67] Orshansky worked to remedy the deficiencies in the CEA poverty measurement by developing two measures (i.e., poverty thresholds) of need based on income data from the Current Population Survey: the Poor and the Near-Poor based on the "minimum money income that could support an average family of given composition at the lowest level consistent with the standards of living prevailing in this country ... to purchase a nutritionally adequate diet on the assumption that no more than a third of family income is used for food."[68] The lower measure (most often used) yielded almost same as the $3,000 adopted by the CEA, but differed qualitatively in that fewer families with more children were substituted for a larger number of older families without children.[69] Fisher summarizes Orshansky's changes to the CEA measure:

> The three steps Orshansky followed in moving from the cost of food for a family to minimum costs for all family requirements were (1) to define the family size and composition prototypes for which food costs would be computed, (2) to decide on the amount of additional income to allow for items other than food, and (3) to relate the cash needs of farm families to those of comparable nonfarm families.[70]

Orshansky's designation of poverty thresholds came to be known as an *absolute* measure of poverty as opposed to a *relative* measure of poverty.[71] Fisher argues, "In the dichotomy between relative and absolute definitions of poverty, one of the essential

---

64. Mollie Orshansky, *How Poverty Is Measured*, 92 Monthly Lab. Rev. 37, 37 (1969).
65. *Id.*
66. *Id.*
67. *Id.*
68. *Id.* at 38.
69. *Id.*
70. Fisher, *supra* note 45, at 4.
71. *Id.* at 6.

[handwritten: absolute v. relative poverty]

characteristics of a purely 'absolute' definition is that it is derived without any reference to the consumption patterns or income levels of the population as a whole."[72] Absolute poverty sets a "poverty line" at a certain income amount or consumption amount per year, based on the estimated value of a "basket of goods" (food, shelter, water, etc.) necessary for proper living.[73] Relative poverty is when the entire population is ranked in order of income per capita.[74] The bottom 10% (or whatever percentage the government chooses to use) is then considered "poor" or "impoverished."[75] Poverty thresholds (issued by the Bureau of the Census) are used for statistical purposes to estimate the number of people in poverty and demographics of the poor.[76] Poverty guidelines (issued by the Department of Health and Human Services) are used for administrative purposes in determining eligibility for assistance from federal programs.[77]

[handwritten: poverty thresholds v. poverty guidelines]

Eligibility for accessing benefits is driven by what measure of poverty the granting agency is using. Cancian and Meyer examine economic success among TANF participants and how variations in measurement, including poverty measures, tell different stories.[78] They argue:

> The measurement of poverty is not straightforward, but generally includes a comparison of resources to a threshold. For resources, income measures are easier to calculate than consumption measures, but decisions must still be made about what sources of income to count, whose income to count, whether subtractions from income are allowed (and for what), and whether adjustments are made for cost of living, standard of living, family size, etc. Thresholds can be determined by measures of the resources of others (relative, median-income based measures, for example), average" family expenditures (the proposed poverty measure; Citro and Michael, 1995), or what is thought to be needed (the official measure).[79]

Other scholars, including Meyer and Sullivan,[80] support a consumption-based model to measure poverty, as opposed to the more traditional income-based measure. Another strain of thought, as proposed by Rebecca Blank, suggests looking to lessons learned in other countries:

---

72. *Id.*

73. *Id.*

74. *Id.*

75. *Id.*

76. *See* U.S. Census Bureau, *Poverty Thresholds,* https://www.census.gov/data/tables/time-series/demo/income-poverty/historical-poverty-thresholds.html (last visited Apr. 4, 2018).

77. U.S. Dep't of Health and Hum. Serv., *U.S. Federal Poverty Guidelines Used to Determine Financial Eligibility for Certain Federal Programs,* https://aspe.hhs.gov/poverty-guidelines (last visited Apr. 4, 2018).

78. Maria Cancian & Daniel R. Meyer, *Alternative Measures of Economic Success among TANF Participants: Avoiding Poverty, Hardship, and Dependence on Public Assistance,* 23 J. Pol'y Analysis & Mgmt. 531, 531 (2004).

79. *Id.* at 538.

80. Bruce D. Meyer & James X. Sullivan, *Identifying the Disadvantaged: Official Poverty, Consumption Poverty, and the New Supplemental Poverty Measure,* 26 J. Econ. Persp. 111, 111 (2012).

Relative poverty lines do have a major advantage in that they are easy to calculate when based on median incomes, and they avoid the extended U.S. debate about how to calculate an appropriate threshold. One disadvantage of a relative measure based on share of median income is that it is harder to make progress against poverty because the poverty threshold rises as incomes rise.[81]

As can be seen through these suggested approaches, there is large debate concerning how poverty should be measured in the United States and many scholars question whether the federal poverty threshold and the federal poverty guidelines are the best approaches.

Official poverty measure is based on cash resources

ii. Criticisms of the Official Poverty Measure

Although the official poverty measure remains the poverty statistic utilized by the United States Census Bureau, scholars have criticized the measure since its inception. Over the last three decades, the Census Bureau has responded to these criticisms by promoting research and discussion into ways through which this measure could be improved.[82] The Bureau's efforts has led to "hundreds of papers, dozens of official Census Bureau publications, and two National Academy of Science Reports."[83] Nonetheless, the official poverty measure has remained largely unchanged since the 1960s, rendering its criticisms as relevant as ever.

5 criticisms of official poverty measure

There are many criticisms of the official poverty measure. One of the main concerns with the official poverty measure is that it "defines resources as pretax money income, failing to reflect the full resources at a family's disposal."[84] The use of pretax money income is considered a weak representation of the reality of the poor since it does not capture tax liabilities, tax credits, or noncash benefits (food stamps, public health insurance, etc.).[85] Another concern with the official poverty measure is that its "headcount" approach only determines the number of individuals who fall below the poverty threshold, but fails to determine the depth of poverty experienced by these individuals.[86] Furthermore, the official poverty measure fails to account for geographic differences in the cost of living.[87] In addition, the official measure defines a unit under the confines of a more traditional family and fails to account for more modern households, in which individuals reside with unrelated children, foster children, or an unmarried partner.[88] Finally, the measure fails to adequately reflect how the standard of living, and its associated cost, has changed since the 1960s.[89] For example, the

---

81. Rebecca M. Blank, *Presidential Address: How to Improve Poverty Measurement in the United States*, 27 J. Pol'y Analysis & Mgmt. 233, 244 (2008).

82. Meyer & Sullivan, *supra* note 80, at 111.

83. *Id.*

84. *Id.* at 114.

85. *Id.*

86. Inst. for Res. on Poverty, How Is Poverty Measured in the United States, https://www.irp.wisc.edu/faqs/faq2.htm#fn8 (last visited Apr. 5, 2018).

87. *Id.*

88. *Id.*

89. *Id.*

official poverty measure was based on a minimum food diet in the 1963, when Americans were believed to spend about one-third of their income on food, but today American families only spend, on average, one-seventh of their income on food.[90]

In response to some of the earlier criticisms of the official poverty measure, Congress requested that the National Academy of Sciences form the Panel on Poverty and Family Assistance to analyze the concerns expressed about the measure.[91] The Panel released a report in 1995 containing numerous recommendations to improve the official poverty measure.[92] For one, the panel recommended that the threshold include a budget for at least three categories of necessary expenditures: food, clothing, and shelter.[93] In addition, the panel believed that the thresholds should be based on actual data from the previous three years to determine the amount of expenditures that are necessary for the various sizes of families.[94] These expenditures should continue to be updated every year and should be adjusted to better reflect the composition of modern families and the geographical differences across the nation.[95] Furthermore, the panel recommended that the measure calculate a family's resources, rather than their pretax income, to reflect taxes and some noncash benefits.[96] In the end, none of these recommendations were adopted to change the official poverty measure, but the Census Bureau did begin to release experimental poverty measures to supplement the official measure.

Almost a decade later, the U.S. Office of Management and Budget asked the Committee on National Statistics of the National Research Council to analyze alternative approaches to measure poverty and to review the progress in adopting the recommendations put forth by the Panel on Poverty and Family Assistance in 1995.[97] The Committee noted that although official poverty measure is updated yearly to account for inflation, little else has changed about the measure in the last 40 years, and overall it has become "increasingly outdated."[98] The Committee echoed the sentiment of the 1995 report and even reissued the original recommendation:

> Our major conclusion is that the current measure needs to be revised: it no longer provides an accurate picture of the differences in the extent of economic poverty among population groups or geographic areas of the country, nor an accurate picture of trends over time. The current measure has remained virtually unchanged over the past 30 years. Yet during that time,

---

90. Nancy K. Cauthen & Sarah Foss, Nat'l Ctr. for Child. in Poverty, Measuring Poverty in the United States, http://www.nccp.org/publications/pdf/text_825.pdf (last visited Apr. 4, 2018).

91. Nat'l Res. Council, Measuring Poverty: A New Approach, 18 (1995).

92. *Id.*

93. *Id.* at 40.

94. *Id.*

95. *Id.*

96. *Id.*

97. *See generally* John Iceland, Comm. on Nat'l Stat., Experimental Poverty Measures (2005).

98. *Id.* at 3.

there have been marked changes in the nation's economy and society and in public policies that have affected families' economic well-being, which are not reflected in the measure.[99]

The Census Bureau has yet to adopt the recommendations put forth by the 1995 panel or the 2004 committee, and has continued to calculate the nation's official poverty measure based on cash resources. Nonetheless, in 2011 the Census Bureau began to release an additional measure of poverty in the United States, the Supplemental Poverty Measure.

iii. The Supplemental Poverty Measure

Under President Obama, the Census Bureau decided to publish an additional poverty measure that, as indicated by the name, would supplement the official poverty measure. Accordingly, the supplemental measure was not meant to replace the official measure, which continues to serve as the official poverty statistic and the determinant for assistance programs.[100] As can be seen through its calculation method, the supplemental measure takes into account many of the suggestions put forth by the Panel on Poverty and Family Assistance in 1995.[101] For example, the supplemental measure expands the definition of a family "unit" by including unrelated children, foster children, unmarried partners, and additional relatives that reside in the same household.[102] In addition, the level of need budgeted for each family is expanded to include food, shelter, clothing, and utilities.[103] The supplemental measure also accounts for geographical differences and the cost associated with the type of residence, such as a rental property or a house with a mortgage.[104] Finally, the supplemental measure calculates beyond an individual's cash income and adds any benefits received by individuals through government programs and subtracts specified expenses, including taxes, medical expenses, child care, and more.[105]

In every year since the supplemental poverty measure has been published, it has identified a slightly larger percentage of the U.S. population as poor than the official poverty measure.[106] The supplemental measure has "ranged from 0.6 to 1.3 percentage points higher than the official measure since 2009."[107] For example, according to the official measure published in 2016, 12.7% of the U.S. population was considered "poor," whereas, according to the supplemental measure, 14% of the U.S. population

[handwritten margin note: things supp poverty measure added to official pov measure]

---

99. *Id.* at 1.

100. U.S. Census Bureau, P60-261 (RV), *The Supplemental Poverty Measure: 2016*, at 1 (2017).

101. *See* U.S. Census Bureau, *How the U.S. Census Bureau Measures Poverty*, https://www.census.gov/library/visualizations/2017/demo/poverty_measure-how.html (last visited Apr. 7, 2018).

102. *Id.*

103. *Id.*

104. *Id.*

105. *Id.*

106. U.S. Census Bureau, *supra* note 100, at 6.

107. *Id.*

was considered "poor."[108] Although this discrepancy may not seem significant, it should be noted that, under the supplemental measure, an additional 4.2 million individuals are considered to have lived in poverty in 2016.[109]

iv. The Measure of Basic Needs and the Goal of Economic Self-Sufficiency

Somewhat incongruously, the question of how much income is needed for a family to achieve economic self-sufficiency stands apart from how poverty is defined or measured. While the official poverty measure marks a threshold below which a family is determined to be eligible for public benefits, the official measure does not calculate the amount of income needed to purchase the goods and services needed for daily living. The Basic Income Approach responds to these limitations. This approach is noted here to establish the ecology of poverty for families who live and work within a few dollars of the minimum wage.

v. The Basic Income Approach and the Family Economic Self-Sufficiency Standard

Economic self-sufficiency has been a stated goal of U.S. poverty policy since 1996, when the Personal Responsibility and Work Opportunity Act ("PWROA") was enacted, and implicitly before then.[110] One goal of the PWROA is to reform welfare policy to ensure that it is the obligation of every U.S. citizen to engage in work, yet this goal may not recognize what is involved in attaining self-sufficiency. Created by Dr. Diana Pearce in the 1990s, the Self-Sufficiency Standard was developed to serve as a performance measure for the goal of enabling self-sufficiency in federal job training programs.[111] The Self-Sufficiency Standard provides realistic and detailed assessments on what an individual or family must earn to achieve economic self-sufficiency. According to the Center for Women's Welfare, "the Self-Sufficiency Standard defines the amount of income necessary to meet basic needs (including taxes) without public subsidies (e.g., public housing, food stamps, Medicaid. or child care) and without private/informal assistance (e.g., free babysitting by a relative or friend, food provided by churches or local food banks, or shared housing)."[112] The Standard is also tailored to the different family types, from one adult with no children to two-adult families with three teenagers.[113]

---

108. *Id.*

109. U.S. Census Bureau, *How the U.S. Census Bureau Measures Poverty*, https://www.census.gov/library/visualizations/2017/demo/poverty_measure-how.html (last visited Apr. 7, 2018).

110. The Personal Responsibility and Work Opportunity Act, Pub. L. 104-193 (1996). *See also* Assistant Sec'y for Plan. & Evaluation, The Personal Responsibility and Work Opportunity Reconciliation Act of 1996, https://aspe.hhs.gov/report/personal-responsibility-and-work-opportunity-reconciliation-act-1996 (last visited Apr. 8, 2018).

111. *See* Ctr. for Women's Welfare, The Self-Sufficiency Standard, http://www.selfsufficiencystandard.org/node/3 (last visited Apr. 8, 2018).

112. *Id.*

113. *Id.*

The Self-Sufficiency Standard differs from the Federal Poverty Measure in several significant ways.[114] As stated by Dr. Pearce:

> *The Self-Sufficiency Standard* is based on ALL major budget items faced by working adults, not just food. These basic needs include housing, child care, food, health care, transportation, taxes, and miscellaneous costs.

> *The Self-Sufficiency Standard* calculates the most recent local or regional costs of each basic need. Accounting for regional or local variation is particularly important for housing because housing costs vary widely (e.g., the most expensive areas of the country, such as Manhattan, can cost four times as much as in the least expensive areas, such as Mississippi, for equivalent size units).

> *The Self-Sufficiency Standard* varies costs by age groups of children (infants, preschoolers, school agers, and teenagers). This is especially important for child care, which varies substantially by age.

> *The Self-Sufficiency Standard* reflects modern family practices, and assumes that all adults (whether married or single) work full-time. Thus, the Standard includes the employment-related costs of transportation, taxes, and child care (when needed). (Note that the Federal Poverty Level assumes a two-parent household with a stay-at-home parent, or single parents relying on welfare or family support. Therefore, work-related expenses such as child care, taxes, and transportation are not considered.)

> *The Self-Sufficiency Standard* includes the net effect of federal and state taxes and tax credits, as well as any local taxes and tax credits. The Standard's real-world assumptions allow the costs of all basic needs—not just food—to vary over time and across geographic locations. With this up-dated and detailed approach, the Standard is able to develop a realistic measurement of the income requirements for 700 different family types across each county in a given state.[115]

The resulting difference between the Federal Poverty Measure and the calculated Family Economic Self-Sufficiency can be striking. For example, a family with one adult, one preschooler, and one school-age child living in Logan County, Colorado, in 2015 would reach above the Federal Poverty Measure with an income of $20,090.[116] At the same time, this family would need an annual income of at least $45,058 to achieve economic self-sufficiency.[117]

Welfare policy begins with how poverty is defined, including the level of income needed to rise above poverty, and then attempts to create a policy that reflects these goals and the many core/shared values of the United States. The prescribed definition

---

114. *Id.*

115. *Id.*

116. CTR. FOR WOMEN'S WELFARE, MEASURING POVERTY, http://www.selfsufficiencystandard.org/measuring-poverty (last visited Apr. 8, 2018).

117. *Id.*

of "poverty" plays a crucial role in all welfare policies since it acts as a barrier to entry for individuals to qualify for welfare assistance.[118] Likewise, the purported values held by Americans also impact how the poor are viewed and, in turn, impact where resources are directed based on the differences attributed to various impoverished individuals.[119]

Perhaps one of the most common misconceptions surrounding poverty is the belief that those who work are not poor.[120] This belief reflects what amounts to a core principal of what many people believe about the American social contract and is incorporated within U.S. welfare policy through the TANF work requirements and time limitations.[121] While this ethic captures popular feelings about the relationship between poverty and work, the reality can be quite different.

---

118. Leonard J. Long, *Optimum Poverty, Character, and the Non-Relevance of Poverty Law*, 47 Rutgers L. Rev. 693, 758–59 (1995).

119. *Id.* at 736.

120. *See infra* Chapter 5.

121. *See infra* Chapter 5.

Chapter Two

Spatial Dimensions of Poverty

A. Place Matters

Millions of people, in areas that include parts of Africa and Asia, die each year from starvation and easily treated illness that comes with extreme deprivation associated with poverty.[1] For these people, poverty is profound.[2] It is difficult to imagine such poverty in the United States and, indeed, absolute poverty is rare in the United States, although areas of extreme deprivation do exist throughout the country.[3] For the most part, and in contrast to the absolute poverty of the developing world, poverty in the United States is often understood in relative terms — in how an individual or family is doing relative to others and perhaps a shared notion of what is expected for citizens of the United States.[4]

Poverty became a matter of broad public awareness in the United States in recent decades during the early years of the 1960s when books such as Michael Harrington's *The Other America*, along with accounts of poverty reported in *The New York Times* and other national papers, brought the realities of poverty into the public light.[5] In 1964, President Johnson used his State of the Union address to focus national attention on poverty and committed his administration to a "war on poverty."[6]

The anti-poverty programs that were launched during the years of the Johnson administration represent the most sweeping and comprehensive efforts in the history of the United States since the Great Depression to address poverty through policies that provide resources to families and build the resilience of communities.[7] By 2018, these programs provided food, medical care, shelter, and income to roughly 17% of the population, with a cost of more than $916 billion.[8] More than $20 trillion dollars

---

1. *See* Philip Stevens, Int'l Pol'y Network, Diseases of Poverty and the 10/90 Gap (2004).

2. *See id.*

3. Mark R. Rank & Thomas A. Hirschl, *The Occurrence of Poverty across the Life Cycle: Evidence from the PSID*, 20 J. Pol'y Analysis and Mgmt. 737, 742–43 (2001).

4. *See id.* at 738.

5. Maurice Isserman, *50 Years Later: Poverty and* The Other America, Dissent Magazine, Winter 2012.

6. Gordon M. Fisher, *The Development and History of the Poverty Thresholds*, 55 Soc. Sec. Bull. 3, 3 (1992).

7. *See generally id.*

8. Robert Rector, *How the War on Poverty Was Lost,* Wall St. J., Jan. 7, 2014, http://www.wsj.com/articles/SB10001424052702303345104579282760272285556.

have been invested in these programs in the 50 years that followed Pres. Johnson's 1964 State of the Union.[9] As a result, nearly all Americans have a degree of economic security, or at least access to a bundle of goods that can provide a very modest quality of life.[10] Nearly all Americans today have access to basic necessities including housing, food, and education; as well as other modern necessities, such as televisions and refrigeration.[11] The access to these things has drawn criticism from some who argue that the definition of poverty in the United States is not what most nonpoor people expect.

While most families do have access to modern necessities, there is a stark lack of economic mobility across generations.[12] For example, a child born in the bottom 20% of income during the time between the mid-1960s and 1980s had a 30% chance of reaching the top 20% of earners by adulthood.[13] A child born in the top 20% of earners had an 80% chance of remaining at that income level through adulthood.[14] In short, the poor may have more things, but they remain ever.

B. The Experiences of Poverty

While data present an overall image of poverty, reports do not provide much insight into the experience of poverty for the individuals and families who live there. These insights are most powerfully provided in personal accounts. Some constants emerge in both the fictional and nonfiction accounts of poverty: Life becomes a series of trade-offs for the poor who are forced to make difficult choices; the poor are made to feel "unworthy" or to have failed in some way; and personal autonomy is lost. In *Down and Out in Paris and London*, for example, George Orwell writes about his experience with poverty and describes the "lowness" of poverty where every financial and social transaction is surrounded by secrecy, where the poor seek to conceal both themselves and their financial condition.[15] In *Bastard Out of Carolina*, Dorothy Allison explores the pain a mother feels as she watches her children suffer from hunger, and the extent to which she will go to end her children's distress, even to the point of prostituting herself to buy her children groceries.[16] These writers capture a sense of

---

9. *Id.*

10. *See id.*

11. *Id.*

12. Julia B. Isaacs et al., Brookings Inst., Getting Ahead of Losing Ground: Economic Mobility in America, 17–21 (2008).

13. *Id.*

14. *Id.* at 21.

15. *See generally* George Orwell, Down and Out in Paris and London (1933). *Down and Out in Paris and London* is an autobiographical account of Orwell's time living and working in Paris and London between the wars. Orwell struggled to find adequate work as a writer during the European depression and in this book he recounts his experiences of deprivation and poverty.

16. *See generally* Dorothy Allison, Bastard Out of Carolina (1992). Dorothy Allison was born in Greenville, South Carolina, and writes about the American experience of class. *Bastard Out of Carolina* was a finalist for the 1992 National Book Award and was later adapted into a movie.

isolation and vulnerability of being poor, even when surrounded by great resources and wealth. Such feelings may be seen as expected given how onerous and harsh life can be made for the poor.

For many people who live in poverty, life is experienced as a series of challenges and burdens.[17] From the beginning of life, where a child born in poverty faces lower birth weight and higher mortality risk, to the end of life, where poverty correlates to shorter life expectancy and higher mortality rates across other demographics, the presence of poverty lessens life's quality.[18]

Women in poverty access prenatal care less frequently than the nonpoor and child abuse and neglect occur more frequently among poor families; perhaps due to the stress associated with poverty and lack of resources.[19] Poor children later in life, during school years, display higher levels of conduct and disciplinary problems along related social adaption delays, when compared with nonpoor children.[20] Poverty contributes to malnourishment and hunger, as well as related health delays and risks.[21] These include obesity, health impacts from environmental exposures, and mental health issues—all of which are experienced in higher regularity among the poor than the nonpoor.[22] Adult health quality is also affected, due to a combination of lack of access to healthful food, adequate preventative treatment, dangerous and demanding labor, and stress.[23] Perhaps the abundance of these stressors explains the prevalence of mental illness among the poor, including mental illness that goes undiagnosed and untreated, resulting in more significant life-altering illnesses among children and adults.[24]

Inadequate housing reduces quality of life for the poor in numerous ways.[25] The presence of lead paint stunts childhood development and leads to cognitive and emotional problems throughout life.[26] The proximity of low-income housing and industrial uses, superfund sites, major traffic arteries, and other undesirable land uses leads to respiratory illnesses, including asthma and emphysema.[27] Polluted water, including public and private water supplies, expose the poor to known carcinogens and

---

17. Leonard J. Long, *Optimum Poverty, Character, and the Non-Relevance of Poverty Law*, 47 RUTGERS L. REV. 693, 702–11 (1995).

18. Kate W. Strully et al., *Effects of Prenatal Poverty on Infant Health: State Earned Income Tax Credits and Birth Weight*, 75 AM. SOC. REV. 534, 534–35 (2011).

19. Long, *supra* note 17, at 752.

20. Jeanne Brooks-Gunn & Greg J. Duncan, *The Effects of Poverty on Children*, 7 THE FUTURE OF CHILD. 55, 57–63 (1997).

21. *Id.* at 57, 60.

22. *Id.* at 57–63.

23. Vijaya Murali & Femi Oyebode, *Poverty, Social Inequality and Mental Health*, 10 ADVANCES IN PSYCH. TREATMENT 216, 221 (2004).

24. *Id.* at 217–20.

25. *See generally* James Krieger & Donna L. Higgins, *Housing and Health: Time Again for Public Health Action*, 92 AM. J. PUB. HEALTH 758 (2002).

26. *Id.* at 761.

27. *Id.* at 758.

poverty rate +
prevelance of cancers
due to prolonged exposure to
carcinogens

pathogens.[28] The poverty rate and prevalence of cancers has been established, and perhaps is not an unforeseeable outcome under such circumstances.[29]

Within the communities where poor people live, the outlook remains as bleak. Crime is more prevalent in low-income communities, particularly violent crimes against others, such as murder.[30] Crimes committed against poor families often leaves these families without the resources that are needed to advance economically, perpetuating poverty.[31] In addition to being directly victimized by criminals, the poor are further subjected to politically motivated criminal prosecutions that are driven by a desire to "get tough on crime," resulting in a disproportionate number of poor people being imprisoned; which further cements an individual's life in poverty.[32]

Beyond the health, housing and crime that disproportionately impacts the poor, the poor are routinely subjected to usurious rents, interest rates, and transaction fees.[33] Common banking transactions, such as cashing a check or writing a check, that cost the nonpoor a few cents cost the poor hundreds of times more.[34] Buy-here/pay-here stores, paycheck cashers, fringe banking outlets, payday lenders, loan sharks, pawn shops, rent-to-own schemes, and sub-sub-prime home lenders are all in place to exact fees and interests from those who lack any alternative — the poor.[35]

The experience of being poor is the true story of poverty, not the statistics that result in an abstraction that is distant and removed from where and how people live. On a day-to-day basis, the experience of poverty is more than difficult. It is crushing. This sense is driven home even more when the choices that the poor must make are compared with the life of the nonpoor. For the poor, a $6.00 ticket to a high school football game can be unaffordable, making it impossible for a mother to see her son play. An unexpected $80 utility bill may mean that a family loses heat or electricity. Even working full-time, a worker cannot earn enough to pay for the basic goods and services needed to support a child without assistance.[36] Minimum wage jobs, which were once reserved for students or those first entering the workforce, are now mostly filled with people older than 25 years of age who are educated with at least a high

---

28. *Id.*

29. *Id.*

30. Benjamin H. Harris & Melissa S. Kearney, Brookings Inst., The Unequal Burden of Crime and Incarceration on America's Poor, https://www.brookings.edu/blog/up-front/2014/04/28/the-unequal-burden-of-crime-and-incarceration-on-americas-poor/ (last visited Nov. 7, 2019).

31. *Id.*

32. *Id.*

33. *See generally The High Cost of Poverty: Rent to Own*, Minn. Pub. Radio (Jan. 1 1997), http://news.minnesota.publicradio.org/features/199701/01_biewenj_poverty/rent.htm.

34. *See generally id.*

35. *See generally id.*

36. Steven Greenhouse, *Low-Wage Workers are Finding Poverty Harder to Escape*, N.Y. Times, Mar. 16, 2014, http://www.nytimes.com/2014/03/17/business/economy/low-wage-workers-finding-its-easier-to-fall-into-poverty-and-harder-to-get-out.html.

SNAP = modern "food stamps"

school diploma and, not uncommonly, college graduates.[37] All of these factors weigh more heavily on women, especially women of color.[38]

Programs run by the state and federal governments do exist to assist the poor. Access to food is provided through the Supplemental Nutrition Assistance Program (SNAP), what was formerly known as "food stamps."[39] According to the U.S. Department of Agriculture, the agency that administers the SNAP program, more than 46 million people received SNAP benefits during any given month in 2014.[40] The average SNAP benefit equaled slightly more than $125 per person ($126 in 2017), with a total cost to the federal government of $74.1 billion in 2014 ($68 billion in 2017).[41] For this money, more than 15% of the U.S. population is provided with food, including roughly 23 million children.[42] In 2014, the SNAP program budget was reduced by $5 billion for 2015, although this amount was indexed to increase to $6 billion the following year and going forward.[43] Average reduction of SNAP benefits equaled between $9 and $10 per recipient.[44] *SNAP benefits have been reduced*

According to the USDA, the average moderate cost food budget for a family of four is $976 a month.[45] For families spending this much on food each month, a $10 to $40 food budget reduction would be absorbed without notice. For many poor people, however, the reduction creates a series of difficult choices. While $10 may seem like a minor amount, here are the things a family could buy with $10 a month:

- Two to three gallons of milk[46]

- Five days of the USDA recommended amount of fresh fruits and vegetables[47]

- Ten pounds of pasta or rice[48]

---

37. *Id.*

38. *Id.*

39. Judith Bartfield, SNAP Matters: How Food Stamps Affect Health and Well-Being 1 (2015).

40. *Supplemental Nutrition Assistance Program Participation and Costs*, https://fns-prod.azureedge.net/sites/default/files/pd/SNAPsummary.pdf (last visited Jan. 10, 2018).

41. *Id.*

42. *Id.*

43. Stacy Dean & Dottie Rosenbaum, Ctr. on Budget and Pol'y Priorities, SNAP Benefits Will Be Cut for Nearly All Participants in November 2013, https://www.cbpp.org/research/snap-benefits-will-be-cut-for-nearly-all-participants-in-november-2013 (last visited Nov. 7, 2019).

44. *Id.*

45. U.S. Dep't of Agr., *Official USDA Food Plans: Cost of Food at Home at Four Levels*, https://fns-prod.azureedge.net/sites/default/files/media/file/CostofFoodSep2019.pdf (last visited Nov. 7, 2019).

46. 126 U.S. Dep't of Agr., *Retail Milk Prices Report*, https://www.ams.usda.gov/sites/default/files/media/RetailMilkPrices2018.pdf (last visited Nov. 5, 2019).

47. U.S. Dep't of Agr. Econ. Res. Serv., *How Much Do Fruits and Vegetables Cost?*, https://www.ers.usda.gov/publications/pub-details/?pubid=44520 (last visited Mar. 20, 2016).

48. *Retail Price of Spaghetti and Macaroni in the United States from 1995 to 2018 (in U.S. dollars per pound)*, Statista, https://www.statista.com/statistics/236634/retail-price-of-spaghetti-in-the-united-states/ (last visited Nov. 7, 2019); *Retail Price of White Rice (Long Grain, Uncooked) in the United States from 1995 to 2018 (in U.S. dollars per pound)*, Statista, https://www.statista.com/statistics/236628/retail-price-of-white-rice-in-the-united-states/ (last visited Nov. 7, 2019).

For families receiving an average benefit of $125 a person each month, the SNAP benefit reductions in 2014 meant fewer dollars for food in each month's budget, and increased reliance on private, nonprofit food pantries. In 2013, more than 46.5 million people accessed private food pantries in the United States.[49] For poor people struggling to eat, what may be seen as a meager cut to food benefits can lead to painful choices that threaten health or even survival.[50]

Small reductions in food benefits have outsized impacts on their recipients. Choices must be made about housing as well. Housing is considered to be affordable for a family if it costs no more than 35% of the family's income.[51] In many communities across the United States, housing costs have skyrocketed far beyond affordability.[52] In San Francisco and the Bay area, the average cost for a two-bedroom rental is more than $4,750 per month.[53] In Manhattan, rents for the same apartment average more than $3,370.[54] In Vail, Colorado, two-bedroom apartments are available for $2,200 a month in rent.[55] Even while rental prices are so high, the economy in each of these cities requires workers at all levels of experience and skill. A worker would need to earn more than $85 an hour to afford the average rent for a two-bedroom apartment in San Francisco, $60 in Manhattan and $40 in Vail. Housing is still unaffordable even when wages are lifted to the levels being called a "living wage" of $15.00 an hour.[56]

Priced out of the housing market in these cities, the poor are forced to choose between not working in the jobs that are available to them in the economy or finding an alternative to local housing. That alternative is often housing in suburbs and far

---

49. Feeding America, Hunger and Poverty Facts and Statistics, http://www.feedingamerica. org/hunger-in-america/impact-of-hunger/hunger-and-poverty/hunger-and-poverty-fact-sheet.html (last visited Mar. 24, 2016).

50. Kim Severson & Winnie Hu, *Cut in Food Stamps Forces Hard Choices on Poor*, N.Y. Times, Nov. 7, 2013, http://www.nytimes.com/2013/11/08/us/cut-in-food-stamps-forces-hard-choices-on-poor.html.

51. U.S. Dep't of Hous. & Urban Dev., *Affordable Housing*, http://portal.hud.gov/hudportal/HUD? src=/program_offices/comm_planning/affordablehousing/ (last visited Mar. 20, 2016). Families who pay more than 30 percent of their income for housing are considered cost-burdened and may have difficulty affording necessities such as food, clothing, transportation, and medical care.

52. Matthew Desmond, *Heavy Is the House: Rent Burden among the American Urban Poor*, 42 Int'l J. Urb. & Reg'l Res. 160, 160 (2018).

53. Crystal Chen, *Zumper National Rent Report: October 2019*, Zumper, https://www.zumper. com/blog/2019/09/zumper-national-rent-report-october-2019/ (last visited Nov. 7, 2019).

54. *Id.*

55. Emily Alligood, *Study: Average Vail 2-Bedroom Rent Is $2,200; Aspen is $3,660*, Vail Daily, https://www.vaildaily.com/news/vail-average-2-bedroom-rent-is-2200/ (last visited Nov. 7, 2019).

56. *See, e.g.*, Gene Balk, *$15 Wage Makes Many Cities Affordable, But Not Seattle*, Seattle Times, Jun. 3, 2013, http://www.seattletimes.com/business/real-estate/15-wage-would-make-big-difference-to-renters-across-us/; *It's Officially Impossible to Afford NYC Rents on the Minimum Wage*, N.Y. Daily News, Sept. 10, 2015, https://www.nydailynews.com/life-style/real-estate/impossible-afford-nyc-rents-minimum-wage-article-1.2352294.

distant communities, requiring long commutes.[57] Costs come with each minute spent commuting, including gas, car repair, and the time spent each day sitting in traffic. The movement of poor families out of the city has also reshaped the suburbs, areas once considered to be the enclave of the middle-class American Dream.[58]

C. The Spaces of Poverty in the United States

Place matters. As anyone who has bought a home will tell you, location has more to do with price than just about any other factor. Community amenities, including such things as access to public transportation, green space, shopping, diversity, public schools, and culture, improves the quality of life residents can expect to enjoy, and as a result prices increase. Conversely, a lack of such amenities, or even the disproportionate placement of burdens, can lessen the quality of life for residents. The place where one lives can be either a blessing or a challenge. Poverty is not evenly distributed. For many people living in poverty, place shapes the opportunities that arise in life, many times in negative ways. Added to this is the fact that people living in poverty tend to live in clustered areas, rural regions, counties, or neighborhoods with a high density of poor people, leaving the poor with limited opportunity for social or economic advancement.

1. Where Poor People Live

Most people can describe a low-income neighborhood, if asked, regardless of whether they have lived in one or not, just as they can describe a wealthy neighborhood and its amenities. These images arise from personal experiences to media portrayals to documentary films as well as research studies. Images shape perceptions that guide behaviors. For example, certain spaces are recognized as "safe" or "unsafe" and individuals in these become symbols of trust or fear.[59] Harvard researchers James Wilson and George Kelling speculate on the criminalization of urban spaces through a *broken windows* theory:[60]

> [I]ts anonymity, the frequency with which cars are abandoned and things are stolen or broken, the past experience of "no one caring"—vandalism begins much more quickly than it does in staid Palo Alto, where people have

---

57. Sheila Dewan, *In Many Cities, Rent Is Rising Out of Reach of Middle Class*, N.Y. Times, Apr.14, 2014, http://www.nytimes.com/2014/04/15/business/more-renters-find-30-affordability-ratio-unattainable.html.

58. Jennifer Medina, *Hardship Makes a New Home in the Suburbs*, N.Y. Times, May 9, 2014, http://www.nytimes.com/2014/05/10/us/hardship-makes-a-new-home-in-the-suburbs.html.

59. *See* George L. Kelling & James Q. Wilson, *Broken Windows*, Atlantic, Mar. 1982.

60. *Id.*

come to believe that private possessions are cared for, and that mischievous behavior is costly. But vandalism can occur anywhere once communal barriers—the sense of mutual regard and the obligations of civility—are lowered by actions that seem to signal that "no one cares."

We suggest that "untended" behavior also leads to the breakdown of community controls. A stable neighborhood of families who care for their homes, mind each other's children, and confidently frown on unwanted intruders can change, in a few years or even a few months, to an inhospitable and frightening jungle. A piece of property is abandoned, weeds grow up, a window is smashed. Adults stop scolding rowdy children; the children, emboldened, become more rowdy. Families move out, unattached adults move in. Teenagers gather in front of the corner store. The merchant asks them to move; they refuse. Fights occur. Litter accumulates. People start drinking in front of the grocery; in time, an inebriant slumps to the sidewalk and is allowed to sleep it off. Pedestrians are approached by panhandlers.

At this point it is not inevitable that serious crime will flourish or violent attacks on strangers will occur. But many residents will think that crime, especially violent crime, is on the rise, and they will modify their behavior accordingly. They will use the streets less often, and when on the streets will stay apart from their fellows, moving with averted eyes, silent lips, and hurried steps. "Don't get involved." For some residents, this growing atomization will matter little, because the neighborhood is not their "home" but "the place where they live." Their interests are elsewhere; they are cosmopolitans. But it will matter greatly to other people, whose lives derive meaning and satisfaction from local attachments rather than worldly involvement; for them, the neighborhood will cease to exist except for a few reliable friends whom they arrange to meet.

Such an area is vulnerable to criminal invasion. Though it is not inevitable, it is more likely that here, rather than in places where people are confident, they can regulate public behavior by informal controls, drugs will change hands, prostitutes will solicit, and cars will be stripped. That the drunks will be robbed by boys who do it as a lark and the prostitutes' customers will be robbed by men who do it purposefully and perhaps violently. That muggings will occur.[61]

More recent social science research counters Wilson and Kelling's *broken windows* theory, arguing that crime and disorder coexist and can be explained by other structural factors, such as unemployment and economic growth.[62] And others have argued that "social disorder is a social construct, rather than a concrete phenomenon."[63]

---

61. *Id.*

62. Robert J. Sampson & Stephen W. Raudenbush, *Systematic Social Observation of Public Spaces: A New Look at Disorder in Urban Neighborhoods*, 105 Am. J. Soc. 603, 609 (1999).

63. Lauren Kirchner, *Breaking Down the Broken Windows Theory*, Pacific Standard (Jan. 7, 2014), http://www.psmag.com/navigation/politics-and-law/breaking-broken-windows-theory-72310/.

Regardless of the direct relationship between the environment and crime rates, it is hard not to see the economic inequalities in our built environment.[64] The built environment includes:

> [O]ur homes, schools, workplaces, parks/recreation areas, business areas and roads. It extends overhead in the form of electric transmission lines, underground in the form of waste disposal sites and subway trains, and across the country in the form of highways. The built environment encompasses all buildings, spaces and products that are created or modified by people. It impacts indoor and outdoor physical environments (e.g., climatic conditions and indoor/outdoor air quality), as well as social environments (e.g., civic participation, community capacity and investment) and subsequently our health and quality of life.[65]

Because the built environment is conceived and constructed by humans, the built environment reflects human biases. It is highly stratified whereby those who are disadvantaged live, work, go to school, shop, and play in areas that are of poor quality, polluted, ill-resourced, and criminalized. In contrast, the nonpoor benefit from public resources that selectively serve communities, spaces that are privatized through gates, security companies and homeowners' associations, comparative safety, and better schools. The built environment also shapes ideas about who inhabits particular spaces as well as the expected and deviant behaviors allowed in a specific space. Spatial distributions of poverty occur across the urban-rural spectrum, ultimately reflecting the places where poor people live as dystopic and lacking.

2. Urban Poverty[66]

The spatial distribution of poverty is shaped by economic restructuring and public policies, as well as social and cultural factors. Historically, the poor have been concentrated in alley dwellings and inner-city enclaves, rural hamlets, federal Indian reservations, and more recently, working class suburbs hard struck by the 2008 economic crisis. After the Civil War, many northern cities experienced massive migrations of blacks into small urban enclaves. As the black population grew and housing became more scarce, racial segregation became the norm. At first whites simply moved out of areas where blacks had migrated. Restrictive covenants in the early 1900s to redlining and zoning regulations in the 1950s and 1960s, to present-day gentrification and urban dislocations physically and socially isolated poor blacks in inner city enclaves. While employment opportunities surged after World War II, civil rights legislation had yet to be enacted; thus, most blacks seeking employment experienced discrim-

---

64. Shobha Srinivasan et al., *Creating Healthy Communities, Healthy Homes, Healthy People: Initiating a Research Agenda on the Built Environment and Public Health*, 93 Am. J. Pub. Health 1446, 1446 (2003).

65. *Id.*

66. *See generally* Sherri Lawson Clark, *Where the Poor Live: How Federal Housing Policy Shapes Residential Communities*, 31 Urb. Anthropology & Stud. of Cultural Sys. & World Econ. Dev. 69 (2002).

ination throughout both the public and private sectors, and if employed, struggled to break through job ceilings. Low wage employment became scarcer as manufacturing jobs moved out of urban cores in the 1970s.

a. Urban Renewal

Urban renewal is a process of land redevelopment in U.S. cities. Established by the Housing Act of 1949, the urban renewal process empowered local government, through access to state and federal funds, to identify, obtain, and redevelop "blighted" or "decaying" property within the urban core. The policy sounds appealing and necessary. Many cities, particularly those in the Northeast corridor, had experienced a decline in housing and infrastructure in the decades between the Great Depression and the end of World War II. Using federal money to revitalize and redevelop the most affected areas had great appeal. New housing and commercial real estate, new road systems, new schools, and utilities would all seamlessly lead to new, vital cities with greater opportunity for the people who lived there. But central to the Urban Renewal process was the movement of people. Those people who lived and worked in areas declared to be blighted or decayed would be relocated to allow for the demolition of existing buildings along with the rebuilding efforts that would follow. The consequences, in hindsight, should have been expected. The burden of urban redevelopment fell most heavily on African American and poor communities Through the process, millions of families were displaced from their homes, minority business districts were disrupted, and communities were disbanded, all with most of the burden falling on the poor.

The process of Urban Renewal did not work alone. In many cities, "redlining," the policy that restricted home sales and lending for African American families to only certain communities, played an equally invidious role. Redlining, which had been sanctioned by federal housing laws from the 1930s, limited where African Americans could live. As civil rights laws expanded, redlining was outlawed. Urban Renewal, however, gave local government a new tool to effectively shape the racial and economic composition of urban communities in its place. Using publicly available data on how Urban Renewal funding was used and the communities where Urban Renewal projects were developed, the University of Richmond's Digital Scholarship Lab generates interactive GIS maps that illustrate these interactions during the crucial decade of 1955–1965.[67] Named *Renewing Inequality*, the tool overlays data on redlining with that on Urban Renewal and shows how closely the power of Urban Renewal was used to shape the places where African Americans and the poor live within U.S. cities.[68] The advent of expanded public housing as part of the Johnson administration's Great Society initiative created further structural barriers facing the poor.

The 1949 Housing Act cleared the way for the very poor to move into public housing by "requiring that the highest rents be 20 percent lower than the lowest prevailing rents for decent housing in the private market and by authorizing the eviction of

---

67. Robert K. Nelson & Edward L. Ayers, *Renewing Inequality*, AMERICAN PANORAMA, https://dsl.richmond.edu/panorama/renewal/#view=0/0/1&viz=cartogram (last visited Sept. 18, 2019).

68. *Id.*

above-income families." Public housing now changed into a place to permanently house the very poor, instead of a place to house those who needed temporary help. Camille Jeffers, who conducted an ethnographic study in public housing during the 1960s, describes the differences—

> By 1960 ... the image, the aura and some of the functions of public housing had changed markedly ... During the Depression and probably as recently as the 1940's, many people could identify their counterparts in public housing and might even envy them to some degree. Recent developments [circa 1960] have apparently walled off those who live in public housing from those who do not. Whether these walls are economic, social psychological, cultural or just plain brick and mortar, it is important to look behind them.

From 1944 to 1951, minorities represented between 26 percent and 39 percent of all public housing tenants. By 1978, the figure reached over 60 percent.[69] From 1950 to 1970, the median income of public residents fell from 64 percent to 37 percent of the national median. By 1988, the average income of public housing households was $6,539, one-fifth of the national average ($32,144). Today only about 40 percent of non-elderly households in public housing have a wage earner. Among big cities, the percentage of working poor is highest in New York City—about 60 percent—which perhaps explains why, with some exceptions, its public housing projects are among the best in the country.[70]

There are more than 1.3 million units of public housing in the United States, which are managed by more than 3,000 housing agencies.[71] In 2016, more than 750,000 children lived in public housing and nearly two million children lived in Section 8 housing.[72] The isolation of the poor who live in public housing, which is often located in areas with fewer job opportunities and that are underserved by public services, limits social and economic advancement for these residents.

Moore v. City of East Cleveland
431 U.S. 494 (1977)

JUSTICE POWELL announced the judgment of the Court.

East Cleveland's housing ordinance, like many throughout the country, limits occupancy of a dwelling unit to members of a single family. § 1351.02. But the ordinance contains an unusual and complicated definitional section that recognizes as a "family"

---

69. Sherri Lawson Clark, Policy, Perceptions, and Place: An Ethnography of the Complexities of Implementing a Federal Housing Program (Nov. 15, 2002) (unpublished Ph.D. dissertation, American University) (on file with the Digital Research Archives, American University) https://dra.american.edu/islandora/object/thesesdissertations:3064/datastream/PDF/view.

70. Peter Dreier & John Atlas, *Public Housing: What Went Wrong?*, SHELTER FORCE (Sept. 1, 1994), https://shelterforce.org/1994/09/01/public-housing-what-went-wrong/.

71. *Id.*

72. NAT'L CTR. FOR HEALTH IN PUB. HOUSING, DEMOGRAPHIC FACTS RESIDENTS LIVING IN PUBLIC HOUSING (May 31, 2016), https://nchph.org/wp-content/uploads/2016/07/Demographics-Fact-Sheet-2016.pdf.

only a few categories of related individuals. § 1341.08. Because her family, living together in her home, fits none of those categories, appellant stands convicted of a criminal offense. The question in this case is whether the ordinance violates the Due Process Clause of the Fourteenth Amendment.

I

Appellant, Mrs. Inez Moore, lives in her East Cleveland home together with her son, Dale Moore, Sr., and her two grandsons, Dale, Jr., and John Moore, Jr. The two boys are first cousins, rather than brothers; we are told that John came to live with his grandmother and with the elder and younger Dale Moores after his mother's death.

In early 1973, Mrs. Moore received a notice of violation from the city, stating that John was an "illegal occupant" and directing her to comply with the ordinance. When she failed to remove him from her home, the city filed a criminal charge. Mrs. Moore moved to dismiss, claiming that the ordinance was constitutionally invalid on its face. Her motion was overruled, and, upon conviction, she was sentenced to five days in jail and a $25 fine. The Ohio Court of Appeals affirmed after giving full consideration to her constitutional claims, and the Ohio Supreme Court denied review. We noted probable jurisdiction of her appeal, 425 U.S. 949 (1976).

II

The city argues that our decision in *Village of Belle Terre v. Boraas*, 416 U.S. 1 (1974), requires us to sustain the ordinance attacked here. Belle Terre, like East Cleveland, imposed limits on the types of groups that could occupy a single dwelling unit. Applying the constitutional standard announced in this Court's leading land use case, *Euclid v. Ambler Realty Co.*, 272 U.S. 365 (1926), we sustained the Belle Terre ordinance on the ground that it bore a rational relationship to permissible state objectives.

But one overriding factor sets this case apart from *Belle Terre*. The ordinance there affected only unrelated individuals. It expressly allowed all who were related by "blood, adoption, or marriage" to live together, and, in sustaining the ordinance, we were careful to note that it promoted "family needs" and "family values." 416 U.S. at 9. East Cleveland, in contrast, has chosen to regulate the occupancy of its housing by slicing deeply into the family itself. This is no mere incidental result of the ordinance. On its face, it selects certain categories of relatives who may live together and declares that others may not. In particular, it makes a crime of a grandmother's choice to live with her grandson in circumstances like those presented here.

When a city undertakes such intrusive regulation of the family, neither *Belle Terre* nor *Euclid* governs; the usual judicial deference to the legislature is inappropriate.

"This Court has long recognized that freedom of personal choice in matters of marriage and family life is one of the liberties protected by the Due Process Clause of the Fourteenth Amendment." *Cleveland Board of Education v. LaFleur*, 414 U.S. 632 (1974). A host of cases, tracing their lineage to *Meyer v. Nebraska*, 262 U.S. 390 (1923), and *Pierce v. Society of Sisters*, 268 U.S. 510 (1925), have consistently acknowledged a "private realm of family life which the state cannot enter." (Citations omitted.) Of course, the family is not beyond regulation. But when the government intrudes on choices concerning family living arrangements, this Court must examine carefully the importance of the governmental interests advanced and the extent to which they are served by the challenged regulation.

When thus examined, this ordinance cannot survive. The city seeks to justify it as a means of preventing overcrowding minimizing traffic and parking congestion, and avoiding an undue financial burden on East Cleveland's school system. Although these are legitimate goals, the ordinance before us serves them marginally, at best. For example, the ordinance permits any family consisting only of husband, wife, and unmarried children to live together, even if the family contains a half dozen licensed drivers, each with his or her own car. At the same time, it forbids an adult brother and sister to share a household, even if both faithfully use public transportation. The ordinance would permit a grandmother to live with a single dependent son and children, even if his school-age children number a dozen, yet it forces Mrs. Moore to find another dwelling for her grandson John, simply because of the presence of his uncle and cousin in the same household. We need not labor the point. Section 1341.08 has but a tenuous relation to alleviation of the conditions mentioned by the city.

III

The city would distinguish the cases based on *Meyer* and *Pierce*. It points out that none of them "gives grandmothers any fundamental rights with respect to grandsons, and suggests that any constitutional right to live together as a family extends only to the nuclear family—essentially a couple and their dependent children.

To be sure, these cases did not expressly consider the family relationship presented here. They were immediately concerned with freedom of choice with respect to childbearing, *e.g., LaFleur, Roe v. Wade, Griswold, supra,* or with the rights of parents to the custody and companionship of their own children, *Stanley v. Illinois, supra,* or with traditional parental authority in matters of childrearing and education. *Yoder, Ginsberg, Pierce, Meyer, supra.* But unless we close our eyes to the basic reasons why certain rights associated with the family have been accorded shelter under the Fourteenth Amendment's Due Process Clause, we cannot avoid applying the force and rationale of these precedents to the family choice involved in this case.

Understanding those reasons requires careful attention to this Court's function under the Due Process Clause. Mr. Justice Harlan described it eloquently:

"Due process has not been reduced to any formula; its content cannot be determined by reference to any code. The best that can be said is that through the course of this Court's decisions it has represented the balance which our Nation, built upon postulates of respect for the liberty of the individual, has struck between that liberty and the demands of organized society. If the supplying of content to this Constitutional concept has of necessity been a rational process, it certainly has not been one where judges have felt free to roam where unguided speculation might take them. The balance of which I speak is the balance struck by this country, having regard to what history teaches are the traditions from which it developed, as well as the traditions from which it broke. That tradition is a living thing. A decision of this Court which radically departs from it could not long survive, while a decision which builds on what has survived is likely to be sound. No formula could serve as a substitute, in this area, for judgment and restraint."

"... [T]he full scope of the liberty guaranteed by the Due Process Clause cannot be found in or limited by the precise terms of the specific guarantees elsewhere provided in the Constitution. This 'liberty' is not a series of isolated points pricked out in terms of the taking of property; the freedom of speech, press, and religion; the right to keep and bear arms; the freedom from unreasonable searches and seizures; and so on. It is a rational continuum which, broadly speaking, includes a freedom from all substantial arbitrary impositions and purposeless restraints, ... and which also recognizes what a reasonable and sensitive judgment must, that certain interests require particularly careful scrutiny of the state needs asserted to justify their abridgment."

Poe v. Ullman, supra at 367 U.S. 542–43 (dissenting opinion).

Substantive due process has at times been a treacherous field for this Court. There are risks when the judicial branch gives enhanced protection to certain substantive liberties without the guidance of the more specific provisions of the Bill of Rights. As the history of the *Lochner* era demonstrates, there is reason for concern lest the only limits to such judicial intervention become the predilections of those who happen at the time to be Members of this Court. That history counsels caution and restraint. But it does not counsel abandonment, nor does it require what the city urges here: cutting off any protection of family rights at the first convenient, if arbitrary bound-ary—the boundary of the nuclear family.

Appropriate limits on substantive due process come not from drawing arbitrary lines, but rather from careful "respect for the teachings of history [and] solid recog-nition of the basic values that underlie our society." *Griswold v. Connecticut,* 381 U.S. at 501 Our decisions establish that the Constitution protects the sanctity of the family precisely because the institution of the family is deeply rooted in this Nation's history and tradition. It is through the family that we inculcate and pass down many of our most cherished values, moral and cultural.

Ours is by no means a tradition limited to respect for the bonds uniting the mem-bers of the nuclear family. The tradition of uncles, aunts, cousins, and especially grandparents sharing a household along with parents and children has roots equally venerable and equally deserving of constitutional recognition. Over the years, millions of our citizens have grown up in just such an environment, and most, surely, have profited from it. Even if conditions of modern society have brought about a decline in extended family households, they have not erased the accumulated wisdom of civ-ilization, gained over the centuries and honored throughout our history, that supports a larger conception of the family. Out of choice, necessity, or a sense of family re-sponsibility, it has been common for close relatives to draw together and participate in the duties and the satisfactions of a common home. Decisions concerning chil-drearing, which *Yoder, Meyer, Pierce* and other cases have recognized as entitled to constitutional protection, long have been shared with grandparents or other relatives who occupy the same household—indeed who may take on major responsibility for the rearing of the children. Especially in times of adversity, such as the death of a spouse or economic need, the broader family has tended to come together for mutual sustenance and to maintain or rebuild a secure home life. This is apparently what happened here.

Whether or not such a household is established because of personal tragedy, the choice of relatives in this degree of kinship to live together may not lightly be denied by the State. *Pierce* struck down an Oregon law requiring all children to attend the State's public schools, holding that the Constitution "excludes any general power of the State to standardize its children by forcing them to accept instruction from public teachers only." 268 U.S. at 535. By the same token, the Constitution prevents East Cleveland from standardizing its children—and its adults—by forcing all to live in certain narrowly defined family patterns.

Reversed.

3. Rural Poverty

Poverty is often presented as a metropolitan issue. In popular culture, television shows often portray metropolitan areas as places with entrenched poverty and crumbling infrastructure. Poverty is certainly a significant concern for cities, but overall, poverty rates are higher and more entrenched in rural, nonmetropolitan communities. Overall, between 2000 and 2015, poverty rates in U.S. rural areas were 1.5% to 2% higher than the national average, ranging between 14.7 and 17.2%.[73] Regional differences are even more pronounced. Over a two-decade period between 1990 and 2010, rural poverty in the South region of the United States averaged 16%, almost 5% percentage points higher than poverty in the South's metropolitan regions.[74] Given that more than 43% of the entire nonmetro population found in the United States lived in the South, this poverty rate is particularly important.[75] Rural counties in the South contain a high incidence of concentrated poverty, with the most severe incidents

---

73. Tracey Farrigan, USDA, *Rural Poverty & Well-Being* (Aug. 20, 2019), https://www.ers.usda.gov/topics/rural-economy-population/rural-poverty-well-being/#historic. Over time, the difference between nonmetro and metro poverty rates has generally narrowed, falling from an average difference of 4.5 percentage points in the 1980s to an average gap of about 3.1 percentage points over the last 10 years. According to the most recent estimates from the 2017 American Community Survey (ACS), the nonmetro poverty rate was 16.4% in 2017, compared with 12.9% for metro areas. Nonmetro poverty fell two percentage points from 2013, when it reached its 30-year peak of 18.4%. That translates to 925,000 fewer rural residents in poverty in just four years. Metro poverty rates declined at a higher rate between 2013 and 2017, causing an increase in the metro-nonmetro poverty rate gap, which was 3.5 percentage points in 2017. *Id.*

74. U.S. Dep't Agric. Econ. Res. Serv., *Rural Poverty Remains Regionally Concentrated*, https://www.ers.usda.gov/data-products/chart-gallery/gallery/chart-detail/?chartId=89187 (last updated June 11, 2018).

75. U.S. Dep't Agric. Econ. Res. Serv., *Rural Poverty & Well-Being*, https://www.ers.usda.gov/topics/rural-economy-population/rural-poverty-well-being/ (last updated Aug. 20, 2019).

of poverty being found in the Mississippi Delta and Appalachia—even more than 50 years after broad-based interventions were begun through the Appalachian Regional Commission.[76] The South is by no means alone. Poverty is more concentrated in rural counties across all other regions, including the Southwest, North Central Midwest, Midwest, Pacific, and Northeast.[77]

In addition to concentration, rural poverty is highly persistent. "Persistent poverty" describes those counties where 20% or more of their population have lived in poverty over the last 30 years, as measured by the decennial census.[78] In 2017, 353 counties across the United States, approximately 11.2% of all U.S. counties, qualified as communities of persistent poverty.[79] The majority of these, 301, or 85.3%, were nonmetro rural counties.[80] As with rural poverty overall, persistent poverty is grouped in tight regional patterns, with nearly 84% of all persistently poor counties being located in the South, where more than 20% of all counties are persistently poor.[81]

The correlation between high poverty rates and rural areas impact children even more harshly. One-fifth of the United States' poor children live in rural communities, where childhood poverty rates have been between 5 and 12 percentage points higher since 1970 than in metropolitan communities.[82] In addition, children living in rural communities are nearly twice as likely to live in extreme poverty, which describes families living on less than 50% of the federal poverty threshold.[83] The rural children living in poverty tend more often to be in white families (57%) overall, while the number of African American children living in rural communities and below the federal poverty level are concentrated in the South.[84] Rural poor Latino children are also concentrated in the South, along with the Southwest and West.[85] Large concentrations of rural poor white children are concentrated in Appalachia, a region that stretches from New Hampshire to Mississippi, consistent with rural poverty overall.[86] Consistent with the placement of tribal lands through the U.S. reservation system, rural Native American children are concentrated in the Southwest and Northern Plains states where large reservations are found.[87] Perhaps predictably, the nature of rural communities makes it extremely difficult for rural poor families to advance economically.

76. U.S. Dep't Agric. Econ. Res. Serv., *supra* note 74.

77. U.S. Dep't Agric. Econ. Res. Serv., *supra* note 75.

78. *Id.*

79. *Id.*

80. *Id.*

81. *Id.*

82. WILLIAM O'HARE, POPULATION REFERENCE BUREAU, POVERTY IS A PERSISTENT REALITY FOR MANY RURAL CHILDREN IN U.S. (Sept. 10, 2009), https://www.prb.org/ruralchildpoverty/.

83. *Id.*

84. *Id.*

85. *Id.*

86. *Id.*

87. *Id.*

The largest and longest economic expansions of the last 30 years have largely over-looked rural communities across the United States, which have seen the least benefit as shown by increased incomes or assets following the economic expansions of the 1990s and early 2000s.[88] Lack of education and job opportunities fuel a cycle of poverty—parents tend to have less education and are more likely to be underem-ployed, leading to children living in scarcity with higher chances for poverty, which in turn leads to longer-term, intergenerational poverty, and so on. How the rural United States ended up in this situation is the result of large and small-scale forces that have shaped rural communities for decades.

For the rural poor, welfare reform, enacted in the atmosphere of personal self-re-liance and criminal law reform championed by the Republican party leading up to the 1994 election, led to increased economic disenfranchisement.

> The Personal Responsibility and Work Opportunity Reconciliation Act of 1996 moved millions of rural poor families off government assistance and into inadequate job prospects. The increased work participation rates found in metropolitan and suburban communities was not seen in rural commu-nities, leaving rural poor families disconnected from both work and the eco-nomic supports that had previously been available through welfare.[89]

The dislocation of workers resulting from broadened free trade agreements created additional pressures on rural employment.

> Rural labor markets tend to be less diversified that metropolitan labor markets. When an employer leaves a rural community, the impact is often amplified by the lack of other employers in the area capable of absorbing the dislocated workers. Because these jobs are most often lost to other commu-nities, it is usually not the case that dislocated workers move to higher paying, higher skilled jobs. They simply stop working or fall into lower paying jobs when available. Rural communities are thus left with lower paying, unskilled jobs concentrated in labor markets that offer few options for economic ad-vancement.... Those workers that are left behind find that they now live in communities that offer few jobs as well as few of the features necessary to find and maintain employment, such as transportation systems, social serv-ices, childcare and health care facilities.[90]

And if this were not enough, rural communities face increased costs of housing and real estate driven by the in-migration of commuters and long distance workers who seek the idyllic vision of rural America at a low cost, made even more affordable by metropolitan income levels, resulting in increased housing costs for the poor.[91]

---

88. *Id.*
89. Sherri Lawson Clark, *In Search of Housing: Urban Families in Rural Contexts*, 77 RURAL SOC. 110, 114–15 (2012).
90. *Id.* at 115.
91. *Id.*

4. Another Way Poor Places Differ: Environmental Justice

Significant differences associated with income and wealth are found across the places where people live in America. Environmental quality is perhaps one difference that goes unnoticed in communities with higher income levels.

"Environmental justice" encompasses issues surrounding environmental racism and discriminatory actions against those with lower socioeconomic status. It is best illustrated through the experiences of those people. Notable examples of environmental justice issues include the crisis in Flint, Michigan, as well as the response, or lack thereof, to Hurricane Maria in Puerto Rico. Examples also exist in the laws passed by the North Carolina legislature aimed at protecting the status quo in confined hog feeding at the expense of neighboring communities and restricting access to justice by people most negatively affected. Advocates for environmental justice argue for "the fair treatment and meaningful involvement of all people regardless of race, color, national origin, or income with respect to the development, implementation, and enforcement of environmental laws, regulations, and policies."[92] Concern for the environment moved to broader public awareness following the publication of *Silent Spring* by Rachel Carson in 1962. *Silent Spring* brought to the public awareness the impact of unregulated use of chemicals on plant and animal life. For the next two decades, the environmentalist movement worked to enhance state and federal policy protecting the environment as a largely middle- and upper-class, mainly white movement, notwithstanding the policy intersection between environmental protections and the civil rights movement.[93] Activism around environmental quality achieved significant results, including the creation of the Environmental Protection Agency and passage of nearly all of the major environmental protection legislation that remains in force nearly five decades later.[94] Communities of color and low-wealth communities were, for the most part, not largely engaged in this movement.[95] By the mid-1980s, however, this changed.

In 1983, the U.S. General Accounting Office (GAO) examined the racial and socioeconomic status of communities surrounding four hazardous waste landfills in the southeastern United States.[96] The GAO study found that African Americans comprised the majority of the population living in three of these communities and marked the first study to confirm the correlation between environmental risk and race or socioeconomic status.[97] Since publication of the 1983 GAO study previously mentioned,

---

92. EPA, *Environmental Justice*, https://www.epa.gov/environmentaljustice (last updated Aug. 19, 2019).

93. *Id.*

94. John R. Kyte, Comment, *Environmental Justice: The Need for Equal Enforcement and Sound Science*, 11 J. Contemp. Health L. & Pol'y 253, 258 (1995).

95. *Id.*

96. *Id.* at 260.

97. *Id.*

several additional studies and reports have been conducted on relationship between the racial and socioeconomic composition of communities and the placement of waste, along with enforcement of environmental regulations in those communities. In 1987, the United Church of Christ ("UCC") began a "comprehensive, national analysis of the relationship between hazardous wastes and the racial and ethnic composition of affected communities."[98] The study used U.S. Census data and looked at the location of hazardous waste sites along with the racial and ethnic composition of the surrounding communities.[99] The study showed that "the percentage of minority residents in communities surrounding hazardous waste sites ranged from two to more than three times the average for communities without such sites" and the statistical analysis indicated that the "probability of this association occurring purely by chance is less than one in ten thousand."[100] However, the UCC study failed to mention specific concerns or health effects on populations and communities situated close to waste disposal facilities.[101]

Recently, researchers at the EPA's National Center for Environmental Assessment published the results of a study on air pollution in the United States. The study concluded that regardless of wealth, black Americans were subjected to higher levels of air pollution than white Americans.[102] Published in the *American Journal of Public Health*, the study found that "black people are exposed to about 1.5 times more particulate matter than white people, and that Hispanics had about 1.2 times the exposure of non-Hispanic whites. The study found that people in poverty had about 1.3 times more exposure than people above poverty."[103] Particulate matter is an air pollutant that is a known carcinogen and has been identified as contributing to upper respiratory conditions, among other health concerns.[104] The authors conclude the study noting that it has "shown that a focus on poverty to the exclusion of race may be insufficient to meet the needs of all burdened populations."[105] Thus, the actions have real and measurable impacts on the health of minority communities; and while poverty plays a factor at some level, there are racial implications as well.

---

98. *Id.*

99. *Id.*

100. *Id.* at 261.

101. *Id.*

102. Ihab Mikati et al., *Disparities in Distribution of Particulate Matter Emission Sources by Race and Poverty Status*, 108 Am. J. Pub. Health 480, 480–85 (2018); *see also* Phil McKenna, *EPA Finds Black Americans Face More Health-Threatening Air Pollution*, Inside Climate News (Mar. 2, 2018), https://insideclimatenews.org/news/01032018/air-pollution-data-african-american-race-health-epa-research.

103. Vann R. Newkirk II, *Trump's EPA Concludes Environmental Racism Is Real*, Atlantic (Feb. 28, 2018), https://www.theatlantic.com/politics/archive/2018/02/the-trump-administration-finds-that-environmental-racism-is-real/554315/.

104. *Id.*

105. Mikati et al., *supra* note 102, at 485.

a. The "Right" to a Clean Environment

There is no "right" to a clean and healthy environment granted to any citizen by the Constitution of the United States.[106] Furthermore, only a few states have granted citizens the right to a healthy environment in their state constitution.[107] Even though the right to a healthy environment is not recognized in the U.S. Constitution, access to clean air, water, and an environment free of other environmental toxins is a pre-requisite for access to all civil and human rights. Moreover, various recognized rights within the Constitution are already implicated in the context of the environment, including the right to assemble, petition government, and free speech, all of which underpin effective environmental policymaking and good governance. However, there exists clear evidence that low-wealth communities and communities of color experience much higher occurrences of environmental exposures.

Recently, the United Nations called for the addition of the right to a healthy environment as a human right.[108] At least 177 nations have protections for rights to a healthy environment in their constitutions, but the United States does not.[109] Scholars debate the value of a constitutional right to a healthy environment, and some states have adopted such provisions. For example, the Constitution of the state of Hawaii provides that:

> Each person has the right to a clean and healthful environment, as defined by laws relating to environmental quality, including control of pollution and conservation, protection and enhancement of natural resources. Any person may enforce this right against any party, public or private, through appro-priate legal proceedings, subject to reasonable limitations and regulation as provided by law.[110]

The legislature, in adopting this amendment, granted the public standing to enforce the state's environmental regulations.[111] Granting citizens standing to sue to can help hold regulatory agencies accountable, at both the state and federal levels. However, the Hawaii legislature also noted that granting citizens standing to sue does not

---

106. *See generally* U.S. CONST. amends. I–X (lacking any protections for a human right to a healthy environment).

107. David R. Boyd, *The Constitutional Right to a Healthy Environment*, ENV'T, July–Aug. 2012, at 3, 4, 13, https://www.tandfonline.com/doi/full/10.1080/00139157.2012.691392 (noting that six states have a right to a healthy environment provided in their constitutions: Hawaii, Illinois, Massa-chusetts, Montana, Pennsylvania, and Rhode Island).

108. Jonathan Watts, *UN Moves Towards Recognising Human Right to a Healthy Environment*, GUARDIAN (Mar. 9, 2018, 3:00 AM), https://www.theguardian.com/environment/2018/mar/09/un-moves-towards-recognising-human-right-to-a-healthy-environment.

109. Boyd, *supra* note 107, at 4.

110. HAW. CONST. art. XI, §9.

111. *See* Kahana Sunset Owners Ass'n v. Maui Cty. Council, 948 P.2d 122, 134 (Haw. 1997) ("The legislature finds that article XI, section 9, of the Constitution of the State of [Hawai'i] has given the public standing to use the courts to enforce laws intended to protect the environment.").

[handwritten note: no right in Constitution to clean + healthy environment — only guaranteed by some state constitutions]

guarantee that they will exercise that right.[112] Constitutional provisions can trigger waves of additional environmental legislation.[113]

The majority of environmental justice claims come from the Civil Rights Act of 1964 or the National Environmental Policy Act. The Clean Water Act and the Clean Air Act both have citizen suit provisions that grant citizens standing to sue for violations of the standards provided; however, they do not specifically address concerns of disparate impact on regulation and enforcement in minority and low-income populations.[114]

b. Executive Response

In response to growing public awareness of environmental justice during the early 1990s, President Clinton moved the federal government toward greater accountability for environmental equity in 1994 when he issued Executive Order 12898, titled *Federal Actions to Address Environmental Justice in Minority Population and Low-Income Populations*.[115] Executive Order 12898 set forth that "each Federal agency shall make achieving environmental justice part of its mission by identifying and addressing, as appropriate, disproportionately high and adverse human health or environmental effects of its programs, policies, and activities on minority populations and low-income populations in the United States and its territories ..."[116]

In E.O. 12898, President Clinton directed federal agencies to develop agency-wide environmental justice strategies that "identif[y] and address[] disproportionately high and adverse human health or environmental effects of its programs, policies, and activities on minority populations and low-income populations."[117] The E.O. elaborated that these strategies should "list programs, policies, planning and public participation processes, enforcement, and/or rulemakings related to human health or the environment that should be revised ..."[118] The intended purpose of the revisions is to:

> (1) promote enforcement of all health and environmental statutes in areas with minority populations and low-income populations; (2) ensure greater public participation; (3) improve research and data collection relating to the health of and environment of minority populations and low-income populations; and (4) identify differential patterns of consumption of natural resources among minority populations and low-income populations.[119]

---

112. *Id.*

113. Boyd, *supra* note 107, at 6 ("In 78 out of 92 nations, environmental laws were strengthened after the right to a healthy environment gained constitutional status. Laws were amended to specifically focus on environmental rights, as well as access to environmental information, participation in decision making, and access to justice.").

114. *Id.*

115. Exec. Order No. 12,898, 59 Fed. Reg. 7629 (Feb. 11, 1994).

116. *Id.*

117. *Id.*

118. *Id.*

119. *Id.*

Agencies are then directed to provide the President and other officials with a report of efforts and strategies adopted to implement the directives set out in E.O. 12898.

Executive Order 12898 directs agencies to ensure that their programs, policies, and activities are conducted in a manner that ensures that they are not excluding persons or populations from participation, denying any persons or populations benefits conferred from the programs, or subjecting persons or populations to discrimination under such programs.[120] The E.O. expressly includes that agencies should accept recommendations from the public on including environmental justice principles in agency programs and policies, should make important public documents "concise, understandable, and readily accessible" and translated whenever "practicable and appropriate" and "relating to human health or the environment."[121]

Accompanying E.O. 12898, President Clinton issued a separate "Memorandum on Environmental Justice."[122] There, the former President reiterated the purposes and goals of the E.O., explaining that it "is designed to focus Federal attention on the environmental and human health conditions in minority communities and low-income communities with the goal of achieving environmental justice."[123] He also underscored existing portions of the law that may be useful in enforcing the directives of the E.O. and "ensure that all communities and persons across this Nation live in a safe and healthful environment."[124] Two important Acts mentioned in the memorandum include the National Environmental Policy Act of 1969 and the Civil Rights Act of 1964.[125]

c. Applying Existing Laws to Environmental Justice

The National Environmental Policy Act of 1969 ("NEPA") requires federal agencies completing significant federal actions to prepare either an environmental assessment or an environmental impact statement that analyzes the environmental impact of the proposed action.[126] When feasible, environmental assessments and environmental impact statements should "address significant and adverse environmental effects of proposed Federal actions on minority communities and low-income communities."[127] Furthermore, the NEPA process requires that agencies make available draft environmental impact statements for public notice and comment.[128] The White House Council on Environmental Quality ("CEQ") issued Guidance Under the National Environmental Policy Act to agencies in 1997 that outlined six principles for environmental

---

120. *Id.*

121. *Id.*

122. *See generally* Memorandum on Executive Order on Federal Actions to Address Environmental Justice in Minority Populations and Low-Income Populations, 1 Pub. Papers 241(Feb. 11, 1994).

123. *Id.*

124. *Id.*

125. *Id.*

126. *See* National Environmental Policy Act of 1969, 14 U.S.C. §§ 4321–4347 (1969).

127. *Id.*

128. EPA Public Participation, 40 C.F.R. § 6.203 (2007).

justice analyses.[129] This followed E.O. 12898 and clarified the responsibilities of agencies for compliance with NEPA.[130]

Under the six principles, agencies are first directed to consider the composition of the affected area. This includes determining whether low-income, minority, or tribal populations are present and if the result of the federal action under NEPA will cause disproportionately high and adverse human or environmental health concerns in the population. Agencies should consider current and historical public health and industry data for cumulative and multiple exposures to environmental and health hazards and recognize the "interrelated cultural, social, occupational, historical, or economic factors that may amplify the natural and physical environmental effects of the proposed action."[131] The guidance emphasizes the importance of having effective strategies for public participation and for seeking tribal representation when possible.

While NEPA provides for the consideration of environmental justice concerns in the preparation of the relevant environmental documents, it is only a procedural statute.[132] The major critique of the Act is that it does not require the agency completing the evaluation to make any changes to the proposed plans concerning the results of the environmental assessment or impact statement.[133] Environmental justice claims brought under NEPA typically challenge the adequacy of consideration of environmental justice in an agency's environmental impact statement.[134] An example of this procedural challenge can be seen with the legal battle over the infamous Dakota Access Pipeline. Plaintiffs successfully challenged the adequacy of the Army Corps EIS's considerations of environmental justice.[135] However, holding that an EIS is inadequate in some regard does not require the court to vacate the decision.[136] Instead, as the D.C. Circuit did here, the court may order additional briefing by the affected parties to determine if vacatur is the appropriate remedy "in light of the deficiencies herein identified and any disruptive consequences that would result given the current

---

129. THE WHITE HOUSE COUNCIL ON ENVIRONMENTAL QUALITY, ENVIRONMENTAL JUSTICE: GUIDANCE UNDER THE NATIONAL ENVIRONMENTAL POLICY ACT, EPA (Dec. 10, 1997), https://www.epa.gov/sites/production/files/2015-02/documents/ej_guidance_nepa_ceq1297.pdf.

130. *Id.*

131. *Id.*

132. *See* Robert L. Fischman, *The EPA's NEPA Duties and Ecosystem Services*, 20 STAN. ENVTL. L.J. 497, 516–19 (2001).

133. Helen Leanne Serassio, *Legislative and Executive Efforts to Modernize NEPA and Create Efficiencies in Environmental Review*, 45 TEX. ENVTL L.J. 317, 319 (2015).

134. *See, e.g.*, Standing Rock Sioux Tribe v. U.S. Army Corps of Eng'rs, 255 F. Supp. 3d 101 (D.C. Cir. 2017).

135. *Id.* at 140.
The Corps need not necessarily have addressed that particular issue, but it needed to offer more than a bare-bones conclusion that Standing Rock would not be disproportionately harmed by a spill. Given the cursory nature of this aspect of the EA's analysis, the Court agrees with the Tribe that the Corps did not properly consider the environmental-justice implications of the project and thus failed to take a hard look at its environmental consequences.

136. *Id.* at 147 ("[C]ourts have discretion to depart from that presumptive remedy and decide not to vacate an EA, FONSI, and corresponding authorizations pending NEPA compliance.")

stage of the pipeline's operation."[137] After further briefing, the Court did not vacate the EIS.[138] The Dakota Access Pipeline continued to flow and the environmental justice claim, while considered, did not prevent the injury.[139]

This decision illustrates the issues and difficulties in bringing environmental justice claims under NEPA. The Court recognized the limitation in its opinion, stating that "the Court's role here is not to determine the wisdom of agency action or to opine on its substantive effects … Instead, it must consider only the Corps' likelihood on remand of fulfilling NEPA's procedural environmental justice requirements and justifying its prior decision."[140] The Court cites to Supreme Court precedent from *Robertson v. Methow Valley Citizens Council,* providing that "NEPA itself does not mandate particular results, but simply prescribes the necessary process."[141] Thus, the burden of proof on a plaintiff challenging the adequacy of environmental justice considerations in an agency's environmental assessments or environmental impact statements is very high, and courts have the discretion to determine whether or not the deficiency should result in vacatur. NEPA's procedural basis makes it an unlikely avenue to achieve success for plaintiffs. Moreover, because the burden is so high, it will not likely be brought independently; instead, attorneys will tack the inadequacy claim to additional proceedings.[142] Therefore, the plaintiffs in a potential environmental justice claim likely need more than a procedural violation of NEPA to challenge the action because alone it is likely insufficient.

The Civil Rights of Act of 1964 was passed to prohibit discrimination on the basis of race, color, or national origin, under any program receiving federal financial assistance.[143] Section 601 sets out the general prohibition of discrimination, while section 602 directs federal agencies to promulgate regulations that prevent agencies receiving funding from engaging in discriminatory practices.[144] Complaints of alleged violations of environmental justice under the Civil Rights Act usually implicate the U.S. EPA. In 1993, the EPA created the Office of Civil Rights,[145] which was reorganized in December 2016 to create the External Civil Rights Compliance Office, which is housed under the EPA Office of General Counsel.[146]

---

137. *Id.* at 148.

138. Standing Rock Sioux Tribe v. U.S. Army Corps of Engineers, 282 F. Supp. 3d 91, 100 (D.C. Cir. 2017) ("Although it is a closer call than the first two issues, the Court concludes that the flaws in the Corps' environmental-justice analysis do not support vacatur.").

139. *See* Merrit Kennedy, *Crude Oil Begins to Flow Through Controversial Dakota Access Pipeline,* NPR (June 1, 2017, 5:23 PM), https://www.npr.org/sections/thetwo-way/2017/06/01/531097758/crude-oil-begins-to-flow-through-controversial-dakota-access-pipeline.

140. *Standing Rock Sioux Tribe,* 282 F. Supp. 3d at 102–03.

141. 490 U.S. 332, 351 (1989).

142. *See, e.g.,* Standing Rock Sioux Tribe v. U.S. Army Corps of Eng'rs, 255 F. Supp. 3d 101 (D.C. Cir. 2017).

143. Civil Rights Act of 1964, Pub. L. No. 88-352, 78 Stat. 241.

144. *See id.* §§ 601–602.

145. EPA, *Civil Rights,* https://www.epa.gov/ocr (last updated Aug. 6, 2018).

146. EPA, *External Civil Rights Compliance Office (Title VI),* https://www.epa.gov/ogc/external-civil-rights-compliance-office-title-vi (last updated Apr. 22, 2019).

The reorganization of the EPA's Office of Civil Rights came after intense criticism of the handling of environmental justice claims under the Civil Rights Act.[147] Environmental justice causes of action began arising under the Civil Rights Act in the 1990s; however, Supreme Court precedent that made the evidentiary bar for discrimination difficult to overcome was set early.[148] First, in *Guardians Association v. Civil Service Commission*, the Court held that section 601 of the Civil Rights Act requires proof of intentional discrimination.[149] Then, in *Alexander v. Sandoval*, the Court was presented with the question of "whether private individuals may sue to enforce disparate-impact regulations promulgated under Title VI of the Civil Rights Act of 1964."[150] The Court in *Alexander* read section 602 to preclude private rights of action for claims of disparate impact.[151] Thus, only section 601 remains to provide plaintiffs with a private right of action and requires under *Guardians* that the plaintiffs show intentional discrimination.

The practical result of both of these holdings has discouraged claims under the Civil Rights Act in court and instead shifted to administrative complaints.[152] The majority of these were directed to the EPA's Office of Civil Rights ("OCR"), but very little was accomplished.[153] In 2011, Deloitte issued an Evaluation of the EPA Office of Civil Rights[154] that concluded the adjudication of Title VI administrative complaints inadequate, with a backlog of cases back to 2001 and only six percent of cases accepted or dismissed within the Agency's 20-day time limit.[155] The Evaluation found that OCR was not well managed, that staff operated without clear expectations or guidelines, and that there were inadequate infrastructure and operating procedures to sustain performance.[156] The Evaluation addressed OCR's deficits and provided recommendations for each concern it identified.[157]

---

147. See *EPA Civil Rights Office Takes Steps to Enforce Civil Rights Laws*, Earthjustice (Jan. 24, 2017), https://earthjustice.org/news/press/2017/epa-civil-rights-office-takes-steps-to-enforce-civil-rights-laws.

148. Albert Huang, *Environmental Justice and Title VI of the Civil Rights Act: A Critical Crossroads*, Am. Bar Ass'n (Mar. 1, 2012), https://www.americanbar.org/groups/environment_energy_resources/publications/trends/2011_12/march_april/environmental_justice_title_vi_civil_rights_act/.

149. 463 U.S. 582 (1983).

150. 532 U.S. 275, 278 (2001); *see also* Scott Michael Edson, *Title VI or Bust? A Practical Evaluation of Title VI of the 1964 Civil Rights Act as an Environmental Justice Remedy*, 16 Fordham Envtl. L. Rev. 141, 155 (2004).

151. *Alexander*, 532 U.S. at 288.

We therefore begin (and find that we can end) our search for Congress's intent with the text and structure of Title VI. Section 602 authorizes federal agencies "to effectuate the provisions of [§ 601] ... by issuing rules, regulations, or orders of general applicability." It is immediately clear that the "rights-creating" language ... of § 601 ... is completely absent from § 602.

152. Huang, *supra* note 148.

153. *See generally id.*

154. Deloitte, Evaluation of the EPA Office of Civil Rights 1 (2011), https://archive.epa.gov/epahome/ocr-statement/web/pdf/epa-ocr_20110321_finalreport.pdf.

155. *Id.* at 1–2.

156. *Id.* at 18.

157. *See, e.g., id.* at 20–24.

In September 2016, the U.S. Commission on Civil Rights issued another report suggesting that the OCR had largely failed to protect against violations of environmental justice.[158] The 200-plus page report examined EPA's compliance with Title VI and E.O. 12898. It concluded that since OCR was established in 1993, EPA received almost 300 Title VI complaints.[159] Of those almost 300 complaints, the report concluded that EPA never made a formal finding of discrimination and never denied or withdrew funding from a recipient.[160] Thus, the following December, EPA restructured OCR and created the "External Civil Rights Compliance Office" under the Office of General Counsel to "strengthen the agency's ability to carry out its external civil rights enforcement responsibilities ..."[161]

Thus, even under both NEPA and the Civil Rights Act, plaintiffs are met with extreme procedural burdens as well as high burdens of proof. Recent restructuring by the EPA has attempted to remedy the crisis and backlog of Title VI complaints, but it will take time to determine if this strategy is effective.

5. Poverty Beyond the United States

Poverty in the specific context of the United States looks very different from that in other parts of the world, particularly in the developing nations. While nearly all people in the United States have access to basic necessities that include clean drinking water and access to literacy along with housing and food, such basic necessities are unavailable to more than two billion people living in extreme poverty around the world. It may be easy to consider poverty in the United States as an exception to the poverty found in other parts of the world, an exception that would make meaningful comparisons unlikely.

Whether or not there is an absolute measure of poverty that would make such comparisons meaningful, poverty outside the United States may play a crucial role in understanding the dynamics of poverty within the United States. The U.S. poor are at once set apart from the poor in other countries and yet still live with the social dynamics of poverty that make it difficult for them to realize their full potential over the course of their lives. This dynamic, which reduces outcomes in education, health, life expectancy, and asset development, is closely linked to being poor regardless of the country or context of poverty.

Recent data shows that despite the prevalent idea that poverty within the United States is "better" than poverty outside of it, this idea might be mistaken. While one cannot deny the difference in the poverty found in "poor" countries, and the inherently different lifestyles it forces, the societal norms of living in the United States does not

---

158. Vann R. Newkirk II, *The EPA's Failure to Protect People from the Environment*, ATLANTIC (Sep. 30, 2016) https://www.theatlantic.com/politics/archive/2016/09/epa-civil-rights-environmental-justice-report/502427/.

159. DELOITTE, *supra* note 154, at 40.

160. *Id.*

161. EPA, *supra* note 146.

diminish the level of poverty the poor experience. Comparisons to other countries may lead to a dangerous minimization of poverty in the United States.

a. Measuring Global Poverty

i. How We Measure It: The Statistics

Poverty is defined in gradations across the developing world. The World Bank defines "extreme poverty" as those living below the international poverty line of U.S. $1.90 per person per day.[162] According to the 2015 comprehensive data, about ten percent of the world's population falls under this category.[163] This amounts to almost ten out of every hundred people in the world. Although this declined by one percent from 2013, this only accounts for the world's poorest of the poor given the extremely low metric of only $1.90 per day.[164]

The outcomes of such devastating need are stark. People living at this level of poverty in the developing world must commit immense amounts of time and energy to the basic needs of life. Here are just a few examples from the United Nations of the outcomes and effects of living at extreme poverty:[165]

- More than 750 million people do not have access to clean drinking water. This leads to illness and disease that kills an estimated 842,000 people every year, or about 2,300 people per day.

- In 2011, 165 million children under the age of five had reduced growth and development due to malnutrition.

- Approximately 1.6 billion people (¼ of all humans) live without electricity.

- Approximately 80% of the world's population lives on roughly $10 a day.

Prior to 2017, the World Bank measured poverty at a single poverty-line measure: the extreme poverty-line measure. This created a wide range of issues surrounding both the explanation and perception of poverty.[166] For example, more than half of those in the "extreme poverty" category do not live in the lowest income countries.[167] Conversely, someone can have much more than $1.90 per day and still live in poverty relative to their country's environment.[168] To address the disparity in measuring

---

162. WORLD BANK, ENDING EXTREME POVERTY (June 8, 2016), https://www.worldbank.org/en/news/feature/2016/06/08/ending-extreme-poverty.

163. Press Release, Decline of Global Extreme Poverty Continues But Has Slowed: World Bank (Sept. 19, 2018), https://www.worldbank.org/en/news/press-release/2018/09/19/decline-of-global-extreme-poverty-continues-but-has-slowed-world-bank.

164. Id.

165. DoSOMETHING.ORG, 11 FACTS ABOUT GLOBAL POVERTY, https://www.dosomething.org/us/facts/11-facts-about-global-poverty (last visited Oct. 1, 2019).

166. CHRIS FLEISHER, AM. ECON. ASS'N, RECONSIDERING THE POVERTY LINE (Dec. 22, 2017), https://www.aeaweb.org/research/world-bank-poverty-line-basic-needs-allen.

167. Marc Silver & Malaka Gharib, *What's the Meaning of the World Bank's New Poverty Lines?*, NPR (Oct. 25, 2017, 1:51 PM), https://www.npr.org/sections/goatsandsoda/2017/10/25/558068646/whats-the-meaning-of-the-world-banks-new-poverty-lines.

168. Id.

poverty across countries with widely different economic realities, the World Bank developed two new "poverty line" figures.[169] The poverty line for a lower-middle-income country, such as India, is $3.20 per day, while for an upper-middle-income country, such as Brazil, it comes in at $5.50 per day.[170] In creating these new metrics for middle-income countries, the World Bank hoped to give those countries a better index for both viewing their own realities of poverty, as well as allowing the international community to assess whether poverty is rising or falling according to a fixed standard.

ii. The Framework of Global Poverty

The effects of extreme poverty are well-known to most people. No one would argue that there is devastating poverty in the world that causes incredible pain for many millions of people. That there is great poverty, however, is a different question from the question of why poverty exists or how to best respond. If extreme poverty results from individual choices or actions by a government accountable to its citizens, those who are not poor may distance themselves by seeing the poverty as an unfortunate situation that could be corrected without also feeling responsible. If extreme poverty goes deeper than this, implicating human rights secured for all people, then the required response changes. There is no human right not to be poor, even extremely poor. This is so even though the conditions of poverty inevitably result in both a cause and a consequence of recognized human rights not being realized. Should extreme poverty—the level of poverty that leads to malnourishment and death for millions of children each year—rise to the level of violating a human right or some international norm?

Amnesty International has for more than a decade campaigned to consider extreme poverty as a human rights issue.[171] The reasons for this position are compelling. More than six million children die from hunger each year, more than 16,000 each day and more than 800 million children suffer malnutrition.[172] A woman living in poverty dies during child birth or pregnancy every minute.[173] Poverty not only limits life outcomes, extreme poverty prevents millions of people from living in dignity or at all. Certainly, these conditions of deprivation must be seen as a human rights issue.

One challenge to seeing extreme poverty in terms of human rights is how blame and responsibility are allocated for poverty—in contrast to other issues of human rights, such as political repression, including such things as torture or execution. The agents of torture in a political regime are most often known, as are their actions. The victims of human rights abuses are also clearly known, they are people who are arrested or murdered. For example, the people who were enslaved in the southern states of the United States were victims of human rights abuses. The government officers and

---

169. *Id.*

170. *Id.*

171. Amnesty Int'l, Poverty Is a Human Rights Issue, https://www.amnestyusa.org/poverty-is-a-human-rights-issue/ (last visited Oct. 1, 2019).

172. *Id.*

173. *Id.*

private slaveholders caused these abuses. The conditions of slavery and human rights abuse could be ended through direct action against the officers and slaveholders.[174] For people living in poverty, however, the situation is starkly different. It is not clear who causes poverty. Poverty results from many factors, including economic conditions that not only lead to differences in how resources are distributed, but that also create great wealth, and along with it a higher standard of living and human dignity, for several billion people. In this context, marking poverty as a human rights violation does little to enable concrete action to end poverty or address its impact.

If extreme poverty is seen in context, however, it may be easier to view lack of income as a human rights violation due to the life necessities that are denied the poor. The extreme lack of income experienced by the one to two billion people in the world who live in extreme poverty effectively denies these people access to clean water, adequate food, education, housing, employment, and more. Denial of these basic human needs amounts to a denial of several international agreements that exist to protect individual human rights, including the Universal Declaration of Human Rights and the International Covenant on Economic, Social and Cultural Rights.[175] Deaths among the poor that result from hunger or lack of medical care violate these foundational agreements are directly attributable to poverty and thus amount to human rights violations. Any remedy addressing extreme poverty must not only ameliorate the symptoms of poverty, but must also consider how poverty impacts human rights as a result.[176]

One challenge to addressing poverty as a human rights violation, or even of effectively considering the context of extreme poverty, is the role played by free markets and trade in creating and perpetuating unequal economic conditions. Writers, including Thomas Friedman, recognize the power of free trade while Nobel laureate Amartya Sen argues that free trade in fact promotes human dignity and freedom.[177] Such insights are appealing. Consider the reality that China has lifted more than 850 million people from poverty since 1978.[178] The lives of these people are undoubtedly better than they were prior to the massive explosion in production that has fueled China's rise since 1990. But even as conditions for these workers have improved, global rates of extreme poverty have remained fairly constant and deeper, entrenched poverty has expanded in the developing and developed countries. The paradox of

---

174. William Easterly, *Amnesty International Confuses Poverty and Human Rights*, HuffPost (July 9, 2009, 5:12 AM), https://www.huffingtonpost.com/william-easterly/amnesty-international-con_b_211804.html.

175. Sameer Dossani, *Amnesty International Responds to "Poverty Is Not a Human Rights Violation*, Dev. Res. Inst.: Aid Watch Blog, http://www.nyudri.org/aidwatcharchive/2009/06/amnesty-international-responds-to-poverty-is-not-a-human-rights-violation (last visited Oct. 1, 2019).

176. *Id.*

177. In his book, *Development as Freedom*, Sen asserts that the solutions to the problems of global inequality, grinding poverty, and environmental degradation "will almost certainly call for institutions that take us *beyond the capitalist market economy*." Amartya Sen, Development as Freedom 267 (1999).

178. World Bank, The World Bank in China, https://www.worldbank.org/en/country/china/overview (last updated Oct. 1, 2019).

capitalism observed by Polyani, that rising prosperity is accompanied by increased pauperism, seems to be maintained.[179] Some would argue that poverty, even extreme poverty, is necessary in a capitalist system.[180] We cannot effectively discuss extreme poverty without also discussing the role that trade and capitalism play in creating and maintaining such deprivation among so many people, but at the same time we cannot do so without having a viable alternative to the existing economic system.

b. Comparing Global Poverty to Poverty within the United States

How does poverty in the United States compare to poverty in other parts of the world? The tragic dynamics of international poverty stand in sharp contrast to many aspects of poverty in the United States. The differences between poverty in the developing world and poverty in the United States has led some commentators to consider poverty in the United States as more of an inconvenience to those who are poor, and substantially different from a level of deprivation warranting significant public policy interventions. The difficulty with comparison begins at the start. Several different methods are used to measure poverty in the United States and these measures generally are not used to measure poverty outside the United States. The Federal Poverty Measure is an example. Using the Federal Poverty Measure to measure poverty in Honduras, for example, would be less than helpful as the poverty line under the FPL is so much higher than the incomes of nearly all families in Honduras and the costs of necessary goods and services is lower in that country. Even in developing countries a number of measurements are used to assess poverty levels. This makes a meaningful comparison difficult even across these countries. One measure of poverty that has received wide acceptance for measuring poverty in the developing work is the $2-a-day threshold. The $2-a-day threshold measures family income per member. Those families with cash income below $2 per day per member live in poverty based on this measure. Using this measure, global poverty has experienced large increases over time.[181] Because this level of income is so low, only $730.00 per year per family member, and families in the United States consume so many goods and services, it may seem that being poor in the United States is not poverty at all.

Robert Rector makes such arguments. Drawing on U.S. Census data that reports details regarding the goods and services that are consumed by the poor, Rector has argued that the number of "truly poor" families in the United States is a mere fraction of the percentage of families defined as poor using the Federal Poverty Measure.[182]

---

179. Robert Kuttner, *Karl Polanyi Explains It All*, The Am. Prospect (Apr. 15, 2014), https://prospect.org/power/karl-polanyi-explains/.

180. David Schweickart, *Global Poverty: Alternative Perspectives on What We Should Do—and Why*, 39 J. Soc. Phil. 471 (2008).

181. H. Luke Shaefer & Kathryn Edin, *Rising Extreme Poverty in the United States and the Response of Federal Means-Tested Transfer Programs*, 87 Soc. Serv. Rev. 250, 250–68 (2013).

182. Rachel Sheffield & Robert Rector, The Heritage Found., Understanding Poverty in the United States: Surprising Facts About America's Poor (Sept. 13, 2011), https://www.

Rector reports that 80% of those families below the Federal Poverty Line live in housing with air conditioning, 92% have microwaves and nearly 80% have a car or truck.[183] Other amenities abound in the lives of the poor, including: televisions, DVD players, VCRs, personal computers, video game systems, and cell phones. Rector reports that the majority of poor families have adequate nutrition and housing, as well as access to medical care and education. Rector reports that images of U.S. poverty are not aligned with the reality.[184] The poor in the United States are, in fact, in much better situation than the poor in other countries and, indeed, in much better situations than the nonpoor often believe them to be. And this leads to poverty policies that miss the point. "[W]elfare policy needs to address the causes of poverty, not merely the symptoms. Among families with children, the collapse of marriage and erosion of the work ethic are the principal long-term causes of poverty," Rector argues.[185] Concentrating resources and attention on poverty that does not bring hardships misses the point.

In December 2017, Philip Alston, United Nations Special Rapporteur on extreme poverty and human rights, visited the United States to investigate the existence of extreme poverty and whether its presence had an effect on the human rights of Americans. In his report, he noted that while the United States was one of the richest, most powerful, and most technologically advanced countries, "neither its wealth nor its power nor its technology is being harnessed to address the situation in which 40 million people continue to live in poverty."[186] In the context of international human rights, Alston goes onto say: "In practice, the United States is alone among developed countries in insisting that while human rights are of fundamental importance, they do not include rights that guard against dying of hunger, dying from a lack of access to affordable healthcare, or growing up in a context of total deprivation."[187]

Here are some statistical observations recorded in the report about how poverty in the United States compares with the rest of the world:

- By most indicators, the United States is one of the world's wealthiest countries. It spends more on national defense than China, Saudi Arabia, Russia, the United Kingdom, India, France, and Japan combined.

- U.S. healthcare expenditures per capita are double the OECD average and much higher than in all other countries. But there are many fewer doctors and hospital beds per person than the OECD average.

- U.S. infant mortality rates in 2013 were the highest in the developed world.

---

heritage.org/poverty-and-inequality/report/understanding-poverty-the-united-states-surprising-facts-about.

183. *Id.*

184. *Id.*

185. *Id.*

186. PHILIP ALSTON, UNITED NATIONS HUM. RTS. OFF. OF THE HIGH COMM'R, STATEMENT ON VISIT TO THE USA (Dec. 15, 2017), https://www.ohchr.org/EN/NewsEvents/Pages/DisplayNews.aspx?NewsID=22533&LangID=E.

187. *Id.*

- Americans can expect to live shorter and sicker lives, compared to people living in any other rich democracy, and the "health gap" between the United States. and its peer countries continues to grow.

United States inequality levels are far higher than those in most European countries

- Neglected tropical diseases, including Zika, are increasingly common in the United States. It has been estimated that 12 million Americans live with a neglected parasitic infection. A 2017 report documents the prevalence of hookworm in Lowndes County, Alabama.

- The United States has the highest prevalence of obesity in the developed world.

- In terms of access to water and sanitation, the United States ranks 36th in the world.

- America has the highest incarceration rate in the world, ahead of Turkmenistan, El Salvador, Cuba, Thailand, and the Russian Federation. Its rate is nearly five times the OECD average.

- The youth poverty rate in the United States is the highest across the OECD with one quarter of youth living in poverty compared to less than 14% across the OECD.

- The Stanford Center on Inequality and Poverty ranks the most well-off countries in terms of labor markets, poverty, safety net, wealth inequality, and economic mobility. The US comes in last of the top 10 most well-off countries, and 18th amongst the top 21.

- In the OECD, the United States ranks 35th out of 37 in terms of poverty and inequality.

- According to the World Income Inequality Database, the United States has the highest Gini rate (measuring inequality) of all Western Countries

- The Stanford Center on Poverty and Inequality characterizes the United States as "a clear and constant outlier in the child poverty league." United States child poverty rates are the highest amongst the six richest countries — Canada, the United Kingdom, Ireland, Sweden, and Norway.

- About 55.7% of the U.S. voting-age population cast ballots in the 2016 presidential election. In the OECD, the United States placed 28th in voter turnout, compared with an OECD average of 75%. Registered voters represent a much smaller share of potential voters in the United States than just about any other OECD country. Only about 64% of the U.S. voting-age population (and 70% of voting-age citizens) was registered in 2016, compared with 91% in Canada (2015) and the UK (2016), 96% in Sweden (2014), and nearly 99% in Japan (2014).

Chapter Three

A History of Poverty
Policy in the United States

A. The Origins and Causes of Poverty

How is it that poverty is part of the experience of millions of people living and working in the United States? There is perhaps no single answer to this question. Just as the discussion of poverty itself involves discussing many discrete topics, including welfare reform, gender bias, access to education, and living wage versus low-wage workforce development. The explanation of poverty is often framed in one of two narratives; poverty results from individual behavior within a fair economic system or poverty is the natural result of how our economic system is structured.

1. The Individual Behavior Argument

The U.S. economy is like no other. The market system creates more wealth for more people than any other system that has ever existed. Most people in the United States have a standard of living that is the envy of the rest of the world. Nearly everyone in the United States has access to adequate housing, food, education, entertainment, travel, and personal safety. Innovation abounds, driven by the incentives provided by the market economy. Personal freedom is enabled through the wealth and exchange that results from a market economy. There are certainly valid concerns with the market economy. There are times of overproduction and resulting corrections that lead to slight increases in unemployment. Externalities are not always adequately captured by producers, leading to losses in other areas like the environment or community. The market also encourages consumption, which may result in poor individual decision making, and creates feelings of desire that are based at times on emotions. But for enabling individual development and social and economic advancement, there is no better system than the market economy. Amartya Sen has argued as much—the advancement of economic exchange in a market system leads to greater individual freedom and economic gain.[1] So then, in such a system, if there is poverty it must be due to either individual behaviors or government systems that enable individual decision making that leads to poverty. In other words, the market system works if it is allowed to.

---

1. Amartya Sen, Development as Freedom (1999).

It is not the market, but government welfare programs that force individual decisions to be made in ways that encourage poverty. There is always work for those who want to work. Unemployment has been at historically low levels for decades. Work of any type leads to skill development, social networks, and individual behavior that can lead to advancing to better jobs with higher wages. Even part-time, low-wage summer employment in high school has lifelong positive impacts on income and stability. The question should be why poverty exists when work is abundant and available. This is in part due to the perverse incentives to not work created by government welfare programs. Individuals make rational decisions about how to use their time. When faced with the choice between work, and the accompanying loss of freedom to spend your time as you please, and not working, many people would choose to not work. When government welfare programs, such as TANF, public housing, and food stamps, provide for your basic human needs, the rational decision would be not to work.[2] Poverty results not from the market, but instead from the influence of government welfare programs that enable individuals to take themselves out of the workforce without any meaningful consequence.

Moreover, the expansion of civil rights laws removed barriers to employment for most groups. Discrimination in the workplace, education, or public accommodation is not only contrary to the idea of a free market, it is also illegal. As these barriers have been removed, economic advancement has increased among previously disenfranchised groups. One most look to the culture of poverty that exists within groups that have higher poverty rates than others.[3] Decision making in such a culture leads to predictable outcomes for families and individuals.

2. The Structural and Systemic Inequalities Argument

Significance differences are found between the opportunities that are available to the poor and those available to the nonpoor in the United States. Historically, the United States was a place of relatively expansive opportunity. Children born into poverty could advance socially and economically through the benefits of an education system that enabled them to enter the workforce with marketable skills or directly through work alone. The growth of the labor movement, the expansion of the industrial economy, the advancement of the civil rights movement and the enhancement of public education at all levels created a widespread path of opportunity for more people. By the 1970s, however, the paths of opportunity began to narrow.[4] Increased economic globalization, which started in the 1970s accelerated throughout the 1980s and 1990s. Wages and savings during these decades stagnated for many low-income

---

2. Lawrence Mead, Government Matters: Welfare Reform in Wisconsin (2004).

3. See, for example, Ruby Payne, A Framework for Understanding Poverty (3d ed. 2003), where Payne described a set of "hidden rules" about poverty.

4. Lane Kenworthy, *It's Hard to Make It in America: How the United States Stopped Being the Land of Opportunity*, Foreign Aff., Nov.–Dec. 2012, at 97, 99–103.

families, even as unemployment levels dropped. Millions of manufacturing jobs, which had enabled millions of families to rise from poverty over the preceding decades, became obsolete. Wages for low-skill workers dropped, while income for workers in skilled or professional positions increased.[5] The resulting gap between the poor and the nonpoor increased steadily during the 1980s and 1990s and then accelerated rapidly into the early twenty-first century, increasing to levels of inequality that have not been seen in the United States in more than a century.[6]

Over the same period when work was reshaped for many low-income families, family life itself underwent significant change. Children living in poor families became increasingly less likely to live with both biological parents. Fewer than 40% of poor children were living with both biological parents as of 2016, less than half the rate for nonpoor children.[7] Living with both biological parents correlate with better school performance, lower crime rates, and higher earnings as an adult, leaving more and more children behind. Moreover, the disparity in wealth and income puts poor children at a further disadvantage compared to the nonpoor, who are able to supplement their children's' educational and development experiences. Nonpoor parents can send their children to higher quality child care and pre-K, in addition to summer camps, athletic camps, music lessons, tutoring, and cultural experiences. Children of the poor lack access to similar resources and must live in the stress of their family's poverty as well.

What results are disparities that remain lifelong challenges. For example, poor children enter kindergarten with deficits across both cognitive and noncognitive skills that remain with them for life.[8] Once in the public school system, poor children are provided with an education that fails to compare in quality to the education provided to nonpoor children. School funding, which relies heavily on local property tax value, causes much of this disparity, but so does an overall shift in public education. During the 1980s through the early 2000s, public schools adopted more punitive discipline schemes, leading to higher expulsion rates for high school and even middle school children. Advanced Placement classes gained prominence, taking resources and skilled teachers away from many standard classrooms and establishing a further barrier for poor children to succeed. As poor children graduate high school in this environment, they are less likely to attend college than children from nonpoor families.[9] The cost of college, however, increased dramatically over the same period.[10] In the 1970s and 1980s, a poor student could afford most public and private colleges through the com-

---

5. Josh Bivens, *Using Standard Models to Benchmark the Costs of Globalization for American Workers without a College Degree*, Econ. Pol'y Inst. (Mar. 22, 2013), https://www.epi.org/publication/standard-models-benchmark-costs-globalization/.

6. *Id.*

7. *Id.*

8. *See, e.g.*, James J. Heckman, Giving Kids a Fair Chance 13–14 (2013).

9. *Id.* at 7–11.

10. Camilo Maldonado, *Price of College Increasing Almost 8 Times Faster Than Wages*, Forbes (Jul. 24, 2018, 8:23 AM), https://www.forbes.com/sites/camilomaldonado/2018/07/24/price-of-college-increasing-almost-8-times-faster-than-wages/#53373e5166c1.

bination of the Pell Grant, summer work, work study, and modest student loans. Tuition increases, however, made this impossible 30 years later.

Entering the job market, these young people find they lack the social networks that often lead to employment and end up locked into low-wage, low-skill jobs that fail to provide more than an opportunity to live paycheck to paycheck.[11] Despite work and effort, the poor are left out with few opportunities and little hope for a better economic future.

B. A Brief History of Anti-Poverty Efforts in the United States

1. Introduction

Poverty has been part of the American experience throughout the history of the United States. United States poverty policies have been shaped by the forces one would expect: specific events, economic restructuring, political and religious ideologies, and social movements. Regardless of differences in specific policies, U.S. poverty policy over time has been driven largely by views of the poor held by the nonpoor. Most often these views rest more on bias and intolerance than on the actual needs of the poor. The history of poverty policy in the United States may be seen as a history of intolerance that is implemented through welfare programs and mandates that attempt to shape individual behavior. Oftentimes, the subclass of the poor is further categorized into those "deserving" and "non-deserving" of societal assistance. Note that the boundaries holding these divisions are dynamic in nature, driven by repressive and ideological state apparatuses;[12] thus, they are detached from an individual's actual need for assistance. These subjective aspects of poverty are built upon to demonstrate the purposiveness of social welfare policies that target the poor while creating mechanisms of profitability for the nonpoor.

Ideology plays a significant role in how society thinks about poverty and those who are poor. The works of the French Marxist philosopher, Louis Althusser, unravels this process—

> This narrative of subjectification was intended to help advance Althusser's argument that regimes or states are able to maintain control by reproducing subjects who believe that their position within the social structure is a natural one. Ideology, or the background ideas that we possess about the way in which the world must function and of how we function within it is, in this account, understood to be always present. Specific socio-economic structures,

---

11. *See, e.g.*, Steven Greenhouse, *Low-Wage Workers Are Finding Poverty Harder to Escape*, N.Y. Times (Mar. 16, 2014), http://www.nytimes.com/2014/03/17/business/economy/low-wage-workers-finding-its-easier-to-fall-into-poverty-and-harder-to-get-out.html.

12. *See* Louis Althusser, *Ideology and Ideological State Apparatuses*, *in* Lenin and Philosophy and Other Essays (1970).

however, require particular ideologies. These ideologies are instantiated by institutions or "Ideological State Apparatuses" like family, schools, church, etc., which provide the developing subject with categories in which she can recognize herself. Inasmuch as a person does so and embraces the practices associated with those institutions, she has been successfully "hailed" or "interpellated" and recognized herself as that subject who does those kinds of things.[13]

In the end, throughout every era, poverty policy becomes more about what the nonpoor think about the poor, than about the desire to enable human capacity or development. Ultimately, the history of poverty policy in the United States is a history of enabling one group, the nonpoor, to act on another, the poor, through the state apparatus of welfare programs that shape individual behavior.

a. Poverty and Citizenship in the Early United States

During the Colonial Era, poverty was largely seen as the result of individual behavior, in contrast to structural economic or social conditions. The cause of poverty, and therefore the response, lay in addressing individual behavior that was believed to lead to poverty and need.[14] Early colonial legislation reflects such a perspective, as well as the belief that individual behavior can be addressed through punitive acts and sanctions that force people to act in productive ways.[15] Early sanctions on the poor included forced work and imprisonment, and anti-poverty measures were included in the first laws enacted by the First General Assembly of Virginia in 1619:

> By this present General Assembly be it enacted that ... Against idleness, gaming, drunkenness, and excess in apparel the assembly has enacted as follows.

> First, in detestation of idlers, be it enacted that if any man be found to live as an idler or renegade, though a freed man, it shall be lawful for that incorporation or plantation to which he belongs to appoint him a master to serve for wages till he shows apparent signs of amendment.[16]

In 1633, the General Court of Massachusetts allowed "idlers" to be arrested and brought before the magistrate who was empowered to force the idler to labor or the paying of a fine.[17] Idlers would simply not be tolerated.

---

13. William Lewis, *Louis Althusser*, Stanford Encyclopedia of Philosophy (2018), https://plato.stanford.edu/entries/althusser/ (last accessed April 19, 2018).

14. Michale Katz, *The Urban Underclass*, *in* The "Underclass" Debate: Views from History 3–23 (Princeton University Press, 1993).

15. For more information on colonial legislation regarding the poor, see John E. Hansan, Social Welfare History Project, Poor Relief in Early America (2011), https://socialwelfare.library.vcu.edu/programs/poor-relief-early-amer/ (last accessed April 19, 2018).

16. H.R. McIlwaine & John P. Kennedy (eds.), Journals of the House of Burgesses of Virginia, vol. 1, at 9–14 (1905).

17. Studies in History, Economics, and Public Law, Vol. 3 (2015).

Consistent with this, in the years following the Revolutionary War, poverty policy focused largely on forcing the poor into work, but other laws worked together with these laws to restrict equal access to the vote and political representation. Prior to the Revolution, nearly all colonies had adopted laws that denied the right to vote to individuals who owned no property.[18] Such voting restrictions were explained by their supporters, who argued that those without property lacked the ability to act as free agents, the propertyless were beholden to others, and therefore could be expected to vote at someone else's direction.

The diminishment of political rights among the poor may be seen as an anachronism in the context of the expanding democracy of the United States, but it is also a continuation of a peculiar view of political agency. In the seventeenth and eighteenth centuries in the United States, property ownership was explicitly bound to the idea of citizenship and social life. Those who did not have property were relegated to a lesser degree of citizenship and were, perhaps more significantly, relegated to a lesser form of personhood. Legislators at both the federal and state levels adopted poor laws during the time between 1790 and 1830, with some common policies and requirements for the poor.

b. Early Public Poor Relief

Public poor relief systems first emerged in the United States during the 1790s. These systems were enacted and maintained by local or state governments and provided limited assistance to those individuals, mostly widowed women and orphaned children, who were seem as deserving of public assistance. By the 1840s, most states had enacted some method for providing public relief to the poor, although none of these methods involved direct cash or food assistance to the nonworking poor. Acceptable methods of poor relief during this time period included: providing assistance to the poor in their homes; hiring caretakers for the poor through a lowest-bidder method; placing poor children into apprenticeships; building poorhouses or poorfarms where the poor would live and be placed in work; jailing the poor and forced work; and contracting out the care of the poor to contractors who would themselves develop a way to provide for them.[19]

• Home assistance

Many, perhaps most, states enacted laws enabling poor assistance to be provided to poor families in their own homes. Usually a general grant of authority was provided by the state legislature to provide the poor with assistance — including housing, medical care, and other life necessities. Because the poor remained in their own homes and were not required to come into a poorhouse or poor farm to access the relief,

---

18. Robert J. Steinfeld, *Property and Suffrage in the Early American Republic*, 41 Stan. L. Rev. 335, 339–342 (Jan. 1989).

19. Prof. Quigley provides an exhaustive historical account of early poverty law in William P. Quigley, *The Quicksands of the Poor Law: Poor Relief Legislation in a Growing Nation, 1790–1820*, 18 N. Ill. U. L. Rev. 1, 61–75 (1997). The following history draws from Quigley's text.

this type of assistance is often called "outdoor relief," referencing the houses and farms. Assistance that was available to the poor only once the entered the poorhouse is often called "indoor relief" in contrast. Many of the types of assistance available to the poor at the state level prior to the Civil War continue to be provided, only in different forms, including; waiver of taxes and licensing fee (Tennessee), *in forma pauperis* access to the courts (Tennessee, Kentucky, and Indiana) and medical care (Alabama, Illinois, Indiana, Kentucky, and Mississippi).

• **Apprenticeship of poor children**[20]

Poor children were commonly hired out into apprenticeships, where they were to work until attaining adulthood. Under this arrangement, the child's care and support was paid by the party to whom the child was apprenticed in exchange for all of the child's labor. Apprenticeships of poor children had become the traditional method for caring for the poor in England, and was made part of the social safety net in the United States as well. Apprenticeships could be voluntary or involuntary under most state laws. Voluntary apprenticeships included the parent's consent, or that of the child if they had reached the age of consent in some states. Involuntary apprenticeships could occur if the child were orphaned or the child's family sought poor relief or were found to be inadequate caretakers.

• **Contracting out poor relief**[21]

A variation of the forced work requirements in the colonies is found in the public contracting methods for placing the poor in private work in many states during this time. In the states and territories that contracted out the poor, a public overseer was appointed to care for the poor. These private parties would bid among themselves to provide care to the poor, with the contract awarded to the lowest bidder. The contractor who accepted the work would then take on the task of providing for the poor, and had the power to put the poor to work as well. Contracting out the poor served to force the poor into labor, as had been done in the past, but without state administrative involvement.

• **Poorhouses**[22]

Many states, particularly states in the Northeast, built and ran poorhouses. Also called almshouses or workhouses, poorhouses were administered by local governments and provided what is known as "indoor relief"—assistance that could only be accessed by the poor once the poor were inside the poorhouse. Poorhouses enabled policy makers to accomplish several goals. Relief was provided in a controlled setting that allowed costs to be managed. Poorhouses forced the poor to work and controlled nonwork hours, enabling the state to discourage behaviors such as drinking or what was seen as laziness. The presence of the poorhouse also served to encourage work effort; one could be placed in the poorhouse by force due to diminished work effort.

---

20. *Id.*
21. *Id.*
22. *Id.*

By the start of the nineteenth century, poverty policy thus served to reinforce distinctions along economic lines that ultimately shape the individual's ability to live equal to all others in the community. From the 1830s to the 1890s, a new paradigm regarding poverty emerged in the United States.

c. Teaching the Poor to Help Themselves[23]

The end of the nineteenth century poverty policy had begun to move toward efforts to help the poor avoid poverty and improve their lives.

2. 1890s–1920s: Progressive Era

During the Progressive Era, an awareness of the needs of working families and the poor began to emerge in public opinion. Progressives saw a role for regulatory reform, believing that regulatory intervention could address poverty by improving working conditions and ending deprivation for millions of Americans.[24] The notion of poverty as the result of economic conditions, instead of individual moral failings and Social Darwinism, emerged during the Progressive Era.[25] Within this construct, poverty was seen as resulting from economic and social conditions that limited access to employment or provided employment on unfair terms. Government, therefore, could play a significant role in addressing such problems, while grassroots advocates played a crucial role in shaping and directing that regulatory policy.[26]

Academic and political leaders, including Jane Addams,[27] George Mead,[28] Paul Douglas,[29] and John Dewey[30] led efforts to turn government toward a common commitment focused on active, moral engagement. These individuals viewed economic and political institutions as having been corrupted by forces that were in need of constraint through elimination of corruption. These newfound beliefs coincided with the adoption of antitrust laws, which were put into place to regulate businesses to promote fair competition.

The social welfare consequence of the Progressive movement was great in three areas: prevention through "social insurance," the use of government regulation, and

---

23. *Id.*

24. *See* SOCIAL WELFARE HISTORY PROJECT, THE PROGRESSIVE ERA (2017), https://socialwelfare. library.vcu.edu/eras/civil-war-reconstruction/progressive-era/ (last accessed April 19, 2018).

25. *Id.*

26. *Id.*

27. *See Jane Addams: The Nobel Peace Prize 1931,* NOBEL PRIZES AND LAUREATES, https://www. nobelprize.org/nobel_prizes/peace/laureates/1931/addams-bio.html (last accessed April 19, 2018).

28. *See George Herbert Mead,* INTERNET ENCYC. OF PHIL., https://www.iep.utm.edu/mead/ (last accessed April 19, 2018).

29. *See* Jonathan Bell, *The Changing Dynamics of American Liberalism: Paul Douglas and the Elections of 1948,* 96 J. ILL. STATE HIST. SOC. (Winter 2004).

30. *See John Dewey,* INTERNET ENCYC. OF PHIL., http://www.iep.utm.edu/dewey/ (last accessed April 19, 2018).

the role of professions in society.[31] The programs put into place through Progressive pressure established a social welfare presence in every state and set into motion the steady expansion of public welfare programs, benefits, and recipients—an expansion that would set the stage for the federal government's assumption of funding for state programs and the development of a genuine social insurance system nationally.[32]

Established during this era were the Interstate Commerce Commission, antitrust regulation, civil service and merit system requirements for employment, the Federal Trade Commission, banking regulation, and the Food and Drug Administration.[33] At the state and local levels, regulatory advances included the areas of child and women's labor, wages, housing and fire codes, public health, food processing, merit employment requirements, property zoning, and many political reforms, including referendum and recall. Child labor, women's suffrage, immigration, and temperance were all major national issues and attracted the involvement of many prominent social workers.[34] The extension of suffrage to women occurred in 1919, as did the passage of another constitutional amendment to prohibit the manufacture, sale, importation, and consumption of alcohol.[35] Prohibition was promoted by its supporters as a social welfare policy that would protect women and children and promote employment and productivity.[36] Likewise, immigration controls passed in 1921 were promoted not as nativism, but as rational planning for improved wages and working conditions, and the stabilization of cities.[37] As can be noted from all of these advances, the Progressive era oversaw the rise of social activism.

3. Early Twentieth Century: The Depression and the Rise of the Welfare State

a. The New Deal

Between 1929 and 1933, the number of people living in poverty in the United States increased dramatically with unemployment levels reached nearly 25% of the

---

31. *See* Soc. Sec'y. Admin., *The Evolution of Medicare: The First Round—1912 to 1920*, https://www.ssa.gov/history/corningchap1.html (last accessed April 19, 2018).

32. *See* Theda Skocpol, *State Formation and Social Policy in the United States*, 35 Am. Behav. Sci. 559 (1992).

33. *See* Ronald Pestritto, *The Birth of the Administrative State: Where It Came From and What It Means for Limited Government*, The Heritage Found. (Nov. 20, 2007), https://www.heritage.org/political-process/report/the-birth-the-administrative-state-where-it-came-and-what-it-means-limited (last accessed April 19, 2018).

34. *See Reform Movements of the Progressive Era*, The Gilder Lehrman Inst. of Am. Hist., https://www.gilderlehrman.org/content/infographic-reform-movements-progressive-era (last accessed April 19, 2018).

35. *See Prohibition, United States History*, 1920–193, Encyc. Britannica, https://www.britannica.com/event/Prohibition-United-States-history- (last accessed April 19, 2018).

36. *Id.*

37. The Emergency Quota Act of 1921, Pub. L. 67-5 (May 19, 1921).

workforce and remained at exceptionally high levels until the start of World War II.[38] In 1933, to deal with the immediate effects of the economic crisis, President Roosevelt established the Federal Emergency Relief Administration (FERA), headed by Harry Hopkins, a social worker whom he had used in New York State in a similar capacity.[39] FERA provided direct cash funds and administrative directives to states for the purpose of providing relief to unemployed workers.[40] Numerous work programs, including the Works Progress Administration and the Civilian Conservation Corps, were launched by FERA. These programs put more than 300,000 people to work by the middle of the decade and became the principle means of providing assistance to un-employed workers.[41] Economic reform was also part of the overall strategy, and in-cluded the National Recovery Act, with its codes for industry that sought to establish wage and price controls and to ensure labor rights in a "planned economy," and the Agricultural Adjustment Act, which sought to reform the agricultural side of the economy through allotments for farm production and the stabilization of market prices.[42] Both acts had substantial political effect and helped to shape later New Deal social policies.[43] In many ways, the federal government's response to the Great De-pression laid the foundation for the federal government's increased role in directing poverty policy in partnership with state agencies.

b. Social Security

In 1934, the Roosevelt administration moved to develop a more dramatic and long-term program for social reform, including a new program for individual eco-nomic security, which was begun with the appointment of a Committee on Social Security in June 1934, leading to passage of the Social Security Act in January 1935.[44] The Social Security Act is the basic document of the American social welfare system. It establishes a federal social insurance system for old age, unemployment, disability, and a state-federal public assistance system, including aid for dependent children and for needy elderly and disabled persons.[45] In addition, the act established a system of federal grants to states in related social services areas.[46] To the Social Security system must be added the Wagner Act, which substantially increased the rights of organized labor;[47] the Fair Labor Standards Act, which regulated wages and hours;

---

38. Richard H. Pells & Christina D. Romer, *Great Depression Economy*, ENCYC. BRITANNICA (Oct. 16, 2019), https://www.britannica.com/event/Great-Depression.

39. *See* WILLIAM E. LEUCHTENBURG, UVA MILLER CENTER, FRANKLIN D. ROOSEVELT: DOMESTIC AFFAIRS (2017), https://millercenter.org/president/fdroosevelt/domestic-affairs (last accessed April 19, 2018).

40. *Id.*

41. *Id.*

42. *Id.*

43. *See* A.L.A. Schechter Poultry Corporation v. U.S., 295 U.S. 495 (1935); *see also* U.S. v. Butler, 297 U.S. 1 (1936).

44. LEUCHTENBURG, *supra* note 39.

45. The Social Security Act, Pub. L. 74-271 (1935).

46. *Id.*

47. The Wagner Act, Pub. L. 74-198 (1935).

and a collection of programs in vocational rehabilitation, public health, housing, and child welfare.[48]

4. The Mid-Twentieth Century and the War on Poverty

Despite the broad reach of the New Deal programs, poverty remained a persistent concern in America following World War II and the Korean Conflict. During the first years of the 1960s, poverty rates remained above 19% overall, with poverty reaching more than 50% of the African American population.[49] As Lyndon B. Johnson considered his priorities following his election in 1964, poverty policy became a significant part of his administration's agenda. On January 20, 1965, as part of his inaugural address, which is excerpted below, President Johnson articulated the underpinnings for a group of policies that would collectively be known as the "War on Poverty."

INAUGURAL ADDRESS OF LYNDON BAINES JOHNSON

Wednesday, January 20, 1965[50]

My fellow countrymen, on this occasion, the oath I have taken before you and before God is not mine alone, but ours together. We are one nation and one people. Our fate as a nation and our future as a people rest not upon one citizen, but upon all citizens.

This is the majesty and the meaning of this moment.

For every generation, there is a destiny. For some, history decides. For this generation, the choice must be our own. Even now, a rocket moves toward Mars. It reminds us that the world will not be the same for our children, or even for ourselves m a short span of years. The next man to stand here will look out on a scene different from our own, because ours is a time of change—rapid and fantastic change bearing the secrets of nature, multiplying the nations, placing in uncertain hands new weapons for mastery and destruction, shaking old values, and uprooting old ways. Our destiny in the midst of change will rest on the unchanged character of our people, and on their faith.

The American Covenant

They came here—the exile and the stranger, brave but frightened—to find a place where a man could be his own man. They made a covenant with this land. Conceived in justice, written in liberty, bound in union, it was meant one day to inspire the hopes of all mankind; and it binds us still. If we keep its terms, we shall flourish.

---

48. The Fair Labor Standards Act, Pub. L. 75-718 (1938).

49. *See Poverty in the United States 1959–1968,* CURRENT POPULATION REPORTS (Dec. 31, 1969), https://www.census.gov/library/publications/1969/demo/p60-68.html (last accessed April 20, 2018).

50. Lyndon Baines Johnson, Inaugural Address (Jan. 20, 1965).

Justice and Change

First, justice was the promise that all who made the journey would share in the fruits of the land. In a land of great wealth, families must not live in hopeless poverty. In a land rich in harvest, children just must not go hungry. In a land of healing miracles, neighbors must not suffer and die unattended. In a great land of learning and scholars, young people must be taught to read and write.

For the more than 30 years that I have served this Nation, I have believed that this injustice to our people, this waste of our resources, was our real enemy. For 30 years or more, with the resources I have had, I have vigilantly fought against it. I have learned, and I know, that it will not surrender easily.

But change has given us new weapons. Before this generation of Americans is finished, this enemy will not only retreat—it will be conquered. Justice requires us to remember that when any citizen denies his fellow, saying, "His color is not mine," or "His beliefs are strange and different," in that moment he betrays America, though his forebears created this Nation.

Between 1964 and 1965, the Johnson administration launched an astonishing number of significant anti-poverty programs, including the following: the Foodstamps Act of 1964,[51] which expanded access to the Foodstamps program; the Economic Opportunity Act of 1964,[52] which established the Community Action Program, Job Corps and VISTA; The Social Security Act of 1965,[53] which established Medicaid; and the Elementary and Secondary Education Act of 1965,[54] which launched Headstart and the community college system. Across the breadth of these initiatives can be found the common belief that the voice of the local community and those being served by federal policy should be incorporated into the decision-making process. "[T]he hallmark of the Great Society ... was the direct relationship between the national government and the ghettoes, a relationship in which both state and local governments were undercut."[55]

Driven by a belief in the role of the federal government in addressing poverty, the Johnson Administration positioned itself as a force for change that began at the local, grassroots level and that was supported with resources and capacity of the federal government and its agencies.[56] The Community Action Program dramatically reflects how fundamental a change was brought about by the War on Poverty programs.[57]

---

51. The Food Stamp Act, Pub. L. 88-525 (1964).

52. The Economic Opportunity Act, Pub. L. 88-452 (1964).

53. The Social Security Amendments of 1965, Pub. L. 89-97 (1965).

54. The Elementary and Secondary Education Act, Pub. L. 89-10 (1965).

55. Francis Fox Piven & Richard A. Cloward, Regulating the Poor: The Functions of Public Welfare 261 (1971) (emphasis omitted).

56. *See* Kent Germany, UVA Miller Center, Lyndon B. Johnson: Domestic Affairs, https://millercenter.org/president/lbjohnson/domestic-affairs (last accessed April 20, 2018).

57. *Id.*

The Economic Opportunity Act and its Community Action Program set "maximum feasible participation" by the poor as a goal for implementing policy at all levels.[58] While looking back on his time as President, Lyndon B. Johnson described the Community Action Program as a plan that had "the sound of something brand new and even faintly radical. Actually, it was based on one of the oldest ideas of our democracy … self-determination at the local level."[59] The mandated participation requirements contained in the Economic Opportunity Act were a completely new direction for poverty policy in the United States.[60] By including participation requirements, the Economic Opportunity Act intended to lift the political voice of the poor, establishing a greater democratic sense in the process, and in stark contrast to more than 200 years of poverty policy, promote the inclusion of those who are served by anti-poverty efforts in determining the most effective and impactful strategy for addressing poverty.[61] Contained in Section 202(a)(3) of the Economic Opportunity Act, federal mandates for political participation by the poor, challenged the status quo in communities across the United States.[62]

5. The Welfare Debate: Poverty Policy Since the 1980s

Community action efforts and maximum public participation by the poor were short-lived strategies. By the early 1970s the maximum participation mandate had been abandoned by federal policy makers.[63] A few years later, mainstream discussion of poverty and the appropriate response returned to a narrative that focused largely on the individual and individual shortcomings. At times polemical and rarely focused on the need for systemically addressing the causes of poverty, consideration of poverty policy once again focused largely on individual behavior and the role of "culture" in maintaining poverty.[64] Public policy debate rarely considered the economic and social conditions that result in poverty.

The return to what has become the traditional narrative on poverty in the United States was highlighted during the 1980 president campaign of then-Governor Ronald Reagan.[65] As governor of California, Reagan initiated several efforts to scale back or

---

58. The Economic Opportunity Act, Pub. L. 88-452 (1964).

59. George Adler, *Community Action and Maximum Feasible Participation: An Opportunity Lost but Not Forgotten for Expanding Democracy at Home*, 8 NOTRE DAME J.L. ETHICS & PUB. POL'Y 547, 547 (1994).

60. *Id.*

61. *Participation of the Poor: Section 202(a)(3) Organizations Under the Economic Opportunity Act of 1964*, 75 YALE L. J. 599, 599–602 (1966).

62. *Id.* at §202(a)(3).

63. JERRY D. MARX, VCU SOC. WELFARE HIST. PROJECT, AMERICAN SOCIAL POLICY IN THE 1960's AND 1970's (2011), https://socialwelfare.library.vcu.edu/war-on-poverty/american-social-policy-in-the-60s-and-70s/.

64. *Id.*

65. *See* Gene Demby, *The Truth Behind the Lies of the Original Welfare Queen*, NPR (Dec. 20, 2013), https://www.npr.org/sections/codeswitch/2013/12/20/255819681/the-truth-behind-the-lies-

eliminate programs serving the poor.[66] Frequently, these efforts were framed in a narrative of the undeserving poor or, going further, the fraudulent acts of some individuals who blatantly took advantage of government assistance programs. Reagan is often credited with coining the term "welfare queen" due to his repeated telling of the story of Linda Taylor, a Chicago woman who fraudulently obtained AFDC benefits for several years.[67] Reagan made a simple and clear point during his presidential campaigns in 1976 and 1980 that poor people were taking advantage of a broken welfare system at the expense of the middle class.[68] Late in his 1980 Presidential campaign, Reagan highlighted his work as governor in California, stating that he had worked "closely with the legislature in constructing a welfare program that put cheaters off the rolls, reducing them by 350,000, while it increased benefits to the truly needy,"[69] a strategy he offered to bring to the federal government when elected. Once in office, President Reagan worked to dismantle the existing welfare system and shift to the poor more responsibility for work and moving to financial self-sufficiency.

Reagan sought to radically change the welfare system during his first term as president and called, in his 1986 State of the Union address, for broad waivers from federal AFDC requirements for every state.[70] Under the waiver program, states were given room to develop policies aimed at moving families off welfare and into the workforce. Wisconsin took the lead with waiver programs that capped benefit levels, tied benefits to school or work preparedness and incentivized family formation.[71] While the waiver program expanded following Reagan's leadership on the issue, federal welfare policy remained largely intact for the next 10 years.

In 1992 Bill Clinton entered the White House promising to "end welfare as we know it."[72] Clinton's remarks suggest two things. First, that he would in fact alter the federal government-centered welfare policies of the previous five decades. Reform would occur on administrative levels as well as in the area of policy mechanics. Administratively, Clinton promoted greater state autonomy and independence from

---

of-the-original-welfare-queen (referencing the many Ronald Reagan campaign speeches concentrated on the "welfare queen").

66. *See* David E. Keefe, *Governor Reagan, Welfare Reform, and AFDC Fertility,* 57 Soc. Serv. Rev. 234, 234 (Jun., 1983).

67. John Levin, *The Welfare Queen,* SLATE (Dec. 19, 2013), http://www.slate.com/articles/news_and_politics/history/2013/12/linda_taylor_welfare_queen_ronald_reagan_made_her_a_notorious_american_villain.html.

68. *See* Ronald Reagan, *A Vision for America* (Nov. 3, 1980).

69. *Id.*

70. *See Ronald Reagan: Address Before a Joint Session of Congress on the State of the Union,* The Am. Pres. Project (Feb. 4, 1986), http://www.presidency.ucsb.edu/ws/index.php?pid=36646.

71. *See* John Pawasarat & Lois M Quinn, *Wisconsin Welfare Employment Experiments: An Evaluation of the WEJT and CWEP Programs,* Emp. and Training Inst. U. of Wis. (Sept. 1993), https://www4.uwm.edu/eti/reprints/WEJT2.pdf (last accessed April 20, 2018).

72. *See* Jason Deparle, *From Pledge to Plan: The Campaign to End Welfare,* N.Y. Times (1994), https://www.nytimes.com/1994/07/15/us/pledge-plan-campaign-end-welfare-special-report-clinton-welfare-bill-long-stormy.html.

centralized policies.[73] In many ways, this was the realization of President Reagan's focus on waivers. The mechanics themselves were also altered as the role of welfare shifted to ending "dependency" through work preparation and proposals to "make work pay."[74] The second thing suggested by Clinton's language is that there was a general consensus on the need to make changes to welfare. The presentation of the need for welfare reform as a keystone issue for President Clinton signaled to the U.S. public that welfare was flawed and specifically challenged due to the dependency that the programs were said to promote. With one phrase, President Clinton both promised reform for a better poverty policy, and also reinforced the public view of the poor as dependent and separate from the nonpoor.

Clinton's pledge to "end welfare as we know it" appealed to conservative lawmakers who had previously sought welfare proposals for such things as time limits on benefits, family cap, school attendance incentives, and penalties for having children outside of marriage.[75] As the discussion of welfare reform focused more heavily on these types of behavior modification efforts, the rhetoric of welfare reform subtly took on the role of blaming the poor for their own situation.

President Clinton's promise to end "welfare as we know it" assumed that there was a common starting point regarding what welfare is and how poor people interact with it. What do most Americans really "know" about welfare at all? For many Americans, their idea of welfare is shaped by beliefs about poverty and its causes, as well as the moral values they apply to individual behavior of the poor.[76] In the public discourse, the rhetoric surrounding welfare policy is reduced to considering individual behavior and the idea of "welfare dependency."[77] Public discourse regularly suggests that poverty is self-inflicted and that receiving welfare benefits leads to continuing poverty, instead of alleviating need at all. What most Americans refer to when they use the term "welfare," is only one part of a larger system of social provision, meaning cash assistance to the poor. The central role of cash benefit welfare programs for the poor in the United States has been to reinforce broadly held distinctions about who is deserving of assistance. In many instances during the history of poverty policy in the United States, who is deserving of public assis-

---

73. *See* Frances X. Clines, *Clinton Signs Bill Cutting Welfare; States In New Role*, N.Y. Times (Aug. 23, 1996), https://www.nytimes.com/1996/08/23/us/clinton-signs-bill-cutting-welfare-states-in-new-role.html.

74. *See* Ron Haskins, Brookings Inst., Making Work Pay—Again (Sept. 15, 2008), https://www.brookings.edu/research/making-work-pay-again/.

75. *See* Barbara Vobejda, *Clinton Signs Welfare Bill Amid Division*, Wash. Post (Aug. 23, 1996) (reporting on the Clinton's welfare bill and stating that "Republican presidential nominee Robert J. Dole praised the bill and said it would be remembered as a Republican victory"), http://www.washingtonpost.com/wp-srv/politics/special/welfare/stories/wf082396.htm.

76. *See, e.g.*, Jason Le Miere, *Why Are People Poor? Because They Are Lazy, Say Almost Half of Christians in the U.S.*, Newsweek (Aug. 3, 2018), http://www.newsweek.com/why-are-people-poor-lazy-646062.

77. *See On the Issues*, http://www.ontheissues.org/Welfare_+_Poverty.htm (last accessed April 20, 2018) (the 2016 presidential candidates on issues of poverty and welfare).

tance is often decided based on race, gender, personal behavior, or family status. In short, welfare policy reflects societal bias that burdens some at the benefit of others.[78]

6. Poverty Policy Today—
Welfare Reform 2.0

The years following the 2016 election promise to be active around welfare policy. The Republican candidate provided few details on welfare policy during the campaign, but other candidates in his party did and it is likely that these proposals will shape policy and create an even further reduced role for the federal government.[79] For example, Congressman Paul Ryan introduced his "Expanding Opportunity in America" proposal in July 2014.[80] Core to the proposal is the consolidation of more than $700 billion annual spending for anti-poverty programs into "Opportunity Block Grants" that will be made available for states to use to fund a series of anti-poverty efforts.[81] In addition to the shift to a block grant program, the proposal would increase the work requirement and expand access to the EITC.[82] Mr. Ryan once again described welfare as a temporary assistance program limited to the working poor: "Hardworking taxpayers deserve a break in this country. Too many people are working hard to get ahead, and yet they're falling further behind. We have an obligation to expand opportunity in this country—to deliver real change and real results. In that spirit, this proposal, Expanding Opportunity in America, offers a number of commonsense ideas to help working families get ahead."[83] Ryan's plan proposed expanded access to the Earned Income Tax Credit, expanded state control over higher education, criminal justice reform and, perhaps unexpectedly, regulation reform in the energy sector.[84]

On April 10, 2018, President Donald Trump signed an Executive Order that seeks to reform the nation's welfare policies.[85] In the Order, Trump describes the current welfare system as set of policies that have "delayed economic independence, perpetuated poverty, and weakened family bonds."[86] The Order emphasizes the fact that the federal government has "spent more than $700 billion on low-income assistance ... [and] the welfare system has grown into a large bureaucracy that might be susceptible to measuring success how many people are enrolled in a program rather than by how

---

78. *See* Matthew O. Hunt & Heather E. Bullock, *Ideologies and Beliefs about Poverty*, THE OXFORD HANDBOOK OF THE SOC. SCI. OF POV. (May 2016), http://www.oxfordhandbooks.com/view/10.1093/oxfordhb/9780199914050.001.0001/oxfordhb-9780199914050-e-6 (last accessed April 20, 2018).

79. *On the Issues, supra* note 77.

80. *See* NAT'L COUNCIL OF STATE HOUSING AGENCIES, EXPANDING OPPORTUNITY IN AMERICA: A DISCUSSION DRAFT FROM THE HOUSE BUDGET COMMITTEE (July 24, 2014), https://www.ncsha.org/blog/house-budget-committee-chair-releases-proposal-to-reform-federal-anti-poverty-programs/.

81. *Id.*

82. *Id.*

83. NAT'L COUNCIL OF STATE HOUSING AGENCIES, *supra* note 80.

84. *Id.*

85. Exec. Order No. 13828, 83 FR 15941 (2018).

86. *Id.*

many have moved from poverty into financial independence."[87] The Order's main objective is to create a stronger tie between welfare and work. The Order directs federal agencies to enforce the work requirements that are already required by law and to increase the work requirements for individuals who receive benefits from government assistance programs.[88] The Order also commands federal agencies to abide by the nine "Principles of Economic Mobility," a list that includes ideas such as reducing the size of bureaucracy, reserving benefits for individuals with low income, and reducing wasteful spending by eliminating duplicative programs.[89] The Order has no immediate effect, and only time will tell what agencies will do in accordance with this new set of instructions.

---

87. *Id.*
88. *Id.*
89. *Id.*

Chapter Four

The Anomaly of Poverty Law

"… the intractable economic, social, and even philosophical problems presented by public welfare assistance programs are not the business of this Court."

Supreme Court of the United States,
Dandridge v. Williams

A. Introduction

Poverty in the United States is defined and measured almost exclusively along income lines. Ostensibly morally neutral, numerous social and political considerations in fact underlie the use of an income measure of poverty. For example, determining the appropriate standard of living for someone who is considered "poor" involves decisions about what is necessary to live and what is a luxury. Similarly, requiring work effort implicates feelings about leisure and deservedness. Ultimately, while definitions of poverty center on economics, poverty is never divorced of the distinctly sociopolitical dimensions that surround it and that stem from the process of determining what an individual or family needs to survive and whether a person "deserves" to be poor.

Although discussed in the context of economics and income, the measure and definition of poverty and enabling of poverty policy in the United States occurs through laws and regulations, beginning with the Federal Poverty Standard and the Federal Poverty Measure, which serve as integral parts of policy at all levels. For the nonpoor, laws are seen as neutral enablers of societal goals. For the poor, however, laws may be seen as an effort to shape the most intimate aspects of life. For those living in poverty, the law becomes a system of control. As one person described the experience, "For me the law is all over. I am caught, you know; there is always some rule that I'm supposed to follow, some rule I don't even know about that they say. It's just different and you can't really understand."[1]

The feeling that the law is "all-over" reflects what may be an underlying distinction about quality of life. Being poor in the United States carries with it significant distinctions that affect individual life and liberty. The poor encounter the law as they engage the agencies and systems that have been put in place to alleviate the effects of poverty. In contrast to the nonpoor, who may be seen as having limited contact

---

1. Austin Sarat, "… *The Law Is All Over*": *Power, Resistance and the Legal Consciousness of the Welfare Poor* 2 YALE J. L. & THE HUMAN. Art. 6 (1990).

with legal structures, the poor must navigate a legal environment that intends to shape individual behavior at a very intimate level. Would it then be reasonable to assume that government actions directed to the poor should be reviewed by the courts with a heightened degree of criticism or review? The Supreme Court has said "No" — the U.S. Constitution is said to be "neutral" on economic matters, including poverty. In *Dandridge v. Williams*, the Court carved such matters out from judicial constitutional review, establishing that the Constitution expresses neither hostility nor preference for an individual solely based upon their economic status and enabling broad government action when it is directed to the poor.

The notion of neutrality of the law as applied to the poor is challenged, however, by the real differences between the poor and nonpoor in education, housing, safety, personal liberty, or asset development. In these areas the poor live in a world with distinctly different and fewer prospects than the nonpoor and in a place where the law serves as a mechanism for control. As early as 1619, the poor were regulated through state laws that subjected individuals to forced work, imprisonment and exclusion. And while history has moved away from forced labor, laws still subject the most intimate aspects of individual and family life to interference through state intrusion. Both public and private laws have developed in ways that reflect substantive differences between what the poor may expect from the rule of law in comparison to what the nonpoor receive. Consequently, poverty in the United States may be seen as existing within a framework that provides a different, less than equal, set of individual protections for those who are poor. While the nonpoor live in a liberal legal framework, the poor confront a context of rules that first move away from being grounded in constitutional protections and then toward efforts to shape individual behavior at the most personal levels.

B. The Supreme Court Carve Out for Social and Economic Legislation

Poverty policy is engaged through laws such as TANF, SNAP, and Section 8. In *Dandridge v. Williams* (1970), the Supreme Court considered an equal protection challenge to how Maryland administered its welfare program, and in particular how the state of Maryland computed the "standard of need" for families.

Dandridge v. Williams
397 U.S. 471 (1970)

This case involves the validity of a method used by Maryland, in the administration of an aspect of its public welfare program, to reconcile the demands of its needy citizens with the finite resources available to meet those demands. Like every other State in the Union, Maryland participates in the Federal Aid to Families with Dependent Children (AFDC program, 42 U.S.C. § 601 et seq., which originated with the Social Security Act of 1935. Under this jointly financed program, a State computes the so-called 'standard of need' of each eligible family unit within its borders. Some States provide that every family shall receive grants sufficient to meet fully the determined standard of need. Other States provide that each family unit shall receive a percentage of the determined need. Still others provide grants to most families in full accord with the ascertained standard of need, but impose an upper limit on the total amount of money any one family unit may receive. Maryland, through administrative adoption of a 'maximum grant regulation,' has followed this last course. This suit was brought by several AFDC recipients to enjoin the application of the Maryland maximum grant regulation on the ground that it is in conflict with the Social Security Act of 1935 and with the Equal Protection Clause of the Fourteenth Amendment. A three-judge District Court, convened pursuant, held that the Maryland regulation violates the Equal Protection Clause. This direct appeal followed.

The operation of the Maryland welfare system is not complex. By statute the State participates in the AFDC program. It computes the standard of need for each eligible family based on the number of children in the family and the circumstances under which the family lives. In general, the standard of need increases with each additional person in the household, but the increments become proportionately smaller. The regulation here in issue imposes upon the grant that any single family may receive an upper limit of $250 per month in certain counties and Baltimore City, and of $240 per month elsewhere in the State. The appellees all have large families, so that their standards of need as computed by the State substantially exceed the maximum grants that they actually receive under the regulation. The appellees urged in the District Court that the maximum grant limitation operates to discriminate against them merely because of the size of their families, in violation of the Equal Protection Clause of the Fourteenth Amendment. They claimed further that the regulation is incompatible with the purpose of the Social Security Act of 1935, as well as in conflict with its explicit provisions.

In its original opinion the District Court held that the Maryland regulation does conflict with the federal statute, and also concluded that it violates the Fourteenth Amendment's equal protection guarantee. After reconsideration on motion, the court issued a new opinion resting its determination of the regulation's invalidity entirely on the constitutional ground. Both the statutory and constitutional issues have been fully briefed and argued here, and the judgment of the District Court must, of course, be affirmed if the Maryland regulation is in conflict with either the federal statute or the Constitution. We consider the statutory question first, because if the appellees' position on this question is correct, there is no occasion to reach the constitutional issues.

I

[Note—in Part 1, the Court considered whether Maryland's maximum grant system was contrary to section 402(a)(10) of the Social Security Act, as amended, which requires that a state plan shall "provide … that all individuals wishing to make application for aid to families with dependent children shall have opportunity to do so, and that aid to families with dependent children shall be furnished with reasonable promptness to all eligible individuals." The Court determined the Maryland system was not contrary to the Act.]

II

Although a State may adopt a maximum grant system in allocating its funds available for AFDC payments without violating the Act, it may not, of course, impose a regime of invidious discrimination in violation of the Equal Protection Clause of the Fourteenth Amendment. Maryland says that its maximum grant regulation is wholly free of any invidiously discriminatory purpose or effect, and that the regulation is rationally supportable on at least four entirely valid grounds. The regulation can be clearly justified, Maryland argues, in terms of legitimate state interests in encouraging gainful employment, in maintaining an equitable balance in economic status as between welfare families and those supported by a wage-earner, in providing incentives for family planning, and in allocating available public funds in such a way as fully to meet the needs of the largest possible number of families. The District Court, while apparently recognizing the validity of at least some of these state concerns, nonetheless held that the regulation 'is invalid on its face for overreaching' and that it violates the Equal Protection Clause '(b)ecause it cuts too broad a swath on an indiscriminate basis as applied to the entire group of AFDC eligible to which it purports to apply.'

If this were a case involving government action claimed to violate the First Amendment guarantee of free speech, a finding of 'overreaching' would be significant and might be crucial. For when otherwise valid governmental regulation sweeps so broadly as to impinge upon activity protected by the First Amendment, its very overbreadth may make it unconstitutional. But the concept of 'overreaching' has no place in this case. For here we deal with state regulation in the social and economic field, not affecting freedoms guaranteed by the Bill of Rights, and claimed to violate the Fourteenth Amendment only because the regulation results in some disparity in grants of welfare payments to the largest AFDC families. For this Court to approve the invalidation of state economic or social regulation as 'overreaching' would be far too reminiscent of an era when the Court thought the Fourteenth Amendment gave it power to strike down state laws 'because they may be unwise, improvident, or out of harmony with a particular school of thought.' That era long ago passed into history.

In the area of economics and social welfare, a State does not violate the Equal Protection Clause merely because the classifications made by its laws are imperfect. If the classification has some 'reasonable basis,' it does not offend the Constitution simply because the classification 'is not made with mathematical nicety or because in practice it results in some inequality.' 'The problems of government are practical ones and may justify, if they do not require, rough accommodations—illogical, it may be, and unscientific.' 'A statutory discrimination will not be set aside if any state of facts reasonably may be conceived to justify it.'

To be sure, the cases cited, and many others enunciating this fundamental standard under the Equal Protection Clause, have in the main involved state regulation of business or industry. The administration of public welfare assistance, by contrast, involves the most basic economic needs of impoverished human beings. We recognize the dramatically real factual difference between the cited cases and this one, but we can find no basis for applying a different constitutional standard. It is a standard that has consistently been applied to state legislation restricting the availability of employment opportunities. And it is a standard that is true to the principle that the Fourteenth Amendment gives the federal courts no power to impose upon the States their views of what constitutes wise economic or social policy.

Under this long-established meaning of the Equal Protection Clause, it is clear that the Maryland Maximum grant regulation is constitutionally valid. We need not explore all the reasons that the State advances in justification of the regulation. It is enough that a solid foundation for the regulation can be found in the State's legitimate interest in encouraging employment and in avoiding discrimination between welfare families and the families of the working poor. By combining a limit on the recipient's grant with permission to retain money earned, without reduction in the amount of the grant, Maryland provides an incentive to seek gainful employment. And by keying the maximum family AFDC grants to the minimum wage a steadily employed head of a household receives, the State maintains some semblance of an equitable balance between families on welfare and those supported by an employed breadwinner.

It is true that in some AFDC families there may be no person who is employable. It is also true that with respect to AFDC families whose determined standard of need is below the regulatory maximum, and who therefore receive grants equal to the determined standard, the employment incentive is absent. But the Equal Protection Clause does not require that a State must choose between attacking every aspect of a problem or not attacking the problem at all. It is enough that the State's action be rationally based and free from invidious discrimination. The regulation before us meets that test.

We do not decide today that the Maryland regulation is wise, that it best fulfills the relevant social and economic objectives that Maryland might ideally espouse, or that a more just and humane system could not be devised. Conflicting claims of morality and intelligence are raised by opponents and proponents of almost every measure, certainly including the one before us. But the intractable economic, social, and even philosophical problems presented by public welfare assistance programs are not the business of this Court. The Constitution may impose certain procedural safeguards upon systems of welfare administration, Goldberg v. Kelly. But the Constitution does not empower this Court to second-guess state officials charged with the difficult responsibility of allocating limited public welfare funds among the myriad of potential recipients.

The judgment is reversed.

Mr. Justice MARSHALL, whom Mr. Justice BRENNAN joins, dissenting.

The Court recognizes, as it must, that this case involves 'the most basic economic needs of impoverished human beings,' and that there is therefore a 'dramatically real factual difference' between the instant case and those decisions upon which the Court relies. The acknowledgment that these dramatic differences exist is a candid recognition that the Court's decision today is wholly without precedent. I cannot subscribe to the Court's sweeping refusal to accord the Equal Protection Clause any role in this entire area of the law, and I therefore dissent from both parts of the Court's decision.

III

Having decided that the injunction issued by the District Court was proper as a matter of statutory construction, I would affirm on that ground alone. However, the majority has of necessity passed on the constitutional issues. I believe that in overruling the decision of this and every other district court that has passed on the validity of the maximum grant device, the Court both reaches the wrong result and lays down an insupportable test for determining whether a State has denied its citizens the equal protection of the laws.

The Maryland AFDC program in its basic structure operates uniformly with regard to all needy children by taking into account the basic subsistence needs of all eligible individuals in the formulation of the standards of need for families of various sizes. However, superimposed upon this uniform system is the maximum grant regulation, the operative effect of which is to create two classes of needy children and two classes of eligible families: those small families and their members who receive payments to cover their subsistence needs and those large families who do not.

This classification process effected by the maximum grant regulation produces a basic denial of equal treatment. Persons who are concededly similarly situated (dependent children and their families), are not afforded equal, or even approximately equal, treatment under the maximum grant regulation. Subsistence benefits are paid with respect to some needy dependent children; nothing is paid with respect to others. Some needy families receive full subsistence assistance as calculated by the State; the assistance paid to other families is grossly below their similarly calculated needs.

Yet, as a general principle, individuals should not be afforded different treatment by the State unless there is a relevant distinction between them and 'a statutory discrimination must be based on differences that are reasonably related to the purposes of the Act in which it is found. Consequently, the State may not, in the provision of important services or the distribution of governmental payments, supply benefits to some individuals while denying them to others who are similarly situated.

In the instant case, the only distinction between those children with respect to whom assistance is granted and those children who are denied such assistance is the size of the family into which the child permits himself to be born. The class of individuals with respect to whom payments are actually made (the first four or five eligible dependent children in a family), is grossly under-inclusive in terms of the class that the AFDC program was designed to assist, namely, all needy dependent children. Such under-inclusiveness manifests 'a prima facie violation of the equal protection requirement of reasonable classification,' compelling the State to come forward with a persuasive justification for the classification.

The Court never undertakes to inquire for such a justification; rather it avoids the task by focusing upon the abstract dichotomy between two different approaches to equal protection problems that have been utilized by this Court.

Under the so-called 'traditional test,' a classification is said to be permissible under the Equal Protection Clause unless it is 'without any reasonable basis.' On the other hand, if the classification affects a 'fundamental right,' then the state interest in perpetuating the classification must be 'compelling' in order to be sustained. This case simply defies easy characterization in terms of one or the other of these 'tests.' The cases relied on by the Court, in which a 'mere rationality' test was used, are most accurately described as involving the application of equal protection reasoning to the regulation of business interests. This case, involving the literally vital interests of a powerless minority—poor families without breadwinners—is far removed from the area of business regulation, as the Court concedes. Why then is the standard used in those cases imposed here? We are told no more than that this case falls in 'the area of economics and social welfare,' with the implication that from there the answer is obvious.

It is the individual interests here at stake that, as the Court concedes, most clearly distinguish this case from the 'business regulation' equal protection cases. AFDC support to needy dependent children provides the stuff that sustains those children's lives: food, clothing, shelter. And this Court has already recognized several times that when a benefit, even a 'gratuitous' benefit, is necessary to sustain life, stricter constitutional standards, both procedural and substantive, are applied to the deprivation of that benefit.

Nor is the distinction upon which the deprivation is here based—the distinction between large and small families—one that readily commends itself as a basis for determining which children are to have support approximating subsistence and which are not. Indeed, governmental discrimination between children on the basis of a factor over which they have no control—the number of their brothers and sisters—bears some resemblance to the classification between legitimate and illegitimate children which we condemned as a violation of the Equal Protection Clause in *Levy v. Louisiana*, 391 U.S. 68, 88 S.Ct. 1509, 20 L.Ed.2d 436 (1968).

The only question presented here is whether, having once undertaken such a program, the State may arbitrarily select from among the concededly eligible those to whom it will provide benefits. And it is too late to argue that political expediency will sustain discrimination not otherwise supportable.

Not only has the State failed to establish that there is a substantial or even a significant proportion of AFDC heads of households as to whom the maximum grant regulation arguably serves as a viable and logical work incentive, but it is also indisputable that the regulation at best is drastically over-inclusive since it applies with equal vigor to a very substantial number of persons who like appellees are completely disabled from working.

Finally, it should be noted that, to the extent there is a legitimate state interest in encouraging heads of AFDC households to find employment, application of the maximum grant regulation is also grossly under-inclusive because it singles out and affects only large families. No reason is suggested why this particular group should be carved out for the purpose of having unusually harsh 'work incentives' imposed upon them. Not only has the State selected for special treatment a small group from among similarly situated families, but it has done so on a basis—family size—that bears no re-lation to the evil that the State claims the regulation was designed to correct. There is simply no indication whatever that heads of large families, as opposed to heads of small families, are particularly prone to refuse to seek or to maintain employment.

Appellees are not a gas company or an optical dispenser; they are needy dependent children and families who are discriminated against by the State. The basis of that discrimination—the classification of individuals into large and small families—is too arbitrary and too unconnected to the asserted rationale, the impact on those dis-criminated against—the denial of even a subsistence existence—too great, and the supposed interests served too contrived and attenuated to meet the requirements of the Constitution. In my view Maryland's maximum grant regulation is invalid under the Equal Protection Clause of the Fourteenth Amendment.

I would affirm the judgment of the District Court.

C. Is Deferential Review Adequate?

State poverty laws have been given substantial deference following *Dandridge*, with courts regularly deferring to state and federal policy makers on economic and social matters. While the Supreme Court in *Dandridge* applied a deferential level of scrutiny to economic and social legislation, the line between what is economic and what is not—and something that infringes on a fundamental right—is subject to becoming blurred. Recent efforts to establish pre-benefit drug testing programs for individuals applying for welfare benefits illustrate how far poverty policy impinges on individual rights and the willingness of legislators to do so.

1. Drug Testing the Poor

The Fourth Amendment to the U.S. Constitution protects individuals from un-reasonable searches and seizures[2] and has been said to recognize an "individual's le-gitimate expectation that in certain places and at certain times [the individual] has the right to be let alone—the most comprehensive of rights and the most valued by civilized men."[3] Between 2010 and 2015 numerous state legislators enacted laws man-dating drug testing of families applying for welfare benefits on the premise that adults in families receiving welfare benefits were engaged in drug abuse. Testing is generally conducted through the collection of bodily fluid samples in connection with an ap-plication for benefits being filed and thus implicates the Fourth Amendment. *Lebron v. Sec'y, Fla. Dep't of Children & Families* addresses the constitutional implications

---

2. "[T]he right of the people to be secure in their persons, houses, papers and effects, against un-reasonable searches and seizures, shall not be violated, and no Warrants shall issue, but upon probably cause, supported by Oath or affirmation, and particularly describing the place to be searched and the person or things to be seized."

3. Winston v. Lee, 470 U.S. 753, 758 (1985).

that arise when a state requires Temporary Assistance for Needy Families program ("TANF") applicants to submit to suspicionless drug testing.

Lebron v. Sec'y, Fla. Dep't of Children & Families
710 F.3d 1202, 1204–21 (11th Cir. 2013)

The Secretary of the Florida Department of Children and Families ("State") appeals from the district court's order enjoining the State of Florida from requiring Luis W. Lebron to submit to a suspicionless drug test pursuant to Section 414.0652 of the Florida Statutes, as a condition for receipt of government-provided monetary assistance for which he was otherwise qualified.

Lebron is an honorably discharged veteran of the United States Navy, college student, single unmarried father and sole caretaker of his young child. Lebron resides with and also cares for his disabled mother, who subsists on Social Security Disability benefits. In July 2011, Lebron applied for financial assistance benefits for himself and his son through Florida's Temporary Assistance for Needy Families program ("TANF"), which, if he were eligible, would have provided him with a maximum of $241 per month to assist in the support of himself and his child.

TANF is a block grant program in which the federal government provides states with funds to assist needy families with short term financial assistance and with finding employment. The State, through the Department of Children and Families ("DCF"), has been administering the TANF program since its creation as part of the Personal Responsibility and Work Opportunity Reconciliation Act in 1996. Lebron met all of the program's eligibility requirements, but DCF ultimately denied his application because Lebron refused to submit to Florida's newly-enacted, mandatory drug testing, which is a final condition of eligibility for TANF benefits in Florida.

Florida's mandatory drug-testing requirement for all TANF applicants was enacted in May 2011. Under the statute, when an individual applies, he is notified that he will be required to submit to and pay for drug testing as a condition of receiving TANF benefits. If the applicant submits to the drug testing and tests negative, the cost of the test will be reimbursed to the applicant through a one-time increase in his TANF benefits. If the applicant tests positive for controlled substances, he is ineligible to receive TANF benefits for one year, id. § 414.0652(1)(b), but can reapply in six months if he completes a substance abuse treatment program and passes another drug test, both at his own expense, id. § 414.0652(1)(j). Although an adult applicant who fails the drug test is ineligible for TANF benefits, the applicant's dependent child may still receive TANF benefits so long as the adult designates an appropriate protective payee to receive the child's benefits. However, the individual who wishes to serve as the protective payee must also submit to and pass mandatory drug testing to receive benefits for the child, even though he is not requesting any TANF benefits for himself.

In addition to the mandatory drug test, applicants are required to sign a release acknowledging their consent to be tested. At the time Lebron applied for TANF benefits, he was notified of Florida's mandatory drug testing requirement and that he was required to sign the release before DCF would allow him to proceed with the application process. Lebron signed the release, completed the application process and was found eligible for TANF benefits. However, he did not submit to the drug test, but instead filed this lawsuit seeking to enjoin the enforcement of Florida's mandatory suspicionless drug testing as a violation of his and all other TANF applicants' Fourth Amendment right to be free from unreasonable searches and seizures. The district court granted a preliminary injunction against the enforcement of the drug testing statute against Lebron and the State agreed to discontinue its drug testing regime as to all TANF applicants until this litigation is fully resolved.

I Standard of Review

Here, the State challenges only the district court's conclusion that Lebron has shown a "substantial likelihood of success on the merits" of his claim that Florida's mandatory suspicionless drug testing of TANF applicants violates his Fourth Amendment right against unreasonable searches. Accordingly, in reviewing the district court's grant of the preliminary injunction, we do not resolve the merits of the constitutional claim, but instead address whether the district court abused its discretion in concluding that Lebron is substantially likely to succeed in establishing that Florida's drug testing regime for TANF applicants violates his Fourth Amendment rights.

II Discussion

The Fourth Amendment protects the rights of individuals "to be secure in their persons, houses, papers, and effects, against unreasonable searches and seizures." U.S. Const. amend. IV. It is undisputed and well-established that government-mandated drug testing is a "search" within the meaning of the Fourth Amendment Thus, the question before us is whether Florida's mandatory, suspicionless drug-testing of all TANF applicants is a constitutionally reasonable search under the Fourth Amendment.

Ordinarily, to be reasonable, a search must be based on individualized suspicion of wrongdoing. In most cases, this standard is met only when a search "is accomplished pursuant to a judicial warrant issued upon probable cause."

However, the Supreme Court has upheld as reasonable searches without a showing of individualized suspicion in certain very limited and exceptional circumstances. But to establish these limited and exceptional circumstances that justify the suspension of Fourth Amendment protections, the Supreme Court has required the government to make a threshold showing that there are "special needs, beyond the normal need for law enforcement, [which] make the warrant and probable-cause requirement impracticable." Not only must the government identify the special needs that make the warrant and probable-cause requirement impracticable but it must establish that those special needs are "substantial" only if the government is able to make a showing of substantial special needs will the court thereafter "undertake a context-specific inquiry, examining closely the competing private and public interests advanced by the parties," to determine the reasonableness of the search.

In the specific context of government-mandated drug testing programs, the Supreme Court has exempted such programs from the Fourth Amendment's warrant and probable cause requirement only where such testing "fit[s] within the closely guarded category of constitutionally permissible suspicionless searches." To fall within this "closely guarded category," the Court has made clear that its "precedents establish that the proffered special need for drug testing must be substantial." The Court has recognized two concerns that present such "exceptional circumstances," which are sufficiently "substantial" to qualify as special needs meriting an exemption to the Fourth Amendment's warrant and probable cause requirement: the specific risk to public safety by employees engaged in inherently dangerous jobs and the protection of children entrusted to the public-school system's care and tutelage. In contrast, this "closely guarded category" does not include a policy requiring candidates for public office to submit to drug testing because the Court concluded that the state's asserted need to "signify that candidates, if elected, will be fit to serve their constituents free from the influence of illegal drugs" was merely "symbolic" and not substantially special to warrant an exemption from the Fourth Amendment.

With reference to ensuring public safety in well-defined circumstances, the Court, in Skinner and Von Raab, recognized a special need where "[railroad] employees are engaged in safety-sensitive tasks," and where the "sensitive positions" of certain United States Customs employees present "extraordinary safety and national security hazards."

Other than the certain well-defined public safety concerns, the "closely guarded category" includes suspicionless drug testing only in one other context—the public-school setting. In Vernonia and Earls, the Court upheld as reasonable under the Fourth Amendment school district policies that provided for random drug testing of public school children who participated in the school systems' athletics programs and non-athletic extracurricular activities, respectively. The Court noted that "'special needs' inhere in the public-school context," given the need for "swift and informal disciplinary procedures" and "the substantial need of teachers and administrators for freedom to maintain order in the schools." The Court also explained that schools have an important concern with deterring drug use by schoolchildren "for whom it has undertaken a special responsibility of care and direction."

In Vernonia, in permitting the drug testing of student athletes, the Court emphasized the findings that "athletes were the leaders of the drug culture" in this school district, which was fueling a "rebellion" that led to an increase in disciplinary problems that "had reached epidemic proportions." The deleterious effects of drug use were of particular concern in the specific context of student athletics, which the Court noted "increases the risk of sports-related injury" and affects "motivation, memory, judgment, reaction, coordination, and performance Likewise in Earls, the Court reiterated "the importance of the governmental concern in preventing drug use by schoolchildren" and determined that the "health and safety risks identified in Vernonia" applied with "equal force" in the context of school children participating in extracurricular activities.

In both Vernonia and Earls, the government's special need in the unique context of the public-school setting was found to outweigh the individual privacy rights of the students—rights which the Court concluded are "limited in a public-school environment where the State is responsible for maintaining discipline, health, and safety." Although the Court in both Vernonia and Earls had before it evidence of a genuine drug problem among the covered students, the Court cautioned that "[t]he most significant element ... is ... that the Policy was undertaken in furtherance of the government's responsibilities, under a public-school system, as guardian and tutor of children entrusted to its care."

Thus in the context of government mandated drug testing, when the Court has permitted the suspension of the Fourth Amendment protections requiring individualized suspicion it has done so only in the "closely guarded categor[ies]" enumerated above where the asserted special need addresses a substantial concern for public safety or where the state is fulfilling its well-recognized role as the guardian and tutor of public school children. That is not to say that there cannot be other governmental needs that are sufficiently substantial to qualify as a special need for Fourth Amendment purposes. Moreover, in subsequently weighing the competing government and individual interests, the Court has noted that the affected individuals have a diminished expectation of privacy given the nature of their employment or status as a public-school student.

Here, the State argues that there is a "special need" to test TANF applicants because TANF funds should not be used for drugs as drug use undermines the program's goals of moving applicants into employment and promoting child welfare and family stability. But this argument, which assumes drug use, begs the question. The question is not whether drug use is detrimental to the goals of the TANF program, which it might be. Instead, the only pertinent inquiry is whether there is a substantial special need for mandatory, suspicionless drug testing of TANF recipients when there is no immediate or direct threat to public safety, when those being searched are not directly involved in the frontlines of drug interdiction, when there is no public school setting where the government has a responsibility for the care and tutelage of its young students, or when there are no dire consequences or grave risk of imminent physical harm as a result of waiting to obtain a warrant if a TANF recipient, or anyone else for that matter, is suspected of violating the law. We conclude that, on this record, the answer to that question of whether there is a substantial special need for mandatory suspicionless drug testing is "no."

The evidence in this record does not suggest that the population of TANF recipients engages in illegal drug use or that they misappropriate government funds for drugs at the expense of their own and their children's basic subsistence. The State has presented no evidence that simply because an applicant for TANF benefits is having financial problems, he is also drug addicted or prone to fraudulent and neglectful behavior.

There is nothing so special or immediate about the government's interest in ensuring that TANF recipients are drug free so as to warrant suspension of the Fourth

Amendment. The only known and shared characteristic of the individuals who would be subjected to Florida's mandatory drug testing program is that they are financially needy families with children. Yet, there is nothing inherent to the condition of being impoverished that supports the conclusion that there is a "concrete danger" that impoverished individuals are prone to drug use or that should drug use occur, that the lives of TANF recipients are "fraught with such risks of injury to others that even a momentary lapse of attention can have disastrous consequences. Thus, the State's argument that it has a special need to ensure that the goals of the TANF program are not jeopardized by the effects of drug use seems to rest on the presumption of unlawful drug use. But the Supreme Court has required that a state must present adequate factual support that there exists a "concrete danger," not simply conjecture that there is a substantial "special need" that cannot be met by ordinary law enforcement methods warranting the drastic action of abrogating an individual's constitutional right to be free from unreasonable government searches.

Moreover, none of the State's asserted concerns will be ameliorated by drug testing. While we recognize that Florida has a significant interest in promoting child welfare, the State has presented no evidence that the general welfare of the children in the TANF program is at greater risk absent its drug testing. Nor has the State shown that Florida's children will be better protected because of mandatory drug testing of TANF applicants. As the district court noted, even if a parent tests positive for drugs and is precluded from receiving TANF funds, the TANF program has no impact on the familial and custodial relationships of its would-be participants. Again, there is no evidence that there is greater drug use and child abuse within the population of economically disadvantaged families who participate in the TANF program. However, even if child neglect or abuse, for whatever reasons, impacts the lives of families in the TANF program, Florida has a separate, well-established and comprehensive statutory, administrative and judicial scheme codified in Chapter 39 of the Florida Statutes, which governs Florida's obligation to protect children from child abuse, abandonment and neglect.

In short, we cannot say that the district court erred in determining that the State failed to meet its burden of showing a substantial special need permitting the suspension of the Fourth Amendment's protections. The simple fact of seeking public assistance does not deprive a TANF applicant of the same constitutional protection from unreasonable searches that all other citizens enjoy. Because we agree with the district court that the State failed to meet its burden in establishing a special need for its mandatory, suspicionless drug testing of TANF applicants, that ends our inquiry into the testing regime's validity for Fourth Amendment purposes, and thus, we need not weigh any competing individual and governmental interests.

We turn then to the State's alternative argument that even if we find no substantial special need supporting Florida's mandatory drug testing of TANF recipients, the drug testing program is still constitutionally valid because it is based on consent. The State's assertion that the "consent" that is provided by TANF applicants renders the drug testing reasonable for Fourth Amendment purposes is belied by Supreme Court precedent, which has invalidated searches premised on consent where it has been shown that consent "was granted in submission to authority rather than as an understanding and intentional waiver of a constitutional right."

By informing TANF applicants that the drug test is one of many conditions to receiving this government-issued benefit and that the applicant's refusal to give consent means that he is ineligible to receive TANF assistance, the State conveys a message that it has the unfettered lawful authority to require such drug testing—period. But it does not and can only do so upon a showing of individualized suspicion or a special need beyond the need for normal law enforcement, both of which are absent in Florida's drug testing program. Accordingly, a TANF applicant's "consent" to the testing by signing a form waiving his constitutional rights amounts to nothing more than "submission to authority rather than ... an understanding and intentional waiver of a constitutional right."

We note that even though each of the drug testing regimes in Skinner, Von Raab, Vernonia, Chandler, and Earls required the affected employees, students or political office candidates to "consent" to the drug testing in order to maintain employment, participate in school activities or gain access to the ballot, the Supreme Court has never held that such drug testing regimes were constitutionally reasonable because of consent. Instead, every time that the Supreme Court has been asked to address the validity of a government mandated drug testing policy, it has applied the same special needs analysis and reasonableness balancing, whether upholding or rejecting those policies. Simply put, we have no reason to conclude that the constitutional validity of a mandated drug testing regime is satisfied by the fact that a state requires the affected population to "consent" to the testing in order to gain access or retain a desired benefit. Moreover, the mandated "consent" the State relies on here, which is not freely and voluntarily given, runs afoul of the Supreme Court's long-standing admonition that the government "may not deny a benefit to a person on a basis that infringes his constitutionally protected interests.

Here, because the state of Florida cannot drug test TANF applicants absent individualized suspicion or a showing of a governmental substantial special need that outweighs the applicant's privacy rights, it cannot do so indirectly by conditioning the receipt of this government benefit on the applicant's forced waiver of his Fourth Amendment right. The State cannot mandate "consent" to drug testing, which essentially requires a TANF applicant to choose between exercising his Fourth Amendment right against unreasonable searches at the expense of life-sustaining financial assistance for his family or, on the other hand, abandoning his right against unreasonable government searches in order to access desperately needed financial assistance, without unconstitutionally burdening a TANF applicant's Fourth Amendment right to be free from unreasonable searches. Accordingly, we cannot say that the district court abused its discretion in rejecting the State's "consent" argument as a violation of the unconstitutional conditions doctrine.

III Conclusion

Because we conclude that the State has failed to establish a substantial special need to support its mandatory suspicionless drug testing of TANF recipients, the district court did not abuse its discretion in granting the preliminary injunction enjoining the State from enforcing § 414.0652, Fla. Stat.

AFFIRMED.

2. Drug Testing the Poor to Qualify for Subsidized Housing

Peery v. Chicago Hous. Auth.

No. 13-CV-5819, 2014 WL 4913565 (N.D. Ill. Sept. 30, 2014),
aff'd, 791 F.3d 788 (7th Cir. 2015)

Plaintiffs seek entry of a preliminary injunction enjoining the defendants from drug screening as a condition of residency in Chicago Housing Authority ("CHA") subsidized units in mixed-income developments. The defendants argue that the drug testing policy is solely the work of the private developers (The Company of Builders "TCB" and Holsten Management Company "HMC"), who are not state actors for purposes of the Fourth Amendment prohibition of suspicionless drug searches, and even if they were, plaintiffs have consented to the searches. For the reasons set forth herein, the Court denies the motions.

I Background

Plaintiff Joseph Peery:

The CHA razed the Cabrini-Green complex as part of the "Plan for Transformation." Residents obtained Section 8 housing vouchers to relocate to private housing. Peery successfully completed the application process, including drug testing, and signed his lease on July 23, 2010. Peery has complied with the drug testing policy each year for renewal of his lease.

HMC is a private real estate developer that owns/manages [various Cabrini Green buildings]. HMC began using drug screening in the mid-1990s at several of its properties. HMC asserts that the drug screening policy at issue here is identical to the one it employs for all its buildings whether housing CHA tenants or not. According to HMC, it administers all aspects of the drug screening, including paying all costs. HMC also attests that results of the tests are not reported to CHA and there is no policy to advise CHA of any objections to the drug testing.

. . .

Joanne Boy of the CHA testified that each site's private developer is responsible for drafting proposed lease agreements and a tenant selection plan. The CHA has minimum requirements for the tenant selection plans. The CHA's minimum tenant selection plan does not contain a drug screening policy.

Defendant the Community Builders ("TCB") is the management agent for the private owners of the [property]. TCB represents that none of the documents for the development and management [the property] define TCB or any other owner entity as an agent of CHA. TCB asserts that all Oakwood Shores tenants sign an identical lease that includes the drug testing policy regardless of whether they are CHA residents or market rate tenants. TCB decided to include the drug screening policy in its lease and tenant selection plan. The CHA did not take a position, except requiring all the sites and units have the same requirements.

II Legal Standard

In order to obtain a preliminary injunction, the plaintiff must show that (1) he has no adequate remedy at law, (2) will suffer irreparable harm if a preliminary injunction is denied, (3) some likelihood of success on the merits, and (4) the balance of harms favors the moving party or whether the harm to the non-moving party or the public is sufficiently weighty that the injunction should be denied.

III Discussion

A. Likelihood of Success on the Merits

Plaintiffs assert that the Chicago Housing Authority imposed, either directly or indirectly, the drug testing requirement, resulting in suspicionless searches in violation of the plaintiffs' Fourth Amendment rights. In order to succeed on the merits of their Section 1983 claims, plaintiffs must prove (1) action under color of law; (2) a search or seizure under the Fourth Amendment; and (3) that the search or seizure was unreasonable in the face of the government interests at stake and the circumstances of the search." Only the first two elements are at issue here: the existence of state action and consent to the search (taking the suspicionless drug testing outside the reach of the Fourth Amendment).

The facts demonstrate that it is the private developers that administered the actual drug testing. Generally, the conduct of private parties lies beyond the scope of the Constitution. Therefore, plaintiffs must demonstrate with clear evidence that the drug testing conducted by the private developers as part of the lease execution and renewal process constitutes state action. Even if plaintiffs demonstrate that the private developer's actions should be treated as state action, if any of the plaintiffs consented to the drug testing then there can be no constitutional violation.

1. State Action

The determination of whether a private entity is a state actor is "necessarily a fact-bound inquiry." This fact-based inquiry comes down to a matter of degree of involvement. Furthermore, the relationship/nexus/entanglement/entwinement between the state and the private entity must be on the precise issue of which the plaintiffs complain, i.e. the drug testing policy.

Plaintiffs make two main arguments for why this Court should treat the drug testing policy as State action. First, they argue that CHA has direct involvement in the challenged conduct because CHA has "absolute and ultimate control over tenant selection criteria" and has used this control to impose drug testing at Parkside and other developments. Second, plaintiffs argue that CHA and the private developers have a "symbiotic relationship" such that the action of the private developers may be said to be that of the CHA. Plaintiffs rely on the following to support their argument: The CHA's membership in the Working Groups; CHA's Board approval of the tenant selection plans and leases; the three-party leases between CHA tenants, the private developers and the CHA; the CHA's ownership of the land; the enforceability of CHA tenant relocation rights; and the CHA's duty to ensure the developments comply with federal law (HUD regulations).

Here, plaintiffs cannot show a sufficiently close nexus between the CHA and the private developers to establish state action. While the CHA is a voting member of both the Near North Working Group (Parkside) and the Madden/Wells Area Working Group (Oakwood Shores), the CHA is not the only member and there is nothing in the record to show that the CHA had greater voting power than any other voting member. In the case of the Near North Working Group, the same working group approved tenant selection plans and leases that did not include drug screening at nine out of eleven mixed-income developments. The only two to include testing are managed by HMC. Further, the record shows that HMC has used drug testing in its developments since the mid-1990s; long before HMC developed mixed-income housing that included CHA subsidized units.

Additionally, the record demonstrates that CHA had minimum tenant selection requirements, but that the private developers were tasked with establishing their own tenant selection plans and lease packages. Plaintiffs assert that CHA requires plaintiffs to enter three-party leases with the CHA and the private management companies under which they can be evicted for drug-use. Yet, this provision, which is required under federal law, simply allows a landlord to terminate a public housing tenant's lease because of illegal drug-use. The provision is not a part of the drug screening policies imposed by HMC and TCB.

Plaintiffs' alternative argument that CHA is indirectly responsible for the drug testing policies, based on a "symbiotic relationship" argument also fails to show sufficient evidence that CHA is behind the testing. The evidence in the record demonstrates that CHA acquiesced in the inclusion of the drug testing policy, but that it otherwise took no affirmative position. Rather than mandating the drug testing as argued by plaintiffs, the CHA took the position that if a private developer wanted to require any additional requirements beyond the minimum TSP, such as drug testing as a condition of occupancy, then CHA required only that the additional conditions apply to all tenants regardless of whether they were CHA residents, affordable rate, or market rate tenants. The record demonstrates that CHA was not driving the drug testing policies of the mixed-income developments nor did it administer or enforce the policies.

2. Consent

Even if the Court were to find state action, if plaintiffs consented to the drug testing then no constitutional violation occurred. "[A] search conducted pursuant to valid consent is constitutionally permissible." Plaintiffs contend that any consent was not voluntary, but was necessarily coerced because their submission to the testing meant they could stay in their current home. Defendants focus on the fact that plaintiffs agreed to the testing, repeatedly, and in the case of Peery signed a waiver. Defendants also argue that each plaintiff acknowledged that they had options of where to live within CHA's relocation program, including units within their target locations that did not mandate drug testing as a condition of lease. CHA asserts that plaintiffs could (and still can) apply for transfer to units in other developments. CHA personnel testified that they would have approved Peery's request for a transfer had he made one.

CHA distinguishes the case Lebron v. Sec'y, Fla. Dep't of Children & Families, on which plaintiffs heavily rely. In Lebron, the court affirmed the district court's order enjoining the State of Florida from requiring the plaintiff to submit to a suspicionless drug test as a condition of the receipt of government-provided monetary assistance for which he was otherwise qualified. There, Florida enacted a statute that mandated drug testing for participation in the State's Temporary Assistance for Needy Families program. In Lebron, unlike here, not only was there no question of state action (it was a Florida statute), but the requirement was only imposed on low-income individuals and the result of refusal was denial of benefits.

Here, the private developers' drug testing policies are applied to all tenants, not just CHA tenants, and the consequence of refusing to submit to the test is not the loss of CHA housing subsidies but only eviction from that particular unit. There is no constitutional right to public housing at any particular location. The record here indicates that plaintiffs' choice to remain at Parkside and Oakwood Shores despite the drug testing policies at each when they had options for units in nearby developments without the drug screening was not coerced or the product of duress. None of the plaintiffs sought a transfer or formally complained of the drug screening. Instead, they consented to the annual testing.

B. The Remaining Elements of a Preliminary Injunction

The remaining elements of a preliminary injunction are: no adequate remedy at law; irreparable harm if no injunction imposed; and balance of harms. Here, the Court finds that plaintiffs fail to meet their burden to show a likelihood of success on the merits. Therefore, the Court need not address the remaining factors.

IV Conclusion

Based on the foregoing, this Court finds that plaintiffs failed to meet their burden to persuade this to impose a preliminary injunction. This Court therefore denies plaintiffs' motions for preliminary injunction.

IT IS SO ORDERED.

3. Poverty as Cause when Reducing the Procedural Rights for the Poor in the Landlord-Tenant Relationship

Poor people living in public housing or subsidized private housing are subject to eviction procedures that are separate and distinct from eviction proceedings in other contexts. The rationale for these differences is found in the seeming correlation between poverty and specific types of crime.

With drug dealers "increasingly imposing a reign of terror on public and other federally assisted low-income housing tenants," Congress passed the Anti-Drug Abuse Act of 1988. The Act, as later amended, provides that each "public housing agency shall utilize leases which ... provide that any criminal activity that threatens the health, safety, or right to peaceful enjoyment of the premises by other tenants or any drug-related criminal activity on or off such premises, engaged in by a public housing tenant, any member of the tenant's household, or any guest or other person under the tenant's control, shall be cause for termination of tenancy." This statute requires lease terms that allow a local public housing authority to evict a tenant when a member of the tenant's household or a guest engages in drug-related criminal activity, regardless of whether the tenant knew, or had reason to know, of that activity. This means that a tenant living in public housing may face eviction if the tenant's guest engages in illegal drug activity even if the tenant did not know about the activity. Such a policy stands in stark contrast to well accepted tenants' rights in most all other contexts.

The Uniform Residential Landlord Tenant Act was drafted between 1969 and 1972 with the goal of equalizing the bargaining power between the landlord and tenant. The drafting committee noted that too many landlords asserted their rights under the law when dealing with tenants and that the tenant's bargaining power was substantially reduced in comparison to that of the landlord. The URLTA has been adopted by the majority of states since then.

Prior to the modern URLTA, landlords enjoyed great power to engage in self-help evictions, where residential tenants could be forcibly dispossessed of their home without any judicial process. Due process is a key concern for the URLTA. While the eviction order may be obtained through summary proceedings, the landlord must still provide notice that allows the tenant either an opportunity to cure or a reasonable amount of time to respond to the eviction complaint, or to relocate.

Dep't of Housing and Urban Dev. v. Rucker

535 U.S. 125 (2002)

Chief Justice REHNQUIST delivered the opinion of the Court.

With drug dealers "increasingly imposing a reign of terror on public and other federally assisted low-income housing tenants," Congress passed the Anti-Drug Abuse Act of 1988. The Act, as later amended, provides that each "public housing agency shall utilize leases which ... provide that any criminal activity that threatens the health, safety, or right to peaceful enjoyment of the premises by other tenants or any drug-related criminal activity on or off such premises, engaged in by a public housing tenant, any member of the tenant's household, or any guest or other person under the tenant's control, shall be cause for termination of tenancy." Petitioners say that this statute requires lease terms that allow a local public housing authority to evict a tenant when a member of the tenant's household or a guest engages in drug-related criminal activity, regardless of whether the tenant knew, or had reason to know, of that activity. Respondents say it does not. We agree with petitioners.

Respondents are four public housing tenants of the Oakland Housing Authority (OHA). Respondents' leases obligate the tenants to "assure that the tenant, any member of the household, a guest, or another person under the tenant's control, shall not engage in ... [a]ny drug-related criminal activity on or near the premise[s]." Respondents also signed an agreement stating that the tenant "understand[s] that if I or any member of my household or guests should violate this lease provision, my tenancy may be terminated and I may be evicted."

In late 1997 and early 1998, OHA instituted eviction proceedings in state court against respondents, alleging violations of this lease provision. The complaint alleged: (1) that the respective grandsons of respondents William Lee and Barbara Hill, both of whom were listed as residents on the leases, were caught in the apartment complex parking lot smoking marijuana; (2) that the daughter of respondent Pearlie Rucker, who resides with her and is listed on the lease as a resident, was found with cocaine and a crack cocaine pipe three blocks from Rucker's apartment; and (3) that on three instances within a 2-month period, respondent Herman Walker's caregiver and two others were found with cocaine in Walker's apartment. OHA had issued Walker notices of a lease violation on the first two occasions, before initiating the eviction action after the third violation.

United States Department of Housing and Urban Development (HUD) regulations require lease terms authorizing evictions in these circumstances. The HUD regulations closely track the statutory language, and provide that "[i]n deciding to evict for criminal activity, the [public housing authority] shall have discretion to consider all of the circumstances of the case...." The agency made clear that local public housing authorities' discretion to evict for drug-related activity includes those situations in which "[the] tenant did not know, could not foresee, or could not control behavior by other occupants of the unit."

After OHA initiated the eviction proceedings in state court, respondents commenced actions against HUD, OHA, and OHA's director in United States District Court. They challenged HUD's interpretation of the statute under the Administrative Procedure Act, 5 U.S.C. §706(2)(A), arguing that 42 U.S.C. §1437d(*l*)(6) does not require lease terms authorizing the eviction of so-called "innocent" tenants, and, in the alternative, that if it does, then the statute is unconstitutional. The District Court issued a preliminary injunction, enjoining OHA from "terminating the leases of tenants pursuant to paragraph 9(m) of the 'Tenant Lease' for drug-related criminal activity that does not occur within the tenant's apartment unit when the tenant did not know of and had no reason to know of, the drug-related criminal activity."

A panel of the Court of Appeals reversed, holding that § 1437d (*l*)(6) unambiguously permits the eviction of tenants who violate the lease provision, regardless of whether the tenant was personally aware of the drug activity, and that the statute is constitutional. An en banc panel of the Court of Appeals reversed and affirmed the District Court's grant of the preliminary injunction. That court held that HUD's interpretation permitting the eviction of so-called "innocent" tenants "is inconsistent with Congressional intent and must be rejected" under the first step of *Chevron U.S.A. Inc. v. Natural Resources Defense Council, Inc.*

We granted certiorari, and now reverse, holding that 42 U.S.C. § 1437d(*l*)(6) unambiguously requires lease terms that vest local public housing authorities with the discretion to evict tenants for the drug-related activity of household members and guests whether or not the tenant knew, or should have known, about the activity.

That this is so seems evident from the plain language of the statute. It provides that "[e]ach public housing agency shall utilize leases which ... provide that ... any drug-related criminal activity on or off such premises, engaged in by a public housing tenant, any member of the tenant's household, or any guest or other person under the tenant's control, shall be cause for termination of tenancy." Congress' decision not to impose any qualification in the statute, combined with its use of the term "any" to modify "drug-related criminal activity," precludes any knowledge requirement.

The statute does not *require* the eviction of any tenant who violated the lease provision. Instead, it entrusts that decision to the local public housing authorities, who are in the best position to take account of, among other things, the degree to which the housing project suffers from "rampant drug-related or violent crime," "the seriousness of the offending action," and "the extent to which the leaseholder has ... taken all reasonable steps to prevent or mitigate the offending action," *ibid.* It is not "absurd" that a local housing authority may sometimes evict a tenant who had no knowledge of the drug-related activity. Such "no-fault" eviction is a common "incident of tenant responsibility under normal landlord-tenant law and practice." Strict liability maximizes deterrence and eases enforcement difficulties.

And, of course, there is an obvious reason why Congress would have permitted local public housing authorities to conduct no-fault evictions: Regardless of knowledge, a tenant who "cannot control drug crime, or other criminal activities by a household member which threaten health or safety of other residents, is a threat to other residents and the project." With drugs leading to "murders, muggings, and other forms of violence against tenants," and to the "deterioration of the physical environment that requires substantial government expenditures," it was reasonable for Congress to permit no-fault evictions in order to "provide public and other federally assisted low-income housing that is decent, safe, and free from illegal drugs," § 11901(1) (1994 ed.).

The government is not attempting to criminally punish or civilly regulate respondents as members of the general populace. It is instead acting as a landlord of property that it owns, invoking a clause in a lease to which respondents have agreed and which Congress has expressly required.

There is no indication that notice has not been given by OHA in the past, or that it will not be given in the future. Any individual factual disputes about whether the lease provision was actually violated can, of course, be resolved in these proceedings.

We hold that "Congress has directly spoken to the precise question at issue." Section 1437d(*l*)(6) requires lease terms that give local public housing authorities the discretion to terminate the lease of a tenant when a member of the household or a guest engages in drug-related activity, regardless of whether the tenant knew, or should have known, of the drug-related activity.

Accordingly, the judgment of the Court of Appeals is reversed, and the cases are remanded for further proceedings consistent with this opinion.

It is so ordered.

4. Drug Abuse Is Not the Real Barrier to Economic Self-Sufficiency; The Real Barrier Is Social Inequality— Which Is Reinforced by Drug Testing Programs

While substance abuse is a barrier to economic self-sufficiency, it is not the only barrier to economic and social advancement. Racial division, structural inequality, inadequate education opportunities and lack of entry-level jobs are more significant barriers for far more people, particularly children. The real barrier to economic self-sufficiency is social inequality.

State policies that subject families seeking assistance from TANF programs to drug testing are inconsistent with the 4th Amendment and violate fundamental notions of individual privacy. Federal housing policy that summarily evicts tenants who do not participate in drug activity seems unfair and inconsistent with our system of justice. Whether in the form or blanket testing requirements, such as Florida's, or efforts that attempt to tailor testing through a "reasonable suspicion" requirement that is applied through administrative case workers, such as in North Carolina, these policies disregard individual liberty in the guise of advancing a legitimate governmental interest. Such interests, however, are minimal at best. As the Lebron court observed, economic means are the only distinction between the individuals being tested in these programs and those that are not. Subjecting the poor to such a reduced level of individual rights only furthers their alienation and disenfranchisement. Such disenfranchisement is, however, consistent with the broader context of welfare reform and the historical treatment of the poor as individuals with fewer rights than the nonpoor. And in the context of policies that marginalize the poor, warrantless drug testing programs fit very well. The testing regime enacted by the State of Florida seems suspect in light of the Supreme Court's assessment of the Constitutionality of pre-suspicion testing requirement prior to *Lebron*.

Further Reading and Research

Skinner v. Railway Lab. Exec. Assoc., 489 U.S. 602 (1988).

National Treasury Emp. Union v. Von Raab, 489 U.S. 656 (1989).

Vernonia Sch. Dist. 47J v. Acton., 515 U.S. 646 (1995).

Lebron v. Sec'y, Florida Dept. of Children and Families, 710 F.3d 1202 (11th Cir. 2013).

Department of Housing and Urban Dev. v. Rucker, 535 U.S. 125 (2002).

Jordan C. Budd, *Pledge Your Body For Your Bread: Welfare, Drug Testing and the Inferior Fourth Amendment* 19 WM. & MARY BILL RTS. J. 751 (2011).

MATTHEW DESMOND, EVICTED: POVERTY AND PROFIT IN THE AMERICAN CITY (New York: Crown, 2016).

Part Two

Anti-Poverty
Programs and Interventions

Chapter Five

Income Assistance[1]

"We should measure welfare's success by how many people leave welfare, not by how many are added."

Ronald Reagan

When, and under what circumstances, should a person who is poor be given money by the government? As discussed in earlier materials, in the United States, poverty is defined by an inability to buy the goods and services that are needed to meet a person's or family's basic needs.[2] While some of these goods and services can be provided through direct government transfers, such as government-provided housing[3] or food and nutrition services,[4] money transfers are needed and remain an important part of any anti-poverty policy. Cash assistance enables individuals to purchase goods tailored to specific needs and is the most efficient and easiest way to provide assistance in many instances.

Few poverty policies, however, generate as much debate and are as generally disliked as direct cash transfer programs that serve the poor.[5] Consequently, these programs highlight the deepest tensions in a community around poverty. While there may be several reasons for this, the autonomy and decision-making power money provides its holder on what to purchase and what to prioritize are perhaps the most problematic. There are few ways to ensure that the cash assistance will not be used for something objectionable and such freedom may cause ambiguity for policy makers. Since money can equally be used to buy bread or beer, as well as other things, anti-poverty programs that transfer money to the poor face the valid concern of control from the start.

---

1. *See* Robert Moffitt, *A Primer on U.S. Welfare Reform*, 26 Inst. for Res. on Poverty 15, 15–16 (2008) (The federal government provides "income assistance," cash assistance to people with low income and limited assets, through various programs, including Aid to Families with Dependent Children (AFDC), Temporary Aid to Needy Families (TANF), and Supplemental Security Income (SSI).).

2. For more information on defining poverty, *see supra* Chapter One, Section B.

3. *See* HUD, *HUD's Public Housing Program*, https://www.hud.gov/topics/rental_assistance/phprog (last visited April 20, 2018).

4. *See* USDA, *Supplemental Nutrition Assistance Program (SNAP)*, https://www.fns.usda.gov/snap/supplemental-nutrition-assistance-program-snap (last published Feb. 5, 2018).

5. David Lauter, *How Do Americans View Poverty? Many Blue-Collar Whites, Key to Trump, Criticize the Poor as Lazy and Content to Stay on Welfare*, L.A. Times (Aug. 14, 2016), http://www.latimes.com/projects/la-na-pol-poverty-poll.

Money transfer payments may also create disincentives to work.[6] If a person will receive the same income through government assistance from *not* working as they would if they worked 40 hours per week, it is fair to assume the person would prefer the freedom of not working.[7] Due to this dynamic, welfare[8] programs play a balancing act in this field of concern.

Three conflicting considerations run across all poverty policies and are heightened when talking about welfare. First, welfare must consider how well cash transfer efforts relieve poverty. Second, welfare policy cannot erode the work incentive and (more importantly) must encourage work. Third, the government must control costs and maintain an effective budgeting process. While welfare policy in the United States may be seen as a continuing effort to balance all of these concerns, the balance significantly shifted toward the second and third concerns in the mid-1990s.[9]

The Aid to Families with Dependent Children (AFDC) program was the first federal anti-poverty policy, enacted as part of the Social Security Act of 1935.[10] AFDC remained the primary source of cash assistance to the poor until passage of the Personal Responsibility and Work Opportunity Act of 1996, which ended "welfare as we kn[e]w it"[11] at the time and established the Temporary Aid to Needy Families (TANF) program.[12] TANF was a significant shift in welfare policy.[13] Where AFDC's purpose was initially described as delivering assistance to families and children who were found to be eligible,[14] TANF overtly shifted focus to behavior modification with the stated goal of reducing welfare caseloads by altering individual behavior.[15]

---

6. *See* Michael D. Tanner & Charles Hughes, CATO Inst., The Work versus Welfare Trade-Off: 2013 (Aug. 19, 2013), https://www.cato.org/publications/white-paper/work-versus-welfare-trade ("The current welfare system provides such a high level of benefits that it acts as a disincentive for work. Welfare currently pays more than a minimum-wage job in 35 states, even after accounting for the Earned Income Tax Credit, and in 13 states it pays more than $15 per hour.").

7. *Id.*

8. Here, the term "welfare" is used to refer to cash assistance programs for the nonworking poor.

9. *See* Moffitt, *supra* note 1, at 18–23.

10. *See* Moffitt, *supra* note 1, at 16.

11. William J. Clinton, President of the United States, Statement on Signing the Personal Responsibility and Work Opportunity Reconciliation Act of 1996, II Pub. Papers 1328 (Aug. 22, 1996), https://www.presidency.ucsb.edu/documents/statement-signing-the-personal-responsibility-and-work-opportunity-reconciliation-act-1996 ("Today, I have signed into law H.R. 3734, the Personal Responsibility and Work Opportunity Reconciliation Act of 1996. While far from perfect, this legislation provides an historic opportunity to *end welfare as we know it* and transform our broken welfare system by promoting the fundamental values of work, responsibility, and family.") (emphasis added).

12. *See* Moffitt, *supra* note 1, at 19–20.

13. *See* Moffitt, *supra* note 1, at 20.

14. *See* Moffitt, *supra* note 1, at 16–17 ("AFDC provided cash financial support to low-income families with "dependent" children, defined as those who were deprived of the support or care of one biological parent by reason of death, disability, or absence from the home, and who were under the care of the other parent or another relative.").

15. *See* Jill Adams, *Family Reform through Welfare Reform: How TANF Violates Constitutional Rights to Volitional Family Formation*, Berkeley L. 1, 10–11 (2006), https://www.law.berkeley.edu/sugarman/Family_seminar_Jill_for_website.doc ("PRWORA represents a re-commitment to the preservation of the moral order—the work ethic and family, gender, race, and ethnic relations. The pro-

Significant questions regarding the relationship between the state and the individual are raised in this context: At what point does poverty empower the state to interfere in individual autonomy? Should individuals in need find that accepting aid means loss of some autonomy? What can an individual expect from his or her society, and what does society owe to an individual? Instead of addressing systematic or structural realities that lead to poverty, welfare policies have evolved to shape a relationship between the poor and the state that is based largely on economic class, where the poor live under a regime that works to control individual behavior.[16]

A. A History of Cash Welfare Programs

Cash assistance programs for the poor are a fairly recent intervention that began in a uniform way at the state and federal levels in the 1930s.[17] The idea is perhaps deceptively easy: If poor people are given cash, they can be lifted from poverty. Direct transfers of cash to individuals create a number of significant concerns, however. For example, why would someone choose to work if he or she did not need to? How do we ensure that money is used for worthwhile reasons, like food and housing, instead of alcohol or another vice? The state has an interest in ensuring that cash assistance is used for legitimate purposes, but the limits of state power to ensure that the recipients of cash assistance follow behavioral requirements are not unbounded.

1. Aid to Families with Dependent Children

The term "welfare" is often used to describe cash assistance programs for the non-working adult poor with dependent children.[18] The first federal welfare program, Aid to Families with Dependent Children ("AFDC"), was enacted as part of the Social Security Act of 1935 and administered by the federal government.[19] The AFDC program was one of many significant safety net programs contained within the Social Security Act of 1935, which also included the Old Age Social Security and Unemployment Insurance programs.[20] AFDC largely retained its original structure from

---

visions and manner of enforcement of welfare have traditionally signaled, at least somewhat subtly, which behaviors are deviant and which are virtuous.") (internal citations omitted).

16. *Id.*

17. CONST. RTS. FOUND., HOW WELFARE BEGAN IN THE UNITED STATES (1998), http://www.crf-usa.org/bill-of-rights-in-action/bria-14-3-a-how-welfare-began-in-the-united-states.html.

18. Stephen B. Page & Mary B. Larner, *Introduction to the AFDC Program*, 7 FUTURE OF CHILD. 20, 20 (1999).

19. *See* ASPE, *Aid to Families with Dependent Children (AFDC) and Temporary Assistance for Needy Families (TANF) Overview* (Nov. 20, 2009), https://aspe.hhs.gov/aid-families-dependent-children-afdc-and-temporary-assistance-needy-families-tanf-overview-0.

20. *See* Moffitt, *supra* note 1, at 16.

1935 through 1996, when Congress made significant changes to federal anti-poverty policies as part of broad "welfare reform."[21]

Although the AFDC program relied on both state and federal funding, the federal government gave states "a large degree of latitude" to set eligibility requirements for families who received AFDC benefits.[22] Eligibility for AFDC was determined based on an applicant family's combined available assets and family income. AFDC was available to families whose combined assets and income fell below a set eligibility line that was well below the federal poverty level, and less than a worker would earn if working a minimum wage job.[23] The AFDC program was an "entitlement" program, meaning that families were entitled to receive certain benefits if they fell within a class of people defined by the government.[24] AFDC provided cash support to families with "dependent children," those who were "deprived of parental support or care because their father or mother is absent from the home continuously, is incapacitated, is deceased, or is unemployed."[25] In addition to cash grants, many families who enrolled in AFDC were also eligible for Medicaid, child care assistance, food stamps, and subsidized housing due to their low incomes.[26] With states setting their own eligibility requirements and assistance amounts, benefit and support levels varied across states.[27] During the program's lifespan, the majority of beneficiaries were single mothers and their children, because eligibility depended on the deprivation of "parental support."[28] While the presence of a father was possible, if he was disabled or the single parent, the caseloads were overwhelmingly families in which the father was not present.[29]

Between 1935 and 1965, funding for AFDC grew in line with population growth, but from 1965 to 1975 AFDC budgets expanded at a disproportionate rate.[30] What caused growth in AFDC during the 10-year period from 1965 to 1975 is subject to some debate. For example, expanded advocacy efforts by lawyers and welfare rights organizations increased access to the system for groups that had been systematically excluded prior to the civil rights movement. In a series of cases, lawyers obtained

---

21. *See* Moffitt, *supra* note 1, at 19.

22. Moffitt, *supra* note 1, at 17 ("In keeping with the "federal" system in the United States, the AFDC program was created as a shared federal-state responsibility, with the federal government subsidizing state payments and setting certain restrictions on eligibility requirements and benefit determination, but leaving states with a large degree of latitude in both of these areas. This led to wide variation in benefit levels among states.").

23. *Id.*

24. *See* Page & Larner, *supra* note 18, at 21 ("Federal legislation required states to provide cash assistance to *all* eligible families.").

25. Page & Larner, *supra* note 18, at 21.

26. Page & Larner, *supra* note 18, at 22.

27. *See* Moffitt, *supra* note 1, at 17.

28. *See* Page & Larner, *supra* note 18, at 21.

29. Page & Larner, *supra* note 18, at 21.

30. HHS, *Indicators of Welfare Dependence: Annual Report to Congress* (Mar. 1, 2002), https://aspe.hhs.gov/report/indicators-welfare-dependence-annual-report-congress-2002; HHS, *Aid to Families with Dependent Children (AFDC) and Temporary Assistance For Needy Families (TANF)* (Mar. 1, 2002), https://aspe.hhs.gov/report/indicators-welfare-dependence-annual-report-congress-2002/aid-families-dependent-children-afdc-and-temporary-assistance-needy-families-tanf.

significant results for the poor that included access to due process (*Goldberg v. Kelly*[31]) and elimination of racially biased exclusionary rules (*King v. Smith*[32]). At the same time, the U.S. economy faced significant recession with accompanying high unemployment levels during most of this period. Finally, the prolonged war in Vietnam may also have contributed to higher numbers of families in need of assistance.

During the growth of AFDC caseloads over this period,[33] public debate on the proper role and scope of welfare also grew. When then-governor of California, Ronald Reagan, first introduced his apocryphal story of the "welfare queen" in the early 1970s, public discourse began to include open discussions on the need to reform a program that was seen as enabling the poor at exceptional public expense.[34] In 1984, Charles Murray published his book, *Losing Ground: American Social Policy 1950–1980*, supporting a narrative of rational economic decision making by the poor that ironically leads to poverty, largely due to the presence of government welfare programs. Since the 1960s, the history of AFDC in this context shows a steady movement away from welfare as an entitlement and toward suspicion of the poor and possible abuses of cash assistance programs.[35] Thus, welfare has been seen more as a problem than as a response to significant societal needs.

2. Welfare "Rights" and the Limits of State Intervention in the Lives of Welfare Beneficiaries

Goldberg v. Kelly
397 U.S. 254 (1970)

The question for decision is whether a State that terminates public assistance payments to a particular recipient without affording him the opportunity for an evidentiary hearing prior to termination denies the recipient procedural due process in violation of the Due Process Clause of the Fourteenth Amendment.

[Residents of New York City who received financial aid under AFDC or New York's State's general Home Relief Program brought this action, alleging that the New York State and New York City officials who administering these programs terminated, or were about to terminate, aid without prior notice and hearing. The plaintiffs claimed that this denied them due process of law. At the time the suit was filed, prior notice or a hearing was not required, but the state and city adopted these procedures soon after. On appeal, the plaintiffs challenged the constitutional adequacy of those procedures.

---

31. Goldberg v. Kelly, 397 U.S. 254 (1970).

32. King v. Smith, 392 U.S. 309 (1968).

33. *See* Moffitt, *supra* note 1, at 18.

34. Gene Demby, *The Truth Behind the Lies of the Original "Welfare Queen,"* NPR (Dec. 20, 2013), https://www.npr.org/sections/codeswitch/2013/12/20/255819681/the-truth-behind-the-lies-of-the-original-welfare-queen ("To people who were opposed to welfare, Taylor's colorful transgressions were evidence of just how little oversight there was in the program and how easily it could be abused.").

35. *See* Lauter, *supra* note 5.

The adopted provisions required giving notice to the recipient of benefits at least seven days prior to a proposed discontinuance or suspension. The notice must also include that, upon request, the recipient may have the proposal reviewed by a local welfare official holding a position that is superior to that of the supervisor who approved the discontinuance or suspension. Further, the recipient may submit a written statement to demonstrate why his grant should not be discontinued or suspended.]

The decision by the reviewing official whether to discontinue or suspend aid must be made expeditiously, with written notice of the decision to the recipient. The section further expressly provides that '(a)ssistance shall not be discontinued or suspended prior to the date such notice of decision is sent to the recipient and his representative, if any, or prior to the proposed effective date of discontinuance or suspension, whichever occurs later.'

...

The constitutional issue to be decided, therefore, is the narrow one whether the Due Process Clause requires that the recipient be afforded an evidentiary hearing before the termination of benefits. The District Court held that only a predetermination evidentiary hearing would satisfy the constitutional command, and rejected the argument of the state and city officials that the combination of the post-termination 'fair hearing' with the informal pre-termination review disposed of all due process claims. The court said: 'While post-termination review is relevant, there is one overpowering fact which controls here. By hypothesis, a welfare recipient is destitute, without funds or assets. * * * Suffice it to say that to cut off a welfare recipient in the face of * * * 'brutal need' without a prior hearing of some sort is unconscionable, unless overwhelming considerations justify it.' *Kelly v. Wyman*, 294 F.Supp. 893, 899, 900 (1968). The court rejected the argument that the need to protect the public's tax revenues supplied the requisite 'overwhelming consideration.' 'Against the justified desire to protect public funds must be weighed the individual's overpowering need in this unique situation not to be wrongfully deprived of assistance. * * * While the problem of additional expense must be kept in mind, it does not justify denying a hearing meeting the ordinary standards of due process. Under all the circumstances, we hold that due process requires an adequate hearing before termination of welfare benefits, and the fact that there is a later constitutionally fair proceeding does not alter the result.' ... We affirm.

Appellant does not contend that procedural due process is not applicable to the termination of welfare benefits. Such benefits are a matter of statutory entitlement for persons qualified to receive them. Their termination involves state action that adjudicates important rights. The constitutional challenge cannot be answered by an argument that public assistance benefits are "a 'privilege' and not a 'right.' Relevant constitutional restraints apply as much to the withdrawal of public assistance benefits as to disqualification for unemployment compensation; or to denial of a tax exemption; or to discharge from public employment. The extent to which procedural due process must be afforded the recipient is influenced by the extent to which he may be 'condemned to suffer grievous loss,' and depends upon whether the recipient's interest in avoiding that loss outweighs the governmental interest in summary adjudication. Accordingly, as we said in *Cafeteria & Restaurant Workers Union, etc. v. McElroy*, 367 U.S. 886 'consideration of what procedures due process may require under any given set of circumstances must begin with a determination of the precise nature of the government function involved as well as of the private interest that has been affected by governmental action.'

[While some government benefits may be terminated without a pretermination hearing, when welfare is discontinued only a pretermination hearing can protect the recipient's due process rights.]

For qualified recipients, welfare provides the means to obtain essential food, clothing, housing, and medical care. Thus the crucial factor in this context — a factor not present in the case of the blacklisted government contractor, the discharged government employee, the taxpayer denied a tax exemption, or virtually anyone else whose governmental entitlements are ended — is that termination of aid pending resolution of a controversy over eligibility may deprive an eligible recipient of the very means by which to live while he waits. Since he lacks independent resources, his situation becomes immediately desperate. His need to concentrate upon finding the means for daily subsistence, in turn, adversely affects his ability to seek redress from the welfare bureaucracy.

[Moreover, important government interests are promoted by pretermination evidentiary hearings, such as fostering dignity and well-being of all persons.]

We have come to recognize that forces not within the control of the poor contribute to their poverty. This perception, against the background of our traditions, has significantly influenced the development of the contemporary public assistance system. Welfare, by meeting the basic demands of subsistence, can help bring within the reach of the poor the same opportunities that are available to others to participate meaningfully in the life of the community. At the same time, welfare guards against the societal malaise that may flow from a widespread sense of unjustified frustration and insecurity. Public assistance, then, is not mere charity, but a means to 'promote the general Welfare, and secure the Blessings of Liberty to ourselves and our Posterity.' The same governmental interests that counsel the provision of welfare, counsel as well its uninterrupted provision to those eligible to receive it; pre-termination evidentiary hearings are indispensable to that end.

[While the Appellant argued that fiscal and administrative time is saved by not providing pretermination hearings, the Court held that these government interests did not override in the welfare context because the state has "weapons" to minimize these costs, such as prompt pretermination hearings and the skillful use of personnel and facilities.]

II

[The pretermination hearing does not have to be judicial or quasi-judicial. Instead, the hearing only serves to determine the validity of the grounds for termination of benefits. Because welfare authorities and recipients have an interest in a speedy resolution, pretermination hearings may be limited to minimum procedural safeguards.]

The fundamental requisite of due process of law is the opportunity to be heard.' In the present context these principles require that a recipient have timely and adequate notice detailing the reasons for a proposed termination, and an effective opportunity to defend by confronting any adverse witnesses and by presenting his own arguments and evidence orally. These rights are important in cases such as those before us, where recipients have challenged proposed terminations as resting on incorrect or misleading factual premises or on misapplication of rules or policies to the facts of particular cases.

[While the Court declined to address New York City's seven-day notice, it concluded that some situations would require a longer notice period in the interest of fairness.]

The opportunity to be heard must be tailored to the capacities and circumstances of those who are to be heard. It is not enough that a welfare recipient may present his position to the decision maker in writing or second-hand through his caseworker. Written submissions are an unrealistic option for most recipients, who lack the educational attainment necessary to write effectively and who cannot obtain professional assistance. Moreover, written submissions do not afford the flexibility of oral presentations; they do not permit the recipient to mold his argument to the issues the decision maker appears to regard as important. Particularly where credibility and veracity are at issue, as they must be in many termination proceedings, written submissions are a wholly unsatisfactory basis for decision. The second-hand presentation to the decision maker by the caseworker has its own deficiencies; since the caseworker usually gathers the facts upon which the charge of ineligibility rests, the presentation of the recipient's side of the controversy cannot safely be left to him. Therefore a recipient must be allowed to state his position orally. Informal procedures will suffice; in this context due process does not require a particular order of proof or mode of offering evidence.

In almost every setting where important decisions turn on questions of fact, due process requires an opportunity to confront and cross-examine adverse witnesses.... Welfare recipients must therefore be given an opportunity to confront and cross-examine the witnesses relied on by the department.

'The right to be heard would be, in many cases, of little avail if it did not comprehend the right to be heard by counsel.' *Powell v. Alabama*, 287 U.S. 45, 68–69 (1932). We do not say that counsel must be provided at the pre-termination hearing, but only that the recipient must be allowed to retain an attorney if he so desires. Counsel can help delineate the issues, present the factual contentions in an orderly manner, conduct cross-examination, and generally safeguard the interests of the recipient. We do not anticipate that this assistance will unduly prolong or otherwise encumber the hearing.

Finally, the decisionmaker's conclusion as to a recipient's eligibility must rest solely on the legal rules and evidence adduced at the hearing. To demonstrate compliance with this elementary requirement, the decision maker should state the reasons for his determination and indicate the evidence he relied on, though his statement need not amount to a full opinion or even formal findings of fact and conclusions of law. And, of course, an impartial decision maker is essential. We agree with the District Court that prior involvement in some aspects of a case will not necessarily bar a welfare official from acting as a decision maker. He should not, however, have participated in making the determination under review.

Affirmed.

Mr. Justice BLACK, dissenting.

In the last half century the United States, along with many, perhaps most, other nations of the world, has moved far toward becoming a welfare state, that is, a nation that for one reason or another taxes its most affluent people to help support, feed, clothe, and shelter its less fortunate citizens. The result is that today more than nine million men, women, and children in the United States receive some kind of state or federally financed public assistance in the form of allowances or gratuities, generally paid them periodically, usually by the week, month, or quarter.1 Since these gratuities are paid on the basis of need, the list of recipients is not static, and some people go off the lists and others are added from time to time. These ever-changing lists put a constant administrative burden on government and it certainly could not have reasonably anticipated that this burden would include the additional procedural expense imposed by the Court today.

The dilemma of the ever-increasing poor in the midst of constantly growing affluence presses upon us and must inevitably be met within the framework of our democratic constitutional government, if our system is to survive as such. It was largely to escape just such pressing economic problems and attendant government repression that people from Europe, Asia, and other areas settled this country and formed our Nation.

...

Representatives of the people of the Thirteen Original Colonies spent long, hot months in the summer of 1787 in Philadelphia, Pennsylvania, creating a government of limited powers. They divided it into three departments — Legislative, Judicial, and Executive. The Judicial Department was to have no part whatever in making any laws.... True, *Marbury v. Madison*, 1 Cranch 137, 2 L.Ed. 60 (1803), held, and properly, I think, that courts must be the final interpreters of the Constitution, and I recognize that the holding can provide an opportunity to slide imperceptibly into constitutional amendment and law making. But when federal judges use this judicial power for legislative purposes, I think they wander out of their field of vested powers and transgress into the area constitutionally assigned to the Congress and the people. That is precisely what I believe the Court is doing in this case. Hence my dissent.

The more than a million names on the relief rolls in New York,5 and the more than nine million names on the rolls of all the 50 States were not put there at random.... Doubtless some draw relief checks from time to time who know they are not eligible, either because they are not actually in need or for some other reason. Many of those who thus draw undeserved gratuities are without sufficient property to enable the government to collect back from them any money they wrongfully receive. But the Court today holds that it would violate the Due Process Clause of the Fourteenth Amendment to stop paying those people weekly or monthly allowances unless the government first affords them a full 'evidentiary hearing' even though welfare officials are persuaded that the recipients are not rightfully entitled to receive a penny under the law. In other words, although some recipients might be on the lists for payment wholly because of deliberate fraud on their part, the Court holds that the government is helpless and must continue, until after an evidentiary hearing, to pay money that it does not owe, never has owed, and never could owe. I do not believe there is any provision in our Constitution that should thus paralyze the government's efforts to protect itself against making payments to people who are not entitled to them.

...

It somewhat strains credulity to say that the government's promise of charity to an individual is property belonging to that individual when the government denies that the individual is honestly entitled to receive such a payment.

...

This decision is thus only another variant of the view often expressed by some members of this Court that the Due Process Clause forbids any conduct that a majority of the Court believes 'unfair,' 'indecent,' or 'shocking to their consciences.' Neither these words nor any like them appear anywhere in the Due Process Clause. If they did, they would leave the majority of Justices free to hold any conduct unconstitutional that they should conclude on their own to be unfair or shocking to them.6 ... I regret very much to be compelled to say that the Court today makes a drastic and dangerous departure from a Constitution written to control and limit the government and the judges and moves toward a constitution designed to be no more and no less than what the judges of a particular social and economic philosophy declare on the one hand to be fair or on the other hand to be shocking and unconscionable.

...

The Court apparently feels that this decision will benefit the poor and needy. In my judgment the eventual result will be just the opposite. While today's decision requires only an administrative, evidentiary hearing, the inevitable logic of the approach taken will lead to constitutionally imposed, time-consuming delays of a full adversary process of administrative and judicial review.... Thus the end result of today's decision may well be that the government, once it decides to give welfare benefits, cannot reverse that decision until the recipient has had the benefits of full administrative and judicial review, including, of course, the opportunity to present his case to this Court. Since this process will usually entail a delay of several years, the inevitable result of such a constitutionally imposed burden will be that the government will not put a claimant on the rolls initially until it has made an exhaustive investigation to determine his eligibility. While this Court will perhaps have insured that no needy person will be taken off the rolls without a full 'due process' proceeding, it will also have insured that many will never get on the rolls, or at least that they will remain destitute during the lengthy proceedings followed to determine initial eligibility.

For the foregoing reasons I dissent from the Court's holding. The operation of a welfare state is a new experiment for our Nation. For this reason, among others, I feel that new experiments in carrying out a welfare program should not be frozen into our constitutional structure. They should be left, as are other legislative determinations, to the Congress and the legislatures that the people elect to make our laws.

King v. Smith
392 U.S. 309(1968)

[Alabama participates in AFDC. This appeal asks whether Alabama's "substitute father" regulation, which denies AFDC payments to the children of a mother who "cohabits" in or outside her home with any single or married "able-bodied man," is consistent with the Social Security Act and with the Equal Protection Clause of the Fourteenth Amendment.]

I.

The AFDC program is one of three major categorical public assistance programs established by the Social Security Act of 1935. The category singled out for welfare assistance by AFDC is the 'dependent child,' who is defined in § 406 of the Act, as an age-qualified 'needy child * * * who has been deprived of parental support or care by reason of the death, continued absence from the home or physical or mental incapacity of a parent, and who is living with' any one of several listed relatives. Under this provision, and, insofar as relevant here, aid can be granted only if 'a parent' of the needy child is continually absent from the home. Alabama considers a man who qualifies as a 'substitute father' under its regulation to be a nonabsent parent within the federal statute. The State therefore denies aid to an otherwise eligible needy child on the basis that his substitute parent is not absent from the home.

Under the Alabama regulation, an 'able-bodied man, married or single, is considered a substitute father of all the children of the applicant * * * mother' in three different situations: (1) if 'he lives in the home with the child's natural or adoptive mother for the purpose of cohabitation'; or (2) if 'he visits (the home) frequently for the purpose of cohabiting with the child's natural or adoptive mother'; or (3) if 'he does not frequent the home but cohabits with the child's natural or adoptive mother elsewhere.' Whether the substitute father is actually the father of the children is irrelevant. It is also irrelevant whether he is legally obligated to support the children, and whether he does in fact contribute to their support. What is determinative is simply whether he 'cohabits' with the mother.

[Testimony by Alabama administrative officials established that "cohabitation" essentially means that the man and woman have "frequent" or "continuing" sexual relations.]

Between June 1964, when Alabama's substitute father regulation became effective, and January 1967, the total number of AFDC recipients in the State declined by about 20,000 persons, and the number of children recipients by about 16,000 or 22%. As applied in this case, the regulation has caused the termination of all AFDC payments to the appellees, Mrs. Sylvester Smith and her four minor children.

[Mrs. Smith and her four children were removed from the list of eligible recipients pursuant to the substitute father regulation because she was sexually involved with Mr. Williams on the weekends. The family was not receiving any other type of public assistance. Mr. Williams had nine children and lived at home with his wife. He had not fathered any of Mrs. Smith's children and was not legally obligated, willing, or able to support her children.]

II.

[While states are not required to participate in AFDC, those who choose to do so must comply with the requirements of the Social Security Act and regulations promulgated by the Secretary of Health, Education, and Welfare. The Act clearly requires participating states to furnish aid to families with children who have a parent absent from the home.]

The State argues that its substitute father regulation simply defines who is a non-absent 'parent' under § 406(a) of the Social Security Act. The State submits that the regulation is a legitimate way of allocating its limited resources available for AFDC assistance, in that it reduces the caseload of its social workers and provides increased benefits to those still eligible for assistance. Two state interests are asserted in support of the allocation of AFDC assistance achieved by the regulation: first, it discourages illicit sexual relationships and illegitimate births; second, it puts families in which there is an informal 'marital' relationship on a part with those in which there is an ordinary marital relationship, because families of the latter sort are not eligible for AFDC assistance.

[While states can set their own standard of need, including whether contributions by a substitute father determine whether a child is needy, Mrs. Smith and her four children do not receive any financial assistance from Mr. Williams. Further, the regulation itself is unrelated to need because the financial status of the family is irrelevant when determining the existence of a substitute father. Finally, Alabama's general power to deal with "immoral" conduct and "illegitimacy" is unquestioned. This appeal only raises whether the State may deal with these problems through denying AFDC benefits to otherwise eligible families.]

Alabama's argument based on its interests in discouraging immorality and illegitimacy would have been quite relevant at one time in the history of the AFDC program. However, subsequent developments clearly establish that these state interests are not presently legitimate justifications for AFDC disqualification. Insofar as this or any similar regulation is based on the State's asserted interest in discouraging illicit sexual behavior and illegitimacy, it plainly conflicts with federal law and policy.

[For example, in the 1850s, public welfare programs exerted preference for the "worthy" poor. This concept characterized the mothers' pension programs, which were restricted to widows considered "morally fit." This context allowed Congress to impose eligibility requirements relating to moral character on AFDC eligibility, including provisions that made children not living in "suitable homes" ineligible for benefits. In the 1940s, these provisions were criticized and abolished by 15 states. In the 1950s, pressure to disqualify illegitimate children from AFDC assistance complicated the matter further, but the federal agency strongly disapproved of these proposed provisions by the 1960s.

When Louisiana adopted conflicting legislation in 1960, HEW issued the "Flemming Rule," which declared that a "state plan may not impose an eligibility condition that would deny assistance with respect to a needy child on the basis of an [unsuitable home]." Congress memorialized this idea in 1962 by providing that dependent children would receive AFDC assistance if they were placed in foster homes after a court determined that their home was unsuitable because of the "immoral or negligence behavior of the parent." Thus, states are permitted to remove a child from a home that is judicially determined to be so unsuitable as to be "contrary to the welfare of such child," but a state may not preclude assistance to dependent children "on the basis of their mother's alleged immorality or to discourage illegitimate births."]

The most recent congressional amendments to the Social Security Act further corroborate that federal public welfare policy now rests on a basis considerably more sophisticated and enlightened than the 'worthy-person' concept of earlier times. State plans are now required to provide for a rehabilitative program of improving and correcting unsuitable homes; to provide voluntary family planning services for the purpose of reducing illegitimate births; and to provide a program for establishing the paternity of illegitimate children and securing support for them.

In sum, Congress has determined that immorality and illegitimacy should be dealt with through rehabilitative measures rather than measures that punish dependent children, and that protection of such children is the paramount goal of AFDC. In light of the Flemming Ruling and the 1961, 1962, and 1968 amendments to the Social Security Act, it is simply inconceivable, as HEW has recognized, that Alabama is free to discourage immorality and illegitimacy by the device of absolute disqualification of needy children. Alabama may deal with these problems by several different methods under the Social Security Act. But the method it has chosen plainly conflicts with the Act.

III.

Alabama's second justification for its substitute father regulation is that ... that since in Alabama the needy children of married couples are not eligible for AFDC aid so long as their father is in the home, it is only fair that children of a mother who cohabits with a man not her husband and not their father be treated similarly. The difficulty with this argument is that it fails to take account of the circumstance that children of fathers living in the home are in a very different position from children of mothers who cohabit with men not their fathers: the child's father has a legal duty to support him, while the unrelated substitute father, at least in Alabama, does not. We believe Congress intended the term 'parent' in § 406(a) of the Act, to include only those persons with a legal duty of support.

...

The AFDC program was designed to meet a need unmet by programs providing employment for breadwinners. It was designed to protect what the House Report characterized as '(o)ne clearly distinguishable group of children.' This group was composed of children in families without a 'breadwinner,' 'wage earner,' or 'father,' as the repeated use of these terms throughout the Report of the President's Committee, Committee Hearings and Reports and the floor debates makes perfectly clear. To describe the sort of breadwinner that it had in mind, Congress employed the word 'parent.' A child would be eligible for assistance if his parent was deceased, incapacitated or continually absent.

The question for decision here is whether Congress could have intended that a man was to be regarded as a child's parent so as to deprive the child of AFDC eligibility despite the circumstances: (1) that the man did not in fact support the child; and (2) that he was not legally obligated to support the child. The State correctly observes that the fact that the man in question does not actually support the child cannot be determinative, because a natural father at home may fail actually to support his child but his presence will still render the child ineligible for assistance. On the question whether the man must be legally obligated to provide support before he can be regarded as the child's parent, the State has no such cogent answer. We think the answer is quite clear: Congress must have meant by the term 'parent' an individual who owed to the child a state-imposed legal duty of support.

It is clear, as we have noted, that Congress expected 'breadwinners' who secured employment would support their children. This congressional expectation is most reasonably explained on the basis that the kind of breadwinner Congress had in mind was one who was legally obligated to support his children. We think it beyond reason to believe that Congress would have considered that providing employment for the paramour of a deserted mother would benefit the mother's children whom he was not obligated to support.

By a parity of reasoning, we think that Congress must have intended that the children in such a situation remain eligible for AFDC assistance notwithstanding their mother's impropriety. AFDC was intended to provide economic security for children whom Congress could not reasonably expect would be provided for by simply securing employment for family breadwinners. We think it apparent that neither Congress nor any reasonable person would believe that providing employment for some man who is under no legal duty to support a child would in any way provide meaningful economic security for that child.

...

The pattern of this legislation could not be clearer. Every effort is to be made to locate and secure support payments from persons legally obligated to support a deserted child. The underlying policy and consistency in statutory interpretation dictate that the 'parent' referred to in these statutory provisions is the same parent as that in § 406(a). The provisions seek to secure parental support in lieu of AFDC support for dependent children. Such parental support can be secured only where the parent is under a state-imposed legal duty to support the child. Children with alleged substitute parents who owe them no duty of support are entirely unprotected by these provisions. We think that these provisions corroborate the intent of Congress that the only kind of 'parent,' under § 406(a), whose presence in the home would provide adequate economic protection for a dependent child is one who is legally obligated to support him. Consequently, if Alabama believes it necessary that it be able to disqualify a child on the basis of a man who is not under such a duty of support, its arguments should be addressed to Congress and not this Court.

IV.

Alabama's substitute father regulation, as written and as applied in this case, requires the disqualification of otherwise eligible dependent children if their mother 'cohabits' with a man who is not obligated by Alabama law to support the children. The regulation is therefore invalid because it defines 'parent' in a manner that is inconsistent with § 406(a) of the Social Security Act. In denying AFDC assistance to appellees on the basis of this invalid regulation, Alabama has breached its federally imposed obligation to furnish 'aid to families with dependent children * * * with reasonable promptness to all eligible individuals.' Our conclusion makes unnecessary consideration of appellees' equal-protection claim, upon which we intimate no views.

. . .

Affirmed.

a. AFDC Reform Efforts Prior to 1996

The passage of the Social Security Act as part of the New Deal reflected two perhaps competing value systems related to poverty. The SSA maintained many of the poverty relief structures that had previously existed, including, for example, work requirements to qualify for old age benefits or other "earned" benefits that were dependent on contributions from wages.[36] These benefits were administered through federal programs and agencies. At the same time, benefits for the poor who fell outside the "deserving" category were funded through federal agencies, yet were administered at the state and local levels.[37] These benefits included AFDC and Unemployment Insurance.[38] Thus, while the modern welfare state was substantially expanded, perhaps even created

---

36. Kathleen Kost & Frank W. Munger, *Fooling All of the People Some of the Time: 1990s Welfare Reform and the Exploitation of American Values*, 4 VA. J. SOC. POL'Y & L. 3, 17–24 (1996) (internal citations omitted).

37. *Id.*

38. *Id.*

by the Social Security Act, to the extent the federal government did provide for the poor it maintained the moral framework that preceded it—a framework that was built upon the notion of deserving and undeserving poor as a means to determine the appropriateness of societal response.

The AFDC program remained relatively unchanged from its enactment in 1935 until the passage of the PRWORA of 1996.[39] During this time, its structure focused resources on dependent children and distributed benefits through an entitlement program.[40] Nevertheless, several revisions were made. While none of these efforts significantly impacted the AFDC program, they may be seen as a continuing reflection on reaching the proper relationship between the state and the family. Noteworthy amendments to the AFDC program included:

> 1961:[41] The AFDC UP program. This 1961 program expanded eligibility for AFDC to include families in which both parents were present but where the primary earner was unemployed, with unemployment defined as "the inability to find work in excess of 100 hours a month." Income and eligibility guidelines were the same as in AFDC, but the program enabled families to receive AFDC benefits while two parents lived in the home.

> 1962:[42] In 1962 the Social Security Act was amended to allow for the "waiver" of specific requirements under the Act. The relevant section of the Social Security Act was section 1115, which allowed the Secretary of Health, Education and Welfare to waive federal requirements for state programs that would be likely to promote the objectives of AFDC. Waivers received support from every administration for the next 35 years and may be seen as the model for what would later become welfare reform.

> 1967:[43] In 1967 the Social Security Act was amended to establish the AFDC "Work Incentive Program," or WIN. WIN required women whose youngest child was older than six and who did not fall within a limited set of exemptions, including disability, to register for work or education activities. WIN was not proven to be effective in increasing work participation among AFDC families, largely due to failure at the state level to establish programs to move registered recipients into the workforce.

> 1988:[44] In 1988 the Social Security Act was amended to create the JOBS program. JOBS replaced the WIN program and required larger numbers of welfare recipients to engage in work-related activities. JOBS did this by reducing

---

39. Robert A. Moffitt, *The Temporary Assistance for Needy Families Program*, Nat'l Bureau Econ. Res. 291, 294 (2003), http://www.nber.org/chapters/c10258.pdf.

40. *Id.*

41. *Id.*

42. Willbur J. Cohen & Robert M. Ball, Social Security Administration, *Public Welfare Amendments of 1962 and Proposals for Health Insurance for the Aged* 3, 13 (1962), https://www.ssa.gov/policy/docs/ssb/v25n10/v25n10p3.pdf.

43. Moffitt, *supra* note 39, at 294.

44. Moffitt, *supra* note 39, at 297.

exemptions from work available to AFDC recipients and mandating that states engage a minimum portion of eligible AFDC recipients in some type of work activity

Through a series of amendments to the Social Security Act over nearly 30 years, federal policy around the AFDC program had changed in significant ways by the late 1980s. First, the program placed increasing emphasis on moving families off AFDC and into the workforce. Second, the program began to devolve to state authority, a relationship seen in the 1961 amendments. These shifts were memorialized in the 1996 Personal Responsibility and Work Reconciliation Act that effectively abolished AFDC and established the Temporary Aid to Needy Families (TANF).[45] This completed the devolution of welfare to the states and redefined the relationship between the poor and their government. After 1996, poor families with children could no longer expect to receive welfare benefits without engaging in work or work preparation activities, and the state had a stronger voice in determining how welfare benefits would be delivered.[46] Thus, the waiver programs and their experimentation reveal the contours of what the poor might expect when accessing benefits.

b. The AFDC Waiver Program

Section 1115 of the Social Security Act granted the Department of Health and Human Services the power to "waive" requirements under the AFDC program, a power that was originally developed during the Kennedy administration in the early 1960s.[47] During the 1960s and 1970s states made use of the waiver program to experiment with developing new welfare policies aimed at moving families off of assistance and into economic self-sufficiency. Notwithstanding the federal government's experimentation with the AFDC program during the 1980s, welfare rolls continued to climb. By 1993, more than 10% of all mothers in the United States (approximately 3.7 million) received cash benefits from the AFDC program.[48] State governments began to take advantage of the AFDC waiver program to promote new efforts to reduce AFDC levels through new policy initiatives. Under the cooperative model of the AFDC program, states could devise their own schemes to address poverty as long as the state's initiative did not conflict with the requirements of the federally established AFDC scheme. If a state wished to adopt a policy or program that conflicted with the federal AFDC scheme, the state had the option of seeking federal approval by submitting a waiver request to the Department of Health and Human Services.[49] President Bush expressed strong support for state requests for waivers during his 1992

---

45. Moffitt, *supra* note 39, at 299.

46. Moffitt, *supra* note 39, at 299 ("[N]o federal definition of who is to be included in the assistance unit is imposed; the AFDC-UP program is abolished, and states cover two-parent families at their own discretion. States are free to impose family caps. In addition, and importantly, the entitlement nature of the program is abolished and states are not required to serve all eligible.").

47. Susan Bennett & Kathleen A. Sullivan, *Disentitling the Poor: Waivers and Welfare "Reform,"* 26 U. MICH. J.L. REF. 741, 746–47 (1993).

48. Moffitt, *supra* note 39, at 309.

49. 42 U.S.C. § 1310 (1988).

State of the Union Address and clearly signaled his administration's support for waiving many of the AFDC program's requirements.[50]

By the early 1990s, the federal government increased the number and range of waivers granted to state AFDC programs.[51] The waiver program allowed states to develop experiments within the AFDC program with the goal of enhancing outcomes for families who received benefits. Experimental efforts were wide-ranging, including family cap measures, incentives to promote marriage, and incentives for school attendance.[52] Efforts to limit family size as a means of reforming the welfare program were widely adopted. Eighteen states enacted programs under the federal waiver program that denied incremental increases in AFDC benefits for families that had additional children while receiving benefits.[53] Such policies became known as "Family Cap" provision and were adopted by states across the country, including Arkansas, California, Connecticut, New Jersey, Virginia, and Wisconsin.[54] The majority of Family Cap policies eliminated any AFDC benefit increase for families that added children. A minority allowed benefits for additional children, but at a very reduced rate, which was most often set at 50% of scheduled benefits coupled with vouchers for additional goods. While ostensibly rigid in application, all Family Cap programs provided a grace period, usually 10 months from the date a family first received AFDC benefits, as well as an exception to the limit in instances of rape or the disability of the child.[55]

Similar to the overall benefit cap addressed by the Supreme Court in *Dandridge v. Williams*,[56] Family Cap programs reduced the overall amount of assistance provided to families. Oddly, this reduction occurred when the family needed more resources to care and provide for the new child. Moreover, under the AFDC waiver program, all states adopting Family Cap policies were required to provide family planning services to recipients.[57] This requirement was not incorporated into the TANF program. Thus, TANF enabled states to adopt Family Cap programs as part of their overall

---

50. President George Bush, Address Before a Joint Session of the Congress on the State of the Union (Jan. 28, 1992), http://www.presidency.ucsb.edu/ws/index.php?pid=20544 ("States throughout the country are beginning to operate with new assumptions that when able-bodied people receive Government assistance, they have responsibilities to the taxpayer: A responsibility to seek work, education, or job training; a responsibility to get their lives in order; a responsibility to hold their families together and refrain from having children out of wedlock; and a responsibility to obey the law. We are going to help this movement. Often, State reform requires waiving certain Federal regulations. I will act to make that process easier and quicker for every State that asks for our help.").

51. Amy Clary & Trish Riley, *States Could Gain More Flexibility to Manage Medicaid Programs— What Can They Learn from the 1990s AFDC Flexibility Experience?*, NAT'L ACAD. ST. HEALTH POL'Y (Oct. 10, 2017), https://nashp.org/states-could-gain-more-flexibility-to-manage-medicaid-programs-what-can-they-learn-from-the-1990s-afdc-flexibility-experience/.

52. *Id.*

53. Robyn Bender, *Implementation of The Family Cap: Models for Integrating Family Planning Services*, 4 GEO. J. ON FIGHTING POVERTY 379, 383 (1997).

54. *Id.* at 392–94.

55. *Id.* at 383.

56. Dandridge v. Williams, 397 U.S. 471, 90 S. Ct. 1153, 25 L. Ed. 2d 491 (1970).

57. *See* Bender, *supra* note 53, at 386.

plan, without previously required components. The waiver program provided important context for the welfare reform of 1996.

c. The Earned Income Tax Credit (EITC)

While the Personal Responsibility and Work Opportunity Act of 1996 ("PRWORA") signaled an overt recognition that the system of transfer payments and centralized government administration was over, a subtle shift in our social welfare policies had already taken place by the time welfare reform became law. Beginning in the mid-1970s, U.S. anti-poverty policy moved toward tax system delivery programs that rely on the market to both define and deliver benefits to the poor. The first iteration of the EITC, presently the largest U.S. anti-poverty program, was enacted in 1972. The EITC program relies on the federal tax system as a mechanism for delivering assistance to poor Americans. Although an income support for the working poor, the EITC is included in these materials on advocacy because of the unique appeal the program has to both liberals and conservatives.[58] The credit seems to be a compelling example of creative policy.

The EITC is the largest anti-poverty program for the non-elderly in the United States. In 2015, working, low-income families received more than $49.0 billion under the EITC, roughly twice the amount spent on TANF. Despite being a cash transfer program, the EITC has found wide support across the entire political spectrum. Enacted in 1975, the EITC has been expanded five times — in 1978, 1984, 1986, 1990, 1993, and 2001[59] under support across political parties. While governor of California, Ronald Reagan supported a state EITC, and his administration was responsible for a substantial expansion of the credit under the 1986 rewrite of the tax code. The next largest expansion of the EITC occurred under President Clinton in 1993. Perhaps accounting for this broad support is the EITC's requirement that makes the credit available only to those who work — the benefit is linked to earned wages. This makes the credit appealing to those who emphasize individual accountability.

The EITC is a fully refundable tax credit, which means that the size of the credit received by the taxpayer does not depend on the taxpayer's tax liability, as it is not an offset of a tax liability. The EITC varies by family type and is conditioned on the family having earned income.

The EITC targets low- and middle-income working families with children, although individuals without children also qualify for a smaller credit. Benefits for the EITC are phased in with earnings at 40% of each dollar of income, up to $11,340 where the beneficiary is entitled to a maximum EITC of $4,824 for a family with two children and joint filers. The EITC then phases out to approximately 21% for each dollar of income up to a maximum of $41,686.

---

58. An additional policy supporting the EITC relates to minimum wage law. Dick Armey in 1996 and Charles Grassley in 2006 each argued that the EITC was preferable to an increased minimum wage.

59. Dennis Ventry, *The Collision of Tax and Welfare Politics: The Political History of the EITC, 1969–1999*, 53 NAT'L TAX J. 983 (2000).

The I.R.S. has developed a suite of marketing materials for the program in an effort to increase participation. Visit https://www.irs.gov/credits-deductions/individuals/earned-income-tax-credit for more information.

When first enacted, the EITC was promoted as providing an incentive for individuals to move from welfare to work. While research has shown that the EITC does increase overall employment, especially among single mothers,[60] employment in itself does not lead to higher standards of living for most women leaving TANF.

The range of work activities that qualify a beneficiary for the EITC is narrow. While TANF recognizes job preparedness and other steps toward economic self-sufficiency as adequate to entitle a family for benefits, the EITC limits eligibility based on wage employment. Moreover, excluding other activities related to economic self-sufficiency from the EITC benefit does not provide for long-term prospects for economic self-sufficiency.

In comparison to other anti-poverty programs, the EITC does enjoy higher participation levels among eligible beneficiaries, indicating that many low-income workers may select the path supported by the credit, although there seems to be no research on whether the disincentives in TANF artificially suppress participation rates in a way that makes such a conclusion invalid.

The EITC's success, at least as an anti-poverty policy acceptable to both liberal and conservative politicians, has been followed at the state level, with state earned income tax credits having been enacted in 17 states and the District of Columbia. Generally, state EITCs are indexed to the federal EITC and allow for a fully or partially refundable credit to be gained by the low-income worker.

Notwithstanding their broad political appeal, tax-based delivery programs face several limitations, particularly during times of severe recession. In the best of times, tax-based delivery systems tend to reach individuals who are participating in some sort of work activity, but who are not earning enough to rise above the poverty line. A large portion, 60 to 65%, of the EITC goes to low-wage, high-hour workers not high-wage, low-hour workers (Scholz 1996); and for more than 50% of filing taxpayers, the EITC directly reduces the poverty gap. While they may be low-income, these families are better off than others in the class of eligible people for the anti-poverty benefit, resulting in a lack of horizontal equity across the EITC program.

Tax-based systems also provide a limited range of supports and are in some cases unable to provide the wraparound supports that are needed to move people from poverty. The poor receive resources through the EITC even though the program is divorced from other support. In addition, tax-based anti-poverty programs do not operate in a uniform efficiency across both urban and rural areas. Finally, in what is perhaps the strongest criticism, the EITC actually provides significant benefits to

---

60. Bruce Meyer & Dan Rosenbaum, *Welfare, the EITC and the Labor Supply of Single Mothers*, 116 Q.J. Econ. 1063 (2001).

the nonpoor. The ETIC does this because the EITC underwrites labor costs for employers who hire low-wage workers. While this may not be as relevant of an issue during times of high unemployment, in times when the labor market is more competitive for low-wage workers, the availability of the EITC provides the employer with a subsidy that allows him to hire workers at lower costs.

The EITC also suffers from potential coordination problems. Because tax-based delivery systems deliver benefits in one lump sum one time each year, a large value of the benefits are lost. The problem is one of coordinating the need with the benefit that is delivered to address it. The needs addressed by anti-poverty and social welfare programs are consistent, and in many cases persistent, over time. Families living below the poverty line face a range of needs each day and week until their situation fundamentally changes, but in most cases even improved standards of living are not long-lasting and a large portion of families move between poverty and low-income status many times over the course of years, but never move beyond this relatively narrow range.

The tax system is premised on an annual accounting, either at the end of the calendar year or fiscal year, and it is at this time that the reckoning is made. Following the reckoning, the benefits available through the tax system are realized. For example, personal income taxes are filed once a year and following the April 15 deadline, millions of families across the United States experience the stimulating effect of receiving hundreds or thousands of dollars in rebates, the cumulative effect of which provides marked benefits to our overall economy. The benefit of the tax refund check, however, has little impact on the overall standard of living for the family during the months before the refund was realized.

Tax-based delivery systems are not "smooth" in allocating resources. Resources are dropped in lump sums following predefined events, instead of being made available over time in a way that smooths the inevitable burdens of poverty that the policies are intended to address. In the context of the EITC, the vast majority of beneficiaries receive the EITC in one lump sum at the end of the tax year. What this means is that the 51 weeks of the year preceding the EITC refund, the family was poor and had a range of challenges when addressing their basic needs. While the EITC provides a bump to the family's annual budget that may lift them out of poverty, it does so in a particularly inefficient way. Instead of having benefits available that allow for a steady and consistent lifting out of poverty, the lump-sum EITC drops in at the end of the year and only when averaged over time changes the families' economic condition.

Few families are able to effectively manage the budgeting issues involved with such lump-sum benefit payments. The majority of families who claim the EITC use these benefits to address credit problems, caused by the preceding 51 months of deprivation, or to invest in needed items, such as cars or appliances, all of which could have been purchased earlier in the year with saved earnings or on consumer credit. The EITC creates a 'jerk' in the family budget that might pull the family above the poverty line, but in reality masks the family's true economic situation.

B. TANF and Welfare Reform

1. The Personal Responsibility and Work Opportunity Reconciliation Act of 1996

President Clinton signed into law the Personal Responsibility and Work Opportunity Act of 1996 ("PRWORA") in 1996.[61] At the time, President Clinton said that he had fulfilled a campaign promise from the same year to "end welfare as we know it."[62] PRWORA ultimately displaced many key elements of the AFDC program and effectively ended the welfare policy that had been established in the United States for more than six decades. PRWORA did this by replacing the AFDC entitlement program with a new program named Temporary Aid to Need Families (TANF). Although TANF remained the primary federal anti-poverty program available to deliver cash assistance to the poor, there were significant changes to policy. No individual or family is *entitled* to receive TANF benefits under the PRWORA.[63] PRWORA also set time limits on TANF and conditioned receipt of support on individual behaviors, including work preparation and required participation in paternity proceedings. PRWORA also changed how cash assistance programs were administered. In contrast to the centralized AFDC funding, under PRWORA the federal government provides block funding to the states and recognized tribes who operate their own TANF programs that then pass cash on to families. The state-level administration gives great power to state and local administrators, who create their own rules for operating the program and using the TANF funds. Although states must use TANF funds to serve needy families with children, states are given wide discretion to determine eligibility for TANF funds and benefits, and to allocate available funding. TANF remains the largest cash transfer program serving non-working, non-disabled families with children.

2. TANF Overview — Federal Block Grant

Under TANF, the federal government, through the Department of Health and Human Services, provides funding to states and federally recognized tribes who operate their own TANF programs. This funding mechanism is known as the "TANF Block Grant" and provides annual funding for the TANF program.[64] The amount of the TANF Block Grant was set equal to the amount spent by the federal and state programs in 1996 and has not increased since then. Roughly $16.5 billion is made available by the federal government every year through the TANF Block Grant.[65] This equals the federal government's highest funding level for the AFDC program prior

---

61. 42 U.S.C. § 1305 (2012).

62. *See* Statement on Signing the Personal Responsibility and Work Opportunity Reconciliation Act of 1996, *supra* note 11.

63. 42 U.S.C. § 601(b) (2012).

64. Moffitt, *supra* note 39, at 299.

65. Liz Schott, Ife Floyd & Ashley Burnside, *How States Use Funds Under the TANF Block Grant*, Ctr. on Budget & Pol'y Priorities, https://www.cbpp.org/research/family-income-support/how-states-use-funds-under-the-tanf-block-grant (last updated Feb. 19, 2019).

to 1996. Because the TANF Block Grant is a static number, the actual worth of the grant has significantly decreased since 1996, resulting in reduced purchasing power of roughly 30% by 2016.[66] This means that resources available to assist the poor actually decrease despite increases in the number of people living in poverty during this time.

There are several conditions placed upon states and tribal governments that accept TANF Block Grant funds. First, TANF Block Grant funds may only be used by programs to serve one of four purposes stated in PRWORA:

(1) Provide assistance to needy families so that children may be cared for in their own homes;

(2) End dependence of needy parents on government benefits by promoting job preparations, work, and marriage;

(3) Prevent and reduce ... out-of-wedlock pregnancies ...

(4) Encourage the formation and maintenance of two-parent families.[67]

Since TANF funds may be used to meet any or all of these purposes, not all TANF funds are restricted to assisting needy families meet their basic needs. Since 1996, TANF Block Grant funds have been used for cash assistance, job training and education, child care, transportation, services to address barriers to work including domestic violence, as well as other services that promise to assist families as they move off welfare and to work.[68] Funds may also be used for pregnancy prevention and encouraging family formation. Even though the TANF Block Grant was budgeted based on the AFDC spending level, the ability to use funding that would once have gone to supporting non-working poor families was effectively reduced by the additional uses to which funding could be put following PRWORA.[69]

3. TANF Funding—State Funding

The TANF program has two funding components: the federal and state governments. Together, these components provide roughly $26.5 billion each year to the program.[70] Federal funding is set at $16.5 billion each year, which is passed through to the states and tribal governments in the form of the TANF Block Grant. The $16.5 billion is a fixed amount that is not adjusted for inflation or, with few exceptions,

---

66. Liz Schott, *Lessons from TANF: Block-Granting a Safety-Net Program Has Significantly Reduced Its Effectiveness*, Ctr. on Budget & Pol'y Priorities (Feb. 22, 2017), https://www.cbpp.org/research/family-income-support/lessons-from-tanf-block-granting-a-safety-net-program-has ("As with most other block grants, TANF funding has lost much of its value over time, with its funding falling by more than a third since it was created, after adjusting for inflation.").

67. 42 U.S.C. §601(a) (2012).

68. *See* Schott, Floyd & Burnside, *supra* note 65.

69. *See* Schott, *supra* note 66 ("TANF highlights how giving states too much flexibility through block grants can undercut accountability.").

70. *See* Schott, Floyd & Burnside, *supra* note 65.

changes in the level of need in a state.[71] In addition to federal TANF Block Grant funds, states are required to contribute an amount to the program that is indexed to each state's pre-1996 spending on AFDC. Under the formula, each state must contribute 80% of their 1994 contribution to the AFDC and AFDC-related program expenses each year.[72] This 80% requirement is reduced to 75%, however, for states that have met overall TANF work participation or two-parent family rates, giving states a clear incentive to move families off TANF and into the workforce. The state component of TANF funding is known as the "maintenance of effort" (MOE) requirement and under this component TANF receives another $15 billion each year.[73]

While seemingly set at $26.5 billion, several factors contribute to reduce the total amount of funding available to poor families under the TANF program. First, the flat funding mechanism effectively reduces the value of cash resources available under the program. Each year the purchasing power of the set block grant is reduced due to inflation.[74] Second, TANF funds can be spent "in any manner that is reasonably calculated to accomplish the purpose of TANF."[75] With funding no longer restricted to providing cash assistance to the poor (like the AFDC program mandated), funds are available for a range of programs that may only serve the poor in indirect ways, such as childcare, transportation, or marriage promotion.[76] Third, TANF's state-imposed categorical and behavioral restrictions limit access to benefits to large groups of people who had previously been entitled to assistance. These included families restricted due to the time limits, work participation requirements, or failure to assign child support. Overall, the value of the TANF system is less than the value of AFDC.

4. TANF as an Entitlement Program

The AFDC was an entitlement program, but the PRWORA expressly declared that there is no "entitlement" to TANF.[77] In contrast to the AFDC program that committed states to provide some level of assistance to all eligible beneficiaries, the dis-entitlement within TANF means that states are not obligated to provide assistance to any person who is eligible under the criteria stated in the law. States have the power, therefore, to deny benefits to any category of persons who would otherwise receive TANF benefits.

Although states have broad discretion to determine eligibility, states must provide criteria for eligibility as well as access to a hearing following denial. Further, states must also use TANF funds to serve needy families with children, including pregnant women.[78] States are obligated to "set forth criteria for the delivery of benefits and the determination of eligibility and for fair and equitable treatment," including an op-

---

71. *See id.*
72. 42 U.S.C. §609(a)(7) (2012); *see* Schott, *supra* note 66.
73. *See* Schott, *supra* note 66.
74. *See id.*
75. 42 U.S.C. §604(a)(1) (2012).
76. *See* Schott, *supra* note 66.
77. 42 U.S.C. §601(b) (2012).
78. 42 U.S.C. §602(a)(1)(A)(i) (2012).

portunity to be heard in an administrative hearing or appeal following the denial of a claim for benefits.[79]

Despite the end of the AFDC entitlement program, a majority of states have adopted language in their TANF statutes that establishes an entitlement to TANF funds (although this individual right is contingent on available state funding in most cases). Ultimately, all state and tribal government programs recognize the rights of all people to file an application for TANF benefits, be notified prior to termination or reduction in TANF benefits, and to be informed of a right to appeal the agency decision.

5. Eligibility Criteria

TANF contains three eligibility criteria; each of these has numerous individual requirements:

Financial Eligibility: Families must be found financially eligible to receive TANF benefits. Financial eligibility is determined at the state level and takes into account both earnings and the assets that are available to the family. States have broad discretion when setting both maximum income and asset eligibility criteria and as a result there is great variation between states. For example, Hawaii typically offers the highest benefit levels and Mississippi offers among the lowest.[80]

Categorical Criteria: Only members of certain categories of applicants may receive TANF benefits:

Families with dependent children or women who are pregnant. Families, known as "applicant assistance units" under the program, receiving TANF must include at least one dependent child or a pregnant woman. This means that childless adults may not receive assistance through the TANF program. As with many other eligibility criteria, states have discretion when defining who will be considered part of the assistance unit, and thus a beneficiary of TANF. Whether other individuals living with a minor child or pregnant woman, for example a grandparent, will be included as part of the assistance unit, and thereby entitled to TANF benefits, is left to the state. This group includes other children, parents, nonparent caretakers, minors who are parents, other adults in the home who are not related by blood.[81]

Immigrants. Immigrants in the United States under a valid VISA or permanent resident status are denied access to TANF as a class until they have lived in the United States for a minimum of five years. Undocumented immigrants are denied access to TANF.[82]

---

79. 42 U.S.C. §602(a)(1)(B)(iii) (2012).

80. Gene Falk, *Temporary Assistance for Needy Families (TANF): Eligibility and Benefit Amounts in State TANF Cash Assistance Programs*, 7-5700 CONG. RES. SERV. 1, 2–6 (July 22, 2014).

81. *Id.*

82. HHS, *Overview of Immigrants' Eligibility for SNAP, TANF, Medicaid, and CHIP* (Mar. 27, 2012), https://aspe.hhs.gov/basic-report/overview-immigrants-eligibility-snap-tanf-medicaid-and-chip.

Behavioral Criteria: Those who find themselves in a needy family are required to behave in well-defined ways to maintain eligibility. TANF directs individual behavior prior to beginning the application process and direction continues during the entire time the family receives benefits. Under TANF, beneficiaries must:

- Take part in an initial application assessment where the applicant may be "diverted" to other programs

- Submit to post-benefit, and in some case pre-benefit, drug screening

- Commit to immunize children

- Cooperate with paternity establishment and child support enforcement efforts, even if those efforts do not provide a financial benefit to the family

- Agree to adhere to what is known as an individual responsibility plan, which contains various goals and action steps for the beneficiary to follow in order to receive TANF, with the ultimate goal of entering the workforce.

6. Time Limits

TANF is intended to be transitional and is designed to move people off welfare and into the workforce through a time-limited, behavior-focused system. The time limits within TANF are very strict. As a general rule, no family that includes an adult who has received TANF assistance funded in whole or in part with federal funds may receive assistance for more than 60 months during their lifetime.[83] The months need not be consecutive and the state where TANF assistance was received is irrelevant. Moreover, the age of the children living with the adult is not considered. Once the 60-month cumulative limit is reached, the adult is no longer eligible to receive TANF benefits.

Consistent with other aspects that retain state autonomy in the welfare program, states are free to impose more restrictive time limits under TANF, but states are not allowed to create less restrictive limits. Thus, a state may reduce eligibility to 48 months but may not expand eligibility to 72 months.

TANF provides a few limited exceptions to the 60-month time limit. For example, states with extremely high unemployment may request a "hardship exception," which allows states to extend eligibility beyond the 60-month time limit for up to 20% of the average monthly TANF caseload.[84] This later limit may be extended beyond 20% based upon a showing that domestic violence is preventing families from moving into the workforce. Such waivers of the 20% extended eligibility option are known as the Family Violence Option. Finally, several types of families are disregarded for purposes of determining whether states are complying with the 60-month time limit, including:

---

83. 42 U.S.C. §608(a)(7)(A) (2012).
84. 42 U.S.C. §608(a)(7)(C) (2012).

- Child-only cases where no adult received assistance[85]
- Cases where a pregnant minor or minor parent is not the head of household or married to the head of household[86]
- Cases where the adult lives in Indian Country with 50% or higher unemployment.[87]

7. Work Requirements

Participation in the paid workforce is central to TANF. Families that receive TANF benefits are expected to work or actively engage in work related activities.[88] "Engaged in work" is defined to encompass a list of discrete activities, including:

- Conducting an active job search
- Being engaged in paid employment or unpaid work
- Taking part in on-the-job training
- Taking part in vocational training[89]

Ending dependency through work is one of the stated purposes of TANF, and this purpose is advanced through a strategy of compelling states to move families into the workforce through two separate work participation rates. These participation rates measure the number of families that receive TANF benefit who participate in work. The "all-families participation" rate includes all families receiving TANF benefits with an adult or minor child head of household. It requires work-eligible individuals to engage in work activities for at least 30 hours per week, but the requirement is reduced for a single custodial parent with child younger than six.[90] The "two-parent-families participation" rate is separate and slightly higher than the broader rate.[91] It requires work-eligible individuals to participate in 35 hours per week or 55 hours per week if they receive federally funded child care subsidies.[92]

8. Sanctions

The sanctions component of TANF is perhaps the most striking element of the law. Under the sanction regulations, if an individual refuses to engage in work without good cause, the family can be sanctioned (through a reduction) or terminated from

---

85. 42 U.S.C. §608(a)(7)(B)(i) (2012).
86. 42 U.S.C. §608(a)(7)(B)(ii) (2012).
87. 42 U.S.C. §§608(a)(7)(D)(i)–(ii) (2012).
88. HEATHER HAHN ET AL., URBAN INST., TANF WORK REQUIREMENTS AND STATE STRATEGIES TO FULFILL THEM 1, at 2 (2012), https://www.acf.hhs.gov/sites/default/files/opre/work_requirements_0.pdf.
89. *Id.* at 3.
90. *Id.* at 2.
91. *Id.*
92. *Id.*

assistance.[93] While there are exceptions to the imposition of sanctions, these are very few.[94] In addition, sanctions are mandatorily imposed by PRWORA even if the state would prefer not to have them.

Studies show that sanctions contribute to the decline in the TANF caseload and significantly affect the size and composition of the population because the probability of being sanctioned is related to a recipient's race, marital status, age, family size, education level, and job experience.[95] Further, while some experts consider sanctions to be the "new paternalism," there is hardly any evidence showing a positive effect on employment and earnings.[96] In fact, researchers consistently estimate that sanctions have a negative impact on recipient earnings with the impact severely worsening for individuals who receive more than one sanction. Even more interesting, a 2013 study shows that sanctions impact individuals with higher levels of education more than others.[97] This finding is particularly problematic because these individuals usually have more job prospects and mobility to leave TANF. Thus, the controversy that TANF's sanctions has produced is not unfounded.

C. The Impact of TANF on Welfare Caseloads

There is little debate that welfare reform and TANF has coincided with a significant reduction in welfare caseloads. Welfare caseloads fell by more than 50% between 1996 and 2011,[98] a stunning reduction. These numbers, however, do not necessarily show how well the welfare program works to alleviate poverty or move people to self-sufficiency. For example, under the AFDC program, 80% of eligible families received benefits, while under TANF only 40% of eligible families receive TANF benefits.[99] In addition, TANF does not provide the same level of support for the nonworking poor — with lower payments that have been devalued over time.

While caseloads have been reduced, families leaving welfare are not better off financially. There is no evidence that families who have received TANF secure long-term employment or remain engaged in the workforce on a consistent basis.

---

93. *See* 42 U.S.C. §607(e)(1) (2012); 45 C.F.R. §261.14.

94. *See* 42 U.S.C. §607(e)(2) (2012); 45 C.F.R. §261.15. For example, if a family consists of a single parent caring for a child under six in a location where appropriate and affordable childcare is not available, work requirements can be altered.

95. Richard C. Fording et al., *Do Welfare Sanctions Help or Hurt the Poor? Estimating the Casual Effect of Sanctioning on Client Earnings*, 87 Soc. Serv. Rev. 641, 645 (2013).

96. *Id.*

97. *Id.* at 669.

98. Danilo Trisi & Ladonna Pavetti, Ctr. on Budget & Pol'y Priorities, TANF Weakening as a Safety Net for Poor Families (Mar. 14, 2012), https://www.cbpp.org/research/tanf-weakening-as-a-safety-net-for-poor-families (See Figure 1).

99. Liz Schott, Ctr. on Budget & Pol'y Priorities, Policy Basics: An Introduction to TANF, https://www.cbpp.org/research/policy-basics-an-introduction-to-tanf (last updated June 15, 2015).

D. What Do People Owe
Each Other?

TANF welfare reform reshaped the idea of what a poor person can expect from the broader community. In doing so, TANF left several questions unanswered: What may a poor person expect from their government? How far may the government push into the private lives of the poor? What legitimizes governmental efforts to direct individual behavior of those who are poor? Who are welfare's true beneficiaries? While the AFDC program explicitly took the position that poor children were the program's intended beneficiaries, TANF focuses more broadly on the family as a whole. And, instead of emphasizing the provision of *welfare*, TANF shifts focus to a wider range of considerations, including nurturing family composition, and addressing employment behavior. With limited funding for TANF and increased programmatic goals beyond the delivery of financial assistance to the poor, TANF serves more interests that go beyond providing for the immediate needs of the poor.

1. Leavers

TANF is time-limited by design. TANF's work requirements, time limits, and sanctions reflect the program's goal of moving people into the workforce.[100] While setting a clear limit on benefits appeals to the public at large, it is not clear that the realities of life for the poor adult heads of a family that receive TANF are always capable of navigating the move from TANF to economic self-sufficiency. The emphasis on reducing the number of TANF beneficiaries through programs designed to move people into the workforce, however, overlooks several important questions. For instance, TANF's work requirements assume that TANF recipients are capable of first finding employment and then effectively participating in the workforce, but local workforces are not necessarily capable of absorbing large numbers of TANF leavers at any given time. Research suggests that many TANF recipients face multiple barriers to employment, and often *more* barriers than families who have not received TANF benefits, including: lower education levels, less work experience, more children, exposure to domestic violence, and limited access to transportation.[101] Research further shows, perhaps unsurprisingly, that TANF recipients with these employment barriers are less likely to find full-time employment.[102] Large numbers of post-TANF families are unable to consistently meet their families' basic needs, including food, shelter, and utilities. Due to this, many families do not have enough food to eat, face eminent eviction or homelessness, and utility cutoffs.

---

100. Office of Family Assistance, *About TANF*, https://www.acf.hhs.gov/ofa/programs/tanf/about (last visited Oct. 31, 2019).

101. Maria Cancian et al., *After the Welfare Revolution: Welfare Patterns since TANF Implementation*, 29 Soc. Work Res. 199, 200 (2005).

102. Heidi Goldberg, Ctr. on Budget & Pol'y Priorities, Improving TANF Program Outcomes for Families with Barriers to Employment (Jan. 22, 2002), https://www.cbpp.org/research/improving-tanf-program-outcomes-for-families-with-barriers-to-employment.

Additionally, physical and mental health conditions create significant barriers to work for TANF recipients. Nearly one-half of TANF recipients reported having physical or mental conditions that would impair function, compared with a much lower 19% of the general population.[103] This means that TANF recipients are at least three times more likely to suffer from a physical or mental impairment that would limit work than other adults in the United States who do not receive TANF assistance.[104] Physical impairments result in limited work ability for one-fifth of TANF recipients, and mental impairments, such as depression and anxiety, limit approximately one-third.[105] Other research has reported that nearly 40% of TANF recipients suffer from severe impairments that render them completely unable to perform one or more activity required for daily life, such as climbing a flight of stairs or balancing a checkbook, without assistance.[106] While a meaningful part of the general population of TANF recipients suffer a physical or mental impairment that limits work, only 20% of those with impairments report any gainful work activity.[107]

Furthermore, limited or low education levels add to the barriers facing TANF recipients as they move to the workforce. In 2015, approximately 38.6% of TANF recipients had less than a high school diploma or its equivalent.[108] Without a high school diploma, job prospects are severely limited either because the diploma is a requirement for the job or because the job requires skills that are developed during high school.[109] In addition, a significant number of TANF recipients suffer from learning disabilities that limit their ability to pursue higher education. Some studies have reported that between 20% and 35% of adult TANF recipients have learning disabilities of a neurological origin that negatively impact learning and cognitive processing associated with understanding.[110] A large portion of the TANF recipient population, shown to be as high as 25% in one study, have IQs below 80.[111]

Mental and physical impairments, low education, and learning disabilities create significant barriers to employment for TANF recipients that are only worsened by individualized challenges. For example, the lack of work experience significantly

---

103. GAO, *Welfare Reform: Outcomes for TANF Recipient with Impairments* 1, 2 (2002), https://www.gao.gov/assets/240/235064.pdf.

104. GAO, *Welfare Reform: More Coordinated Federal Effort Could Help States and Localities Move TANF Recipients with Impairments Toward Employment* 1, 2 (2001), https://www.gao.gov/assets/240/232971.pdf.

105. Eileen P. Sweeny, Ctr. on Budget & Pol'y Priorities, Recent Studies Indicate that Many Parents who are Current or Former Welfare Recipients Have Disabilities or Other Medical Conditions (Feb 29, 2000), https://www.cbpp.org/archiveSite/2-29-00wel.pdf.

106. *See* GAO, *supra* note 103, at 9.

107. *See* GAO, *supra* note 104, at 4.

108. OFA, *Of FY2015 TANF Recipients* (Aug. 23, 2016), https://www.acf.hhs.gov/ofa/quick-fact/education.

109. *See* Goldberg, *supra* note 102.

110. *See id.*

111. *See* Sweeney, *supra* note 105, at 3.

limits an applicant's ability to secure a job, particularly when an employer seeks prior relevant work experience in a position.[112] Between 20% and 25% of TANF recipients have low work experience or have worked in fewer than four jobs,[113] and nearly half (43%) of TANF recipients report a lack of recent work experience within the last two years.[114]

Family dynamics add further barriers to employment for many TANF recipients. For example, up to one-quarter of TANF recipients who are unemployed mothers have a child with an illness or disability that requires significant medical attention, which disrupts the normal workday and limits the parent's ability to work or attend school.[115] As many parents know, even a child who is healthy often interrupts the regular workday.

In addition to barriers that arise due to parenting, TANF recipients face barriers that are often created by their partners. Domestic violence further limits TANF recipients' work prospects. Exposure to domestic violence is a barrier to employment due to the physical and psychological toll that violence exacts from the victim.[116] Domestic violence is more prevalent among TANF recipients at 74% than the general population at 31%.[117] Thus, TANF recipients must learn to cope with elements, such as domestic violence and abuse, that many people in the general population may never experience.[118]

TANF recipients, however, like many people, also carry the stigma of past behavior. Substance abuse and criminal behavior limit employment options for between 5% and 20% of the TANF recipient population.[119] Past criminal activity can also limit work prospects due to employer concerns about safety or liability.[120] TANF recipients

---

112. Sheila R. Zedlewski, The Urban Inst., Work-Related Activities and Limitations of Current Welfare Recipients, Assessing the New Federalism, 1, 8 (1999), https://www.urban.org/sites/default/files/publication/66341/409169-Work-Related-Activities-and-Limitations-of-Current-Welfare-Recipients.PDF.

113. Susan Hauan & Sarah Douglas, HHS, *Potential Employment Liabilities Among TANF Recipients: A Synthesis of Data from Six State TANF Caseload Studies* 1, 2 (2004), https://aspe.hhs.gov/system/files/pdf/178371/rb.pdf.

114. *See* Zedlewski, *supra* note 112, at 8–9.

115. *See* Goldberg, *supra* note 102, at 3.

116. *See* Goldberg, *supra* note 102, at 4.

117. OFA, *TANF-ACF-IM-2014-03 (Domestic Violence Awareness Month: Opportunities and TANF Resources for Prevention and Action)* (Oct. 20, 2014), https://www.acf.hhs.gov/ofa/resource/tanf-acf-im-2014-03.

118. For additional information and annually updated statistics, visit the Office of Family Assistance at https://www.acf.hhs.gov/ofa/programs/tanf/data-reports.

119. Lisa R. Metsch & Harold A. Pollack, Robert Wood Johnson Found., Substance Abuse and Welfare Reform (Jul. 1, 2017), https://www.rwjf.org/en/library/research/2007/07/substance-abuse-welfare-reform.html.

120. Pamela Ovwigho et al., *Removing Criminal Records as a Barrier for TANF Recipients, Family Welfare Research Training Group*, U. Md. Balt. Sch. Soc. Work (Mar. 2009), https://pdfs.semanticscholar.org/2c12/a0663bd8249586c000a82122cc2e6c796e23.pdf.

face ancillary punishments due to criminal behavior that further limit job prospects because federal law requires that convicted drug felons be banned for life from receiving TANF benefits—unless exempted by state law.[121]

Moving from the family and individual behavior, TANF recipients next face barriers to work from within their own communities, beginning with finding a way to commute to work. The Federal Transit Administration has found the 94% of TANF recipients do not own a car,[122] which forces the majority of TANF recipients to rely on public transportation to get to work. At the same time, many cities lack adequate, let alone convenient, public transportation systems to move TANF recipients to a workplace.[123] Despite a seeming prevalence of public transportation options, public transportation systems lack adequate schedules to serve working people, are not affordable, do not provide routes that serve areas with high job growth (which often occurs on the built fringe of a city), require impractically long commutes, and involve risk to personal safety.[124]

While any of these barriers noted here would be significant alone, TANF recipients experience multiple barriers to employment, each of which is significant in itself. The Urban Institute, for example, has shown that 44% of TANF recipients report having at least two of the above barriers to work, with 17% reporting three or more.[125] A mere 23% of all adult TANF recipients describe themselves as having no barriers to employment.[126]

Overall, TANF's focus on work unfortunately ignores the realities facing its recipients as they attempt to enter the job market. Sadly, at the same time, TANF caseload numbers have been reduced, long-term economic self-sufficiency among TANF recipients has not increased, and poverty levels among TANF leavers increased.[127] Studies of TANF leavers over the 10-year period between 1996 and 2005 showed that most families who left welfare during this time were "disconnected" workers who had neither income from work nor welfare post-TANF, that the share of families post-TANF without any source of income increased over time and that workers who left TANF faced significant barriers to employment or education.[128] Studies during this

---

121. GAO, *Drug Offenders: Various Factors May Limit the Impact of Federal Laws That Provide for Denial of Selected Benefits*, GAO (Sept. 26, 2005), https://www.gao.gov/assets/250/247940.pdf.

122. Eileen S. Stommes & Dennis M. Brown, Econ. Res. Ser., USDA, *Moving Rural Residents to Work: Lessons Learned from Implementation of Eight Job Access and Reverse Commute Projects*, Food and Rural Economic Division (2002), https://naldc-legacy.nal.usda.gov/naldc/download.xhtml?id=38805&content=PDF.

123. April Kaplan, *Transportation: The Essential Need to Address the 'To' in Welfare-to-Work* (Washington DC: Welfare Information Network, Issue Notes, vol. 2, No. 10, June 1998).

124. *Id.*

125. Zedlewski, *supra* note 112, at 11.

126. *Id.*

127. Liz Schott, Ctr. on Budget & Pol'y Priorities, Policy Basics: An Introduction to TANF (Dec. 4, 2012), http://cbpp.org/files/7-22-10tanf2.pdf.

128. Shawn Fremstad, Ctr. on Budget & Pol'y Priorities, Recent Welfare Reform Research Findings: Implications for TANF Reauthorization and State TANF Policies 1, 2 (Jan. 30, 2004), https://www.cbpp.org/archiveSite/1-30-04wel.pdf (internal citations omitted).

same period found that between 50% and 75% of families post-TANF remained poor three years after losing benefits.[129] Moreover, hardship was found uniformly across the United States, whether in rural or urban areas and in states from New York to California. Families who left TANF due to sanctions experienced higher rates of hardship and deeper poverty.[130]

2. Barriers to Economic Self-Sufficiency[131]

States struggle to put TANF adults in work activities because most adults receiving TANF have at least one barrier to work, while about four in ten TANF eligible adults face multiple barriers. These barriers to work include lack of education, mental or physical disabilities, substance abuse or alcoholism, limited work experience, and caregiving responsibilities for disabled children. For those who are working, income gains from employment are often reduced by the loss of public benefits and are eaten up by the very costs of working, such as childcare, transportation, uniforms, and other expenses. Thus, "even among the least disadvantaged sample members, those with more than a high school education, substantial recent work histories, and consistently good health, steady economic progress is far from certain."[132]

Moreover, as a result of sanctions, time limits, diversion tactics, and other discouraging practices, at least one in five families that leave TANF are disconnected from the social safety net, and these families tend to be poorer than other single-parent families. Ironically, sanctions do not incentivize finding work. Instead, as they increase in severity and duration, welfare leavers are more likely to end up jobless and with lower earnings. In short, the employment rate of welfare parents has decreased, TANF caseloads remain low despite increasing need caused by the recession,[133] and current and former welfare recipients remain mired in poverty.

E. Challenging Welfare Reform and Behavior Modification

TANF completed a transition to a welfare system that moved away from supporting children and, instead, focused heavily on modifying the behavior of the poor. Underlying TANF and the PRWORA was the belief that poverty results from individual choices instead of structural or societal inequities. In most areas of public policy, in-

---

129. *Id.*
130. *Id.*
131. *See* Sunshine Rote & Jill Quadagno, *Depression and Alcohol Dependence Among Poor Women: Before and After Welfare Reform*, 85 Soc. Serv. Rev. 229, 231 (2011).
132. Robert G. Wood et al., *Two Steps Forward, One Step Back: The Uneven Economic Progress of TANF Recipients*, 82 Soc. Serv. Rev. 3, 24 (2012).
133. *See* Randi Hall, CLASP, TANF 101: TANF During the Great Recession (July 2015), https://www.clasp.org/sites/default/files/publications/2017/04/TANF-101-TANF-in-the-Great-Recession.pdf.

dividual liberties are protected from government intrusion through a system of constitutional controls and legislative prudence. However, this does not seem to be the case in poverty policy. Instead, welfare reform explicitly adopted an ideology focused on the perceived lack of work ethic and responsibility among the poor and the political will to address this perception.

1. TANF and Family Composition

Perhaps one of the most intrusive elements of TANF are policies directed to limit family size among welfare recipients under what is called the "Family Cap" provision. Several states used the AFDC waiver process to enact Family Cap regulations that limited benefits for additional children born into a family receiving AFDC. The Family Cap policy was made part of TANF as enacted.[134] In a society that values families and individual liberty, these policies seem to be a stark departure from widely held opinions concerning the proper role of government.

Williams v. Martin

283 F. Supp. 2d 1286 (N.D. Ga. 2003)

I. BACKGROUND

[Defendant Jim Martin is the administrator of Georgia's TANF program. The plaintiffs are minor children of former recipients of TANF benefits.] The Defendant Jim Martin is the Commissioner of the Georgia Department of Human Resources and administrator of the Temporary Assistance to Needy Families ("TANF") program. He is sued in his official capacity as administrator of the program. TANF is Georgia's current welfare program for families. The Plaintiffs are minor children of former recipients of benefits under the program.

In order to receive this federal block grant, a state must submit a plan demonstrating compliance with federal law to the United States Department of Health and Human Services for approval. The state must also certify that it operates a child support enforcement program consistent with the requirements of Title IV-D of the Social Security Act. As a condition of eligibility for TANF benefits, an applicant must assign to the state any right to collect child support payments for all persons for whom TANF is sought.

Georgia is a participant in the TANF block grant program. With some limited exceptions, families receiving TANF assistance in Georgia are subject to a "family cap" under which TANF benefits do not increase as a result of a birth of additional children during the time that the family is receiving TANF assistance. The state requires TANF recipients to assign to the state the right to establish and collect child support for any child who is subject to the family cap even though inclusion of the "capped" child

---

134. MARK GREENBERG & STEVE SAVNER, CTR. FOR L. AND SOC. POL'Y, A DETAILED SUMMARY OF KEY PROVISIONS OF THE TEMPORARY ASSISTANCE FOR NEEDY FAMILIES BLOCK GRANT OF H.R. 3734, at 1, 2–4 (1996).

does not increase the family's TANF benefits. Plaintiffs contend that this policy and practice violate federal law and the due process and equal protection clauses of the Constitution.

The Plaintiff Brendan Williams was born on May 9, 1998. At the time, his mother, Michelle Pait, was receiving Georgia TANF benefits for herself and Brendan's half-brother Byron. Michelle Pait does not receive child support for Byron. Ms. Pait reported Brendan's birth to the Department of Family and Children Services ("DFCS") and signed papers to assign to the state her rights to child support for Brendan. Brendan was excluded from the TANF benefits under Georgia's "family cap". In January 1999, Brendan's father began to pay child support in the amount of $161 per month. Because Brendan is a "capped" child, Ms. Pait continued to receive TANF benefits at the level of a family of two, even after Brendan was born.

The Plaintiff Zon'tarrio' Q. Boston was born on January 10, 2000. At the time, his mother, Audrey Boston, was receiving TANF benefits for her daughter Yerdua and herself. Yerdua's father was paying child support. When Ms. Boston reported Zon'tarrio's birth to DFCS, her social worker had her assign Zon'tarrio's right to child support to DFCS. Zon'tarrio's father began paying child support through the State Office of Child Support Enforcement in August 2000. Plaintiff Zon'tarrio' Q. Boston is also a "capped" child, and a portion of the child support paid by his father has been kept by the state, pursuant to the policy set forth above. The state continued to receive child support payments made by the fathers of Brendan Williams and Zon'tarrio' Q. Boston after the families stopped receiving TANF benefits. For Plaintiff Zon'tarrio' Q. Boston, the assignments remain in effect and offset public assistance which he alleges he is no longer receiving. For Plaintiff Brendan Williams, the challenged policy keeps him and the Pait family from electing to reapply for TANF benefits.

The Plaintiffs claim that the Georgia TANF program violates federal law, by requiring assignment of child support payments for "capped" children. The Plaintiffs also claim that this mandatory assignment of child support constitutes a taking in violation of the Fourteenth Amendment. In their Amended Complaint, Plaintiffs sought both retroactive monetary relief and prospective injunctive relief. Defendant moved this Court to dismiss these claims on the grounds that the suit is barred by the Eleventh Amendment.

III. *DISCUSSION*

C. *Plaintiffs' Statutory Claim*

The Plaintiffs assert that federal law prohibits Defendant's policy requiring assignment of "capped" children's court-ordered child support. The statute, 42 U.S.C. § 608(a)(3), mandates that states require children who receive TANF assistance to assign their child support payments to the state.

. . .

They argue that the assignments mandated by Section 608(a)(3) are limited to assignments for family members receiving TANF assistance. The Defendant contends that "capped" children are in fact receiving TANF assistance and that the state's child support assignment requirement is not barred by Section 608(a)(3).

Setting aside for the moment the issue of whether the "capped" children receive TANF assistance, the Court holds that the assignment requirement is not prohibited by Section 608(a)(3).... The statute contains no explicit prohibition, and the Court sees no statutory or other basis for implying one. As Georgia's child support assignment requirement does not violate 42 U.S.C. §608(a)(3), summary judgment for Defendant on Plaintiffs' statutory claim is proper.

D. *Plaintiffs' Constitutional Takings Claim*

The Plaintiffs also contend that Georgia's policy of requiring families to assign the child support rights of "capped" children to the state takes private property for a public purpose without compensation, in violation of the Fourteenth Amendment. In *Bowen v. Gilliard*, 483 U.S. 587, 107 S.Ct. 3008, 97 L.Ed.2d 485 (1987), the Supreme Court upheld the constitutionality of a North Carolina regulation requiring families receiving public assistance to assign child support payments to the state for each child living in the same home. In evaluating whether the North Carolina regulation constituted a "taking," the Court relied on an ad hoc factual inquiry into the circumstances of the case. To aid in this determination, the Court employed the three-factor analysis developed in *Penn Central Transportation Co. v. City of New York*, 438 U.S. 104, 98 S.Ct. 2646, 57 L.Ed.2d 631 (1978).

The first *Penn Central* factor is the economic impact of the regulation on the claimant. *Bowen*, 483 U.S. at 606, 107 S.Ct. 3008. With respect to the North Carolina regulation, the Supreme Court held that any reduction in the value of support payments received by a child was mitigated by the benefits received by the child due to his inclusion in the family assistance unit. *Id.* at 607, 107 S.Ct. 3008. The benefits provided to the child by the North Carolina regulation included an extra $50 received by the family, extra AFDC benefits based on an additional family member, the state's enforcement power to collect support payments, and the state's bearing the risk of the parent's failure to pay. *Id.*

Plaintiffs contend that, pursuant to Georgia's family cap, the state has, unlike North Carolina in *Bowen*, withheld their child support payments without providing them any TANF assistance in return. Defendant concedes that the "capped" children are not included in calculation of monthly maximum TANF grants. Before Plaintiff Zon'tarrio' Q. Boston was added to the Boston TANF family assistance unit, the Boston's' maximum monthly TANF grant amount was $155. After Zon'tarrio' was added to the family assistance unit, the maximum TANF grant amount remained $155. Before Plaintiff Brendan Williams was added to the Pait TANF family assistance unit, the Pait family's maximum monthly TANF grant was $235. After Brendan was added to the family assistance unit, the maximum TANF grant amount remained $235.

However, the aid that the state grants to a family assistance unit is not limited to TANF monthly grants. Families may also receive GAP payments. These GAP payments reflect the difference between the family's Standard of Need and the TANF monthly grant they receive. As the family's Standard of Need increases, the family's potential GAP payments also increase. The addition of "capped" children to a family assistance unit increases that family's Standard of Need and, thus, increases the family's potential GAP payments. The additions of Zon'tarrio' Q. Boston and Brendan Williams to their families' assistance units are no exception. Before Zon'tarrio' was added to the Boston TANF unit, the Bostons' Standard of Need was $235. After Zon'tarrio' was added, this Standard of Need was raised to $356. As their TANF monthly maximum grant remained constant at $155, the Bostons' potential GAP payments increased from $80 to $201, an increase of $121 per month. The Boston family received $2,030 in the form of GAP payments while receiving TANF benefits. Similarly, before Brendan was added to the Pait TANF unit, the Paits' Standard of Need was $356. After Brendan was added, the Standard of Need was raised to $424. As their TANF monthly maximum grant remained constant at $235, the Paits' potential GAP payments increased from $121 to $189, an increase of $68 per month. The Pait family assistance unit received $1,122 in GAP payments while receiving TANF benefits. Plaintiffs' families' receipt of GAP payments mitigates the adverse economic impact on Plaintiffs of the assignment of their child support to the state.

Moreover, any economic harm to Plaintiffs stemming from the assignment of their child support to the state is also mitigated by the state's role in collecting these support payments. Though the state, unlike North Carolina in *Bowen,* does not bear the risk of nonpayment of child support (as GAP payments are not made when child support funds are not received), the state does use its own enforcement resources to collect these payments. As the state provides significant assistance to Plaintiffs and their families in exchange for assignment of Plaintiffs' child support payments, the economic impact of the TANF regulation on Plaintiffs does not justify finding an unconstitutional taking.

The second *Penn Central* factor is the extent to which the regulation interferes with the claimant's investment-backed expectations. *Penn Central,* 438 U.S. at 124, 98 S.Ct. 2646. In *Bowen,* the Supreme Court held this factor largely inapplicable, as the child receiving support payments "holds no vested protectable expectation that his or her parent will continue to receive identical support payments on the child's behalf, and that the child will enjoy the same rights with respect to them." *Bowen,* 483 U.S. at 607, 107 S.Ct. 3008. The Court supported this contention with a decision of the Supreme Court of North Carolina asserting that, in North Carolina, child support is not a property right of the child. *Id.* By contrast, Georgia recognizes a child's property interest in child support. *Georgia Dept. of Human Resources ex rel. Holland v. Holland,* 263 Ga. 885, 886, 440 S.E.2d 9 (1994); *Stewart v. Stewart,* 217 Ga. 509, 510, 123 S.E.2d 547 (1962). However, as this right may be modified by parental election or by law, it similarly does not give the child a vested expectation in continued identical child support payments.

Child support payments may be modified at the custodial parent's election. In Georgia, custodial parents are not owners but mere trustees of the funds paid for a child's benefit. *Holland,* 263 Ga. at 886, 440 S.E.2d 9; *Stewart,* 217 Ga. at 510, 123

S.E.2d 547. They are charged with the duty of ensuring that child support is applied for the benefit of the children. *Law Office of Tony Center v. Baker*, 185 Ga.App. 809, 810, 366 S.E.2d 167 (1988). A custodial parent may, however, exercise the child's right to child support at her election. One way in which a parent may modify child support payments is through assignment of child support rights in return for temporary need-based assistance. *Wehunt v. Ledbetter*, 875 F.2d 1558, 1566 (11th Cir.1989). This gives states the opportunity to recoup the financial drain imposed by the welfare system on the state and federal treasuries. *Id.* As custodial parents have the ability to assign child support payments, the child cannot have any vested expectations in continued child support.

The prospective right to child support payments may also be modified by law. O.C.G.A. § 19-6-19 outlines the grounds upon which child support payments may be revised. A child support award may be amended based on changes in income or financial status of either parent. O.C.G.A. § 19-6-19(a). Child support payments may also be revised due to remarriage or voluntary cohabitation of the former spouse. O.C.G.A. § 19-6-19(b). Any right to have the state force a noncustodial parent to make payments, is, like so many other legal rights, subject to modification by the "public acts of government." *Bowen*, 483 U.S. at 608, 107 S.Ct. 3008 (quoting *Reichelderfer v. Quinn*, 287 U.S. 315, 319, 53 S.Ct. 177, 77 L.Ed. 331 (1932)). As child support payments may be prospectively modified for myriad reasons, a parent's election to modify these payments by assigning them to the state does not unduly interfere with the recipient child's expectations. Thus, as the Supreme Court notes, "[t]his prospective change in the child's expectations concerning future use of support payments is far from anything we have ever deemed a taking." *Bowen*, 483 U.S. at 608, 107 S.Ct. 3008.

The third and final *Penn Central* factor is the character of the governmental action. *Penn Central*, 438 U.S. at 124, 98 S.Ct. 2646. In *Bowen*, the Court recognized that the government is required to make hard choices and balance various incentives in deciding how to allocate benefits in welfare programs. *Id.* at 608, 107 S.Ct. 3008. The Court held that a "decision to include child support as part of family income certainly does not implicate the type of concerns that the Takings Clause protects." *Id.*

...

Moreover, as acknowledged by the Supreme Court in *Bowen*, involvement in the TANF program, and the subsequent assignment of child support payments, is *voluntary*. The law does not require any custodial parent to apply for TANF benefits. A parent, the law must presume, would only apply for benefits when he or she believes that the family as a whole—and each child committed to his or her custody—will be better off with the family receiving benefits than without. *Bowen*, 483 U.S. at 608–09, 107 S.Ct. 3008. Plaintiffs' custodial parents deny that their assignment of child support payments was voluntary, as they assert that they did not understand the terms of the application for TANF benefits. Specifically, Boston and Pait assert that they did not know that child support for their "capped" children would be assigned to and ultimately kept by the state. Any misunderstanding of these terms is unfortunate. However, the language of an application for TANF benefits clearly states that by accepting assistance, the parent assigns to Georgia the right to any child support. Boston and Pait signed statements acknowledging that they agreed to this condition and to Georgia's family cap Thus, their failure to comprehend the terms of the applications for TANF benefits do not make their participation in the program or its child support assignment requirement involuntary. A custodial parent's voluntary decision to enter the program, and thereby assign child support payments to the state, does not create an unconstitutional taking by the state.

...

Application of the three *Penn Central* factors counsel the Court to find that the assignment of child support payments for "capped" children does not constitute a taking in violation of the Fourteenth Amendment. Summary judgment for the Defendant is proper.

IV. *CONCLUSION*

For the reasons set forth above, Plaintiffs' Motion for Summary Judgment is DENIED, and Defendant's Motion for Summary Judgment is GRANTED.

2. TANF Benefits and Criminal Behavior

Despite an individual's need, criminal acts can categorically disqualifying a person from receiving TANF benefits under 21 U.S.C. § 862a(a)(1)–(2):

> An individual convicted (under Federal or State law) of any offense which is classified as a felony by the law of the jurisdiction involved and which has as an element the possession, use, or distribution of a controlled substance (as defined in section 802(6) of this title) shall not be eligible for—
>
> (1) assistance under any State program funded under part A of title IV of the Social Security Act [42 U.S.C.A. § 601 et seq.], or
>
> (2) benefits under the supplemental nutrition assistance program (as defined in section 3 of the Food and Nutrition Act of 2008 (7 U.S.C. § 2012)) or any State program carried out under that Act.

While poverty and crime rates have a comingled effect on one another, poverty does not necessarily cause crime. Since the 1990s, crime rates have decreased[135] despite an increase in poverty.[136] Though poverty rates among poorer communities may be slightly higher than the national average, tying eligibility for TANF benefits to convictions disregards need but could provide an incentive for good behavior. For more information regarding criminal justice issues in the poverty context, see Chapter 11, Access to Justice.

---

135. MATTHEW FRIEDMAN, AMES GRAWERT & JAMES CULLEN, BRENNAN CTR. FOR JUST., CRIME TRENDS: 1990–2016 (Apr. 18, 2017), https://www.brennancenter.org/publication/crime-trends1990-2016.

136. *Poverty Rate in the United States from 1990 to 2016*, STATISTA, https://www.statista.com/statistics/200463/us-poverty-rate-since-1990/ (last visited Nov. 20, 2019).

United States v. Littlejohn

224 F.3d 960 (9th Cir. 2000)

[Littlejohn pleaded guilty to one count of cocaine base distribution and gave up his right to appeal in exchange for, among other things, the government's agreement to stipulate to, and recommend, that Littlejohn receive a 240-month sentence instead of the possibility of life in prison.]

...

Littlejohn's Pre-Sentencing Report ("PSR") included a section on the "Denial of Federal Benefits," an issue discussed neither in the plea agreement nor at Littlejohn's plea hearing. The PSR stated that, ... the court "may deny eligibility for certain Federal benefits of any individual convicted of distribution or possession of a controlled substance," and that, "[p]ursuant to 21 U.S.C. § 862(a)(1)(C), upon a third or subsequent conviction for distribution of a controlled substance, the defendant shall be permanently ineligible" for such benefits, unless ineligibility is suspended by the court under 21 U.S.C. § 862(c). Elsewhere, the PSR listed Littlejohn's three prior California convictions for "possession of a controlled substance for sale," and two prior California convictions for "possession of a controlled substance."

At sentencing, the district court noted that "[t]here is a recommendation in here [that] the defendant, having sustained a third conviction for distribution of a controlled substance, is permanently ineligible for all federal benefits as defined at 21 U.S.C. 862(d) until such time as the Court may suspend the ineligibility." However, the court and both parties expressed uncertainty about the issue of federal benefit ineligibility, and the court stated that it was reluctant to impose the ineligibility. Ultimately, the court concluded that it did not have to include the ineligibility in the judgment and commitment order and refused to do so. The court closed its discussion of the issue by stating that "[i]f I had the discretion—we haven't fully plumbed this issue—I would suspend the ineligibility because I think it's counterproductive to rehabilitation." Littlejohn made no attempt to argue before the district court that the failure to mention federal benefit ineligibility at the time of the plea hearing or in the text of the plea agreement affected the voluntariness of either his entrance into the plea agreement or his eventual guilty plea.

The district court sentenced Littlejohn to 240 months of imprisonment—in accord with the parties' agreement—but gave little explanation of its sentencing decision.

DISCUSSION

[The voluntariness of Littlejohn's guilty plea, the validity of Littlejohn's waiver of his right to appeal, and whether the trial court satisfied Federal Rules of Criminal Procedure 11 are reviewed de novo.]

On appeal, Littlejohn argues that his lack of warning concerning ineligibility for federal benefits rendered involuntary his entrance into the plea agreement, the waiver of appeal included therein, and his eventual guilty plea. This question appears to be one of first impression in this circuit. He also argues that the court failed to satisfy the mandate of 18 U.S.C. § 3553(c) in its selection of a 240-month sentence. He seeks a remand for re-pleading or, in the alternative, re-sentencing. The government responds by asserting that this court should review Littlejohn's claims, at most, under a plain error review, that the district court was not required to warn Littlejohn of ineligibility for federal benefits, that any error was harmless under Fed.R.Crim.P. 11(h), and that Littlejohn waived any appeal of his sentence by entering into the plea agreement.

...

Section 862a, on the other hand, is a separate benefit ineligibility provision for certain drug offenders. It provides that

[a]n individual convicted (under Federal or State law) of any offense which is classified as a felony by the law of the jurisdiction involved and which has as an element the possession, use, or distribution of a controlled substance (as defined in section 802(6) of this title) shall not be eligible for ... assistance under any state program funded under part A of title IV of the Social Security Act [42 U.S.C.A. § 601 et seq.], or ... benefits under the food stamp program (as defined in section 3(h) of the Food Stamp Act of 1977 [7 U.S.C.A. § 2012(h)]) or any State program carried out under the Food Stamp Act of 1977 [7 U.S.C.A. § 2011 et seq.].

21 U.S.C. § 862a(a) (1999). Although neither the PSR nor the district court mentioned the applicability of section 862a at any time in the proceedings below,3 both it and subsection 862(a) plainly apply to Littlejohn.

As should be clear from the language of both subsection 862(a) and section 862a, Littlejohn's conviction automatically strips him of benefits under both sections. In the case of subsection 862(a), this is so because Littlejohn has three prior state convictions for possession of a controlled substance for sale. *See* 21 U.S.C. § 862(a)(1)(C). With regards to section 862a, he is stripped of benefits through his conviction for distribution of cocaine base at issue in this case, irrespective of his prior state law convictions. Because these sections automatically affect the range of Littlejohn's punishment, they are "direct" consequences.

CONCLUSION

The district court was not required, when it took Littlejohn's plea, to inform him of the effects of subsection 862(a). The district court *was* required to inform Littlejohn of the direct consequences implicated by section 862a, but the court's failure to do so in this case was harmless error. As such, Littlejohn's conviction is AFFIRMED. His appeal of his sentence is DISMISSED.

F. TANF, Immigration, and the Right to Travel

Title IV of the PRWORA law contains provisions that address the eligibility of "unqualified aliens" to receive benefits from state and federal government agencies and reflects a desire to restrict benefits for undocumented children in the United States. The PRWORA set out specific findings in support of these restrictions:

The Congress makes the following statements concerning national policy with respect to welfare and immigration:

(1) Self-sufficiency has been a basic principle of United States immigration law since this country's earliest immigration statutes.

(2) It continues to be the immigration policy of the United States that—

(A) aliens within the Nation's borders not depend on public resources to meet their needs, but rather rely on their own capabilities and the resources of their families, their sponsors, and private organizations, and

(B) the availability of public benefits not constitute an incentive for immigration to the United States.

(3) Despite the principle of self-sufficiency, aliens have been applying for and receiving public benefits from Federal, State, and local governments at increasing rates.

(4) Current eligibility rules for public assistance and unenforceable financial agreements have proved wholly incapable of assuring that individual aliens not burden the public benefits system.

(5) It is a compelling government interest to enact new rules for eligibility and sponsorship agreements in order to assure that aliens be self-reliant in accordance with national immigration policy.

(6) It is a compelling government interest to remove the incentive for illegal immigration provided by the availability of public benefits.

(7) With respect to the state authority to make determinations concerning the eligibility of qualified aliens for public benefits in this chapter, a state that chooses to follow the federal classification in determining the eligibility of such aliens for public assistance shall be considered to have chosen the least restrictive means available for achieving the compelling governmental interest of assuring that aliens be self-reliant in accordance with national immigration policy.

These findings reflect a belief that immigrants are motivated by public benefit programs instead of other factors, such as human rights conditions or persecution. As such, the PRWORA limits benefits to "qualified aliens" who are defined by 8 U.S.C. § 1641(b) as:

(1) an alien who is lawfully admitted for permanent residence under the Immigration and Nationality Act,

(2) an alien who is granted asylum under section 208 of such Act,

(3) a refugee who is admitted to the United States under section 207 of such Act,

(4) an alien who is paroled into the United States under section 212(d)(5) of such Act for a period of at least 1 year,

(5) an alien whose deportation is being withheld under section 243(h) of such Act,

(6) an alien who is granted conditional entry pursuant to section 203(a)(7) of such Act as in effect prior to April 1, 1980, or

(7) an alien who is a Cuban and Haitian entrant (as defined in section 501(e) of the Refugee Education Assistance Act of 1980).

In 2014, tens of thousands of women and unaccompanied children ventured from Honduras, El Salvador, and Guatemala (the "Northern Triangle Region" of Central America) to the United States seeking asylum.[137] While President Obama considered this a "humanitarian crisis," his office and the DHS launched a "deterrence strategy" that aimed to spread a message that prospective immigrants that migrating to the United States "was not worth the risk."[138] The U.S. immigration agencies, USCIS and DHS, expanded detention and removal efforts following the 2016 elections.

While the Obama administration and DHS' efforts may have deterred some immigrants from entering the United States in 2014, immigration from the Northern Triangle Region has steadily increased since 2015.[139] In fact, half the unaccompanied children and family units apprehended in *all* of 2015 were from Mexico and the Northern Triangle.[140] These deterrence efforts are particularly disheartening because the Northern Triangle Region is crippled with violence perpetrated by criminal gangs, poverty, and the lack of economic opportunity.[141] Thus, immigrants from the Northern Triangle seek asylum due to the "failed state" of their home countries.

Because TANF and other public benefit programs do not extend to undocumented immigrants, these individuals face hurdles beyond the border. These barriers include language and cultural sensitivity issues, fear of adverse immigration consequences, and confusion about the programs themselves.[142] Complicating the matter further,

---

137. JONATHAN T. HISKEY ET AL., AM. IMMIGR. COUNCIL, UNDERSTANDING THE CENTRAL AMERICAN REFUGEE CRISIS (Feb. 1, 2016), https://www.americanimmigrationcouncil.org/research/understanding-central-american-refugee-crisis.

138. *Id.*

139. MUZAFFAR CHISTI & FAYE HIPSMAN, MIGRATION POL'Y INST., INCREASED CENTRAL AMERICAN MIGRATION TO THE UNITED STATES MAY PROVE AN ENDURING PHENOMENON (Feb. 18, 2016), https://www.migrationpolicy.org/article/increased-central-american-migration-united-states-may-prove-enduring-phenomenon.

140. *Id.*

141. *Id.*

142. ASPE, *Overview of Immigrant Eligibility for SNAP, TANF, Medicaid, and CHIP* (Mar. 2012), https://aspe.hhs.gov/basic-report/overview-immigrants-eligibility-snap-tanf-medicaid-and-chip.

eligibility standards among states vary widely.[143] Thus, immigrants who seek asylum from violent conditions after journeying from afar are met with little aid once arriving in the United States.

In addition to immigrants, the PRWORA provided for interstate movement of TANF applicants. There is great variation in TANF benefit levels across the United States. In an effort to limit the gaming of the TANF program, the PRWORA expressly authorizes any state receiving TANF funds to "apply to a family the rules (including benefit amounts) of the [TANF] program ... of another State if the family has moved to the State from the other State and has resided in the State for less than 12 months."[144]

In 1997, the state of California issued an "All County Letter,"[145] announcing that the Department of Health and Human Services would begin to enforce a durational residency requirement on April 1, 1997. Under the residency requirement, if members of an eligible family had lived in California all of their lives, but left the state "on January 29th, intending to reside in another state, and returned on April 15th," their benefits would be determined by the law of their state of residence from January 29 to April 15, assuming that that level was lower than California's. Moreover, the lower level of benefits would apply regardless of whether the family was on welfare in the state of prior residence and regardless of the family's motive for moving to California. The instructions also explain that the residency requirement is inapplicable to families that recently arrived from another country. The Supreme Court considered this durational residency requirement in *Saenz v. Roe*.

Saenz v. Roe
526 U.S. 489 (1999)

In 1992, California enacted a statute limiting the maximum welfare benefits available to newly arrived residents. The scheme limits the amount payable to a family that has resided in the State for less than 12 months to the amount payable by the State of the family's prior residence. The questions presented by this case are whether the 1992 statute was constitutional when it was enacted and, if not, whether an amendment to the Social Security Act enacted by Congress in 1996 affects that determination.

II

On April 1, 1997, the two respondents filed this action in the Eastern District of California ... challenging the constitutionality of PRWORA's approval of the durational residency requirement.

...

[Judge Levi] comment[ed] on the parties' factual contentions. He noted that the State did not challenge plaintiffs' evidence indicating that, although California benefit

---

143. *Id.*

144. 42 U.S.C. §604(c) (2012).

145. Dep't Soc. Servs., *All County Letter* (Feb. 28, 1997), http://www.cdss.ca.gov/lettersnotices/entres/getinfo/acl97/97-11.PDF.

levels were the sixth highest in the Nation in absolute terms, when housing costs are factored in, they rank 18th; that new residents coming from 43 States would face higher costs of living in California; and that welfare benefit levels actually have little, if any, impact on the residential choices made by poor people. On the other hand, he noted that the availability of other programs such as homeless assistance and an additional food stamp allowance of $1 in stamps for every $3 in reduced welfare benefits partially offset the disparity between the benefits for new and old residents. Notwithstanding those ameliorating facts, the State did not disagree with plaintiffs' contention that § 11450.03 would create significant disparities between newcomers and welfare recipients who have resided in the State for over one year.

The State relied squarely on the undisputed fact that the statute would save some $10.9 million in annual welfare costs — an amount that is surely significant even though only a relatively small part of its annual expenditures of approximately $2.9 billion for the entire program. It contended that this cost saving was an appropriate exercise of budgetary authority as long as the residency requirement did not penalize the right to travel. The State reasoned that the payment of the same benefits that would have been received in the State of prior residency eliminated any potentially punitive aspects of the measure. Judge Levi concluded, however, that the relevant comparison was not between new residents of California and the residents of their former States, but rather between the new residents and longer term residents of California. He therefore again enjoined the implementation of the statute.

Without finally deciding the merits, the Court of Appeals affirmed[.] We now affirm.

III

The word "travel" is not found in the text of the Constitution. Yet the "constitutional right to travel from one State to another" is firmly embedded in our jurisprudence. Indeed, as Justice Stewart reminded us in *Shapiro v. Thompson*, 394 U.S. 618, 89 S.Ct. 1322, 22 L.Ed.2d 600 (1969), the right is so important that it is "assertable against private interference as well as governmental action ... a virtually unconditional personal right, guaranteed by the Constitution to us all."

...

[In *Shapiro*,] we squarely held that it was "constitutionally impermissible" for a State to enact durational residency requirements for the purpose of inhibiting the migration by needy persons into the State. We further held that a classification that had the effect of imposing a penalty on the exercise of the right to travel violated the Equal Protection Clause "unless shown to be necessary to promote a *compelling* governmental interest," *id.*, at 634, 89 S.Ct. 1322, and that no such showing had been made.

In this case California argues that § 11450.03 was not enacted for the impermissible purpose of inhibiting migration by needy persons and that, unlike the legislation reviewed in *Shapiro*, it does not penalize the right to travel because new arrivals are not ineligible for benefits during their first year of residence. California submits that, instead of being subjected to the strictest scrutiny, the statute should be upheld if it is supported by a rational basis and that the State's legitimate interest in saving over $10 million a year satisfies that test.

...

IV

The "right to travel" discussed in our cases embraces at least three different components. It protects the right of a citizen of one State to enter and to leave another State, the right to be treated as a welcome visitor rather than an unfriendly alien when temporarily present in the second State, and, for those travelers who elect to become permanent residents, the right to be treated like other citizens of that State.

It was the right to go from one place to another, including the right to cross state borders while en route, that was vindicated in *Edwards v. California,* 314 U.S. 160, 62 S.Ct. 164, 86 L.Ed. 119 (1941), which invalidated a state law that impeded the free interstate passage of the indigent. We reaffirmed that right in *United States v. Guest,* 383 U.S. 745, 86 S.Ct. 1170, 16 L.Ed.2d 239 (1966), which afforded protection to the "'right to travel freely to and from the State of Georgia and to use highway facilities and other instrumentalities of interstate commerce within the State of Georgia.'" Given that § 11450.03 imposed no obstacle to respondents' entry into California, we think the State is correct when it argues that the statute does not directly impair the exercise of the right to free interstate movement.... The right of "free ingress and regress to and from" neighboring States, which was expressly mentioned in the text of the Articles of Confederation, may simply have been "conceived from the beginning to be a necessary concomitant of the stronger Union the Constitution created."

The second component of the right to travel is, however, expressly protected by the text of the Constitution. The first sentence of Article IV, § 2, provides:

> "The Citizens of each State shall be entitled to all Privileges and Immunities of Citizens in the several States."

Thus, by virtue of a person's state citizenship, a citizen of one State who travels in other States, intending to return home at the end of his journey, is entitled to enjoy the "Privileges and Immunities of Citizens in the several States" that he visits.... It provides important protections for nonresidents who enter a State whether to obtain employment, to procure medical services, or even to engage in commercial shrimp fishing. Those protections are not "absolute," but the Clause "does bar discrimination against citizens of other States where there is no substantial reason for the discrimination beyond the mere fact that they are citizens of other States." There may be a substantial reason for requiring the nonresident to pay more than the resident for a hunting license, or to enroll in the state university, but our cases have not identified any acceptable reason for ... for discrimination between residents and nonresidents.

...

What is at issue in this case, then, is this third aspect of the right to travel—the right of the newly arrived citizen to the same privileges and immunities enjoyed by other citizens of the same State. That right is protected not only by the new arrival's status as a state citizen, but also by her status as a citizen of the United States. That additional source of protection is plainly identified in the opening words of the Fourteenth Amendment[.]

...

[O]ne of the privileges conferred by this Clause "is that a citizen of the United States can, of his own volition, become a citizen of any State of the Union by a *bonâ fide* residence therein, with the same rights as other citizens of that State." *Id.*, at 80.

...

Neither mere rationality nor some intermediate standard of review should be used to judge the constitutionality of a state rule that discriminates against some of its citizens because they have been domiciled in the State for less than a year. The appropriate standard may be more categorical than that articulated in *Shapiro*, see *supra*, at 1524–1525, but it is surely no less strict.

V

Because this case involves discrimination against citizens who have completed their interstate travel, the State's argument that its welfare scheme affects the right to travel only "incidentally" is beside the point. Were we concerned solely with actual deterrence to migration, we might be persuaded that a partial withholding of benefits constitutes a lesser incursion on the right to travel than an outright denial of all benefits. See *Dunn v. Blumstein*, 405 U.S. 330, 339, 92 S.Ct. 995, 31 L.Ed.2d 274 (1972). But since the right to travel embraces the citizen's right to be treated equally in her new State of residence, the discriminatory classification is itself a penalty.

It is undisputed that respondents and the members of the class that they represent are citizens of California and that their need for welfare benefits is unrelated to the length of time that they have resided in California. We thus have no occasion to consider what weight might be given to a citizen's length of residence if the bona fides of her claim to state citizenship were questioned. Moreover, because whatever benefits they receive will be consumed while they remain in California, there is no danger that recognition of their claim will encourage citizens of other States to establish residency for just long enough to acquire some readily portable benefit, such as a divorce or a college education, that will be enjoyed after they return to their original domicile.

...

To justify § 11450.03, California must therefore explain not only why it is sound fiscal policy to discriminate against those who have been citizens for less than a year, but also why it is permissible to apply such a variety of rules within that class.

These classifications may not be justified by a purpose to deter welfare applicants from migrating to California for three reasons. First, although it is reasonable to assume that some persons may be motivated to move for the purpose of obtaining higher benefits, the empirical evidence reviewed by the District Judge, which takes into account the high cost of living in California, indicates that the number of such persons is quite small—surely not large enough to justify a burden on those who had no such motive. Second, California has represented to the Court that the legislation was not enacted for any such reason. Third, even if it were, as we squarely held in *Shapiro v. Thompson*, such a purpose would be unequivocally impermissible.

Disavowing any desire to fence out the indigent, California has instead advanced an entirely fiscal justification for its multi-tiered scheme. The enforcement of § 11450.03 will save the State approximately $10.9 million a year. The question is not whether such saving is a legitimate purpose but whether the State may accomplish that end by the discriminatory means it has chosen. An evenhanded, across-the-board reduction of about 72 cents per month for every beneficiary would produce the same result. But our negative answer to the question does not rest on the weakness of the State's purported fiscal justification. It rests on the fact that the Citizenship Clause of the Fourteenth Amendment expressly equates citizenship with residence: "That Clause does not provide for, and does not allow for, degrees of citizenship based on length of residence." *Zobel*, 457 U.S., at 69, 102 S.Ct. 2309. It is equally clear that the Clause does not tolerate a hierarchy of 45 subclasses of similarly situated citizens based on the location of their prior residence. Thus § 1145.03 is doubly vulnerable: Neither the duration of respondents' California residence, nor the identity of their prior States of residence, has any relevance to their need for benefits. Nor do those factors bear any relationship to the State's interest in making an equitable allocation of the funds to be distributed among its needy citizens.

...

In short, the State's legitimate interest in saving money provides no justification for its decision to discriminate among equally eligible citizens.

VI

The question that remains is whether congressional approval of durational residency requirements in the 1996 amendment to the Social Security Act somehow resuscitates the constitutionality of § 11450.03. That question is readily answered, for we have consistently held that Congress may not authorize the States to violate the Fourteenth Amendment. Moreover, the protection afforded to the citizen by the Citizenship Clause of that Amendment is a limitation on the powers of the National Government as well as the States.

...

Citizens of the United States, whether rich or poor, have the right to choose to be citizens "of the State wherein they reside." U.S. Const., Amdt. 14, § 1. The States, however, do not have any right to select their citizens. The Fourteenth Amendment, like the Constitution itself, was, as Justice Cardozo put it, "framed upon the theory that the peoples of the several states must sink or swim together, and that in the long run prosperity and salvation are in union and not division." The judgment of the Court of Appeals is affirmed.

G. TANF and the Devolution of Poverty Policy

Perhaps the greatest shift brought by PRWORA is the shift from a program that recognized federal level benefits and entitlement, which carry the benefits of centralized administration and decision-making authority, to a decentralized system with expanded state oversight and policy-making power. With respect to welfare policy, welfare reform restated the relationship of state and the federal governments. This new model of administration gave large amounts of discretionary authority to local government, and the many thousands of government workers who implement welfare policy at the state level. When a family applies for TANF benefits, or other benefits such as public housing, a caseworker begins the process with them.[146] The caseworker walks the applicant through the benefits that are available, eligibility, work obligations, and the diversion process. At each point, this caseworker, most often a worker with a college or high school education, will exercise great discretion when explaining benefits, directing the applicant and determining eligibility for benefits. Whether this discretion is subject to abuse and random application may be open to some debate. Some commentators argue that decentralized control leads to more regularized and predictable application of welfare policy.[147] Nevertheless, there exists a significant power deferential between the welfare applicant and caseworkers from the very start of the application process and throughout the term of benefits.

---

146. HHS, *Screening and Assessment in TANF/Welfare-to-Work: Local Answers to Difficult Questions. TANF Case Managers: Responsibilities, Skills and Training, and Caseload Size* (Dec. 1, 2001), https://aspe.hhs.gov/report/screening-and-assessment-tanfwelfare-work-local-answers-difficult-questions/tanf-case-managers-responsibilities-skills-and-training-and-caseload-sizes.

147. Matthew Diller, *The Revolution in Welfare Administration: Rules, Discretion, and Entrepreneurial Government*, 75 N.Y.U. L. Rev. 1121, 1172–86 (2000).

Chapter Six

Food

United States farmers produce an astonishing amount of the world's food. The United States is by far the largest producer of corn, growing up to one-third of the world's corn crop.[1] United States farmers are also the largest producers of beef and the second largest producers of pork in the world. Overall, the United States is a net exporter of food.[2] Nevertheless, in the face of such abundance, hunger remains.

A. Hunger and Food Insecurity in the United States

Hunger is a present and real challenge for millions of Americans.[3] In any given year, tens of millions of people in the United States live in "food insecurity," lacking reliable access to nutritious, affordable food. The USDA divides food insecurity into two categories: low food security and very low food security.[4] Those that fall under the first category report reduced quality, variety, or desirability of diet with little or no indication of reduced food intake. People who are classified as very low food secure report multiple indications of disrupted eating patterns and reduced food intake. The number of people facing very low food insecurity also runs into the tens of millions, with slight distinctions between families with and without children. The Economic Research Service within the U.S. Department of Agriculture provides annually updated data that reveals details about hunger and food insecurity within the United States each year.[5]

The U.S.D.A. operates the Supplement Nutrition Access Program (SNAP), a successor to the Food Stamp program, which provides the poor with resources to purchase food. SNAP is widely seen as being effective in reaching the poor and alleviating

---

1. M. Shahbandeh, *Corn Production by Country 2018/19*, Statista (Feb. 13, 2019), https://www.statista.com/statistics/254292/global-corn-production-by-country-2012/.

2. USDA, *Agricultural Trade* (Aug. 20, 2019), https://www.ers.usda.gov/data-products/ag-and-food-statistics-charting-the-essentials/agricultural-trade/.

3. USDA, *Food Security in the U.S.* (Sept. 4, 2019), https://www.ers.usda.gov/topics/food-nutrition-assistance/food-security-in-the-us/.

4. *Food Security Status of U.S. Households in 2018*, USDA (Sept. 4, 2019), https://www.ers.usda.gov/topics/food-nutrition-assistance/food-security-in-the-us/key-statistics-graphics.aspx; *see, e.g.*, Tracie McMillan, *The New Face of Hunger*, Nat'l Geographic, https://www.nationalgeographic.com/food features/hunger/ (last visited Nov. 6, 2019).

5. *See, e.g.*, USDA, *supra* note 3.

hunger. For example, the number of people living with hunger increased significantly during the first decade and a half of the twenty-first century, with a sharp escalation during and after the 2008 recession.[6] The SNAP program expanded with the growth in the number of families facing food insecurity and hunger.

The effects of hunger and undernutrition on child development are immediate and long-lasting. Maternal undernutrition during pregnancy increases risks of premature birth, low birth weight, smaller head size, and lower brain weight.[7] Babies born prematurely are at an increased risk of developing learning disabilities when they reach school age. Undernutrition during the first three years of life can lead to lasting cognitive, social, and emotional deficits.[8] Significant iron, iodine, zinc, or other vitamin deficiencies in early childhood can cause brain impairment while hunger reduces motor skills and motivation to explore the environment.[9]

During childhood, hungry children are significantly more likely to receive special education services, to have repeated a grade in school, and to have received mental health counseling during their school years. Hungry children also exhibited several times as many symptoms of conduct disorders, including fighting, than non-hungry students and showed increased anxiety, irritability, aggression, and oppositional behavior when compared with their peers. In addition, the stressors associated with poverty will result in significantly increased risks for developing psychiatric disorders.[10] Children living with severe hunger experience increased risk for multiple negative outcomes; including: homelessness; chronic physical and mental health issues, including depression and anxiety; and low self-esteem.[11] While hunger is an immediate concern, it brings with it long-term impacts for those who are hungry. How hunger exists in the United States reveals much about how the poor and nonpoor live together in America.

1. Food Deserts

Food production in the United States is a highly industrialized endeavor. Most row crops, such as corn, wheat, and soybeans, are grown using environmentally intensive methods that demand genetically modified plants, and substantial nutrient,

---

6. Ned Resnikoff, *The Return of American Hunger: An Uneven Recovery and the New Food-Stamp Restrictions Have Left Millions More People Short on Food*, ATLANTIC (July 19, 2016), https://www.the atlantic.com/business/archive/2016/07/the-return-of-american-hunger/492062/.

7. *See* Goodwin S. Ashiabi & Keri K. O'Neal, *A Framework for Understanding the Association between Food Insecurity and Children's Developmental Outcomes*, 2 CHILD DEV. PERSPS. 71, 71 (July 11, 2008); *see also* Elizabeth L. Prado & Kathryn G. Dewey, *Nutrition and Brain Development in Early Life*, 72 NUTRITION REVS. OXFORD ACAD. 267, 267 (Apr. 1, 2014), https://academic.oup.com/nutrition reviews/article/72/4/267/1859597.

8. Prado & Dewey, *supra* note 7, at 271.

9. Naresh Kumar et al., *Micronutrient Deficiency Status in Children Below 2 Years of Age With Delayed Milestones*, 4 INT. J. CONTEMP. PEDIATRICS 1542, 1543 (2018).

10. Kevin M. Simon et al., *Addressing Poverty and Mental Illness*, PSYCHIATRIC TIMES (June 29, 2018), https://www.psychiatrictimes.com/special-reports/addressing-poverty-and-mental-illness.

11. *See id. See, e.g.,* Kumar, *supra* note 9; *see also* Prado & Dewey, *supra* note 7.

pesticide, and herbicide applications. Once produced, food is then distributed through a commodity-based system that involves multinational corporations and worldwide distribution networks. There are profound levels of efficiency across these systems, as shown by the increased food production by fewer farmers each year since the late 1940s.[12] In 1945, farmers produced an average of 28 bushels of corn per acre, a number that rose to 175 bushels per acre by 2015.[13] In the context of these systems, places have emerged where food is neither abundant nor healthy. These areas have been named "food deserts." Food deserts are defined as urban neighborhoods and rural towns that lack ready access to fresh, healthy, and affordable food.[14] These areas do not have access to supermarkets that offer a range of fresh, healthy, and affordable food and are most often served by convenience stores and fast-food restaurants. As a result, the people who live in food deserts often suffer a range of diet-related health diseases, including heart disease and obesity. An estimated 25 million people across the United States live in food deserts where fresh, healthy, and affordable food is difficult to find.[15] More than one-half of these people are poor and more than 85% live in urban areas.[16]

2. Federal Food Access Programs

The federal government has maintained food access programs for more than 80 years and these programs provide a substantial number of families with uninterrupted access to food. At the same time, these programs provide a ready stream of revenue to millions of grocers, enhancing the stability of local economies. The most well-known food access program is the Supplement Nutrition Assistance Program ("SNAP"), the successor to the Food Stamps program, but several other programs also provide food access for the poor.

a. Food Stamps and SNAP

Federal entitlement programs for food include the Food Stamps Program, created in 1939 as part of the Social Security Act and significantly expanded in 1964 before being converted to the Supplemental Nutrition Assistance Program (SNAP) in 1996.[17] Each of these programs is housed within the U.S. Department of Agriculture. The

---

12. R.L. Nielsen, *Historical Corn Grain Yields for the U.S.*, AGRONOMY DEPT. PURDUE UNIV. (May 2017), https://www.agry.purdue.edu/ext/corn/news/timeless/yieldtrends.html; *see, e.g.*, Bill Ganzel, *The Productivity Revolution*, LIVING HIST. FARM, https://livinghistoryfarm.org/farminginthe40s/money_01.html (last visited Nov. 7, 2019).

13. Nielsen, *supra* note 12.

14. Michele Ver Ploeg, USDA, *Access to Affordable, Nutritious Food Is Limited in "Food Deserts"* (Mar. 1, 2010), https://www.ers.usda.gov/amber-waves/2010/march/access-to-affordable-nutritious-food-is-limited-in-food-deserts/.

15. *Id.*

16. *Id.*

17. USDA, *A Short History of SNAP* (Sept. 11, 2018), https://www.fns.usda.gov/snap/short-history-snap.

Food Stamp program operated as an entitlement program that provided benefits to poor individuals and families that could be spent on unprepared food.[18] Food Stamps were aptly named as they were distributed to beneficiaries as coupons that corresponded to the U.S. currency denominations. Food Stamps could be used to buy most food items, but not prepared foods or alcohol, tobacco, soap, paper products, pet food, or other nonfood items. Food Stamp coupons were printed in very bright colors that varied based on the value of the coupon. A $5.00 Food Stamp coupon, for example, was printed in a vibrant yellow while a $10.00 coupon was printed in orange. The coupon system was abandoned during the 1990s and replaced with a stored value card known as the Electronic Benefit Transfer, or "EBT," card.[19] Stores that participated in the food stamp program accepted the EBT card, which was used in a way like a credit or debit card. EBT remains the delivery method for the Supplemental Nutritional Assistance Program, or "SNAP," which replaced Food Stamps.[20]

Nearly anyone who met federal income, resource, and work requirements was eligible for food stamps, with some exceptions. Unemployed, able-bodied adults without children were limited to three months of benefits within a 36-month period and those who intentionally violated the food stamp programs rules were disqualified, along with those on strike and college students.[21] Adults convicted of a drug felony after August 1996 were not able to receive food stamps unless the state where they applied pass legislation allowing them to do so.[22] A range of rules applied to immigrants before October 2002 when all qualified immigrant children became eligible for food stamp benefits.[23]

The "household" is an important concept within the Food Stamp system. A household consists of a person living alone or a group of people living together who purchase and prepare meals together. As such, more than one household could live together in a shared living space while each received Food Stamps.[24]

The application for food stamps required that a print application be filed with the state administrative office, which could be done in person or through the mail. Verification of income, resources, and work status, along with an interview and registration for work, were mandatory. Generally, any money or financial assets available to the applicant were counted as resources when assessing food stamp eligibility, as were vehicles, land, buildings other that the applicant's home, and other property.[25] Income included work and passive income, subject to numerous deductions. Expe-

---

18. *Id.*

19. *Id.*

20. *Id.*

21. *See generally id. See also* MASS. LEGAL SERVS., SNAP DISQUALIFICATIONS AND SANCTIONS (Oct. 20, 2014), https://www.masslegalservices.org/WebHelp/SNAP/DisqualificationsSanctions/IPV/SNAPD isquailificationsandSanctions.htm.

22. *Id.*

23. Nat'l Immigr. Forum, *Fact Sheet: Immigrants and Public Benefits* (Aug. 21, 2018), https:// immigrationforum.org/article/fact-sheet-immigrants-and-public-benefits.

24. *See* USDA, *supra* note 17; *see also SNAP Disqualifications and Sanctions, supra* note 21.

25. *Id.*

dited food stamps were available for applicants who lacked food or money to obtain food at the time of application.

The Food Stamp program became the Supplemental Nutrition Assistance Program (SNAP) in October 2008.[26] The name change was premised on a desire to fight the stigma of food stamps, while most aspects of the program remained largely intact. SNAP is the largest anti-hunger program in the United States. While large, SNAP remains highly efficient and is able to reach nearly 85% of the individuals and families who are eligible to receive SNAP benefits.[27] SNAP is also highly responsive to need, with 92% of its benefits reaching families below the Federal Poverty Line and 56% of SNAP benefits reaching families in extreme poverty with income below one-half of the federal poverty line.[28] As with food stamps before it, SNAP operates as an entitlement program, meaning that anyone who meets eligibility criteria qualifies to receive the benefit. This makes SNAP quick and effective in meeting the needs of the poor. Because SNAP benefits offset the costs of food, families that receive SNAP benefits have more money for other needs, such as housing and childcare. The Center for Budget and Policy Priorities has found that SNAP lifts nearly 8.5 million people out of poverty each year, which is more than any other single program.[29]

SNAP households include a large number of worker families with earned income. Roughly one-third of all families receiving SNAP benefits have income from work, from as much as 14% to 20% in take-home income.[30] SNAP's economic benefits extend beyond the family. SNAP benefits, once distributed to families, are then used in local commerce, with more than 97% of all SNAP benefits being spent within one month of a recipient receiving them.[31] This means that local merchants, such as grocery stores, and farmers markets, receive the economic benefits of consumers shopping in their shops, buying their products, and supporting the food producers they buy from. Large grocery stores end up redeeming huge amounts of SNAP benefits—Walmart alone redeems more than $13 billion each year.[32]

Qualifying for SNAP eligibility is a straightforward process. SNAP eligibility rules and benefits are set at the federal level and apply uniformly across the United States. There are three qualification criteria a household must meet to qualify for SNAP benefits:[33]

---

26. USDA, *supra* note 17.

27. Ctr. on Budget & Pol'y Priorities, Policy Basics: The Supplemental Nutrition Assistance Program (SNAP), (June 25, 2019), https://www.cbpp.org/research/food-assistance/policy-basics-the-supplemental-nutrition-assistance-program-snap.

28. *Id.*

29. *Id.*

30. *Id.*

31. *Id.*

32. Krissy Clark, *The Secret Life of a Food Stamp Might Become a Little Less Secret*, Slate Bus. (Aug. 5, 2014), https://slate.com/business/2014/08/how-much-walmart-gets-in-food-stamp-dollars-the-answer-may-be-forthcoming.html.

33. USDA, *SNAP Eligibility*, https://www.fns.usda.gov/snap/recipient/eligibility (last visited Nov. 7, 2019).

1. Household gross monthly income must fall below 130% of the Federal Poverty Line

2. Household net monthly income (which takes into account deductions for child-care and other needs) must fall below 100% of the Federal Poverty Line

3. The household must have assets that fall below set limits, for example, $2,250 for a household without an elderly or disabled family member.

Certain groups are categorically ineligible, however, and these include college students, undocumented immigrants, and some legal immigrants. In addition, work obligations may be imposed at the state level. Childless unemployed adults are limited to three months of benefits unless they are working at least 20 hours a week in most states.

Once eligibility is determined, the household will apply for SNAP benefits at the local social services or welfare benefit office. These offices are run at the state and county levels and the applicant will be asked to present numerous documents establishing eligibility, residency, family composition, immigration status, income, and expenses.[34] There is a reapplication process that is performed every six months for most families, or 12 months for families with disabled members or the elderly.[35] Once eligibility and benefit levels are established, the family will receive an Electronic Benefit Transfer (EBT) card. The EBT card is a stored value card through which SNAP benefits are distributed. The EBT card can only be used to purchase approved food items and cannot be used to purchase things such as prepared food, alcohol, cigarettes and non-grocery items. Counties may request waivers for the purchase of prepared food as well.[36] In addition, EBT cards can only be used at approved outlets, such as grocery stores, but counties may allow EBT to be used at farmers markets.[37]

The average SNAP benefit is $126 per month, roughly $4.15 per day or $1.40 per meal, and is based on the USDA Thrifty Meal Plan, which assumes that families spend 30% of their net income on food.[38] SNAP benefits are scaled to income, so a family with zero income will receive the maximum benefit allowed under the program while a family with income will have that maximum reduced.[39] Significantly, the reduction is not dollar for dollar, which means that a family who earns one dollar in income will see their SNAP benefit decrease by 24 cents up to the eligibility ceiling. This provides an important work incentive, as well as an indirect subsidy to employers. SNAP costs the federal government between $70 and $80 billion a year, although administrative costs are very low for the program, at roughly seven percent, meaning that nearly all SNAP benefits support nutritional needs and food producers.[40]

---

34. *Id.*
35. *Id.*
36. *Id.*
37. *Id.*
38. *Id.*
39. *Id.*
40. *Id.*

Despite SNAP's efficacy and ability to lift families out of poverty, large numbers of families continue to experience hunger and do not have enough to eat post-TANF even when they are able to access SNAP.[41] SNAP alone is not enough to address hunger and food access for at least one-quarter of poor families after they no longer receive TANF.

President Trump signed an executive order in April 2018 that would force low-income recipients of SNAP, Medicaid, and low-income housing to comply with new work requirements or risk losing their benefits. Trump's executive order called on several different departments to review their existing waivers and mandates to work requirements and submit recommended policy changes. Not only does the order plan to impose work requirements on able-bodied recipients, but also aims to block ineligible immigrants from receiving aid.

Earlier in the year, the House farm bill proposed there be a 20-hour per week work requirement and expand the age to 59 for low-income to receive SNAP benefits. The new age requirements would begin in 2021. The SNAP program currently requires able-bodied adults without dependents between 18 and 49 years of age to either work 20 hours per week or participate in 20 hours a week of education and training to receive benefits. Those who do not comply would lose benefits for one year after the first violation and for three years after future violations. To regain program eligibility under the proposal, recipients must either meet the work requirement for a full month or receive an exemption for disability or other reasons.

These requirements, however, do not match the reality of the job market for many low-income individuals. According to the Center for American Progress, in households that receive SNAP and have at least one non-disabled adult, 58% are employed and 82% worked in the year prior to or after enrollment. Also, most able-bodied adults receiving benefits who do not already have a job are unemployed because of other obstacles, which include mental problems, criminal records, complicated family situations, and lack of access to transportation.

b. School Lunch Program

The National School Lunch Program (NSLP) is administered by the Department of Agriculture. Through the NSLP, low-income children receive hot meals while at school. Meals include both breakfast and lunch. Eligibility is determined by the student's family's income. In school year 2017–2018, a student whose family income was at or below 185% of the federal poverty level was entitled to a reduced costs meal. A student with family income below 130% of the FPL was entitled to a free meal through the NSLP.

The U.S. government has provided hot meals to low-income students in public schools across the United States since 1946 and passage of the Russell National Lunch

---

41. Mary E. Corcoran et al., *Food Insufficiency and Material Hardship in Post-TANF Welfare Families*, 60 OHIO ST. L.J. 1395 (1999).

Act. In 1966 the National School Lunch Program was revitalized with the passage of the Child Nutrition Act of 1966, with a stated purpose: "In recognition of the demonstrated relationship between food and good nutrition and the capacity of children to develop and learn, based on the years of cumulative successful experience under the National School Lunch Program with its significant contributions in the field of applied nutrition research, it is hereby declared to be the policy of Congress that these efforts shall be extended, expanded, and strengthened under the authority of the Secretary of Agriculture as a measure to safeguard the health and well-being of the Nation's children, and to encourage the domestic consumption of agricultural and other foods, by assisting States, through grants-in-aid and other means, to meet more effectively the nutritional needs of our children."

In 1966, a pilot breakfast program was added for two years, although the program remains an integral part of the federal feeding policy. In 1970, the Special Milk Program, which had operated within the Department of Agriculture since 1954, was extended and made part of the NSLP. Nonprofit schools, including nursery schools, childcare, and "similar" institutions, were made eligible to receive NSLP benefits.

The NSLP provides funding for a range of activities connected to feeding low-income children, including the partial purchase of food and the purchase of food preparation equipment. In states where state funding is inadequate to finance the lunch program, federal NSLP funding can be allocated to state administrative costs associated with hiring and training additional state personnel.

c. Effect of NSLP on Food Insecurity

There are relatively few studies that examine the impact of the NSLP on food insecurity among school-age children. There are two identification problems that may contribute to this difficulty. First, children receiving free or reduced-price meals are likely to differ from eligible nonparticipants in ways that are not observed in the data. Second, the association between participation in the NSLP and food insecurity may be, at least partly, an artifact of household misreporting of program participation. Controlling for these differences, Gundersen, Kreider, and Pepper have found persuasive evidence that the NSLP leads to substantial reductions in food insecurity.[42]

B. State Determinations Regarding Access to Food Stamps and SNAP

Despite the primacy of food, state agencies have enacted numerous policies limiting access to federal feeding programs, such as food stamps and SNAP. In some instances, the reduction in access can only be seen as a penalty. In others, the dis-

---

42. Craig Gunderson et al., *The Economics of Food Insecurity in the United States*, 33 APPLIED ECON. PERSPS. & POL'Y 281 (2011).

tinction between who may and who may not benefit from feeding programs seems to be arbitrarily made.

Turner v. Glickman
207 F.3d 419 (7th Cir. 2000)

The class representative, Henry Turner, on his own behalf and on behalf of all those similarly situated, challenges the constitutionality of 21 U.S.C. 862a. That statute provides that individuals convicted of certain drug-related felonies are permanently ineligible for benefits under the federal food stamp and Temporary Assistance for Needy Families("TANF") programs. The plaintiffs-appellants allege that this statute violates the Due Process Clauses of the Fifth and Fourteenth Amendments, the equal protection component of the Fifth Amendment's Due Process Clause and the Equal Protection Clause of the Fourteenth Amendment, and the Double Jeopardy Clause of the Fifth Amendment to the United States Constitution. The district court rejected these constitutional claims and entered judgment for the defendants-appellees. For the reasons stated below, we affirm the decision of the district court.

I. Facts

The statutory provision at issue in this case, 21 U.S.C. 862a, was enacted by Congress as part of the Personal Responsibility and Work Opportunity Reconciliation Act of 1996. The statute was passed in response to growing concerns about the escalating costs of federal welfare programs. In particular, Section 862a was an attempt to address what many members of Congress regarded as increasing and costly incidences of fraud in the food stamp program. Section 862a attempts to reach the problem of fraud by permanently disqualifying individuals convicted of certain drug-related felonies from receiving benefits under either the federal foodstamp program or the TANF program. Although Congress did not specify where this provision was to be codified, the Office of Law Revision Counsel placed the statute in Title 21 of the United States Code. The statute applies to all convictions occurring on or after August 22, 1996. The law provides that states may exempt recipients from disqualification under Section 862a, but the State of Indiana has chosen not to provide such an exemption to its citizens.

The class representative, Henry Turner, is an Indiana resident and former recipient of food stamps. As part of an annual review of his foodstamp eligibility, Turner was required to reapply for that program in January 1998. Subsequent to this reapplication, Turner was convicted of felony possession of heroin and cocaine based on conduct that occurred in April 1997. Solely because of this conviction, Turner's pending reapplication for food stamps was denied under Section 862a.

In August 1998, Turner commenced a class action suit for declaratory and injunctive relief in federal district court, challenging the constitutionality of Section 862a. Following a hearing on the parties' cross-motions for summary judgment, the district court entered judgment for the defendants-appellees. The plaintiffs-appellants now appeal the decision of the district court, arguing that permanent disqualification from participation in the foodstamp and TANF programs of those convicted of certain drug-related felonies violates the Due Process Clauses of the Fifth and Fourteenth Amendments, the equal protection component of the Fifth Amendment's Due Process Clause and the Equal Protection Clause of the Fourteenth Amendment, and the Double Jeopardy Clause of the Fifth Amendment to the United States Constitution.

II. Analysis

A.

The plaintiffs-appellants first contend that Section 862a violates the equal protection component of the Fifth Amendment's Due Process Clause and the Equal Protection Clause of the Fourteenth Amendment because it lacks any rational basis connected to a legitimate government interest. Because the statute at issue does not implicate any fundamental rights or involve any suspect classifications, the question before us is whether the stated reasons proffered by the government are a sufficient justification to survive rational basis review. In rejecting the plaintiffs-appellants' equal protection challenge, the district court found three rational bases for the legislation: (1) deterring drug use; (2) reducing fraud in the food stamp program; and (3) curbing welfare spending. The defendants-appellees assert these same three bases for the statute now, and argue that they all represent legitimate government interests.

In attempting to show that the classification in Section 862a has no rational basis, the plaintiffs-appellants must meet a heavy burden. Rational basis review "is not a license for courts to judge the wisdom, fairness, or logic of legislative choices." Rather, we must uphold the challenged classification if "there is a rational relationship between the disparity of treatment and some legitimate government purpose." Heller, 509 U.S. at 320. In order to show that Section 862a is irrational, the plaintiffs-appellants must "'negative every conceivable basis which might support it,' ... whether or not the basis has a foundation in the record." *Id.* at 320–21, However, "the relationship of the classification to its goal [must] not [be] so attenuated as to render the distinction arbitrary or irrational".

The plaintiffs-appellants argue that Section 862a is exactly the kind of arbitrary and irrational government sanction that the equal protection guaranties forbid. As the plaintiffs-appellants correctly point out, one of the express purposes of the Food Stamp Act is "[t]o alleviate ... hunger and malnutrition ... [by] permit[ting] low-income households to obtain a more nutritious diet through normal channels of trade." 7 U.S.C. 2011. According to the plaintiffs-appellants, Section 862a is not relevant to this purpose because it deprives individuals convicted of drug-related felonies of food stamps despite their continuing financial and nutritional needs. Furthermore, the plaintiffs-appellants contend that Section 862a has no rational connection to the three justifications accepted by the district court: deterring drug use, reducing fraud in the foodstamp program, and curbing welfare spending.

Ordinarily, an argument as to the actual purpose of a legislature in passing a law would not be relevant to the question of whether the challenged classification had a rational connection to a legitimate government interest. However, as we understand it, the plaintiffs-appellants' argument does not rest on their ability to prove that Congress acted with an unconstitutional motive. Rather, the plaintiffs-appellants argue that because no possible motive exists for passing this law other than punishment, Congress must have acted out of animus toward individuals convicted of drug-related felonies and that the district court's assertion that the law functions to reduce welfare fraud, deter drug abuse, and decrease welfare expenditures is therefore implausible. If this is true, and the plaintiffs-appellants can " 'negative every conceivable basis which might support [862a] ... whether or not the basis has a foundation in the record," *id.* at 320–21, then the challenged statute would lack a rational relation to a legitimate state interest.

After a consideration of Section 862a in light of the proffered government interests, we reject the plaintiffs-appellants' equal protection challenge. First, as the district correctly found, there is a rational connection between the disqualification of drug felons from eligibility for food stamps and TANF and the government's desire to deter drug use. Rendering those convicted of drug-related felony crimes ineligible to receive food stamps or aid under TANF is a potentially serious sanction, and individuals who are currently eligible for such assistance would undoubtedly consider potential disqualification from federal benefits before engaging in crimes involving illegal drugs. It was not irrational for Congress to conclude that the disqualification of drug felons from receiving certain kinds of federal aid under Section 862a would deter drug use among the population eligible to receive that aid. This is all that is required to sustain a classification in the face of an equal protection challenge when the challenged classification is subject to rational basis review. See *Heller*, ("[A] classification 'must be upheld against equal protection challenge if there is any reasonably conceivable state of facts that could provide a rational basis for the classification.' ").

Similarly, the district court was correct in finding a rational connection between Section 862a and the government's desire to reduce fraud in the food stamp program. As we noted above, Congress passed this law at a time when serious concerns had arisen regarding rising welfare costs and increasing fraud in the food stamp program. The legislative record in this case contains testimony that food stamps were being traded for drugs. In light of this testimony, it was not irrational for Congress to conclude that denying food stamps and TANF aid to those convicted of a drug felony would decrease the overall incidences of fraud in those programs. The challenged classification thus survives rational basis review on this ground as well.

B.

The plaintiffs-appellants next contend that Section 862a unconstitutionally burdens their rights under the Due Process Clauses of the Fifth and Fourteenth Amendments. Because Section 862a does not implicate a fundamental right, substantive due process requires only that the statutory imposition not be completely arbitrary and lacking any rational connection to a legitimate government interest. The plaintiffs-appellants' due process claim, like their equal protection claim, is thus subject to highly-deferential rational basis review.

For the same reasons that the plaintiffs-appellants cannot make out an equal protection claim, their due process argument fails as well. In order for us to uphold this statute, the government need only show a rational connection between Section 862a and a legitimate government interest. Here, as we discussed at length above, the challenged statute has a rational basis in both the government's desire to deter drug use and to reduce the incidences of fraud in the food stamp program. In light of these rational bases proffered by the government, the plaintiffs-appellants have not made the kind of showing necessary for us to invalidate the statute under the deferential standard of rational basis review.

C.

Lastly, the plaintiffs-appellants contend that Section 862a inflicts a second punishment on those convicted of drug-related felonies in violation of the Double Jeopardy Clause. The representative plaintiff in this case was convicted of possession of cocaine and heroin, and was sentenced to one year in prison and one year of probation. According to the plaintiffs-appellants, this punishment was followed by a second punishment for the same conduct when, through the effect of Section 862a, he was permanently disqualified from receiving federal assistance under the food stamp and TANF programs. The plaintiffs-appellants allege that because Congress intended to punish those convicted of drug-related felonies when it passed Section 862a, that statute's sanction is an unconstitutional second punishment based on the same underlying conduct from which his prison sentence and probation stemmed.

The Double Jeopardy Clause provides that no "person [shall] be subject for the same offence to be twice put in jeopardy of life or limb." U.S. Const. amend. V. While "[t]he Clause protects … against the imposition of multiple criminal punishments for the same offense," it has long been "recognized that the Double Jeopardy Clause does not prohibit the imposition of any additional sanction that could 'in common parlance' be described as punishment." *Id.* The question, then, is whether Section 862a functions as the kind of criminal punishment covered by the Double Jeopardy Clause, or whether the statute is a civil penalty not subject to the prohibitions of that Clause.

Our analysis as to whether the penalty is properly deemed criminal or civil involves two steps: (1) an examination of congressional intent; and (2) a consideration of the effect and purpose of the statute. As to congressional intent, our inquiry is "at least initially, a matter of statutory construction." *Hudson.* We look to whether Congress "indicated either expressly or impliedly" that Section 862a was a criminal or civil penalty. If we determine that Congress intended the statute to be a criminal punishment of those convicted of drug-related felonies, our inquiry is at an end and the statute would constitute criminal punishment for purposes of the Double Jeopardy Clause. However, if we conclude that Congress intended a punishment to be civil in nature, we then turn to the purpose and effect of the statute to determine whether a penalty Congress intended to be civil in nature actually functions as a criminal one.

Because 21 USC 862a is rationally related to legitimate government interests in deterring drug use and reducing welfare fraud, and because the challenged statute imposes only a civil sanction on individuals convicted of drug-related felonies, we affirm the decision of the district court.

Walton v. Hammons

192 F.3d 590 (6th Cir. 1999)

Defendant-Appellant Marva Livingston Hammons, in her capacity as director of the Michigan Family Independence Agency ("MFIA"), contests the district court's grant of summary judgment to Plaintiff-Appellee Ethan Walton. Specifically, the district court concluded that Hammons exceeded her authority under the Food Stamp Act ("FSA") by denying food stamps to the entire Walton family because Ethan Walton's mother was found to be non-cooperative in establishing the legal paternity of one of her children. Because the district court's holding comports with the text and legislative intent of the statutory provisions in question, we AFFIRM.

I.

A.

In 1996, Congress and President Clinton embarked on the latest phase of this effort by passing and signing into law the Personal Responsibility and Work Opportunity Reconciliation Act of 1996 ("PRWORA").... PRWORA also amended certain sections of the FSA, which has been in place since 1964 to "safeguard the health and well-being of the Nation's population by raising levels of nutrition among low-income households." 7 U.S.C. 2011 (1988). While offering reforms which would allow states to "harmonize" food stamp with other assistance programs, Congress rejected the proposed utilization of a block grant scheme in administering the federal food stamp program. Instead, Congress opted to retain general federal government control to ensure that a "'safety net' at the federal level" remained in place. In the case *sub judice*, the parties dispute two provisions introduced by PRWORA that together permit states to impose sanctions with respect to TANF and food stamp benefits when a custodial parent fails to cooperate in establishing the paternity of her child or children.

Relying on the newly enacted TANF, the MFIA—the state agency responsible for administering the FSA program in Michigan—restructured the operation of Michigan's welfare system in 1997. As part of that restructuring, the MFIA implemented an administrative rule, Mich. Admin. Code. R. 400.3125 (1997), requiring the termination of a household's Family Independence Program ("FIP") cash assistance benefits when a member of the household has failed (without "good cause") for at least four consecutive months to cooperate in establishing the paternity of a child. Claiming that it has statutory authority to do so, Michigan also applies that cash assistance disqualification "rule" to its administration of food stamps through the FSA, thereby terminating household food stamp assistance for the same acts of non-cooperation. Both FIP benefits and food stamps resume if the household member begins cooperating.

B.

The plaintiffs in this class action lawsuit are children in danger of losing their food stamp support under the MFIA policy described above. The plaintiffs contend that the 1996 federal welfare reforms do not endow the State with the power to terminate food stamp benefits to an entire household for an individual member's non-cooperation in establishing paternity or obtaining child support.

Plaintiff Ethan Walton (the lead plaintiff) is three years old. His mother, Antoinette Walton, also has a daughter — Te'Asha Walton, age five — by another father. Ethan's father has acknowledged paternity and pays child support pursuant to a court order obtained with the cooperation of Antoinette. Unfortunately, the identity of Te'Asha's father is not as clear. Shortly after Te'Asha's birth in May 1992, Antoinette informed the state that Te'Asha's father was a "Mr. Jackson." However, in March 1993, she told the state that Te'Asha's father was Randle Mooring. In June 1996, a state court dismissed a paternity action against Mooring because a blood test had excluded him as a possible father of Te'Asha. Based on its determination that Antoinette did not cooperate in establishing Te'Asha's paternity, the MFIA terminated her then-AFDC grant in August 1996. The test of Mooring having proven negative, Antoinette again asserted in August and October 1996 that "Mr. Jackson" was Te'Asha's father. Although Antoinette notified the MFIA that she had little information about the purported father, she stated that she had seen him in a store and given him a picture of the child, and also knew that he lived on the same block as she did during her pregnancy. Neither the State nor Antoinette has successfully located him or further identified him.

Pursuant to the MFIA's administrative rule change, the MFIA in April 1997 notified Antoinette that her failure to cooperate regarding Te'Asha's paternity would compel the MFIA to terminate her family's FIP and food stamp benefits effective November 1, 1997 — in other words, the MFIA would terminate both her own allotments and the allotments to Ethan and Te'Asha. Antoinette requested a hearing regarding the MFIA's decision. On November 10, 1997, a state administrative judge held that she had failed to cooperate with the MFIA in establishing the paternity of Te'Asha.

Ethan Walton filed this action on December 9, 1997, claiming that the defendant was denying him and other minor children food stamp benefits in violation of the FSA. Specifically, the plaintiffs allege that PRWORA does not permit states to terminate FSA benefits due to parents' failure to cooperate in establishing paternity or child support payments, and that accordingly, FIA's termination of their food stamps would directly contravene the FSA. The district court granted Walton's motion for class certification on December 11, 1997, ordering a class under Fed.R.Civ.P. 23(b)(2) comprising "all past, present, and future Michigan Food Stamp recipients whose Food Stamps have been or will be terminated because of the [MFIA non-cooperation policy]." J.A. at 190. The parties filed cross-motions for summary judgment on January 21, 1998. On March 20, 1998, the district court granted Walton's motion for summary judgment, and denied the defendant's motion as moot. On June 2, 1998, the court ordered defendant to revise its food stamp termination policy to comply with its March 20th opinion. This timely appeal followed.

III.

Looking anew at the text, structure and legislative history of the statutory provisions to derive Congress's purpose regarding the relevant language, we affirm the district court's summary judgment in favor of plaintiffs.

The outcome of this case hinges on the interplay of two distinct statutory provisions enacted in 1996: (1) § 6(i)(2) of the FSA and (2) Part A of Title IV of TANF. First, we must construe the meaning of § 6(i)(2) of the FSA, 7 U.S.C. 2015(i)(2). Section 6(i)(2) allows for the application of rules and procedures enumerated under Part A of Title IV of TANF to the administration of disqualifications under the food stamp program:

(i) Comparable treatment for disqualification

(1) In general

If a disqualification is imposed on a member of a household for a failure of the member to perform an action required under a Federal, state, or local law relating to a means-tested public assistance program, the *State agency may impose the same disqualification on the member of the household under the food stamp program.*

(2) Rules and procedures

If a disqualification is imposed under paragraph (1) for a failure of an individual to perform an action required under part A of Title IV of the Social Security Act, *the State agency may use the rules and procedures that apply under part A of Title IV of the Act to impose the same disqualification under the food stamp program.*

7 U.S.C. 2015(i)(1), (i)(2).

We also must scrutinize part A of Title IV of TANF itself, referenced by the provision above, which sets forth penalties for a parent's non-cooperation in establishing paternity for her minor child or children:

(a) In General

(2) Reduction or elimination of assistance for noncooperation in establishing paternity or obtaining child support

If the agency responsible for administering the State plan ... determines that an individual is not cooperating with the state in establishing paternity or in establishing, modifying or enforcing a support order with respect to a child of the individual, and the individual does not qualify for any good cause or other exception established by the State pursuant to section 654(29) of this title, then the State—

(A) shall deduct from the assistance that would otherwise be provided to the family of the individual under the State program funded under

> this part an amount equal to not less than 25 percent of the amount of such assistance; and
>
> **(B)** *may deny the family any assistance under the State program.*

42 U.S.S. 608(a)

Defendant argues that together, these statutes allow Michigan to disqualify the Walton household from receiving all FIP (TANF) benefits, as well as all FSA benefits, due to the finding that Antoinette failed to cooperate in establishing Te'Asha's paternity. Although the statute is not altogether clear on its face, in light of the textual evidence that does exist, as well as legislative history that we find persuasive, we disagree with defendant's construction of these provisions.

A. Statutory Text and Structure

"The best evidence of [a statute's] purpose is the statutory text adopted by both Houses of Congress and submitted to the President." The meaning of a statute's words can also be "enlightened by their context and the contemporaneous legislative history," as well as the "historical context of the statute." Using these tools of interpretation, we find that the text of the statutory provisions involved weighs heavily in favor of the plaintiffs. Where the provisions are ambiguous on their face, we find that the legislative history conclusively shows that the MFIA's termination policy contravenes Congressional intent.

Defendant's textual arguments largely fail to pass muster. First, the crucial provision involved, nowhere expressly provides for disqualification of an entire family's food stamp benefits because of one family member's failure to meet a Federal, state or local law. To the contrary, the language of that provision explicitly applies to individual members of a household. The first paragraph of that provision provides that if a disqualification is imposed "on a *member* of a household for a failure of the *member* to perform an action required under Federal, state, or local law," then the State "may impose the same disqualification on the *member* of the household under the food stamp program." 7 U.S.C. 2015(i)(1).

An ambiguity remains on the statute's face. Defendant correctly points out that Part A of Title IV of TANF, referenced by paragraph (2), indeed allows the outright elimination of household benefits for the failure of a member to cooperate in establishing paternity.... The provision thus contradicts the clear textual evidence against household disqualifications discussed *infra*. It also contradicts 7 U.S.C. 2015(l), the specific FSA provision addressing non-cooperation in establishing paternity. In sec 2015(l), Congress provided that no individual *parent* who was non-cooperative in establishing paternity or obtaining child support could be eligible for child support allotments, leaving the rest of the household's FSA benefits intact.

B. Legislative History

Given this latent ambiguity, we must turn to a consideration of legislative history and intent to divine Congressional purposes. Examining the textual ambiguity in light of this broader context and legislative history, we hold that Congress did not mean for states to eliminate household food stamp allotments in the fashion undertaken by defendant.

PRWORA's reform of the FSA comprised a delicate balancing act. Among the goals listed by the House Committee on Agriculture designing the reforms was "the retention of the Food Stamp Program as a *'safety net'* at the *federal level.*" At the same time, the committee stated that the reforms were intended to expand states' role in administering the FSA "by broadening their authority to harmonize the [program] with other welfare programs." *Id.* Clearly, Congress sought to balance this added state discretion to "harmonize" with the preservation of a federal "safety net" for food assistance, girded by federally imposed rules and guidelines. Neither goal absolutely trumps the other and, indeed, much of the complexity of the provisions in question arises from this difficult balancing effort. For instance, unlike the PRWORA's wholesale replacement of the federally-controlled AFDC with a block-grant regime, PRWORA did not alter the basic national standards of eligibility for FSA assistance that have long been in place, and gave no control over such standards to states. Congress also left intact the complex array of federally-imposed administrative requirements to which states must adhere.

Most importantly for this case, a crucial aspect of the "safety net" that Congress retained is the concern for the well-being of dependent minor children under the FSA. Numerous FSA provisions carve out safeguards for these children's interests — safeguards states cannot trammel. In determining eligibility for assistance, for instance, the FSA provides added benefits to support families with children. Likewise, in rendering disqualifications, FSA pursues policies intended to benefit dependent children. Of course, the very rationale for which Antoinette is being penalized in this case — failing to protect adequately the interests of Te'Asha by identifying her father in order to secure child support — stems from a concern for the welfare of the children who depend on her. Just as under TANF, Congress disqualifies from FSA assistance any custodial parent who is non-cooperative in establishing paternity or obtaining child support for the child. Unlike under TANF, however, family allotments are not affected by this provision....

Finally, Congress's concern for innocent minor children can be seen in the care Congress took in discerning between individual sanctions and household sanctions, which deprive innocent, dependent children of FSA benefits. As described *supra,* the FSA carefully distinguishes provisions which affect individual members from those affecting whole households, and erects safeguards when it does intend for the transgressions of a member of a household to render ineligible the entire household. See. E.g. 7 U.S.C. 2015(d)(1)(B), 7 U.S.C. 2017(d)(1)(B). This care is warranted given the general principle, expressed by the Supreme Court in different contexts, that "visiting [ ] condemnation on the head of an infant" is generally ineffectual and unjust, because while "parents have the ability to conform their conduct to societal norms, [ ] their [ ] children can affect neither their parents' conduct nor their own status."

The legislative history demonstrates that Congress adhered to these broader concerns when it considered and enacted the language of 2015(i)(2) in particular.

C. Agency Deference

Plaintiffs and defendant have argued that interpretations of the relevant provisions by the United States Department of Agriculture ("USDA") and by the implementing state agency merit our deference under *Chevron* principles. Because the "traditional tools of statutory construction" have allowed us to derive a clear meaning to the statute, the USDA statements interpreting the food stamp provisions consistent with our reading are not relevant to our holding, and therefore receive no *Chevron* deference.

IV.

Because we conclude that the text and legislative history of the PRWORA reforms indicate clear Congressional intent against permitting the disqualification of a household's FSA benefits when a member of that household is found non-cooperative regarding issues of paternity, we **AFFIRM** the district court's decision.

Alvarino v. Wing

261 A.D.2d 255

Order, Supreme Court, New York County entered January 7, 1999, which, in an action by plaintiffs' lawful resident aliens challenging the constitutionality of Social Services Law § 95.10 insofar as it restricts food assistance to certain categories of aliens, denied plaintiffs' motion for a preliminary injunction prohibiting the State and its local social services districts from implementing Social Services Law § 95.10(a) and (b)(ii–v), and for class certification, unanimously affirmed, without costs.

Plaintiffs' argument that they are being denied assistance for reasons unrelated to need in violation of N.Y. Const. art. XVII 1 addresses the manner and level of assistance, not the denial of any assistance, and indeed all but one of the named plaintiffs is currently receiving public assistance. In actuality, the argument is an equal protection claim, to which the IAS court properly applied rational basis rather than strict scrutiny review. Although State classification of aliens is subject to strict scrutiny, the classification challenged here was enacted in direct response to a Federal supplemental appropriations bill authorizing the States to provide food assistance to aliens no longer eligible for Federally funded food stamps by reason of the enactment of the Personal Responsibility and Work Opportunity and Reconciliation Act of 1996 (8 U.S.C. 1612). The challenged provisions are therefore entitled to the same rational basis review as would a Federally-enacted law classifying aliens No argument is made challenging the rationality of any of the five requirements an alien must satisfy in order to qualify for food assistance — under the age of 18 or elderly or disabled; resident in a social services district that has opted to participate in the program; resident in the same social services district since August 22, 1996, the effective date of the Personal Responsibility and Work Opportunity and Reconciliation Act of 1996; not have been away from the United States for more than 90 days within the 12-month period preceding the application for food assistance; and apply for citizenship within 30 days of applying for food assistance. Class certification is unwarranted since "governmental operations are involved, and ... subsequent petitioners will be adequately protected under the principles of *stare decisis*."

Chapter Seven

Housing

Housing plays many roles in our society. At a basic level, housing provides a place (ideally a safe place) for families to live and at least a modest degree of dignity for its residents. Home is also a place where families can expect a degree of privacy that is not found elsewhere. Perhaps because of such unique benefits, housing conditions and quality have been shown to have numerous positive benefits for families, including higher educational achievement, better physical and mental health, greater financial stability, and enhanced interpersonal relationships.

Housing also plays a significant role in the U.S. economy. Taking all aspects of housing together, housing accounts for more than 40% of the U.S. economy, including construction, durable goods, services, and finance. Given the dominance of housing in our economy and as part of nearly all social structures, it would not be possible to consider housing outside of an economic and political context. What, then, does housing mean for the poor, who do not have full economic and social participation? While a fair amount of literature discusses how the poverty rate has dropped in recent years, the U.S. Census Bureau's 2017 estimates report that at least 39.7 million Americans still live in poverty.[1] Unfortunately, many of these Americans living in poverty are unable to provide housing for themselves.

Lindsey v. Normet
405 U.S. 56 (1972)

[In this case the United States Supreme Court considered whether Oregon's forcible entry and detainer statute violated Constitutional guarantees of due process and equal protection. The plaintiffs were tenants of Mr. Normet and paid $100.00 a month to live in a home that was declared unfit for habitation. Because the house was condemned, the Lindseys asked Normet to make repairs to bring the property up to a habitable state. Normet threatened eviction, or, as described by his attorney, to "have papers drawn up" in response to Lindsey's complaints. Lindsey then filed a civil rights action in United States District Court basing the claim on two aspects of the FED statute. First, the statute required that a trial on the landlord's eviction action be held within 5 days of notice to the tenant. Lindsey argued that the extremely short notice

---

1. CTR. FOR POVERTY RES., WHAT IS THE CURRENT POVERTY RATE IN THE UNITED STATES? (Oct. 15, 2018), https://poverty.ucdavis.edu/faq/what-current-poverty-rate-united-states.

time between service of the complaint and the trial violated the right to due process by effectively denying any meaningful process at all. Second, the FED statute required that respondents in eviction proceedings post a "double bond" if they sought to extend the time allowed for trial beyond five days after service. No other appellants were required to post a "double bond" to perfect an appeal or stay a proceeding, only respondents in FED proceedings. The Court's analysis of the Equal Protection argument follows.]

We also cannot agree that the FED Statute is invalid on its face under the Equal Protection Clause. It is true that Oregon FED suits differ substantially from other litigation, where the time between complaint and trial is substantially longer, and where a broader range of issues may be considered. But it does not follow that the Oregon statute invidiously discriminates against defendants in FED actions.

The statute potentially applies to all tenants, rich and poor, commercial and non-commercial; it cannot be faulted for over-exclusiveness or under-exclusiveness. And classifying tenants of real property differently from other tenants for purposes of possessory actions will offend the equal protection safeguard 'only if the classification rests on grounds wholly irrelevant to the achievement of the State's objective,' or if the objective itself is beyond the State's power to achieve. It is readily apparent that prompt as well as peaceful resolution of disputes over the right to possession of real property is the end sought by the Oregon statute. It is also clear that the provisions for early trial and simplification of issues are closely related to that purpose. The equal protection claim with respect to these provisions thus depends on whether the State may validly single out possessory disputes between landlord and tenant for especially prompt judicial settlement. In making such an inquiry a State is 'presumed to have acted within (its) constitutional power despite the fact that, in practice, (its) laws result in some inequality.'

At common law, one with the right to possession could bring an action for ejectment, a 'relatively slow, fairly complex, and substantially expensive procedure.' But, as Oregon cases have recognized, the common law also permitted the landlord to 'enter and expel the tenant by force, without being liable to an action of tort for damages, either for his entry upon the premises, or for an assault in expelling the tenant, provided he uses no more force than is necessary, and do(es) no wanton damage.' Smith v. Reeder, 21 Or. 541, 546, 28 P. 890, 891 (1892). The landlord-tenant relationship was one of the few areas where the right to self-help was recognized by the common law of most States, and the implementation of this right has been fraught with 'violence and quarrels and bloodshed.' Entelman v. Hagood, 95 Ga. 390, 392, 22 S.E. 545 (1895). An alternative legal remedy to prevent such breaches of the peace has appeared to be an overriding necessity to many legislators and judges.

Hence, the Oregon statute was enacted in 1866 to alter the common law and obviate resort to self-help and violence. The statute, intended to protect tenants as well as landlords, provided a speedy, judicially supervised proceeding to settle the possessory issue in a peaceful manner:

'But if (the landlord) forcibly enter and expels the tenant, while he may not be liable to him in an action of tort, he is guilty of a violation of the forcible entry and detainer act, which is designed to protect the public peace; and in such case the law will award restitution to the tenant, not because it recognizes any rights in him, but for the reason that, out of regard for the peace and good order of society, it does not permit a person, in the quiet and peaceable possession of land, to be disturbed by force, even by one lawfully entitled to the possession.'

Before a tenant is forcibly evicted from property the Oregon statute requires a judicial determination that he is not legally entitled to possession. 'The action of forcible entry and detainer is intended for the benefit of him whose possession is invaded.' Taylor v. Scott, 10 Or. 483, 485 (1883). The objective of achieving rapid and peaceful settlement of possessory disputes between landlord and tenant has ample historical explanation and support. It is not beyond the State's power to implement that purpose by enacting special provisions applicable only to possessory disputes between landlord and tenant.

There are unique factual and legal characteristics of the landlord-tenant relationship that justify special statutory treatment inapplicable to other litigants. The tenant is, by definition, in possession of the property of the landlord; unless a judicially supervised mechanism is provided for what would otherwise be swift repossession by the landlord himself, the tenant would be able to deny the landlord the rights of income incident to ownership by refusing to pay rent and by preventing sale or rental to someone else. Many expenses of the landlord continue to accrue whether a tenant pays his rent or not. Speedy adjudication is desirable to prevent subjecting the landlord to undeserved economic loss and the tenant to unmerited harassment and dispossession when his lease or rental agreement gives him the right to peaceful and undisturbed possession of the property. Holding over by the tenant beyond the term of his agreement or holding without payment of rent has proved a virulent source of friction and dispute. We think Oregon was well within its constitutional powers in providing for rapid and peaceful settlement of these disputes.

Appellants argue, however, that a more stringent standard than mere rationality should be applied both to the challenged classification and its stated purpose. They contend that the 'need for decent shelter' and the 'right to retain peaceful possession of one's home' are fundamental interests which are particularly important to the poor and which may be trenched upon only after the State demonstrates some superior interest. They invoke those cases holding that certain classifications based on unalterable traits such as race and lineage are inherently suspect and must be justified by some 'overriding statutory purpose.' They also rely on cases where classifications burdening or infringing constitutionally protected rights were required to be justified as 'necessary to promote a compelling governmental interest.'

We do not denigrate the importance of decent, safe, and sanitary housing. But the Constitution does not provide judicial remedies for every social and economic ill. We are unable to perceive in that document any constitutional guarantee of access to dwellings of a particular quality, or any recognition of the right of a tenant to occupy the real property of his landlord beyond the term of his lease without the payment of rent or otherwise contrary to the terms of the relevant agreement. Absent constitutional mandate, the assurance of adequate housing and the definition of land-lord-tenant relationships are legislative, not judicial, functions. Nor should we forget that the Constitution expressly protects against confiscation of private property or the income therefrom.

Since the purpose of the Oregon Forcible Entry and Wrongful Detainer Statute is constitutionally permissible and since the classification under attack is rationally related to that purpose, the statute is not repugnant to the Equal Protection Clause of the Fourteenth Amendment.

Village of Belle Terre v. Boraas
416 U.S. 1 (1974)

[In Village of Bell Terre v. Boraas, the Supreme Court was confronted with the question of whether a local zoning ordinance could limit the number of unrelated adults who live together in a home. The ordinance at issue limited the number of families that could live together in the same home to one and defined family to include"[o]ne or more persons related by blood, adoption, or marriage, living and cooking together as a single housekeeping unit." In addition to families under this definition, a maximum of two people who were not related by blood or marriage could occupy the same home. The plaintiffs in Belle Terre were a group of students and a homeowner who made a number of constitutional arguments, including: (1) the ordinance interferes with a person's right to travel; (2) it interferes with the right to migrate to and settle within a state; (3) it bars people who are uncongenial to the present residents; (4) it expressed social preferences of the residents for groups that will be congenial to them; (5) social homogeneity is not a legitimate interest of government; (6) the restriction of those whom the neighbors do not like trenches on the newcomers' right to privacy; (7) it is not rightful concern to the villages whether the residents are married or unmarried; (8) the ordinance is antithetical to the egalitarian, open, and integrated ideology of the nation. Group and co-housing is often relied upon by the poor as sharing a home is less expensive than maintaining a separate home. The Supreme Court was presented an opportunity to consider the economic barriers to adequate housing that can be created through prohibitive zoning ordinances.]

This case brings to this Court a different phase of local zoning regulations from those we have previously reviewed. Village of Euclid v. Ambler Realty Co., 272 U.S. 365, 47 S.Ct. 114,71 L.Ed. 303, involved a zoning ordinance classifying land use in a given area into six categories. The Dickmans' tracts fell under three classifications: U-2, which included two-family dwellings; U-3, which included apartments, hotels, churches, schools, private clubs, hospitals, city hall and the like; and U-6, which included sewage disposal plants, incinerators, scrap storage, cemeteries, oil and gas storage and so on. Heights of buildings were prescribed for each zone; also, the size of land areas required for each kind of use was specified. The land in litigation was vacant and being held for industrial development; and evidence was introduced showing that under the restricted-use ordinance the land would be greatly reduced in value. The claim was that the landowner was being deprived of liberty and property without due process within the meaning of the Fourteenth Amendment.

The Court sustained the zoning ordinance under the police power of the State, saying that the line 'which in this field separates the legitimate from the illegitimate assumption of power is not capable of precise delimitation. It varies with circumstances and conditions.' Id., at 387, 47 S.Ct., at 118. And the Court added: 'A nuisance may be merely a right thing in the wrong place, like a pig in the parlor instead of the barnyard. If the validity of the legislative classification for zoning purposes be fairly debatable, the legislative judgment must be allowed to control.' Id., at 388, 47 S.Ct., at 118. The Court listed as considerations bearing on the constitutionality of zoning ordinances the danger of fire or collapse of buildings, the evils of overcrowding people, and the possibility that 'offensive trades, industries, and structures' might 'create nuisance' to residential sections. Ibid. But even those historic police power problems need not loom large or actually be existent in a given case. For the exclusion of 'all industrial establishments' does not mean that 'only offensive or dangerous industries will be excluded.' Ibid. That fact does not invalidate the ordinance; the Court held:

'The inclusion of a reasonable margin to insure effective enforcement, will not put upon a law, otherwise valid, the stamp of invalidity. Such laws may also find their justification in the fact that, in some fields, the bad fades into the good by such insensible degrees that the two are not capable of being readily distinguished and separated in terms of legislation.' Id., at 388–389, 47 S.Ct., at 118.

The main thrust of the case in the mind of the Court was in the exclusion of industries and apartments, and as respects that it commented on the desire to keep residential areas free of 'disturbing noises'; 'increased traffic'; the hazard of 'moving and parked automobiles'; the 'depriving children of the privilege of quiet and open spaces for play, enjoyed by those in more favored localities.' Id., at 394, 47 S.Ct., at 120. The ordinance was sanctioned because the validity of the legislative classification was 'fairly debatable' and therefore could not be said to be wholly arbitrary. Id., at 388, 47 S.Ct., at 118.

Our decision in Berman v. Parker, 348 U.S. 26, 75 S.Ct. 98, 99 L.Ed. 27, sustained a land use project in the District of Columbia against a landowner's claim that the taking violated the Due Process Clause and the Just Compensation Clause of the Fifth Amendment. The essence of the argument against the law was, while taking property for ridding an area of slums was permissible, taking it 'merely to develop a better balanced, more attractive community' was not, id., at 31, 75 S.Ct., at 102. We refused to limit the concept of public welfare that may be enhanced by zoning regulations. We said:

'Miserable and disreputable housing conditions may do more than spread disease and crime and immorality. They may also suffocate the spirit by reducing the people who live there to the status of cattle. They may indeed make living an almost insufferable burden. They may also be an ugly sore, a blight on the community which robs it of charm, which makes it a place from which men turn. The misery of housing may despoil a community as an open sewer may ruin a river.

'We do not sit to determine whether a particular housing project is or is not desirable. The concept of the public welfare is broad and inclusive.... The values it represents are spiritual as well as physical, aesthetic as well as monetary. It is within the power of the legislature to determine that the community should be beautiful as well as healthy, spacious as well as clean, well-balanced as well as carefully patrolled.' Id., at 32–33, 75 S.Ct., at 102.

If the ordinance segregated one area only for one race, it would immediately be suspect ...

In Seattle Title Trust Co. v. Roberge, 278 U.S. 116, 49 S.Ct. 50, 73 L.Ed. 210, Seattle had a zoning ordinance that permitted a "philanthropic home for children or for old people" in a particular district "when the written consent shall have been obtained of the owners of two-thirds of the property within four hundred (400) feet of the proposed building." Id., at 118, 49 S.Ct., at 50. The Court held that provision of the ordinance unconstitutional, saying that the existing owners could 'withhold consent for selfish reasons or arbitrarily and may subject the trustee (owner) to their will or caprice.' Id., at 122, 49 S.Ct., at 52. Unlike the billboard cases (e.g., Cusack Co. v. City of Chicago, 242 U.S. 526, 37 S.Ct. 190, 61 L.Ed. 472), the Court concluded that the Seattle ordinance was invalid since the proposed home for the aged poor was not shown by its maintenance and construction 'to work any injury, inconvenience or annoyance to the community, the district or any person.' 278 U.S., at 122, 49 S.Ct., at 52.

The present ordinance is challenged on several grounds: that it interferes with a person's right to travel; that it interferes with the right to migrate to and settle within a State; that it bars people who are uncongenial to the present residents; that it expresses the social preferences of the residents for groups that will be congenial to them; that social homogeneity is not a legitimate interest of government; that the restriction of those whom the neighbors do not like trenches on the newcomers' rights of privacy; that it is of no rightful concern to villagers whether the residents are married or unmarried; that the ordinance is antithetical to the Nation's experience, ideology, and self-perception as an open, egalitarian, and integrated society.

We find none of these reasons in the record before us. It is not aimed at transients. It involves no procedural disparity inflicted on some but not on others such as was presented by Griffin v. Illinois, 351 U.S. 12, 76 S.Ct. 585, 100 L.Ed. 891. It involves no 'fundamental' right guaranteed by the Constitution, such as voting, the right of association, the right of access to the courts, or any rights of privacy, We deal with economic and social legislation where legislatures have historically drawn lines which we respect against the charge of violation of the Equal Protection Clause if the law be "reasonable, not arbitrary."

A. Homelessness Defined

What does it mean to be homeless? Oftentimes, the word "homeless" brings to mind panhandlers and signs saying, "anything helps," someone pushing a grocery cart full of what is obviously all that they possess, or someone sleeping on a park bench late at night in the cold. However, so much more defines the people we see so frequently and what it actually means to be homeless. Homelessness resonates in communities across the United States. A homeless individual is defined as one who:

> lacks a fixed, regular, and adequate night-time residence; and ... has a primary night time residency that is: (A) a supervised publicly or privately operated shelter designed to provide temporary living accommodations ... (B) An institution that provides a temporary residence for individuals intended to be institutionalized, or (C) a public or private place not designed for, or ordinarily used as, a regular sleeping accommodation for human beings." The term "homeless individual" does not include any individual imprisoned or otherwise detained pursuant to an Act of Congress or a state law.[2]

In short, a homeless person lacks permanent housing and may live on the streets, stay in shelters, or in any other non-permanent, unstable situation.

There is a healthy debate about the causes of homelessness, and there are certainly numerous reasons why people end up homeless. Homelessness can be the result of disability, dependency or disaster, lack of affordable housing, unemployment, and poverty. These numerous factors contribute to homelessness, and they should not be understated. For example, the National Survey of Homeless Assistance Providers and Clients (NSHAPC) found that more than 35% of the homeless population suffer from some combination of alcohol, drug, and mental illness (ADM).[3] For these people, homelessness becomes a long-term situation where more than 35% experience homelessness for more than two years.[4] Untreated mental illness has been found to be a factor in homelessness for more than 25% of homeless adults.[5] While mental illness, addiction, and unemployment are serious causes of homelessness, for the majority of the homeless population, the biggest factor leading to homelessness is affordability. Families and individuals that end up homeless simply cannot afford to secure housing.

1. The Affordable Housing Crisis

The U.S. Census uses a 30% of income standard to determine affordability. This means that housing is deemed affordable if a family can acquire it with no more than 30% of their income (Note: The Department of Health and Human Services issues poverty guidelines for each family to determine if they fall below the poverty line. For example, in 2018 the poverty level for a family of four is an annual income of

---

2. 42 U.S.C. § 11302(c).

3. Nat'l Survey of Homeless Assistance Providers & Clients, Homelessness: Programs and the People They Serve 8-1 (1999), https://www.huduser.gov/portal/publications/pdf/home_tech/tchap-08.pdf.

4. *Id.* at 4-17, 4-20, https://www.huduser.gov/portal/publications/pdf/home_tech/tchap-04.pdf.

5. Jonathan L. Hafetz, *Homeless Legal Advocacy: New Challenges and Directions for the Future*, 30 Fordham Urb. L. J. 1215, 1216–21 (2003).

$24,600, meaning that of that meager salary a family of four would spend $7,380 to acquire "affordable housing.") Workers making within a few dollars of the minimum wage find it difficult to secure affordable housing in almost all markets in the United States. In Los Angeles, for example, a worker in 2019 would have needed to earn more than $124,000 a year to afford a median-priced home in that market.[6] In Houston that same year a worker would have needed to earn more than $58,800, or roughly $29.00 an hour.[7] In Philadelphia, a worker would need more than $58,900 a year in income for a median-priced home.[8] There is a striking disconnect between the cost of a modest home in all of these examples and the real earnings of many millions of working families.

Despite common perceptions, many homeless people, perhaps up to 50%, are gainfully employed but lack adequate income to afford housing.[9] While poverty or near poverty does not in itself cause homelessness, it does tend to make the poor more susceptible to homelessness due to the lack of available financial resources when an emergency arises.[10] For these families, homelessness is the result of the razor-thin margins they live on every day when income is simply not enough to afford adequate housing as well as other needed goods and services.

In the fall of each year the Department of Housing and Urban Development ("HUD") releases its Annual Homeless Assessment report to Congress. This report, compiled from information collected throughout the year and that includes individualized counts of homeless people, contains the most current and accurate information regarding homelessness in the United States.[11] For example, in January 2018, 552,830 people were homeless on any given night. Most (65%) were staying in residential programs for homeless people, and 35% were found in unsheltered locations. Nearly one-quarter of all homeless people were children, under the age of 18 (20.2% or 111,592). Slightly less than nine percent (8.7% or 48,139) were between the ages of 18 and 24, and 71.1% (or 392,919) were 25 years or older.

Several defined terms are widely used when discussing homelessness, including:

Continuums of Care (CoC) are local planning bodies responsible for coordinating the full range of homelessness services in a geographic area, which may cover a city, county, metropolitan area, or an entire state.

---

6. THE SALARY YOU MUST EARN TO BUY A HOME IN THE 50 LARGEST METROS (2019), https://www.hsh.com/finance/mortgage/salary-home-buying-25-cities.html#l.

7. *Id.*

8. *Id.*

9. *See* NAT'L SURVEY OF HOMELESS ASSISTANCE PROVIDERS & CLIENTS, *supra* note 3, at 5-1 https://www.huduser.gov/portal/publications/pdf/home_tech/tchap-05.pdf (noting 65% of homeless participants worked most or all of the time since age 16).

10. *See* Hafetz, *supra* note 5, at 1216–27 (collecting research on the causes of homelessness and the role the lack of affordable housing plays in maintain homelessness in a community).

11. MEGHAN HENRY ET AL., THE 2018 ANNUAL HOMELESSNESS ASSESSMENT REPORT (AHAR) TO CONGRESS (2018) https://www.wpr.org/sites/default/files/2018-ahar-part-1-compressed.pdf.

Chronically Homeless People in Families are people experiencing homelessness in families (with at least one adult and one child) in which the head of household has a disability and has either been continuously homeless for a year or more or has experienced at least four episodes of homelessness in the last three years.

Chronically Homeless Individuals are homeless individuals with disabilities who have either been continuously homeless for a year or more or have experienced at least four episodes of homelessness in the last three years.

Emergency Shelter is a facility with the primary purpose of providing temporary shelter for homeless persons.

Individuals are people who are not part of a family with children during their episode of homelessness. They are homeless as single adults, unaccompanied youth, or in multiple-adult or multiple-child households.

Other Permanent Housing is housing with or without services that is specifically for formerly homeless people, but that does not require people to have a disability.

Parenting Youth are people under 25 who are the parents or legal guardians of one or more children who are present with or sleeping in the same place as that youth parent, where there is no person over age 24 in the household.

Permanent Supportive Housing is designed to provide housing and supportive services on a long-term basis for formerly homeless people who have disabilities.

People in Families with Children are people who are homeless as part of households that have at least one adult and one child.

Point-in-Time Counts are unduplicated one-night estimates of both sheltered and unsheltered homeless populations. The one-night counts are conducted by Continuums of Care nationwide and occur during the last week in January of each year.

Safe Havens provide private or semi-private long-term housing for people with severe mental illness and are limited to serving no more than 25 people within a facility.

Sheltered Homeless People are individuals who are staying in emergency shelters, transitional housing programs, or safe havens.

Transitional Housing Program provides homeless people a place to stay combined with supportive services for up to 24 months in order to help them overcome barriers to moving into and retaining permanent housing.

Unaccompanied Youth (under 18) are people who are not part of a family with children during their episode of homelessness, and who are under the age of 18.

Unaccompanied Youth (18–24) are people who are not homeless as a part of a family with children, and who are not accompanied by their parent or guardian during their episode of homelessness and who are between the ages of 18 and 24.

Unsheltered Homeless People are people who stay in places not meant for human habitation.

2. Homelessness and the Criminal Justice System

It is sadly a common sight to see the homeless who live on America's streets, but it is almost sadder (and increasingly more common) that many communities have taken action to limit them by passing ordinances that prohibit homeless activity. For example, in Gore Park in New York City, the city redesigned benches and added arm rests to them two-thirds of the way down the length of the bench.[12] These design features have been nicknamed as features of "defensive architecture" which is the "term [that has been given to design techniques] that are meant to deter or prevent homeless people from sleeping or otherwise congregating in a certain place."[13] Another example can be seen when homeless people engage in subsistence activities within the places they live. This activity has been described as:

> Hunting-gathering subsistence strategy, in which mainstream society's detritus — abandoned buildings, scavenged food, discarded clothing, or recyclable goods — is mined for its subsistence potential, or in which urban fixtures, not intended for subsistence use — freeway overpasses, dumpsters, and transportation waiting rooms — are put to this end.[14]

These types of subsistence activities are increasingly regulated by local governments, leading to ticketing and arrests of homeless individuals. Sizeable numbers of cities across the country have passed ordinances that prohibit sitting or lying in public places (30%), loitering in certain public areas (47%), and completely banning panhandling (23%), while others have instituted panhandling licensing schemes.[15] Not satisfied with these methods, other cities have considered privatizing public sidewalks, which has not been adopted.[16]

---

12. Kelly Bennett, *No Sleeping in Redesigned Gore Park, Thanks to New Benches*, CBC News (Nov. 10, 2016 4:36 PM), http://www.cbc.ca/news/canada/hamilton/no-sleeping-in-redesigned-gore-park-thanks-to-new-benches-1.3845405.

13. *Id.*

14. Paul Koegel et al., *Subsistence Adaptation among Homeless Adults in the Inner City of Los Angeles*, 46 J. Soc. Issues, Winter 1990, at 83, 102.

15. Nat'l Law Ctr. on Homeless & Poverty, Homes Not Handcuffs: The Criminalization of Homelessness in U.S. Cities (2009), http://www.nationalhomeless.org/publications/crimreport/CrimzReport_2009.pdf.

16. *See* Mary Ellen Hombs, American Homelessness: A Reference Handbook 190 (3d ed. 2001).

B. Policy Efforts and Early Public Housing

In 1949, the United States declared "a decent home and suitable living environment for every American family" as a stated goal of our federal housing policy.[17] If, as the Supreme Court states in *Lindsey v. Normet*, access to housing is an economic and political matter and not a question of constitutional right, how does our political system address issues of housing and housing access when given this goal? The Housing Act of 1949, and the Act of 1937 that preceded it, reflect a fundamental tension between the lofty goals of federal housing policy and the limitations of what is possible when addressing economic and social issues.

1. Housing Acts of 1937 and 1949

Housing the poor in the United States has challenged policymakers since the beginning of the New Deal. The conflicts have centered around predictable concerns: increasing costs of subsidized housing and decreasing budgets to maintain housing programs; the eligibility requirements of housing authorities that define whether or not housing in the United States should be considered a human right or just another commodity to be bought and sold; and the precarious position of public housing residents that positions them against real estate speculators who want to develop the land on which public housing developments stand. The National Housing Act of 1937 paved the way for millions of people to obtain safe and affordable housing in the United States by making low-interest loans over a 60-year period to local governments. The impetus for government intervention was the increasing visibility of the nation's poorly housed, particularly in Washington, D.C. "In a short period of time [after the enactment of New Deal legislation], tens of thousands of new employees joined the government work force, construction accelerated, and public relief programs blossomed."[18] With so many new residents pouring into Washington, housing continued to be one of the biggest problems in the District—one that could not be ignored especially since many battered shanties, mostly housed by poor blacks, were in direct view of the Capitol, including one of the most sordid group of alley dwellings, the Navy Place Slums, on which the present-day Townhomes on Capitol Hill, Arthur Capper, and Carrollsburg Dwellings sit.

The public housing program was created with the passing of the United States Housing Act of 1937 ("1937 Housing Act").[19] Congress intended the 1937 Housing

---

17. Housing Act of 1949, Pub. L. No. 81-171, 63 Stat. 413 (codified as amended in 42 U.S.C. § 1441).

18. FREDERIC M. MILLER & HOWARD GILLETTE JR., WASHINGTON SEEN: A PHOTOGRAPHIC HISTORY, 1875–1965 135 (1995).

19. U.S. Housing Act of 1937, Pub. L. No. 75-412, 50 Stat. 888 (codified as amended in scattered sections of 42 U.S.C.).

Act to provide decent and safe rental housing for a "huge, new, submerged middle class" during the Depression by providing for subsidies that the U.S. government would pay out to local public housing agencies and would in turn improve living conditions for these new, low-income residents. Congress intended public housing to specifically serve eligible low-income working families. While public housing may have become synonymous with extreme poverty, it did not begin as housing for very low-income households. Instead, the program was intended to provide direct financial support for the construction and operation of housing serving low-income working families. Over time, large concentrations of the very poor living in public housing, often under extreme conditions, resulted in the displacement of the working poor from public housing, as families who could afford to move often did.

While Franklin D. Roosevelt initially gained support for his first round of New Deal programs from the Left, many, including his previous supporters, thought the programs were not doing enough to help the elderly, farmers, workers, and the urban poor. Upon implementing a second round of relief programs, Roosevelt experienced a great deal of opposition, especially from special interest groups. He reluctantly supported a public housing program against opposition from bankers and real estate developers who saw public housing as an infringement on their market capabilities. As conciliation, the Housing Act of 1937 sought to appeal to a wide audience by "serv[ing] only those people who could not compete for housing on the private market ... The program therefore targeted those who could not find decent, affordable housing on the private market, but not the so-called unworthy poor and those with no means to pay rent."[20] It was also mandated that the physical appearance of public housing developments would differ dramatically from private market housing, and for each new public housing unit built, an equivalent number of substandard dwellings had to be eliminated.[21] While the federal government supplied the funding for the construction of public housing developments, local housing authorities were responsible for managing the properties and collecting tenant rents, which covered the operating expenses.

The 1937 Housing Act authorized the federal government to enter into Annual Contributions Contracts ("ACC") with local public housing authorities. ("PHAs"). The ACC commits the federal government to pay annual principal and interest costs associated with long-term bonds, which may have a term of up to 40 years. The proceeds of these bonds are used to finance the costs of constructing new rental housing for low-income families. Because the ACC is an obligation of the federal government, it carries the full faith and credit of the United States and, as a result, bonds issued to finance new public housing enjoy very favorable interest rates.

Unfortunately, New Deal government expansion further exacerbated the housing problems for most of the poor. In our nation's capital, for example, blacks continued to be pushed out of Georgetown and Foggy Bottom so that new accommodations

---

20. Rachel Bratt, Rebuilding a Low-Income Housing Policy 56–57 (1989).
21. *Id.* at 56.

could be built for the onslaught of federal workers coming to the District.[22] New public housing was also built in southwest and southeast D.C. and in Arlington, Virginia; however, this housing was built for whites, who were working at federal government locations near the Potomac River. Public housing construction for blacks occurred sporadically throughout the city, but the numbers were insufficient to house the growing numbers of displaced alley dwellers. To make matters worse, as the war approached and anti-New Deal congressional leaders came to power, all funding for public housing ended and the Alley Dwelling Authority was directed to shift its attention to the construction of temporary, de-mountable housing units for war workers in open spaces.[23] Black migration from the South increased throughout the years of World War II as families moved to Washington to take advantage of the growing labor market. Federal government and domestic service employment lured many blacks to D.C., where opportunities for well-paying work were often countered by a lack of affordable housing options. Miss Maggie[24] states:

> I got married after high school in 1952. I went down and took all the civil service tests. The main thing everybody wanted to do at that particular time was try to get a government job because that was about the best a black person could do back then. I took the civil service test and I got little jobs ... and I finally got a job working at a hotel ... as a maid, because everybody was ... yeah, that's one job you could always get ... cleaning hotel rooms, and setting up for the new people coming in. Sometimes we had to set up like a dining room ... so, it was various work, not just cleaning the bedrooms. So, my mother hated it. That hurt her ... but it was a job ... and all this time, I was studying and taking all these civil service tests ... A lot of my friends got called, but I never got called ... and I passed. I think the lowest score I made was about 70-something. Quite a few of my friends got called in. You know, back then if you got a grade two, you were doin' good ... you were doin' real good ... and black, too? And they start you off as a clerk, you know, just file papers and xerox and stuff ... and twice I got called for temporary stuff, but I never got in a full-time, permanent [position].

The condition of the alley dwellings and the health of its residents further deteriorated throughout the 1940s. After the Second World War, the United States entered a period of economic growth and Washington, D.C., along with other major urban centers grew at exponential rates.[25] This growth spurred development. During this period, the demographics of public housing, as well as the nation's major cities, began to change. Those working-class residents who lived in public housing in the 1930s and 1940s took advantage of the New Deal Federal Housing Administration

22. MILLER & GILLETTE, *supra* note 18, at 141.

23. *Id.* at 146.

24. Respondent participated in a HUD-funded research study. SHERRI LAWSON CLARK, POLICY, PERCEPTIONS, AND PLACE: AN ETHNOGRAPHY OF THE COMPLEXITIES OF IMPLEMENTING A FEDERAL HOUSING PROGRAM (2002).

25. MILLER & GILLETTE, *supra* note 18, at 151.

(FHA) and Veterans Administration (VA) mortgage guarantee programs and moved out of public housing developments and into surrounding suburbs, leaving in the nation's urban cores a growing number of mostly black and poor residents who were in desperate need of sanitary housing. Throughout the 1940s, government officials lobbied back and forth to come up with a solution to the urban blight that threatened tax revenues and the survival of American cities (von Hoffman 2000).

Thus, on July 15, 1949, Congress enacted the Housing Act of 1949, which provided federal aid for slum-clearance, community development, and redevelopment programs. The Housing Act of 1949 states that it was Congress' goal to provide "a decent home and suitable living environment for every American family" as a matter of national public policy.[26]

The 1937 Housing Act was amended significantly following World War II, with the passage of the 1949 Housing Act. The Preamble to the 1949 Housing Act stated a lofty vision for the federal government's role in housing:

> The Congress declares that the general welfare and security of the Nation and the health and living standards of its people require housing production and related community development sufficient to remedy the serious housing shortage, the elimination of substandard and other inadequate housing through the clearance of slums and blighted areas, and the realization as soon as feasible of the goal of a decent home and a suitable living environment for every American family, thus contributing to the development and redevelopment of communities and to the advancement of the growth, wealth, and security of the Nation.

Despite a clear statement of policy and mandate from Congress, it took more than 20 years to complete construction on the housing units originally authorized under the Act of 1949.[27] It was finally in 1972 when all of the housing authorized under the Act of 1949 was completed,[28] and during these more the two decades, housing projects across the United States became associated with "urban decay, rampant crime and social isolation,"[29] a perception that would later drive changes to housing policy.

In 1949, however, the Act cleared the way for the very poor to move into public housing by "requiring that the highest rents be 20% lower than the lowest prevailing

---

26. Housing Act of 1949, Pub. L. No. 81-171, 63 Stat. 413 (codified as amended in scattered sections of 42 U.S.C.)

27. Thomas C. Kost, Note, *Hope After HOPE VI? Reaffirming Racial Integration as the Primary Goal in Housing Policy Prescriptions*, 106 Nw. U.L. Rev. 1379, 1384 (2010); *see also* Paul Mitchell, *Historical Overview of Direct Federal Housing Assistance*, in Federal Housing Policy & Programs: Past and Present 187, 195 (J. Paul Mitchell ed., 1985).

28. Michael H. Schill, *Privatizing Federal Low-Income Housing Assistance: The Case of Public Housing*, 75 Cornell L. Rev. 877, 895–96 (1990).

29. Kost, *supra* note 27, at 1384–85; *see also* Alexander von Hoffman, *A Study in Contradictions: The Origins and Legacy of the Housing Act of 1949*, 11 Housing Pol'y Debate 299, 315–20 (2000).

rents for decent housing in the private market and by authorizing the eviction of above-income families."[30] Public housing now changed into a place to permanently house the very poor; instead of a place to house those who temporarily needed help to pull themselves out of the Depression. Camille Jeffers, who conducted an ethnographic study in public housing during the 1960s, describes the differences:

> By 1960 ... the image, the aura and some of the functions of public housing had changed markedly ... During the Depression and probably as recently as the 1940's, many people could identify their counterparts in public housing and might even envy them to some degree. Recent developments [circa 1960] have apparently walled off those who live in public housing from those who do not. Whether these walls are economic, social psychological, cultural or just plain brick and mortar, it is important to look behind them.[31]

The racial composition of public housing developments also began to change in the 1950s. Bratt states that "by 1978, over 60% of the residents of public housing were minority-group members (HUD, 1980), whereas from 1944 to 1951 nonwhite families represented between 26 and 39% of all public housing tenants."[32] It was not until 1955 that segregation in public housing developments would be eradicated. As more blacks moved into public housing, whites moved out. The contemporary idiom used to describe public housing residents as "socially isolated" is a direct result of the 1949 Housing Act, which forced working-class families out of public housing. Over her 20 adult years living in public housing raising her four children while employed, Miss Maggie (quoted earlier) exclaims, "It wasn't no welfare coming in that house! We were working mothers ... then, over time, more and more women with children and no jobs and a lot of problems moved in."[33]

Public Housing Authorities ("PHAs"), the local body of government empowered to implement public housing, soon became unable to stop to quick downward spiral of public housing.[34] In a significant change to pre-1949 policy, following the Act of 1949 public housing residents were enabled to pay little to no monthly rental fees, fees that had previously covered the operating expenses of the development. As the numbers of extremely poor tenants unable to pay rent rose, PHAs' operating and maintenance budgets shrank.[35] Thus, over time, housing authorities had to rely more on federal subsidies to manage and maintain their developments, which, during periods of federal devolution of social services, added to the rapid deterioration of public housing developments. During these years, Congress repeatedly refused to

---

30. BRATT, *supra* note 20, at 58.

31. Camille Jeffers, *Child Rearing Practices among Low Income Families in the District of Columbia*, Regional Training Institute, Project Enable, Miami, FL (1966).

32. BRATT, *supra* note 20, at 58.

33. LAWSON CLARK, *supra* note 24.

34. Kost, *supra* note 27, at 1383, 1385.

35. *Id.*

provide operational subsidies for public housing.[36] By 1972, the public perception of public housing as a failure, together with the financial challenges of a revenue model that collected ever lessening amounts of rental income, along with a persistent opposition to integration, culminated in a moratorium, announced by President Nixon, on the construction of new housing units under the Act of 1949.[37]

The moratorium of 1972 brought significant change to public housing policy and ushered in new strategies for housing the poor. The new era was characterized by a move from centralized government housing development led by federal and local partnerships, to a free market and private development strategy that encouraged private developers and real estate owners to house the poor, primarily through the Section 8 program.[38]

2. Rent Subsidies and Section 8 Tenant Assistance

The Housing and Community Development Act of 1974, which took effect in January 1975, represents the most significant national legislation on community development since the Housing Act of 1949. The Act is the product of a four-year national debate on housing and represents compromises and concessions developed among the administration, Congress, and national interest groups. The Act has the potential to inject new vitality into local government's ability to provide for physical and social needs. The objective of the legislation, as it is articulated in the Act, is "the development of viable urban communities" through provision of "decent housing and a suitable living environment and expanding economic opportunities principally for persons of low and moderate income."[39] Consistent with this objective, the provisions of this omnibus legislation alter significantly the pattern of federal-local relationships in a wide range of housing and community development activities. Unlike prior community development programs in which control was maintained by the federal bureaucracy, the theory of development that underlies the new Act is that local jurisdictions can best determine and meet local needs. With this shift in control and responsibility, whereby local government becomes a focal point for community planning, major challenges await professionals engaged in social welfare policy analysis and planning with local governmental and voluntary community organizations.

The Act is composed of eight titles, with Title I (Community Development) providing the foundation for the future federal role in supporting local housing and community development activities. Title I is based philosophically on the "new fed-

---

36. *Id.*; *see also* R. ALLEN HAYS, THE FEDERAL GOVERNMENT AND URBAN HOUSING 99–100 (3d ed. 2012) (describing the twin forces of reduced revenue from lower rent income and increased costs associated with deteriorating buildings).

37. Kost, *supra* note 27, at 1385.

38. *Id.*; *see also* Housing Community Development Act of 1974, Pub. L. No. 93-383, § 8, 88 Stat. 633, 662–66 (codified as amended at 42 U.S.C. § 1437f (2015)).

39. Housing and Community Development Act of 1974, *supra* note 38.

eralism," which seeks to decentralize control, maximize local participation in the planning and programming of federal resources, and ensure the design of comprehensive strategies to meet community needs and guide community development. Community development block grants, available under Title I, will provide significant federal resources for urban physical development programs.[40]

Title II of the Housing Act provides for Assisted Housing. The title replaced Section 23 of the public housing law, leased-housing subsidy program, with a new leasing program referred to as Section 8. Initially, the Section 8 program housed three subprograms: New Construction, Substantial Rehabilitation, and Existing Housing Certificate programs. The Moderate Rehabilitation Program was added in 1978, the Voucher Program in 1983, and the Project-based Certificate program in 1991. The Quality Housing and Work Responsibility Act of 1998 is one of the most "comprehensive" efforts to reform public housing. This Act made the following changes to the Section 8 program, now called the Housing Choice Voucher program:

> Merges and consolidates the Section 8 certificate and voucher programs. Allows PHAs to establish a set of local preferences based on local housing needs and priorities. The screening and selection of tenants shall be the responsibility of the owner. PHAs are given the power to terminate contracts with owners who fail to evict tenants that engage in activity which threatens the health, safety or peaceful enjoyment of the premises of other tenants or that is drug-related or violent criminal activity.[41]

Public housing authorities oversee the occupancy and eligibility of both public housing residents and Section 8 residents. Each year HUD posts income guidelines for eligibility. Section 8 participants must have incomes below 50% of the area median income; while public housing participants must have incomes below 80% of the area median.

The Rural Housing Service (RHS) administers direct loans, loan guarantees, and grants. Direct loans are made and serviced by USDA staff; loan guarantees are made to banks or other private lenders, and grants are made directly to a person or organization. RHS provides homeownership options to individuals; housing rehabilitation and preservation funding; rental assistance to tenants of RHS-funded multi-family housing complexes; farm labor housing; help to developers of multifamily housing projects, i.e., assisted housing for the elderly and disabled, or apartment buildings; and community facilities, such as libraries, child care centers, schools, municipal buildings, and firefighting equipment to Indian groups, nonprofit organizations, communities, and local governments.

The housing choice voucher program is the federal government's major program for assisting very low-income families, the elderly, and the disabled to afford decent,

---

40. William Frej & Harry Specht, *The Housing and Community Development Act of 1974: Implications for Policy and Planning*, 50 Soc. Serv. Rev. 275 (1976).

41. Subtitle C—Section 8 Rental and Homeownership Assistance (October 6, 1998), https://www.congress.gov/crec/1998/10/06/CREC-1998-10-06-pt1-PgH9597-3.pdf.

safe, and sanitary housing in the private market. Since housing assistance is provided on behalf of the family or individual, participants are able to find their own housing, including single-family homes, townhouses, and apartments.

The participant is free to choose any housing that meets the requirements of the program and is not limited to units located in subsidized housing projects. Housing choice vouchers are administered locally by PHAs The PHAs receive federal funds from the U.S. Department of Housing and Urban Development to administer the voucher program.

A family that is issued a housing voucher is responsible for finding a suitable housing unit of the family's choice where the owner agrees to rent under the program. This unit may include the family's present residence. Rental units must meet minimum standards of health and safety, as determined by the PHA.

A housing subsidy is paid to the landlord directly by the PHA on behalf of the participating family. The family then pays the difference between the actual rent charged by the landlord and the amount subsidized by the program. Under certain circumstances, if authorized by the PHA, a family may use its voucher to purchase a modest home. Below is a list of voucher programs currently funded by HUD:[42]

1. **Housing Choice Voucher program** — Tenant-based voucher assistance, providing rental subsidies for standard-quality units that are chosen by the tenant in the private market.

2. **Project-based voucher assistance** — a PHA may use up to 20% of its voucher assistance to implement a project-based voucher program.

3. **Homeownership voucher assistance** — A PHA may choose to use tenant-based housing choice voucher assistance to help eligible first-time homeowners with their monthly homeownership expenses.

4. **Enhanced voucher assistance** — These are special vouchers available to tenants who would otherwise be adversely affected by HUD program decisions. Enhanced vouchers are generally issued to provide continued assistance for a family at the termination of project-based rental assistance. If the family stays in the same project, the voucher payment standard covers the full market rent. Enhanced vouchers have several special requirements but in all other respects are subject to rules of the tenant-based voucher program. Differences include a special statutory minimum rent requirement and a special payment standard, applicable to a family receiving enhanced voucher assistance that elects to stay in the same unit, which can sometimes result in a PHA approving a unit that would otherwise be unaffordable to a family with regular tenant-based assistance. If the family moves, all normal voucher rules apply.

"[Voucher Programs] help families afford decent, stable housing, avoid homelessness, and make ends meet. They also enable children to grow up in better neighborhoods

---

42. Housing Choice Voucher Program, https://www.hud.gov/hudprograms/hcvp.

and thereby enhance their chances of long-term health and success."[43] Further, it is clear that location can mean just about everything for a family in poverty. Harvard economists Raj Chetty, Nathaniel Hendren, and Lawrence Katz "found that young children in families that used housing vouchers to move to better neighborhoods fared much better as young adults than similar children who remained in extremely poor neighborhoods."[44] With such statistics as these, why is it, then, that recent funding bills for HUD would cut the number of Housing Choice Vouchers by 30,000 and 110,000? Housing policies are obviously still troubling policymakers today.[45]

C. Housing Authorities and Annual Contribution Contracts

Federal housing policy is largely implemented through partnerships between local and federal agencies. Public housing is a creature of three parts: the local housing authority or public housing agency; the Department of Housing and Urban Development; and the tenant. The public housing agency is a quasi-governmental entity that is responsible for building, financing, operating, and managing public housing within its jurisdiction. As creatures of state law, PHAs rely on state enabling legislation to exist, although they must still comply with federal law and regulation. This means that local law, or intentions, may sometimes conflict with federal law, as will be seen in the Cuyahoga County case below. State enabling statutes contain provisions regarding the power, purposes and limitations for the PHA as well as the procedure for establishing the PHA. The process is somewhere between an act of government and acts of individual citizens. For example, in North Carolina any 25 residents of a city may file a petition with the city clerk setting forth that a PHA is needed. A public hearing follows, at which the city council shall determine:

(1) Whether insanitary or unsafe inhabited dwelling accommodations exist in the city and said surrounding area; and/or

(2) Whether there is a lack of safe or sanitary dwelling accommodations in the city and said surrounding area available for all the inhabitants thereof.

If the council determines that either unsanitary dwellings exist or that there is a need for sanitary dwellings, then the council shall establish a commission with the responsibility for filing articles of incorporation with the secretary of state, thereby creating the PHA. The articles of incorporation must state the public hearing process that

---

43. Barbara Sard & Douglas Rice, Ctr. on Budget & Pol'y Priorities, Realizing the Housing Voucher Program's Potential to Enable Families to Move to Better Neighborhoods (Jan. 12, 2016), https://www.cbpp.org/research/housing/realizing-the-housing-voucher-programs-potential-to-enable-families-to-move-to.

44. Id.

45. See Douglas Rice & Lissette Flores, Ctr. on Budget & Pol'y Priorities, Congress Should Add Funding to Prevent 2018 Housing Voucher Cuts (Nov. 27, 2017) https://www.cbpp.org/research/housing/congress-should-add-funding-to-prevent-2018-housing-voucher-cuts.

was followed establishing the PHA commission and be signed by each commissioner. In North Carolina, for example, "When the application has been made, filed and recorded, as herein provided, the authority shall constitute a public body and a body corporate and politic under the name proposed in the application; the Secretary of State shall make and issue to the said commissioners a certificate of incorporation pursuant to this Article, under the seal of the State, and shall record the same with the application."[46]

Because the state enabling statute does not reflect numerous regulatory requirements under the Housing Act, PHAs are required to enter into contractual agreements with HUD that mandate operation of the housing agency in a manner that complies with federal law. Two agreements ensure that local PHAs comply with federal law when administering their public housing programs: the Annual Contributions Contract and the Cooperation Agreement.

> **The Annual Contributions Contract** — Under the Housing Act, the federal government ultimately pays for the costs of constructing and operating public housing, but before that happens the local PHA is responsible for actually constructing, owning, and managing the development. The federal financial support for the development is distributed to the PHA through the Annual Contributions Contract.[47] The Annual Contributions Contract obligates the federal government to pay the cost of development, but not in one lump sum. Due to the significant budget impact that would have been associated with a one-time payment for construction cost, the ACC provides for regular annual payments that offset the cost of 40 year bonds issued by the PHA. These bonds are sold on the market to private investors. This financing method provides huge benefits to the federal government. First, it allows for the development cost to be amortized over a very long term, lessening the initial capital outlay and reducing the impact on the federal budget. Furthermore, these are tax-exempt, thus lowering the costs of borrowing.
>
> Second, because the annual payment from the federal government is contingent on the PHA's compliance with the ACC, and the requirements under the Housing Act, the federal government maintains a degree of control over the development, and thus can ensure that the development complies with the Housing Act. Such compliance extends to such matters as tenant income limits, housing quality standards, and safety.

The Housing Act was amended in 1969, 1970, and 1974 to place restrictions on the amount of rent that could be charged for public housing, authorized contributions under the ACC to be used to cover some of the PHA's operating costs and permitted tenants to be elected or appointed to the governing boards of the PHA.[48]

---

46. N.C. Gen. Stat. § 157-4 (2018).

47. 42 U.S.C. § 1437c(a) (2018).

48. U.S. Housing Act, 42 U.S.C. §§ 1437a, 1437g (2018).

Historically, compliance with HUD requirements was a frequent basis of litigation on behalf of the poor. In *Thorpe v. Housing Authority of the City of Durham,*[49] for example, attorneys were successful in protecting a family's housing based on HUD's pre-eviction requirements, which were inconsistent with state eviction requirements. The strategy of using federal public housing requirements to protect access to appropriate housing was pursued in numerous courts with some success, such as in *Henry Horner v. City of Chicago.*

With *Thorpe,* the Court established the role of federal law, and due process protections, in the administration and management of public housing financed by the federal government. After *Thorpe,* a tenant in public housing would receive the due process and other administrative benefits provided by HUD's regulatory scheme even if those procedures were greater than what was required under state law. Advocates for tenants of public housing developed a strategy focused those regulatory requirements. As the Henry Horner Mothers Guild litigation reflects, the conditions in public housing were sometimes very poor.

The Annual Contributions Contract provided a minimum set of standards for public housing that was often used to compel change in public housing conditions. The potential of using the ACC to establish a basis for litigating conditions of public housing shifted, however, with *Blessing v. Freestone,* 520 U.S. 329 (1997); *Sandoval v. Hagan,* 7 F. Supp. 2d 1234 (M.D. Ala. 1998); and *Wright v. Roanoke Redevelopment Auth.,* 479 U.S. 418 (1987).

1. Other Aspects of the ACC

The ACC may also obligate the federal government to pay an annual amount for operating and maintenance costs, as well as reserve funds.[50] In 1998, partly in response to cases such as *Henry Horner,* which publicized the realities of public housing, HUD took significant steps to reform aspects of public housing. These included steps to reduce segregation by race and income, encourage and reward work, and increase the number of subsidized units for very poor families. Congress also ordered a consolidation of funds for PHAs into two basic funds, one for capital expenses and one for operating expenses. Operating expenses were expanded to allow for social services, anti-crime, policy, and management provisions.[51] The range of expenses that may be paid by HUD is now very broad, including:

Capital Fund (1) In general The Secretary shall establish a Capital Fund for the purpose of making assistance available to public housing agencies to carry out capital and management activities, including:

> (A) the development, financing, and modernization of public housing projects, including the redesign, reconstruction, and reconfiguration of public

---

49. 393 U.S. 268 (1969).
50. 42 U.S.C. § 1437g (2018).
51. Pub. L. No. 105-276, § 519, 112 Stat. 2461, 2551 (1998) (amending 42 U.S.C. §§ 1437g(a)–(e)).

housing sites and buildings (including accessibility improvements) and the development of mixed-finance projects;

(B) vacancy reduction;

(C) addressing deferred maintenance needs and the replacement of obsolete utility systems and dwelling equipment;

(D) planned code compliance;

(E) management improvements, including the establishment and initial operation of computer centers in and around public housing through a Neighborhood Networks initiative, for the purpose of enhancing the self-sufficiency, employability, and economic self-reliance of public housing residents by providing them with onsite computer access and training resources;

(F) demolition and replacement;

(G) resident relocation;

(H) capital expenditures to facilitate programs to improve the empowerment and economic self-sufficiency of public housing residents and to improve resident participation;

(I) capital expenditures to improve the security and safety of residents;

(J) homeownership activities, including programs under section 1437z-4 of this title;

(K) improvement of energy and water-use efficiency by installing fixtures and fittings that conform to the American Society of Mechanical Engineers/ American National Standards Institute standards A112.19.2-1998 and A112.18.1-2000, or any revision thereto, applicable at the time of installation, and by increasing energy efficiency and water conservation by such other means as the Secretary determines are appropriate; and

(L) integrated utility management and capital planning to maximize energy conservation and efficiency measures.

Seen as a whole, the ACC provides a mechanism to fund the ongoing provision of housing as well as supportive services that might successfully move families out of subsidized housing.

2. The Cooperation Agreement

In addition to the ACC, the local PHA must enter into a Cooperation Agreement with the federal government.[52] This agreement must provide:

(2) the Secretary shall not make any contract for loans (other than preliminary loans) or for contributions pursuant to this chapter unless the governing body of the locality involved has entered into an agreement with the public housing agency providing for the local cooperation required by the Secretary

---

52. 42 U.S.C. § 1437c(e)(2) (2018).

pursuant to this chapter; the Secretary shall require that each such agreement shall provide that, notwithstanding any order, judgment, or decree of any court (including any settlement order), before making any amounts that are provided pursuant to any contract for contributions under this subchapter available for use for the development of any housing or other property not previously used as public housing, the public housing agency shall (A) notify the chief executive officer (or other appropriate official) of the unit of general local government in which the public housing for which such amounts are to be so used is located (or to be located) of such use, and

(B) pursuant to the request of such unit of general local government, provide such information as may reasonably be requested by such unit of general local government regarding the public housing to be so assisted (except to the extent otherwise prohibited by law).

Under the Cooperation Agreement, the local PHA agrees to a number of provisions that allow for the ongoing operation of the public housing development. These include a requirement to make a payment in lieu of taxes, to provide usual municipal services, and services on the same terms as they are provided to nonpublic housing units.[53] For example:

LEGAL AUTHORITY. A PHA must demonstrate to the Area Office that it has the required legal authority. The PHA demonstration shall include the organization documents which evidence that it was created pursuant to a state housing authority law which authorizes the establishment of a PHA and gives it the legal authority to develop, own, and operate public housing projects under an Annual Contributions Contract (ACC) with HUD.

LOCAL COOPERATION. The Act requires the local governing body for the area in which the public housing project will be located to enter into an agreement (i.e., a Cooperation Agreement) with the PHA to provide the local cooperation required by HUD pursuant to the Act. This local cooperation includes exemption from real and personal property taxes, acceptance of PHA payments in lieu of taxes (PILOT), and the provision at no cost or at no greater cost by the governing body of the same public services and facilities normally furnished to others in the community.

D. Public Housing — The Intersection of a Lack of Right and an Economic Policy

Public housing is a complex partnership among the federal government, local housing agencies, and private interests. In simplest forms, public housing operates as a partnership between federal and local agencies, with federal agencies providing operating funds, the receipt of which is contingent on certain standards being satisfied,

---

53. 42 U.S.C. § 1437d(d) (2018).

and local agencies serving as operating arms in the planning, construction, and operation of housing projects or as a conduit of funds for private landlords. Public housing offers benefits through this relationship by providing the resources of the federal government to serve local needs and conditions. However, the model is not without challenges.

The history of housing policy shows a move to privatization. The primary structures for financing the construction and operation of housing for low-income people remained largely intact from 1937 until 1974, when the 1937 Housing Act was again significantly amended by the Housing and Community Development Act of 1974 ("1974 Act"). The 1974 Act expanded options for public housing through the Section 8 voucher program. Twelve years later, in 1986, as part of a significant overhaul of the Internal Revenue Code, the Low Income Housing Tax Credit (LIHTC) program (discussed further below) was created and shifted the provision of housing for the poor even further into private developers' control.[54] During the same decade, federal funding for public housing dropped dramatically, leaving "the nation saddled with a deteriorated physical stock of public housing, poor on-site management, and frayed relationship between many PHAs and their residents."[55] In addition, poor public administration during the Reagan presidency resulted in a loss of more than $2 billion due to fraud, influence peddling, and misappropriate of funds from HUD.[56] Thus, public housing policy prior to the 1990s may be seen as moving in a continuum from hope at the start, to failed efforts and loss five decades later. Constant throughout this time, despite early promise, is racial discrimination, which was present from the beginning of the 1937 Housing Act and maintained following, driven largely by local interests.[57] Given the power of the local PHAs, public housing was often operated in conformity with local segregationist norms, a practice that was implicit from the start of public housing.[58] Even though *de jure* discrimination ended in 1962, *de facto* racial segregation remained within public housing,[59] a fact that the Civil Rights Commission recognized as early as 1975.[60] Consequently, by the late 1980s public housing is widely viewed to be an "abject failure"[61] on many fronts, setting the stage for new policies that re-envisioned public housing in the United States and ultimately HOPE VI, which was enacted in 1992.

---

54. Tax Reform Act of 1986, Pub. L. No. 99-514, § 252, 100 Stat. 2085, 2189–2208 (codified as amended at I.R.C. § 42); Florence Wagman Roisman, *Mandates Unsatisfied: The Low Income Housing Tax Credit Program and the Civil Rights Laws*, 52 U. MIAMI L. REV. 1011, 1012 (1998).

55. Kost, *supra* note 27, at 1386; *see also* HAYS, *supra* note 36, at 235–37.

56. Opinion, *The Reagan Scandals*, WASH. POST, July 30, 1989, at C6.

57. Ngai Pindell, *Is There Hope for HOPE VI?: Community Economic Development and Localism*, 35 CONN. L. REV. 385, 389 (2003).

58. Kost, *supra* note 27, at 1386.

59. Danielle Palfrey Duryea, *Gendering the Gentrification of Public Housing: Hope VI's Disparate Impact on the Lowest-Income African American Women*, 13 GEO. J. ON POVERTY L. POL'Y 567, 572–73 (2006).

60. U.S. COMM'N ON CIVIL RTS., TWENTY YEARS AFTER BROWN: EQUAL OPPORTUNITY IN HOUSING 39 (1975).

61. Duryea, *supra* note 59, at 573.

1. Public Housing: Who Gets It Right and Have We Gotten It Wrong?

Homelessness and public housing, where the federal and state governments have to work together, is certainly not unique to the United States. Affordable housing programs have been widely successful in other countries. For example, in Vienna, Austria, the city built a housing system and to this day they provide 400 million euros to maintain it. The city owns 25% of the housing stock, and they do not restrict the public housing to low-income residents. Instead as a family moves up the income ladder, [they are not] expelled from public housing.[62] Because of this, Vienna has garnered huge support from the public because it is serving the needs of many. Successful programs have also been found in Texas and Colorado.[63] Boulder, Colorado, and Austin, Texas, have been successful because the private and nonprofit sectors have collaborated to meet the demands of their respective cities. In Boulder, their housing program requires developers to make at a minimum 20% of total housing units to be "built permanently affordable for low-income households," which is defined in Boulder as anyone learning less than 80% of AM.[64] "The program ... requires developers to either create affordable units on or offsite, dedicate land for affordable housing, or pay a fee to the Affordable Housing Trust Fund of $18,000 per unit.... Developers who provide more than 20% of affordable units ... get their land use review and building permit fees reduced."[65]

Anastasia Kalugina says it best: "Addressing the lack of affordable housing in the United States requires long-term thinking, political determination, and behavioral changes. Cities must prioritize an acceptance of mixed-income communities, and tolerance for more social diversity within areas historically absent of households with a variety of socio-economic statuses."[66]

E. HOPE VI: Homeownership and Opportunity for People Everywhere Program

1. Theory Guiding HOPE VI Policy

Since 1987, William J. Wilson's *The Truly Disadvantaged: The Inner City, The Underclass, and Public Policy*[67] has been one of the most widely cited studies on poor, inner-city blacks. Wilson argues that there is a growing number of poor, urban

---

62. Anastasia Kalugina, *Affordable Housing Policies: An Overview*, 14 CORNELL REAL EST. REV. 76 (2016), https://scholarship.sha.cornell.edu/cgi/viewcontent.cgi?article=1156&context=crer.

63. *Id.*

64. *Id.*

65. *Id.*

66. *Id.*

67. WILLIAM J. WILSON, THE TRULY DISADVANTAGED: THE INNER CITY, THE UNDERCLASS, AND PUBLIC POLICY (reprint ed. 1990).

blacks who are both spatially and socially isolated from mainstream society despite advances made by many middle-class blacks as a result of the civil rights and affirmative action legislation of the late 1960s. The basis for this argument is an analysis of the changes in the U.S. economic structure. He argues that, beginning in the mid-1970s, U.S. factories sought cheaper labor overseas and opened sweatshops here at home that employed recent immigrants, many of whom were eager to work for less than minimum wage. Government, food services, sales, and maintenance jobs replaced factory jobs. Unfortunately, only the skilled and educated among the factory workers were able to take advantage of the new service sector employment. This change from a manufacturing-based economy to a service-centered economy, along with the enactment of new civil rights laws, opened doors to many middle- and working-class blacks who were then able to move away from inner cities and into suburbs.

This middle- and working-class black exodus removed:

> ... an important 'social buffer' that could deflect the full impact of the kind of prolonged and increasing joblessness that plagued inner-city neighborhoods in the 1970s and early 1980s, joblessness created by uneven economic growth and periodic recessions. This argument is based on the assumption that even if the truly disadvantaged segments of an inner-city area experience a significant increase in long-term spells of joblessness, the basic institutions in that area (churches, schools, stores, recreational facilities, etc.) would remain viable if much of the base of their support comes from the more economically stable and secure families. Moreover, the very presence of these families during such periods provides mainstream role models that help keep alive the perception that education is meaningful, that steady employment is a viable alternative to welfare, and that family stability is the norm, not the exception.[68]

With little to no employment prospects or upwardly mobile social networks, poor, inner-city blacks had become socially and economically isolated from the mainstream dominant culture. This isolation, Wilson continues, also creates a ripple effect in the children who grow up in the inner city, who "will seldom interact on a sustained basis with people who are employed or with families that have a steady breadwinner," which results in a "vicious cycle ... perpetuated through the family, through the community, and through the schools."[69] Wilson uses census data and school attainment records to support his arguments of social isolation and the ensuing tangle of pathology associated with poor, inner-city residents. The physical and social isolation of public housing developments and the behavioral pathologies that have been associated with public housing living have been the major reasons given by HUD administrators to revamp public housing throughout the nation.

While Wilson positions his arguments within an economic restructuring framework, many have argued that his work focuses on resulting behaviors such as

---

68. *Id.* at 56.
69. *Id.* at 57.

out-of-wedlock births, drugs, crime, and lack of role models.[70] Even within an economic restructuring framework, however, some theorists, have argued that the marginalization of poor inner-city residents cannot be explained by the structure of the economy alone. Castells argues that:

> ... technology *per se* or the structure of the economy itself are *not* the driving force behind the process of urbanization. Economic factors and technological progress do play a major role in establishing the shape and meaning of space. But this role is determined, as well as the economy and technology themselves, by the social process through which humankind appropriates space and time and constructs a social organization, relentlessly challenged by the production of new values and the emergence of new social interests.[71]

He presents a theory of urban social movements defined as: "a collective conscious action aimed at the transformation of the institutionalized urban meaning against the logic, interest, and values of the dominant class."[72] His work is a collection of case studies from urban centers around the world. The researchers identified grassroots organizations and analyzed their goals and the effects they had on the communities that they were actively trying to change. Thus, Castells might argue that the process of making an underclass in the inner city is the result of "conflicting social interests and values" between the dominant class and grassroots mobilizations[73] in addition to changes in the economic structure. He cautions, however, that the "autonomous role of the state, the gender relationships, the ethnic and national movements, and movements that define themselves as citizen ... are among other alternative sources of urban social change."[74] Thus, many factors must be taken into consideration when conceptualizing urban class inequities.

Hirsch presents another theoretical perspective that relies upon a race-specific analysis of urban culture change. He argues that "after World War II, however, government urban redevelopment and renewal policies, as well as a massive public housing program, had a direct and enormous impact on the evolution of the [second]

---

70. Larry Bennett & Adolph Reed Jr., *The New Face of Urban Renewal: The Near North Redevelopment Initiative and the Cabrini-Green Neighborhood, in* WITHOUT JUSTICE FOR ALL: THE NEW LIBERALISM AND OUR RETREAT FROM RACIAL EQUALITY 175–214 (Adolph Reed Jr. ed., 1999); Micaela di Leonardo, *"Why Can't They Be Like Our Grandparents?" and Other Racial Fairy Tales, in* WITHOUT JUSTICE FOR ALL: THE NEW LIBERALISM AND OUR RETREAT FROM RACIAL EQUALITY 29–64 (Adolph Reed Jr. ed., 1999); Brett Williams, *The Great Family Fraud of Postwar America, in* WITHOUT JUSTICE FOR ALL: THE NEW LIBERALISM AND OUR RETREAT FROM RACIAL EQUALITY (Adolph Reed Jr. ed., 1999); Susan Wright, *Blaming the Victim, Blaming Society or Blaming the Discipline: Fixing Responsibility for Poverty and Homelessness,* 34 Soc. Q. 1, 1–16 (1993); Katherine Newman, *Culture and Structure in The Truly Disadvantaged,* 6 CITY & SOC'Y 3, 3–25 (1992).

71. MANUEL CASTELLS, THE CITY AND THE GRASSROOTS: A CROSS-CULTURAL THEORY OF URBAN SOCIAL MOVEMENTS (1983).

72. *Id.*

73. *Id.*

74. *Id.*

ghetto."[75] During the 1940s and 1950s, Chicago, like other northern cities, experienced large-scale black migration due to increased wartime employment opportunities. The housing stock, however, especially in the segregated black enclaves, did not keep up with the influx of individuals. Overcrowding, increased rodent infestations, and devastating fires became a major problem. The Black Belt expanded its borders and many whites sought housing farther outside the inner city while others implored city administrators to take action. Racial tensions rose quickly and became more violent.

After the war, cities like Chicago acted fast in taking advantage of federal funds to ease overcrowding and avoid racially integrated communities. Humanitarian aid to the poor before the 1940s had changed in the 1950s to preservation of other areas not affected by the overcrowding problems of the inner city. Between 1945 and 1960, Chicago experienced a construction boom of single-family homes located mostly in the white suburbs. More affluent blacks were then able to move from the Black Belt into previously white neighborhoods. Poor blacks, however, remained in the inner city where public housing developments were built, or were relocated to other parts of the city. Thus, new public housing developments located in isolated black neighborhoods furthered the reconstruction goals of private developers after the war. Hirsch argues that "the high degree of residential segregation in Chicago produced a dual housing market: one for whites and one for blacks."[76] In her study of the dual housing market in the United States, Susan Greenbaum also finds that, "the dual housing market defines neighborhoods as either black or white, and by tacit agreement real estate brokers 'steer' their clients to one or the other, depending on their race ..." and that "... less powerful constituents are spatially bundled and bounded by [this] dual housing market."[77]

2. Legislative History

During the eight years of the Reagan administration and the subsequent four years of the Bush administration, funding for public housing authorities (PHAs) decreased steadily. PHAs and the developments that they managed had to rely on even fewer government subsidies to upgrade or simply maintain buildings, provide for resident social service needs, and retain qualified staff.[78] However, toward the end of the Bush administration, the Department of Housing and Urban Development Reform Act of 1989 was passed. The legislation "intended to help eliminate the systemic flaws that have allowed a number of Housing and Urban Development (HUD) programs to be

---

75. Arnold R. Hirsch, Making the Second Ghetto: Race and Housing in Chicago 1940–1960 10 (U. Chicago Press ed. 1998) (1983).

76. *Id.* at 29.

77. Susan D. Greenbaum, *Housing Abandonment in Inner-City Black Neighborhoods: A Case Study of the Effects of the Dual Housing Market, in* The Cultural Meaning of Urban Space 139, 141 (Robert Rotenberg & Gary McDonogh eds., 1994).

78. Harry J. Wexler, *HOPE VI: Market Means/Public Ends* 1–49. (Yale Sch. of Mgmt., Working Paper No. PM-1, 2000).

abused for political purposes or personal gain at the expense of those in need."[79] As part of these reform measures, President Bush announced the HOPE Initiative: Home-ownership and Opportunity for People Everywhere on November 10, 1989. The principles of the initiative included:[80]

> Empowering low-income families to achieve self-sufficiency and have a stake in their communities by promoting resident management and urban homesteading;

> Expanding homeownership and affordable housing opportunities for low- to moderate-income families and young families just starting out;

> Helping to end the tragedy of homelessness and to provide special emphasis on the long-term homeless who are in need of social services or health care;

> Creating jobs and economic opportunities in our nation's distressed inner cities and rural areas.

From these principles, three homeownership programs were adopted:

HOPE I—for tenants of public and Indian housing units; HOPE II—the sale of units in multifamily projects owned by HUD, the Farmers Home Administration, the Resolution Trust Corporation, or state or local governments; and HOPE III—the sale of single-family units in scattered site projects owned by HUD, the Veterans' Administration, or the Resolution Trust Corporation, among others. The 1990 Act also contained HOPE IV, a demonstration program to test ways to combine Section 8 certificates and vouchers with support services to help the frail elderly live independently. HOPE V, the Youthbuild Program, was enacted as part of the Housing and Community Development Act of 1992 to expand job opportunities for disadvantaged youth by training them to construct housing for low- and moderate-income families.[81, 82]

After a year of parleying through Congress, President Bush signed the "Cranston-Gonzalez National Affordable Housing Act" on November 28, 1990. The Act received its name from then-Chairman of the House Banking Committee, Congressman Henry Gonzalez (D-TX), and then-Senate Banking Committee member, Senator Alan Cranston (D-CA) and symbolized its support from Democrats and the Republican leadership.

Another outcome of the HUD Reform Act of 1989 was the formation of the National Commission on Severely Distressed Public Housing. A major task of the Commission was "to identify public-housing projects in severe distress, identify and assess strategies for dealing with these conditions, and come up with a plan for eliminating

---

79. George H. W. Bush, President of the United States, Statement on Signing the Department of Housing and Urban Development Reform Act of 1989 (Dec. 15, 1989).

80. Press Release, The White House, President Bush's Hope Initiative Homeownership and Opportunity for People Everywhere (Nov. 10, 1989) (on file with the Dole Archives, University of Kansas) https://dolearchives.ku.edu/sites/ dolearchive.drupal.ku.edu/files/files/historyday/originals/hd15_ghwbush_083.pdf.

81. Wexler, *supra* note 78.

82. Although HOPE VI carries the acronym, HOPE, it was not part of the original HOPE programs.

distressed conditions by 2000."[83] The results of the Commission found in 1992 that of the approximately 1.3 million public housing units, at least 86,000 units [6.62%] of urban public housing were in immediate need of demolition or revitalization. Approximately 80 percent of these distressed units were occupied, the rest had deteriorated to such a degree that they lay vacant, unfit for habitation. Several studies[84] concurred with the Commission's findings and argued that the majority of public housing in the United States is in fair condition and is part of the solution, not the problem, to housing our nation's poor. Nevertheless, the Commission found high unemployment among residents who had limited employment opportunities overall. Residents also faced fear of unemployment as well as fear of other residents and housing authority administrations, who failed to maintain the physical condition of the public housing or to promote self-sufficiency among residents.[85] Overall, residents in public housing were found to live in greater distress than residents in other housing, had lower incomes and lower education levels compared to the income and education levels of the area where they lived, and faced higher incidents of crime.[86]

Thus, the Commission recommended a 10-year National Action Plan to eliminate all distressed public housing developments by the year 2000. The plan, named the Urban Revitalization Demonstration (URD), focused on "revitalization in three general areas: physical improvements, management improvements, and social and community services to address resident needs," and estimated $750 million per year would cover these costs.[87] The Departments of Veterans Affairs and Housing and Urban Development, and the Independent Agencies Appropriations Act approved the URD, later renamed the Homeownership and Opportunity for People Everywhere (HOPE VI) Program on October 6, 1992.

The key goals of the HOPE VI program include:

- Changing the physical shape of public housing;
- Establishing positive incentives for resident self-sufficiency and comprehensive services that empower residents;
- Lessening concentrations of poverty by placing public housing in non-poverty neighborhoods and promoting mixed-income communities; and

---

83. Wexler, *supra* note 78, at 4.

84. Terry Williams & William Kornblum, *Public-Housing Projects as Successful Environments for Adolescent Development*, 749 ANNALS N.Y. ACAD. SCI. 153 (1995); BRATT, *supra* note 20.

85. THE FINAL REPORT OF THE NATIONAL COMMISSION ON SEVERELY DISTRESSED PUBLIC HOUSING: A REPORT TO THE CONGRESS AND THE SECRETARY OF HOUSING AND URBAN DEVELOPMENT xiii–xiv (1992).

86. HUD, *Case Study and Site Examination Reports of the National Commission on Severely Distressed Public Housing* 14-3 to -6 (1992).

87. HUD, *Revitalization of Severely Distressed Public Housing (HOPE VI)*, https://www.hud.gov/hudprograms/hopevi (last visited Nov. 20, 2019).

- Forging partnerships with other agencies, local governments, nonprofit organizations, and private businesses to leverage support and resources.[88]

When President Clinton came to office in 1993, his administration supported the HOPE VI program. The program was congruent with his administration's "reinventing government" efforts that sought to make government more efficient by borrowing from the best business practices in the private sector. The program has been funded by appropriation since its inception in 1993. Most programs, however, are both authorized and appropriated by Congress; it was not until the passage of the Quality Housing and Work Responsibility Act of 1998 when HOPE VI was authorized. Before authorization, each fiscal year the Federal Register publishes a Notice of Funding Availability (NOFA) that details the monies that are available to support the program. Housing authorities are able to submit grant proposals requesting funds for their sites to be demolished and rebuilt or rehabilitated. The support of this program by both Republicans and Democrats, and the billions of dollars that have been budgeted for this program mark a shift in hegemonic ideology that, as Reed argues, favors special interest groups and "well-off, white, and male" constituents over those in need of social reforms.[89]

When the program began in 1993, only 15 cities were to be selected from either the 40 most populous U.S. cities or from any city whose housing authority was considered to have been on HUD's troubled housing authorities list as of March 31, 1992, and no more than 500 units could be funded from each city (FY 1993 Appropriation Act 1992). However, in 1993, the Act allowed for the Secretary of HUD to approve funding for more than 15 cities, and in 1994, the Act allowed funding for more than 500 units for each participating city. The successful transformation of public housing developments via HOPE VI funding have led to the Choice Neighborhoods Planning and Implementation grant program. This program goes beyond the revitalization of public housing developments and seeks to transform distressed neighborhoods and public and assisted projects into viable and sustainable mixed-income neighborhoods. Such goals would be accomplished through linking housing improvements with appropriate services, schools, public assets, transportation, and access to jobs.[90]

3. Who Receives HOPE VI Funds?

Due to the aforementioned changes in the HOPE VI program, any public housing authority (PHA) that operates public housing units is eligible to apply for that public

---

88. HUD, *About HOPE VI*, https://www.hud.gov/program_offices/public_indian_housing/programs/ph/hope6/about (last visited Oct. 25, 2019).

89. Adolph Reed Jr., *Introduction: The New Liberal Orthodoxy on Race and Inequality*, in Without Justice for All: The New Liberalism and Our Retreat from Racial Equality 1–8 (Adolph Reed Jr. ed., 1999).

90. HUD, *Choice Neighborhoods*, https://www.hud.gov/cn (last visited Oct. 25, 2019).

housing, regardless of whether units fall within the distressed facilities criteria. PHAs may apply for Revitalization Grants or Demolition Grants. The revitalization (implementation) grants cover:

- Capital costs of major rehabilitation, new construction, and other physical improvements
- Demolition of severely distressed public housing
- Management improvements
- Planning and technical assistance
- Community and supportive service programs for residents.[91]

Demolition grants cover "the demolition of severely distressed public housing, relocation, and services for relocated residents."[92]

While individuals and organizations are not eligible to apply directly for HOPE VI funds, the program encourages PHAs to work with communities and corporations in creating social and financial partnerships to rebuild safe and affordable mixed-income housing developments. Each HOPE VI grantee is unique in its justification for submitting grant proposals. Some PHAs work hard to leverage private monies to combine with federal funds while others depend solely on HOPE VI funds to redevelop their projects. For example, the Louisville Housing Authority, which received a 1996 HOPE VI grant of $20 million, partnered with the National Equity Fund, Fannie Mae, the Community Development Financial Institutions Fund, the Enterprise Foundation, and the Kentucky Housing Corporation to leverage $89 million in non-HOPE VI funds to support the entire Park Duvalle revitalization. On the other hand, the Ellen Wilson Community Development Corporation (Washington, D.C.) relied solely on its HOPE VI grant to finance the demolition and revitalization of a new development.[93] Once a grant is awarded, however, grantees must abide by the parameters outlined in the HOPE VI Grant Agreement given at the time of the award.

Hope VI had the goal of creating new-urbanist spaces that contained mixed-use developments and diverse economic residents. At the core of the policies that spun from HOPE-VI was the objective of enhancing economic diversity within HOPE-VI communities. The thinking behind these objectives seems compelling. For poor people living in public housing, public housing had become a place of isolation where they were left without access to jobs, meaningful opportunities for education, and little social capital beyond that found within the public housing community. All of these obstacles to economic and social advancement could be mitigated through enhancing economic diversity. In many cases, however, such economic di-

---

91. HUD, *supra* note 88.
92. *Id.*
93. *Id.*

versity resulted in major shifts in community structure, for example as HOPE-VI communities pulled in more nonpoor residents, they shifted to have lower minority population density. For some, the goals of HOPE-VI created real tensions between the desire to develop mixed-income communities against the goal of achieving a robust racial diversity at the same time. Racial integration was seen as a paramount goal of housing policy, and the argument was made that racial diversity should take precedence in instances where diversity would be compromised for higher mixed-income integration.[94] Such preference would reflect many of the core policy objectives within the Housing Act and HOPE VI, including enhancing social capital and improving employment prospects. Absent an explicit mandate protecting racial diversity within HOPE-VI communities, there seem to be few tools to remedy the harms of racial isolation and displacement that has occurred in connection with the HOPE-VI program.

F. The Low-Income Housing Tax Credit — Investor Subsidies for Low-Income Housing Development

Traditionally, federal and state anti-poverty programs provide income or supports directly to the poor through state or federal administrative agencies. TANF, for example, provides a small amount of income support to low-income families by paying this amount directly to the family — although the supports come with significant strings attached. Transfer payment programs bring about a redistribution of resources and are necessary to alleviate poverty. In addition to these programs, a significant part of present-day, anti-poverty policy is implemented through tax systems.

In 1986, as part of the Tax Reform Act of 1986 ("1986 Act") significant changes were made in how federal policy encouraged the creation of low-income housing. The 1986 Act contained a new mechanism, described in section 42 of the tax code, for financing the construction of low-income rental housing. Known as the "Low-Income Housing Tax Credit" or LIHTC, Section 42 provides incentives for developers in the private sector to build new housing for the working poor. The LIHTC does this by establishing a mechanism for the private financing of construction, substantial rehabilitation, moderate rehabilitation, acquisition, and repair of low-income housing.

Section 42 is the longest section of the Internal Revenue Code, running more than 21 single-spaced pages. It is also one of the most complicated sections of the tax code, as you will see. Nonprofit developers play a large role in implementing the LIHTC, and at least one writer has found it necessary to warn potential developers of the com-

---

94. Kost, *supra* note 27.

plexity of the program: "Nonprofit developers should be aware that this LIHTC program is extremely complicated and rife with land mines for those uninitiated in this type of financing. Early in the development process, sponsors who are seriously considering a tax credit project should retain tax counsel experienced in the low-income housing tax credit."[95] What follows is an introduction to the LIHTC and the mechanisms that run through the Internal Revenue Code to finance low-income housing.

1. LIHTC Overview

The LIHTC may be seen as an incentive for private investors to invest in low-income housing. The LIHTC begins with the U.S. Treasury, who issues tax credits to real estate developers. These developers may be either for-profit or nonprofit organizations. After receiving the tax credits, the developers sell them to investors, who can use the credit to offset their federal tax liability. Because the investor uses the tax credit over a 10-year time period when filing their returns, the investor pays a price that reflects present-day value for the tax credit. This short paragraph is a vastly simplified description of the LIHTC program. Below is a graphic description of the program, which illustrates its complexity:[96]

The LIHTC provides developers with a "present value" tax credit equal to 70% of the cost of new construction or 30% of the cost of acquisition of existing low-income housing. In exchange, the developer agrees to limit rents on the properties for a period of up to 30 years. Tax credits are allocated over a 10-year period based upon the Applicable Federal Rate (APR). The value of the credit is nine percent annually for the 70% credit and four percent annually for projects receiving the 30 percent credit. For example, over 10 years the investor annually receives nine percent of the total LIHTC allocated to the project.

The Low-Income Housing Tax Credit is the largest federal program for funding new affordable housing, and as with the EITC, the LIHTC relies on the tax code to identify beneficiaries and place resources—under I.R.C. §42.

The LIHTC Program operates as an indirect federal subsidy and is used to finance the development of affordable rental housing for low-income households. The credit accomplishes this through a complex structure involving the U.S. Treasury, state-sponsored intermediary agencies, private developers (both for-profit and nonprofit) and private investors, nearly all of whom are large financial institutions.

The LIHTC Program was enacted by Congress in 1986 to provide the private market with an incentive to invest in developing affordable rental housing. Since 1986, the program has grown to become the single largest source of funding to finance affordable and low-income housing development, providing nearly $1 billion a year

---

95. Bennett L. Hecht, Developing Affordable Housing: A Practical Guide for Nonprofit Organizations 148 (1994).

96. Press Release, GAO, Tax Credits: Opportunities to Improve Oversight of the Low-Income Housing Program (Apr. 23, 1997) (on file with author), https://www.gao.gov/assets/110/106855.pdf.

in new funding for new development of affordable housing—but this does not take into account previously allocated tax credits, which increases the total amount of tax credits being used in any given year to at least $10 billion.

LIHTCs are allocated by the IRS to state agencies on a per capita basis, subject to a variety of step-ups and boosts. Each state is allocated $1.75 per resident, adjusted for inflation since 2003, which amounted to roughly $2.09 in 2009. Only the first year of the 10-year compliance period counts against the allocation. This means that when the state finance agency allocates $1,000,000 of tax credits over 10 years, only $100,000 count against the state's LIHTC allocation, even though there is an ongoing credit liability to the Treasury.

Having received the allocation from the Treasury, the state agency then passes them through to individual developers who are constructing or substantially remodeling "qualified projects." Developers then sell these credits to investors to raise equity for their projects, which reduces the debt that the developer would otherwise have to borrow. Because the debt is lower, a tax credit property can, in turn, offer lower, more affordable rents.

Provided the property maintains compliance with Section 42, then the investor receives a dollar-for-dollar credit for the amount they invested against their federal tax liability each year over a 10-year period.

To qualify for the LIHTC, the property must be a residential property and the developer must commit to one of two low-income occupancy thresholds. The 20-50 Rule, which requires that 20% of the units financed with LIHTC must be rent restricted and occupied by resident with incomes at or below 50% of the HUD determined area median income. Or the 40-60 Rule, which requires that at least 40% of the units financed with LIHTC must be rent restricted and occupied by households with incomes at or below 60% of the HUD Determined area median income. In each case, the area median income is adjusted for household size.

The developer/manager then agrees to restrict rents, including utilities, to no more than 30% of the tenant's income for those units, for a period of at least 15 years, but in most cases the developer agrees to operate under rent restrictions for 30 years or longer. At the end of the rent-restricted period, the developer has the option to convert the property to "market rate rent."

Tax credits may be claimed directly by the developer. Alternatively, LIHTC may be sold by the developer directly to a single investor, or to a syndicator who in turn markets the tax credits to investors. In many ways it is difficult to imagine a more complex method for financing new low-income housing development.

2. Section 42 — The Details

a. Allocation

Each year the IRS allocates housing tax credits to designated state agencies. These agencies are established by state legislation and organized and operated with the sole purpose of receiving allocated tax credits and then allocating the credits to what are called "qualified projects."

The tax credits that are allocated to each state are limited to $1.75 per resident, adjusted for cost-of-living increases beginning in 2003. Only the first year of the 10-year award is counted against the allocation limit. An example illustrates this dynamic.

Allocation of the tax credit is accomplished through a competitive process. Developers seeking to receive an allocation of credits must submit their application to the state housing finance agency by set deadlines. The applications are extremely detailed and involve hundreds of hours of work to prepare.

States receiving tax credits must develop and publish a plan for determining how to allocate the credits they receive from the federal government. This is known as the Consolidated Plan. Each application for an award of tax credits is assessed against the state finance agency's Consolidated Plan.

The LIHTC program requires that the allocation plan give priority to projects that (a) serve the lowest-income families; and (b) are structured to remain affordable for the longest period. Federal law also requires that 10% of each state's annual housing tax credit allocation be set aside for projects owned by nonprofit organizations. These priorities are published, along with detailed guidance, in the annual Qualified Allocation Plan (QAP). The QAP becomes the tool used to define needed low-income housing development and determine the best allocation of available LIHTC by state.

The amount of tax credits awarded to a project is calculated on the portion of the costs of the development that is defined as the "Qualified Basis" and the number of Qualified Low-Income Units in the development. Tax credits allocated to a state must be awarded to projects within two years of the allocation. Tax credits that are not awarded within this time frame are returned to the federal government.

b. Calculating the Housing Tax Credit

To calculate the amount of tax credits allocated to a development, a somewhat complicated formula is used that follows four steps. The formula reflects Section 42's requirement that the tax credit be connected to low-income housing, as defined by the statute. The following defined terms are integral to calculating the tax credit a project will receive.

- **Eligible Basis** — this is generally the adjusted basis of the new construction to be financed by the LIHTC.

- **Applicable Fraction** — this measure refers to the portion of the building that is financed by the LIHTC allocation.

- **Qualified Basis** — this is the base amount that is multiplied by the credit percentage to determine the annual tax credit that may be claimed by each investor.

There are four steps involved in calculating the qualified basis:

First, the Eligible Basis must be determined. Eligible Basis is the amount of the total depreciable development costs that may be included in calculating the amount of available housing tax credits. Total depreciable development costs generally include all "hard" costs, including costs related to construction of the housing. In addition, most depreciable "soft" costs can be included in Eligible Basis as depreciable development costs. Soft costs include architectural costs, engineering costs, site preparation, and fees for connecting to utilities. Several costs are expressly excluded from Eligible Basis, including, among others, land acquisition costs, costs of permanent financing, and deposits into reserves.

Second, the Applicable Fraction must be determined. This refers to the percentage of qualified low-income units that are part of the total number of developed units. If the owner fails to achieve the projected applicable fraction, the amount of credits is reduced pro rata. The "Applicable Fraction" is the lower of two percentages: the percentage of affordable units to total units, and the percentage of square feet in the affordable units to the total square feet in the project. The IRS monitors Applicable Fraction on a building-by-building basis.

At the time each building is first occupied ("placed in service"), the developer and IRS establish a minimum Applicable Fraction for that building that the developer must maintain for the entire affordability period. Typically, developers prefer to structure their LIHTC projects so that each building has an Applicable Fraction of 100% or 0%, because this makes ongoing compliance much easier.

Third, the "Qualified Basis" is determined. Qualified Basis refers to the dollar amount that is eligible for the housing tax credits.

Fourth, additional credit values are attached to the project under some circumstance. If the development is located in certain HUD-designated high-cost areas, the state housing financing agency may award up to 30% in additional tax credits. This is known as the "basis boost" and provides a further incentive for developments in both Qualified Census Tracts and Difficult Development Areas.

c. Project Eligibility

Not all real estate projects may receive LIHTCs. To be eligible for tax credits under the program, the proposed project must meet the following criteria:

1. Be a residential rental property

2. Follow either the 20-50 or 40-60 occupancy restrictions

3. Restrict rents on the low-income units

4. Operate the project under the occupancy and rent restrictions for 30 years or longer—and commit to a written contract with the state agency that issued the tax credits.

Each of the above criteria has additional detail requiring careful analysis that goes beyond the scope of these materials.

d. Rent Restrictions

The amount of rent that may be collected for LIHTC-financed properties is limited to a percentage of the area median income and cannot exceed established market limits. The LIHTC limitation only applies to the amount of rent paid by the tenant, not the total rent. A tenant's total rent may be subsidized by Section 8 assistance, keeping in mind that rents subsidized by project-based Section 8 may exceed the LIHTC limit but tenant-based Section 8 rents may not.

e. Operation Restrictions and Affordability Requirements

Projects that are financed with the LIHTC are required to maintain their rent restrictions and occupancy requirements for a period of 30 years. This 30-year period is reached by adding the 15-year compliance period with the 15-year use period that follows. This is known as the "Affordability Period." A longer Affordability Period may be required for specific properties or in certain circumstances. These situations will be negotiated individually between the developer and the state agency.

Each year during the Affordability Period the project manager certifies that the restrictions on rent and occupancy are being complied with to the state agency that awarded the tax credits. The state agency that awarded the tax credits is responsible for monitoring compliance under an agreement with the IRS. An annual report is filed with the IRS by the state agency.

At the end of the rent-restricted period, the developer has the option to convert the property to "market rate rent." This means the developer may effectively remove the rent restrictions that had been placed on the LIHTC-financed property, thus possibly making the property unaffordable for low-income tenants.

f. Syndication

Although a developer that receives tax credits may use them directly to offset their tax bill, they usually sell them to either an investor who will use them or to a syndicator who assembles groups of investors who each take a part of the tax credits to reduce their federal tax liability. One of, if not the only, reason for the use of syndicators in the LIHTC arena is the 10-year period that applies to the tax credits. As noted above, the tax credits must be used by the taxpayer over a 10-year period. This creates a challenge for the developer, who needs money to pay the costs of the development immediately, as bills are presented. By selling the tax credits, or more precisely the right to participate in the tax credits over the 10-year period, the developer can assemble the money that is needed for the development. To accomplish this, a few complicated structures are used.

The most common structure used to sell the LIHTC is a Limited Liability Partnership ("LLP") or Limited Liability Company ("LLC"), which is functionally the same. Under this arrangement, an investor buys a partnership interest in the LLP or a membership interest in the LLC and becomes part of the ownership. Typically, 99.99% of the ownership of these LLPs or LLCs is by investors with .01% owned by the developer, who serves as the General Partner or Managing Member for management and tax purposes. The General Partner or Managing Member is responsible for the day-to-day management of the development and the partnership, and usually serves as the tax partner, the person designated for IRS correspondence and to serve as an agent with the IRS for tax matters. (The Form 1065 is used to designate the tax matters partner.) The investors serve in a purely passive role.

Profits, of which there are rarely any, and losses, of which there are usually some, and depreciation are shared among the partners based upon their percentage ownership interest. The project must have positive cash flow to operate, and this is generated from rents. From this cash flow the costs of maintaining the property, paying utilities, and covering vacancies will be paid. These costs are usually paid to a management company, which is selected by the General Partner in a partnership or Managing Member in an LLC.

For many years, the LLP was the preferred entity for LIHTC transactions. More recently, LLCs have become the most common entity for such transactions.

A Note on Structure:

Limited partnerships were the most common ownership structure for multifamily properties in the 1960s and continuing through much of the 1990s. A typical LIHTC limited partnership consists of the developer (or an affiliate) as the general partner, and the credit purchaser as the limited partner. The general partner has a small percentage ownership interest (often below one percent) but has the responsibility for managing the affairs of the partnership, arrange for management of the property, and make most of the day-to-day operating decisions. The limited partner has a large percentage ownership interest (often well above 99 percent), has a passive role, and has liability that is limited to the amount invested. That is, if a disaster occurs, the most the limited partner can lose is the amount invested; however, the general partner can lose many times the amount invested. The rights and obligations of the partners are outlined in a Limited Partnership Agreement. Typically, the limited partners do not participate in day-to-day operating decisions, but do participate in major decisions such as whether to sell or refinance the property.

Limited liability companies (LLCs) are an increasingly common ownership structure for multifamily properties. A typical LIHTC LLC consists of the developer (or an affiliate) as the managing member, and the credit purchaser as an additional (non-managing) member. The managing member has a small percentage ownership interest (often below one percent) but has the responsibility for managing the affairs of the partnership, arrange for the management of the property, and make most of the day-to-day operating decisions. The non-managing member has a large percentage ownership interest (often well above 99 percent) and has a passive investor role. All members of an LLC have liability that is limited to the amount invested. That is, if a disaster occurs, the most they can lose is the amount invested. The rights and obligations of the partners are described in an LLC Operating Agreement. Typically, the non-managing members do not participate in day-to-day operating decisions, but do participate in major decisions such as whether to sell or refinance the property.

g. Recapture

Once the development is built and in use, the developer is responsible for maintaining continued compliance with Section 42 and the LIHTC program. This means that rent restrictions must be maintained and occupancy restrictions must be observed. The state agency is responsible for ensuring these requirements are met for the entire 15-year compliance period.

If a project fails to comply with the LIHTC rent and occupancy restrictions, the tax credits may be subject to recapture. Recapture allows the IRS to pull the tax credits back, with a resulting payment by the taxpayers/investors who financed the deal at the beginning. Such a process will subject a taxpayer to significant tax liability for past due taxes and penalties.

While the potential for recapture is real, there has never been a reported instance of either a state agency or the IRS recapturing credits awarded to a project. If a project should be subject to the recapture provisions, the investors who purchased the tax credit would be required to repay income taxes previously off set with the tax credits, along with penalties and interest. The amount subject to recapture is calculated as the difference in the amount of credits that would have been available over the 15-year period minus the amount claimed according to the 10-year schedule.

h. Tenant Protections

Owners of LIHTC properties must have "good cause" in order to evict their tenants. This "good cause" requirement is an important tool for low-income individuals or families looking for stable housing. Some states, such as California, have implemented the good cause requirement by requiring all LIHTC properties to have a good cause lease rider and providing all tenants with a letter informing them of their rights. Other states, such as Massachusetts and Wisconsin, reference good cause in LIHTC regulatory agreements.

A few courts have addressed the "good cause" requirement issue. In *Carter v. Maryland Mgmt. Co.*, an LIHTC landlord was attempting to evict a holdover tenant. The court held, in part, that a landlord participating in the Federal Low-Income Housing Tax Credit Program could not terminate the tenancy of low-income tenant other than for good cause.[97] Similarly in *Cimarron Village Townhomes, Ltd. v. Washington*, an LIHTC landlord declined to renew the lease of a low-income housing tenant. The court here held that the plain meaning of the statutory language prohibits the eviction

---

97. Carter v. Md. Mgmt. Co., 835 A.2d 158, 165, 377 Md. 596, 608 (Md. Ct. App. 2003) (holding good cause required for termination of LIHTC/Voucher tenancy).

of tenants without good cause at any time within the 30-year extended low-income housing commitment.[98]

Although courts have consistently held that the Internal Revenue Code requires "good cause" for eviction of low-income tenants, many state tax credit allocating agencies have failed to implement and enforce the good cause requirement. Lawyers from groups like the National Housing Law Project are currently engaged in advocacy efforts to implement "good cause" eviction standards because of the important due process protections it provides to tax credit tenants. These efforts include informing tenants of their rights under the Internal Revenue Code, working with state agencies to include good cause lease riders, and letters to owners of their obligations to tenants under LIHTC requirements.

3. Tax Credit Allocation and Bid Process

The federal Low-Income Housing Tax Credit program requires each state agency that allocates tax credits, generally called a state housing agency, to have a Qualified Allocation Plan (QAP). The QAP sets out the state's criteria and priorities for awarding federal tax credits to developers. The QAP is a tool low-income housing advocates can use to influence how their state's share of annual low-income housing tax credits is allocated to affordable housing properties.[99]

Each QAP must set out the state agency's priorities, with local conditions factored in, and specify the criteria it will use to evaluate tax credit allocation bids. The QAP must give preference to projects serving residents with the lowest income, serving income-eligible residents for the longest period, and located in qualified census tracts (QCTs) or difficult development areas (DDAs).[100]

> The QAP selection criteria must address 10 items: (1) location; (2) housing needs; (3) public housing waiting lists; (4) individuals with children; (5) special needs populations; (6) whether a project includes the use of existing housing as part of a community revitalization plan; (7) project sponsor characteristics; (8) projects intended for eventual tenant ownership; (9) energy efficiency; and (10) historic nature. These requirements are minimums; states can adopt more rigorous criteria that target advocates' priority populations

---

98. Cimarron Vill. Townhomes, Ltd. v. Wash., No. C3-99-118, 1999 WL 538110 (Minn. Ct. App. July 27, 1999) (holding good cause eviction protection required under LIHTC statute).

99. Ed Gramlich, Director of Regulatory Affairs for the National Low-Income Housing Coalition, suggests that advocates use the public hearing and comment requirements to convince their housing finance agency to better target tax credits to properties that house people with extremely low incomes, locate projects in priority areas, and preserve the existing stock of affordable housing. Ed Gramlich, *Low-Income Housing Tax Credits, in* ADVOCATES' GUIDE TO HOUSING AND COMMUNITY DEVELOPMENT POLICY 5-19 (2019), https://nlihc.org/sites/default/files/AG-2019/05-05_LIHTC.pdf.

100. QCTs are census tracts with a poverty rate of 25% or in which 50% of the households have incomes below 60% of the area median income (AMI). DDAs are areas in which construction, land, and utility costs are high relative to incomes. *Id.* at 5-18.

and locations. Most states establish detailed QAP selection criteria and set-asides based on the characteristics of their state's needs.[101]

North Carolina's QAP judges tax credit site evaluations via point system with 60 points being the maximum score.[102] The majority of these 60 points (38) is distributed based upon the proposed sites' proximity to tenant amenities. The closer an amenity is located to the proposed development, and the more essential the amenity is deemed, the more points are granted to the proposed project. North Carolina deems grocery, pharmacy, and shopping to be the most essential, or "primary," amenities. For example, if a developer's proposed project is less than one mile from a Walmart Supercenter, which qualifies under the grocery, pharmacy, and shopping categories, the project would receive the maximum 26 "primary amenities points." However, if the project were located three miles from the Walmart Supercenter, it would only be eligible to receive 14 "primary amenities points." The rationale for awarding tax credits based on proximity to amenities is twofold. First, low-income tenants, by and large, have less access to reliable transportation so having "primary amenities" within a one-mile radius puts them in convenient walking distance. Second, having these amenities in convenient walking distance not only ensures no LIHTC developments are built in food deserts, but also provides nearby sources of employment for tenants.

Along with positive site characteristics mentioned above, QAPs also lay out detrimental site characteristics or even disqualifying site characteristics. One might argue that the local housing authority maintains a high degree of control over where LIHTC projects are being built in their states and metropolitan areas. Further, nonprofit and for-profit developers looking to break into LIHTC as a financing mechanism often need to engage with legal counsel not only to walk through the tax allocations and program requirements of LIHTC, but to interact with local housing agencies to stay abreast of allocation preferences and requirements.

4. A Critique

An enduring critique of the LIHTC system is housing that is subsidized through tax credits is more suited to the needs of the investor/developer than it is to poor renters. LIHTC was implemented during the rise of Reagan-era economics, a period where governmental actors were withdrawing from the role of providing social services. The development and subsequent management of low-income rental housing is a vivid example of functions once monopolized by the government becoming largely privatized.

When Congress adopted the tax credit, as result of the 1986 Tax Reform Act, competition between for-profit and nonprofit developers began to emerge. For-profit real estate developers wanted LIHTC to compensate developers for losses of

---

101. *Id.* at 5-19.

102. N.C. Hous. Fin. Agency, The 2019 Low-Income Housing Tax Credit Qualified Action Plan For the State of North Carolina 11 (2019), https://www.nchfa.com/rental-housing-partners/rental-developers/qualified-allocation-plan/2019-qualified-allocation-plan-qap.

tax advantages eliminated by the 1986 Tax Reform Act. Nonprofit organizations primarily saw LIHTC as a mechanism to supply very low to moderate-income housing. These nonprofit organizations play a pivotal role in the supply of low-income housing because of their willingness to serve the poorest tenants, in the poorest neighborhoods, and embark on deals with far less financial security than their for-profit counterparts would.

LIHTC statutory provisions incorporate very little incentive for developers to rent to very poor people. Developers applying for the tax credit must agree to either dedicate 20% of their rental units to tenants living at or below 50% of the area median income, or alternatively dedicate 40% of their units to tenants making 60% of the area median income. Rents in these tax credit funded developments are capped at 30% of the of either 50% or 60% of the area median income—depending on which option the developer selected from above. Eighty-eight percent of developers choose the 40-60 option, meaning they choose to dedicate a larger number of rental units for higher-income tenants than choosing fewer units to low-income tenants. Because of this, LIHTC has been criticized as system that benefits the developers foremost, people on the fringes of poverty next, while ignoring the housing needs of the poorest among us.

5. LIHTC Selection Processes and the Fair Housing Act

Like HOPE VI, Section 8, and Public Housing, the LIHTC program implicates fair housing and other civil rights concerns. In 2015, the Supreme Court considered whether LIHTC property siting decisions were subject to Fair Housing Act challenges based on a disparate impact theory.

a. Texas Department of Housing & Community Affairs v. Inclusive Communities Project, Inc.

i. Case Background and Relation to LIHTC[103]

As explained earlier, the federal government provides tax credits through the states to promote low-income housing development.[104] In Texas, the state's Department of Housing and Community Affairs (the Department) distributes these credits directly to developers based on a number of criteria articulated in federal and state statutes.[105] From 1999 to 2008, the Department approved tax credits for 49.7% of proposed nonelderly, low-income housing developments in areas where less than 10% of the pop-

---

103. *See* Recent Case, Texas Department of Housing & Community Affairs v. Inclusive Communities Project, Inc., 129 Harv. L. Rev. 321 (2015) for a more in-depth analysis of the Court's opinion and disparate impact claims based on race.

104. *See* 26 U.S.C. § 42 (2018).

105. Inclusive Cmtys. Project, Inc. v. Tex. Dep't of Hous. & Cmty. Affairs (*Inclusive II*), 860 F. Supp. 2d 312, 314–16 (N.D. Tex. 2012).

ulation was made up by whites.[106] During the same period, the Department approved credits for only 37.4% of non-elderly, low-income housing development in areas where whites made up 90% or more of the population.[107] In Dallas, 92.29% of all housing units built using low-income tax credits were located in majority-minority census tracts.[108]

The Inclusive Communities Project (ICP), a nonprofit organization that assists low-income voucher recipients in finding affordable housing, sued the Department over concerns that the Department's practices were having the effect of denying minorities the opportunity to live in white neighborhoods; and therefore contributing to housing segregation in Dallas.[109] ICP alleged that the Department was engaging in intentional discrimination against African Americans in violation of the Fourteenth Amendment, 42 U.S.C. § 1982, and created a disparate impact under the Fair Housing Act (FHA).

The district court held that ICP failed to prove its claims of intentional discrimination.[110] The court nevertheless ruled in favor of ICP on their disparate impact claim.[111] The trial court, having previously ruled that the disparity in tax credit approvals established a *prima facie* case of disparate impact,[112] examined the agency's defense that the tax credits were distributed in an "objective, transparent, predictable, and race-neutral manner."[113] The court determined that the Department "failed to meet [its] burden of proving that there are no less discriminatory alternatives."[114] The Fifth Circuit reversed and remanded, adopting a "burden shifting framework," holding that the district court should have required the ICP to demonstrate the availability of less discriminatory alternatives.[115]

ii. The Supreme Court's Disparate Impact Analysis

The Supreme Court held that disparate impact claims are cognizable under the FHA.[116] First established in *Griggs v. Duke Power Co.,* disparate impact doctrine prohibits facially neutral practices that have discriminatory effects on protected classes (for example, race) if the government cannot provide a "legitimate interest" in the

---

106. Inclusive Cmtys. Project, Inc. v. Tex. Dep't of Hous. & Cmty. Affairs (*Inclusive I*), 749 F. Supp. 2d 486, 499 (N.D. Tex. 2010).

107. *Id.*

108. *Id.*

109. *Id.* at 492–93.

110. *Inclusive II*, 860 F. Supp. 2d at 317.

111. *Id.* at 331.

112. *Inclusive I,* 749 F. Supp. 2d at 486, 499–500.

113. *Inclusive II*, 860 F. Supp. 2d at 323.

114. *Id.* at 331.

115. *See* Inclusive Cmtys. Project, Inc. v. Tex. Dep't of Hous. & Cmty. Affairs (*Inclusive III*), 747 F.3d 275, 282–83 (5th Cir. 2014).

116. Tex. Dep't of Hous. & Cmty. Affairs v. Inclusive Cmtys Project, Inc. (*Inclusive IV*), 135 S. Ct. 2507, 2525 (2015).

practice.[117] Justice Kennedy, writing for the majority,[118] prefaced the Court's disparate impact analysis with a survey of the legislative and social history of the passage of the FHA. Justice Kennedy summarized decades of discriminatory housing practices by both state and private entities,[119] described President Johnson's establishment of the Kerner Commission and the Commission's subsequent recommendation for fair housing laws,[120] and observed that Congress passed the FHA in response to the social unrest in inner cities following the assassination of Dr. Martin Luther King Jr.[121]

The bulwark of the Court's opinion is concerned with statutory interpretation of the FHA. Looking at the Court's precedent, Justice Kennedy examined both *Griggs v. Duke Power Co.*[122] and *Smith v. City of Jackson*,[123] which held disparate impact claims cognizable under Title VII of the Civil Rights Act of 1964[124] and the Age Discrimination in Employment Act (ADEA).[125] Justice Kennedy read these cases as establishing that "antidiscrimination laws must be construed to encompass disparate impact claims when their text refers to the consequences of actions."[126] Both Title VII and the ADEA share language prohibiting actions that "other-wise adversely affect" a person's employment opportunities. In Justice Kennedy's view, the FHA provision prohibiting actions that "otherwise make unavailable" housing because of race serves a similar purpose.[127] In all three statutes, Congress utilizes language that focuses on the consequences of an action rather than the actor's intent. The Court held that this "results-oriented language" counseled in favor of recognizing disparate impact liability.[128]

After comparing the operative language of the FHA to both Title VII and the ADEA, Justice Kennedy further contends that the FHA's 1988 amendments supported the Court's interpretation. At the time the amendments to the FHA passed, every circuit court that examined the issue had held that the FHA created disparate impact liability.[129] Justice Kennedy contends that by leaving the FHA's operative language untouched, Congress had "accepted and ratified" the unanimous interpretation of the statute by the circuit courts.[130]

---

117. *See* Griggs v. Duke Power Co., 401 U.S. 424, 431 (1971); *see also* Ricci v. DeStefano, 557 U.S. 557, 558 (2009).

118. Justice Kennedy's majority opinion was joined by Justices Ginsburg, Breyer, Sotomayor, and Kagan. *Inclusive IV*, 135 S. Ct. at 2512.

119. *Id.* at 2515.

120. *Id.*

121. *Id.* at 2516.

122. 401 U.S. 424 (1971).

123. 544 U.S. 228 (2005).

124. 42 U.S.C. §§ 2000e to 2000e-17 (2018).

125. 29 U.S.C. §§ 621–34 (2018).

126. *Inclusive IV*, 135 S. Ct. at 2518.

127. *Id.* at 2519.

128. *Id.*

129. *Id.*

130. *Id.* at 2520.

Further, the Court contended that disparate impact liability furthers the FHA's "central purpose ... to eradicate discriminatory practices within a sector of our Nation's economy."[131] Disparate impact liability accomplishes this goal in two ways: First, by rooting out systemic issues that further engrain segregation. Disparate impact liability would provide a legal mechanism to strip away "zoning laws and other housing restrictions that function unfairly to exclude minorities from certain neighborhoods without any sufficient justification."[132] Second, the recognition of disparate impact claims under the FHA would "uncover[] discriminatory intent" and "counteract unconscious prejudices and disguised animus that escape easy classification as disparate treatment."[133]

After recognizing the ability to bring disparate impact claims under the FHA, Justice Kennedy goes on to limit the doctrine to "avoid the serious constitutional questions that might arise."[134] He notes that there are a variety of legitimate reasons potential defendants may assert as a justification for their policies. This could include entrepreneurial reasons like cost and other market factors, or, for zoning officials, objective criteria like traffic patterns, as well as subjective desires for historic preservation.[135] A statistical disparity alone would not be sufficient to succeed on a disparate impact claim; instead the claimant must identify "a policy or policies causing that disparity."[136]

Texas Department of Housing and Community Affairs v. The Inclusive Communities Project, Inc.
576 U.S. 519 (2015)

The underlying dispute in this case concerns where housing for low-income persons should be constructed in Dallas, Texas — that is, whether the housing should be built in the inner city or in the suburbs. This dispute comes to the Court on a disparate-impact theory of liability. In contrast to a disparate-treatment case, where a "plaintiff must establish that the defendant had a discriminatory intent or motive," a plaintiff bringing a disparate-impact claim challenges practices that have a "disproportionately adverse effect on minorities" and are otherwise unjustified by a legitimate rationale. *Ricci v. DeStefano*, 557 U.S. 557, 577, 129 S.Ct. 2658, 174 L.Ed.2d 490 (2009). The question presented for the Court's determination is whether disparate-impact claims are cognizable under the Fair Housing Act (or FHA), 82 Stat. 81, as amended, 42 U.S.C. § 3601 *et seq.*

I

A

Before turning to the question presented, it is necessary to discuss a different federal statute that gives rise to this dispute. The Federal Government provides low-income

---

131. *Id.* at 2521.
132. *Id.* at 2521–22.
133. *Id.* at 2522.
134. *Id.*
135. *Id.* at 2522–23.
136. *Id.* at 2523.

housing tax credits that are distributed to developers through designated state agencies. 26 U.S.C. § 42. Congress has directed States to develop plans identifying selection criteria for distributing the credits. § 42(m)(1). Those plans must include certain criteria, such as public housing waiting lists, § 42(m)(1)(C), as well as certain preferences, including that low-income housing units "contribut[e] to a concerted community revitalization plan" and be built in census tracts populated predominantly by low-income residents. §§ 42(m)(1)(B)(ii)(III), 42(d)(5)(ii)(I). Federal law thus favors the distribution of these tax credits for the development of housing units in low-income areas.

In the State of Texas these federal credits are distributed by the Texas Department of Housing and Community Affairs (Department). Under Texas law, a developer's application for the tax credits is scored under a point system that gives priority to statutory criteria, such as the financial feasibility of the development project and the income level of tenants. Tex. Govt.Code Ann. §§ 2306.6710(a)–(b) (West 2008). The Texas Attorney General has interpreted state law to permit the consideration of additional criteria, such as whether the housing units will be built in a neighborhood with good schools. Those criteria cannot be awarded more points than statutorily mandated criteria.

The Inclusive Communities Project, Inc. (ICP), is a Texas-based nonprofit corporation that assists low-income families in obtaining affordable housing. In 2008, the ICP brought this suit against the Department and its officers in the United States District Court for the Northern District of Texas. As relevant here, it brought a disparate-impact claim under §§ 804(a) and 805(a) of the FHA. The ICP alleged the Department has caused continued segregated housing patterns by its disproportionate allocation of the tax credits, granting too many credits for housing in predominantly black inner-city areas and too few in predominantly white suburban neighborhoods. The ICP contended that the Department must modify its selection criteria in order to encourage the construction of low-income housing in suburban communities.

B

De jure residential segregation by race was declared unconstitutional almost a century ago, *Buchanan v. Warley,* 245 U.S. 60, 38 S.Ct. 16, 62 L.Ed. 149 (1917), but its vestiges remain today, intertwined with the country's economic and social life. Some segregated housing patterns can be traced to conditions that arose in the mid-20th century. Rapid urbanization, concomitant with the rise of suburban developments accessible by car, led many white families to leave the inner cities. This often left minority families concentrated in the center of the Nation's cities. During this time, various practices were followed, sometimes with governmental support, to encourage and maintain the separation of the races: Racially restrictive covenants prevented the conveyance of property to minorities, see *Shelley v. Kraemer,* 334 U.S. 1, 68 S.Ct. 836, 92 L.Ed. 1161 (1948); steering by real-estate agents led potential buyers to consider homes in racially homogenous areas; and discriminatory lending practices, often referred to as redlining, precluded minority families from purchasing homes in affluent areas. By the 1960's, these policies, practices, and prejudices had created many predominantly black inner cities surrounded by mostly white suburbs.

The mid-1960's was a period of considerable social unrest; and, in response, President Lyndon Johnson established the National Advisory Commission on Civil Disorders, commonly known as the Kerner Commission. After extensive fact finding the Commission identified residential segregation and unequal housing and economic conditions in the inner cities as significant, underlying causes of the social unrest. The Commission found that "[n]early two-thirds of all nonwhite families living in the central cities today live in neighborhoods marked by substandard housing and general urban blight." *Id.*, at 13. The Commission further found that both open and covert racial discrimination prevented black families from obtaining better housing and moving to integrated communities. *Ibid.* The Commission concluded that "[o]ur Nation is moving toward two societies, one black, one white—separate and unequal." *Id.*, at 1. To reverse "[t]his deepening racial division," *ibid.*, it recommended enactment of "a comprehensive and enforceable open-occupancy law making it an offense to discriminate in the sale or rental of any housing ... on the basis of race, creed, color, or national origin." *Id.*, at 263.

In April 1968, Dr. Martin Luther King, Jr., was assassinated in Memphis, Tennessee, and the Nation faced a new urgency to resolve the social unrest in the inner cities. Congress responded by adopting the Kerner Commission's recommendation and passing the Fair Housing Act. The statute addressed the denial of housing opportunities on the basis of "race, color, religion, or national origin." Civil Rights Act of 1968, § 804, 82 Stat. 83. Then, in 1988, Congress amended the FHA. Among other provisions, it created certain exemptions from liability and added "familial status" as a protected characteristic.

II

The issue here is whether, under a proper interpretation of the FHA, housing decisions with a disparate impact are prohibited. Before turning to the FHA, however, it is necessary to consider two other antidiscrimination statutes that preceded it.

The first relevant statute is § 703(a) of Title VII of the Civil Rights Act of 1964, 78 Stat. 255. The Court addressed the concept of disparate impact under this statute in *Griggs v. Duke Power Co.*, 401 U.S. 424, 91 S.Ct. 849, 28 L.Ed.2d 158 (1971). There, the employer had a policy requiring its manual laborers to possess a high school diploma and to obtain satisfactory scores on two intelligence tests. The Court of Appeals held the employer had not adopted these job requirements for a racially discriminatory purpose, and the plaintiffs did not challenge that holding in this Court. Instead, the plaintiffs argued § 703(a)(2) covers the discriminatory effect of a practice as well as the motivation behind the practice. Section 703(a), as amended, provides as follows:

"It shall be an unlawful employer practice for an employer—

"(1) to fail or refuse to hire or to discharge any individual, or otherwise to discriminate against any individual with respect to his compensation, terms, conditions, or privileges of employment, because of such individual's race, color, religion, sex, or national origin; or

"(2) to limit, segregate, or classify his employees or applicants for employment in any way which would deprive or tend to deprive any individual of employment opportunities or otherwise adversely affect his status as an employee, because of such individual's race, color, religion, sex, or national origin." 42 U.S.C. § 2000e-2(a).

The Court did not quote or cite the full statute, but rather relied solely on § 703(a)(2).

In interpreting § 703(a)(2), the Court reasoned that disparate-impact liability furthered the purpose and design of the statute. The Court explained that, in § 703(a)(2), Congress "proscribe[d] not only overt discrimination but also practices that are fair in form, but discriminatory in operation." *Id.,* at 431, 91 S.Ct. 849. For that reason, as the Court noted, "Congress directed the thrust of [§ 703(a)(2)] to the consequences of employment practices, not simply the motivation." *Id.,* at 432, 91 S.Ct. 849. In light of the statute's goal of achieving "equality of employment opportunities and remov[ing] barriers that have operated in the past" to favor some races over others, the Court held § 703(a)(2) of Title VII must be interpreted to allow disparate-impact claims. *Id.,* at 429–430, 91 S.Ct. 849.

The Court put important limits on its holding: namely, not all employment practices causing a disparate impact impose liability under § 703(a)(2). In this respect, the Court held that "business necessity" constitutes a defense to disparate-impact claims. *Id.,* at 431, 91 S.Ct. 849. This rule provides, for example, that in a disparate-impact case, § 703(a)(2) does not prohibit hiring criteria with a "manifest relationship" to job performance. *Id.,* at 432, 91 S.Ct. 849; see also *Ricci,* 557 U.S., at 587–589, 129 S.Ct. 2658 (emphasizing the importance of the business necessity defense to disparate-impact liability). On the facts before it, the Court in *Griggs* found a violation of Title VII because the employer could not establish that high school diplomas and general intelligence tests were related to the job performance of its manual laborers. See 401 U.S., at 431–432, 91 S.Ct. 849.

The second relevant statute that bears on the proper interpretation of the FHA is the Age Discrimination in Employment Act of 1967 (ADEA), 81 Stat. 602 *et seq.,* as amended. Section 4(a) of the ADEA provides:

"It shall be unlawful for an employer—

"(1) to fail or refuse to hire or to discharge any individual or otherwise discriminate against any individual with respect to his compensation, terms, conditions, or privileges of employment, because of such individual's age;

"(2) to limit, segregate, or classify his employees in any way which would deprive or tend to deprive any individual of employment opportunities or otherwise adversely affect his status as an employee, because of such individual's age; or

"(3) to reduce the wage rate of any employee in order to comply with this chapter." 29 U.S.C. § 623(a).

The Court first addressed whether this provision allows disparate-impact claims in *Smith v. City of Jackson,* 544 U.S. 228, 125 S.Ct. 1536, 161 L.Ed.2d 410 (2005). There, a group of older employees challenged their employer's decision to give proportionately greater raises to employees with less than five years of experience.

Explaining that *Griggs* "represented the better reading of [Title VII's] statutory text," 544 U.S., at 235, 125 S.Ct. 1536 a plurality of the Court concluded that the same reasoning pertained to § 4(a)(2) of the ADEA. The *Smith* plurality emphasized that both § 703(a)(2) of Title VII and § 4(a)(2) of the ADEA contain language "prohibit[ing] such actions that 'deprive any individual of employment opportunities or *otherwise adversely affect* his status as an employee, because of such individual's' race or age." 544 U.S., at 235, 125 S.Ct. 1536. As the plurality observed, the text of these provisions "focuses on the *effects* of the action on the employee rather than the motivation for the action of the employer" and therefore compels recognition of disparate-impact liability. *Id.*, at 236, 125 S.Ct. 1536. In a separate opinion, Justice SCALIA found the ADEA's text ambiguous and thus deferred under *Chevron, U.S.A. Inc. v. Natural Resources Defense Council, Inc.*, 467 U.S. 837, 104 S.Ct. 2778, 81 L.Ed.2d 694 (1984), to an Equal Employment Opportunity Commission regulation interpreting the ADEA to impose disparate-impact liability.

Together, *Griggs* holds and the plurality in *Smith* instructs that antidiscrimination laws must be construed to encompass disparate-impact claims when their text refers to the consequences of actions and not just to the mindset of actors, and where that interpretation is consistent with statutory purpose. These cases also teach that disparate-impact liability must be limited so employers and other regulated entities are able to make the practical business choices and profit-related decisions that sustain a vibrant and dynamic free-enterprise system. And before rejecting a business justification — or, in the case of a governmental entity, an analogous public interest — a court must determine that a plaintiff has shown that there is "an available alternative ... practice that has less disparate impact and serves the [entity's] legitimate needs." *Ricci, supra*, at 578, 129 S.Ct. 2658. The cases interpreting Title VII and the ADEA provide essential background and instruction in the case now before the Court.

Turning to the FHA, the ICP relies on two provisions. Section 804(a) provides that it shall be unlawful:

> "To refuse to sell or rent after the making of a bona fide offer, or to refuse to negotiate for the sale or rental of, or otherwise make unavailable or deny, a dwelling to any person because of race, color, religion, sex, familial status, or national origin." 42 U.S.C. § 3604(a).

Here, the phrase "otherwise make unavailable" is of central importance to the analysis that follows.

Section 805(a), in turn, provides:

> "It shall be unlawful for any person or other entity whose business includes engaging in real estate-related transactions to discriminate against any person in making available such a transaction, or in the terms or conditions of such a transaction, because of race, color, religion, sex, handicap, familial status, or national origin." § 3605(a).

Applied here, the logic of *Griggs* and *Smith* provides strong support for the conclusion that the FHA encompasses disparate-impact claims. Congress' use of the phrase "otherwise make unavailable" refers to the consequences of an action rather than the actor's intent. See *United States v. Giles,* 300 U.S. 41, 48, 57 S.Ct. 340, 81 L.Ed. 493 (1937). This results-oriented language counsels in favor of recognizing disparate-impact liability. The Court has construed statutory language similar to §805(a) to include disparate-impact liability.

A comparison to the antidiscrimination statutes examined in *Griggs* and *Smith* is useful. Title VII's and the ADEA's "otherwise adversely affect" language is equivalent in function and purpose to the FHA's "otherwise make unavailable" language. In these three statutes the operative text looks to results. The relevant statutory phrases, moreover, play an identical role in the structure common to all three statutes: Located at the end of lengthy sentences that begin with prohibitions on disparate treatment, they serve as catchall phrases looking to consequences, not intent. And all three statutes use the word "otherwise" to introduce the results-oriented phrase. "Otherwise" means "in a different way or manner," thus signaling a shift in emphasis from an actor's intent to the consequences of his actions. Webster's Third New International Dictionary 1598 (1971). This similarity in text and structure is all the more compelling given that Congress passed the FHA in 1968—only four years after passing Title VII and only four months after enacting the ADEA.

It is true that Congress did not reiterate Title VII's exact language in the FHA, but that is because to do so would have made the relevant sentence awkward and unclear. A provision making it unlawful to "refuse to sell [,] ... or otherwise [adversely affect], a dwelling to any person" because of a protected trait would be grammatically obtuse, difficult to interpret, and far more expansive in scope than Congress likely intended. Congress thus chose words that serve the same purpose and bear the same basic meaning but are consistent with the structure and objectives of the FHA.

Emphasizing that the FHA uses the phrase "because of race," the Department argues this language forecloses disparate-impact liability since "[a]n action is not taken 'because of race' unless race is a *reason* for the action." Brief for Petitioners 26. *Griggs* and *Smith,* however, dispose of this argument. Both Title VII and the ADEA contain identical "because of" language, see 42 U.S.C. §2000e-2(a)(2); 29 U.S.C. §623(a)(2), and the Court nonetheless held those statutes impose disparate-impact liability.

In addition, it is of crucial importance that the existence of disparate-impact liability is supported by amendments to the FHA that Congress enacted in 1988. By that time, all nine Courts of Appeals to have addressed the question had concluded the Fair Housing Act encompassed disparate-impact claims.

When it amended the FHA, Congress was aware of this unanimous precedent. And with that understanding, it made a considered judgment to retain the relevant statutory text. Indeed, Congress rejected a proposed amendment that would have eliminated disparate-impact liability for certain zoning decisions.

Against this background understanding in the legal and regulatory system, Congress' decision in 1988 to amend the FHA while still adhering to the operative language in §§ 804(a) and 805(a) is convincing support for the conclusion that Congress accepted and ratified the unanimous holdings of the Courts of Appeals finding disparate-impact liability. "If a word or phrase has been ... given a uniform interpretation by inferior courts..., a later version of that act perpetuating the wording is presumed to carry forward that interpretation."

Further and convincing confirmation of Congress' understanding that disparate-impact liability exists under the FHA is revealed by the substance of the 1988 amendments. The amendments included three exemptions from liability that assume the existence of disparate-impact claims. The most logical conclusion is that the three amendments were deemed necessary because Congress presupposed disparate impact under the FHA as it had been enacted in 1968.

The relevant 1988 amendments were as follows. First, Congress added a clarifying provision: "Nothing in [the FHA] prohibits a person engaged in the business of furnishing appraisals of real property to take into consideration factors other than race, color, religion, national origin, sex, handicap, or familial status." 42 U.S.C. § 3605(c). Second, Congress provided: "Nothing in [the FHA] prohibits conduct against a person because such person has been convicted by any court of competent jurisdiction of the illegal manufacture or distribution of a controlled substance." § 3607(b)(4). And finally, Congress specified: "Nothing in [the FHA] limits the applicability of any reasonable ... restrictions regarding the maximum number of occupants permitted to occupy a dwelling." § 3607(b)(1).

The exemptions embodied in these amendments would be superfluous if Congress had assumed that disparate-impact liability did not exist under the FHA. Indeed, none of these amendments would make sense if the FHA encompassed only disparate-treatment claims. If that were the sole ground for liability, the amendments merely restate black-letter law. If an actor makes a decision based on reasons other than a protected category, there is no disparate-treatment liability. But the amendments do constrain disparate-impact liability. For instance, certain criminal convictions are correlated with sex and race. By adding an exemption from liability for exclusionary practices aimed at individuals with drug convictions, Congress ensured disparate-impact liability would not lie if a landlord excluded tenants with such convictions. The same is true of the provision allowing for reasonable restrictions on occupancy. And the exemption from liability for real-estate appraisers is in the same section as § 805(a)'s prohibition of discriminatory practices in real-estate transactions, thus indicating Congress' recognition that disparate-impact liability arose under § 805(a). In short, the 1988 amendments signal that Congress ratified disparate-impact liability.

A comparison to *Smith*'s discussion of the ADEA further demonstrates why the Department's interpretation would render the 1988 amendments superfluous. Under the ADEA's reasonable-factor-other-than-age (RFOA) provision, an employer is permitted to take an otherwise prohibited action where "the differentiation is based on reasonable factors other than age." 29 U.S.C. §623(f)(1). In other words, if an employer makes a decision based on a reasonable factor other than age, it cannot be said to have made a decision on the basis of an employee's age. According to the *Smith* plurality, the RFOA provision "plays its principal role" "in cases involving disparate-impact claims" "by precluding liability if the adverse impact was attributable to a nonage factor that was 'reasonable.'" 544 U.S., at 239, 125 S.Ct. 1536. The plurality thus reasoned that the RFOA provision would be "simply unnecessary to avoid liability under the ADEA" if liability were limited to disparate-treatment claims. *Id.*, at 238, 125 S.Ct. 1536.

A similar logic applies here. If a real-estate appraiser took into account a neighborhood's schools, one could not say the appraiser acted because of race. And by embedding 42 U.S.C. §3605(c)'s exemption in the statutory text, Congress ensured that disparate-impact liability would not be allowed either. Indeed, the inference of disparate-impact liability is even stronger here than it was in *Smith*. As originally enacted, the ADEA included the RFOA provision, see §4(f)(1), 81 Stat. 603, whereas here Congress added the relevant exemptions in the 1988 amendments against the backdrop of the uniform view of the Courts of Appeals that the FHA imposed disparate-impact liability.

Recognition of disparate-impact claims is consistent with the FHA's central purpose. The FHA, like Title VII and the ADEA, was enacted to eradicate discriminatory practices within a sector of our Nation's economy. See 42 U.S.C. §3601 ("It is the policy of the United States to provide, within constitutional limitations, for fair housing throughout the United States"); H.R. Rep., at 15 (explaining the FHA "provides a clear national policy against discrimination in housing").

These unlawful practices include zoning laws and other housing restrictions that function unfairly to exclude minorities from certain neighborhoods without any sufficient justification. Suits targeting such practices reside at the heartland of disparate-impact liability. The availability of disparate-impact liability, furthermore, has allowed private developers to vindicate the FHA's objectives and to protect their property rights by stopping municipalities from enforcing arbitrary and, in practice, discriminatory ordinances barring the construction of certain types of housing units. See, *e.g.*, *Huntington, supra*, at 18, 109 S.Ct. 276. Recognition of disparate-impact liability under the FHA also plays a role in uncovering discriminatory intent: It permits plaintiffs to counteract unconscious prejudices and disguised animus that escape easy classification as disparate treatment. In this way disparate-impact liability may prevent segregated housing patterns that might otherwise result from covert and illicit stereotyping.

But disparate-impact liability has always been properly limited in key respects that avoid the serious constitutional questions that might arise under the FHA, for instance, if such liability were imposed based solely on a showing of a statistical disparity. Disparate-impact liability mandates the "removal of artificial, arbitrary, and unnecessary barriers," not the displacement of valid governmental policies. *Griggs, supra*, at 431, 91 S.Ct. 849. The FHA is not an instrument to force housing authorities to reorder their priorities. Rather, the FHA aims to ensure that those priorities can be achieved without arbitrarily creating discriminatory effects or perpetuating segregation.

Unlike the heartland of disparate-impact suits targeting artificial barriers to housing, the underlying dispute in this case involves a novel theory of liability. This case, on remand, may be seen simply as an attempt to second-guess which of two reasonable approaches a housing authority should follow in the sound exercise of its discretion in allocating tax credits for low-income housing.

An important and appropriate means of ensuring that disparate-impact liability is properly limited is to give housing authorities and private developers leeway to state and explain the valid interest served by their policies. This step of the analysis is analogous to the business necessity standard under Title VII and provides a defense against disparate-impact liability. See 78 Fed.Reg. 11470 (explaining that HUD did not use the phrase "business necessity" because that "phrase may not be easily understood to cover the full scope of practices covered by the Fair Housing Act, which applies to individuals, businesses, nonprofit organizations, and public entities"). As the Court explained in *Ricci*, an entity "could be liable for disparate-impact discrimination only if the [challenged practices] were not job related and consistent with business necessity." 557 U.S., at 587, 129 S.Ct. 2658. Just as an employer may maintain a workplace requirement that causes a disparate impact if that requirement is a "reasonable measure[ment] of job performance," *Griggs, supra*, at 436, 91 S.Ct. 849 so too must housing authorities and private developers be allowed to maintain a policy if they can prove it is necessary to achieve a valid interest. To be sure, the Title VII framework may not transfer exactly to the fair-housing context, but the comparison suffices for present purposes.

It would be paradoxical to construe the FHA to impose onerous costs on actors who encourage revitalizing dilapidated housing in our Nation's cities merely because some other priority might seem preferable. Entrepreneurs must be given latitude to consider market factors. Zoning officials, moreover, must often make decisions based on a mix of factors, both objective (such as cost and traffic patterns) and, at least to some extent, subjective (such as preserving historic architecture). These factors contribute to a community's quality of life and are legitimate concerns for housing authorities. The FHA does not decree a particular vision of urban development; and it does not put housing authorities and private developers in a double bind of liability, subject to suit whether they choose to rejuvenate a city core or to promote new low-income housing in suburban communities. As HUD itself recognized in its recent rulemaking, disparate-impact liability "does not mandate that affordable housing be located in neighborhoods with any particular characteristic." 78 Fed.Reg. 11476.

In a similar vein, a disparate-impact claim that relies on a statistical disparity must fail if the plaintiff cannot point to a defendant's policy or policies causing that disparity. A robust causality requirement ensures that "[r]acial imbalance ... does not, without more, establish a prima facie case of disparate impact" and thus protects defendants from being held liable for racial disparities they did not create. *Wards Cove Packing Co. v. Atonio*, 490 U.S. 642, 653, 109 S.Ct. 2115, 104 L.Ed.2d 733 (1989), superseded by statute on other grounds, 42 U.S.C. § 2000e-2(k). Without adequate safeguards at the prima facie stage, disparate-impact liability might cause race to be used and considered in a pervasive way and "would almost inexorably lead" governmental or private entities to use "numerical quotas," and serious constitutional questions then could arise. 490 U.S., at 653, 109 S.Ct. 2115.

The litigation at issue here provides an example. From the standpoint of determining advantage or disadvantage to racial minorities, it seems difficult to say as a general matter that a decision to build low-income housing in a blighted inner-city neighborhood instead of a suburb is discriminatory, or vice versa. If those sorts of judgments are subject to challenge without adequate safeguards, then there is a danger that potential defendants may adopt racial quotas—a circumstance that itself raises serious constitutional concerns.

Courts must therefore examine with care whether a plaintiff has made out a prima facie case of disparate impact and prompt resolution of these cases is important. A plaintiff who fails to allege facts at the pleading stage or produce statistical evidence demonstrating a causal connection cannot make out a prima facie case of disparate impact. For instance, a plaintiff challenging the decision of a private developer to construct a new building in one location rather than another will not easily be able to show this is a policy causing a disparate impact because such a one-time decision may not be a policy at all. It may also be difficult to establish causation because of the multiple factors that go into investment decisions about where to construct or renovate housing units. And as Judge Jones observed below, if the ICP cannot show a causal connection between the Department's policy and a disparate impact—for instance, because federal law substantially limits the Department's discretion—that should result in dismissal of this case.

The FHA imposes a command with respect to disparate-impact liability. Here, that command goes to a state entity. In other cases, the command will go to a private person or entity. Governmental or private policies are not contrary to the disparate-impact requirement unless they are "artificial, arbitrary, and unnecessary barriers." *Griggs*, 401 U.S., at 431, 91 S.Ct. 849. Difficult questions might arise if disparate-impact liability under the FHA caused race to be used and considered in a pervasive and explicit manner to justify governmental or private actions that, in fact, tend to perpetuate race-based considerations rather than move beyond them. Courts should avoid interpreting disparate-impact liability to be so expansive as to inject racial considerations into every housing decision.

The limitations on disparate-impact liability discussed here are also necessary to protect potential defendants against abusive disparate-impact claims. If the specter of disparate-impact litigation causes private developers to no longer construct or renovate housing units for low-income individuals, then the FHA would have undermined its own purpose as well as the free-market system. And as to governmental entities, they must not be prevented from achieving legitimate objectives, such as ensuring compliance with health and safety codes. The Department's *amici,* in addition to the well-stated principal dissenting opinion in this case, see *post,* at 2532–2533, 2548–2549 (opinion of ALITO, J.), call attention to the decision by the Court of Appeals for the Eighth Circuit in *Gallagher v. Magner,* 619 F.3d 823 (2010). Although the

Court is reluctant to approve or disapprove a case that is not pending, it should be noted that *Magner* was decided without the cautionary standards announced in this opinion and, in all events, the case was settled by the parties before an ultimate determination of disparate-impact liability.

Were standards for proceeding with disparate-impact suits not to incorporate at least the safeguards discussed here, then disparate-impact liability might displace valid governmental and private priorities, rather than solely "remov[ing] ... artificial, arbitrary, and unnecessary barriers." *Griggs*, 401 U.S., at 431, 91 S.Ct. 849. And that, in turn, would set our Nation back in its quest to reduce the salience of race in our social and economic system.

It must be noted further that, even when courts do find liability under a disparate-impact theory, their remedial orders must be consistent with the Constitution. Remedial orders in disparate-impact cases should concentrate on the elimination of the offending practice that "arbitrar [ily] ... operate[s] invidiously to discriminate on the basis of rac[e]." *Ibid.* If additional measures are adopted, courts should strive to design them to eliminate racial disparities through race-neutral means. See *Richmond v. J.A. Croson Co.*, 488 U.S. 469, 510, 109 S.Ct. 706, 102 L.Ed.2d 854 (1989) (plurality opinion) ("[T]he city has at its disposal a whole array of race-neutral devices to increase the accessibility of city contracting opportunities to small entrepreneurs of all races"). Remedial orders that impose racial targets or quotas might raise more difficult constitutional questions.

While the automatic or pervasive injection of race into public and private transactions covered by the FHA has special dangers, it is also true that race may be considered in certain circumstances and in a proper fashion. Just as this Court has not "question[ed] an employer's affirmative efforts to ensure that all groups have a fair opportunity to apply for promotions and to participate in the [promotion] process," *Ricci*, 557 U.S., at 585, 129 S.Ct. 2658 it likewise does not impugn housing authorities' race-neutral efforts to encourage revitalization of communities that have long suffered the harsh consequences of segregated housing patterns. When setting their larger goals, local housing authorities may choose to foster diversity and combat racial isolation with race-neutral tools, and mere awareness of race in attempting to solve the problems facing inner cities does not doom that endeavor at the outset.

The Court holds that disparate-impact claims are cognizable under the Fair Housing Act upon considering its results-oriented language, the Court's interpretation of similar language in Title VII and the ADEA, Congress' ratification of disparate-impact claims in 1988 against the backdrop of the unanimous view of nine Courts of Appeals, and the statutory purpose.

III

In light of the longstanding judicial interpretation of the FHA to encompass disparate-impact claims and congressional reaffirmation of that result, residents and policymakers have come to rely on the availability of disparate-impact claims. See Brief for Massachusetts et al. as *Amici Curiae* 2 ("Without disparate impact claims,

States and others will be left with fewer crucial tools to combat the kinds of systemic discrimination that the FHA was intended to address"). Indeed, many of our Nation's largest cities—entities that are potential defendants in disparate-impact suits—have submitted an *amicus* brief in this case supporting disparate-impact liability under the FHA. See Brief for City of San Francisco et al. as *Amici Curiae* 3–6. The existence of disparate-impact liability in the substantial majority of the Courts of Appeals for the last several decades "has not given rise to ... dire consequences." *Hosanna-Tabor Evangelical Lutheran Church and School v. EEOC*, 565 U.S. ___, ___, 132 S.Ct. 694, 710, 181 L.Ed.2d 650 (2012).

Much progress remains to be made in our Nation's continuing struggle against racial isolation. In striving to achieve our "historic commitment to creating an integrated society," *Parents Involved, supra,* at 797, 127 S.Ct. 2738 (KENNEDY, J., concurring in part and concurring in judgment), we must remain wary of policies that reduce homeowners to nothing more than their race. But since the passage of the Fair Housing Act in 1968 and against the backdrop of disparate-impact liability in nearly every jurisdiction, many cities have become more diverse. The FHA must play an important part in avoiding the Kerner Commission's grim prophecy that "[o]ur Nation is moving toward two societies, one black, one white—separate and unequal." Kerner Commission Report 1. The Court acknowledges the Fair Housing Act's continuing role in moving the Nation toward a more integrated society.

The judgment of the Court of Appeals for the Fifth Circuit is affirmed, and the case is remanded for further proceedings consistent with this opinion.

It is so ordered.

G. Housing as a Fundamental Right

Despite the relationship between access to adequate housing and a wide range of civil liberties, U.S. courts have failed to recognize housing as a "right." Instead, access to housing is seen as an economic question, albeit one that often involves many of our civil rights laws, including the Civil Rights Act of 1964 and the Fair Housing Act Amendments of 1991. The U.S. Supreme Court has consistently refused to classify housing as a fundamental right entitled to higher levels of judicial scrutiny. In the cases that follow, the Court draws a clear line that classifies access to adequate housing as a matter of social and economic policy that is left to the legislative arena, while not implicating a fundamental right.

In *Village of Belle Terre v. Boraas*,[137] for example, the Supreme Court was asked to consider a zoning ordinance that limited the occupancy of single-family homes to traditional families or a group of unrelated adults of no more than two. Co-housing among low-income families provides obvious economic benefits to the poor, particularly in communities with high real estate costs. In *Village of Belle Terre*, the

---

137. 416 U.S. 1 (1974).

Court pointed out that limiting occupancy under a zoning ordinance involved no fundamental right guaranteed by the Constitution. The Court went on to say: "We deal with economic and social legislation where legislatures have historically drawn lines which we respect against the charge of violation of the Equal Protection Clause if the law be 'reasonable, not arbitrary' and bears 'a rational relationship to a [permissible] state objective.'"[138] The Court ruled that the protection of surrounding properties from depreciation and the preservation of the zoning ordinance were permissible objectives.

In *Lindsey v. Normet*,[139] the Court recognized the importance of decent, safe, and sanitary housing, but went on to point out that there was no constitutional guarantee of access to dwellings of a particular quality or any recognition of the right of a tenant to occupy any particular dwellings. The Court concluded that, absent constitutional mandate, the assurance of adequate housing is a legislative—not a judicial—function.

Again, in *James v. Valtierra*,[140] the Court held that a legal requirement in the housing context may have a greater impact upon the poor or other minority, but that in itself does not render the requirement invalid under the Fourteenth Amendment. And in *San Antonio Independent School District v. Rodriguez*,[141] the Supreme Court specifically held, citing *Lindsey*, that there was no fundamental right to housing guaranteed by the Constitution. "As in the case of housing, the central importance of welfare benefits to the poor was not an adequate foundation for requiring the State to justify its law by showing some compelling state interest. *See also, Jefferson v. Hackney*, 406 U.S. 535 (1972); *Richardsen v. Belcher*, 404 U.S. 78 (1971)."[142] Under the current state of the Supreme Court's consideration of the question, the right to housing, even though socially of great significance, does not implicant a fundamental constitutional right or involve a civil or human right in the broadest sense. The Supreme Court's reticence to define a right to housing may be explained by the Court's unwillingness to attempt to define the parameters of such a right that would by necessity involve considerations of individual actions and property rights more than limits on governmental power.[143]

H. Fair Housing and Group Homes

Group homes offer many benefits to the poor. Obvious benefits include reduced housing costs, but in some circumstances group homes are necessary to achieve other goals. This occurs when groups decide to live together for therapeutic reasons. People

---

138. *Id.* at 8.

139. 405 U.S. 56 (1972).

140. 402 U.S. 137 (1971).

141. 411 U.S. 1 (1973).

142. *Id.* at 33.

143. Shelby D. Green, *Imagining a Right to Housing, Lying in the Interstices*, 19 GEO. J. ON POVERTY L. & POL'Y 393 (2012)

living with disabilities or those recovering from addiction all may benefit from living in a group community. The issue then becomes determining the point at which the community interest in limiting occupancy must yield to the needs of those who benefit from living in a group home environment.

City of Edmonds v. Oxford House, Inc.
514 U.S. 725 (1995)

The Fair Housing Act (FHA or Act) prohibits discrimination in housing against, *inter alios*, persons with handicaps. Section 807(b)(1) of the Act entirely exempts from the FHA's compass "any reasonable local, State, or Federal restrictions regarding the maximum number of occupants permitted to occupy a dwelling." 42 U.S.C. § 3607(b)(1). This case presents the question whether a provision in petitioner City of Edmonds' zoning code qualifies for § 3607(b)(1)'s complete exemption from FHA scrutiny. The provision, governing areas zoned for single-family dwelling units, defines "family" as "persons [without regard to number] related by genetics, adoption, or marriage, or a group of five or fewer [unrelated] persons." Edmonds Community Development Code (ECDC) § 21.30.010 (1991).

The defining provision at issue describes who may compose a family unit; it does not prescribe "*the* maximum number of occupants" a dwelling unit may house. We hold that § 3607(b)(1) does not exempt prescriptions of the family-defining kind, *i.e.*, provisions designed to foster the family character of a neighborhood. Instead, § 3607(b)(1)'s absolute exemption removes from the FHA's scope only total occupancy limits, *i.e.*, numerical ceilings that serve to prevent overcrowding in living quarters.

I

In the summer of 1990, respondent Oxford House opened a group home in the City of Edmonds, Washington (City), for 10 to 12 adults recovering from alcoholism and drug addiction. The group home, called Oxford House-Edmonds, is located in a neighborhood zoned for single-family residences. Upon learning that Oxford House had leased and was operating a home in Edmonds, the City issued criminal citations to the owner and a resident of the house. The citations charged violation of the zoning code rule that defines who may live in single-family dwelling units. The occupants of such units must compose a "family," and family, under the City's defining rule, "means an individual or two or more persons related by genetics, adoption, or marriage, or a group of five or fewer persons who are not related by genetics, adoption, or marriage." ECDC § 21.30.010. Oxford House-Edmonds houses more than five unrelated persons, and therefore does not conform to the code.

Oxford House asserted reliance on the Fair Housing Act, 102 Stat. 1619, 42 U.S.C. § 3601 *et seq.*, which declares it unlawful "[t]o discriminate in the sale or rental, or to otherwise make unavailable or deny, a dwelling to any buyer or renter because of a handicap of … that buyer or renter." § 3604(f)(1)(A). The parties have stipulated, for purposes of this litigation, that the residents of Oxford House-Edmonds "are recovering alcoholics and drug addicts and are handicapped persons within the meaning" of the Act. App. 106.

Discrimination covered by the FHA includes "a refusal to make reasonable accommodations in rules, policies, practices, or services, when such accommodations may be necessary to afford [handicapped] person[s] equal opportunity to use and enjoy a dwelling." § 3604(f)(3)(B). Oxford House asked Edmonds to make a "reasonable accommodation" by allowing it to remain in the single-family dwelling it had leased. Group homes for recovering substance abusers, Oxford urged, need 8 to 12 residents to be financially and therapeutically viable. Edmonds declined to permit Oxford House to stay in a single-family residential zone, but passed an ordinance listing group homes as permitted uses in multifamily and general commercial zones.

Edmonds sued Oxford House in the United States District Court for the Western District of Washington, seeking a declaration that the FHA does not constrain the City's zoning code family definition rule. Oxford House counterclaimed under the FHA, charging the City with failure to make a "reasonable accommodation" permitting maintenance of the group home in a single-family zone. The United States filed a separate action on the same FHA "reasonable accommodation" ground, and the two cases were consolidated. Edmonds suspended its criminal enforcement actions pending resolution of the federal litigation.

On cross-motions for summary judgment, the District Court held that ECDC § 21.30.010, defining "family," is exempt from the FHA under § 3607(b)(1) as a "reasonable ... restrictio[n] regarding the maximum number of occupants permitted to occupy a dwelling." App. to Pet. for Cert. B-7. The United States Court of Appeals for the Ninth Circuit reversed; holding § 3607(b)(1)'s absolute exemption inapplicable, the Court of Appeals remanded the cases for further consideration of the claims asserted by Oxford House and the United States. *Edmonds v. Washington State Building Code Council,* 18 F.3d 802 (1994).

The Ninth Circuit's decision conflicts with an Eleventh Circuit decision declaring exempt under § 3607(b)(1) a family definition provision similar to the Edmonds prescription. See *Elliott v. Athens,* 960 F.2d 975 (1992).2 We granted certiorari to resolve the conflict, 513 U.S. 959, 115 S.Ct. 417, 130 L.Ed.2d 332 (1994), and we now affirm the Ninth Circuit's judgment.3

II

The sole question before the Court is whether Edmonds' family composition rule qualifies as a "restrictio[n] regarding the maximum number of occupants permitted to occupy a dwelling" within the meaning of the FHA's absolute exemption. 42 U.S.C. § 3607(b)(1).4 In answering this question, we are mindful of the Act's stated policy "to provide, within constitutional limitations, for fair housing throughout the United States." § 3601. We also note precedent recognizing the FHA's "broad and inclusive" compass, and therefore according a "generous construction" to the Act's complaint-filing provision. *Trafficante v. Metropolitan Life Ins. Co.,* 409 U.S. 205, 209, 212, 93

S.Ct. 364, 366–367, 368, 34 L.Ed.2d 415 (1972). Accordingly, we regard this case as an instance in which an exception to "a general statement of policy" is sensibly read "narrowly in order to preserve the primary operation of the [policy]." *Commissioner v. Clark*, 489 U.S. 726, 739, 109 S.Ct. 1455, 1463, 103 L.Ed.2d 753 (1989).

A

Congress enacted § 3607(b)(1) against the backdrop of an evident distinction between municipal land-use restrictions and maximum occupancy restrictions.

Land-use restrictions designate "districts in which only compatible uses are allowed and incompatible uses are excluded." These restrictions typically categorize uses as single-family residential, multiple-family residential, commercial, or industrial.

Land use restrictions aim to prevent problems caused by the "pig in the parlor instead of the barnyard." *Village of Euclid v. Ambler Realty Co.*, 272 U.S. 365, 388, 47 S.Ct. 114, 118, 71 L.Ed. 303 (1926). In particular, reserving land for single-family residences preserves the character of neighborhoods, securing "zones where family values, youth values, and the blessings of quiet seclusion and clean air make the area a sanctuary for people." *Village of Belle Terre v. Boraas*, 416 U.S. 1, 9, 94 S.Ct. 1536, 1541, 39 L.Ed.2d 797 (1974)To limit land use to single-family residences, a municipality must define the term "family"; thus family composition rules are an essential component of single-family residential use restrictions.

Maximum occupancy restrictions, in contradistinction, cap the number of occupants per dwelling, typically in relation to available floor space or the number and type of rooms. See, *e.g.*, International Conference of Building Officials, Uniform Housing Code § 503(b) (1988); Building Officials and Code Administrators International, Inc., BOCA National Property Maintenance Code §§ PM-405.3, PM-405.5 (1993) (hereinafter BOCA Code); Southern Building Code Congress, International, Inc., Standard Housing Code §§ 306.1, 306.2 (1991); E. Mood, APHA-CDC Recommended Minimum Housing Standards § 9.02, p. 37 (1986) (hereinafter APHA-CDC Standards).6 These restrictions ordinarily apply uniformly to *all* residents of *all* dwelling units. Their purpose is to protect health and safety by preventing dwelling overcrowding. See, *e.g.*, BOCA Code §§ PM-101.3, PM-405.3, PM-405.5 and commentary; Abbott, Housing Policy, Housing Codes and Tenant Remedies, 56 B.U.L.Rev. 1, 41–45 (1976).

We recognized this distinction between maximum occupancy restrictions and land-use restrictions in *Moore v. East Cleveland*, 431 U.S. 494, 97 S.Ct. 1932, 52 L.Ed.2d 531 (1977). In *Moore*, the Court held unconstitutional the constricted definition of "family" contained in East Cleveland's housing ordinance. East Cleveland's ordinance "select[ed] certain categories of relatives who may live together and declare[d] that others may not"; in particular, East Cleveland's definition of "family" made "a crime of a grandmother's choice to live with her grandson." *Id.*, at 498–499, 97 S.Ct., at 1935 (plurality opinion). In response to East Cleveland's argument that its aim was to prevent overcrowded dwellings, streets, and schools, we observed that the municipality's restrictive definition of family served the asserted, and undeniably legitimate, goals "marginally, at best." *Id.*, at 500, 97 S.Ct., at 1936 (footnote omitted). Another East Cleveland ordinance, we noted, "specifically addressed ... the problem of overcrowding"; that ordinance tied "the maximum permissible occupancy of a dwelling to the habitable floor area." *Id.*, at 500, n. 7, 97 S.Ct., at 1936, n. 7; accord, *id.*, at 520, n. 16, 97 S.Ct., at 1939, n. 16 (STEVENS, J., concurring in judgment). Justice Stewart, in dissent, also distinguished restrictions designed to "preserv[e] the character of a residential area," from prescription of "a minimum habitable floor area per person," *id.*, at 539, n. 9, 97 S.Ct., at 1937, n. 9, in the interest of community health and safety.7

Section 3607(b)(1)'s language — "restrictions regarding the maximum number of occupants permitted to occupy a dwelling" — surely encompasses maximum occupancy restrictions. But the formulation does not fit family composition rules typically tied to land-use restrictions. In sum, rules that cap the total number of occupants in order to prevent overcrowding of a dwelling "plainly and unmistakably," fall within § 3607(b)(1)'s absolute exemption from the FHA's governance; rules designed to preserve the family character of a neighborhood, fastening on the composition of households rather than on the total number of occupants living quarters can contain, do not.9

B

Turning specifically to the City's Community Development Code, we note that the provisions Edmonds invoked against Oxford House, ECDC §§ 16.20.010 and 21.30.010, are classic examples of a use restriction and complementing family composition rule. These provisions do not cap the number of people who may live in a dwelling. In plain terms, they direct that dwellings be used only to house families. Captioned "USES," ECDC § 16.20.010 provides that the sole "Permitted Primary Us[e]" in a single-family residential zone is "[s]ingle-family dwelling units." Edmonds itself recognizes that this provision simply "defines those uses permitted in a single family residential zone." Pet. for Cert. 3.

A separate provision caps the number of occupants a dwelling may house, based on floor area:

> "Floor Area. Every dwelling unit shall have at least one room which shall have not less than 120 square feet of floor area. Other habitable rooms, except kitchens, shall have an area of not less than 70 square feet. Where more than two persons occupy a room used for sleeping purposes, the required floor area shall be increased at the rate of 50 square feet for each occupant in excess of two." ECDC § 19.10.000 (adopting Uniform Housing Code § 503(b) (1988)).10

This space and occupancy standard is a prototypical maximum occupancy restriction.

Edmonds nevertheless argues that its family composition rule, ECDC § 21.30.010, falls within § 3607(b)(1), the FHA exemption for maximum occupancy restrictions, because the rule caps at five the number of unrelated persons allowed to occupy a single-family dwelling. But Edmonds' family composition rule surely does not answer the question: "What is the maximum number of occupants permitted to occupy a house?" So long as they are related "by genetics, adoption, or marriage," any number of people can live in a house. Ten siblings, their parents and grandparents, for example, could dwell in a house in Edmonds' single-family residential zone without offending Edmonds' family composition rule.

Family living, not living space per occupant, is what ECDC § 21.30.010 describes. Defining family primarily by biological and legal relationships, the provision also accommodates another group association: Five or fewer unrelated people are allowed to live together as though they were family. This accommodation is the peg on which Edmonds rests its plea for § 3607(b)(1) exemption. Had the City defined a family solely by biological and legal links, § 3607(b)(1) would not have been the ground on which Edmonds staked its case. See Tr. of Oral Arg. 11–12, 16. It is curious reasoning indeed that converts a family values preserver into a maximum occupancy restriction once a town adds to a related persons prescription "and also two unrelated persons."11

Edmonds additionally contends that subjecting single-family zoning to FHA scrutiny will "overturn Euclidian zoning" and "destroy the effectiveness and purpose of single-family zoning." Brief for Petitioner 11, 25. This contention both ignores the limited scope of the issue before us and exaggerates the force of the FHA's antidiscrimination provisions. We address only whether Edmonds' family composition rule qualifies for § 3607(b)(1) exemption. Moreover, the FHA antidiscrimination provisions, when applicable, require only "reasonable" accommodations to afford persons with handicaps "equal opportunity to use and enjoy" housing. §§ 3604(f)(1)(A) and (f)(3)(B).

The parties have presented, and we have decided, only a threshold question: Edmonds' zoning code provision describing who may compose a "family" is not a maximum occupancy restriction exempt from the FHA under § 3607(b)(1). It remains for the lower courts to decide whether Edmonds' actions against Oxford House violate the FHA's prohibitions against discrimination set out in §§ 3604(f)(1)(A) and (f)(3)(B). For the reasons stated, the judgment of the United States Court of Appeals for the Ninth Circuit is AFFIRMED.

Chapter Eight

Health

Healthcare is largely a private enterprise in the United States. Slightly more than half (56%) of all Americans receive health insurance coverage from their employers or purchase their own coverage.[1] About one-third (36%) receive health insurance coverage through one of several public insurance programs, including Medicaid and Medicare, leaving roughly nine percent (approximately 41 million people) of Americans uninsured.[2] Per capita spending on healthcare in the United States equaled $10,739 in 2017 and totaled more than $3.5 trillion, more than 17% of GDP.[3] This level of spending far exceeds spending on healthcare in any other nation. Access to healthcare has a significant impact on quality of life and longevity. What level of healthcare should the poor expect to receive and at what cost to the individual and the broader public?

A. The Health of the Poor

Poverty is closely correlated with a variety of negative health outcomes, mortality, and behavioral risks.[4] Much of the difference in health outcomes can be explained by the stark difference in health outcomes of minority groups, who experience much higher poverty rates than the general population.

Poverty heavily impacts a person's social and physical environment, with attendant disparities in morbidity and mortality between the poor and nonpoor. The differences are quite stark. There is a six-year gap between the state with the highest life expectancy (Hawai'i) and that with the lowest (Mississippi). Disparities at the local level are even more pronounced, including a 20-year life expectancy difference between two neighborhoods in Baltimore that are less than five miles apart. Where one lives is a significant indicator of health outcomes and life expectancy, and people who live in

1. Kaiser Fam. Found., Health Insurance Coverage of the Total Population, http://kff.org/other/state-indicator/total-population/ (last visited Oct. 31, 2019).

2. *Id.*

3. Ctrs. for Disease Control, Nat'l Ctr. For Health Statistics, Health Expenditures, http://www.cdc.gov/nchs/fastats/health-expenditures.htm (last visited Oct. 31, 2019).

4. George A. Kaplan et al., *Inequality in Income and Mortality in the United States: Analysis of Mortality and Potential Pathways*, The BMJ (Apr. 20, 1996), http://www.bmj.com/content/312/7037/999.

areas with high concentrations of poverty and in areas with high minority populations have a shorter life expectancy than wealthier, less minority communities. Marginalized and socially excluded communities tend to have worse health outcomes overall.[5] Differences in spending for healthcare infrastructure, access to healthcare, public spending on prevention and social supports explains many of these differences. Health outcomes are better in communities that offer the poor easier access to healthcare and preventative measures and that offer supportive services for those who are sick or disabled. This may be an intuitive outcome in a country that prefers market access to healthcare. In the United States, the commodification of healthcare means that individuals who lack resources to acquire healthcare are denied access to the benefits healthcare provides. The foundations of health are found in people's social resources, including income, wealth education, employment, food security, housing, transportation, social inclusion, and access to care.[6] Improving health outcomes for the poor requires resources to be directed toward these fundamental causes.

B. Medicaid and Medicare

Access to medical care has been provided to the poor for more than 50 years through the Medicaid and Medicare programs. Spending on these programs accounted for an astonishing $1.288 trillion dollars in 2017, with approximately 55% of this directed toward Medicare.[7] Following passage of the Affordable Care Act, Medicaid was expanded to provide medical insurance coverage to a larger portion of the U.S. population, building upon the infrastructure developed over five decades. In addition to these programs, the poor receive medical care through a number of other providers, including the Veterans Administration and private nonprofit charitable care, neither of whose budget is included in these numbers.

Medicaid is a public health insurance program that was created by Congress in 1965 to provide health coverage to low-income families and individuals with disabilities. Medicaid is sometimes confused with Medicare. Medicare is a health insurance program for people over 65 and those who have disabilities. Medicaid is jointly funded by the federal government and each state, following the same joint funding arrangement found in other poverty programs. Under a model of federal-state cooperation, each state operates its own Medicaid program along federal guidelines, which allows for broad flexibility at the state level. As a result, Medicaid benefits vary from state to state. About 43% of all people covered by Medicaid are under the age of 16, al-

---

5. James Teufel et al., *Legal Aid Inequities Predict Health Disparities*, 38 Hamline L. Rev. 329 (2015).

6. *Id.*

7. Ctrs. for Medicare & Medicaid Servs., *NHE Fact Sheet* (Apr. 26, 2019), https://www.cms.gov/research-statistics-data-and-systems/statistics-trends-and-reports/nationalhealthexpenddata/nhe-fact-sheet.html.

though more than 50% of Medicaid's cost is spent on the elderly and disabled individuals covered by the program.[8]

Eligibility for Medicaid varies widely from state to state because states have broad flexibility for setting eligibility criteria for optional populations and income levels. The Affordable Care Act gave states the option to expand Medicaid to provide health insurance to poor, nondisabled adults without children. States have the option to expand Medicaid but were not obligated to do so.

1. Eligibility

Medicaid operates as an entitlement program. Anyone who meets eligibility criteria has a right to enroll in Medicaid and receive healthcare coverage. The federal government guarantees funding to states for part of the costs of their Medicaid program. States must provide coverage to defined "mandatory" populations, which include:

- Children under 18 years of age and pregnant women who are below 138% of the Federal Poverty Line
- Parents whose income was within the state's eligibility criteria for assistance under the AFDC program prior to TANF; and
- Seniors and people with disabilities who receive Supplemental Security Income (SSI) benefits.[9]

States have the option to receive additional Medicaid funding to cover the costs of additional "optional" groups, including individuals with incomes above "mandatory" coverage income limits, "medically needy" people (those whose income exceeds the Medicaid eligibility limit, but who have high medical expenses that reduce disposable income below the eligibility limit), and poor nondisabled adults without children if the state has elected expansion under the Affordable Care Act. In the typical nonexpansion state, Medicaid eligibility is limited to working parents with incomes at 45%of the poverty line and is not available to nondisabled adults without children. Childless adults between 21 and 65 who are not disabled and not pregnant are not eligible for Medicaid in states that have not expanded eligibility. Moreover, legal immigrants are barred from Medicaid for the first five years of residency, even if they meet all other eligibility requirements.[10]

2. Services Provided by Medicaid

Medicaid pays hospitals, physicians, nursing homes, managed care plans, and other healthcare providers for covered services delivered to eligible patients. Not all

---

8. Ctr. on Budget & Pol'y Priorities, Policy Basics: Introduction to Medicaid (Aug. 16, 2016), https://www.cbpp.org/research/health/policy-basics-introduction-to-medicaid.

9. *Id.*

10. *Id.*

healthcare providers are required to participate in the Medicaid program, and some hospitals, physicians, and others do not. But for those who do, Medicaid pays for the delivery of hospital and physician services, prescription drugs, nursing homes, and rehabilitative care. Roughly one-quarter of Medicaid spending goes to nursing home and other long-term care services and supports.[11]

Medicaid requires states to cover certain "mandatory" services, including: physician, midwife, and certified nurse practitioner services; inpatient and outpatient hospital services; laboratory and diagnostic services; family planning services; rural health clinic services; nursing facility and home healthcare for adults over 21; and Early and Periodic Screening, Diagnostic, and Treatment (EPSDT) services for children under 21. States may elect to cover certain additional services, including prescription drugs, dental care, vision services, hearing aids, and personal care services for the elderly or those with disabilities.[12]

3. Medicaid's Costs and Funding

Medicaid is funded with both state and federal money. In any given year, the total funding for the Medicaid program will exceed $430 billion. Although Medicaid may be seen as an expensive program, Medicaid costs substantially less than private insurance to cover people with similar health status and needs. This is because of Medicaid's lower payment rates to healthcare providers and lower administrative costs overall. States may also limit costs by setting lower limits on the amount, duration, and scope of services provided to patients under the Medicaid program; states must, however, continue to provide services that are sufficient to achieve the purposes of the Medicaid program.

The federal government contributes at least $1 in funds for every $1 spent by a state on the state's Medicaid program. As an entitlement program, the federal government is obligated to make these payments regardless of whatever the costs may be. The percentage of each state's Medicaid costs paid by the federal government varies and, in some states, the federal government pays more than 70% of the state's total costs, although the national average is 57%.[13]

Flexibility at the state level allows states to reduce provider reimbursement rates as state spending on Medicaid increases, particularly in times of high unemployment. This may lead to reducing access to healthcare for many poor people as lower reimbursement rates cause correspondingly lower provider participation rates.[14] Lower Medicaid reimbursement rates have a detrimental effect on access to healthcare for

---

11. *Id.*
12. *Id.*
13. *Id.*
14. Daniel J. Sheffner, *Rate Setting After* Douglas, 38 HAMLINE L. REV. 57, 59–61 (2015).

the poor, as well as affecting quality of healthcare that is delivered. Lower rates lead to low nursing home staffing levels, for example, with a reduction in quality of care.

C. Medicaid and the Affordable Care Act

Medicaid works in tandem with the Affordable Care Act. The Affordable Care Act provides healthcare coverage for able-bodied poor and low-income adults by expanding Medicaid eligibility to 138% of the federal poverty line. In 2012, the Supreme Court ruled that states had the choice of whether to expand their Medicaid programs to align with the Affordable Care Act's policy objectives. The majority of states decided to expand Medicaid under the ACA, although 22 states failed to do so as of 2018. More than 14 million more adults and children will receive healthcare coverage under Medicaid by 2025 as a result of the Affordable Care Act.

1. Medicaid and Work

Since its inception more than five decades ago, Medicaid has operated as an entitlement program. There are benefits to treating access to healthcare as an entitlement. First, providing healthcare to the poor improves the lives of many millions of individuals, enabling them to heal and live with dignity. More than this, however, Medicaid actually works to lower overall healthcare costs by creating conditions that avoid emergency care or treating conditions that have grown to require significant interventions. Access to healthcare also enables workers to rejoin the workforce, and advance economically and socially. In April 2018, the federal government mandated, through Executive Order, that states require Medicaid recipients to engage in work activity to access benefits.[15] Several states, including Arizona, Arkansas, Indiana, Kansas, Kentucky, Maine, New Hampshire, North Carolina, Utah, and Wisconsin, received waivers from the federal government prior to April 2018 and had already included work requirements as part of their Medicaid program.

2. The Affordable Care Act

Expanding healthcare coverage was an early initiative of President Obama. In 2010, Congress passed two separate pieces of legislation—the Patient Protection and Affordable Care Act (P.L. 111-148) and the Health Care and Education Reconciliation Act of 2010 (P.L. 111-152)—collectively referred to as the Affordable Care Act. The Affordable Care Act expanded Medicaid coverage to millions of low-income Americans

---

15. Tami Luhby, *Trump Signs Executive Order Pushing Work Requirements for the Poor*, CNN Bus. (Apr. 2018, 8:41 PM), http://money.cnn.com/2018/04/10/news/economy/trump-executive-order-work-requirements/index.html.

and made significant changes to both Medicaid and the Child Health Insurance Program (CHIP).

The Patient Protection and Affordable Care Act (ACA) represented a sweeping reform to how healthcare is provided in the United States and satisfied nearly no one. The ACA extended healthcare coverage to many millions of Americans who would otherwise lack access to affordable, quality healthcare. This extension was accomplished through two mechanisms. First, an expansion of eligibility under the Medicaid program to include all citizens and legal immigrants with incomes up to 133% of the federal poverty level. Medicaid coverage is extended to these individuals and families regardless of whether the beneficiary is working or has children. The extension of Medicaid benefits to this class of low-wage workers was a significant shift in poverty policy in many ways. The embedded preference for working, deserving poor people and parents with dependent children was eroded by a preference for coverage in all instances. Next, the ACA established state-sponsored "American Health Benefit Exchanges" through which all individuals without health insurance could purchase affordable, quality health insurance coverage through state sponsored "exchanges." Exchanges were intended to operate as clearinghouses for insurance coverage for those seeking coverage. could. The Congressional Budget Office estimated that the ACA would extend healthcare coverage to more than 32 million people who would otherwise lack access to affordable, quality health insurance. Even with the greatly expanded coverage, however, more than 20 million Americans were still expected to lack coverage after the ACA was fully implemented. This group was comprised primarily of undocumented immigrants and low-wage workers who could not afford coverage even through the state exchanges.

State exchanges were required to provide insureds with a basic set of services, including emergency care, hospitalization, prescription drugs, maternity care, mental health treatment, pediatric services, preventive care, and wellness services. State exchanges were available to provide cost-sharing credits for individuals with incomes between 133% and 400% of the federal poverty level. In addition to expanding coverage for those who previously lacked health insurance, the ACA removed barriers to coverage for all insureds. For example, the ACA prohibits coverage exclusions based on "pre-existing conditions."[16] The ACA also bans lifetime and annual coverage limits and prohibits insurers from refusing additional coverage should an insured individual become ill. Children up to the age of 26 must also remain covered under their parent's policy and policies are required to cover preventive services, such as annual physicals and preventive screening, without patient cost sharing. While expanding coverage for both the previously uninsured as well as the insured, the ACA maintained a preference for market-based delivery of healthcare insurance by protecting the established system of private health insurance linked to employment. Given such a panacea of benefits to both those who were once uninsured and those who once provided healthcare insurance, how could substantial opposition to the ACA exist?

---

16. HealthCare.gov, *Coverage for Pre-existing Conditions*, https://www.healthcare.gov/coverage/pre-existing-conditions/ (last visited Nov. 20, 2019).

National Federation of Independent Business v. Sebelius
567 U.S. 519 (2015)

Today we resolve constitutional challenges to two provisions of the Patient Protection and Affordable Care Act of 2010: the individual mandate, which requires individuals to purchase a health insurance policy providing a minimum level of coverage; and the Medicaid expansion, which gives funds to the States on the condition that they provide specified health care to all citizens whose income falls below a certain threshold. We do not consider whether the Act embodies sound policies. That judgment is entrusted to the Nation's elected leaders. We ask only whether Congress has the power under the Constitution to enact the challenged provisions.

In our federal system, the National Government possesses only limited powers; the States and the people retain the remainder. Nearly two centuries ago, Chief Justice Marshall observed that "the question respecting the extent of the powers actually granted" to the Federal Government "is perpetually arising, and will probably continue to arise, as long as our system shall exist." *McCulloch v. Maryland*, 4 Wheat. 316, 405, 4 L.Ed. 579 (1819). In this case we must again determine whether the Constitution grants Congress powers it now asserts, but which many States and individuals believe it does not possess. Resolving this controversy requires us to examine both the limits of the Government's power, and our own limited role in policing those boundaries.

The Federal Government "is acknowledged by all to be one of enumerated powers." *Ibid.* That is, rather than granting general authority to perform all the conceivable functions of government, the Constitution lists, or enumerates, the Federal Government's powers. Congress may, for example, "coin Money," "establish Post Offices," and "raise and support Armies." Art. I, §8, cls. 5, 7, 12. The enumeration of powers is also a limitation of powers, because "[t]he enumeration presupposes something not enumerated." *Gibbons v. Ogden*, 9 Wheat. 1, 195, 6 L.Ed. 23 (1824). The Constitution's express conferral of some powers makes clear that it does not grant others. And the Federal Government "can exercise only the powers granted to it." *McCulloch, supra,* at 405.

Today, the restrictions on government power foremost in many Americans' minds are likely to be affirmative prohibitions, such as contained in the Bill of Rights. These affirmative prohibitions come into play, however, only where the Government possesses authority to act in the first place. If no enumerated power authorizes Congress to pass a certain law, that law may not be enacted, even if it would not violate any of the express prohibitions in the Bill of Rights or elsewhere in the Constitution.

Indeed, the Constitution did not initially include a Bill of Rights at least partly because the Framers felt the enumeration of powers sufficed to restrain the Government. As Alexander Hamilton put it, "the Constitution is itself, in every rational sense, and to every useful purpose, A BILL OF RIGHTS." The Federalist No. 84, p. 515 (C. Rossiter ed. 1961). And when the Bill of Rights was ratified, it made express what the enumeration of powers necessarily implied: "The powers not delegated to the United States by the Constitution ... are reserved to the States respectively, or to the people." U.S. Const., Amdt. 10. The Federal Government has expanded dramatically over the past two centuries, but it still must show that a constitutional grant of power authorizes each of its actions.

The same does not apply to the States, because the Constitution is not the source of their power. The Constitution may restrict state governments—as it does, for example, by forbidding them to deny any person the equal protection of the laws. But where such prohibitions do not apply, state governments do not need constitutional authorization to act. The States thus can and do perform many of the vital functions of modern government—punishing street crime, running public schools, and zoning property for development, to name but a few—even though the Constitution's text does not authorize any government to do so. Our cases refer to this general power of governing, possessed by the States but not by the Federal Government, as the "police power."

"State sovereignty is not just an end in itself: Rather, federalism secures to citizens the liberties that derive from the diffusion of sovereign power." Because the police power is controlled by 50 different States instead of one national sovereign, the facets of governing that touch on citizens' daily lives are normally administered by smaller governments closer to the governed. The Framers thus ensured that powers which "in the ordinary course of affairs, concern the lives, liberties, and properties of the people" were held by governments more local and more accountable than a distant federal bureaucracy. The Federalist No. 45, at 293 (J. Madison). The independent power of the States also serves as a check on the power of the Federal Government: "By denying any one government complete jurisdiction over all the concerns of public life, federalism protects the liberty of the individual from arbitrary power." *Bond v. United States*, 564 U.S. ___, ___, 131 S.Ct. 2355, 2364, 180 L.Ed.2d 269 (2011).

This case concerns two powers that the Constitution does grant the Federal Government, but which must be read carefully to avoid creating a general federal authority akin to the police power. The Constitution authorizes Congress to "regulate Commerce with foreign Nations, and among the several States, and with the Indian Tribes." Art. I, §8, cl. 3. Our precedents read that to mean that Congress may regulate "the channels of interstate commerce," "persons or things in interstate commerce," and "those activities that substantially affect interstate commerce." *Morrison, supra*, at 609, 120 S.Ct. 1740 (internal quotation marks omitted). The power over activities that substantially affect interstate commerce can be expansive. That power has been held to authorize federal regulation of such seemingly local matters as a farmer's decision to grow wheat for himself and his livestock, and a loan shark's extortionate collections from a neighborhood butcher shop. See *Wickard v. Filburn*, 317 U.S. 111, 63 S.Ct. 82, 87 L.Ed. 122 (1942); *Perez v. United States*, 402 U.S. 146, 91 S.Ct. 1357, 28 L.Ed.2d 686 (1971).

Congress may also "lay and collect Taxes, Duties, Imposts and Excises, to pay the Debts and provide for the common Defence and general Welfare of the United States." U.S. Const., Art. I, §8, cl. 1. Put simply, Congress may tax and spend. This grant gives the Federal Government considerable influence even in areas where it cannot directly regulate. The Federal Government may enact a tax on an activity that it cannot authorize, forbid, or otherwise control. See, *e.g., License Tax Cases,* 5 Wall. 462, 471, 18 L.Ed. 497 (1867). And in exercising its spending power, Congress may offer funds to the States, and may condition those offers on compliance with specified conditions. These offers may well induce the States to adopt policies that the Federal Government itself could not impose. See, *e.g., South Dakota v. Dole,* 483 U.S. 203, 205–206, 107 S.Ct. 2793, 97 L.Ed.2d 171 (1987) (conditioning federal highway funds on States raising their drinking age to 21).

The reach of the Federal Government's enumerated powers is broader still because the Constitution authorizes Congress to "make all Laws which shall be necessary and proper for carrying into Execution the foregoing Powers." Art. I, § 8, cl. 18. We have long read this provision to give Congress great latitude in exercising its powers: "Let the end be legitimate, let it be within the scope of the constitution, and all means which are appropriate, which are plainly adapted to that end, which are not prohibited, but consist with the letter and spirit of the constitution, are constitutional." *McCulloch,* 4 Wheat., at 421.

Our permissive reading of these powers is explained in part by a general reticence to invalidate the acts of the Nation's elected leaders. "Proper respect for a coordinate branch of the government" requires that we strike down an Act of Congress only if "the lack of constitutional authority to pass [the] act in question is clearly demonstrated." *United States v. Harris,* 106 U.S. 629, 635, 1 S.Ct. 601, 27 L.Ed. 290 (1883). Members of this Court are vested with the authority to interpret the law; we possess neither the expertise nor the prerogative to make policy judgments. Those decisions are entrusted to our Nation's elected leaders, who can be thrown out of office if the people disagree with them. It is not our job to protect the people from the consequences of their political choices.

Our deference in matters of policy cannot, however, become abdication in matters of law. "The powers of the legislature are defined and limited; and that those limits may not be mistaken, or forgotten, the constitution is written." *Marbury v. Madison,* 1 Cranch 137, 176, 2 L.Ed. 60 (1803). Our respect for Congress's policy judgments thus can never extend so far as to disavow restraints on federal power that the Constitution carefully constructed. "The peculiar circumstances of the moment may render a measure more or less wise, but cannot render it more or less constitutional." Chief Justice John Marshall, A Friend of the Constitution No. V, Alexandria Gazette, July 5, 1819, in John Marshall's Defense of *McCulloch v. Maryland* 190–191 (G. Gunther ed. 1969). And there can be no question that it is the responsibility of this Court to enforce the limits on federal power by striking down acts of Congress that transgress those limits. *Marbury v. Madison, supra,* at 175–176.

The questions before us must be considered against the background of these basic principles.

I

In 2010, Congress enacted the Patient Protection and Affordable Care Act, 124 Stat. 119. The Act aims to increase the number of Americans covered by health insurance and decrease the cost of health care. The Act's 10 titles stretch over 900 pages and contain hundreds of provisions. This case concerns constitutional challenges to two key provisions, commonly referred to as the individual mandate and the Medicaid expansion.

The individual mandate requires most Americans to maintain "minimum essential" health insurance coverage. 26 U.S.C. § 5000A. The mandate does not apply to some individuals, such as prisoners and undocumented aliens. § 5000A(d). Many individuals will receive the required coverage through their employer, or from a government program such as Medicaid or Medicare. See § 5000A(f). But for individuals who are not exempt and do not receive health insurance through a third party, the means of satisfying the requirement is to purchase insurance from a private company.

Beginning in 2014, those who do not comply with the mandate must make a "[s]hared responsibility payment" to the Federal Government. § 5000A(b)(1). That payment, which the Act describes as a "penalty," is calculated as a percentage of household income, subject to a floor based on a specified dollar amount and a ceiling based on the average annual premium the individual would have to pay for qualifying private health insurance. § 5000A(c). In 2016, for example, the penalty will be 2.5 percent of an individual's household income, but no less than $695 and no more than the average yearly premium for insurance that covers 60 percent of the cost of 10 specified services (*e.g.*, prescription drugs and hospitalization). *Ibid.*; 42 U.S.C. § 18022. The Act provides that the penalty will be paid to the Internal Revenue Service with an individual's taxes, and "shall be assessed and collected in the same manner" as tax penalties, such as the penalty for claiming too large an income tax refund. 26 U.S.C. § 5000A(g)(1). The Act, however, bars the IRS from using several of its normal enforcement tools, such as criminal prosecutions and levies. § 5000A(g)(2). And some individuals who are subject to the mandate are nonetheless exempt from the penalty—for example, those with income below a certain threshold and members of Indian tribes. § 5000A(e).

On the day the President signed the Act into law, Florida and 12 other States filed a complaint in the Federal District Court for the Northern District of Florida. Those plaintiffs—who are both respondents and petitioners here, depending on the issue— were subsequently joined by 13 more States, several individuals, and the National Federation of Independent Business. The plaintiffs alleged, among other things, that the individual mandate provisions of the Act exceeded Congress's powers under Article I of the Constitution. The District Court agreed, holding that Congress lacked constitutional power to enact the individual mandate. 780 F.Supp.2d 1256 (N.D.Fla.2011). The District Court determined that the individual mandate could not be severed from the remainder of the Act, and therefore struck down the Act in its entirety. *Id.,* at 1305–1306.

* * *

The second provision of the Affordable Care Act directly challenged here is the Medicaid expansion. Enacted in 1965, Medicaid offers federal funding to States to assist pregnant women, children, needy families, the blind, the elderly, and the disabled in obtaining medical care. See 42 U.S.C. § 1396a(a)(10). In order to receive that funding, States must comply with federal criteria governing matters such as who receives care and what services are provided at what cost. By 1982 every State had chosen to participate in Medicaid. Federal funds received through the Medicaid program have become a substantial part of state budgets, now constituting over 10 percent of most States' total revenue.

The Affordable Care Act expands the scope of the Medicaid program and increases the number of individuals the States must cover. For example, the Act requires state programs to provide Medicaid coverage to adults with incomes up to 133 percent of the federal poverty level, whereas many States now cover adults with children only if their income is considerably lower, and do not cover childless adults at all. See § 1396a(a)(10)(A)(i)(VIII). The Act increases federal funding to cover the States' costs in expanding Medicaid coverage, although States will bear a portion of the costs on their own. § 1396d(y)(1). If a State does not comply with the Act's new coverage requirements, it may lose not only the federal funding for those requirements, but all of its federal Medicaid funds. See § 1396c.

* * *

III

The Government advances two theories for the proposition that Congress had constitutional authority to enact the individual mandate. First, the Government argues that Congress had the power to enact the mandate under the Commerce Clause. Under that theory, Congress may order individuals to buy health insurance because the failure to do so affects interstate commerce, and could undercut the Affordable Care Act's other reforms. Second, the Government argues that if the commerce power does not support the mandate, we should nonetheless uphold it as an exercise of Congress's power to tax. According to the Government, even if Congress lacks the power to direct individuals to buy insurance, the only effect of the individual mandate is to raise taxes on those who do not do so, and thus the law may be upheld as a tax.

A

The Government's first argument is that the individual mandate is a valid exercise of Congress's power under the Commerce Clause and the Necessary and Proper Clause. According to the Government, the health care market is characterized by a significant cost-shifting problem. Everyone will eventually need health care at a time and to an extent they cannot predict, but if they do not have insurance, they often will not be able to pay for it. Because state and federal laws nonetheless require hospitals to provide a certain degree of care to individuals without regard to their ability to pay, see, e.g., 42 U.S.C. § 1395dd; Fla. Stat. Ann. § 395.1041, hospitals end up receiving compensation for only a portion of the services they provide. To recoup the losses, hospitals pass on the cost to insurers through higher rates, and insurers, in turn, pass on the cost to policy holders in the form of higher premiums. Congress estimated that the cost of uncompensated care raises family health insurance premiums, on average, by over $1,000 per year. 42 U.S.C. § 18091(2)(F).

* * *

The Government claims that Congress has power under the Commerce and Necessary and Proper Clauses to enact this solution.

1

The Government contends that the individual mandate is within Congress's power because the failure to purchase insurance "has a substantial and deleterious effect on interstate commerce" by creating the cost-shifting problem. Brief for United States 34. The path of our Commerce Clause decisions has not always run smooth, see *United States v. Lopez*, 514 U.S. 549, 552–559, 115 S.Ct. 1624, 131 L.Ed.2d 626 (1995), but it is now well established that Congress has broad authority under the Clause. We have recognized, for example, that "[t]he power of Congress over interstate commerce is not confined to the regulation of commerce among the states," but extends to activities that "have a substantial effect on interstate commerce." *United States v. Darby*, 312 U.S. 100, 118–119, 61 S.Ct. 451, 85 L.Ed. 609 (1941). Congress's power, moreover, is not limited to regulation of an activity that by itself substantially affects interstate commerce, but also extends to activities that do so only when aggregated with similar activities of others. See *Wickard*, 317 U.S., at 127–128, 63 S.Ct. 82.

Given its expansive scope, it is no surprise that Congress has employed the commerce power in a wide variety of ways to address the pressing needs of the time. But Congress has never attempted to rely on that power to compel individuals not engaged in commerce to purchase an unwanted product. Legislative novelty is not necessarily fatal; there is a first time for everything. But sometimes "the most telling indication of [a] severe constitutional problem ... is the lack of historical precedent" for Congress's action. *Free Enterprise Fund v. Public Company Accounting Oversight Bd.*, 561 U.S. ___, ___, 130 S.Ct. 3138, 3159, 177 L.Ed.2d 706 (2010) (internal quotation marks omitted). At the very least, we should "pause to consider the implications of the Government's arguments" when confronted with such new conceptions of federal power. *Lopez, supra*, at 564, 115 S.Ct. 1624.

The Constitution grants Congress the power to "*regulate* Commerce." Art. I, § 8, cl. 3 (emphasis added). The power to *regulate* commerce presupposes the existence of commercial activity to be regulated. If the power to "regulate" something included the power to create it, many of the provisions in the Constitution would be superfluous. For example, the Constitution gives Congress the power to "coin Money," in addition to the power to "regulate the Value thereof." *Id.*, cl. 5. And it gives Congress the power to "raise and support Armies" and to "provide and maintain a Navy," in addition to the power to "make Rules for the Government and Regulation of the land and naval Forces." *Id.*, cls. 12–14. If the power to regulate the armed forces or the value of money included the power to bring the subject of the regulation into existence, the specific grant of such powers would have been unnecessary. The language of the Constitution reflects the natural understanding that the power to regulate assumes there is already something to be regulated. See *Gibbons*, 9 Wheat., at 188 ("[T]he enlightened patriots who framed our constitution, and the people who adopted it, must be understood to have employed words in their natural sense, and to have intended what they have said").

Our precedent also reflects this understanding. As expansive as our cases construing the scope of the commerce power have been, they all have one thing in common: They uniformly describe the power as reaching "activity." It is nearly impossible to avoid the word when quoting them. See, *e.g., Lopez, supra,* at 560, 115 S.Ct. 1624 ("Where economic activity substantially affects interstate commerce, legislation regulating that activity will be sustained"); *Perez,* 402 U.S., at 154, 91 S.Ct. 1357 ("Where the *class of activities* is regulated and that *class* is within the reach of federal power, the courts have no power to excise, as trivial, individual instances of the class" (emphasis in original; internal quotation marks omitted)); *Wickard, supra,* at 125, 63 S.Ct. 82 ("[E]ven if appellee's activity be local and though it may not be regarded as commerce, it may still, whatever its nature, be reached by Congress if it exerts a substantial economic effect on interstate commerce"); *NLRB v. Jones & Laughlin Steel Corp.,* 301 U.S. 1, 37, 57 S.Ct. 615, 81 L.Ed. 893 (1937) ("Although activities may be intrastate in character when separately considered, if they have such a close and substantial relation to interstate commerce that their control is essential or appropriate to protect that commerce from burdens and obstructions, Congress cannot be denied the power to exercise that control"); see also *post,* at 2616, 2621–2623, 2623, 2625 (GINSBURG, J., concurring in part, concurring in judgment in part, and dissenting in part).

The individual mandate, however, does not regulate existing commercial activity. It instead compels individuals to *become* active in commerce by purchasing a product, on the ground that their failure to do so affects interstate commerce. Construing the Commerce Clause to permit Congress to regulate individuals precisely *because* they are doing nothing would open a new and potentially vast domain to congressional authority. Every day individuals do not do an infinite number of things. In some cases they decide not to do something; in others they simply fail to do it. Allowing Congress to justify federal regulation by pointing to the effect of inaction on commerce would bring countless decisions an individual could *potentially* make within the scope of federal regulation, and — under the Government's theory — empower Congress to make those decisions for him.

* * *

Indeed, the Government's logic would justify a mandatory purchase to solve almost any problem. See *Seven-Sky,* 661 F.3d, at 14–15 (noting the Government's inability to "identify any mandate to purchase a product or service in interstate commerce that would be unconstitutional" under its theory of the commerce power). To consider a different example in the health care market, many Americans do not eat a balanced diet. That group makes up a larger percentage of the total population than those without health insurance. See, *e.g.,* Dept. of Agriculture and Dept. of Health and Human Services, Dietary Guidelines for Americans 1 (2010). The failure of that group to have a healthy diet increases health care costs, to a greater extent than the failure of the uninsured to purchase insurance. See, *e.g.,* Finkelstein, Trogdon, Cohen,

& Dietz, Annual Medical Spending Attributable to Obesity: Payer- and Service-Specific Estimates, 28 Health Affairs w822 (2009) (detailing the "undeniable link between rising rates of obesity and rising medical spending," and estimating that "the annual medical burden of obesity has risen to almost 10 percent of all medical spending and could amount to $147 billion per year in 2008"). Those increased costs are borne in part by other Americans who must pay more, just as the uninsured shift costs to the insured. Congress addressed the insurance problem by ordering everyone to buy insurance. Under the Government's theory, Congress could address the diet problem by ordering everyone to buy vegetables. See Dietary Guidelines, *supra,* at 19 ("Improved nutrition, appropriate eating behaviors, and increased physical activity have tremendous potential to ... reduce health care costs").

People, for reasons of their own, often fail to do things that would be good for them or good for society. Those failures—joined with the similar failures of others—can readily have a substantial effect on interstate commerce. Under the Government's logic, that authorizes Congress to use its commerce power to compel citizens to act as the Government would have them act.

*** The individual mandate's regulation of the uninsured as a class is, in fact, particularly divorced from any link to existing commercial activity. The mandate primarily affects healthy, often young adults who are less likely to need significant health care and have other priorities for spending their money. It is precisely because these individuals, as an actuarial class, incur relatively low health care costs that the mandate helps counter the effect of forcing insurance companies to cover others who impose greater costs than their premiums are allowed to reflect. See 42 U.S.C. § 18091(2)(I) (recognizing that the mandate would "broaden the health insurance risk pool to include healthy individuals, which will lower health insurance premiums"). If the individual mandate is targeted at a class, it is a class whose commercial inactivity rather than activity is its defining feature.

*** The proximity and degree of connection between the mandate and the subsequent commercial activity is too lacking to justify an exception of the sort urged by the Government. The individual mandate forces individuals into commerce precisely because they elected to refrain from commercial activity. Such a law cannot be sustained under a clause authorizing Congress to "regulate Commerce."

B

That is not the end of the matter. Because the Commerce Clause does not support the individual mandate, it is necessary to turn to the Government's second argument: that the mandate may be upheld as within Congress's enumerated power to "lay and collect Taxes." Art. I, §8, cl. 1.

The Government's tax power argument asks us to view the statute differently than we did in considering its commerce power theory. In making its Commerce Clause argument, the Government defended the mandate as a regulation requiring individuals to purchase health insurance. The Government does not claim that the taxing power allows Congress to issue such a command. Instead, the Government asks us to read the mandate not as ordering individuals to buy insurance, but rather as imposing a tax on those who do not buy that product.

The text of a statute can sometimes have more than one possible meaning. To take a familiar example, a law that reads "no vehicles in the park" might, or might not, ban bicycles in the park. And it is well established that if a statute has two possible meanings, one of which violates the Constitution, courts should adopt the meaning that does not do so. Justice Story said that 180 years ago: "No court ought, unless the terms of an act rendered it unavoidable, to give a construction to it which should involve a violation, however unintentional, of the constitution." *Parsons v. Bedford*, 3 Pet. 433, 448–449, 7 L.Ed. 732 (1830). Justice Holmes made the same point a century later: "[T]he rule is settled that as between two possible interpretations of a statute, by one of which it would be unconstitutional and by the other valid, our plain duty is to adopt that which will save the Act." *Blodgett v. Holden*, 275 U.S. 142, 148, 48 S.Ct. 105, 72 L.Ed. 206 (1927) (concurring opinion).

The most straightforward reading of the mandate is that it commands individuals to purchase insurance. After all, it states that individuals "shall" maintain health insurance. 26 U.S.C. § 5000A(a). Congress thought it could enact such a command under the Commerce Clause, and the Government primarily defended the law on that basis. But, for the reasons explained above, the Commerce Clause does not give Congress that power. Under our precedent, it is therefore necessary to ask whether the Government's alternative reading of the statute—that it only imposes a tax on those without insurance—is a reasonable one.

Under the mandate, if an individual does not maintain health insurance, the only consequence is that he must make an additional payment to the IRS when he pays his taxes. See § 5000A(b). That, according to the Government, means the mandate can be regarded as establishing a condition—not owning health insurance—that triggers a tax—the required payment to the IRS. Under that theory, the mandate is not a legal command to buy insurance. Rather, it makes going without insurance just another thing the Government taxes, like buying gasoline or earning income. And if the mandate is in effect just a tax hike on certain taxpayers who do not have health insurance, it may be within Congress's constitutional power to tax.

The question is not whether that is the most natural interpretation of the mandate, but only whether it is a "fairly possible" one. *Crowell v. Benson*, 285 U.S. 22, 62, 52 S.Ct. 285, 76 L.Ed. 598 (1932). As we have explained, "every reasonable construction must be resorted to, in order to save a statute from unconstitutionality." *Hooper v. California*, 155 U.S. 648, 657, 15 S.Ct. 207, 39 L.Ed. 297 (1895). The Government asks us to interpret the mandate as imposing a tax, if it would otherwise violate the Constitution. Granting the Act the full measure of deference owed to federal statutes, it can be so read, for the reasons set forth below.

C

The exaction the Affordable Care Act imposes on those without health insurance looks like a tax in many respects. The "[s]hared responsibility payment," as the statute entitles it, is paid into the Treasury by "taxpayer[s]" when they file their tax returns. 26 U.S.C. § 5000A(b). It does not apply to individuals who do not pay federal income taxes because their household income is less than the filing threshold in the Internal Revenue Code. § 5000A(e)(2). For taxpayers who do owe the payment, its amount is determined by such familiar factors as taxable income, number of dependents, and joint filing status. §§ 5000A(b)(3), (c)(2), (c)(4). The requirement to pay is found in the Internal Revenue Code and enforced by the IRS, which—as we previously explained—must assess and collect it "in the same manner as taxes." *Supra*, at 2583–2584. This process yields the essential feature of any tax: it produces at least some revenue for the Government. *United States v. Kahriger*, 345 U.S. 22, 28, n. 4, 73 S.Ct. 510, 97 L.Ed. 754 (1953). Indeed, the payment is expected to raise about $4 billion per year by 2017. Congressional Budget Office, Payments of Penalties for Being Uninsured Under the Patient Protection and Affordable Care Act (Apr. 30, 2010), in Selected CBO Publications Related to Health Care Legislation, 2009–2010, p. 71 (rev. 2010).

It is of course true that the Act describes the payment as a "penalty," not a "tax." But while that label is fatal to the application of the Anti-Injunction Act, *supra*, at 2582–2583, it does not determine whether the payment may be viewed as an exercise of Congress's taxing power. It is up to Congress whether to apply the Anti-Injunction Act to any particular statute, so it makes sense to be guided by Congress's choice of label on that question. That choice does not, however, control whether an exaction is within Congress's constitutional power to tax.

*** Our cases confirm this functional approach. For example, in *Drexel Furniture*, we focused on three practical characteristics of the so-called tax on employing child laborers that convinced us the "tax" was actually a penalty. First, the tax imposed an exceedingly heavy burden—10 percent of a company's net income—on those who employed children, no matter how small their infraction. Second, it imposed that exaction only on those who knowingly employed underage laborers. Such scienter requirements are typical of punitive statutes, because Congress often wishes to punish only those who intentionally break the law. Third, this "tax" was enforced in part by the Department of Labor, an agency responsible for punishing violations of labor laws, not collecting revenue. 259 U.S., at 36–37, 42 S.Ct. 449; see also, *e.g., Kurth Ranch*, 511 U.S., at 780–782, 114 S.Ct. 1937 (considering, *inter alia,* the amount of the exaction, and the fact that it was imposed for violation of a separate criminal law); *Constantine, supra,* at 295, 56 S.Ct. 223 (same).

The same analysis here suggests that the shared responsibility payment may for constitutional purposes be considered a tax, not a penalty: First, for most Americans the amount due will be far less than the price of insurance, and, by statute, it can never be more. It may often be a reasonable financial decision to make the payment rather than purchase insurance, unlike the "prohibitory" financial punishment in *Drexel Furniture*. 259 U.S., at 37, 42 S.Ct. 449. Second, the individual mandate contains no scienter requirement. Third, the payment is collected solely by the IRS through the normal means of taxation—except that the Service is *not* allowed to use those means most suggestive of a punitive sanction, such as criminal prosecution.

See § 5000A(g)(2). The reasons the Court in *Drexel Furniture* held that what was called a "tax" there was a penalty support the conclusion that what is called a "penalty" here may be viewed as a tax.

None of this is to say that the payment is not intended to affect individual conduct. Although the payment will raise considerable revenue, it is plainly designed to expand health insurance coverage. But taxes that seek to influence conduct are nothing new. Some of our earliest federal taxes sought to deter the purchase of imported manufactured goods in order to foster the growth of domestic industry. Today, federal and state taxes can compose more than half the retail price of cigarettes, not just to raise more money, but to encourage people to quit smoking. And we have upheld such obviously regulatory measures as taxes on selling marijuana and sawed-off shotguns. See *United States v. Sanchez*, 340 U.S. 42, 44–45, 71 S.Ct. 108, 95 L.Ed. 47 (1950); *Sonzinsky v. United States*, 300 U.S. 506, 513, 57 S.Ct. 554, 81 L.Ed. 772 (1937). Indeed, "[e]very tax is in some measure regulatory. To some extent it interposes an economic impediment to the activity taxed as compared with others not taxed." *Sonzinsky, supra*, at 513, 57 S.Ct. 554. That § 5000A seeks to shape decisions about whether to buy health insurance does not mean that it cannot be a valid exercise of the taxing power.

In distinguishing penalties from taxes, this Court has explained that "if the concept of penalty means anything, it means punishment for an unlawful act or omission." *United States v. Reorganized CF & I Fabricators of Utah, Inc.*, 518 U.S. 213, 224, 116 S.Ct. 2106, 135 L.Ed.2d 506 (1996); see also *United States v. La Franca*, 282 U.S. 568, 572, 51 S.Ct. 278, 75 L.Ed. 551 (1931) ("[A] penalty, as the word is here used, is an exaction imposed by statute as punishment for an unlawful act"). While the individual mandate clearly aims to induce the purchase of health insurance, it need not be read to declare that failing to do so is unlawful. Neither the Act nor any other law attaches negative legal consequences to not buying health insurance, beyond requiring a payment to the IRS. The Government agrees with that reading, confirming that if someone chooses to pay rather than obtain health insurance, they have fully complied with the law.

*** Our precedent demonstrates that Congress had the power to impose the exaction in § 5000A under the taxing power, and that § 5000A need not be read to do more than impose a tax. That is sufficient to sustain it. The "question of the constitutionality of action taken by Congress does not depend on recitals of the power which it undertakes to exercise." *Woods v. Cloyd W. Miller Co.*, 333 U.S. 138, 144, 68 S.Ct. 421, 92 L.Ed. 596 (1948).

Even if the taxing power enables Congress to impose a tax on not obtaining health insurance, any tax must still comply with other requirements in the Constitution. Plaintiffs argue that the shared responsibility payment does not do so, citing Article I, § 9, clause 4. That clause provides: "No Capitation, or other direct, Tax shall be laid, unless in Proportion to the Census or Enumeration herein before directed to be taken." This requirement means that any "direct Tax" must be apportioned so that each State pays in proportion to its population. According to the plaintiffs, if the individual mandate imposes a tax, it is a direct tax, and it is unconstitutional because Congress made no effort to apportion it among the States.

Even when the Direct Tax Clause was written it was unclear what else, other than a capitation (also known as a "head tax" or a "poll tax"), might be a direct tax. See *Springer v. United States*, 102 U.S. 586, 596–598, 26 L.Ed. 253 (1881). Soon after the framing, Congress passed a tax on ownership of carriages, over James Madison's objection that it was an unapportioned direct tax. *Id.*, at 597. This Court upheld the tax, in part reasoning that apportioning such a tax would make little sense, because it would have required taxing carriage owners at dramatically different rates depending on how many carriages were in their home State. See *Hylton v. United States*, 3 Dall. 171, 174, 1 L.Ed. 556 (1796) (opinion of Chase, J.). The Court was unanimous, and those Justices who wrote opinions either directly asserted or strongly suggested that only two forms of taxation were direct: capitations and land taxes. See *id.*, at 175; *id.*, at 177 (opinion of Paterson, J.); *id.*, at 183 (opinion of Iredell, J.).

*** There may, however, be a more fundamental objection to a tax on those who lack health insurance. Even if only a tax, the payment under § 5000A(b) remains a burden that the Federal Government imposes for an omission, not an act. If it is troubling to interpret the Commerce Clause as authorizing Congress to regulate those who abstain from commerce, perhaps it should be similarly troubling to permit Congress to impose a tax for not doing something.

Three considerations allay this concern. First, and most importantly, it is abundantly clear the Constitution does not guarantee that individuals may avoid taxation through inactivity. A capitation, after all, is a tax that everyone must pay simply for existing, and capitations are expressly contemplated by the Constitution. The Court today holds that our Constitution protects us from federal regulation under the Commerce Clause so long as we abstain from the regulated activity. But from its creation, the Constitution has made no such promise with respect to taxes. See Letter from Benjamin Franklin to M. Le Roy (Nov. 13, 1789) ("Our new Constitution is now established … but in this world nothing can be said to be certain, except death and taxes").

Whether the mandate can be upheld under the Commerce Clause is a question about the scope of federal authority. Its answer depends on whether Congress can exercise what all acknowledge to be the novel course of directing individuals to purchase insurance. Congress's use of the Taxing Clause to encourage buying something is, by contrast, not new. Tax incentives already promote, for example, purchasing homes and professional educations. See 26 U.S.C. §§ 163(h), 25A. Sustaining the mandate as a tax depends only on whether Congress *has* properly exercised its taxing power to encourage purchasing health insurance, not whether it *can*. Upholding the individual mandate under the Taxing Clause thus does not recognize any new federal power. It determines that Congress has used an existing one.

Second, Congress's ability to use its taxing power to influence conduct is not without limits. A few of our cases policed these limits aggressively, invalidating punitive exactions obviously designed to regulate behavior otherwise regarded at the time as beyond federal authority. See, *e.g.*, *United States v. Butler*, 297 U.S. 1, 56 S.Ct. 312, 80 L.Ed. 477 (1936); *Drexel Furniture*, 259 U.S. 20, 42 S.Ct. 449, 66 L.Ed. 817. More often and more recently we have declined to closely examine the regulatory motive or effect of revenue-raising measures. See *Kahriger*, 345 U.S., at 27–31, 73 S.Ct. 510 (collecting cases). We have nonetheless maintained that "'there comes a time in the extension of the penalizing features of the so-called tax when it loses its character as such and becomes a mere penalty with the characteristics of regulation and punishment.'" *Kurth Ranch*, 511 U.S., at 779, 114 S.Ct. 1937 (quoting *Drexel Furniture*, *supra*, at 38, 42 S.Ct. 449).

We have already explained that the shared responsibility payment's practical characteristics pass muster as a tax under our narrowest interpretations of the taxing power. *Supra*, at 2595–2596. Because the tax at hand is within even those strict limits, we need not here decide the precise point at which an exaction becomes so punitive that the taxing power does not authorize it. It remains true, however, that the "'power to tax is not the power to destroy while this Court sits.'" *Oklahoma Tax Comm'n v. Texas Co.*, 336 U.S. 342, 364, 69 S.Ct. 561, 93 L.Ed. 721 (1949) (quoting *Panhandle Oil Co. v. Mississippi ex rel. Knox*, 277 U.S. 218, 223, 48 S.Ct. 451, 72 L.Ed. 857 (1928) (Holmes, J., dissenting)).

Third, although the breadth of Congress's power to tax is greater than its power to regulate commerce, the taxing power does not give Congress the same degree of control over individual behavior. Once we recognize that Congress may regulate a particular decision under the Commerce Clause, the Federal Government can bring its full weight to bear. Congress may simply command individuals to do as it directs. An individual who disobeys may be subjected to criminal sanctions. Those sanctions can include not only fines and imprisonment, but all the attendant consequences of being branded a criminal: deprivation of otherwise protected civil rights, such as the right to bear arms or vote in elections; loss of employment opportunities; social stigma; and severe disabilities in other controversies, such as custody or immigration disputes.

By contrast, Congress's authority under the taxing power is limited to requiring an individual to pay money into the Federal Treasury, no more. If a tax is properly paid, the Government has no power to compel or punish individuals subject to it. We do not make light of the severe burden that taxation — especially taxation motivated by a regulatory purpose — can impose. But imposition of a tax nonetheless leaves an individual with a lawful choice to do or not do a certain act, so long as he is willing to pay a tax levied on that choice.

The Affordable Care Act's requirement that certain individuals pay a financial penalty for not obtaining health insurance may reasonably be characterized as a tax. Because the Constitution permits such a tax, it is not our role to forbid it, or to pass upon its wisdom or fairness.

IV

A

The States also contend that the Medicaid expansion exceeds Congress's authority under the Spending Clause. They claim that Congress is coercing the States to adopt the changes it wants by threatening to withhold all of a State's Medicaid grants, unless the State accepts the new expanded funding and complies with the conditions that come with it. This, they argue, violates the basic principle that the "Federal Government may not compel the States to enact or administer a federal regulatory program." *New York,* 505 U.S., at 188, 112 S.Ct. 2408.

There is no doubt that the Act dramatically increases state obligations under Medicaid. The current Medicaid program requires States to cover only certain discrete categories of needy individuals—pregnant women, children, needy families, the blind, the elderly, and the disabled. 42 U.S.C. § 1396a(a)(10). There is no mandatory coverage for most childless adults, and the States typically do not offer any such coverage. The States also enjoy considerable flexibility with respect to the coverage levels for parents of needy families. § 1396a(a)(10)(A)(ii). On average States cover only those unemployed parents who make less than 37 percent of the federal poverty level, and only those employed parents who make less than 63 percent of the poverty line. Kaiser Comm'n on Medicaid and the Uninsured, Performing Under Pressure 11, and fig. 11 (2012).

The Medicaid provisions of the Affordable Care Act, in contrast, require States to expand their Medicaid programs by 2014 to cover *all* individuals under the age of 65 with incomes below 133 percent of the federal poverty line. § 1396a(a)(10)(A)(i)(VIII). The Act also establishes a new "[e]ssential health benefits" package, which States must provide to all new Medicaid recipients—a level sufficient to satisfy a recipient's obligations under the individual mandate. §§ 1396a(k)(1), 1396u-7(b)(5), 18022(b). The Affordable Care Act provides that the Federal Government will pay 100 percent of the costs of covering these newly eligible individuals through 2016. § 1396d(y)(1). In the following years, the federal payment level gradually decreases, to a minimum of 90 percent. *Ibid.* In light of the expansion in coverage mandated by the Act, the Federal Government estimates that its Medicaid spending will increase by approximately $100 billion per year, nearly 40 percent above current levels. Statement of Douglas W. Elmendorf, CBO's Analysis of the Major Health Care Legislation Enacted in March 2010, p. 14, Table 2 (Mar. 30, 2011).

The Spending Clause grants Congress the power "to pay the Debts and provide for the ... general Welfare of the United States." U.S. Const., Art. I, § 8, cl. 1. We have long recognized that Congress may use this power to grant federal funds to the States, and may condition such a grant upon the States' "taking certain actions that Congress could not require them to take." *College Savings Bank,* 527 U.S., at 686, 119 S.Ct. 2219. Such measures "encourage a State to regulate in a particular way, [and] influenc[e] a State's policy choices." *New York, supra,* at 166, 112 S.Ct. 2408. The conditions imposed by Congress ensure that the funds are used by the States to "provide for the ... general Welfare" in the manner Congress intended.

At the same time, our cases have recognized limits on Congress's power under the Spending Clause to secure state compliance with federal objectives. "We have repeatedly characterized ... Spending Clause legislation as 'much in the nature of a *contract.*'" *Barnes v. Gorman*, 536 U.S. 181, 186, 122 S.Ct. 2097, 153 L.Ed.2d 230 (2002) (quoting *Pennhurst State School and Hospital v. Halderman*, 451 U.S. 1, 17, 101 S.Ct. 1531, 67 L.Ed.2d 694 (1981)). The legitimacy of Congress's exercise of the spending power "thus rests on whether the State voluntarily and knowingly accepts the terms of the 'contract.'" *Pennhurst, supra*, at 17, 101 S.Ct. 1531. Respecting this limitation is critical to ensuring that Spending Clause legislation does not undermine the status of the States as independent sovereigns in our federal system. That system "rests on what might at first seem a counter-intuitive insight, that 'freedom is enhanced by the creation of two governments, not one.'" *Bond*, 564 U.S., at ___, 131 S.Ct., at 2364 (quoting *Alden v. Maine*, 527 U.S. 706, 758, 119 S.Ct. 2240, 144 L.Ed.2d 636 (1999)). For this reason, "the Constitution has never been understood to confer upon Congress the ability to require the States to govern according to Congress' instructions." *New York, supra*, at 162, 112 S.Ct. 2408. Otherwise the two-government system established by the Framers would give way to a system that vests power in one central government, and individual liberty would suffer.

That insight has led this Court to strike down federal legislation that commandeers a State's legislative or administrative apparatus for federal purposes. See, *e.g.*, *Printz*, 521 U.S., at 933, 117 S.Ct. 2365 (striking down federal legislation compelling state law enforcement officers to perform federally mandated background checks on handgun purchasers); *New York, supra*, at 174–175, 112 S.Ct. 2408 (invalidating provisions of an Act that would compel a State to either take title to nuclear waste or enact particular state waste regulations). It has also led us to scrutinize Spending Clause legislation to ensure that Congress is not using financial inducements to exert a "power akin to undue influence." *Steward Machine Co. v. Davis*, 301 U.S. 548, 590, 57 S.Ct. 883, 81 L.Ed. 1279 (1937). Congress may use its spending power to create incentives for States to act in accordance with federal policies. But when "pressure turns into compulsion," *ibid.*, the legislation runs contrary to our system of federalism. "[T]he Constitution simply does not give Congress the authority to require the States to regulate." *New York*, 505 U.S., at 178, 112 S.Ct. 2408. That is true whether Congress directly commands a State to regulate or indirectly coerces a State to adopt a federal regulatory system as its own.

Permitting the Federal Government to force the States to implement a federal program would threaten the political accountability key to our federal system. "[W]here the Federal Government directs the States to regulate, it may be state officials who will bear the brunt of public disapproval, while the federal officials who devised the regulatory program may remain insulated from the electoral ramifications of their decision." *Id.*, at 169, 112 S.Ct. 2408. Spending Clause programs do not pose this danger when a State has a legitimate choice whether to accept the federal conditions in exchange for federal funds. In such a situation, state officials can fairly be held politically accountable for choosing to accept or refuse the federal offer. But when the State has no choice, the Federal Government can achieve its objectives without accountability, just as in *New York* and *Printz*. Indeed, this danger is heightened when Congress acts under the Spending Clause, because Congress can use that power to implement federal policy it could not impose directly under its enumerated powers.

*** As our decision in *Steward Machine* confirms, Congress may attach appropriate conditions to federal taxing and spending programs to preserve its control over the use of federal funds. In the typical case we look to the States to defend their prerogatives by adopting "the simple expedient of not yielding" to federal blandishments when they do not want to embrace the federal policies as their own. *Massachusetts v. Mellon*, 262 U.S. 447, 482, 43 S.Ct. 597, 67 L.Ed. 1078 (1923). The States are separate and independent sovereigns. Sometimes they have to act like it.

The States, however, argue that the Medicaid expansion is far from the typical case. They object that Congress has "crossed the line distinguishing encouragement from coercion," *New York, supra*, at 175, 112 S.Ct. 2408, in the way it has structured the funding: Instead of simply refusing to grant the new funds to States that will not accept the new conditions, Congress has also threatened to withhold those States' existing Medicaid funds. The States claim that this threat serves no purpose other than to force unwilling States to sign up for the dramatic expansion in health care coverage effected by the Act.

Given the nature of the threat and the programs at issue here, we must agree. We have upheld Congress's authority to condition the receipt of funds on the States' complying with restrictions on the use of those funds, because that is the means by which Congress ensures that the funds are spent according to its view of the "general Welfare." Conditions that do not here govern the use of the funds, however, cannot be justified on that basis. When, for example, such conditions take the form of threats to terminate other significant independent grants, the conditions are properly viewed as a means of pressuring the States to accept policy changes.

In *South Dakota v. Dole*, we considered a challenge to a federal law that threatened to withhold five percent of a State's federal highway funds if the State did not raise its drinking age to 21. The Court found that the condition was "directly related to one of the main purposes for which highway funds are expended—safe interstate travel." 483 U.S., at 208, 107 S.Ct. 2793. At the same time, the condition was not a restriction on how the highway funds—set aside for specific highway improvement and maintenance efforts—were to be used.

We accordingly asked whether "the financial inducement offered by Congress" was "so coercive as to pass the point at which 'pressure turns into compulsion.'" *Id.*, at 211, 107 S.Ct. 2793 (quoting *Steward Machine, supra*, at 590, 57 S.Ct. 883). By "financial inducement" the Court meant the threat of losing five percent of highway funds; no new money was offered to the States to raise their drinking ages. We found that the inducement was not impermissibly coercive, because Congress was offering only "relatively mild encouragement to the States." *Dole*, 483 U.S., at 211, 107 S.Ct. 2793. We observed that "all South Dakota would lose if she adheres to her chosen course as to a suitable minimum drinking age is 5%" of her highway funds. *Ibid.* In fact, the federal funds at stake constituted less than half of one percent of South Dakota's budget at the time. See Nat. Assn. of State Budget Officers, The State Expenditure Report 59 (1987); *South Dakota v. Dole*, 791 F.2d 628, 630 (C.A.8 1986). In consequence, "we conclude[d] that [the] encouragement to state action [was] a valid use of the spending power." *Dole*, 483 U.S., at 212, 107 S.Ct. 2793. Whether to accept the drinking age change "remain[ed] the prerogative of the States not merely in theory but in fact." *Id.*, at 211–212, 107 S.Ct. 2793.

In this case, the financial "inducement" Congress has chosen is much more than "relatively mild encouragement"—it is a gun to the head. Section 1396c of the Medicaid Act provides that if a State's Medicaid plan does not comply with the Act's requirements, the Secretary of Health and Human Services may declare that "further payments will not be made to the State." 42 U.S.C. § 1396c. A State that opts out of the Affordable Care Act's expansion in health care coverage thus stands to lose not merely "a relatively small percentage" of its existing Medicaid funding, but *all* of it. *Dole, supra*, at 211, 107 S.Ct. 2793. Medicaid spending accounts for over 20 percent of the average State's total budget, with federal funds covering 50 to 83 percent of those costs. See Nat. Assn. of State Budget Officers, Fiscal Year 2010 State Expenditure Report, p. 11, Table 5 (2011); 42 U.S.C. § 1396d(b). The Federal Government estimates that it will pay out approximately $3.3 trillion between 2010 and 2019 in order to cover the costs of *pre*-expansion Medicaid. Brief for United States 10, n. 6. In addition, the States have developed intricate statutory and administrative regimes over the course of many decades to implement their objectives under existing Medicaid. It is easy to see how the *Dole* Court could conclude that the threatened loss of less than half of one percent of South Dakota's budget left that State with a "prerogative" to reject Congress's desired policy, "not merely in theory but in fact." 483 U.S., at 211–212, 107 S.Ct. 2793. The threatened loss of over 10 percent of a State's overall budget, in contrast, is economic dragooning that leaves the States with no real option but to acquiesce in the Medicaid expansion.

*** As we have explained, "[t]hough Congress' power to legislate under the spending power is broad, it does not include surprising participating States with post-acceptance or 'retroactive' conditions." *Pennhurst, supra*, at 25, 101 S.Ct. 1531. A State could hardly anticipate that Congress's reservation of the right to "alter" or "amend" the Medicaid program included the power to transform it so dramatically.

* * *

B

* * *

The Affordable Care Act is constitutional in part and unconstitutional in part. The individual mandate cannot be upheld as an exercise of Congress's power under the Commerce Clause. That Clause authorizes Congress to regulate interstate commerce, not to order individuals to engage in it. In this case, however, it is reasonable to construe what Congress has done as increasing taxes on those who have a certain amount of income, but choose to go without health insurance. Such legislation is within Congress's power to tax.

As for the Medicaid expansion, that portion of the Affordable Care Act violates the Constitution by threatening existing Medicaid funding. Congress has no authority to order the States to regulate according to its instructions. Congress may offer the States grants and require the States to comply with accompanying conditions, but the States must have a genuine choice whether to accept the offer. The States are given no such choice in this case: They must either accept a basic change in the nature of Medicaid, or risk losing all Medicaid funding. The remedy for that constitutional violation is to preclude the Federal Government from imposing such a sanction. That remedy does not require striking down other portions of the Affordable Care Act.

The Framers created a Federal Government of limited powers, and assigned to this Court the duty of enforcing those limits. The Court does so today. But the Court does not express any opinion on the wisdom of the Affordable Care Act. Under the Constitution, that judgment is reserved to the people.

The judgment of the Court of Appeals for the Eleventh Circuit is affirmed in part and reversed in part.

It is so ordered.

————————

While no longer mandated, states may still choose to expand Medicaid coverage under the ACA following the Supreme Court's decision in *NFIB v. Sebelius*. While the ACA does not mandate expansion, at the risk of lost Medicaid funding for failing to do so, state governors and legislatures may elect to expand coverage to reach the group of people who would otherwise be covered by the ACA. To accomplish this, states may apply for what is known as an "1115 waiver" to the state's administrative plan for Medicaid. As previously noted, Medicaid is a cooperative endeavor between state and federal government. States are allowed some flexibility under Medicaid when shaping their individual Medicaid program, but in order to receive federal Medicaid funding, the state programs must meet established minimum criteria for benefits. While all state plans are obligated to comply with the federal Medicaid minimum criteria, states may request waivers of specific Medicaid standards to implement an "experimental, pilot or demonstration project which, in the judgment of the Secretary, is likely to assist in promoting the objectives of the Social Security Act."[17] The waiver authority is found in Sec. 1115 of the Social Security Act and dates from 1965 when the Social Security Act was amended to establish the Medicaid program. Under Sec. 115, the Secretary of Health and Human Services has the authority to waive specific requirements under the Medicaid program based upon a state showing that the requested waiver will support a test or demonstration project and further the Social Security Act's objectives. The Medicaid program was designed in 1965, *inter alia*, "to furnish (1) medical assistance on behalf of families with dependent children and of

————————

17. 42 U.S.C. § 1315(a) (2018).

aged, blind or disabled individuals, whose income and resources are insufficient to meet the costs of necessary medical services."[18] The ACA expanded the Social Security Act's purpose to include single, childless adults living at or below 133% of the federal poverty line.

The cost of expanding Medicaid under the ACA is largely borne by the federal government, which pays up to 90% of the program's costs. By the end of 2018, 37 states had expanded Medicaid under the ACA to provide healthcare coverage to single, childless adults living at or below 138% of the federal poverty level. Several states have refused to expand coverage.[19] In December 2017, Congress passed a tax reform bill that eliminated the individual mandate penalty for individuals not having health insurance.[20]

The expansion of Medicaid under the ACA represents a significant policy shift for poverty programs.[21] Prior to the ACA, Medicaid retained the entrenched preference for the "deserving" poor and provided benefits only to categories of poor people who were viewed as deserving of assistance—children, pregnant women, elderly, and the disabled. Generally, the class of poor people who received benefits under Medicaid prior to the ACA was limited to those who could not be seen as responsible for their own poverty. Pre-ACA, Medicaid ignored the needs of poor, able-bodied individuals who fell below or near the federal poverty line and who lacked access to healthcare. As with other poverty policies, including AFDC, food stamps, and public housing, the undeserving poor were locked out and left to their own devices when in need. The ACA took a strikingly different approach. In contrast to established preference for the deserving poor, the ACA unconditionally extended benefits to individuals who had traditionally been seen as undeserving of society's support. Concerns over what impact the ACA might have on work effort or whether access to healthcare would create perverse incentives were mitigated by broader concerns surrounding the right to access healthcare and increased societal benefits from expanded access. As the Supreme Court notes, following the ACA, "Medicaid is no longer a program for the neediest among us."

D. The Children's Health Insurance Program (CHIP)

Congress adopted the State Child Health Insurance Program (SCHIP) in 1997 as part of the 1997 Balanced Budget Act. SCHIP was later renamed the Children's Health

---

18. 42 U.S.C. § 1396-1 (2018).

19. Kaiser Fam. Found., Status of State Medicaid Expansion Decisions: Interactive Map (Nov. 15, 2019), https://www.kff.org/medicaid/issue-brief/status-of-state-medicaid-expansion-decisions-interactive-map/.

20. Elizabeth O'Brien, *The GOP Tax Bill Kills Obamacare's Individual Mandate. Here's What That Means*, Money (Dec. 20, 2017, 12:16 PM), http://time.com/money/5067044/gop-tax-plan-individual-mandate-obamacare/.

21. David Orentlicher, *Medicaid at 50: No Longer Limited to the "Deserving" Poor?*, 15 Yale J. Health Pol'y, L. & Ethics 185 (2015).

Insurance Program (CHIP). Originally authorized for 10 years, CHIP was reauthorized in 2009 and again in 2013 and 2015 through September 2017. CHIP provided funding assistance to states to fund healthcare coverage for children in families whose income was too high for Medicaid and too low to afford private health insurance either independently or through an employer.[22] CHIP thereby expanded healthcare coverage for near-poor children. CHIP was not enacted as an entitlement, in contrast to Medicaid, and federal spending on the program could therefore be controlled on an annual basis.

To ensure that states would continue to adequately fund existing Medicaid programs, CHIP required that states commit to "maintenance of effort" requirements.[23] Under the maintenance of effort requirements, states could not use CHIP funding to replace existing programs or funding. States elect to be part of the CHIP program by submitting a plan to the U.S. Secretary of Health and Human Services, which then allocated funding based on each state's share of the total number of low-income, uninsured children. Children in families below 300% (originally 200%) of the federal poverty level qualify for CHIP benefits. States must also agree to provide matching funds for the program, with the federal government paying between 65% and 85% of the overall cost of insuring a child through CHIP. The federal government allocated $25.5 billion to states between 2015 and 2016. CHIP was due to sunset in September 2017. On January 22, 2018 Congress passed a 10-year extension of the program.

E. Access to Reproductive Healthcare

Slightly more than half the population requires reproductive healthcare—gynecological examinations, prenatal and postpartum care, menstrual products, etc.[24]—but do not always have access or affordable access to such care. Homeless women and women living in poverty often have a harder time accessing or affording reproductive healthcare and access to menstrual products.[25] Many low-income women rely on organizations like Planned Parenthood for access to STI testing and treatment, contraception, cancer screenings, wellness exams, prenatal services, and more.[26]

Even among low-income and homeless women, there are further disparities in reproductive healthcare and access to it. Although healthcare spending in the United States is at least twice as much per capita as in almost every other western industrialized

---

22. Robert F. Rich, Cinthia L. Deye & Elizabeth Mazur, Symposium, *The State Children's Health Insurance Program: An Administrative Experiment in Federalism*, 2004 U. ILL. L. REV. 107, 112.

23. Alison Mitchell & Evelyne P. Baumrucker, *CHIP and the ACA Maintenance of Effort (MOE) Requirement: In Brief*, 7-5700 CONG. RES. SERV. 1, 1–6 (Sept. 16, 2019).

24. CDC, *Reproductive Health: About Us*, https://www.cdc.gov/reproductivehealth/drh/about-us/index.htm (last updated Apr. 3, 2019).

25. Abigail Durkin, *Profitable Menstruation: How the Cost of Feminine Hygiene Products Is a Battle Against Reproductive Justice*, 18 GEO. J. GENDER & L. 131, 138 (2017).

26. *Why Trump's Change to Title X Funding Means Fewer Health Choices for Women*, PBS: NewsHour (Aug. 19, 2019, 6:45PM), https://www.pbs.org/newshour/show/why-trumps-change-to-title-x-funding-means-fewer-health-choices-for-women#transcript.

nation, the United States maintains some of the widest disparities in health outcomes, particularly with respect to health outcomes for women and women of color.[27] African American women die in pregnancy or childbirth at a rate of three to four times the rate of white women.[28] Together, African American women and Latinas account for almost 80% of reported female HIV/AIDS diagnoses in 2017, even though they represent only 25% of the U.S. female population.[29] Almost half of all unintended pregnancies in the United States end in abortion; African American women, who are three times as likely as white women to experience an unintended pregnancy, are also three times as likely as white women to obtain abortion services.[30]

The ability of many homeless women and women in poverty to access reproductive and sexual healthcare services impacts more than just their health outcomes. Many women and girls go without menstrual products because they cannot afford them. Consequently, they are forced to miss work and school[31] or risk embarrassment if they are not properly equipped or allowed to use the bathroom regularly at school.[32] There are many organizations and campaigns that seek to ensure that girls in school, especially, have access to menstrual products—if they do not have to stay home every month when they are on their periods, they can focus and thrive in school.[33]

Government assistance programs, such as SNAP and WIC, do not allow for the purchase of feminine hygiene products with the benefits.[34] Menstrual products are considered "nonfood, paper products" that are not covered under either program. Instead, many women resort to illegally selling their food stamps, in order to have cash to buy tampons or pads.[35] Low-income, homeless, and incarcerated women's access to feminine hygiene products is, in fact, a crisis.

---

27. CENT. FOR REPROD. RTS., ADDRESSING DISPARITIES IN REPRODUCTIVE AND SEXUAL HEALTH CARE IN THE U.S., https://reproductiverights.org/addressing-disparities-reproductive-and-sexual-health-care-us (last visited Oct. 30, 2019).

28. Nina Martin & Renee Montagne, *Black Mothers Keep Dying After Giving Birth. Shalon Irving's Story Explains Why*, NPR (Dec. 17, 2017 7:51 PM) https://www.npr.org/2017/12/07/568948782/black-mothers-keep-dying-after-giving-birth-shalon-irvings-story-explains-why.

29. *HIV Among Women*, CDC, https://www.cdc.gov/hiv/group/gender/women/index.html (last updated Nov. 12, 2019).

30. Susan A. Cohen, *Abortion and Women of Color: The Bigger Picture*, GUTTMACHER POL'Y REV., Summer 2008, at 2–5, https://www.guttmacher.org/sites/default/files/article_files/gpr110302.pdf.

31. Durkin, *supra* note 25, at 132.

32. Doha Madani, *Girls Reportedly Bleeding Through Pants Due to Charter School Bathroom Policy*, HUFFPOST (Apr. 30, 2018, 9:44 PM), https://www.huffingtonpost.com/entry/charter-school-bathroom-policy-periods_us_5ae7a19be4b04aa23f26463c.

33. Morgan Smith & Valerie Strauss, *Activists Call on Education Department to Take Action for "Menstrual Equity,"* WASH. POST (Jan. 28, 2019, 7:13 PM), https://www.washingtonpost.com/local/education/activists-call-on-education-department-to-take-action-for-menstrual-equity/2019/01/28/815c6d08-2349-11e9-90cd-dedb0c92dc17_story.html.

34. USDA, *What Can SNAP Buy?*, https://www.fns.usda.gov/snap/eligible-food-items (last updated Sept. 4, 2013); USDA, *WIC Frequently Asked Questions*, https://www.fns.usda.gov/wic/frequently-asked-questions-about-wic (last updated Aug. 28, 2019).

35. Seth Free Wessler, *Selling Food Stamps for Kids' Shoes*, COLORLINES (Feb. 16, 2010, 12:00 PM), https://www.colorlines.com/articles/selling-food-stamps-kids-shoes.

As of 2017, approximately 219,000 women were incarcerated in federal and state prisons and jails.[36] Incarcerated women often face significant challenges getting access to menstrual products, as well as other reproductive healthcare.[37] Depending on individual prison policies and practices, incarcerated women are often only given minimal menstrual products and do not receive regular gynecological care.[38] In August 2017, the Federal Bureau of Prisons adopted a policy to provide women with a variety of menstrual products at no cost to them. Several states have since introduced similar bills to address access to these products for women incarcerated in state prisons and jails—where the majority of women are incarcerated.[39]

---

36. Aleks Kajstura, Women's Mass Incarceration: The Whole Pie 2017, at 2 (2017), https://www.prisonpolicy.org/reports/pie2017women.html.

37. Kate Walsh, *Inadequate Access: Reforming Reproductive Health Care Policies for Women Incarcerated in New York State Correctional Facilities*, 50 Colum. J.L. & Soc. Probs. 45, 46, 48 (2016).

38. *Id.*

39. Kajstura, *supra* note 36, at 3.

Chapter Nine

Education

Education is a key element to significant individual and community benefits throughout a person's lifetime. Early childhood education leads to higher educational achievement later in life, with higher correlating income throughout a lifetime of work. Individuals who complete secondary education access healthcare more efficiently, manage chronic healthcare needs better, and experience better long-term health outcomes.[1] Those who complete high school earn more than those who don't and they face fewer terms of unemployment.[2] Household savings are higher in families led by high school graduates than they are in families led by adults who do not graduate from high school.[3] Incarceration rates are higher for adults who do not finish high school compared to those who do.[4] Life expectancies are lower for those who do not complete high school compared to those who graduate.[5] By any measure, and perhaps by every measure, the individual and societal benefits of both early childhood education and graduating from high school are significant.

Low-wealth families lack access to public education or only have access to public education systems that are insufficiently funded and face significant burdens. This is due in large part to how public education is funded in the United States, where state and local funding supplies the vast majority of funding for public education. Other factors, including historic racial and ethnic disparities, have exacerbated overall funding inequality.

In the materials that follow, the role of education in enhancing social and economic mobility is discussed. The materials then consider an individual's right to a sound basic education under state law and the treatment of claims that education is not equally available to low-wealth students under federal law. In the cases that address

---

1. *See* Robert A. Hahn, *Education Improves Public Health and Promotes Health Equity*, 45 Int. J. Health Servs. 657 (2015).

2. Christopher S. Rugaber, *Pay Gap between College Grads and Everyone Else at a Record*, USA Today (Jan. 2, 2017 1:59 PM), https://www.usatoday.com/story/money/2017/01/12/pay-gap-between-college-grads-and-everyone-else-record/96493348/.

3. *See* Peter G. Peterson Found., Income and Wealth in the United States: An Overview of Recent Data (Oct. 4, 2019), https://www.pgpf.org/blog/2019/10/income-and-wealth-in-the-united-states-an-overview-of-data.

4. Andrew Sum et al., Northeastern U. Ctr. for Labor Market Stud., The Consequences of Dropping Out of High School (Oct. 2009), https://repository.library.northeastern.edu/downloads/neu:376324?datastream_id=content.

5. Robert A. Hummer & Elaine M. Hernandez, *The Effect of Educational Attainment on Adult Mortality in the United States*, Population Bull., June 2013, at 1.

federal claims, the Supreme Court devises a clear analysis of poverty and the role of judicial review when considering the quality of public education available to low-wealth children.

A. Education and Social and Economic Mobility

In the area of education, poverty engages in a powerful feedback loop. First, poverty significantly affects a child's development and educational outcomes beginning at the earliest stages of life. A child's ability to use and profit from school plays a profound role in moving children from poverty in the United States, as witnessed by the outcomes seen in children who participate in Headstart programs prior to formal education.[6] But early experiences with poverty, however, reduce the likelihood a child will be ready for school when they are old enough for kindergarten, leading to critical losses over the course of the child's education.

> The association between poverty and children's development and academic performance has been well documented, beginning as early as the second year of life, and extending through elementary and high school. When these risks occur during preschool years, they can have long-lasting consequences. For example, readiness for school on entry to kindergarten sets the trajectory for future success. School readiness is critical to later academic achievement because differences on school entry have long-term consequences. Lee and Burkman, found that most American students who start school significantly behind their peers can never close the readiness gap. Rather, the gap tends to widen as they move through school. "School readiness has been shown to be predictive of virtually every educational benchmark (e.g., achievement test scores, grade retention, special education placement, dropout, etc.)". The consequences of early school failure are increased likelihood of truancy, drop out, and unhealthy or delinquent behaviors. Between 30 and 40% of children entering kindergarten in the United States are estimated to not be ready for school. The link between poverty and low academic achievement has been well established. Low-income children are at increased risk of leaving school without graduating, resulting in inflation-adjusted earnings in the United States that declined 16% from 1979 to 2005, averaging slightly over $10/hour. Evidence from the National Institute of Child Health and Human Development Early Child Care Research Network has shown that children in chronically impoverished families have lower cognitive and academic performance and more behavior problems than children who are not exposed to poverty, partially explained by a lack of stimulating behaviors and home experiences among low-income families.[7]

---

6. Patrice L. Engle & Maureen M. Black, *The Effect of Poverty on Child Development and Educational Outcomes*, 1136 Ann. N.Y. Acad. Sci. 243, 250 (2008).

7. *Id.* at 244.

In turn, a worker's education level has become an increasingly important factor for obtaining an adequately paying job and mitigating income disparities.[8]

State constitutions have promised some form of public education to their citizens for more than 200 years. Many state governments have been less than successful in fulfilling this promise. The mechanisms for funding public education have created significant challenges to both students and the governments obligated to provide access to education. Traditionally, public education has been financed largely through property taxes, resulting in wide disparities among the education opportunities, quality of instruction, and resources offered to poor and nonpoor children based on the real estate value of the property where the children live. A counter to such differences would be for the courts to recognize a right to a public education. Whether poor children have a right to receive a sound, basic education regardless of the ability of local governments to finance such an education for all children is a question that may have different answers depending on the source of the alleged right.

B. The Right to a Public Education under the U.S. Constitution

San Antonio Independent School District v. Rodriguez
411 U.S. 1 (1972)

This suit attacking the Texas system of financing public education was initiated by Mexican-American parents whose children attend the elementary and secondary schools in the Edgewood Independent School District, an urban school district in San Antonio, Texas. They brought a class action on behalf of schoolchildren throughout the State who are members of minority groups or who are poor and reside in school districts having a low property tax base. Named as defendants were the State Board of Education, the Commissioner of Education, the State Attorney General, and the Bexar County Board of Trustees.... In December 1971 the [District Court] rendered its judgment in a per curiam opinion holding the Texas school finance system unconstitutional under the Equal Protection Clause of the Fourteenth Amendment. The State appealed, and we noted probable jurisdiction to consider the far-reaching constitutional questions presented. For the reasons stated in this opinion, we reverse the decision of the District Court.

I

The first Texas State Constitution, promulgated upon Texas' entry into the Union in 1845, provided for the establishment of a system of free schools. Early in its history, Texas adopted a dual approach to the financing of its schools, relying on mutual participation by the local school districts and the State. As early as 1883, the state con-

---

8. David H. Autor, Lawrence F. Katz & Melissa S. Kearney, *Trends in U.S. Wage Inequality: Revising the Revisionists*, 90 Rev. Econ. & Stat. 300 (2008).

stitution was amended to provide for the creation of local school districts empowered to levy ad valorem taxes with the consent of local taxpayers for the 'erection ... of school buildings' and for the 'further maintenance of public free schools.' Such local funds as were raised were supplemented by funds distributed to each district from the State's Permanent and Available School Funds. The Permanent School Fund, its predecessor established in 1854 with $2,000,000 realized from an annexation settlement, was thereafter endowed with millions of acres of public land set aside to assure a continued source of income for school support. The Available School Fund, which received income from the Permanent School Fund as well as from a state ad valorem property tax and other designated taxes, served as the disbursing arm for most state educational funds throughout the late 1800's and first half of this century. Additionally, in 1918 an increase in state property taxes was used to finance a program providing free textbooks throughout the State.

Until recent times, Texas was a predominantly rural State and its population and property wealth were spread relatively evenly across the State. Sizable differences in the value of assessable property between local school districts became increasingly evident as the State became more industrialized and as rural-to-urban population shifts became more pronounced. The location of commercial and industrial property began to play a significant role in determining the amount of tax resources available to each school district. These growing disparities in population and taxable property between districts were responsible in part for increasingly notable differences in levels of local expenditure for education.

In due time it became apparent to those concerned with financing public education that contributions from the Available School Fund were not sufficient to ameliorate these disparities. Prior to 1939, the Available School Fund contributed money to every school district at a rate of $17.50 per school-age child. Although the amount was increased several times in the early 1940's, the Fund was providing only $46 per student by 1945.

Recognizing the need for increased state funding to help offset disparities in local spending and to meet Texas' changing educational requirements, the state legislature in the late 1940's undertook a thorough evaluation of public education with an eye toward major reform. In 1947, an 18-member committee, composed of educators and legislators, was appointed to explore alternative systems in other States and to propose a funding scheme that would guarantee a minimum or basic educational offering to each child and that would help overcome interdistrict disparities in taxable resources. The Committee's efforts led to the passage of the Gilmer-Aikin bills, named for the Committee's co-chairmen, establishing the Texas Minimum Foundation School Program. Today, this Program accounts for approximately half of the total educational expenditures in Texas.

The Program calls for state and local contributions to a fund earmarked specifically for teacher salaries, operating expenses, and transportation costs. The State, supplying funds from its general revenues, finances approximately 80% of the Program, and the school districts are responsible—as a unit—for providing the remaining 20%.

The districts' share, known as the Local Fund Assignment, is apportioned among the school districts under a formula designed to reflect each district's relative taxpaying ability. The Assignment is first divided among Texas' 254 counties pursuant to a complicated economic index that takes into account the relative value of each county's contribution to the State's total income from manufacturing, mining, and agricultural activities. It also considers each county's relative share of all payrolls paid within the State and, to a lesser extent, considers each county's share of all property in the State. Each county's assignment is then divided among its school districts on the basis of each district's share of assessable property within the county. The district, in turn, finances its share of the Assignment out of revenues from local property taxation.

The design of this complex system was twofold. First, it was an attempt to assure that the Foundation Program would have an equalizing influence on expenditure levels between school districts by placing the heaviest burden on the school districts most capable of paying. Second, the Program's architects sought to establish a Local Fund Assignment that would force every school district to contribute to the education of its children but that would not by itself exhaust any district's resources. Today every school district does impose a property tax from which it derives locally expendable funds in excess of the amount necessary to satisfy its Local Fund Assignment under the Foundation Program.

In the years since this program went into operation in 1949, expenditures for education—from state as well as local sources—have increased steadily. Between 1949 and 1967, expenditures increased approximately 500%. In the last decade alone the total public school budget rose from $750 million to.$2.1 billion and these increases have been reflected in consistently rising per pupil expenditures throughout the State. Teacher salaries, by far the largest item in any school's budget, have increased dramatically—the state-supported minimum salary for teachers possessing college degrees has risen from $2,400 to $6,000 over the last 20 years.

The school district in which appellees reside, the Edgewood Independent School District, has been compared throughout this litigation with the Alamo Heights Independent School District. This comparison between the least and most affluent districts in the San Antonio area serves to illustrate the manner in which the dual system of finance operates and to indicate the extent to which substantial disparities exist despite the State's impressive progress in recent years. Edgewood is one of seven public school districts in the metropolitan area. Approximately 22,000 students are enrolled in its 25 elementary and secondary schools. The district is are enrolled in its 25 elementary situated in the core-city sector of San Antonio in a residential neighborhood that has little commercial or industrial property. The residents are predominantly of Mexican-American descent: approximately 90% of the student population is Mexican-American and over 6% is Negro. The average assessed property value per pupil is $5,960—the lowest in the metropolitan area—and the median family income ($4,686) is also the lowest. At an equalized tax rate of $1.05 per $100 of assessed property—the highest in the metropolitan area—the district contributed $26 to the education of each child for the 1967–1968 school year above its Local Fund Assignment for the Minimum Foundation Program. The Foundation Program contributed $222 per pupil for a state-local total of $248. Federal funds added another $108 for a total of $356 per pupil.

Alamo Heights is the most affluent school district in San Antonio. Its six schools, housing approximately 5,000 students, are situated in a residential community quite unlike the Edgewood District. The school population is predominantly 'Anglo,' having only 18% Mexican-Americans and less than 1% Negroes. The assessed property value per pupil exceeds $49,000, and the median family income is $8,001. In 1967–1968 the local tax rate of $.85 per $100 of valuation yielded $333 per pupil over and above its contribution to the Foundation Program. Coupled with the $225 provided from that Program, the district was able to supply $558 per student. Supplemented by a $36 per-pupil grant from federal sources, Alamo Heights spent $594 per pupil.

Although the 1967–1968 school year figures provide the only complete statistical breakdown for each category of aid, more recent partial statistics indicate that the previously noted trend of increasing state aid has been significant. For the 1970–1971 school year, the Foundation School Program allotment for Edgewood was $356 per pupil, a 62% increase over the 1967–68 school year. Indeed, state aid alone in 1970–1971 equaled Edgewood's entire 1967–1968 school budget from local, state, and federal sources. Alamo Heights enjoyed a similar increase under the Foundation Program, netting $491 per pupil in 1970–1971. These recent figures also reveal the extent to which these two districts' allotments were funded from their own required contributions to the Local Fund Assignment. Alamo Heights, because of its relative wealth, was required to contribute out of its local property tax collections approximately $100 per pupil, or about 20% of its Foundation grant. Edgewood, on the other hand, paid only $8.46 per pupil, which is about 2.4% of its grant. It appears then that, at least as to these two districts, the Local Fund Assignment does reflect a rough approximation of the relative taxpaying potential of each.

Despite these recent increases, substantial interdistrict disparities in school expenditures found by the District Court to prevail in San Antonio and in varying degrees throughout the State still exist. And it was these disparities, largely attributable to differences in the amounts of money collected through local property taxation, that led the District Court to conclude that Texas' dual system of public school financing violated the Equal Protection Clause. The District Court held that the Texas system discriminates on the basis of wealth in the manner in which education is provided for its people. Finding that wealth is a 'suspect' classification and that education is a 'fundamental' interest, the District Court held that the Texas system could be sustained only if the State could show that it was premised upon some compelling state interest. On this issue the court concluded that '(n)ot only are defendants unable to demonstrate compelling state interests ... they fail even to establish a reasonable basis for these classifications.'

Texas virtually concedes that its historically rooted dual system of financing education could not withstanding the strict judicial scrutiny that this Court has found appropriate in reviewing legislative judgments that interfere with fundamental constitutional rights or that involve suspect classifications. If, as previous decisions have indicated, strict scrutiny means that the State's system is not entitled to the usual presumption of validity, that the State rather than the complainants must carry a 'heavy burden of justification,' that the State must demonstrate that its educational system has been structured with 'precision,' and is 'tailored' narrowly to serve legitimate objectives and that it has selected the 'less drastic means' for effectuating its objectives, the Texas financing system and its counterpart in virtually every other State will not pass muster. The State candidly admits that '(n)o one familiar with the Texas system would contend that it has yet achieved perfection.' Apart from its concession that educational financing in Texas has 'defects' and 'imperfections,' the State defends the system's rationality with vigor and disputes the District Court's finding that it lacks a 'reasonable basis.'

This, then, establishes the framework for our analysis. We must decide, first, whether the Texas system of financing public education operates to the disadvantage of some suspect class or impinges upon a fundamental right explicitly or implicitly protected by the Constitution, thereby requiring strict judicial scrutiny. If so, the judgment of the District Court should be affirmed. If not, the Texas scheme must still be examined to determine whether it rationally furthers some legitimate, articulated state purpose and therefore does not constitute an invidious discrimination in violation of the Equal Protection Clause of the Fourteenth Amendment.

II

The District Court's opinion does not reflect the novelty and complexity of the constitutional questions posed by appellees' challenge to Texas' system of school financing. In concluding that strict judicial scrutiny was required, that court relied on decisions dealing with the rights of indigents to equal treatment in the criminal trial and appellate processes, and on cases disapproving wealth restrictions on the right to vote. Those cases, the District Court concluded, established wealth as a suspect classification. Finding that the local property tax system discriminated on the basis of wealth, it regarded those precedents as controlling. It then reasoned, based on decisions of this Court affirming the undeniable importance of education, that there is a fundamental right to education and that, absent some compelling state justification, the Texas system could not stand.

We are unable to agree that this case, which in significant aspects is sui generis, may be so neatly fitted into the conventional mosaic of constitutional analysis under the Equal Protection Clause. Indeed, for the several reasons that follow, we find neither the suspect-classification nor the fundamental-interest analysis persuasive.

A

The wealth discrimination discovered by the District Court in this case, and by several other courts that have recently struck down school-financing laws in other States, is quite unlike any of the forms of wealth discrimination heretofore reviewed by this Court. Rather than focusing on the unique features of the alleged discrimination, the courts in these cases have virtually assumed their findings of a suspect classification through a simplistic process of analysis: since, under the traditional systems of financing public schools, some poorer people receive less expensive educations than other more affluent people, these systems discriminate on the basis of wealth. This approach largely ignores the hard threshold questions, including whether it makes a difference for purposes of consideration under the Constitution that the class of disadvantaged 'poor' cannot be identified or defined in customary equal protection terms, and whether the relative—rather than absolute—nature of the asserted deprivation is of significant consequence. Before a State's laws and the justifications for the classifications they create are subjected to strict judicial scrutiny, we think these threshold considerations must be analyzed more closely than they were in the court below.

The case comes to us with no definitive description of the classifying facts or delineation of the disfavored class. Examination of the District Court's opinion and of appellees' complaint, briefs, and contentions at oral argument suggests, however, at least three ways in which the discrimination claimed here might be described. The Texas system of school financing might be regarded as discriminating (1) against 'poor' persons whose incomes fall below some identifiable level of poverty or who might be characterized as functionally 'indigent,' or (2) against those who are relatively poorer than others, or (3) against all those who, irrespective of their personal incomes, happen to reside in relatively poorer school districts. Our task must be to ascertain whether, in fact, the Texas system has been shown to discriminate on any of these possible bases and, if so, whether the resulting classification may be regarded as suspect.

The precedents of this Court provide the proper starting point. The individuals, or groups of individuals, who constituted the class discriminated against in our prior cases shared two distinguishing characteristics: because of their impecunity they were completely unable to pay for some desired benefit, and as a consequence, they sustained an absolute deprivation of a meaningful opportunity to enjoy that benefit. In Griffin v. Illinois, and its progeny, the Court invalidated state laws that prevented an indigent criminal defendant from acquiring a transcript, or an adequate substitute for a transcript, for use at several stages of the trial and appeal process. The payment requirements in each case were found to occasion de facto discrimination against those who, because of their indigence, were totally unable to pay for transcripts. And the Court in each case emphasized that no constitutional violation would have been shown if the State had provided some 'adequate substitute' for a full stenographic transcript.

* * *

Only appellees' first possible basis for describing the class disadvantaged by the Texas school-financing system—discrimination against a class of definably 'poor' persons—might arguably meet the criteria established in these prior cases. Even a cursory examination, however, demonstrates that neither of the two distinguishing characteristics of wealth classifications can be found here. First, in support of their charge that the system discriminates against the 'poor,' appellees have made no effort to demonstrate that it operates to the peculiar disadvantage of any class fairly definable as indigent, or as composed of persons whose incomes are beneath any designated poverty level. Indeed, there is reason to believe that the poorest families are not necessarily clustered in the poorest property districts. A recent and exhaustive study of school districts in Connecticut concluded that '(i)t is clearly incorrect ... to contend that the 'poor' live in 'poor' districts.... Thus, the major factual assumption of Serrano—that the educational financing system discriminates against the 'poor'—is simply false in Connecticut.' Defining 'poor' families as those below the Bureau of the Census 'poverty level,' the Connecticut study found, not surprisingly, that the poor were clustered around commercial and industrial areas—those same areas that provide the most attractive sources of property tax income for school districts. Whether a similar pattern would be discovered in Texas is not known, but there is no basis on the record in this case for assuming that the poorest people—defined by reference to any level of absolute impecunity—are concentrated in the poorest districts.

Second, neither appellees nor the District Court addressed the fact that, unlike each of the foregoing cases, lack of personal resources has not occasioned an absolute deprivation of the desired benefit. The argument here is not that the children in districts having relatively low assessable property values are receiving no public education; rather, it is that they are receiving a poorer quality education than that available to children in districts having more assessable wealth. Apart from the unsettled and disputed question whether the quality of education may be determined by the amount of money expended for it, a sufficient answer to appellees' argument is that, at least where wealth is involved, the Equal Protection Clause does not require absolute equality or precisely equal advantages. Nor indeed, in view of the infinite variables affecting the educational process, can any system assure equal quality of education except in the most relative sense. Texas asserts that the Minimum Foundation Program provides an 'adequate' education for all children in the State. By providing 12 years of free public-school education, and by assuring teachers, books, transportation, and operating funds, the Texas Legislature has endeavored to 'guarantee, for the welfare of the state as a whole, that all people shall have at least an adequate program of education. This is what is meant by 'A Minimum Foundation Program of Education." The State repeatedly asserted in its briefs in this Court that it has fulfilled this desire and that it now assures 'every child in every school district an adequate education.' No proof was offered at trial persuasively discrediting or refuting the State's assertion.

For these two reasons—the absence of any evidence that the financing system discriminates against any definable category of 'poor' people or that it results in the absolute deprivation of education—the disadvantaged class is not susceptible of identification in traditional terms.

As suggested above, appellees and the District Court may have embraced a second or third approach, the second of which might be characterized as a theory of relative or comparative discrimination based on family income. Appellees sought to prove that a direct correlation exists between the wealth of families within each district and the expenditures therein for education. That is, along a continuum, the poorer the family the lower the dollar amount of education received by the family's children.

The principal evidence adduced in support of this comparative-discrimination claim is an affidavit submitted by Professor Joele S. Berke of Syracuse University's Educational Finance Policy Institute. The District Court, relying in major part upon this affidavit and apparently accepting the substance of appellees' theory, noted, first, a positive correlation between the wealth of school districts, measured in terms of assessable property per pupil, and their levels of per-pupil expenditures. Second, the court found a similar correlation between district wealth and the personal wealth of its residents, measured in terms of median family income.

If, in fact, these correlations could be sustained, then it might be argued that ex-penditures on education — equated by appellees to the quality of education — are dependent on personal wealth. Appellees' comparative-discrimination theory would still face serious unanswered questions, including whether a bare positive correlation or some higher degree of correlation is necessary to provide a basis for concluding that the financing system is designed to operate to the peculiar disadvantage of the comparatively poor, and whether a class of this size and diversity could ever claim the special protection accorded 'suspect' classes. These questions need not be addressed in this case, however, since appellees' proof fails to support their allegations or the District Court's conclusions.

Professor Berke's affidavit is based on a survey of approximately 10% of the school districts in Texas. His findings, previously set out in the margin, show only that the wealthiest few districts in the sample have the highest median family in-comes and spend the most on education, and that the several poorest districts have the lowest family incomes and devote the least amount of money to education. For the remainder of the districts — 96 districts composing almost 90% of the sam-ple — the correlation is inverted, i.e., the districts that spend next to the most money on education are populated by families having next to the lowest median family incomes while the districts spending the least have the highest median family in-comes. It is evident that, even if the conceptual questions were answered favorably to appellees, no factual basis exists upon which to found a claim of comparative wealth discrimination.

This brings us, then, to the third way in which the classification scheme might be defined — district wealth discrimination. Since the only correlation indicated by the evidence is between district property wealth and expenditures, it may be argued that discrimination might be found without regard to the individual income characteristics of district residents. Assuming a perfect correlation between district property wealth and expenditures from top to bottom, the disadvantaged class might be viewed as encompassing every child in every district except the district that has the most as-sessable wealth and spends the most on education....

However described, it is clear that appellees' suit asks this Court to extend its most exacting scrutiny to review a system that allegedly discriminates against a large, diverse, and amorphous class, unified only by the common factor of residence in districts that happen to have less taxable wealth than other districts. The system of alleged discrimination and the class it defines have none of the traditional indicia of suspectness: the class is not saddled with such disabilities, or subjected to such a history of purposeful unequal treatment, or relegated to such a position of political powerlessness as to command extraordinary protection from the majoritarian political process.

We thus conclude that the Texas system does not operate to the peculiar disadvantage of any suspect class. But in recognition of the fact that this Court has never heretofore held that wealth discrimination alone provides an adequate basis for invoking strict scrutiny, appellees have not relied solely on this contention. They also assert that the State's system impermissibly interferes with the exercise of a 'fundamental' right and that accordingly the prior decisions of this Court require the application of the strict standard of judicial review. It is this question—whether education is a fundamental right, in the sense that it is among the rights and liberties protected by the Constitution—which has so consumed the attention of courts and commentators in recent years.

B

In Brown v. Board of Education, a unanimous Court recognized that 'education is perhaps the most important function of state and local governments.' What was said there in the context of racial discrimination has lost none of its vitality with the passage of time: "Compulsory school attendance laws and the great expenditures for education both demonstrate our recognition of the importance of education to our democratic society. It is required in the performance of our most basic public responsibilities, even service in the armed forces. It is the very foundation of good citizenship. Today it is a principal instrument in awakening the child to cultural values, in preparing him for later professional training, and in helping him to adjust normally to his environment. In these days, it is doubtful that any child may reasonably be expected to succeed in life if he is denied the opportunity of an education. Such an opportunity, where the state has undertaken to provide it, is a right which must be made available to all on equal terms." Ibid.

This theme, expressing an abiding respect for the vital role of education in a free society, may be found in numerous opinions of Justices of this Court writing both before and after Brown was decided.

Nothing this Court holds today in any way detracts from our historic dedication to public education. We are in complete agreement with the conclusion of the three-judge panel below that 'the grave significance of education both to the individual and to our society' cannot be doubted. But the importance of a service performed by the State does not determine whether it must be regarded as fundamental for purposes of examination under the Equal Protection Clause. Mr. Justice Harlan, dissenting from the Court's application of strict scrutiny to a law impinging upon the right of interstate travel, admonished that '(v)irtually every state statute affects important rights.' Shapiro v. Thompson. In his view, if the degree of judicial scrutiny of state legislation fluctuated, depending on a majority's view of the importance of the interest affected, we would have gone 'far toward making this Court a 'super-legislature.'" Ibid.

We would, indeed, then be assuming a legislative role and one for which the Court lacks both authority and competence. But Mr. Justice Stewart's response in Shapiro to Mr. Justice Harlan's concern correctly articulates the limits of the fundamental-rights rationale employed in the Court's equal protection decisions:

'The Court today does not 'pick out particular human activities, characterize them as 'fundamental,' and give them added protection.... 'To the contrary, the Court simply recognizes, as it must, an established constitutional right, and gives to that right no less protection than the Constitution itself demands.'

Mr. Justice Stewart's statement serves to underline what the opinion of the Court in Shapiro makes clear. In subjecting to strict judicial scrutiny state welfare eligibility statutes that imposed a one-year durational residency requirement as a precondition to receiving AFDC benefits, the Court explained:

'(I)n moving from State to State ... appellees were exercising a constitutional right, and any classification which serves to penalize the exercise of that right, unless shown to be necessary to promote a compelling governmental interest, is unconstitutional.'

The right to interstate travel had long been recognized as a right of constitutional significance, and the Court's decision, therefore, did not require an ad hoc determination as to the social or economic importance of that right.

Lindsey v. Normet, decided only last Term, firmly reiterates that social importance is not the critical determinant for subjecting state legislation to strict scrutiny. The complainants in that case, involving a challenge to the procedural limitations imposed on tenants in suits brought by landlords under Oregon's Forcible Entry and Wrongful Detainer Law, urged the Court to examine the operation of the statute under 'a more stringent standard than mere rationality.' The tenants argued that the statutory limitations implicated 'fundamental interests which are particularly important to the poor,' such as the "need for decent shelter" and the "right to retain peaceful possession of one's home." Ibid. Mr. Justice White's analysis, in his opinion for the Court is instructive:

'We do not denigrate the importance of decent, safe and sanitary housing. But the Constitution does not provide judicial remedies for every social and economic ill. We are unable to perceive in that document any constitutional guarantee of access to dwellings of a particular quality or any recognition of the right of a tenant to occupy the real property of his landlord beyond the term of his lease, without the payment of rent.... Absent constitutional mandate, the assurance of adequate housing and the definition of landlord-tenant relationships are legislative, not judicial, functions.' (Emphasis supplied.)

Similarly, in Dandridge v. Williams, the Court's explicit recognition of the fact that the 'administration of public welfare assistance ... involves the most basic economic needs of impoverished human beings,' provided no basis for departing from the settled mode of constitutional analysis of legislative classifications involving questions of economic and social policy. As in the case of housing, the central importance of welfare benefits to the poor was not an adequate foundation for requiring the State to justify its law by showing some compelling state interest.

....

Education, of course, is not among the rights afforded explicit protection under our Federal Constitution. Nor do we find any basis for saying it is implicitly so protected. As we have said, the undisputed importance of education will not alone cause this Court to depart from the usual standard for reviewing a State's social and economic legislation. It is appellees' contention, however, that education is distinguishable from other services and benefits provided by the State because it bears a peculiarly close relationship to other rights and liberties accorded protection under the Constitution. Specifically, they insist that education is itself a fundamental personal right because it is essential to the effective exercise of First Amendment freedoms and to intelligent utilization of the right to vote. In asserting a nexus between speech and education, appellees urge that the right to speak is meaningless unless the speaker is capable of articulating his thoughts intelligently and persuasively. The 'marketplace of ideas' is an empty forum for those lacking basic communicative tools. Likewise, they argue that the corollary right to receive information becomes little more than a hollow privilege when the recipient has not been taught to read, assimilate, and utilize available knowledge.

...

We need not dispute any of these propositions. The Court has long afforded zealous protection against unjustifiable governmental interference with the individual's rights to speak and to vote. Yet we have never presumed to possess either the ability or the authority to guarantee to the citizenry the most effective speech or the most informed electoral choice. That these may be desirable goals of a system of freedom of expression and of a representative form of government is not to be doubted. These are indeed goals to be pursued by a people whose thoughts and beliefs are freed from governmental interference. But they are not values to be implemented by judicial instruction into otherwise legitimate state activities.

Even if it were conceded that some identifiable quantum of education is a constitutionally protected prerequisite to the meaningful exercise of either right, we have no indication that the present levels of educational expenditures in Texas provide an education that falls short. Whatever merit appellees' argument might have if a State's financing system occasioned an absolute denial of educational opportunities to any of its children, that argument provides no basis for finding an interference with fundamental rights where only relative differences in spending levels are involved and where—as is true in the present case—no charge fairly could be made that the system fails to provide each child with an opportunity to acquire the basic minimal skills necessary for the enjoyment of the rights of speech and of full participation in the political process.

Furthermore, the logical limitations on appellees' nexus theory are difficult to perceive. How, for instance, is education to be distinguished from the significant personal interests in the basics of decent food and shelter? Empirical examination might well buttress an assumption that the ill-fed, ill-clothed, and ill-housed are among the most ineffective participants in the political process, and that they derive the least enjoyment from the benefits of the First Amendment. If so, appellees' thesis would cast serious doubt on the authority of Dandridge v. Williams, supra and Lindsey v. Normer, supra.

We have carefully considered each of the arguments supportive of the District Court's finding that education is a fundamental right or liberty and have found those arguments unpersuasive. In one further respect we find this a particularly inappropriate case in which to subject state action to strict judicial scrutiny. The present case, in another basic sense, is significantly different from any of the cases in which the Court has applied strict scrutiny to state or federal legislation touching upon constitutionally protected rights. Each of our prior cases involved legislation which 'deprived,' 'infringed,' or 'interfered' with the free exercise of some such fundamental personal right or liberty. A critical distinction between those cases and the one now before us lies in what Texas is endeavoring to do with respect to education. Mr. Justice Brennan, writing for the Court in Katzenbach v. Morgan, expresses well the salient point:

'This is not a complaint that Congress ... has unconstitutionally denied or diluted anyone's right to vote but rather that Congress violated the Constitution by not extending the relief effected (to others similarly situated)....

'(The federal law in question) does not restrict or deny the franchise but in effect extends the franchise to persons who otherwise would be denied it by state law.... We need only decide whether the challenged limitation on the relief effected ... was permissible. In deciding that question, the principle that calls for the closest scrutiny of distinctions in laws denying fundamental rights ... is inapplicable; for the distinction challenged by appellees is presented only as a limitation on a reform measure aimed at eliminating an existing barrier to the exercise of the franchise. Rather, in deciding the constitutional propriety of the limitations in such a reform measure we are guided by the familiar principles that a 'statute is not invalid under the Constitution because it might have gone farther than it did,' ... that a legislature need not 'strike at all evils at the same time,' ... and that 'reform may take one step at a time, addressing itself to the phase of the problem which seems most acute to the legislative mind ...

The Texas system of school financing is not unlike the federal legislation involved in Katzenbach in this regard. Every step leading to the establishment of the system Texas utilizes today—including the decisions permitting localities to tax and expend locally, and creating and continuously expanding the state aid—was implemented in an effort to extend public education and to improve its quality. Of course, every reform that benefits some more than others may be criticized for what it fails to accomplish. But we think it plain that, in substance, the thrust of the Texas system is affirmative and reformatory and, therefore, should be scrutinized under judicial principles sensitive to the nature of the State's efforts and to the rights reserved to the States under the Constitution.

It should be clear, for the reasons stated above and in accord with the prior decisions of this Court, that this is not a case in which the challenged state action must be subjected to the searching judicial scrutiny reserved for laws that create suspect classifications or impinge upon constitutionally protected rights.

We need not rest our decision, however, solely on the inappropriateness of the strict-scrutiny test. A century of Supreme Court adjudication under the Equal Protection Clause affirmatively supports the application of the traditional standard of review, which requires only that the State's system be shown to bear some rational relationship to legitimate state purposes. This case represents far more than a challenge to the manner in which Texas provides for the education of its children. We have here nothing less than a direct attack on the way in which Texas has chosen to raise and disburse state and local tax revenues. We are asked to condemn the State's judgment in conferring on political subdivisions the power to tax local property to supply revenues for local interests. In so doing, appellees would have the Court intrude in an area in which it has traditionally deferred to state legislatures. This Court has often admonished against such interferences with the State's fiscal policies under the Equal Protection Clause:

'The broad discretion as to classification possessed by a legislature in the field of taxation has long been recognized.... (T)he passage of time has only served to underscore the wisdom of that recognition of the large area of discretion which is needed by a legislature in formulating sound tax policies.... It has ... been pointed out that in taxation, even more than in other fields, legislatures possess the greatest freedom in classification. Since the members of a legislature necessarily enjoy a familiarity with local conditions which this Court cannot have, the presumption of constitutionality can be overcome only by the most explicit demonstration that a classification is a hostile and oppressive discrimination against particular persons and classes....' Madden v. Kentucky.

Thus, we stand on familiar grounds when we continue to acknowledge that the Justices of this Court lack both the expertise and the familiarity with local problems so necessary to the making of wise decisions with respect to the raising and disposition of public revenues. Yet, we are urged to direct the States either to alter drastically the present system or to throw out the property tax altogether in favor of some other form of taxation. No scheme of taxation, whether the tax is imposed on property, income, or purchases of goods and services, has yet been devised which is free of all discriminatory impact. In such a complex arena in which no perfect alternatives exist, the Court does well not to impose too rigorous a standard of scrutiny lest all local fiscal schemes become subjects of criticism under the Equal Protection Clause.

In addition to matters of fiscal policy, this case also involves the most persistent and difficult questions of educational policy, another area in which this Court's lack of specialized knowledge and experience counsels against premature interference with the informed judgments made at the state and local levels. Education, perhaps even more than welfare assistance, presents a myriad of 'intractable economic, social, and even philosophical problems.' Dandridge v. Williams, 397 U.S. at 487. The very complexity of the problems of financing and managing a statewide public school system suggests that 'there will be more than one constitutionally permissible method of solving them,' and that, within the limits of rationality, 'the legislature's efforts to tackle the problems' should be entitled to respect. Jefferson v. Hackney. In such circumstances, the judiciary is well advised to refrain from imposing on the States inflexible constitutional restraints that could circumscribe or handicap the continued research and experimentation so vital to finding even partial solutions to educational problems and to keeping abreast of ever-changing conditions.

It must be remembered, also, that every claim arising under the Equal Protection Clause has implications for the relationship between national and state power under our federal system. Questions of federalism are always inherent in the process of determining whether a State's laws are to be accorded the traditional presumption of constitutionality, or are to be subjected instead to rigorous judicial scrutiny. While '(t)he maintenance of the principles of federalism is a foremost consideration in interpreting any of the pertinent constitutional provisions under which this Court examines state action,' it would be difficult to imagine a case having a greater potential impact on our federal system than the one now before us, in which we are urged to abrogate systems of financing public education presently in existence in virtually every State.

The foregoing considerations buttress our conclusion that Texas' system of public school finance is an inappropriate candidate for strict judicial scrutiny. These same considerations are relevant to the determination whether that system, with its conceded imperfections, nevertheless bears some rational relationship to a legitimate state purpose. It is to this question that we next turn our attention.

III

The basic contours of the Texas school finance system have been traced at the outset of this opinion. We will now describe in more detail that system and how it operates, as these facts bear directly upon the demands of the Equal Protection Clause.

. . .

In sum, to the extent that the Texas system of school financing results in unequal expenditures between children who happen to reside in different districts, we cannot say that such disparities are the product of a system that is so irrational as to be invidiously discriminatory. Texas has acknowledged its shortcomings and has persistently endeavored—not without some success—to ameliorate the differences in levels of expenditures without sacrificing the benefits of local participation. The Texas plan is not the result of hurried, ill-conceived legislation. It certainly is not the product of purposeful discrimination against any group or class. On the contrary, it is rooted in decades of experience in Texas and elsewhere, and in major part is the product of responsible studies by qualified people. In giving substance to the presumption of validity to which the Texas system is entitled, Lindsley v. Natural Carbonic Gas Co., it is important to remember that at every stage of its development it has constituted a 'rough accommodation' of interests in an effort to arrive at practical and workable solutions. Metropolis Theatre Co. v. City of Chicago,. One also must remember that the system here challenged is not peculiar to Texas or to any other State. In its essential characteristics, the Texas plan for financing public education reflects what many educators for a half century have thought was an enlightened approach to a problem for which there is no perfect solution. We are unwilling to assume for ourselves a level of wisdom superior to that of legislators, scholars, and educational authorities in 50 States, especially where the alternatives proposed are only recently conceived and nowhere yet tested. The constitutional standard under the Equal Protection Clause is whether the challenged state action rationally furthers a legitimate state purpose or interest. McGinnis v. Royster. We hold that the Texas plan abundantly satisfies this standard.

IV

In light of the considerable attention that has focused on the District Court opinion in this case and on its California predecessor, Serrano v. Priest, 5 Cal.3d 584, 96 Cal.Rptr. 601, 487 P.2d 1241 (1971), a cautionary postscript seems appropriate. It cannot be questioned that the constitutional judgment reached by the District Court and approved by our dissenting Brothers today would occasion in Texas and elsewhere an unprecedented upheaval in public education. Some commentators have concluded that, whatever the contours of the alternative financing programs that might be devised and approved, the result could not avoid being a beneficial one. But, just as there is nothing simple about the constitutional issues involved in these cases, there is nothing simple or certain about predicting the consequences of massive change in the financing and control of public education. Those who have devoted the most thoughtful attention to the practical ramifications of these cases have found no clear or dependable answers and their scholarship reflects no such unqualified confidence in the desirability of completely uprooting the existing system.

The complexity of these problems is demonstrated by the lack of consensus with respect to whether it may be said with any assurance that the poor, the racial minorities, or the children in over-burdened core-city school districts would be benefited by abrogation of traditional modes of financing education. Unless there is to be a substantial increase in state expenditures on education across the board—an event the likelihood of which is open to considerable question—these groups stand to realize gains in terms of increased per-pupil expenditures only if they reside in districts that presently spend at relatively low levels, i.e., in those districts that would benefit from the redistribution of existing resources. Yet, recent studies have indicated that the poorest families are not invariably clustered in the most impecunious school districts. Nor does it now appear that there is any more than a random chance that racial minorities are concentrated in property-poor districts. Additionally, several research projects have concluded that any financing alternative designed to achieve a greater equality of expenditures is likely to lead to higher taxation and lower educational expenditures in the major urban centers, a result that would exacerbate rather than ameliorate existing conditions in those areas.

These practical considerations, of course, play no role in the adjudication of the constitutional issues presented here. But they serve to highlight the wisdom of the traditional limitations on this Court's function. The consideration and initiation of fundamental reforms with respect to state taxation and education are matters reserved for the legislative processes of the various States, and we do no violence to the values of federalism and separation of powers by staying our hand. We hardly need add that this Court's action today is not to be viewed as placing its judicial imprimatur on the status quo. The need is apparent for reform in tax systems which may well have relied too long and too heavily on the local property tax. And certainly innovative thinking as to public education, its methods, and its funding is necessary to assure both a higher level of quality and greater uniformity of opportunity. These matters merit the continued attention of the scholars who already have contributed much by their challenges. But the ultimate solutions must come from the lawmakers and from the democratic pressures of those who elect them.

Reversed.

Plyler v. Doe
457 U.S. 202 (1982)

The question presented by these cases is whether, consistent with the Equal Protection Clause of the Fourteenth Amendment, Texas may deny to undocumented school-age children the free public education that it provides to children who are citizens of the United States or legally admitted aliens.

I

Since the late 19th century, the United States has restricted immigration into this country. Unsanctioned entry into the United States is a crime, 8 U.S.C. § 1325 and those who have entered unlawfully are subject to deportation, 8 U.S.C. §§ 1251, 1252. But despite the existence of these legal restrictions, a substantial number of persons have succeeded in unlawfully entering the United States, and now live within various States, including the State of Texas.

In May 1975, the Texas Legislature revised its education laws to withhold from local school districts any state funds for the education of children who were not "legally admitted" into the United States. The 1975 revision also authorized local school districts to deny enrollment in their public schools to children not "legally admitted" to the country. Tex.Educ.Code Ann. § 21.031 (Vernon Supp.1981). These cases involve constitutional challenges to those provisions.

This is a class action, filed in the United States District Court for the Eastern District of Texas in September 1977, on behalf of certain school-age children of Mexican origin residing in Smith County, Tex., who could not establish that they had been legally admitted into the United States. The action complained of the exclusion of plaintiff children from the public schools of the Tyler Independent School District. The Superintendent and members of the Board of Trustees of the School District were named as defendants; the State of Texas intervened as a party-defendant. After certifying a class consisting of all undocumented school-age children of Mexican origin residing within the School District, the District Court preliminarily enjoined defendants from denying a free education to members of the plaintiff class. In December 1977, the court conducted an extensive hearing on plaintiffs' motion for permanent injunctive relief.

. . . .

The District Court held that illegal aliens were entitled to the protection of the Equal Protection Clause of the Fourteenth Amendment, and that § 21.031 violated that Clause. Suggesting that "the state's exclusion of undocumented children from its public schools ... may well be the type of invidiously motivated state action for which the suspect classification doctrine was designed," the court held that it was unnecessary to decide whether the statute would survive a "strict scrutiny" analysis because, in any event, the discrimination embodied in the statute was not supported by a rational basis. *Id.*, at 585. The District Court also concluded that the Texas statute violated the Supremacy Clause. *Id.*, at 590–592.

The Court of Appeals for the Fifth Circuit upheld the District Court's injunction. 628 F.2d 448 (1980). The Court of Appeals held that the District Court had erred in finding the Texas statute pre-empted by federal law. With respect to equal protection, however, the Court of Appeals affirmed in all essential respects the analysis of the District Court, *id.*, at 454–458, concluding that § 21.031 was "constitutionally infirm regardless of whether it was tested using the mere rational basis standard or some more stringent test," *id.*, at 458. We noted probable jurisdiction.

In re Alien Children Education Litigation

During 1978 and 1979, suits challenging the constitutionality of § 21.031 and various local practices undertaken on the authority of that provision were filed in the United States District Courts for the Southern, Western, and Northern Districts of Texas.... In July 1980, the court entered an opinion and order holding that § 21.031 violated the Equal Protection Clause of the Fourteenth Amendment. The court held that "the absolute deprivation of education should trigger strict judicial scrutiny, particularly when the absolute deprivation is the result of complete inability to pay for the desired benefit." The court determined that the State's concern for fiscal integrity was not a compelling state interest,; that exclusion of these children had not been shown to be necessary to improve education within the State,; and that the educational needs of the children statutorily excluded were not different from the needs of children not excluded, *ibid.* The court therefore concluded that § 21.031 was not carefully tailored to advance the asserted state interest in an acceptable manner. While appeal of the District Court's decision was pending, the Court of Appeals rendered its decision in No. 80-1538. Apparently on the strength of that opinion, the Court of Appeals, on February 23, 1981, summarily affirmed the decision of the Southern District. We noted probable jurisdiction, and consolidated this case with No. 80-1538 for briefing and argument.

III

The Equal Protection Clause directs that "all persons similarly circumstanced shall be treated alike." *F. S. Royster Guano Co. v. Virginia*, 253 U.S. 412, 415, 40 S.Ct. 560, 561, 64 L.Ed. 989 (1920). But so too, "[t]he Constitution does not require things which are different in fact or opinion to be treated in law as though they were the same." *Tigner v. Texas*, 310 U.S. 141, 147, 60 S.Ct. 879, 882, 84 L.Ed. 1124 (1940). The initial discretion to determine what is "different" and what is "the same" resides in the legislatures of the States. A legislature must have substantial latitude to establish classifications that roughly approximate the nature of the problem perceived, that accommodate competing concerns both public and private, and that account for limitations on the practical ability of the State to remedy every ill. In applying the Equal Protection Clause to most forms of state action, we thus seek only the assurance that the classification at issue bears some fair relationship to a legitimate public purpose.

But we would not be faithful to our obligations under the Fourteenth Amendment if we applied so deferential a standard to every classification. The Equal Protection Clause was intended as a restriction on state legislative action inconsistent with elemental constitutional premises. Thus we have treated as presumptively invidious those classifications that disadvantage a "suspect class," or that impinge upon the exercise of a "fundamental right." With respect to such classifications, it is appropriate to enforce the mandate of equal protection by requiring the State to demonstrate that its classification has been precisely tailored to serve a compelling governmental interest. In addition, we have recognized that certain forms of legislative classification, while not facially invidious, nonetheless give rise to recurring constitutional difficulties; in these limited circumstances we have sought the assurance that the classification reflects a reasoned judgment consistent with the ideal of equal protection by inquiring whether it may fairly be viewed as furthering a substantial interest of the State. We turn to a consideration of the standard appropriate for the evaluation of § 21.031.

A

Sheer incapability or lax enforcement of the laws barring entry into this country, coupled with the failure to establish an effective bar to the employment of undocumented aliens, has resulted in the creation of a substantial "shadow population" of illegal migrants — numbering in the millions — within our borders. This situation raises the specter of a permanent caste of undocumented resident aliens, encouraged by some to remain here as a source of cheap labor, but nevertheless denied the benefits that our society makes available to citizens and lawful residents. The existence of such an underclass presents most difficult problems for a Nation that prides itself on adherence to principles of equality under law.

The children who are plaintiffs in these cases are special members of this underclass. Persuasive arguments support the view that a State may withhold its beneficence from those whose very presence within the United States is the product of their own unlawful conduct. These arguments do not apply with the same force to classifications imposing disabilities on the minor *children* of such illegal entrants. At the least, those who elect to enter our territory by stealth and in violation of our law should be prepared to bear the consequences, including, but not limited to, deportation. But the children of those illegal entrants are not comparably situated. Their "parents have the ability to conform their conduct to societal norms," and presumably the ability to remove themselves from the State's jurisdiction; but the children who are plaintiffs in these cases "can affect neither their parents' conduct nor their own status." *Trimble v. Gordon,*). Even if the State found it expedient to control the conduct of adults by acting against their children, legislation directing the onus of a parent's misconduct against his children does not comport with fundamental conceptions of justice.

"[V]isiting ... condemnation on the head of an infant is illogical and unjust. Moreover, imposing disabilities on the ... child is contrary to the basic concept of our system that legal burdens should bear some relationship to individual responsibility or wrongdoing. Obviously, no child is responsible for his birth and penalizing the ... child is an ineffectual—as well as unjust—way of deterring the parent."

Of course, undocumented status is not irrelevant to any proper legislative goal. Nor is undocumented status an absolutely immutable characteristic since it is the product of conscious, indeed unlawful, action. But § 21.031 is directed against children, and imposes its discriminatory burden on the basis of a legal characteristic over which children can have little control. It is thus difficult to conceive of a rational justification for penalizing these children for their presence within the United States. Yet that appears to be precisely the effect of § 21.031.

Public education is not a "right" granted to individuals by the Constitution. But neither is it merely some governmental "benefit" indistinguishable from other forms of social welfare legislation. Both the importance of education in maintaining our basic institutions, and the lasting impact of its deprivation on the life of the child, mark the distinction. The "American people have always regarded education and [the] acquisition of knowledge as matters of supreme importance." *Meyer v. Nebraska,* 262 U.S. 390, 400, 43 S.Ct. 625, 627, 67 L.Ed. 1042 (1923). We have recognized "the public schools as a most vital civic institution for the preservation of a democratic and as the primary vehicle for transmitting "the values on which our society rests." *Ambach v. Norwick,* 441 U.S. 68, 76, 99 S.Ct. 1589, 1594, 60 L.Ed.2d 49 (1979). "[A]s ... pointed out early in our history, ... some degree of education is necessary to prepare citizens to participate effectively and intelligently in our open political system if we are to preserve freedom and independence." *Wisconsin v. Yoder,* 406 U.S. 205, 221, 92 S.Ct. 1526, 1536, 32 L.Ed.2d 15 (1972). And these historic "perceptions of the public schools as inculcating fundamental values necessary to the maintenance of a democratic political system have been confirmed by the observations of social scientists." *Ambach v. Norwick, supra,* 411 U.S., at 77, 99 S.Ct., at 1594. In addition, education provides the basic tools by which individuals might lead economically productive lives to the benefit of us all. In sum, education has a fundamental role in maintaining the fabric of our society. We cannot ignore the significant social costs borne by our Nation when select groups are denied the means to absorb the values and skills upon which our social order rests.

In addition to the pivotal role of education in sustaining our political and cultural heritage, denial of education to some isolated group of children poses an affront to one of the goals of the Equal Protection Clause: the abolition of governmental barriers presenting unreasonable obstacles to advancement on the basis of individual merit. Paradoxically, by depriving the children of any disfavored group of an education, we foreclose the means by which that group might raise the level of esteem in which it is held by the majority. But more directly, "education prepares individuals to be self-reliant and self-sufficient participants in society." *Wisconsin v. Yoder, supra*, 406 U.S., at 221, 92 S.Ct., at 1536. Illiteracy is an enduring disability. The inability to read and write will handicap the individual deprived of a basic education each and every day of his life. The inestimable toll of that deprivation on the social economic, intellectual, and psychological well-being of the individual, and the obstacle it poses to individual achievement, make it most difficult to reconcile the cost or the principle of a status-based denial of basic education with the framework of equality embodied in the Equal Protection Clause. What we said 28 years ago in *Brown v. Board of Education*, 347 U.S. 483, 74 S.Ct. 686, 98 L.Ed. 873 (1954), still holds true:

"Today, education is perhaps the most important function of state and local governments. Compulsory school attendance laws and the great expenditures for education both demonstrate our recognition of the importance of education to our democratic society. It is required in the performance of our most basic public responsibilities, even service in the armed forces. It is the very foundation of good citizenship. Today it is a principal instrument in awakening the child to cultural values, in preparing him for later professional training, and in helping him to adjust normally to his environment. In these days, it is doubtful that any child may reasonably be expected to succeed in life if he is denied the opportunity of an education. Such an opportunity, where the state has undertaken to provide it, is a right which must be made available to all on equal terms." *Id.*, at 493, 74 S.Ct., at 691.

B

These well-settled principles allow us to determine the proper level of deference to be afforded § 21.031. Undocumented aliens cannot be treated as a suspect class because their presence in this country in violation of federal law is not a "constitutional irrelevancy." Nor is education a fundamental right; a State need not justify by compelling necessity every variation in the manner in which education is provided to its population. But more is involved in these cases than the abstract question whether § 21.031 discriminates against a suspect class, or whether education is a fundamental right. Section 21.031 imposes a lifetime hardship on a discrete class of children not accountable for their disabling status. The stigma of illiteracy will mark them for the rest of their lives. By denying these children a basic education, we deny them the ability to live within the structure of our civic institutions, and foreclose any realistic possibility that they will contribute in even the smallest way to the progress of our Nation. In determining the rationality of § 21.031, we may appropriately take into account its costs to the Nation and to the innocent children who are its victims. In light of these countervailing costs, the discrimination contained in § 21.031 can hardly be considered rational unless it furthers some substantial goal of the State.

IV

It is the State's principal argument, and apparently the view of the dissenting Justices, that the undocumented status of these children *vel non* establishes a sufficient rational basis for denying them benefits that a State might choose to afford other residents. The State notes that while other aliens are admitted "on an equality of legal privileges with all citizens under non-discriminatory laws," *Takahashi v. Fish & Game Comm'n*, 334 U.S. 410, 420, 68 S.Ct. 1138, 1143, 92 L.Ed. 1478 (1948), the asserted right of these children to an education can claim no implicit congressional imprimatur. Indeed, in the State's view, Congress' apparent disapproval of the presence of these children within the United States, and the evasion of the federal regulatory program that is the mark of undocumented status, provides authority for its decision to impose upon them special disabilities. Faced with an equal protection challenge respecting the treatment of aliens, we agree that the courts must be attentive to congressional policy; the exercise of congressional power might well affect the State's prerogatives to afford differential treatment to a particular class of aliens. But we are unable to find in the congressional immigration scheme any statement of policy that might weigh significantly in arriving at an equal protection balance concerning the State's authority to deprive these children of an education.

The Constitution grants Congress the power to "establish an uniform Rule of Naturalization." Art. I., § 8, cl. 4. Drawing upon this power, upon its plenary authority with respect to foreign relations and international commerce, and upon the inherent power of a sovereign to close its borders, Congress has developed a complex scheme governing admission to our Nation and status within our borders. The obvious need for delicate policy judgments has counseled the Judicial Branch to avoid intrusion into this field. *Mathews, supra*, at 81, 96 S.Ct., at 1892. But this traditional caution does not persuade us that unusual deference must be shown the classification embodied in § 21.031. The States enjoy no power with respect to the classification of aliens. This power is "committed to the political branches of the Federal Government." *Mathews*, 426 U.S., at 81, 96 S.Ct., at 1892. Although it is "a routine and normally legitimate part" of the business of the Federal Government to classify on the basis of alien status, *id.*, at 85, 96 S.Ct., at 1894, and to "take into account the character of the relationship between the alien and this country," *id.*, at 80, 96 S.Ct., at 1891, only rarely are such matters relevant to legislation by a State.

As we recognized in *DeCanas v. Bica*, 424 U.S. 351, 96 S.Ct. 933, 47 L.Ed.2d 43 (1976), the States do have some authority to act with respect to illegal aliens, at least where such action mirrors federal objectives and furthers a legitimate state goal. In *DeCanas*, the State's program reflected Congress' intention to bar from employment all aliens except those possessing a grant of permission to work in this country. In contrast, there is no indication that the disability imposed by § 21.031 corresponds to any identifiable congressional policy. The State does not claim that the conservation of state educational resources was ever a congressional concern in restricting immigration. More importantly, the classification reflected in § 21.031 does not operate harmoniously within the federal program.

To be sure, like all persons who have entered the United States unlawfully, these children are subject to deportation. 8 U.S.C. §§ 1251, 1252 (1976 ed. and Supp.IV). But there is no assurance that a child subject to deportation will ever be deported. An illegal entrant might be granted federal permission to continue to reside in this country, or even to become a citizen. See, e.g., 8 U.S.C. §§ 1252, 1253(h), 1254 (1976 ed. and Supp.IV). In light of the discretionary federal power to grant relief from deportation, a State cannot realistically determine that any particular undocumented child will in fact be deported until after deportation proceedings have been completed. It would of course be most difficult for the State to justify a denial of education to a child enjoying an inchoate federal permission to remain.

We are reluctant to impute to Congress the intention to withhold from these children, for so long as they are present in this country through no fault of their own, access to a basic education. In other contexts, undocumented status, coupled with some articulable federal policy, might enhance state authority with respect to the treatment of undocumented aliens. But in the area of special constitutional sensitivity presented by these cases, and in the absence of any contrary indication fairly discernible in the present legislative record, we perceive no national policy that supports the State in denying these children an elementary education. The State may borrow the federal classification. But to justify its use as a criterion for its own discriminatory policy, the State must demonstrate that the classification is reasonably adapted to "*the purposes for which the state desires to use it.*" *Oyama v. California*, 332 U.S. 633, 664–665, 68 S.Ct. 269, 284, 92 L.Ed. 249 (1948) (Murphy, J., concurring) (emphasis added). We therefore turn to the state objectives that are said to support § 21.031.

V

Appellants argue that the classification at issue furthers an interest in the "preservation of the state's limited resources for the education of its lawful residents." Of course, a concern for the preservation of resources standing alone can hardly justify the classification used in allocating those resources. The State must do more than justify its classification with a concise expression of an intention to discriminate. Apart from the asserted state prerogative to act against undocumented children solely on the basis of their undocumented status — an asserted prerogative that carries only minimal force in the circumstances of these cases — we discern three colorable state interests that might support § 21.031.

. . .

Finally, appellants suggest that undocumented children are appropriately singled out because their unlawful presence within the United States renders them less likely than other children to remain within the boundaries of the State, and to put their education to productive social or political use within the State. Even assuming that such an interest is legitimate, it is an interest that is most difficult to quantify. The State has no assurance that any child, citizen or not, will employ the education provided by the State within the confines of the State's borders. In any event, the record is clear that many of the undocumented children disabled by this classification will remain in this country indefinitely, and that some will become lawful residents or citizens of the United States. It is difficult to understand precisely what the State hopes to achieve by promoting the creation and perpetuation of a subclass of illiterates within our boundaries, surely adding to the problems and costs of unemployment, welfare, and crime. It is thus clear that whatever savings might be achieved by denying these children an education they are wholly insubstantial in light of the costs involved to these children, the State, and the Nation.

VI

If the State is to deny a discrete group of innocent children the free public education that it offers to other children residing within its borders, that denial must be justified by a showing that it furthers some substantial state interest. No such showing was made here. Accordingly, the judgment of the Court of Appeals in each of these cases is

Affirmed.

Justice MARSHALL, concurring.

While I join the Court's opinion, I do so without in any way retreating from my opinion in San Antonio Ind. School Dist. V Rodriguez. I continue to believe that an individual's interest in education is fundamental, and that this view is amply supported "by the unique status accorded public education by our society, and by the close relationship between education and some of our most basic constitutional values." Furthermore, I believe that the facts of these cases demonstrate the wisdom of rejecting a rigidified approach to equal protection analysis, and of employing an approach that allows for varying levels of scrutiny depending upon "the constitutional and societal importance of the interest adversely affected and the recognized invidiousness of the basis upon which the particular classification is drawn." *Id.*, at 99, 93 S.Ct., at 1330. It continues to be my view that a class-based denial of public education is utterly incompatible with the Equal Protection Clause of the Fourteenth Amendment.

C. The Right to a Sound Basic Education under State Constitutions and Funding Public Education

In contrast to the rights expressed in the U.S. Constitution, all state constitutions contain a right to education, although there is broad division on the scope of such a right and the remedies that are available to litigants to protect the right. Most state constitutions provide citizens with a right to a sound basic education. These state rights reflect a civic philosophy of Jefferson and other founders that public education is an essential keystone to democracy.[9] Jefferson advanced this idea in Virginia as early as 1779 with the "Bill for the General Diffusion of Knowledge," and 20 years later Samuel Knox advocated for a national public education system.[10] In a more classic tradition, Rousseau argued that the aim of a democratic society was not merely

---

9. Areto A. Imoukhuede, *The Fifth Freedom: The Constitutional Duty to Provide Public Education,* 22 U. Fla. J.L. & Pub. Pol'y 45, 60 (2011).

10. *Id.* at 61–62.

the production of goods, but the production of free human beings associated with one another on equal terms.[11] Formal education was therefore a necessity to any democratic system. Although not contained within the U.S. Constitution, there is historical support for the argument that the United States was founded on the idea that all people have a right to an education.

International law provides greater clarity on the right to education. The United States is a party to several United Nations Conventions, beginning with the U.N. Charter, that describe the state duty to advance a higher standard of living for all people and to secure other fundamental freedoms. The United States is party to the Universal Declaration of Human Rights, which, in Article 26, describes the right to a public education as a human right. The status of U.N. Conventions, as well as other international laws, under U.S. law is clear. International laws ratified by the U.S. Congress are to be afforded the same status as federal statutes under the U.S. hierarchy of laws.[12] Several other international laws and agreements recognize a right to education, including the International Covenant on Economic, Social and Cultural Rights. Accordingly, there is an oft-repeated commitment by the United States to the idea that there is a right to a public education. While state supreme courts have repeatedly found such a right to exist,[13] the U.S. Supreme Court ruled in *San Antonio v. Rodriquez* that no such right may be found under the U.S. Constitution. While the Supreme Court has found fundamental rights that are not articulated in the U.S. Constitution, it has consistently been unwilling to extend this reasoning to the right to education.

How is it possible that disparities exist in public education if a right to public education exists under state constitutions? The most direct answer to this question is that such disparities arise because of how public education is funded in the majority of states. Public education throughout the United States is primarily funded through the collection of local property taxes. The majority of funding for K–12 public education comes from local sources, including local and state government. Revenue is drawn from local taxpayers based on formulas that assess tax liability in relation to property value. The dependency on local revenue to finance public education results in significant disparities in the funding available to children in public schools serving low-wealth communities that have a lower overall property tax base. What this means should be obvious. In school districts that have a large number of wealthy families, who own large numbers of expensive homes, tax revenue will be higher than in districts with large numbers of poor families who rent or own more modest homes. Due to this, in most communities for the better part of the last century, students living in school districts with the greatest need had the fewest resources. The loudest

---

11. Matt McManus, *Why We Should Read Rousseau*, QUILLETTE (Mar. 2, 2019), https://quillette.com/2019/03/02/why-we-should-read-rousseau/.

12. *See* The Paquete Habana, 175 U.S. 677 (1900), which supplies the foundation for domestic recognition of international laws that have been ratified by the U.S. Congress.

13. Michael A. Rebell, *Safeguarding the Right to a Sound Basic Education in Times of Fiscal Constraint*, 75 ALB. L. REV. 1855, 1864–68 (2012).

arguments made to retain such a system come from those who want to maintain "local control" over education and seek to keep funding and decision making at the school district level,[14] even though local funding fails to provide an adequate public education to millions of poor children across the United States.

Knight v. Alabama

458 F. Supp. 2d 1273 (N.D. Ala. 2004)

This is a desegregation lawsuit involving all public universities in the State of Alabama and a plaintiff class consisting of all black citizens of the State of Alabama. The case is before the Court on Plaintiffs' Motion for Additional Relief with Respect to State Funding of Public Higher Education.

II. Findings of Fact

A. Property Tax Policies Traceable to *De jure* Segregation

* * *

f. Amendments 325 and 373lin

42. The impact of *Brown v. Board of Education*, 347 U.S. 483, 74 S.Ct. 686, 98 L.Ed. 873 (1954), on white Alabamians' support for public education varied according to how seriously they took the threat of federally mandated school desegregation:

> For many years after *Brown* the feeling was quite widespread in the South that there simply was going to be no way that the federal government would ever have the power to bring integration to the state. There was no sense ... that integration was impending or even very likely. And if you are quite confident that that's true, then you can continue to be an advocate of increased funding for the schools and the confidence that these schools ... will continue segregated.

> If, on the other hand, you believe that there is some real likelihood that schools will be integrated, then you would have very much more substantial doubts because all political leaders at this period said, and some actually believed, that the outcome of the integration of the schools would be the abolition of the schools. Certainly Governor John Patterson was, not merely in rhetoric but actually in his heart, ... to the abolition of the public school system of the state if integration came to the state, or particular school districts, ... if there was no likelihood that it was going to become statewide, he was prepared to close them in particular districts and leave them open elsewhere.

> And Governor Wallace, I think actually welcomed the thought of general conversion to a system ... of private segregated academies if there continued to be some form of public funding that did not go to the school, but instead went

---

14. Debra L. Ireland, *The Price of Education: What Local Control Is Costing American Children*, 6 SCHOLAR 159 (2003).

to the parents in the form of tuition grants or scholarships, … which the parents could then use to send their child to the segregated private academy.

(Thornton Dep. at 163–64.)

g. Summary

76. The 1971 Amendment 325, which established the first classification system for property taxes in Alabama history, and the 1978 Amendment 373, which modified the assessment ratios and added a current use provision for farm and timber land, were the products of a series of contemporaneous events that brought to an end the ability of Black Belt whites to control the Legislature and to block increases in local property taxes. All of the those events revolved around the rise of black political power: (1) school desegregation, which undermined support for public schools; (2) court challenges to the widespread under-assessment of property for tax purposes, culminating in the 1971 federal court decree in *Weissinger v. Boswell,* which required uniform property assessments statewide; (3) corresponding pushes by the Farm Bureau and forestry interests to obtain additional constitutional protection from legislative or local tax initiatives; (4) legislative reapportionment resulting in an increase in the number of black legislators, which created a corresponding growing concern on the part of white property owners about their property taxes being raised; and (5) passage of the 1965 Voting Rights Act, re-enfranchisement of blacks, and corresponding litigation challenging racially discriminatory election structures. (Thornton Dep. at 160–80.)

77. There is a direct line of continuity between the property tax provisions of the 1875 Constitution, the 1901 Constitution, and the amendments up to 1978. (Thornton Dep. at 175–81.) "[T]he fact is, that this is a set of assumptions and a set of institutional relationships and a set of social relationships that … is created by historical events, that is historically created and … interrelated so that the events feed onto each other and it makes a single understandable whole." (*Id.* at 174.) The historical fears of white property owners, particularly those residing in the Black Belt, that black majorities in their counties would eventually become fully enfranchised and raise their property taxes motivated the property tax provisions in the 1901 Constitution and the amendments to it in 1971 and 1978. (*Id.* at 178–80; *accord,* Norrell, May 4, 2004, Tr. at 95 ("The limits are always associated with white supremacist intent, and that occurs in 1875, strongly reinforced in 1901, and essentially uninterrupted, unbroken, … as main public policy commitments of the state through the 1970's.").)

78. Dr. Norrell agreed with another point Dr. Thornton made in his deposition:

[A]ll tax policy made or revised in the 20th century has effectively been made to conform with the commitments of taxation capped by constitutional mandate, reinforced by limits on local control, local authority to tax, and that of course was the result of fears, especially among Black Belt counties, that in the future some re-enfranchised black electorate would raise property taxes, the very fear that Sam Engelhardt acted on starting about 1950. And Thornton then takes us into the more modern period and effectively says, you know, these themes continue right through the important policy decisions made with regard to property taxes in 1971 and shored up to an extent in 1978.

(May 4, 2004, Tr. at 95.) Dr. Norrell summarized his testimony as follows:

[S]tate policies about property taxes were formulated in the context of the racially charged circumstance of Reconstruction and the immediate post Reconstruction years. Those property tax policies were created to maintain the lowest possible taxation because property taxation is associated with funding for education for black children, and ... that's anathema to this very conservative white supremacist group that gains dominance in 1875, that reinforces and sort of strengthens its structure in the 1901 [constitution], the time at which the vast majority of black voters are taken out of the polity in Alabama, and that those policies of minimal property taxes, of white supremacist control of local government, of minimal support for black education in Alabama are effectively uninterrupted even through the various anxieties and concerns that white supremacists had in Alabama as a result of the coming ... civil rights movement and the reality of the civil rights movement. And even after we think of the modern civil rights movement having succeeded with the Civil Rights Act of '64, the Voting Rights Act of '65, that those same forces are able to further reinforce the historic commitment to minimal property taxation, minimal support for education now because of course it ... means education, desegregated or integrated racial education in Alabama. So, ... it's a story for me and for Thornton of powerful continuities established in 1875 or thereabouts and continuing effectively uninterrupted in the making of policy through 1978, and ... folks in Alabama still live very much under policies that were effectively created in 1875 and continuously reinforced up through the years.

Q. And the 1971 and 1978 lid bills reinforced those same policies?

A. That's right.

(May 4, 2004, Tr. at 120–22.) Indeed, Black Belt and urban industrial interests successfully used the argument that it is unfair for white property owners to pay for the education of blacks to produce all the state constitutional barriers to property taxes from 1875 to the present, including the 1971 and 1978 Lid Bill amendments. (Thornton Dep. at 211–12.)

* * *

2. Effect on Funding for Public K–12 and Higher Education

87. The effect of low property tax revenues has had a crippling effect on poor, majority black school districts. (May 4, 2004, Tr. at 27–30.)

88. In rural areas of the state, most local school districts simply do not have a critical mass of valuable commercial property and residential homes—the two types of property shouldering eighty-five percent of the property taxes—to raise adequate funds

for public education. (May 4, 2004, Tr. at 31–32.) Moreover, in areas where the significant source of wealth is timber, the property tax structure bars taxation above ten percent of the current use value of such areas; consequently, that property does not provide much property tax revenue. (*Id.;* Pls.' Ex. 57.)

89. Indeed, even areas boasting valuable commercial and residential property have difficulty in raising adequate revenue because of the Lid Bill's low assessment ratios for all property classifications. (May 4, 2004, Tr. at 32–34.)

* * *

98. One illustration of the strained education budget is Alabama's funding for textbooks:

> I think we have 128 school systems now, or 129 perhaps, but 80 of that number used its textbook monies to some degree to avoid layoffs. In fact, we have had several school systems, 20 some-odd if I remember correctly, that had not purchased textbooks in three years. Now, you have to keep in mind, what's the problem. Well, they have kept the textbooks they have for six years already, so you add three more years on top of that. So you have got textbooks you have been using for nine years. Obviously the condition is bad, pages missing, and in some cases dated, you know, like science and social studies. So that was a tremendous impact, had a tremendous impact, and it was reflective of school systems that had low local support as well.

(Richardson Dep. at 58–59; Pls.' Ex. 37 (Regan Loyola Connolly, *State BOE Closes Books on New Texts,* Montgomery Advertiser (September 12, 2003)).)

99. Additionally, the current underfunding of K–12 public schools has almost entirely eliminated state appropriations for textbooks and remedial programs for students who fail the high school exit exam. (Richardson Dep. at 59–60, 70.)

100. According to Dr. Richardson, by the 2004–05 school year the reserve funds of 100 of the 128 public school systems in Alabama will have been depleted. (Richardson Dep. at 71.)

101. According to a February 23, 2003, "report card" released by the Alabama Board of Education, a "tremendous gulf" exists among differing racial and socioeconomic groups in Alabama. (Richardson Dep. at 67; Pls.' Ex. 38 (Ken L. Spear, *Cash Woes Tax Schools,* Montgomery Advertiser (Feb. 28, 2003)).) The test scores of whites in Alabama's K–12 schools placed them in the 65th percentile nationwide, Hispanics were in the 46th percentile, and blacks in the 39th percentile. (Richardson Dep. at 67; Pls.' Ex. 38 (Ken L. Spear, *Cash Woes Tax Schools,* Montgomery Advertiser (Feb. 28, 2003)).) Likewise, students receiving a free or reduced-price lunch, a common indicator of poverty, ranked in the 40th percentile nationwide, while students who paid for their lunches scored in the 67th percentile. (Richardson Dep. at 75–76; Pls.' Ex. 38 (Ken L. Spear, *Cash Woes Tax Schools,* Montgomery Advertiser (Feb. 28, 2003)).)

102. Importantly, more than a third of Alabama's college freshmen are not prepared for college level classes, and the number is rising, even though high school graduation

exam scores and some elementary scores are improving. Last school year, thirty-five percent of freshmen at the state's public colleges and universities were enrolled in remedial courses. (Richardson Dep. at 76–77; Pls.' Ex. 39 (Regan Loyola Connolly, *Students Lack Readiness for College*, Montgomery Advertiser (Feb. 27, 2004)).) Dr. Richardson expressed concern about the high percentage of college freshman enrolled in remedial classes because "Alabama has the most rigorous requirement for high school graduates of any state in the nation. We require more math and science than any other state. And for us to have that level of remediation was just rather shocking to me." (Richardson Dep. at 77.) Poor school systems must also meet the State Department's minimum requirements, but, according to Dr. Richardson, basic problems cannot be overcome without adequate funding: "The problem is, is that you have, in many cases, difficulty securing teachers with advanced math certification or science in some of your poor and rural—rural really drives that about as much as anything." (*Id.* at 77–78.)

103. During the past few years, Alabama's K–12 students had been making "tremendous progress" increasing their standardized test scores, but recent budget cuts have made that progress "unravel." (Richardson Dep. at 79–80.) For instance, in the past year, the average high school dropout rate for Alabama students was fourteen or fifteen percent, but for black students it was "around the 20 percent range." (*Id.* at 81.)5

104. In 2002, the State Department of Education, responding to the mandate of the state court Equity Funding Case to make a recommendation to the Legislature, performed an analysis that indicated an additional $1.6 billion annually is needed to provide "adequate"6 K–12 education in Alabama. (Richardson Dep. at 94-111.) As of 2004, Dr. Richardson estimates that figure is closer to $2 billion. (*Id.* at 111.)

105. Dr. Richardson concurs with the following opinions expressed by Dr. William Muse in a letter to the editor Dr. Muse wrote when he resigned as President of Auburn University and accepted a position at East Carolina University: (1) Alabama has been hampered by a tax structure that is both inequitable and inadequate; (2) the tax structure places a disproportionate burden on the poor through an over-reliance on sales taxes and does not produce sufficient revenues to fund education, both elementary and secondary and higher education, on levels comparable to that of other Southern states; (3) a critical and necessary step in the process will be rewriting the state's antiquated constitution, because so many of the obstacles to progress, particularly the tax structure, are written into the constitution; and (4) one of the most important changes needed in Alabama is a substantial increase in property taxes because in Alabama, the property tax revenue is so low the state has to pick up the bulk of the cost of the public schools from regressive sales and income taxes; moreover, inasmuch as higher education is funded from the same source as K–12, the monies available to higher education are substantially reduced. (Richardson Dep. at 105–11; Pls.' Ex. 46 (William V. Muse, *State Should Heed North Carolina's Example*, Montgomery Advertiser (Jul. 8, 2001)).)

106. Dr. Sullivan similarly testified that because the ETF funds both K–12 schools and public colleges and universities, the constitutional constraints on property taxes

have required an increasing share of the ETF to be allocated to K–12 schools, so that less state funds are available to public colleges and universities. (May 5, 2004, Tr. at 83–84.) According to Dr. Sullivan, if higher education's share of the ETF had remained constant over the last ten years, public colleges and universities would have received nearly $200 million more than those institutions actually received. (Pls.' Ex. 71 (chart depicting amount, distribution, and change in ETF revenues from 1990–91 to 2002–03).) That decline is most significant in the years following 1995 when the State implemented a new foundation program for K–12:

> In terms of the specific issues related to the impact of the property tax and the relationship between K–12 funding and higher ed. funding, that relationship got a lot tighter after the foundation program was passed in '95, and so that … starting 95–96 and then coming forward, that's where you start to see this sort of steady downward trend. And I would call … to the court's attention [that] we already have a difference which amounts to as much as 200 million dollars between what would have been generated by the share a few years ago and what would be generated by it today…. [T]he trend is fairly steadily in the downward direction, and … so one might anticipate that, absent any change, the higher ed. share could continue to decline.

(May 5, 2004, Tr. at 85–86.)

107. Dr. Sullivan identified that an important consequence of the reduction in the share of ETF revenue appropriated for higher education has been that the gap between what the State appropriates and what ACHE defines as the "need" for the senior institutions, based on the median funding of the SREB7 region, continues to widen. (May 5, 2004, Tr. at 86–88.) Since this case was tried in 1990, Alabama's state appropriations to senior institutions have declined from 84.1% of the ACHE regional standard to 55.8% of the ACHE regional standard. (*Id.* at 88; Pls.' Ex. 72 (chart demonstrating relationship between ETF appropriation for senior institutions and need, as measured by the ACHE standard).) In real dollars, these percentages represent a difference of over $650 million between Alabama's state appropriations and the regional standard of need and $400 million less than the 84% level of need that was being met during the 1990 trial. (May 5, 2004, Tr. at 89.) Moreover, "these data understate the magnitude of that drop because beginning in 95–96 the appropriation includes the retirement benefits that weren't in there in the early years that were separately appropriated. So that we've got some amount of money, somewhere perhaps between 50 and 100 million dollars, that's now imbedded into that—this higher ed. appropriation that wasn't there in the earlier years." (*Id.* at 88.)

108. Dr. Sullivan testified that senior institutions having to cope with budgets that represent a smaller fraction of their need have been adversely impacted in two ways: (1) the institutions have been unable to increase salaries as fast as institutions in other states and thus have fallen further behind their SREB counterparts and the United States as a whole (May 5, 2004, Tr. at 89–90); Pls.' Ex. 74(chart indicating median household in SREB states); and (2) the institutions have been forced to dramatically increase in tuition (May 5, 2004, Tr. at 91).

109. Although the dramatic increase in tuition is certainly not unique to Alabama, the results of the tuition increase are more burdensome in the State because (1) there is not a corresponding increase in need-based scholarship funding to ensure continued access for students from lower income households, and (2) the percent of students in Alabama who would be eligible for such aid (using federal guidelines) is well above average. (May 5, 2004, Tr. at 91–99; Pls.' Exs. 74, 76 (chart comparing need-based financial aid from state sources for students at public institutions) & 77 (chart indicating Pell grant funding in United States, SREB States, and Alabama from 1990–91 to 2000–01).) Those circumstances place considerably more of the burden of increased tuition on low-income students. (May 5, 2004, Tr. at 92.) That is, compared to the situation in other states, it is becoming relatively easier for wealthy students to attend a state university in Alabama and relatively more difficult for poor students to do so.

* * *

114. The total EFT expenditures for higher education have also decreased from 28.5% of total ETF appropriations to 26.1% of ETF appropriations. (May 4, 2004, Tr. at 173–175.) Additionally, although the amount appropriations to higher education from the EFT has increased between FY 1990 and FY 2003, appropriations for K–12, as expected, have grown more quickly. (*Id.* at 178–79); Pls.' Ex. 132 (indicating percentages and actual amounts of appropriations for K–12 and higher education from ETF.)

* * *

III. Conclusions of Law

A. *United States v. Fordice*

1. The *Fordice* Standard

In *United States v. Fordice*, 505 U.S. 717, 112 S.Ct. 2727, 120 L.Ed.2d 575 (1992), the Supreme Court set forth a three-part constitutional analysis governing higher education desegregation lawsuits to determine "whether a state has fully met its remedial obligation" to dismantle policies and practices that inhibit free choice by students with respect to attending institutions of higher education. *Knight v. Alabama*, 14 F.3d 1534, 1540–42 (11th Cir.1994).

2. The first step requires the plaintiff to show that a policy "challenged as segregative is 'traceable' to decisions that were made or practices that were instituted in the past for segregative reasons, thus rendering it a vestige of discrimination." *Knight*, 14 F.3d at 1540. Put differently, "[o]nce it is determined that a particular policy was originally adopted for discriminatory reasons, the *Fordice* test inquires whether the current policy is 'traceable' to the original policy, or is 'rooted' or has 'antecedents' in that original policy." *Id.* at 1550.

3. The burden of proof to satisfy the "traceable to" prong lies on the plaintiff: "Where plaintiffs in a lawsuit contend that a state or other public actor has not discharged its duty to dismantle its former system of *de jure* segregated

higher education, the burden of proof lies with the charging party to show that a challenged contemporary policy is traceable to past segregation." *Knight*, 14 F.3d at 1540–41.

4. The second step in the *Fordice* analysis requires that if the plaintiff successfully demonstrates that a challenged contemporary policy is traceable to past segregation, the burden next shifts to the State to show that the policy no longer has continuing segregative effects. *Knight*, 14 F.3d at 1541. Upon proving that a challenged policy has no segregative effects, the State "is relieved of its duty to eliminate or modify the policy." *Id.* (citing *Fordice*, 505 U.S. at 738–39, 112 S.Ct. 2727).

5. If, on the other hand, the State is unable to show that the challenged policy has no continuing segregative effects, the State may nevertheless escape liability if "the State show[s] that there are no less segregative alternatives which are practicable and educationally sound." *Knight*, 14 F.3d at 1541; *see also Fordice*, 505 U.S. at 743, 112 S.Ct. 2727 ("[T]he State may not leave in place policies rooted in its prior officially segregated system that serve to maintain the racial identifiability of its universities if those policies can practically be eliminated without eroding sound educational policies."). "This examination of the practicability and educational soundness of possible alternatives or modifications to a challenged policy constitutes the third step in the *Fordice* analysis." *Knight*, 14 F.3d at 1541–42. The state's burden to make such a showing, however, is heavy: "a court should consider the full range of alternative remedies, … when determining which would achieve the greatest reduction in the identified segregative effects." *Id.* at 1541 (citing *Fordice*, 505 U.S. at 742–43, 112 S.Ct. 2727.)

6. The Eleventh Circuit has succinctly summarized the *Fordice* standard as follows:

> Where plaintiffs show that a current policy is traceable to past segregation, and defendants fail to demonstrate either (1) that the policy, in combination with other policies, has no current segregative effects, or (2) that none of the full range of less segregative alternative remedies are practicable and educationally sound, defendants must adopt the practicable and educationally sound alternatives that will bring about the greatest possible reduction in the segregative effects. "If the state has not discharged [this remedial] duty, it remains in violation of the Fourteenth Amendment."

Knight, 14 F.3d at 1542 (citing *Fordice*, 505 U.S. at 727, 112 S.Ct. 2727).

2. Step One: Whether the Current Property Tax Structure Is "Traceable To" Alabama's Prior System of Segregation

7. The Court first considers whether Plaintiffs have demonstrated that the constitutional restrictions placed on the property tax authority of both state and local governments are traceable to Alabama's prior *de jure* dual system.

8. Based on the extensive record before the Court, the Court finds that Plaintiffs have met their burden to demonstrate that the current ad valorem tax structure is a vestige of discrimination inasmuch as the constitutional provisions governing the taxation of property are traceable to, rooted in, and have their antecedents in an original segregative, discriminatory policy.

9. It is clear that the current tax structure in Alabama cripples the effectiveness of state and local governments in Alabama to raise funds adequate to support higher education. The Lid Bill and the low assessment ratios impede and restrict the ability of the State and local governments from raising revenue from taxation of property.

3. "Continuing Effects" Step

10. Plaintiffs having satisfied their burden to show that the current tax structure is "traceable to" *de jure* segregation, the burden shifts to Defendants to show that the challenged provisions of the Alabama constitution do not have a continuing segregative effect. Knight v. Alabama, 14 F.3d at 1541.

11. Defendants contend that the property tax is not related to Alabama's system of higher education — i.e., that no nexus exists between the lack of funds derived from state and local property taxation and the effect on student enrollment decisions. Consequently, Defendants submit, the challenged provisions of the Alabama Constitution do not and cannot have a continuing segregative effect.

12. Plaintiffs contend that a causal nexus does indeed exist, arguing that the lack of property tax revenue has financially strained K–12 schools in Alabama, thereby requiring that the State allocate an increased proportion of the ETF to K–12. As a result of this inequitable distribution, Plaintiffs claim that tuition at Alabama's institutions of higher education has skyrocketed and that funds available for need-based financial assistance have plummeted. Consequently, the ability of poorer students, who are disproportionately black, to attend college is adversely affected.

13. The Court appreciates Plaintiffs' argument, and agrees that the current property tax system in Alabama has a crippling effect on the ability of local and state government to raise revenue adequately to fund K–12 schools. Nevertheless, the Court cannot agree that the property tax structure stymies school choice in such a way that results in an unconstitutional denial of a student's right to make a decision unfettered by vestiges of discrimination.

14. The Court finds that the relationship between the funding of higher education and finding of K–12 is marginal insofar as ad valorem property tax is concerned. Put differently, the effect of the state's inability to raise revenue due to the challenged constitutional provisions is simply too attenuated to form a causal connection between the tax policy and any segregative effect on school choice.

15. Additionally, although the proportion of the ETF allocated to higher education has fallen since 1990, the actual amount of money paid to higher education has increased from $820,063,882 to $1,160,033,885 over that same period. (Defs.' Ex. 04-004.)

16. Moreover, insofar as Plaintiffs contend that the lack of funding for property taxes somehow works to frustrate the Court's prior remedial decrees, the Court finds that

argument unavailing. Rather, the State has unbegrudgingly complied with the Court's remedial decrees, meeting all its obligations as ordered by the Court. Along those same lines, between the 1991–92 and 2002–03 academic years, black student enrollment and graduation rates at HWIs have increased considerably.

17. The Court concludes, therefore, that although the ad valorem taxation system in Alabama may be traceable to past discriminatory decisions, Defendants have satisfied their burden to demonstrate that the challenged provisions of the Alabama constitution do not continue to have a segregative effect on student choice.

4. *Hunter v. Erickson*

18. Plaintiffs also argue that the challenged provisions of the Alabama constitution violate the Fourteenth Amendment by restricting blacks' full participation in the political process. Specifically, Plaintiffs contend that those provisions were adopted for the racially discriminatory purpose of restricting the ability of black voters to influence property tax policy through ordinary lawmaking processes both in the Alabama Legislature and in their local governments, especially in majority-black counties, municipalities, and school districts; therefore, the provisions at issue in the instant Motion unconstitutionally burden the ability of blacks to further their political aims.

19. Plaintiffs rely principally on *Hunter v. Erickson*, 393 U.S. 385, 89 S.Ct. 557, 21 L.Ed.2d 616 (1969), in which the Supreme Court struck down an amendment to the Akron, Ohio, city charter that restricted the city counsel's authority to enact an ordinance prohibiting racial, religious, or ancestral discrimination in housing without prior voter approval. *Hunter*, 393 U.S. at 387, 89 S.Ct. 557. All other ordinances, including ordinances preventing housing discrimination on grounds other than race or religion, could be enacted simply with the support of the Akron City Counsel. *Id.* at 389–90, 89 S.Ct. 557.

20. Although the Akron amendment was facially neutral, the real effect of the legislation was to "disadvantage those who would benefit from laws barring racial, religious, or ancestral discriminations as against those who would bar other discriminations or who would otherwise regulate the real estate market in their favor." *Hunter*, 393 U.S. at 391, 89 S.Ct. 557. The Supreme Court further reasoned that "the reality is that the law's impact falls on the minority" in that the amendment "places special burdens on racial minorities within the governmental process." *Id.*

21. Likewise, in *Washington v. Seattle School District No. 1*, 458 U.S. 457, 102 S.Ct. 3187, 73 L.Ed.2d 896 (1982), the Supreme Court, following *Hunter*, struck down an initiative that was "carefully tailored to interfere with desegregative busing." *Washington*, 458 U.S. at 471, 102 S.Ct. 3187. In particular, that initiative prohibited school boards from requiring any student to attend a school other than the school nearest or next nearest to the student's residence. *Id.* at 462, 102 S.Ct. 3187. Like the ordinance in *Hunter*, the challenged initiative in *Washington* sought to frustrate attempts to provide legislation, *i.e.* busing for integration, designed to primarily benefit minorities. *Id.* at 472–74, 102 S.Ct. 3187. The Supreme Court therefore concluded that "[g]iven the

racial focus of [the initiative], this suffices to trigger application of the *Hunter* doctrine." *Id.* at 474, 102 S.Ct. 3187.

22. The Court is unpersuaded that the instant case falls under *Hunter* and its progeny. Specifically, unlike the challenged legislation in *Hunter* and *Washington,* Alabama's property tax structure uniformly affects all citizens of Alabama, regardless of race, burdening all of the constituency by making it difficult to influence or change the property tax structure.

23. Additionally, the purpose underlying the enactment of the legislation in both *Hunter* and *Washington* differs from the instant case. In those cases, the challenged legislation sought to eliminate the possibility of legislation specifically tailored to remedy discrimination and segregation. Here, on the other hand, the challenged constitutional provisions were not ratified with the intent to foreclose legislation specifically tailored to remedy discrimination. Accordingly, the Court does not find that the circumstances of this case trigger the applicability *Hunter* and its progeny.

24. In conclusion, therefore, although the provisions of the Alabama constitution may represent poor public tax policy, the Court finds that those provisions do not violate the Fourteenth Amendment.

Papasan v. Allain
478 U.S. 265 (1986)

In this case, we consider the claims of school officials and schoolchildren in 23 northern Mississippi counties that they are being unlawfully denied the economic benefits of public school lands granted by the United States to the State of Mississippi well over 100 years ago. Specifically, we must determine to what extent these claims are barred by the Eleventh Amendment and, with respect to those claims that are not barred, if any, whether the complaint is sufficient to withstand a motion to dismiss for failure to state a claim.

I

The history of public school lands in the United States stretches back over 200 years. Even before the ratification of the Constitution, the Congress of the Confederation initiated a practice with regard to the Northwest Territory which was followed with most other public lands that eventually became States and were admitted to the Union. In particular, the Land Ordinance of 1785, which provided for the survey and sale of the Northwest Territory, "reserved the lot No. 16, of every township, for the maintenance of public schools within the said township...." In 1802, when the eastern portion of the Northwest Territory became what is now the State of Ohio, Congress granted Ohio the lands that had been previously reserved under the 1785 Ordinance for the use of public schools in the State.

Following the Ohio example of reserving lands for the maintenance of public schools, "'grants were made for common school purposes to each of the public-land States admitted to the Union. Between the years of 1802 and 1846 the grants were of every section sixteen, and, thereafter, of sections sixteen and thirty-six. In some instances, additional sections have been granted.'" Thus, the basic Ohio example has been followed with respect to all but a few of the States admitted since then. In addition to the school lands designated in this manner, Congress made provision for townships in which the pertinent section or sections were not available for one reason or another. Thus, Congress generally indemnified States for the missing designated sections, allowing the States to select lands in an amount equal to and in lieu of the designated but unavailable lands.

Although the basic pattern of school lands grants was generally consistent from State to State in terms of the reservation and grant of the lands, the specific provisions of the grants varied by State and over time. For example, in Indiana and Alabama, the school lands were expressly granted to the inhabitants of the townships directly. In most of the other grants before 1845, the school lands were given instead to the States but were explicitly designated to be for the use of the townships in which they lay. The Michigan grant in 1836, on the other hand, was simply "to the State for the use of schools." See 5 Stat. 59. After 1845, the type of grant used in Michigan, granting the lands to the State for the use of its schools generally, became the norm. Finally, the most recent grants are phrased not as outright gifts to the States for a specific use but instead as express trusts. These grants also are stated to be to the States for the support of the schools in those States generally. In addition, though, under these grants the State is specifically designated a trustee, there are explicit restrictions on the management and disposition of the lands in trust, and the Federal Government expressly retains an ongoing oversight responsibility

The history of the school lands grants in Mississippi generally follows the pattern thus described. In 1798, Congress created the Mississippi Territory, which included what is now about the southern third of the States of Mississippi and Alabama. Congress provided for the sale and survey of all Mississippi Territory lands to which Indian title had been extinguished but excepted "the section number sixteen, which shall be reserved in each township for the support of schools within the same." In 1804, the Mississippi Territory was extended northward to the southern boundary of Tennessee. Two years later, Congress authorized the selection of lands in lieu of unavailable Sixteenth Sections in the Territory. Eventually, in 1817, Mississippi was admitted as a State, and a further Land Sales Act provided for the survey and sale of those lands in the northern part of the new State that had not been covered by the 1803 Act. The 1817 Act provided that these lands were to be "surveyed and divided in the manner provided by law for the surveying of the other public lands of the United States in the Mississippi territory"; thus, the Act required that "the section No. 16 in each township ... shall be reserved for the support of schools therein." The Sixteenth Section lands and lands selected in lieu thereof were granted to the State of Mississippi.

By their own terms, however, these Acts did not apply to the lands in northern Mississippi that were held by the Chickasaw Indian Nation, an area essentially comprising what came to be the northern 23 counties in the State. This land was held by the Chickasaws until 1832, when it was ceded to the United States by the Treaty of

Pontitoc Creek. Although that Treaty provided that the land would be surveyed and sold "in the same manner and on the same terms and conditions as the other public lands," no Sixteenth Section lands were reserved from sale. In 1836, Congress attempted to remedy this oversight by providing for the reservation of lands in lieu of the Sixteenth Section lands and for the vesting of the title to these lands "in the State of Mississippi, for the use of schools within [the Chickasaw Cession] in said State." These Chickasaw Cession Lieu Lands, some 174,555 acres, App. 36, were selected and given to the State. In 1856, however, with authority expressly given by Congress, the state legislature sold these lands and invested the proceeds, approximately $1,047,330, in 8% loans to the State's railroads. These railroads and the State's investment in them, unfortunately, were subsequently destroyed during the Civil War and never replaced.

From these historical circumstances, the current practice in Mississippi with regard to Sixteenth Section lands has evolved directly. Under state law, these lands, which are still apparently held in large part by the State, "constitute property held in trust for the benefit of the public schools and must be treated as such." Miss.Code Ann. § 29-3-1(1) (Supp.1985). In providing for the operation of these trusts, the legislature has retained the historical tie of these lands to particular townships in terms of both trust administration and beneficiary status. Thus, the State has delegated the management of this property to local school boards throughout the State: Where Sixteenth Section lands lie within a school district or where Lieu Lands were originally appropriated for a township that lies within a school district, the board of education of that district has "control and jurisdiction of said school trust lands and of all funds arising from any disposition thereof heretofore or hereafter made." *Ibid.* In this respect, the board of education is "under the general supervision of the state land commissioner." *Ibid.*[6] Further, the State has, by statute, set forth certain prescriptions for the management of these lands. Most important for purposes of this case, however, is Miss.Code Ann. § 29-3-109 (1972 and Supp.1985), which provides:

> "All expendable funds derived from sixteenth section or lieu lands shall be credited to the school districts of the township in which such sixteenth section lands may be located, or to which any sixteenth sections lieu lands may belong. Such funds shall not be expended except for the purpose of education of the educable children of the school district to which they belong, or as otherwise may be provided by law."

Consequently, all proceeds from Sixteenth Section and Lieu Lands are allocated directly to the specific township in which these lands are located or to which those lands apply. With respect to the Chickasaw Cession counties, to which no lands now belong, the state legislature has for over 100 years paid "interest" on the lost principal acquired from the sale of those lands in the form of annual appropriations to the Chickasaw Cession schools. Originally, the rate was 8%, but since 1890 the rate has been 6%. The annual amount until 1985 was $62,191.

The result of this dual treatment has for many years been a disparity in the level of school funds from Sixteenth Section lands that are available to the Chickasaw Cession schools as compared to the schools in the remainder of the State. In 1984, for example, the legislative appropriation for the Chickasaw Cession resulted in an estimated average per pupil income relative to the Sixteenth Section substitute appropriation of $0.63 per pupil. The average Sixteenth Section income in the rest of the State, in comparison, was estimated to be $75.34 per pupil. *Id.*, at 44. It is this disparity which gave rise to the present action.

In 1981, the petitioners, local school officials and schoolchildren from the Chickasaw Cession, filed suit in the United States District Court for the Northern District of Mississippi against the respondents, an assortment of state officials, challenging the disparity in Sixteenth Section funds. The petitioners' complaint traced the history of public school lands in Mississippi, characterizing as illegal several of the actions that resulted in there being now no Sixteenth Section lands in the Chickasaw Cession area. In particular, the petitioners asserted that the sale of the Chickasaw Cession school lands and unwise investment of the proceeds from that sale in the 1850's had abrogated the State's trust obligation to hold those lands for the benefit of Chickasaw Cession schoolchildren in perpetuity. The result of these actions, said the petitioners, was the disparity between the financial support available to the Chickasaw Cession schools and other schools in the State, which disparity in turn allegedly deprived the Chickasaw Cession schoolchildren of a minimally adequate level of education and of the equal protection of the laws.

Based on these allegations, the petitioners sought various forms of relief for breach of the trust regarding the Chickasaw Cession Sixteenth Section lands and for denial of equal protection. Specifically, the complaint sought a declaration that the state legislation purporting to implement the sale of the Chickasaw Cession school lands was void and unenforceable; the establishment by legislative appropriation or otherwise of a fund in a suitable amount to be held in perpetual trust for the benefit of plaintiffs; or in the alternative making available to plaintiffs Lieu Lands of the same value as the original Chickasaw Cession Sixteenth Section lands.

The District Court dismissed the complaint, holding the claims barred by the applicable statute of limitations and by the Eleventh Amendment to the United States Constitution. The Court of Appeals for the Fifth Circuit affirmed, *Papasan v. United States*, 756 F.2d 1087 (1985), agreeing that the relief requested in the complaint was barred by the Eleventh Amendment. Noting that a federal court should not dismiss a constitutional complaint because it "seeks one remedy rather than another plainly appropriate one," however, the Court of Appeals deemed the equal protection claim to assert a current, ongoing, and disparate distribution of state funds for the support of local schools, the remedy for which would not be barred by the Eleventh Amendment. Even so, it found dismissal of the complaint to be proper since such differential funding was not unconstitutional under this Court's decision in *San Antonio Independent School Dist. v. Rodriguez*, 411 U.S. 1, 93 S.Ct. 1278, 36 L.Ed.2d 16 (1973).

We granted certiorari, 474 U.S. 1004, 106 S.Ct. 521, 88 L.Ed.2d 454 (1985), and now vacate the judgment of the Court of Appeals and remand for further proceedings.

II

We first consider whether the Eleventh Amendment bars the petitioners' claims and required dismissal of the complaint.

A

The Amendment provides:

> "The Judicial power of the United States shall not be construed to extend to any suit in law or equity, commenced or prosecuted against one of the United States by Citizens of another State, or by Citizens or Subjects of any Foreign State."

This language expressly encompasses only suits brought against a State by citizens of another State, but this Court long ago held that the Amendment bars suits against a State by citizens of that same State as well. "[I]n the absence of consent a suit in which the State or one of its agencies or departments is named as the defendant is proscribed by the Eleventh Amendment." *Pennhurst State School and Hospital v. Halderman,* 465 U.S. 89, 100, 104 S.Ct. 900, 908, 79 L.Ed.2d 67 (1984). This bar exists whether the relief sought is legal or equitable

Where the State itself or one of its agencies or departments is not named as defendant and where a state official is named instead, the Eleventh Amendment status of the suit is less straightforward. *Ex parte Young,* 209 U.S. 123, 28 S.Ct. 441, 52 L.Ed. 714 (1908), held that a suit to enjoin as unconstitutional a state official's action was not barred by the Amendment. This holding was based on a determination that an unconstitutional state enactment is void and that any action by a state official that is purportedly authorized by that enactment cannot be taken in an official capacity since the state authorization for such action is a nullity. As the Court explained in *Young* itself:

> "If the act which the state Attorney General seeks to enforce be a violation of the Federal Constitution, the officer proceeding under such enactment comes into conflict with the superior authority of that Constitution, and he is in that case stripped of his official or representative character and is subjected in his person to the consequences of his individual conduct. The State has no power to impart to him any immunity from responsibility to the supreme authority of the United States." Id., at 159–160, 28 S.Ct., at 454.

Thus, the official, although acting in his official capacity, may be sued in federal court.

Young, however, does not insulate from Eleventh Amendment challenge every suit in which a state official is the named defendant. In accordance with its original rationale, *Young* applies only where the underlying authorization upon which the named official acts is asserted to be illegal. And it does not foreclose an Eleventh Amendment challenge where the official action is asserted to be illegal as a matter of state law alone. In such a case, federal supremacy is not implicated because the state official is acting contrary to state law only.

* * *

Relief that in essence serves to compensate a party injured in the past by an action of a state official in his official capacity that was illegal under federal law is barred even when the state official is the named defendant. This is true if the relief is expressly denominated as damages. It is also true if the relief is tantamount to an award of damages for a past violation of federal law, even though styled as something else. On the other hand, relief that serves directly to bring an end to a present violation of federal law is not barred by the Eleventh Amendment even though accompanied by a substantial ancillary effect on the state treasury.

For Eleventh Amendment purposes, the line between permitted and prohibited suits will often be indistinct: "[T]he difference between the type of relief barred by the Eleventh Amendment and that permitted under *Ex parte Young* will not in many instances be that between day and night." *Edelman, supra,* at 667, 94 S.Ct., at 1357. In discerning on which side of the line a particular case falls, we look to the substance rather than to the form of the relief sought, and will be guided by the policies underlying the decision in *Ex parte Young.*

B

The petitioners claim that the federal grants of school lands to the State of Mississippi created a perpetual trust, with the State as trustee, for the benefit of the public schools. Relying on *Alamo Land & Cattle Co. v. Arizona,* 424 U.S. 295, 96 S.Ct. 910, 47 L.Ed.2d 1 (1976), and *Lassen v. Arizona ex rel. Arizona Highway Dept.,* 385 U.S. 458, 87 S.Ct. 584, 17 L.Ed.2d 515 (1967), the petitioners contend that "[s]chool lands trusts impose specific burdens and obligations on the states, as well as the state officials who act as trustees, which include preserving the corpus, maximizing income, and, where the corpus is lost or converted wrongfully, continuing the payment of appropriate income indefinitely." The idea that this last obligation exists is gleaned not from any prior judicial construction of school lands grants but instead from alleged federal common-law rules that purportedly govern such trusts. The petitioners rely on this asserted continuing obligation in contending that they seek only a prospective, injunctive remedy, permissible under *Ex parte Young,* requiring state officials to meet that continuing federal obligation by providing the Chickasaw Cession schools with appropriate trust income.

To begin with, it is not at all clear that the school lands grants to Mississippi created a binding trust. The respondents, in fact, contend that the school lands were given to the State in fee simple absolute and that no binding federal obligation was imposed. But even if the petitioners' legal characterization is accepted, their trust claims are barred by the Eleventh Amendment. The distinction between a continuing obligation on the part of the trustee and an ongoing liability for past breach of trust is essentially a formal distinction of the sort we rejected in *Edelman.* There, the Court of Appeals had upheld an award of "equitable restitution" against the state official, requiring the payment to the plaintiff class of "all AABD benefits wrongfully withheld." 415 U.S., at 656, 94 S.Ct., at 1352. We found, to the contrary, that the "retroactive award of monetary relief ... is in practical effect indistinguishable in many aspects from an award of damages against the State."

The characterization in that case of the legal wrong as the continuing withholding of accrued benefits is very similar to the petitioners' characterization of the legal wrong here as the breach of a continuing obligation to comply with the trust obligations. We discern no substantive difference between a not-yet-extinguished liability for a past breach of trust and the continuing obligation to meet trust responsibilities asserted by the petitioners. In both cases, the trustee is required, because of the past loss of the trust corpus, to use its own resources to take the place of the corpus or the lost income from the corpus. Even if the petitioners here were seeking only the payment of an amount equal to the income from the lost corpus, such payment would be merely a substitute for the return of the trust corpus itself. That is, continuing payment of the income from the lost corpus is essentially equivalent in economic terms to a one-time restoration of the lost corpus itself: It is in substance the award, as continuing income rather than as a lump sum, of "'an *accrued* monetary liability.'" *Milliken v. Bradley,* 433 U.S., at 289, 97 S.Ct., at 2762 (quoting *Edelman,* 415 U.S., at 664, 94 S.Ct., at 1356). Thus, we hold that the petitioners' trust claim, like the claim we rejected in *Edelman,* may not be sustained.

C

The Court of Appeals held, however, that the petitioners' equal protection claim was not barred by the Eleventh Amendment. We agree with that ruling. The complaint asserted:

> "By their aforesaid past, present and future deprivations of and to Plaintiffs and the Plaintiff class of the use and benefits of their Sixteenth Section Lands, while at the same time granting to and securing to all other school districts and school children in the State of Mississippi in perpetuity the use and benefit of their Sixteenth Section Lands, the State Defendants have deliberately, intentionally, purposefully, and with design denied to Plaintiffs and the Plaintiff class the equal protection of the laws in violation of their rights secured by the Fourteenth Amendment to the Constitution of the United States." App. 20.

The petitioners also alleged that these same actions denied them "their rights to an interest in a minimally adequate level of education, or reasonable opportunity therefor," *id.,* at 21, while assuring such right to the other schoolchildren in the State. Thus the complaint alleged a present disparity in the distribution of the benefits from the State's Sixteenth Section lands.

This alleged ongoing constitutional violation—the unequal distribution by the State of the benefits of the State's school lands—is precisely the type of continuing violation for which a remedy may permissibly be fashioned under *Young.* It may be that the current disparity results directly from the same actions in the past that are the subject of the petitioners' trust claims, but the essence of the equal protection allegation is the present disparity in the distribution of the benefits of state-held assets and not the past actions of the State. A remedy to eliminate this current disparity, even a remedy that might require the expenditure of state funds, would ensure "'compliance *in the future* with a substantive federal-question determination'" rather than bestow an award for accrued monetary liability. *Milliken, supra* 433 U.S., at 289, 97 S.Ct., at 2762 (quoting *Edelman, supra* 415 U.S., at 668, 94 S.Ct., at 1358). This claim is, in fact, in all essential respects the same as the equal protection claim for which relief was approved in *Milliken*. Consequently, we agree with the Court of Appeals that the Eleventh Amendment would not bar relief necessary to correct a current violation of the Equal Protection Clause and that this claim may not properly be dismissed on this basis.

III

The question remains whether the petitioners' equal protection claim, although not barred by the Eleventh Amendment, is legally insufficient and was properly dismissed for failure to state a claim. We are bound for the purposes of this review to take the well-pleaded factual allegations in the complaint as true. Construing these facts and relevant facts obtained from the public record in the light most favorable to the petitioners, we must ascertain whether they state a claim on which relief could be granted.

A

In *Rodriguez,* the Court upheld against an equal protection challenge Texas' system of financing its public schools, under which funds for the public schools were derived from two main sources. Approximately half of the funds came from the Texas Minimum Foundation School Program, a state program aimed at guaranteeing a certain level of minimum education for all children in the State. Most of the remainder of the funds came from local sources—in particular local property taxes. As a result of this dual funding system, most specifically as a result of differences in amounts collected from local property taxes, "substantial interdistrict disparities in school expenditures [were] found ... in varying degrees throughout the State

In examining the equal protection status of these disparities, the Court declined to apply any heightened scrutiny based either on wealth as a suspect classification or on education as a fundamental right. As to the latter, the Court recognized the importance of public education but noted that education "is not among the rights afforded explicit protection under our Federal Constitution." The Court did not, however, foreclose the possibility "that some identifiable quantum of education is a constitutionally protected prerequisite to the meaningful exercise of either [the right to speak or the right to vote]." Given the absence of such radical denial of educational opportunity, it was concluded that the State's school financing scheme would be constitutional if it bore "some rational relationship to a legitimate state purpose."

Applying this standard, the dual Texas system was deemed reasonably structured to accommodate two separate forces:

> "'[T]he desire by members of society to have educational opportunity for all children, and the desire of each family to provide the best education it can afford for its own children.'

"... While assuring a basic education for every child in the State, it permits and encourages a large measure of participation in and control of each district's schools at the local level

Given this rational basis, the Court concluded that the mere "happenstance" that the quality of education might vary from district to district because of varying property values within the districts did not render the system "so irrational as to be invidiously discriminatory." In particular, the Court found that "any scheme of local taxation—indeed the very existence of identifiable local governmental units—requires the establishment of jurisdictional boundaries that are inevitably arbitrary."

Almost 10 years later, the Court again considered the equal protection status of the administration of the Texas public schools—this time in relation to the State's decision not to expend any state funds on the education of children who were not "legally admitted" to the United States. *Plyler v. Doe,* 457 U.S. 202, 102 S.Ct. 2382, 72 L.Ed.2d 786 (1982). The Court did not, however, measurably change the approach articulated in *Rodriguez.* It reiterated that education is not a fundamental right and concluded that undocumented aliens were not a suspect class. Nevertheless, it concluded that the justifications for the discrimination offered by the State were "wholly insubstantial in light of the costs involved to these children, the State, and the Nation."

B

The complaint in this case asserted not simply that the petitioners had been denied their right to a minimally adequate education but also that such a right was fundamental and that because that right had been infringed the State's action here should be reviewed under strict scrutiny. App. 20. As *Rodriguez* and *Plyler* indicate, this Court has not yet definitively settled the questions whether a minimally adequate education is a fundamental right and whether a statute alleged to discriminatorily infringe that right should be accorded heightened equal protection review.

Nor does this case require resolution of these issues. Although for the purposes of this motion to dismiss we must take all the factual allegations in the complaint as true, we are not bound to accept as true a legal conclusion couched as a factual allegation. The petitioners' allegation that, by reason of the funding disparities relating to the Sixteenth Section lands, they have been deprived of a minimally adequate education is just such an allegation. The petitioners do not allege that schoolchildren in the Chickasaw Counties are not taught to read or write; they do not allege that they receive no instruction on even the educational basics; they allege no actual facts in support of their assertion that they have been deprived of a minimally adequate education. As we see it, we are not bound to credit and may disregard the allegation that the petitioners have been denied a minimally adequate education.

Concentrating instead on the disparities in terms of Sixteenth Section lands benefits that the complaint in fact alleged and that are documented in the public record, we are persuaded that the Court of Appeals properly determined that *Rodriguez* dictates the applicable standard of review. The differential treatment alleged here constitutes an equal protection violation only if it is not rationally related to a legitimate state interest.

Applying this test, the Court of Appeals concluded that, historical roots aside, the essence of the petitioners' claim was an attack on Mississippi's system of financing public education. And it reasoned that the inevitability of disparities in income derived from real estate managed and administered locally, as in *Rodriguez,* supplied a rationale for the disparities alleged. To begin with, we disagree with the Court of Appeals' apparent understanding of the crux of the petitioners' claim. As we read their complaint, the petitioners do not challenge the overall organization of the Mississippi public school financing program. Instead, their challenge is restricted to one aspect of that program: The Sixteenth Section and Lieu Lands funding. All of the allegations in the complaint center around disparities in the distribution of these particular benefits, and no allegations concerning disparities in other public school funding programs are included.

Consequently, this is a very different claim than the claim made in *Rodriguez.* In *Rodriguez,* the contention was that the State's overall system of funding was unconstitutionally discriminatory. There, the Court examined the basic structure of that system and concluded that it was rationally related to a legitimate state purpose. In reaching that conclusion, the Court necessarily found that funding disparities resulting from differences in local taxes were acceptable because related to the state goal of allowing a measure of effective local control over school funding levels. *Rodriguez* did not, however, purport to validate all funding variations that might result from a State's public school funding decision. It held merely that the variations that resulted from allowing local control over local property tax funding of the public schools were constitutionally permissible in that case.

Here, the petitioners' claim goes neither to the overall funding system nor to the local ad valorem component of that system. Instead, it goes solely to the Sixteenth Section and Lieu Lands portion of the State's public school funding. And, as to this claim, we are unpersuaded that *Rodriguez* resolves the equal protection question in favor of the State. The allegations of the complaint are that the State is distributing the income from Sixteenth Section lands or from lieu lands or funds unequally among the school districts, to the detriment of the Chickasaw Cession schools and their students. The Sixteenth Section and Lieu Lands in Mississippi were granted to and held by the State itself. Under state law, these lands "constitute property held in trust for the benefit of the public schools and must be treated as such," but in carrying out the trust, the State has vested the management of these lands in the local school boards throughout the State, under the supervision of the Secretary of State, and has credited the income from these lands to the "school districts of the township in which such sixteenth section lands may be located, or to which any sixteenth section lieu lands may belong," such income to be used for the purpose of educating the children of the school district or as otherwise may be provided by law. This case is therefore very different from *Rodriguez,* where the differential financing available to school districts was traceable to school district funds available from local real estate taxation, not to a state decision to divide state resources unequally among school districts. The rationality of the disparity in *Rodriguez*, therefore, which rested on the fact that funding disparities based on differing local wealth were a necessary adjunct of allowing meaningful local control over school funding, does not settle the constitutionality of disparities alleged in this case, and we differ with the Court of Appeals in this respect.

Nevertheless, the question remains whether the variations in the benefits received by school districts from Sixteenth Section or Lieu Lands are, on the allegations in the complaint and as a matter of law, rationally related to a legitimate state interest. We believe, however, that we should not pursue this issue here but should instead remand the case for further proceedings. Neither the Court of Appeals nor the parties have addressed the equal protection issue as we think it is posed by this case: Given that the State has title to assets granted to it by the Federal Government for the use of the State's schools, does the Equal Protection Clause permit it to distribute the benefit of these assets unequally among the school districts as it now does?

A crucial consideration in resolving this issue is whether the federal law requires the State to allocate the economic benefits of school lands to schools in the townships in which those lands are located. If, as a matter of federal law, the State has no choice in the matter, whether the complaint states an equal protection claim depends on whether the federal policy is itself violative of the Clause. If it is, the State may properly be enjoined from implementing such policy. Contrariwise, if the federal law is valid and the State is bound by it, then it provides a rational reason for the funding disparity. Neither the courts below nor the parties have addressed the equal protection issue in these terms. Another possible consideration in resolving the equal protection issue is that school lands require management and that the State has assigned this task to the individual districts in which the lands are located, subject to supervision by the State. The significance, if any, in equal protection terms of this allocation of duties in justifying assigning the income exclusively to those who perform the management function and none of it to those districts that have no lands to manage is a matter that is best addressed by the lower courts in the first instance.

Accordingly, the judgment of the Court of Appeals is affirmed insofar as it affirmed the dismissal of petitioners' breach of trust and related claims. With respect to the affirmance of the District Court's dismissal of the equal protection claim, the judgment of the Court of Appeals is vacated, and the case is remanded to that court for further proceedings consistent with this opinion.

So ordered.

Leandro v. State
346 N.C. 336, 488 S.E.2d 249 (1997)

Plaintiffs in this action for declaratory and injunctive relief are students and their parents or guardians from the relatively poor school systems in Cumberland, Halifax,

Hoke, Robeson, and Vance Counties and the boards of education for those counties. Plaintiff-intervenors are students and their parents or guardians from the relatively large and wealthy school systems of the City of Asheville and of Buncombe, Wake, Forsyth, Mecklenburg, and Durham Counties and the boards of education for those systems. Both plaintiffs and plaintiff-intervenors (hereinafter "plaintiff-parties" when referred to collectively) allege in their complaints in the case resulting in this appeal that they have a right to adequate educational opportunities which is being denied them by defendants under the current school funding system. Plaintiff-parties also allege that the North Carolina Constitution not only creates a fundamental right to an education, but it also guarantees that every child, no matter where he or she resides, is entitled to equal educational opportunities. Plaintiff-parties allege that defendants have denied them this right.

Plaintiffs allege that children in their poor school districts are not receiving a sufficient education to meet the minimal standard for a constitutionally adequate education. Plaintiffs further allege that children in their districts are denied an equal education because there is a great disparity between the educational opportunities available to children in their districts and those offered in more wealthy districts of our state. Plaintiffs allege that their districts lack the necessary resources to provide fundamental educational opportunities for their children due to the nature of the state's system of financing education and the burden it places on local governments. They allege that the state leaves the funding of capital expenses, as well as twenty-five percent of current school expenses, to local governments. They further allege that although their poor districts are the beneficiaries of higher local tax rates than many wealthy school districts, those higher rates cannot make up for their lack of resources or for the disparities between systems. Plaintiffs also allege that students in their poor school districts are not receiving the education called for by the Basic Education Program, part of the statutory framework for providing education to the children of this state.

Plaintiffs complain of inadequate school facilities with insufficient space, poor lighting, leaking roofs, erratic heating and air conditioning, peeling paint, cracked plaster, and rusting exposed pipes. They allege that their poor districts' media centers have sparse and outdated book collections and lack the technology present in the wealthier school districts. They complain that they are unable to compete for high quality teachers because local salary supplements in their poor districts are well below those provided in wealthy districts. Plaintiffs allege that this relative inability to hire teachers causes the number of students per teacher to be higher in their poor districts than in wealthy districts.

Plaintiffs allege that college admission test scores and yearly aptitude test scores reflect both the inadequacy and the disparity in education received by children in their poor districts. Plaintiffs allege that end-of-grade tests show that the great majority of students in plaintiffs' districts are failing in basic subjects.

Plaintiff-intervenors allege that the current state educational funding system does not sufficiently take into consideration the burdens faced by their urban school districts, which must educate a large number of students with extraordinary educational needs. In particular, plaintiff-intervenors claim that their school districts have a large number of students who require special education services, special English instruction, and academically gifted programs. They allege that providing these services requires plaintiff-intervenor school boards to divert substantial resources from their regular education programs.

Plaintiff-intervenors contend that defendants, the State of North Carolina and the State Board of Education, have violated the North Carolina Constitution and chapter 115C of the North Carolina General Statutes by failing to ensure that their relatively wealthy school districts have sufficient resources to provide all of their students with adequate and equal educational opportunities. In addition, plaintiff-intervenors claim that the state's singling out of certain poor rural districts to receive supplemental state funds, while failing to recognize comparable if not greater needs in the urban school districts, is arbitrary and capricious in violation of the North Carolina Constitution and state law. Plaintiff-intervenors allege that deficiencies in physical facilities and educational materials are particularly significant in their systems because most of the growth in North Carolina's student population is taking place in urban areas such as those served by plaintiff-intervenor school boards. They claim that their urban districts must serve a disproportionate number of children who due to poverty, language barriers, or other handicaps, require special resources. They allege that because urban counties have high levels of poverty, homelessness, crime, unmet health care needs, and unemployment which drain their fiscal resources, they cannot allocate as large a portion of their local tax revenues to public education as can the more rural poor districts.

In response to plaintiffs' and plaintiff-intervenors' complaints seeking declaratory and other relief, defendants filed a motion to dismiss under N.C.G.S.1A-1, Rule 12(b)(1)(2) and (6), asserting that the trial court lacked subject matter and personal jurisdiction and that plaintiff-parties had failed to state any claim upon which relief could be granted. After a hearing, Judge Braswell denied defendants' motion to dismiss. Defendants filed a timely notice of appeal to the Court of Appeals from the order denying their motion to dismiss. Following denial of a joint petition of the parties for discretionary review by this Court prior to determination by the Court of Appeals, defendants filed an alternative petition for writ of certiorari with the Court of Appeals. The petition was allowed, and the matter was heard 24 January 1996 in the Court of Appeals.

The Court of Appeals reversed the trial court's order denying defendants' motion to dismiss. In its opinion, the Court of Appeals concluded that the right to education guaranteed by the North Carolina Constitution is limited to one of equal access to the existing system of education and does not embrace a qualitative standard....

Defendants argued in the Court of Appeals that the trial court had erred by denying their motion to dismiss plaintiff-parties' educational adequacy claims as being "nonjusticiable political questions." Defendants did not raise this defense as to plaintiff-parties' other claims. The Court of Appeals based its decision on other grounds and did not reach the "political question" issue, but defendants maintain that the "political question" issue is a threshold question that must be addressed. We address it now.

It has long been understood that it is the duty of the courts to determine the meaning of the requirements of our Constitution. When a government action is challenged as unconstitutional, the courts have a duty to determine whether that action exceeds constitutional limits. Therefore, it is the duty of this Court to address plaintiff-parties' constitutional challenge to the state's public education system. Defendants' argument is without merit.

Plaintiff-parties first argue that the Court of Appeals erred in holding that no right to a qualitatively adequate education arises under the North Carolina Constitution. We agree.

The right to a free public education is explicitly guaranteed by the North Carolina Constitution: "The people have a right to the privilege of education, and it is the duty of the State to guard and maintain that right." N.C. Const. art. I sec 15. The Constitution also provides:

> The General Assembly shall provide by taxation and otherwise for a general
> and uniform system of free public schools, which shall be maintained at least
> nine months in every year, and wherein equal opportunities shall be provided
> for all students.

Id. art. IX, § 2(1). The principal question presented by this argument is whether the people's constitutional right to education has any qualitative content, that is, whether the state is required to provide children with an education that meets some minimum standard of quality. We answer that question in the affirmative and conclude that the right to education provided in the state constitution is a right to a sound basic education. An education that does not serve the purpose of preparing students to participate and compete in the society in which they live and work is devoid of substance and is constitutionally inadequate.

The Court of Appeals concluded that the right to education guaranteed by the state constitution "is limited to one of equal access to education, and it does not embrace a qualitative standard." ...

This Court has long recognized that there is a qualitative standard inherent in the right to education guaranteed by this state's constitution. In *Board of Educ. v. Board of Comm'rs of Granville County,* 174 N.C. 469, 93 S.E. 1001 (1917), for example, we stated:

> [I]t is manifest that these constitutional provisions were intended to establish
> a system of public education *adequate to the needs of a great and progressive
> people,* affording school facilities of recognized and ever-increasing merit to
> all the children of the State, and to the full extent that our means could afford
> and intelligent direction accomplish.

Id. at 472, 93 S.E. at 1002 (emphasis added).

The General Assembly also seems to have recognized the constitutional right to a sound basic education and to have embraced that right in chapter 115C of the General

Statutes. For example, in a statute governing the use of funds under the control of the State Board of Education, the General Assembly has stated:

> (a) It is the policy of the State of North Carolina to create a public school system that graduates good citizens with the skills demanded in the marketplace, and the skills necessary to cope with contemporary society, using State, local and other funds in the most cost-effective manner....

> (b) To insure a *quality* education for every child in North Carolina, and to assure that the necessary resources are provided, it is the policy of the State of North Carolina to provide from State revenue sources the instructional expenses for current operations of the public school system as defined in the standard course of study.

N.C.G.S. § 115C-408 (1994) (emphasis added). In addition, the legislature has required local boards of education "to provide *adequate* school systems within their respective local school administrative units, as directed by law." N.C.G.S. § 115C-47(1) (Supp.1996) (emphasis added).

We conclude that Article I, Section 15 and Article IX, Section 2 of the North Carolina Constitution combine to guarantee every child of this state an opportunity to receive a sound basic education in our public schools. For purposes of our Constitution, a "sound basic education" is one that will provide the student with at least: (1) sufficient ability to read, write, and speak the English language and a sufficient knowledge of fundamental mathematics and physical science to enable the student to function in a complex and rapidly changing society; (2) sufficient fundamental knowledge of geography, history, and basic economic and political systems to enable the student to make informed choices with regard to issues that affect the student personally or affect the student's community, state, and nation; (3) sufficient academic and vocational skills to enable the student to successfully engage in post-secondary education or vocational training; and (4) sufficient academic and vocational skills to enable the student to compete on an equal basis with others in further formal education or gainful employment in contemporary society.

The trial court properly denied defendants' motion to dismiss this claim for relief. The Court of Appeals erred in concluding otherwise.

By other arguments, plaintiff-parties contend that the Court of Appeals erred in holding that the alleged disparity in the educational opportunities offered by the different school districts in the state does not violate their right to equal opportunities for education. They contend that Article IX, Section 2(1), requiring a "general and uniform system" in which "equal opportunities shall be provided for all students," mandates equality in the educational programs and resources offered the children in all school districts in North Carolina.

Plaintiffs and plaintiff-intervenors make somewhat different arguments in support of their purported rights to equal educational opportunities. Specifically, plaintiffs contend that inequalities in the facilities, equipment, student-teacher ratios, and test results between their poor districts and the wealthy districts compel the conclusion that students in their poor districts are denied equal opportunities for education. Plaintiffs contend that such inequalities arise from great variations in per-pupil expenditures from district to district.

We first look to the North Carolina Constitution itself to determine whether it provides a basis for relief. It places upon the General Assembly the duty of providing for "a general and uniform system of free public schools ... wherein equal opportunities shall be provided for all students." N.C. Const. art. IX, §2(1). We conclude that at the time this provision was originally written in 1868 providing for a "general and uniform" system but without the equal opportunities clause, the intent of the framers was that every child have a fundamental right to a sound basic education which would prepare the child to participate fully in society as it existed in his or her lifetime. *See, e.g., City of Greensboro v. Hodgin,* 106 N.C. 182, 190, 11 S.E. 586, 589 (1890); *Lane v. Stanly,* 65 N.C. 153, 158 (1871). The 1970 amendment adding the equal opportunities clause ensured that all the children of this state would enjoy this right.

The issue here, however, is plaintiffs' contention that North Carolina's system of school funding, based in part on funding by the county in which the district is located, necessarily denies the students in plaintiffs' relatively poor school districts educational opportunities equal to those available in relatively wealthy districts and thereby violates the equal opportunities clause of Article IX, Section 2(1). Although we have concluded that the North Carolina Constitution requires that access to a sound basic education be provided equally in every school district, we are convinced that the equal opportunities clause of Article IX, Section 2(1) does not require substantially equal funding or educational advantages in all school districts. We have considered the language and history underlying this and other constitutional provisions concerned with education as well as former opinions by this Court. As a result, we conclude that provisions of the current state system for funding schools which require or allow counties to help finance their school systems and result in unequal funding among the school districts of the state do not violate constitutional principles.

Article IX, Section 2(2) of the North Carolina Constitution expressly authorizes the General Assembly to require that local governments bear part of the costs of their local public schools. Further, it expressly provides that local governments may add to or supplement their school programs as much as they wish.

> The General Assembly may assign to units of local government such responsibility for the financial support of the free public schools as it may deem appropriate. The governing boards of units of local government with financial responsibility for public education may use local revenues to add to or supplement any public school or post-secondary school program.

N.C. Const. art. IX, §2(2).

...

Because the North Carolina Constitution expressly states that units of local governments with financial responsibility for public education may provide additional funding to supplement the educational programs provided by the state, there can be nothing unconstitutional about their doing so or in any inequality of opportunity occurring as a result. We agree with the reasoning of the Court of Appeals in *Britt* that

> the Constitution itself contains provisions that contradict plaintiffs' arguments. The governing boards of units of local government having financial responsibility for public education are expressly authorized to "use local revenues to add to or supplement any public school or post-secondary school program." N.C. Const., Article IX, § 2(2). Clearly then, a county with greater financial resources will be able to supplement its programs to a greater degree than less wealthy counties, resulting in enhanced educational opportunity for its students.... [This] provision[ ] obviously preclude[s] the possibility that exactly equal educational opportunities can be offered throughout the State.

Britt, 86 N.C.App. at 288, 357 S.E.2d at 435–36.

Further, as the North Carolina Constitution so clearly creates the likelihood of unequal funding among the districts as a result of local supplements, we see no reason to suspect that the framers intended that substantially equal educational opportunities beyond the sound basic education mandated by the Constitution must be available in all districts. A constitutional requirement to provide substantial equality of educational opportunities in every one of the various school districts of the state would almost certainly ensure that no matter how much money was spent on the schools of the state, at any given time some of those districts would be out of compliance. If strong local public support in a given district improved the educational opportunities of that district to the point that they were substantially better than those of any other district, the children of all the other school districts by definition would be denied substantially equal educational opportunities. The result would be a steady stream of litigation which would constantly interfere with the running of the schools of the state and unnecessarily deplete their human and fiscal resources as well as the resources of the courts.

Substantial problems have been experienced in those states in which the courts have held that the state constitution guaranteed the right to a sound basic education.... We conclude that the framers of our Constitution did not intend to set such an impractical or unattainable goal. Instead, their focus was upon ensuring that the children of the state have the opportunity to receive a sound basic education.

For the foregoing reasons, we conclude that Article IX, Section 2(1) of the North Carolina Constitution requires that all children have the opportunity for a sound basic education, but it does not require that equal educational opportunities be afforded students in all of the school districts of the state. The Court of Appeals did not err in reversing the order of the trial court to the extent that order denied defendants' motion to dismiss this claim for relief.

Plaintiff-intervenors make a different argument. They neither allege in their complaint nor argue before this Court that constitutionally mandated educational opportunities require equal funding. Instead, they allege and contend that due to the particular demographics of their urban districts, which include many disadvantaged children, the current state system leaves them unable to provide all of their students a "minimally adequate" basic education. Ironically, if plaintiff-intervenors' argument should prevail, they would be entitled to an unequally large per-pupil allocation of state school funds for their relatively wealthy urban districts. When reduced to its essence, however, this argument by plaintiff-intervenors is merely repetitious of their previous argument that the state must provide all of its children with the opportunity to receive a sound basic education. As we have already concluded that the children of the state enjoy that right and that plaintiff-intervenors may proceed on that claim, we need not and do not address this argument by plaintiff-intervenors.

In another argument, plaintiffs contend that the disparities in the funding provided their poor school districts as compared to the wealthier districts deprive them of equal protection of the laws in violation of Article I, Section 19 of the North Carolina Constitution. Here again, plaintiffs are complaining of the disparities resulting from the local supplements going to the wealthier districts as expressly authorized by Article IX, Section 2(2). Any disparity in school funding among the districts resulting from local subsidies is directly attributable to Article IX, Section 2(2) itself. Plaintiffs are essentially reduced to arguing that one section of the North Carolina Constitution violates another. It is axiomatic that the terms or requirements of a constitution cannot be in violation of the same constitution—a constitution cannot violate itself. This argument is without merit.

In another argument, plaintiff-intervenors contend that their relatively wealthy urban districts have been denied equal protection of the laws because there is no rational nexus between the current allocation of the state's portion of the funding for the school districts and the actual costs of providing students with educational services. This problem is especially acute in plaintiff-intervenors' districts, they contend, because they have greater numbers of students requiring special education programs than other districts. Plaintiff-intervenors complain that the current funding system does not take into consideration the amount of money required to educate particular students with special needs. Plaintiff-intervenors argue, therefore, that the state system providing supplemental state funding to poor and small school districts is arbitrary and denies students in plaintiff-intervenors' wealthy urban districts the equal protection of the laws guaranteed by Article I, Section 19.

Plaintiff-intervenors do not argue that the General Assembly may not provide supplemental state funds to some districts and not others. Instead, they contend that the General Assembly has set up the programs for supplementing some but not all districts from purely state funds arbitrarily and without regard for the actual supplemental educational needs of particular school districts throughout the state.

Because we conclude that the General Assembly, under Article IX, Section 2(1), has the duty of providing the children of every school district with access to a sound basic education, we also conclude that it has inherent power to do those things reasonably related to meeting that constitutionally prescribed duty. This power would include the power to create a supplemental state funding program which has as its purpose the provision of additional state funds to poor districts so that they can provide their students access to a sound basic education. However, a funding system that distributed state funds to the districts in an arbitrary and capricious manner unrelated to such educational objectives simply would not be a valid exercise of that constitutional authority and could result in a denial of equal protection or due process.

We conclude that the Court of Appeals erred in reversing the trial court's denial of the motion to dismiss this claim by plaintiff-intervenors. Plaintiff-intervenors have made sufficient allegations in their complaint to entitle them to proceed to attempt to prove that the state supplemental funding system in question is unrelated to legitimate educational objectives and, therefore, is arbitrary and capricious. The Court of Appeals erred in holding to the contrary and in reversing the trial court's denial of defendants' motion to dismiss this claim for relief.

In other arguments, plaintiff-parties contend that the Court of Appeals erred in holding that they had not made sufficient allegations in their complaints to state a claim for the violation of their rights under chapter 115C of the North Carolina General Statutes. We find it unnecessary to dwell at length on these arguments by plaintiff-parties, as even they agree that most of the sections of the statutes they rely upon do little more than codify a fundamental right guaranteed by our Constitution.

Specifically, plaintiff-parties allege in their complaints that the education system of North Carolina as currently maintained and operated violates the following requirements of chapter 115C: (1) that part of N.C.G.S. § 115C-1 requiring a "general and uniform system of free public schools ... throughout the State, wherein equal opportunities shall be provided for all students"; (2) that part of N.C.G.S. § 115C-81(a1) requiring that the state provide "every student in the State equal access to a Basic Education Program"; (3) that part of N.C.G.S. § 115C-122(3) requiring the state to "prevent denial of equal educational ... opportunity on the basis of ... economic status ... in the provision of services to any child"; and (4) that part of N.C.G.S. § 115C-408(b) requiring that the state "assure that the necessary resources are provided ... from State revenue sources [for] the instructional expenses for current operations of the public school system as defined in the standard course of study." We conclude that none of the statutes relied upon by plaintiff-parties requires that substantially equal educational opportunities be offered in each of the school districts of the state. Instead, those statutes, at most, reiterate the constitutional requirement that every child in the state have equal access to a sound basic education. To the extent that plaintiff-parties can produce evidence tending to show that defendants have committed the violations of chapter 115C alleged in the complaints and that those violations have deprived children of some districts of the opportunity to receive a sound basic education, plaintiff-parties are entitled to do so. The Court of Appeals erred in its conclusion to the contrary.

As we have stated in this opinion, we conclude that the North Carolina Constitution does not guarantee a right to equal educational opportunities in each of the various school districts of the state. Therefore, the Court of Appeals was correct in concluding that the trial court erred in failing to dismiss plaintiff-parties' claims for relief based upon this purported right.

We have concluded, however, that the North Carolina Constitution does guarantee every child of the state the opportunity to receive a "sound basic education" as we have defined that phrase in this opinion. We have announced that definition with some trepidation. We recognize that judges are not experts in education and are not particularly able to identify in detail those curricula best designed to ensure that a child receives a sound basic education. However, it is the duty of this Court under the North Carolina Constitution to be the final authority in interpreting that constitution, and the definition we have given of a "sound basic education" is that which we conclude is the minimum constitutionally permissible.

We acknowledge that the legislative process provides a better forum than the courts for discussing and determining what educational programs and resources are most likely to ensure that each child of the state receives a sound basic education. The members of the General Assembly are popularly elected to represent the public for the purpose of making just such decisions. The legislature, unlike the courts, is not limited to addressing only cases and controversies brought before it by litigants. The legislature can properly conduct public hearings and committee meetings at which it can hear and consider the views of the general public as well as educational experts and permit the full expression of all points of view as to what curricula will best ensure that every child of the state has the opportunity to receive a sound basic education.

We have concluded that some of the allegations in the complaints of plaintiff-parties state claims upon which relief may be granted if they are supported by substantial evidence. Therefore, we must remand this case to the trial court to permit plaintiff-parties to proceed on those claims.

Educational goals and standards adopted by the legislature are factors which may be considered on remand to the trial court for its determination as to whether any of the state's children are being denied their right to a sound basic education. *See generally* William E. Thro, *Judicial Analysis During the Third Wave of School Finance Litigation: The Massachusetts Decision as a Model*, 35 B.C.L.Rev. 597 (1994). They will not be determinative on this issue, however.

Another factor which may properly be considered in this determination is the level of performance of the children of the state and its various districts on standard achievement tests. In fact, such "output" measurements may be more reliable than measurements of "input" such as per-pupil funding or general educational funding provided by the state. *Id.* at 329. It must be recognized, however, that the value of standardized tests is the subject of much debate. Therefore, they may not be treated as absolutely authoritative on this issue.

Another relevant factor which may be considered by the trial court on remand of this case is the level of the state's general educational expenditures and per-pupil expenditures. However, we agree with the observation of the United States Supreme Court that

> [t]he very complexity of the problems of financing and managing a statewide public school system suggests that "there will be more than one constitu-

tionally permissible method of solving them," and that within the limits of rationality, "the legislature's efforts to tackle the problems" should be entitled to respect. *Jefferson v. Hackney*, 406 U.S. [535], 546–547 [92 S.Ct. 1724, 1731–1732, 32 L.Ed.2d 285, 296 (1972)]. *On even the most basic questions in this area the scholars and educational experts are divided.* Indeed, one of the major sources of controversy concerns the extent to which there is a demonstrable correlation between educational expenditures and the quality of education....

San Antonio Indep. Sch. Dist. v. Rodriguez, 411 U.S. 1, 42–43, 93 S.Ct. 1278, 1301–1302, 36 L.Ed.2d 16, 48–49 (1973) (emphasis added).

More recently, one commentator has concluded that "available evidence suggests that substantial increases in funding produce only modest gains in most schools." William H. Clune, *New Answers to Hard Questions Posed by Rodriguez: Ending the Separation of School Finance and Educational Policy by Bridging the Gap Between Wrong and Remedy*, 24 Conn.L.Rev. 721, 726 (1992). The Supreme Court of the United States recently found such suggestions to be supported by the actual experience of the Kansas City, Missouri, schools over several decades. The Supreme Court expressly noted that despite massive court-ordered expenditures in the Kansas City schools which had provided students there with school "facilities and opportunities not available anywhere else in the country," the Kansas City students had not come close to reaching their potential, and "learner outcomes" of those students were "at or below national norms at many grade levels." *Missouri v. Jenkins*, 515 U.S. 70, 70, 115 S.Ct. 2038, 2040, 132 L.Ed.2d 63, 88–89 (1995).

We note that in every fiscal year since 1969–70, the General Assembly has dedicated more than forty percent of its general fund operating appropriations to the public primary and secondary schools. During each of those same years, more than fifty-nine percent of the general fund operating appropriations were dedicated to overall public education, which includes community colleges and higher education. Additionally, the Excellent Schools Act, which became effective when signed by Governor James B. Hunt, Jr., on 24 June 1997, will require additional large appropriations to the primary and secondary schools of the state. S.B. 272, 1997 N.C. Gen. Assembly (enacted June 24, 1997). Courts, however, should not rely upon the single factor of school funding levels in determining whether a state is failing in its constitutional obligation to provide a sound basic education to its children.

Other factors may be relevant for consideration in appropriate circumstances when determining educational adequacy issues under the North Carolina Constitution. The fact that we have mentioned only a few factors here does not indicate our opinion that only those factors mentioned may properly be considered or even that those mentioned will be relevant in every case.

In conclusion, we reemphasize our recognition of the fact that the administration of the public schools of the state is best left to the legislative and executive branches of government. Therefore, the courts of the state must grant every reasonable deference to the legislative and executive branches when considering whether they have established and are administering a system that provides the children of the various school districts of the state a sound basic education. A clear showing to the contrary must be made before the courts may conclude that they have not. Only such a clear showing will justify a judicial intrusion into an area so clearly the province, initially at least, of the legislative and executive branches as the determination of what course of action will lead to a sound basic education.

But like the other branches of government, the judicial branch has its duty under the North Carolina Constitution. If on remand of this case to the trial court, that court makes findings and conclusions from competent evidence to the effect that defendants in this case are denying children of the state a sound basic education, a denial of a fundamental right will have been established. It will then become incumbent upon defendants to establish that their actions denying this fundamental right are "necessary to promote a compelling governmental interest." *Town of Beech Mountain v. County of Watauga*, 324 N.C. 409, 412, 378 S.E.2d 780, 782, *cert. denied*, 493 U.S. 954, 110 S.Ct. 365, 107 L.Ed.2d 351 (1989). If defendants are unable to do so, it will then be the duty of the court to enter a judgment granting declaratory relief and such other relief as needed to correct the wrong while minimizing the encroachment upon the other branches of government. *Corum v. University of N.C.*, 330 N.C. 761, 784, 413 S.E.2d 276, 291, *cert. denied*, 506 U.S. 985, 113 S.Ct. 493, 121 L.Ed.2d 431 (1992).

For the foregoing reasons, the decision of the Court of Appeals is reversed in part and affirmed in part. This case is remanded to the Court of Appeals for further remand to the Superior Court, Wake County, for proceedings not inconsistent with this opinion.

REVERSED IN PART; AFFIRMED IN PART; AND REMANDED.

Part Three
Advocacy

Advocacy is at the center of poverty law. The materials in this part discuss the structures for advocacy in the legal system and the role of lawyers who represent the poor. Up to this point, these materials have focused heavily on anti-poverty programs that provide assistance to the poor. This approach continues here and first considers whether the poor have rights to assistance, the limitations to such rights, and the role of private legal assistance when securing those rights. This section is focused on litigation. While a courtroom provides a well-organized forum to present and discuss an issue, the relief that can be obtained from litigation and secured over time can be limited. In recent decades, new approaches to reducing poverty that focus on building relationships within communities—and changing the economic landscape as a result—have been developed. The materials on community economic development discuss these approaches, followed by a discussion of how tax and other policies may be used to address poverty.

Chapter Ten

The Emergence of a
New Property Right and the
Rise of Legal Advocacy

A. A Right to Welfare

In the cases that follow, lawyers, most often Legal Aid lawyers, challenge government actions that limit access to benefits under welfare programs. What right does a person have to receive benefits under an anti-poverty program in the first place and what are the contours of such a right if it exists? A right is more than a subjective belief in something; it is a claim against the government. When may an individual assert a claim against the government for support or assistance? The writers and cases that follow explore this issue.

1. A New Property Right

In 1964, Charles Reich published his article *The New Property*,[1] Reich's article addressed the growth of government power following the Second World War and the expansion of a Progressive jurisprudence that he saw as "monstrous and oppressive." In Reich's view, government had become the source of wealth for citizens and, as a result, had great power. Reich described a relationship between government and people as a space of unequal powers, where "a man or woman ... has no rights which may not be taken away to serve the public policy." And the dominant example of this relationship for Reich was the administration of public welfare. Prior to *The New Property*, the relationship between the individual and the public administrator of welfare benefits ran one way. Government provided benefits to the poor on the government's terms and conditions. The poor had no claim to demand more. Reich viewed this dynamic as pervasive, allowing government power to invade individual rights to privacy while pronouncing moralism and disrespect for civil liberties. Reich conceived a new property right to counter the imbalance of power between government and individual. Property is the circle around an individual that limits the power of government. *The New Property* argued for the inclusion of welfare benefits within

---

1. Charles A. Reich, *The New Property*, 73 YALE L.J. 733 (1964).

the property rights of the poor, thereby limiting the intrusive power of government and the diminution of civil liberties. The notion that the poor hold a property right that limits government action was later developed by the Supreme Court.

State efforts to control individual behavior through controlling access to public benefits were well established by the early 1960s. Such efforts were limited by the Supreme Court in *King v. Smith*, 88 S. Ct. 2128 (1968), a case that considered an Alabama statute that used AFDC benefits as a means of controlling the sexual behavior of single mothers. Under the Alabama AFDC program at issue in *King v. Smith*, a mother and her children were declared ineligible for AFDC benefits if the mother was found to be in a sexual relationship with a man. The Alabama program essentially treated the mother's partner as a substitute father, thus making the entire family ineligible for AFDC benefits. The Alabama program applied this eligibility restriction even if the couple did not live together or if the man was not the father of the children who were otherwise eligible for AFDC benefits. Mrs. Smith was the mother of four children and had been denied AFDC benefits following a home inspection by a state welfare worker. The worker found evidence of a relationship, specifically men's clothing in the home. The Alabama AFDC program specifically addressed the sexual behavior of mothers who received AFDC benefits in an effort to shape conduct the state of Alabama saw as immoral. The Supreme Court did not address Alabama's power "to deal with conduct it regards as immoral and with problems of illegitimacy," instead finding that Congress "has determined that immorality and illegitimacy should be dealt with through rehabilitative measures rather than measures that punish dependent children." The interest of the children in continuing to receive AFDC benefits thus limited the state of Alabama's efforts.

2. Finding a Right

Goldberg v. Kelly
397 U.S. 254 (1970)

The question for decision is whether a State that terminates public assistance payments to a particular recipient without affording him the opportunity for an evidentiary hearing prior to termination denies the recipient procedural due process in violation of the Due Process Clause of the Fourteenth Amendment.

This action was brought in the District Court for the Southern District of New York by residents of New York City receiving financial aid under the federally assisted program of Aid to Families with Dependent Children (AFDC) or under New York State's general Home Relief program. Their complaint alleged that the New York State and New York City officials administering these programs terminated, or were about to terminate, such aid without prior notice and hearing, thereby denying them due process of law. At the time the suits were filed there was no requirement of prior notice or hearing of any kind before termination of financial aid. However, the State and city adopted procedures for notice and hearing after the suits were brought, and the plaintiffs, appellees here, then challenged the constitutional adequacy of those procedures.

The State Commissioner of Social Services amended the State Department of Social Services' Official Regulations to require that local social services officials proposing to discontinue or suspend a recipient's financial aid do so according to a procedure that conforms to either subdivision (a) or subdivision (b) of § 351.26 of the regulations as amended. The City of New York elected to promulgate a local procedure according to subdivision (b). That subdivision, so far as here pertinent, provides that the local procedure must include the giving of notice to the recipient of the reasons for a proposed discontinuance or suspension at least seven days prior to its effective date, with notice also that upon request the recipient may have the proposal reviewed by a local welfare official holding a position superior to that of the supervisor who approved the proposed discontinuance or suspension, and, further, that the recipient may submit, for purposes of the review, a written statement to demonstrate why his grant should not be discontinued or suspended. The decision by the reviewing official whether to discontinue or suspend aid must be made expeditiously, with written notice of the decision to the recipient. The section further expressly provides that '(a)ssistance shall not be discontinued or suspended prior to the date such notice of decision is sent to the recipient and his representative, if any, or prior to the proposed effective date of discontinuance or suspension, whichever occurs later.'

Pursuant to subdivision (b), the New York City Department of Social Services promulgated Procedure No. 68-18. A caseworker who has doubts about the recipient's continued eligibility must first discuss them with the recipient. If the caseworker concludes that the recipient is no longer eligible, he recommends termination of aid to a unit supervisor. If the latter concurs, he sends the recipient a letter stating the reasons for proposing to terminate aid and notifying him that within seven days he may request that a higher official review the record, and may support the request with a written statement prepared personally or with the aid of an attorney or other person. If the reviewing official affirms the determination of ineligibility, aid is stopped immediately and the recipient is informed by letter of the reasons for the action. Appellees' challenge to this procedure emphasizes the absence of any provisions for the personal appearance of the recipient before the reviewing official, for oral presentation of evidence, and for confrontation and cross-examination of adverse witnesses. However, the letter does inform the recipient that he may request a post-termination 'fair hearing.' This is a proceeding before an independent state hearing officer at which the recipient may appear personally, offer oral evidence, confront and cross-examine the witnesses against him, and have a record made of the hearing. If the recipient prevails at the 'fair hearing' he is paid all funds erroneously withheld. A recipient whose aid is not restored by a 'fair hearing' decision may have judicial review.

I

The constitutional issue to be decided, therefore, is the narrow one whether the Due Process Clause requires that the recipient be afforded an evidentiary hearing before the termination of benefits. The District Court held that only a pre-termination evidentiary hearing would satisfy the constitutional command, and rejected the argument of the state and city officials that the combination of the post-termination 'fair hearing' with the informal pre-termination review disposed of all due process claims. The court said: 'While post-termination review is relevant, there is one overpowering fact which controls here. By hypothesis, a welfare recipient is destitute, without funds or assets. * * * Suffice it to say that to cut off a welfare recipient in the face of * * * 'brutal need' without a prior hearing of some sort is unconscionable, unless overwhelming considerations justify it.' Kelly v. Woman, 294 F. Supp. 898 (1968). The court rejected the argument that the need to protect the public's tax revenues supplied the requisite 'overwhelming consideration.' 'Against the justified desire to protect public funds must be weighed the individual's overpowering need in this unique situation not to be wrongfully deprived of assistance. * * * While the problem of additional expense must be kept in mind, it does not justify denying a hearing meeting the ordinary standards of due process. Under all the circumstances, we hold that due process requires an adequate hearing before termination of welfare benefits, and the fact that there is a later constitutionally fair proceeding does not alter the result.' ... We affirm.

Appellant does not contend that procedural due process is not applicable to the termination of welfare benefits. Such benefits are a matter of statutory entitlement for persons qualified to receive them. Their termination involves state action that adjudicates important rights. The constitutional challenge cannot be answered by an argument that public assistance benefits are "a 'privilege' and not a 'right.'" Relevant constitutional restraints apply as much to the withdrawal of public assistance benefits as to disqualification for unemployment compensation; or to denial of a tax exemption; or to discharge from public employment. The extent to which procedural due process must be afforded the recipient is influenced by the extent to which he may be 'condemned to suffer grievous loss,' and depends upon whether the recipient's interest in avoiding that loss outweighs the governmental interest in summary adjudication. Accordingly, 'consideration of what procedures due process may require under any given set of circumstances must begin with a determination of the precise nature of the government function involved as well as of the private interest that has been affected by governmental action.'

It is true, of course, that some governmental benefits may be administratively terminated without affording the recipient a pre-termination evidentiary hearing. But we agree with the District Court that when welfare is discontinued, only a pre-termination evidentiary hearing provides the recipient with procedural due process. Thus the crucial factor in this context—a factor not present in the case of the blacklisted government contractor, the discharged government employee, the taxpayer denied a tax exemption, or virtually anyone else whose governmental entitlements are ended—is that termination of aid pending resolution of a controversy over eligibility may deprive an eligible recipient of the very means by which to live while he waits. Since he lacks independent resources, his situation becomes immediately desperate.

His need to concentrate upon finding the means for daily subsistence, in turn, adversely affects his ability to seek redress from the welfare bureaucracy.

Moreover, important governmental interests are promoted by affording recipients a pre-termination evidentiary hearing. From its founding the Nation's basic commitment has been to foster the dignity and well-being of all persons within its borders. We have come to recognize that forces not within the control of the poor contribute to their poverty. This perception, against the background of our traditions, has significantly influenced the development of the contemporary public assistance system. Welfare, by meeting the basic demands of subsistence, can help bring within the reach of the poor the same opportunities that are available to others to participate meaningfully in the life of the community. At the same time, welfare guards against the societal malaise that may flow from a widespread sense of unjustified frustration and insecurity. Public assistance, then, is not mere charity, but a means to 'promote the general Welfare, and secure the Blessings of Liberty to ourselves and our Posterity.' The same governmental interests that counsel the provision of welfare, counsel as well its uninterrupted provision to those eligible to receive it; pre-termination evidentiary hearings are indispensable to that end.

Appellant does not challenge the force of these considerations but argues that they are outweighed by countervailing governmental interests in conserving fiscal and administrative resources. These interests, the argument goes, justify the delay of any evidentiary hearing until after discontinuance of the grants. Summary adjudication protects the public fisc by stopping payments promptly upon discovery of reason to believe that a recipient is no longer eligible. Since most terminations are accepted without challenge, summary adjudication also conserves both the fisc and administrative time and energy by reducing the number of evidentiary hearings actually held.

We agree with the District Court, however, that these governmental interests are not overriding in the welfare context. The requirement of a prior hearing doubtless involves some greater expense, and the benefits paid to ineligible recipients pending decision at the hearing probably cannot be recouped, since these recipients are likely to be judgment-proof. But the State is not without weapons to minimize these increased costs. Much of the drain on fiscal and administrative resources can be reduced by developing procedures for prompt pre-termination hearings and by skillful use of personnel and facilities. Indeed, the very provision for a post-termination evidentiary hearing in New York's Home Relief program is itself cogent evidence that the State recognizes the primacy of the public interest in correct eligibility determinations and therefore in the provision of procedural safeguards. Thus, the interest of the eligible recipient in uninterrupted receipt of public assistance, coupled with the State's interest that his payments not be erroneously terminated, clearly outweighs the State's competing concern to prevent any increase in its fiscal and administrative burdens. As the District Court correctly concluded, '(t)he stakes are simply too high for the welfare recipient, and the possibility for honest error or irritable misjudgment too great, to allow termination of aid without giving the recipient a chance, if he so desires, to be fully informed of the case against him so that he may contest its basis and produce evidence in rebuttal.'

II

We also agree with the District Court, however, that the pre-termination hearing need not take the form of a judicial or quasi-judicial trial. We bear in mind that the statutory 'fair hearing' will provide the recipient with a full administrative review. Accordingly, the pre-termination hearing has one function only: to produce an initial determination of the validity of the welfare department's grounds for discontinuance of payments in order to protect a recipient against an erroneous termination of his benefits. Thus, a complete record and a comprehensive opinion, which would serve primarily to facilitate judicial review and to guide future decisions, need not be provided at the pre-termination stage. We recognize, too, that both welfare authorities and recipients have an interest in relatively speedy resolution of questions of eligibility, that they are used to dealing with one another informally, and that some welfare departments have very burdensome caseloads. These considerations justify the limitation of the pre-termination hearing to minimum procedural safeguards, adapted to the particular characteristics of welfare recipients, and to the limited nature of the controversies to be resolved. We wish to add that we, no less than the dissenters, recognize the importance of not imposing upon the States or the Federal Government in this developing field of law any procedural requirements beyond those demanded by rudimentary due process.

'The fundamental requisite of due process of law is the opportunity to be heard.' The hearing must be 'at a meaningful time and in a meaningful manner.' In the present context these principles require that a recipient have timely and adequate notice detailing the reasons for a proposed termination, and an effective opportunity to defend by confronting any adverse witnesses and by presenting his own arguments and evidence orally. These rights are important in cases such as those before us, where recipients have challenged proposed terminations as resting on incorrect or misleading factual premises or on misapplication of rules or policies to the facts of particular cases.

We are not prepared to say that the seven-day notice currently provided by New York City is constitutionally insufficient per se, although there may be cases where fairness would require that a longer time be given. Nor do we see any constitutional deficiency in the content or form of the notice. New York employs both a letter and a personal conference with a caseworker to inform a recipient of the precise questions raised about his continued eligibility. Evidently the recipient is told the legal and factual bases for the Department's doubts. This combination is probably the most effective method of communicating with recipients.

The city's procedures presently do not permit recipients to appear personally with or without counsel before the official who finally determines continued eligibility. Thus a recipient is not permitted to present evidence to that official orally, or to confront or cross-examine adverse witnesses. These omissions are fatal to the constitutional adequacy of the procedures.

The opportunity to be heard must be tailored to the capacities and circumstances of those who are to be heard. It is not enough that a welfare recipient may present his position to the decision maker in writing or second-hand through his caseworker. Written submissions are an unrealistic option for most recipients, who lack the educational attainment necessary to write effectively and who cannot obtain professional assistance. Moreover, written submissions do not afford the flexibility of oral presentations; they do not permit the recipient to mold his argument to the issues the decision maker appears to regard as important. Particularly where credibility and veracity are at issue, as they must be in many termination proceedings, written submissions are a wholly unsatisfactory basis for decision. The second-hand presentation to the decision maker by the caseworker has its own deficiencies; since the caseworker usually gathers the facts upon which the charge of ineligibility rests, the presentation of the recipient's side of the controversy cannot safely be left to him. Therefore a recipient must be allowed to state his position orally. Informal procedures will suffice; in this context due process does not require a particular order of proof or mode of offering evidence.

In almost every setting where important decisions turn on questions of fact, due process requires an opportunity to confront and cross-examine adverse witnesses:

> 'Certain principles have remained relatively immutable in our jurisprudence. One of these is that where governmental action seriously injures an individual, and the reasonableness of the action depends on fact findings, the evidence used to prove the Government's case must be disclosed to the individual so that he has an opportunity to show that it is untrue. While this is important in the case of documentary evidence, it is even more important where the evidence consists of the testimony of individuals whose memory might be faulty or who, in fact, might be perjurers or persons motivated by malice, vindictiveness, intolerance, prejudice, or jealousy. We have formalized these protections in the requirements of confrontation and cross-examination. They have ancient roots. They find expression in the Sixth Amendment * * *. This Court has been zealous to protect these rights from erosion. It has spoken out not only in criminal cases, * * * but also in all types of cases where administrative * * * actions were under scrutiny.'

Welfare recipients must therefore be given an opportunity to confront and cross-examine the witnesses relied on by the department.

'The right to be heard would be, in many cases, of little avail if it did not comprehend the right to be heard by counsel.' *Powell v. Alabama*. We do not say that counsel must be provided at the pre-termination hearing, but only that the recipient must be allowed to retain an attorney if he so desires. Counsel can help delineate the issues, present the factual contentions in an orderly manner, conduct cross-examination, and generally safeguard the interests of the recipient. We do not anticipate that this assistance will unduly prolong or otherwise encumber the hearing. Evidently HEW has reached the same conclusion.

Finally, the decision-maker's conclusion as to a recipient's eligibility must rest solely on the legal rules and evidence adduced at the hearing. To demonstrate compliance with this elementary requirement, the decision maker should state the reasons for his determination and indicate the evidence he relied on, though his statement need not amount to a full opinion or even formal findings of fact and conclusions of law. And, of course, an impartial decision maker is essential. We agree with the District Court that prior involvement in some aspects of a case will not necessarily bar a welfare official from acting as a decision maker. He should not, however, have participated in making the determination under review.

Affirmed.

Jefferson v. Hackney

406 U.S. 535 (1972)

Appellants in this case challenge certain computation procedures that the State of Texas uses in its federally assisted welfare program. Believing that neither the Constitution nor the federal welfare statute prohibits the State from adopting these policies, we affirm the judgment of the three-judge court below upholding the state procedures.

I

Appellants are Texas recipients of Aid to Families With Dependent Children (AFDC). The Texas State Constitution provides a ceiling on the amount the State can spend on welfare assistance grants. In order to allocate this fixed pool of welfare money among the numerous individuals with acknowledged need, the State has adopted a system of percentage grants. Under this system, the State first computes the monetary needs of individuals eligible for relief under each of the federally aided categorical assistance programs. Then, since the constitutional ceiling on welfare is insufficient to bring each recipient up to this full standard of need, the State applies a percentage reduction factor in order to arrive at a reduced standard of need in each category that the State can guarantee.

Appellants challenge the constitutionality of applying a lower percentage reduction factor to AFDC than to the other categorical assistance programs. They claim a violation of equal protection because the proportion of AFDC recipients who are black or Mexican-American is higher than the proportion of the aged, blind, or disabled welfare recipients who fall within these minority groups. Appellants claim that the distinction between the programs is not rationally related to the purposes of the Social Security Act, and violates the Fourteenth Amendment for that reason as well. In their original complaint, appellants also argued that any percentage-reduction reduction system violated § 402(a)(23) of the Social Security Act of 1935, as amended, 81 Stat. 898 42 USC 602(a)(23) which required each State to make certain cost-of-living adjustments to its standard of need.

II

[Note—In this section, the Court considered Appellants' argument that the state method for computing percentage reduction when the recipient had some other income contravened the Social Security Act and concluded that it did not.]

III

We turn, then, to appellants' claim that the Texas system of percentage reductions violates the Fourteenth Amendment. Appellants believe that once the State has computed a standard of need for each recipient, it is arbitrary and discriminatory to provide only 75% of that standard to AFDC recipients, while paying 100% of recognized need to the aged, and 95% to the disabled and the blind. They argue that if the State adopts a percentage-reduction system, it must apply the same percentage to each of its welfare programs.

This claim was properly rejected by the court below. It is clear from the statutory framework that, although the four categories of public assistance found in the Social Security Act have certain common elements, the States were intended by Congress to keep their AFDC plans separate from plans under the other titles of the Act. A State is free to participate in one, several, or all of the categorical assistance programs, as it chooses. It is true that each of the programs is intended to assist the needy, but it does not follow that there is only one constitutionally permissible way for the State to approach this important goal.

This Court emphasized only recently, in *Dandridge v. Williams*, that in 'the area of economics and social welfare, a State does not violate the Equal Protection Clause merely because the classifications made by its laws are imperfect.' A legislature may address a problem 'one step at a time,' or even 'select one phase of one field and apply a remedy there, neglecting the others. So long as its judgments are rational, and not invidious, the legislature's efforts to tackle the problems of the poor and the needy are not subject to a constitutional straitjacket. The very complexity of the problems suggests that there will be more than one constitutionally permissible method of solving them.

The standard of judicial review is not altered because of appellants' unproved allegations of racial discrimination. The three-judge court found that the 'payment by Texas of a lesser percentage of unmet needs to the recipients of the AFDC than to the recipients of other welfare programs is not the result of racial or ethnic prejudice and is not violative of the federal Civil Rights Act or the Equal Protection Clause of the 14th Amendment.' The District Court obviously gave careful consideration to this issue, and we are cited by its opinion to a number of subsidiary facts to support its principal finding quoted above. There has never been a reduction in the amount of money appropriated by the legislature to the AFDC program, and between 1943 and the date of the opinion below there had been five increases in the amount of money appropriated by the legislature for the program, two of them having occurred since 1959. The overall percentage increase in appropriation for the programs between 1943 and the time of the District Court's hearing in this case was 410% for AFDC, as opposed to 211% for OAA and 200% for AB. The court further concluded:

> 'The depositions of Welfare officials conclusively establish that the defendants did not know the racial make-up of the various welfare assistance categories prior to or at the time when the orders here under attack were issued.'

Appellants in their brief in effect abandon any effort to show that these findings of fact were clearly erroneous, and we hold they were not.

Appellants are thus left with their naked statistical argument: that there is a larger percentage of Negroes and Mexican-Americans in AFDC than in the other programs, and that the AFDC is funded at 75% whereas the other programs are funded at 95% and 100% of recognized need. As the statistics cited in the footnote demonstrate, the number of minority members in all categories is substantial. The basic outlines of eligibility for the various categorical grants are established by Congress, not by the States; given the heterogeneity of the Nation's population, it would be only an infrequent coincidence that the racial composition of each grant class was identical to that of the others. The acceptance of appellants' constitutional theory would render suspect each difference in treatment among the grant classes, however lacking in racial motivation and however otherwise rational the treatment might be. Few legislative efforts to deal with the difficult problems posed by current welfare programs could survive such scrutiny, and we do not find it required by the Fourteenth Amendment.

Applying the traditional standard of review under that amendment, we cannot say that Texas' decision to provide somewhat lower welfare benefits for AFDC recipients is invidious or irrational. Since budgetary constraints do not allow the payment of the full standard of need for all welfare recipients, the State may have concluded that the aged and infirm are the least able of the categorical grant recipients to bear the hardships of an inadequate standard of living. While different policy judgments are of course possible, it is not irrational for the State to believe that the young are more adaptable than the sick and elderly, especially because the latter have less hope of improving their situation in the years remaining to them. Whether or not one agrees with this state determination, there is nothing in the Constitution that forbids it.

Similarly, we cannot accept the argument in Mr. Justice MARSHALL'S dissent that the Social Security Act itself requires equal percentages for each categorical assistance program. The dissent concedes that a State might simply refuse to participate in the AFDC program, while continuing to receive federal money for the other categorical programs. Nevertheless, it is argued that Congress intended to prohibit any middle ground—once the State does participate in a program it must do so on the same basis as it participates in every other program. Such an all-or-nothing policy judgment may well be defensible, and the dissenters may be correct that nothing in the statute expressly rejects it. But neither does anything in the statute approve or require it. In conclusion, we re-emphasize what the Court said in *Dandridge*:

> 'We do not decide today that the (state law) is wise, that it best fulfills the relevant social and economic objectives that (the State) might ideally espouse, or that a more just and humane system could not be devised. Conflicting claims of morality and intelligence are raised by opponents and proponents of almost every measure, certainly including the one before us. But the intractable economic, social, and even philosophical problems presented by public welfare assistance programs are not the business of this Court....

(T)he Constitution does not empower this Court to second-guess state officials charged with the difficult responsibility of allocating limited public welfare funds among the myriad of potential recipients.'

Affirmed.

Mathews v. Eldridge
424 U.S. 319 (1976)

The issue in this case is whether the Due Process Clause of the Fifth Amendment requires that prior to the termination of Social Security disability benefit payments the recipient be afforded an opportunity for an evidentiary hearing.

I

Cash benefits are provided to workers during periods in which they are completely disabled under the disability insurance benefits program created by the 1956 amendments to Title II of the Social Security Act. Respondent Eldridge was first awarded benefits in June 1968. In March 1972, he received a questionnaire from the state agency charged with monitoring his medical condition. Eldridge completed the questionnaire, indicating that his condition had not improved and identifying the medical sources, including physicians, from whom he had received treatment recently. The state agency then obtained reports from his physician and a psychiatric consultant. After considering these reports and other information in his file the agency informed Eldridge by letter that it had made a tentative determination that his disability had ceased in May 1972. The letter included a statement of reasons for the proposed termination of benefits, and advised Eldridge that he might request reasonable time in which to obtain and submit additional information pertaining to his condition.

* * *

Instead of requesting reconsideration Eldridge commenced this action challenging the constitutional validity of the administrative procedures established by the Secretary of Health, Education, and Welfare for assessing whether there exists a continuing disability. The Secretary moved to dismiss on the grounds that Eldridge's benefits had been terminated in accordance with valid administrative regulations and procedures and that he had failed to exhaust available remedies. In support of his contention that due process requires a pre-termination hearing, Eldridge relied exclusively upon this Court's decision in Goldberg v. Kelly, which established a right to an "evidentiary hearing" prior to termination of welfare benefits. The Secretary contended that Goldberg was not controlling since eligibility for disability benefits, unlike eligibility for welfare benefits, is not based on financial need and since issues of credibility and veracity do not play a significant role in the disability entitlement decision, which turns primarily on medical evidence.

The District Court concluded that the administrative procedures pursuant to which the Secretary had terminated Eldridge's benefits abridged his right to procedural due process. *** Relying entirely upon the District Court's opinion, the Court of Appeals for the Fourth Circuit affirmed the injunction barring termination of Eldridge's benefits prior to an evidentiary hearing. We reverse.

II

[Note — This section discusses whether the Secretary's decision is a final action supporting the court's jurisdiction.]

III

A

Procedural due process imposes constraints on governmental decisions which deprive individuals of "liberty" or "property" interests within the meaning of the Due Process Clause of the Fifth or Fourteenth Amendment. The Secretary does not contend that procedural due process is inapplicable to terminations of Social Security disability benefits. He recognizes, as has been implicit in our prior decisions, that the interest of an individual in continued receipt of these benefits is a statutorily created "property" interest protected by the Fifth Amendment. Rather, the Secretary contends that the existing administrative procedures, detailed below, provide all the process that is constitutionally due before a recipient can be deprived of that interest.

This Court consistently has held that some form of hearing is required before an individual is finally deprived of a property interest. The "right to be heard before being condemned to suffer grievous loss of any kind, even though it may not involve the stigma and hardships of a criminal conviction, is a principle basic to our society." The fundamental requirement of due process is the opportunity to be heard "at a meaningful time and in a meaningful manner." Eldridge agrees that the review procedures available to a claimant before the initial determination of ineligibility becomes final would be adequate if disability benefits were not terminated until after the evidentiary hearing stage of the administrative process. The dispute centers upon what process is due prior to the initial termination of benefits, pending review.

In recent years this Court increasingly has had occasion to consider the extent to which due process requires an evidentiary hearing prior to the deprivation of some type of property interest even if such a hearing is provided thereafter. In only one case, Goldberg v Kelly, has the Court held that a hearing closely approximating a judicial trial is necessary. In other cases requiring some type of pretermination hearing as a matter of constitutional right the Court has spoken sparingly about the requisite procedures.... More recently, in *Arnett v. Kennedy*, supra, we sustained the validity of procedures by which a federal employee could be dismissed for cause. They included notice of the action sought, a copy of the charge, reasonable time for filing a written response, and an opportunity for an oral appearance. Following dismissal, an evidentiary hearing was provided

These decisions underscore the truism that " '(d)ue process,' unlike some legal rules, is not a technical conception with a fixed content unrelated to time, place and circumstances." "(D)ue process is flexible and calls for such procedural protections as the particular situation demands." Accordingly, resolution of the issue whether the administrative procedures provided here are constitutionally sufficient requires analysis of the governmental and private interests that are affected. More precisely, our prior decisions indicate that identification of the specific dictates of due process generally requires consideration of three distinct factors: First, the private interest that will be affected by the official action; second, the risk of an erroneous deprivation of such interest through the procedures used, and the probable value, if any, of additional or substitute procedural safeguards; and finally, the Government's interest, including the function involved and the fiscal and administrative burdens that the additional or substitute procedural requirement would entail. See, e. g., Goldberg v. Kelly, 397 U.S. at 263–271.

We turn first to a description of the procedures for the termination of Social Security disability benefits and thereafter consider the factors bearing upon the constitutional adequacy of these procedures.

B

The disability insurance program is administered jointly by state and federal agencies. State agencies make the initial determination whether a disability exists, when it began, and when it ceased. The standards applied and the procedures followed are prescribed by the Secretary, who has delegated his responsibilities and powers under the Act to the SSA.

In order to establish initial and continued entitlement to disability benefits a worker must demonstrate that he is unable

"to engage in any substantial gainful activity by reason of any medically determinable physical or mental impairment which can be expected to result in death or which has lasted or can be expected to last for a continuous period of not less than 12 months...." 42 USC 423 (d)(1)(A).

To satisfy this test the worker bears a continuing burden of showing, by means of "medically acceptable clinical and laboratory diagnostic techniques," sec. 423(d)(3), that he has a physical or mental impairment of such severity that "he is not only unable to do his previous work but cannot, considering his age, education, and work experience, engage in any other kind of substantial gainful work which exists in the national economy, regardless of whether such work exists in the immediate area in which he lives, or whether a specific job vacancy exists for him, or whether he would be hired if he applied for work." SEC. 423 (d)(2)(A).

The principal reasons for benefits terminations are that the worker is no longer disabled or has returned to work. As Eldridge's benefits were terminated because he was determined to be no longer disabled, we consider only the sufficiency of the procedures involved in such cases.

The continuing-eligibility investigation is made by a state agency acting through a "team" consisting of a physician and a nonmedical person trained in disability evaluation. The agency periodically communicates with the disabled worker, usually by mail in which case he is sent a detailed questionnaire or by telephone, and requests information concerning his present condition, including current medical restrictions and sources of treatment, and any additional information that he considers relevant to his continued entitlement to benefits.

Information regarding the recipient's current condition is also obtained from his sources of medical treatment. If there is a conflict between the information provided by the beneficiary and that obtained from medical sources such as his physician, or between two sources of treatment, the agency may arrange for an examination by an independent consulting physician. Whenever the agency's tentative assessment of the beneficiary's condition differs from his own assessment, the beneficiary is informed that benefits may be terminated, provided a summary of the evidence upon which the proposed determination to terminate is based, and afforded an opportunity to review the medical reports and other evidence in his case file. He also may respond in writing and submit additional evidence.

The state agency then makes its final determination, which is reviewed by an examiner in the SSA Bureau of Disability Insurance. If, as is usually the case, the SSA accepts the agency determination it notifies the recipient in writing, informing him of the reasons for the decision, and of his right to seek de novo reconsideration by the state agency. Upon acceptance by the SSA, benefits are terminated effective two months after the month in which medical recovery is found to have occurred.

If the recipient seeks reconsideration by the state agency and the determination is adverse, the SSA reviews the reconsideration determination and notifies the recipient of the decision. He then has a right to an evidentiary hearing before an SSA administrative law judge. The hearing is nonadversary, and the SSA is not represented by counsel. As at all prior and subsequent stages of the administrative process, however, the claimant may be represented by counsel or other spokesmen. If this hearing results in an adverse decision, the claimant is entitled to request discretionary review by the SSA Appeals Council, § 404.945, and finally may obtain judicial review. 42 U.S.C. § 405(g).

Should it be determined at any point after termination of benefits, that the claimant's disability extended beyond the date of cessation initially established, the worker is entitled to retroactive payments. If, on the other hand, a beneficiary receives any payments to which he is later determined not to be entitled, the statute authorizes the Secretary to attempt to recoup these funds in specified circumstances.

C

Despite the elaborate character of the administrative procedures provided by the Secretary, the courts below held them to be constitutionally inadequate, concluding that due process requires an evidentiary hearing prior to termination. In light of the private and governmental interests at stake here and the nature of the existing procedures, we think this was error.

Since a recipient whose benefits are terminated is awarded full retroactive relief if he ultimately prevails, his sole interest is in the uninterrupted receipt of this source of income pending final administrative decision on his claim. His potential injury is thus similar in nature to that of the welfare recipient in *Goldberg*, the nonprobationary federal employee in *Arnett* and the wage earner in *Sniadach*.

Only in *Goldberg* has the Court held that due process requires an evidentiary hearing prior to a temporary deprivation. It was emphasized there that welfare assistance is given to persons on the very margin of subsistence:

> "The crucial factor in this context a factor not present in the case of ... virtually anyone else whose governmental entitlements are ended is that termination of aid pending resolution of a controversy over eligibility may deprive an eligible recipient of the very means by which to live while he waits."

Eligibility for disability benefits, in contrast, is not based upon financial need. Indeed, it is wholly unrelated to the worker's income or support from many other sources, such as earnings of other family members, workmen's compensation awards, tort claims awards, savings, private insurance, public or private pensions, veterans' benefits, food stamps, public assistance, or the "many other important programs, both public and private, which contain provisions for disability payments affecting a substantial portion of the work force...."

As *Goldberg* illustrates, the degree of potential deprivation that may be created by a particular decision is a factor to be considered in assessing the validity of any administrative decisionmaking process. The potential deprivation here is generally likely to be less than in *Goldberg*, although the degree of difference can be overstated. As the District Court emphasized, to remain eligible for benefits a recipient must be "unable to engage in substantial gainful activity. Thus, in contrast to the discharged federal employee in *Arnett*, there is little possibility that the terminated recipient will be able to find even temporary employment to ameliorate the interim loss.

As we recognized last Term "the possible length of wrongful deprivation of ... benefits (also) is an important factor in assessing the impact of official action on the private interests." The Secretary concedes that the delay between a request for a hearing before an administrative law judge and a decision on the claim is currently between 10 and 11 months. Since a terminated recipient must first obtain a reconsideration decision as a prerequisite to invoking his right to an evidentiary hearing, the delay between the actual cutoff of benefits and final decision after a hearing exceeds one year.

In view of the torpidity of this administrative review process, and the typically modest resources of the family unit of the physically disabled worker, the hardship imposed upon the erroneously terminated disability recipient may be significant. Still, the disabled worker's need is likely to be less than that of a welfare recipient. In addition to the possibility of access to private resources, other forms of government assistance will become available where the termination of disability benefits places a worker or his family below the subsistence level. In view of these potential sources of temporary income, there is less reason here than in Goldberg to depart from the ordinary principle, established by our decisions, that something less than an evidentiary hearing is sufficient prior to adverse administrative action.

D

An additional factor to be considered here is the fairness and reliability of the existing pretermination procedures, and the probable value, if any, of additional procedural safeguards. Central to the evaluation of any administrative process is the nature of the relevant inquiry. In order to remain eligible for benefits the disabled worker must demonstrate by means of "medically acceptable clinical and laboratory diagnostic techniques," 42 USC 423(d)(3), that he is unable "to engage in any substantial gainful activity by reason of any medically determinable physical or mental impairment...." 42 USC 423(d)(1)(A). In short, a medical assessment of the worker's physical or mental condition is required. This is a more sharply focused and easily documented decision than the typical determination of welfare entitlement. In the latter case, a wide variety of information may be deemed relevant, and issues of witness credibility and veracity often are critical to the decision making process. *Goldberg* noted that in such circumstances "written submissions are a wholly unsatisfactory basis for decision."

By contrast, the decision whether to discontinue disability benefits will turn, in most cases, upon "routine, standard, and unbiased medical reports by physician specialists," concerning a subject whom they have personally examined. In Richardson the Court recognized the "reliability and probative worth of written medical reports," emphasizing that while there may be "professional disagreement with the medical conclusions" the "specter of questionable credibility and veracity is not present To be sure, credibility and veracity may be a factor in the ultimate disability assessment in some cases. But procedural due process rules are shaped by the risk of error inherent in the truth finding process as applied to the generality of cases, not the rare exceptions. The potential value of an evidentiary hearing, or even oral presentation to the decision maker, is substantially less in this context than in Goldberg.

The decision in *Goldberg* also was based on the Court's conclusion that written submissions were an inadequate substitute for oral presentation because they did not provide an effective means for the recipient to communicate his case to the decision maker. Written submissions were viewed as an unrealistic option, for most recipients lacked the "educational attainment necessary to write effectively" and could not afford professional assistance. In addition, such submissions would not provide the "flexibility of oral presentations" or "permit the recipient to mold his argument to the issues the decision maker appears to regard as important." In the context of the disability-benefits-entitlement assessment the administrative procedures under review here fully answer these objections.

The detailed questionnaire which the state agency periodically sends the recipient identifies with particularity the information relevant to the entitlement decision, and the recipient is invited to obtain assistance from the local SSA office in completing the questionnaire. More important, the information critical to the entitlement decision usually is derived from medical sources, such as the treating physician. Such sources are likely to be able to communicate more effectively through written documents than are welfare recipients or the lay witnesses supporting their cause. The conclusions of physicians often are supported by X-rays and the results of clinical or laboratory tests, information typically more amenable to written than to oral presentation.

A further safeguard against mistake is the policy of allowing the disability recipient's representative full access to all information relied upon by the state agency. In addition, prior to the cutoff of benefits the agency informs the recipient of its tentative assessment, the reasons therefor, and provides a summary of the evidence that it considers most relevant. Opportunity is then afforded the recipient to submit additional evidence or arguments, enabling him to challenge directly the accuracy of information in his file as well as the correctness of the agency's tentative conclusions. These procedures, again as contrasted with those before the Court in Goldberg, enable the recipient to "mold" his argument to respond to the precise issues which the decision maker regards as crucial.

Despite these carefully structured procedures, *amici* point to the significant reversal rate for appealed cases as clear evidence that the current process is inadequate. Depending upon the base selected and the line of analysis followed, the relevant reversal rates urged by the contending parties vary from a high of 58.6% For appealed reconsideration decisions to an overall reversal rate of only 3.3%. Bare statistics rarely provide a satisfactory measure of the fairness of a decision making process. Their adequacy is especially suspect here since the administrative review system is operated on an open-file basis. A recipient may always submit new evidence, and such submissions may result in additional medical examinations.... In this context, the value of reversal rate statistics as one means of evaluating the adequacy of the pretermination process is diminished. Thus, although we view such information as relevant, it is certainly not controlling in this case.

E

In striking the appropriate due process balance the final factor to be assessed is the public interest. This includes the administrative burden and other societal costs that would be associated with requiring, as a matter of constitutional right, an evidentiary hearing upon demand in all cases prior to the termination of disability benefits. The most visible burden would be the incremental cost resulting from the increased number of hearings and the expense of providing benefits to ineligible recipients pending decision. No one can predict the extent of the increase, but the fact that full benefits would continue until after such hearings would assure the exhaustion in most cases of this attractive option. Nor would the theoretical right of the Secretary to recover undeserved benefits result, as a practical matter, in any substantial offset to the added outlay of public funds. The parties submit widely varying estimates of the probable additional financial cost. We only need say that experience with the constitutionalizing of government procedures suggests that the ultimate additional cost in terms of money and administrative burden would not be insubstantial.

Financial cost alone is not a controlling weight in determining whether due process requires a particular procedural safeguard prior to some administrative decision. But the Government's interest, and hence that of the public, in conserving scarce fiscal and administrative resources is a factor that must be weighed. At some point the benefit of an additional safeguard to the individual affected by the administrative action and to society in terms of increased assurance that the action is just, may be outweighed by the cost. Significantly, the cost of protecting those whom the preliminary administrative process has identified as likely to be found undeserving may in the end come out of the pockets of the deserving since resources available for any particular program of social welfare are not unlimited. But more is implicated in cases of this type than ad hoc weighing of fiscal and administrative burdens against the interests of a particular category of claimants. The ultimate balance involves a determination as to when, under our constitutional system, judicial-type procedures must be imposed upon administrative action to assure fairness.... The judicial model of an evidentiary hearing is neither a required, nor even the most effective, method of decision making in all circumstances. The essence of due process is the requirement that "a person in jeopardy of serious loss (be given) notice of the case against him and opportunity to meet it." All that is necessary is that the procedures be tailored, in light of the decision to be made, to "the capacities and circumstances of those who are to be heard," *Goldberg*, to insure that they are given a meaningful opportunity to present their case. In assessing what process is due in this case, substantial weight must be given to the good-faith judgments of the individuals charged by Congress with the administration of social welfare programs that the procedures they have provided assure fair consideration of the entitlement claims of individuals. This is especially so where, as here, the prescribed procedures not only provide the claimant with an effective process for asserting his claim prior to any administrative action, but also assure a right to an evidentiary hearing, as well as to subsequent judicial review, before the denial of his claim becomes final.

We conclude that an evidentiary hearing is not required prior to the termination of disability benefits and that the present administrative procedures fully comport with due process.

The judgment of the Court of Appeals is

Reversed.

B. Protecting the Individual
Right to Benefits

The courts of the United States provide the forum for protecting the property rights provided to the poor under federal anti-poverty policies. Significant gains in the fight for economic dignity have been achieved as a result of the tireless work of advocates on behalf of their clients, who themselves face significant risk when challenging the unjust denial or reduction of benefits. Litigation to secure rights provided under established anti-poverty policies is often brought under the Civil Rights Act.

Every person who, under color of any statute, ordinance, regulation, custom, or usage, of any State or Territory or the District of Columbia, subjects, or causes to be subjected, any citizen of the United States or other person within the jurisdiction thereof to the deprivation of any rights, privileges, or immunities secured by the Constitution and laws, shall be liable to the party injured in an action at law, suit in equity, or other proper proceeding for redress, except that in any action brought against a judicial officer for an act or omission taken in such officer's judicial capacity, injunctive relief shall not be granted unless a declaratory decree was violated or declaratory relief was unavailable. For the purposes of this section, any Act of Congress applicable exclusively to the District of Columbia shall be considered to be a statute of the District of Columbia.

42 U.S.C. § 1983.

Wright v. City of Roanoke
Redevelopment and Housing Authority
479 U.S. 418 (1987)

Petitioners in this case, tenants living in low-income housing projects owned by respondent, brought suit under 42 U.S.C. § 1983, alleging that respondent overbilled them for their utilities and thereby violated the rent ceiling imposed by the Brooke Amendment to the Housing Act of 1937, and the implementing regulations of the Department of Housing and Urban Development (HUD). The District Court and the Court of Appeals for the Fourth Circuit concluded that petitioners did not have a cause of action under § 1983. We granted certiorari and now reverse.

I

Respondent is one of many public housing authorities (PHA's) established throughout the country under the United States Housing Act of 1937, to provide affordable housing for low-income people. In 1969, the Housing Act was amended in a fundamental respect: the Brooke Amendment, imposed a ceiling for rents charged to low-income people living in public housing projects, and, as later amended, provides that a low-income family "shall pay as rent" a specified percentage of its income. HUD has consistently considered "rent" to include a reasonable amount for the use of utilities, which is defined by regulation as that amount equal to or less than an amount determined by the PHA to be a reasonable part of the rent paid by low-income tenants.

In their suit against respondent, petitioners alleged that respondent had overcharged them for their utilities by failing to comply with the applicable HUD regulations in establishing the amount of utility service to which petitioners were entitled. Thus, according to petitioners, respondent imposed a surcharge for "excess" utility consumption that should have been part of petitioners' rent4 and deprived them of their statutory right to pay only the prescribed maximum portion of their income as rent. The District Court granted summary judgment for respondent on petitioners' § 1983 claim, holding that a private cause of action was unavailable to enforce the Brooke Amendment. The Court of Appeals for the Fourth Circuit affirmed.

II

Maine v. Thiboutot, 448 U.S. 1, 100 S.Ct. 2502, 65 L.Ed.2d 555 (1980), held that § 1983 was available to enforce violations of federal statutes by agents of the State. *Pennhurst State School and Hospital v. Halderman,* 451 U.S. 1, 101 S.Ct. 1531, 67 L.Ed.2d 694 (1981), and *Middlesex County Sewerage Authority v. National Sea Clammers Assn.,* 453 U.S. 1, 101 S.Ct. 2615, 69 L.Ed.2d 435 (1981), however, recognized two exceptions to the application of § 1983 to remedy statutory violations: where Congress has foreclosed such enforcement of the statute in the enactment itself and where the statute did not create enforceable rights, privileges, or immunities within the meaning of § 1983. In *Pennhurst,* a § 1983 action did not lie because the statutory provisions were thought to be only statements of "findings" indicating no more than a congressional preference — at most a "nudge in the preferred directio[n]," 451 U.S., at 19, 101 S.Ct., at 1541, and not intended to rise to the level of an enforceable right.... Under these cases, if there is a state deprivation of a "right" secured by a federal statute, § 1983 provides a remedial cause of action unless the state actor demonstrates by express provision or other specific evidence from the statute itself that Congress intended to foreclose such private enforcement. "We do not lightly conclude that Congress intended to preclude reliance on § 1983 as a remedy" for the deprivation of a federally secured right. *Id.,* at 1012, 104 S.Ct. 3468.

Here, the Court of Appeals held that the statute and the Brooke Amendment clearly manifested congressional intention to vest in HUD the exclusive power to enforce the benefits due housing project tenants and hence the intention to foreclose both a private cause of action under the Housing Act and any private enforcement under § 1983. For the Court of Appeals, the barrier was not the lack of statutory right or its quality or enforceability — "the plaintiffs under 42 U.S.C. § 1437a have certain rights," 771 F.2d, at 837 — but the fact that Congress had not intended tenants to have the authority themselves to sue: "HUD alone may, as quasi trustee, take legal action, for the right is explicitly tailored not to allow the beneficiaries, the low cost housing tenants, to do so." *Ibid.*

We disagree with the Court of Appeals' rather summary conclusion that the administrative scheme of enforcement foreclosed private enforcement. The Court of Appeals merely relied on one of its prior cases which had referred to HUD's authority to enforce the annual contributions contracts between PHA's and HUD, see 42 U.S.C. § 1437c, to conduct audits and to cut off funds. HUD undoubtedly has considerable authority to oversee the operation of the PHA's. We are unconvinced, however, that respondent has overcome its burden of showing that "the remedial devices provided in [the Housing Act] are sufficiently comprehensive ... to demonstrate congressional intent to preclude the remedy of suits under § 1983." *Sea Clammers, supra,* 453 U.S., at 20, 101 S.Ct., at 2626. They do not show that "Congress specifically foreclosed a remedy under § 1983." *Smith v. Robinson, supra,* 468 U.S., at 1004–1005, n. 9, 104 S.Ct., at 3464 n. 9. Not only are the Brooke Amendment and its legislative history devoid of any express indication that exclusive enforcement authority was vested in HUD, but there have also been both congressional and agency actions indicating that enforcement authority is not centralized and that private actions were anticipated. Neither, in our view, are the remedial mechanisms provided sufficiently comprehensive and effective to raise a clear inference that Congress intended to foreclose a § 1983 cause of action for the enforcement of tenants' rights secured by federal law.

In 1981, Congress changed the maximum percentage of income that could be paid as "rent" from 25 percent to 30 percent. In making this change, Congress gave the Secretary of HUD discretion to raise tenants' rent incrementally over a 5-year period to ease the burden on low-income tenants during the transition. § 322(i), 95 Stat. 404. To avoid a potential multitude of litigation over the way in which the Secretary implemented the phased-in rate increase, Congress specifically made the Secretary's decisions effectuating the phase-in immune from judicial review. § 322(i)(3). At congressional hearings in which this specific and limited exception to judicial review was discussed, HUD representatives explained that this exception had no effect on tenants' ability to enforce their rights under the Housing Act in federal court other than the limited exception concerning the phase-in. Apparently dissatisfied with even a temporary preclusion of judicial review, Congress repealed it two years later.

Also at odds with the holding that HUD has exclusive authority to enforce the Brooke Amendment is the enactment in 1985 of 42 U.S.C. § 1437d(k), which directed HUD to continue its longstanding regulatory requirement that each PHA provide formal grievance procedures for the resolution of tenant disputes with the PHA arising out of their lease or PHA regulations. These procedures, which Congress ordered continued, include informal and formal hearings and administrative appeals, conducted within each PHA by impartial decision makers, to consider adverse decisions taken against tenants by the PHA. Congress' aim was to provide a "decentralized, informal, and relatively non-adversarial administrative process" for resolving tenant-management disputes. The procedures are open to individual grievances but not to class actions. See 24 CFR § 966.51(b) (1986). HUD itself has never provided a procedure by which tenants could complain to it about the alleged failures of PHA's to abide by their annual contribution contracts, the Brooke Amendment, or HUD regulations; nor has it taken unto itself the task of reviewing PHA grievance procedure decisions.

There is other evidence clearly indicating that in HUD's view tenants have the right to bring suit in federal court to challenge housing authorities' calculations of utility allowances. Among HUD's 1982 proposed regulations was § 865.476(d), which would have confined tenant utility-allowance challenges to the procedures available in state court. The final regulation, however, contained no such limitation and contemplated that tenants could challenge PHA actions in federal as well as state courts. 24 CFR § 965.473(e) (1985). As the comment accompanying the final regulation explained, the proposal to limit challenges to state-court actions had been abandoned. The final "provision does not preclude Federal court review." 49 Fed.Reg. 31403 (1984). HUD's opinion as to available tenant remedies under the Housing Act is entitled to some deference by this Court. See *Jean v. Nelson,* 472 U.S. 846, 865, 105

S.Ct. 2992, 3002, 86 L.Ed.2d 664 (1985); *Chevron U.S.A. Inc. v. Natural Resources Defense Council, Inc.,* 467 U.S. 837, 844, 104 S.Ct. 2778, 2782, 81 L.Ed.2d 694 (1984).

* * *

The Court of Appeals and respondents rely on HUD's authority to audit, enforce annual contributions contracts, and cut off federal funds. But these generalized powers are insufficient to indicate a congressional intention to foreclose § 1983 remedies. HUD has the authority to audit, but it does not do so frequently and its own Handbook requires audits only every eight years. There are no other mechanisms provided to enable HUD to effectively oversee the performance of the some 3,000 local PHA's across the country. The statute does not require and HUD has not provided any formal procedure for tenants to bring to HUD's attention alleged PHA failures to abide by the Brooke Amendment and HUD regulations. Hence, there will be little occasion to exercise HUD's power to sue PHA's to enforce the provisions of the annual contributions contracts. Respondent asserts PHA's must annually file their utility allowance schedules with HUD and that HUD must approve them, but the final regulations eliminated HUD's duty to approve these schedules before their effective date. 24 CFR § 965.473(d) (1986). Review of the schedules would be done in the course of audits or reviews of PHA operations.

Lastly, it is said that tenants may sue on their lease in state courts and enforce their Brooke Amendment rights in that litigation. Perhaps they could, but the state-court remedy is hardly a reason to bar an action under § 1983, which was adopted to provide a federal remedy for the enforcement of federal rights.

In sum, we conclude that nothing in the Housing Act or the Brooke Amendment evidences that Congress intended to preclude petitioners' § 1983 claim against respondent.

III

Although the Court of Appeals read the Brooke Amendment as extending to housing project tenants certain rights enforceable only by HUD, respondent asserts that neither the Brooke Amendment nor the interim regulations gave the tenants any specific or definable rights to utilities, that is, no enforceable rights within the meaning of § 1983. We perceive little substance in this claim. The Brooke Amendment could not be clearer: as further amended in 1981, tenants could be charged as rent no more and no less than 30 percent of their income. This was a mandatory limitation focusing on the individual family and its income. The intent to benefit tenants is undeniable. Nor is there any question that HUD interim regulations, in effect when this suit began, expressly required that a "reasonable" amount for utilities be included in rent that a PHA was allowed to charge, an interpretation to which HUD has adhered both before and after the adoption of the Brooke Amendment. HUD's view is entitled to deference as a valid interpretation of the statute, and Congress in the course of amending that provision has not disagreed with it.

Respondent nevertheless asserts that the provision for a "reasonable" allowance for utilities is too vague and amorphous to confer on tenants an enforceable "right" within the meaning of § 1983 and that the whole matter of utility allowances must be left to the discretion of the PHA, subject to supervision by HUD. The regulations, however, defining the statutory concept of "rent" as including utilities, have the force of law, *Chrysler Corp. v. Brown*, 441 U.S. 281, 294–295, 99 S.Ct. 1705, 1713–1714, 60 L.Ed.2d 208 (1979), they specifically set out guidelines that the PHAs were to follow in establishing utility allowances, and they require notice to tenants and an opportunity to comment on proposed allowances. In our view, the benefits Congress intended to confer on tenants are sufficiently specific and definite to qualify as enforceable rights under *Pennhurst* and § 1983, rights that are not, as respondent suggests, beyond the competence of the judiciary to enforce.

The judgment of the Court of Appeals is accordingly

Reversed.

Blessing v. Freestone

520 U.S. 329 (1997)

Justice O'CONNOR delivered the opinion of the Court.

This case concerns a lawsuit brought by five mothers in Arizona whose children are eligible to receive child support services from the State pursuant to Title IV-D of the Social Security Act. These custodial parents sued the director of Arizona's child support agency under Rev. Stat. § 1979, 42 U.S.C. § 1983, claiming that they had an enforceable individual right to have the State's program achieve "substantial compliance" with the requirements of Title IV-D. Without distinguishing among the numerous provisions of this complex program, the Court of Appeals for the Ninth Circuit held that respondents had such a right. We disagree that the statutory scheme can be analyzed so generally, and hold that Title IV-D does not give individuals a federal right to force a state agency to substantially comply with Title IV-D. Accordingly, we vacate and remand with instructions to remand to the District Court.

I

This controversy concerns an interlocking set of cooperative federal-state welfare programs. Arizona participates in the federal Aid to Families with Dependent Children (AFDC) program, which provides subsistence welfare benefits to needy families. Social Security Act, Title IV-A, 42 U.S.C. §§ 601–617. To qualify for federal AFDC funds, the State must certify that it will operate a child support enforcement program that conforms with the numerous requirements set forth in Title IV-D of the Social Security Act, 42 U.S.C. §§ 651–669b (1994 ed. and Supp. II), and will do so pursuant to a detailed plan that has been approved by the Secretary of Health and Human Services (Secretary). § 602(a)(2); see also § 652(a)(3). The Federal Government underwrites roughly two-thirds of the cost of the State's child support efforts. § 655(a). But the State must do more than simply collect overdue support payments; it must also establish a comprehensive system to establish paternity, locate absent parents, and help families obtain support orders. §§ 651, 654.

A State must provide these services free of charge to AFDC recipients and, when requested, for a nominal fee to children and custodial parents who are not receiving AFDC payments. §§ 651, 654(4). AFDC recipients must assign their child support rights to the State and fully cooperate with the State's efforts to establish paternity and obtain support payments. Although the State may keep most of the support payments that it collects on behalf of AFDC families in order to offset the costs of providing welfare benefits, until recently it only had to distribute the first $50 of each payment to the family. 42 U.S.C. § 657(b)(1). The amended version of Title IV-D replaces this $50 pass-through with more generous distributions to families once they leave welfare. 42 U.S.C. § 657(a)(2) (1994 ed., Supp. II). Non-AFDC recipients who request the State's aid are entitled to have all collected funds passed through. § 657(a)(3). In all cases, the State must distribute the family's share of collected support payments within two business days after receipt. § 654b(c)(1).

The structure of each State's Title IV-D agency, like the services it provides, must conform to federal guidelines. For example, States must create separate units to administer the plan, § 654(3), and to disburse collected funds, § 654(27), each of which must be staffed at levels set by the Secretary, 45 CFR § 303.20 (1995). If a State delegates its disbursement function to local governments, it must reward the most efficient local agencies with a share of federal incentive payments. 42 U.S.C. § 654(22). To maintain detailed records of all pending cases, as well as to generate the various reports required by federal authorities, States must set up computer systems that meet numerous federal specifications. § 654a. Finally, in addition to setting up this administrative framework, each participating State must enact laws designed to streamline paternity and child support actions. §§ 654(20), 666.

To oversee this complex federal-state enterprise, Congress created the Office of Child Support Enforcement (OCSE) within the Department of Health and Human Services (HHS). This agency is charged with auditing the States' compliance with their federally approved plans. Audits must occur at least once every three years, or more often if a State's performance falls below certain standards. § 652(a)(4). If a State does not "substantially comply" with the requirements of Title IV-D, the Secretary is authorized to penalize the State by reducing its AFDC grant by up to five percent. § 609(a)(8). The Secretary has interpreted "substantial compliance" as: (a) full compliance with requirements that services be offered statewide and that certain recipients be notified monthly of the support collected, as well as with reporting, recordkeeping, and accounting rules; (b) 90 percent compliance with case opening and case closure criteria; and (c) 75 percent compliance with most remaining program requirements. 45 CFR § 305.20 (1995). The Secretary may suspend a penalty if the State implements an adequate corrective action plan, and if the program achieves "substantial compliance," she may rescind the penalty entirely. 42 U.S.C. § 609(c) (1994 ed., Supp.II).

II

Arizona's record of enforcing child support obligations is less than stellar, particularly compared with those of other States. In a 1992 report, Arizona's Auditor General chronicled many of the State's problems. In the 1989–1990 fiscal year, Arizona failed to collect enough child support payments and federal incentives to cover the administrative costs of its Title IV-D program — 1 of only 10 States to fall below that target. Arizona Auditor General, A Performance Audit of the Arizona Department of Economic Security 2 (1992). The Auditor General also pointed out that the cost effectiveness of Arizona's support enforcement efforts had been "minimal." For every dollar spent on enforcement, the State collected barely two dollars — almost half the nationwide average. *Ibid.* In 1992, nearly three-quarters of Arizona's 275,000 child support cases were still in the earliest stages of the enforcement process. In 42 percent of all cases, paternity had yet to be established. In a further 29 percent, the absent parent had been identified but his or her whereabouts were unknown. *Id.,* at 12. Overall, the Auditor General found that Arizona "obtains regular child support payments for fewer than five percent of the parents it serves." *Id.,* at 9.

Federal audits by OCSE have also identified shortcomings in Arizona's child support system. In several reviews of the State's performance from 1984 to 1989, the Secretary found that Arizona had not substantially complied with significant program requirements, and she repeatedly penalized the State one percent of its AFDC grant. The State developed a corrective action plan after each failed audit, which prompted the Secretary to suspend and — in every instance but one — waive the one-percent reduction in Arizona's AFDC funding.

Respondents are five Arizona mothers (some of whom receive AFDC benefits) whose children are eligible for Title IV-D child support services. They filed this lawsuit in the United States District Court for the District of Arizona against the Director of the Arizona Department of Economic Security, the state agency charged with providing child support services under Title IV-D. In a lengthy complaint, respondents claimed that they had properly applied for child support services but that, despite their good faith efforts to cooperate, the agency never took adequate steps to obtain child support payments from the fathers of their children. These omissions, respondents contended, were largely attributable to structural defects in the State's child support efforts: staff shortages, high caseloads, unmanageable backlogs, and deficiencies in the State's accounting methods and recordkeeping. App. 11, 14–16. Respondents sought to represent a class of all children and custodial parents residing in Arizona who are or will be entitled to Title IV-D services.

Respondents claimed that the State's systemic failures violated their federal rights under Title IV-D. Invoking 42 U.S.C. § 1983, they asked the District Court to grant them the following broad relief:

> "Enter a declaratory judgment determining that operation of the Arizona Title IV-D program violates controlling, substantive provisions of federal law creating rights in plaintiffs and the class enforceable through an action permitted by 42 U.S.C. § 1983.

> "Grant permanent (and as necessary and appropriate, interlocutory) injunctions prohibiting continued adherence to the aforesaid pattern and practices and requiring affirmative measures sufficient to achieve as well as sustain

substantial compliance with federal law, throughout all programmatic operations at issue." App. 42.

The Director immediately moved to dismiss the complaint on several grounds, arguing primarily that Title IV-D creates no individual rights enforceable under § 1983. The District Court treated this motion as one for summary judgment and ruled in favor of the Director. Relying primarily on a decision of the Court of Appeals for the Sixth Circuit, *Carelli v. Howser*, 923 F.2d 1208 (1991), the District Court held that Congress had foreclosed private actions to enforce Title IV-D by authorizing the Secretary to audit and cut off funds to States with programs that do not substantially comply with Title IV-D's requirements.

A divided panel of the Court of Appeals for the Ninth Circuit reversed. 68 F.3d 1141 (1995).... We granted certiorari to resolve disagreement among the Courts of Appeals as to whether individuals may sue state officials under § 1983 for violations of Title IV-D.

III

Section 1983 imposes liability on anyone who, under color of state law, deprives a person "of any rights, privileges, or immunities secured by the Constitution and laws." We have held that this provision safeguards certain rights conferred by federal statutes. In order to seek redress through § 1983, however, a plaintiff must assert the violation of a federal *right*, not merely a violation of federal *law. Golden State Transit Corp. v. Los Angeles*, 493 U.S. 103, 106, 110 S.Ct. 444, 448–449, 107 L.Ed.2d 420 (1989). We have traditionally looked at three factors when determining whether a particular statutory provision gives rise to a federal right. First, Congress must have intended that the provision in question benefit the plaintiff. Second, the plaintiff must demonstrate that the right assertedly protected by the statute is not so "vague and amorphous" that its enforcement would strain judicial competence. Third, the statute must unambiguously impose a binding obligation on the States. In other words, the provision giving rise to the asserted right must be couched in mandatory, rather than precatory, terms

Even if a plaintiff demonstrates that a federal statute creates an individual right, there is only a rebuttable presumption that the right is enforceable under § 1983. Because our inquiry focuses on congressional intent, dismissal is proper if Congress "specifically foreclosed a remedy under § 1983." *Smith v. Robinson*, 468 U.S. 992, 1005, n. 9, 104 S.Ct. 3457, 3464, n. 9, 82 L.Ed.2d 746 (1984). Congress may do so expressly, by forbidding recourse to § 1983 in the statute itself, or impliedly, by creating a comprehensive enforcement scheme that is incompatible with individual enforcement under § 1983. *Livadas v. Bradshaw*, 512 U.S. 107, 133, 114 S.Ct. 2068, 2083, 129 L.Ed.2d 93 (1994).

A

With these principles in mind, we turn first to the question whether respondents have established that Title IV-D gives them federal rights.

In their complaint, respondents argued that federal law granted them "individual rights to all mandated services delivered in substantial compliance with Title IV-D and its implementing regulations." App. 41. They sought a broad injunction requiring the Director of Arizona's child support agency to achieve "substantial compliance ... throughout all programmatic operations." *Id.*, at 42. Attributing the deficiencies in the State's program primarily to staff shortages and other structural defects, respondents essentially invited the District Court to oversee every aspect of Arizona's Title IV-D program.

Without distinguishing among the numerous rights that might have been created by this federally funded welfare program, the Court of Appeals agreed in sweeping terms that "Title IV-D creates enforceable rights in families in need of Title IV-D services." 68 F.3d, at 1150. The Court of Appeals did not specify exactly which "rights" it was purporting to recognize, but it apparently believed that federal law gave respondents the right to have the State substantially comply with Title IV-D in all respects. We disagree.

As an initial matter, the lower court's holding that Title IV-D "creates enforceable rights" paints with too broad a brush. It was incumbent upon respondents to identify with particularity the rights they claimed, since it is impossible to determine whether Title IV-D, as an undifferentiated whole, gives rise to undefined "rights." Only when the complaint is broken down into manageable analytic bites can a court ascertain whether each separate claim satisfies the various criteria we have set forth for determining whether a federal statute creates rights. See, *e.g., Golden State, supra,* at 106, 110 S.Ct., at 448 (asking whether the "provision in question" was designed to benefit the plaintiff).

In prior cases, we have been able to determine whether or not a statute created a given right because the plaintiffs articulated, and lower courts evaluated, well-defined claims. In *Wright,* for example, we held that tenants of public housing projects had a right to have their utility costs included within a rental payment that did not exceed 30 percent of their income. We did not ask whether the federal housing legislation generally gave rise to rights; rather, we focused our analysis on a specific statutory provision limiting "rent" to 30 percent of a tenant's income. 479 U.S., at 430, 107 S.Ct., at 773–774. Similarly, in *Wilder,* we held that health care providers had an enforceable right to reimbursement at "reasonable and adequate rates" as required by a particular provision in the Medicaid statute. 496 U.S., at 511–512, 110 S.Ct., at 2518–2519. And in *Suter v. Artist M.,* 503 U.S. 347, 112 S.Ct. 1360, 118 L.Ed.2d 1 (1992), where we held that Title IV-E of the Social Security Act did not give the plaintiffs the right that they asserted, we again analyzed the claim in very specific terms: whether children had a right to have state authorities undertake "reasonable efforts to prevent removal of children from their homes and to facilitate reunification of families where removal had occurred." *Id.,* at 352, 112 S.Ct., at 1364 (footnote omitted). Finally, in *Livadas, supra,* at 134, 114 S.Ct., at 2083–2084, we discerned in the structure of the National Labor Relations Act (NLRA) the very specific right of employees "to complete the collective-bargaining process and agree to an arbitration clause." See 512 U.S., at 133, n. 27, 114 S.Ct., at 2083, n. 27 (explaining that whether a claim founded on the NLRA is cognizable under § 1983 may depend on whether the claim stems from abridgment of a "protected individual interest"). We did not simply ask whether the NLRA created unspecified "rights."

* * *

The same reasoning applies to the staffing levels of the state agency, which respondents seem to claim are inadequate. Title IV-D generally requires each participating State to establish a separate child support enforcement unit "which meets such staffing and organizational requirements as the Secretary may by regulation prescribe." 42 U.S.C. § 654(3). The regulations, in turn, simply provide that each level of the State's organization must have "sufficient staff" to fulfill specified functions. These mandates do not, however, give rise to federal rights. For one thing, the link between increased staffing and the services provided to any particular individual is far too tenuous to support the notion that Congress meant to give each and every Arizonan who is eligible for Title IV-D the right to have the State Department of Economic Security staffed at a "sufficient" level. Furthermore, neither the statute nor the regulation gives any guidance as to how large a staff would be "sufficient." Cf. *Suter*, 503 U.S., at 360, 112 S.Ct., at 1368 (finding requirement of "reasonable efforts" unenforceable where there was "[n]o further statutory guidance . . . as to how 'reasonable efforts' are to be measured"). Enforcement of such an undefined standard would certainly "strain judicial competence." *Livadas*, 512 U.S., at 132, 114 S.Ct., at 2083.

We do not foreclose the possibility that some provisions of Title IV-D give rise to individual rights. The lower court did not separate out the particular rights it believed arise from the statutory scheme, and we think the complaint is less than clear in this regard. For example, respondent Madrid alleged that the state agency managed to collect some support payments from her ex-husband but failed to pass through the first $50 of each payment, to which she was purportedly entitled under the pre-1996 version of § 657(b)(1). Although § 657 may give her a federal right to receive a specified portion of the money collected on her behalf by Arizona, she did not explicitly request such relief in the complaint.

In any event, it is not at all apparent that respondents sought any relief more specific than a declaration that their "rights" were being violated and an injunction forcing Arizona's child support agency to "substantially comply" with all of the provisions of Title IV-D. We think that this defect is best addressed by sending the case back for the District Court to construe the complaint in the first instance, in order to determine exactly what rights, considered in their most concrete, specific form, respondents are asserting. Only by manageably breaking down the complaint into specific allegations can the District Court proceed to determine whether any specific claim asserts an individual federal right.

B

Because we leave open the possibility that Title IV-D may give rise to some individually enforceable rights, we pause to consider petitioner's final argument that no remand is warranted because the statute contains "a remedial scheme that is 'sufficiently comprehensive . . . to demonstrate congressional intent to preclude the remedy of suits under § 1983.'" *Wilder*, 496 U.S., at 521, 110 S.Ct., at 2523 (quoting *Middlesex County Sewerage Authority v. National Sea Clammers Assn.*, 453 U.S. 1, 20, 101 S.Ct. 2615, 2626–2627, 69 L.Ed.2d 435 (1981)). Because petitioner does not claim that any provision of Title IV-D expressly curtails § 1983 actions, she must make the difficult showing that allowing § 1983 actions to go forward in these circumstances "would be inconsistent with Congress' carefully tailored scheme." *Golden State*, 493 U.S., at 107, 110 S.Ct., at 449 (citation and internal quotation marks omitted).

Only twice have we found a remedial scheme sufficiently comprehensive to supplant § 1983: in *Sea Clammers, supra,* and *Smith v. Robinson,* 468 U.S. 992, 104 S.Ct. 3457, 82 L.Ed.2d 746 (1984). In *Sea Clammers,* we focused on the "unusually elaborate enforcement provisions" of the Federal Water Pollution Control Act, which placed at the disposal of the Environmental Protection Agency a panoply of enforcement options, including noncompliance orders, civil suits, and criminal penalties. 453 U.S., at 13, 101 S.Ct., at 2622–2623. We emphasized that several provisions of the Act authorized private persons to initiate enforcement actions. *Id.,* at 14, 20, 101 S.Ct., at 2623, 2626–2627. We found it "hard to believe that Congress intended to preserve the § 1983 right of action when it created so many specific statutory remedies, including the two citizen-suit provisions." *Id.,* at 20, 101 S.Ct., at 2626. Likewise, in *Smith,* the review scheme in the Education of the Handicapped Act permitted aggrieved individuals to invoke "carefully tailored" local administrative procedures followed by federal judicial review. 468 U.S., at 1009, 104 S.Ct., at 3467. We reasoned that Congress could not possibly have wanted parents to skip these procedures and go straight to court by way of § 1983, since that would have "render[ed] superfluous most of the detailed procedural protections outlined in the statute." *Id.,* at 1011, 104 S.Ct., at 3468.

We have also stressed that a plaintiff's ability to invoke § 1983 cannot be defeated simply by "[t]he availability of administrative mechanisms to protect the plaintiff's interests." *Golden State, supra,* at 106, 110 S.Ct., at 448. Thus, in *Wright,* we rejected the argument that the Secretary of Housing and Urban Development's "generalized powers" to audit local public housing authorities, to enforce annual contributions contracts, and to cut off federal funding demonstrated a congressional intention to prevent public housing tenants from using § 1983 to enforce their rights under the federal Housing Act. 479 U.S., at 428, 107 S.Ct., at 773. We reached much the same conclusion in *Wilder,* where the Secretary of Health and Human Services had power to reject state Medicaid plans or to withhold federal funding to States whose plans did not comply with federal law. 496 U.S., at 521, 110 S.Ct., at 2523–2524. Even though in both cases these oversight powers were accompanied by limited state grievance procedures for individuals, we found that § 1983 was still available. *Wright, supra,* at 427–428, 107 S.Ct., at 772–773; *Wilder, supra,* at 523, 110 S.Ct., at 2524–2525.

The enforcement scheme that Congress created in Title IV-D is far more limited than those in *Sea Clammers* and *Smith.* Unlike the federal programs at issue in those cases, Title IV-D contains no private remedy—either judicial or administrative— through which aggrieved persons can seek redress. The only way that Title IV-D assures that States live up to their child support plans is through the Secretary's oversight. The Secretary can audit only for "substantial compliance" on a programmatic basis. Furthermore, up to 25 percent of eligible children and custodial parents can go without most of the services enumerated in Title IV-D before the Secretary can trim a State's AFDC grant. These limited powers to audit and cut federal funding closely resemble those powers at issue in *Wilder* and *Wright*. Although counsel for the Secretary suggested at oral argument that the Secretary "has the same right under a contract as any other party to seek specific performance," Tr. of Oral Arg. 49, this possibility was not developed in the briefs. Even assuming the Secretary's authority to sue for specific performance, Title IV-D's administrative enforcement arsenal would not compare to those in *Sea Clammers* and *Smith*, especially if, as the Government further contended, see Tr. of Oral Arg. 49–50, no private actor would have standing to force the Secretary to bring suit for specific performance. To the extent that Title IV-D may give rise to individual rights, therefore, we agree with the Court of Appeals that the Secretary's oversight powers are not comprehensive enough to close the door on § 1983 liability. 68 F.3d, at 1151–1156.

IV

The judgment of the Court of Appeals is vacated, and the case is remanded with instructions to remand to the District Court for further proceedings consistent with this opinion.

Alexander v. Sandoval

532 U.S. 275 (2001

This case presents the question whether private individuals may sue to enforce disparate-impact regulations promulgated under Title VI of the Civil Rights Act of 1964.

I

The Alabama Department of Public Safety (Department), of which petitioner James Alexander is the director, accepted grants of financial assistance from the United States Department of Justice (DOJ) and Department of Transportation (DOT) and so subjected itself to the restrictions of Title VI of the Civil Rights Act of 1964. Section 601 of that Title provides that no person shall, "on the ground of race, color, or national origin, be excluded from participation in, be denied the benefits of, or be subjected to discrimination under any program or activity" covered by Title VI. 42 U.S.C. § 2000d. Section 602 authorizes federal agencies "to effectuate the provisions of [§ 601] ... by issuing rules, regulations, or orders of general applicability," 42 U.S.C. § 2000d-1, and the DOJ in an exercise of this authority promulgated a regulation forbidding funding recipients to "utilize criteria or methods of administration which have the effect of subjecting individuals to discrimination because of their race, color, or national origin...." 28 CFR § 42.104(b)(2) (2000). See also 49 CFR § 21.5(b)(2) (2000) (similar DOT regulation).

The State of Alabama amended its Constitution in 1990 to declare English "the official language of the state of Alabama." Amdt. 509. Pursuant to this provision and, petitioners have argued, to advance public safety, the Department decided to administer state driver's license examinations only in English. Respondent Sandoval, as representative of a class, brought suit in the United States District Court for the Middle District of Alabama to enjoin the English-only policy, arguing that it violated the DOJ regulation because it had the effect of subjecting non-English speakers to discrimination based on their national origin. The District Court agreed. It enjoined the policy and ordered the Department to accommodate non-English speakers. *Sandoval v. Hagan*, 7 F.Supp.2d 1234 (M.D.Ala.1998). Petitioners appealed to the Court of Appeals for the Eleventh Circuit, which affirmed. *Sandoval v. Hagan*, 197 F.3d 484 (C.A.11 1999). Both courts rejected petitioners' argument that Title VI did not provide respondents a cause of action to enforce the regulation.

We do not inquire here whether the DOJ regulation was authorized by § 602, or whether the courts below were correct to hold that the English-only policy had the effect of discriminating on the basis of national origin. The petition for writ of certiorari raised, and we agreed to review, only the question posed in the first paragraph of this opinion: whether there is a private cause of action to enforce the regulation. 530 U.S. 1305, 121 S.Ct. 28, 147 L.Ed.2d 1051 (2000).

II

* * *

Implicit in our discussion thus far has been a particular understanding of the genesis of private causes of action. Like substantive federal law itself, private rights of action to enforce federal law must be created by Congress. *Touche Ross & Co. v. Redington*, 442 U.S. 560, 578, 99 S.Ct. 2479, 61 L.Ed.2d 82 (1979) (remedies available are those "that Congress enacted into law"). The judicial task is to interpret the statute Congress has passed to determine whether it displays an intent to create not just a private right but also a private remedy. *Transamerica Mortgage Advisors, Inc. v. Lewis*, 444 U.S. 11, 15, 100 S.Ct. 242, 62 L.Ed.2d 146 (1979). Statutory intent on this latter point is determinative. Without it, a cause of action does not exist and courts may not create one, no matter how desirable that might be as a policy matter, or how compatible with the statute. See, *e.g.*, *Massachusetts Mut. Life Ins. Co. v. Russell*, 473 U.S. 134, 145, 148, 105 S.Ct. 3085, 87 L.Ed.2d 96 (1985); *Transamerica Mortgage Advisors, Inc. v. Lewis, supra*, at 23, 100 S.Ct. 242; *Touche Ross & Co. v. Redington, supra*, at 575–576, 99 S.Ct. 2479. "Raising up causes of action where a statute has not created them may be a proper function for common-law courts, but not for federal tribunals." *Lampf, Pleva, Lipkind, Prupis & Petigrow v. Gilbertson*, 501 U.S. 350, 365, 111 S.Ct. 2773, 115 L.Ed.2d 321 (1991) (SCALIA, J., concurring in part and concurring in judgment).

Respondents would have us revert in this case to the understanding of private causes of action that held sway 40 years ago when Title VI was enacted. That understanding is captured by the Court's statement in *J.I. Case Co. v. Borak*, 377 U.S. 426, 433, 84 S.Ct. 1555, 12 L.Ed.2d 423 (1964), that "it is the duty of the courts to be alert to provide such remedies as are necessary to make effective the congressional purpose" expressed by a statute. We abandoned that understanding in *Cort v. Ash*, 422 U.S. 66, 78, 95 S.Ct. 2080, 45 L.Ed.2d 26 (1975)—which itself interpreted a statute enacted under the *ancien regime*—and have not returned to it since. Not even when interpreting the same Securities Exchange Act of 1934 that was at issue in *Borak* have we applied *Borak's* method for discerning and defining causes of action. Having sworn off the habit of venturing beyond Congress's intent, we will not accept respondents' invitation to have one last drink.

Nor do we agree with the Government that our cases interpreting statutes enacted prior to *Cort v. Ash* have given "dispositive weight" to the "expectations" that the enacting Congress had formed "in light of the 'contemporary legal context.'" Only three of our legion implied-right-of-action cases have found this sort of "contemporary legal context" relevant, and two of those involved Congress's enactment (or reenactment) of the verbatim statutory text that courts had previously interpreted to create a private right of action. In the third case, this sort of "contemporary legal context" simply buttressed a conclusion independently supported by the text of the statute. We have never accorded dispositive weight to context shorn of text. In determining whether statutes create private rights of action, as in interpreting statutes generally, legal context matters only to the extent it clarifies text.

We therefore begin (and find that we can end) our search for Congress's intent with the text and structure of Title VI. Section 602 authorizes federal agencies "to effectuate the provisions of [§ 601] ... by issuing rules, regulations, or orders of general applicability." 42 U.S.C. § 2000d-1. It is immediately clear that the "rights-creating" language so critical to the Court's analysis in *Cannon* of § 601, see 441 U.S., at 690, n. 13, 99 S.Ct. 1946, is completely absent from § 602. Whereas § 601 decrees that "[n]o person ... shall ... be subjected to discrimination," 42 U.S.C. § 2000d, the text of § 602 provides that "[e]ach Federal department and agency ... is authorized and directed to effectuate the provisions of [§ 601]," 42 U.S.C. § 2000d-1. Far from displaying congressional intent to create new rights, § 602 limits agencies to "effectuat[ing]" rights already created by § 601. And the focus of § 602 is twice removed from the individuals who will ultimately benefit from Title VI's protection. Statutes that focus on the person regulated rather than the individuals protected create "no implication of an intent to confer rights on a particular class of persons." *California v. Sierra Club*, 451 U.S. 287, 294, 101 S.Ct. 1775, 68 L.Ed.2d 101 (1981). Section 602 is yet a step further removed: It focuses neither on the individuals protected nor even on the funding recipients being regulated, but on the agencies that will do the regulating. Like the statute found not to create a right of action in *Universities Research Assn., Inc. v. Coutu*, 450 U.S. 754, 101 S.Ct. 1451, 67 L.Ed.2d 662 (1981), § 602 is "phrased as a directive to federal agencies engaged in the distribution of public funds," *id.*, at 772, 101 S.Ct. 1451. When this is true, "[t]here [is] far less reason to infer a private remedy in favor of individual persons," *Cannon v. University of Chicago, supra*, at 690–691, 99 S.Ct. 1946. So far as we can tell, this authorizing portion of § 602 reveals no congressional intent to create a private right of action.

Nor do the methods that § 602 goes on to provide for enforcing its authorized regulations manifest an intent to create a private remedy; if anything, they suggest the opposite. Section 602 empowers agencies to enforce their regulations either by terminating funding to the "particular program, or part thereof," that has violated the regulation or "by any other means authorized by law," 42 U.S.C. § 2000d-1. No enforcement action may be taken, however, "until the department or agency concerned has advised the appropriate person or persons of the failure to comply with the requirement and has determined that compliance cannot be secured by voluntary means." *Ibid.* And every agency enforcement action is subject to judicial review. § 2000d-2. If an agency attempts to terminate program funding, still more restrictions apply. The agency head must "file with the committees of the House and Senate having legislative jurisdiction over the program or activity involved a full written report of the circumstances and the grounds for such action." § 2000d-1. And the termination of funding does not "become effective until thirty days have elapsed after the filing of such report." *Ibid.* Whatever these elaborate restrictions on agency enforcement may imply for the private enforcement of rights created *outside* of § 602, compare *Cannon v. University of Chicago, supra,* at 706, n. 41, 712, n. 49, 99 S.Ct. 1946; *Regents of Univ. of Cal. v. Bakke,* 438 U.S., at 419, n. 26, 98 S.Ct. 2733 (STEVENS, J., concurring in judgment in part and dissenting in part), with *Guardians Assn. v. Civil Serv. Comm'n of New York City,* 463 U.S., at 609–610, 103 S.Ct. 3221 (Powell, J., concurring in judgment); *Regents of Univ. of Cal. v. Bakke, supra,* at 382–383, 98 S.Ct. 2733 (opinion of White, J.), they tend to contradict a congressional intent to create privately enforceable rights through § 602 itself. The express provision of one method of enforcing a substantive rule suggests that Congress intended to preclude others. Sometimes the suggestion is so strong that it precludes a finding of congressional intent to create a private right of action, even though other aspects of the statute (such as language making the would-be plaintiff "a member of the class for whose benefit the statute was enacted") suggest the contrary. *Massachusetts Mut. Life Ins. Co. v. Russell,* 473 U.S., at 145, 105 S.Ct. 3085; see *id.,* at 146–147, 105 S.Ct. 3085. And as our Rev. Stat. § 1979, 42 U.S.C. § 1983, cases show, some remedial schemes foreclose a private cause of action to enforce even those statutes that admittedly create substantive private rights. See, *e.g., Middlesex County Sewerage Authority v. National Sea Clammers Assn.,* 453 U.S. 1(1981). In the present case, the claim of exclusivity for the express remedial scheme does not even have to overcome such obstacles. The question whether § 602's remedial scheme can overbear other evidence of congressional intent is simply not presented, since we have found no evidence anywhere in the text to suggest that Congress intended to create a private right to enforce regulations promulgated under § 602.

Both the Government and respondents argue that the *regulations* contain rights-creating language and so must be privately enforceable, see Brief for United States 19–20; Brief for Respondents 31, but that argument skips an analytical step. Language in a regulation may invoke a private right of action that Congress through statutory text created, but it may not create a right that Congress has not. *Touche Ross & Co. v. Redington,* 442 U.S., at 577, n. 18, 99 S.Ct. 2479 ("[T]he language of the statute and not the rules must control"). Thus, when a statute has provided a general authorization for private enforcement of regulations, it may perhaps be correct that the intent displayed in each regulation can determine whether or not it is privately enforceable. But it is most certainly incorrect to say that language in a regulation can conjure up a private cause of action that has not been authorized by Congress. Agencies may play the sorcerer's apprentice but not the sorcerer himself.

The last string to respondents' and the Government's bow is their argument that two amendments to Title VI "ratified" this Court's decisions finding an implied private right of action to enforce the disparate-impact regulations. See Rehabilitation Act Amendments of 1986, § 1003, 42 U.S.C. § 2000d-7; Civil Rights Restoration Act of 1987, § 6, 102 Stat. 31, 42 U.S.C. § 2000d-4a. One problem with this argument is that, as explained above, none of our decisions establishes (or even assumes) the private right of action at issue here, see *supra*, at 1517–1519, which is why in *Guardians* three Justices were able expressly to reserve the question. See 463 U.S., at 645, n. 18, 103 S.Ct. 3221 (STEVENS, J., dissenting). Incorporating our cases in the amendments would thus not help respondents. Another problem is that the incorporation claim itself is flawed. Section 1003 of the Rehabilitation Act Amendments of 1986, on which only respondents rely, by its terms applies only to suits "for a violation of a *statute*," 42 U.S.C. § 2000d-7(a)(2) (emphasis added). It therefore does not speak to suits for violations of regulations that go beyond the statutory proscription of § 601. Section 6 of the Civil Rights Restoration Act of 1987 is even less on point. That provision amends Title VI to make the term "program or activity" cover larger portions of the institutions receiving federal financial aid than it had previously covered, see *Grove City College v. Bell,* 465 U.S. 555, 104 S.Ct. 1211, 79 L.Ed.2d 516 (1984). It is impossible to understand what this has to do with implied causes of action—which is why we declared in *Franklin v. Gwinnett County Public Schools,* 503 U.S., at 73, 112 S.Ct. 1028, that § 6 did not "in any way alte[r] the existing rights of action and the corresponding remedies permissible under … Title VI." Respondents point to *Merrill Lynch, Pierce, Fenner & Smith, Inc. v. Curran,* 456 U.S., at 381–382, 102 S.Ct. 1825, which inferred congressional intent to ratify lower court decisions regarding a particular statutory provision when Congress comprehensively revised the statutory scheme but did not amend that provision. But we recently criticized *Curran's* reliance on congressional inaction, saying that "[a]s a general matter … [the] argumen[t] deserve[s] little weight in the interpretive process." *Central Bank of Denver, N.A. v. First Interstate Bank of Denver, N. A.,* 511 U.S., at 187, 114 S.Ct. 1439. And when, as here, Congress has not comprehensively revised a statutory scheme but has made only isolated amendments, we have spoken more bluntly: "It is 'impossible to assert with any degree of assurance that congressional failure to act represents' affirmative congressional approval of the Court's statutory interpretation." *Patterson v. McLean Credit Union,* 491 U.S. 164, 175, n. 1, 109 S.Ct. 2363, 105 L.Ed.2d 132 (1989).

Neither as originally enacted nor as later amended does Title VI display an intent to create a freestanding private right of action to enforce regulations promulgated under § 602. We therefore hold that no such right of action exists.

C. Access to Justice and Legal Aid

There is no more powerful place in our society than a U.S. courtroom. For the poor, however, the courts can become places that seem unfair, overreaching, and vengeful. This is because, as the Court recognized in *Gideon*, meaningful access to due process requires a lawyer who is capable of navigating the legal system.

The materials that follow address how the poor can access legal assistance in civil matters, including things like landlord-tenant disputes, consumer law problems, and family law matters. For the right to counsel in criminal matters, *see Gideon v. Wainwright, infra.*

For many decades, the law offices funded through the Legal Services Corporation ("LSC") have provided a first line of assistance to the poor on legal aid matters.[2] Congress established the LSC as a nonprofit corporation in July 1974 when President Nixon signed its enacting legislation. LSC's establishment was the result of years of work led by President Johnson's administration to fundamentally change the poverty environment. Sargent Shriver was appointed by President Johnson to lead the Office of Economic Opportunity in 1964 and launched the first federally funded legal services program in 1965. Lewis Powell, who would later become a Supreme Court Justice, and the American Bar Association advocated for the creation of neighborhood law offices in low-income communities throughout the United States where poor people could find direct assistance with their legal problems. In enacting LSC, Congress found "there is a need to provide equal access to the system of justice in our Nation" and that "there is a need to provide high quality legal assistance to those who would be otherwise unable to afford adequate legal counsel."

LSC receives funds from the federal government and then distributes this money to qualifying state legal services offices, which provide free legal services to income-qualifying clients in civil legal matters. 42 U.S.C. § 2996. At the time LSC was created, Congress attached a number of restrictions to LSC funding that limited some activity of local legal services offices. Restrictions on the use of LSC funds have remained a concern since the founding of LSC. In 1996 Congress attached a set of significant

---

2. In 1974, Congress enacted the Legal Services Corporation Act, 42 U.S.C. § 2996 et seq. The Act established the LSC as a private nonprofit corporation "for the purpose of providing financial support for legal assistance in noncriminal proceedings ... to persons financially unable to afford legal assistance." § 2996b. The LSC receives funds annually from Congress and makes grants directly to local organizations that provide civil legal assistance to indigent persons. *See* LSC, 1994 Annual Report 1, 5. To obtain LSC funding, local organizations must submit applications describing the legal services they intend to provide with LSC funding. *See* 45 C.F.R. 1634.3. In the initial Act creating the LSC, Congress placed restrictions on local organizations who received grants from the LSC. For example, LSC funds could not be used by recipients to provide legal assistance in proceedings concerning abortion, desegregation, or military desertion. § 2996f(b)(8)–(10). With certain exceptions for funds received from tribal, "interest on lawyers trust account," and other nonfederal sources, these restrictions applied even if the organization's activities were funded with non-LSC funds. *See* § 2996i(c); 45 C.F.R. pt. 1610 (1976).

new restrictions on LSC grantees. See Omnibus Consolidated Rescissions and Appropriations Act of 1997, Pub. L 104-208, sec 502, 110 Stat. 3009 (1997). These restrictions had a profound impact on local legal aid offices across the country.

D. Filing Fees and Poverty
Boddie v. Connecticut
401 U.S. 371 (1971)

Appellants, welfare recipients residing in the State of Connecticut, brought this action in the Federal District Court for the District of Connecticut on behalf of themselves and others similarly situated, challenging, as applied to them, certain state procedures for the commencement of litigation, including requirements for payment of court fees and costs for service of process, that restrict their access to the courts in their effort to bring an action for divorce.

It appears from the briefs and oral argument that the average cost to a litigant for bringing an action for divorce is $60. Section 52-259 of the Connecticut General Statutes provides: 'There shall be paid to the clerks of the supreme court or the superior court, for entering each civil cause, forty-five dollars * * *.' An additional $15 is usually required for the service of process by the sheriff, although as much as $40 or $50 may be necessary where notice must be accomplished by publication.

There is no dispute as to the inability of the named appellants in the present case to pay either the court fees required by statute or the cost incurred for the service of process. The affidavits in the record establish that appellants' welfare income in each instance barely suffices to meet the costs of the daily essentials of life and includes no allotment that could be budgeted for the expense to gain access to the courts in order to obtain a divorce. Also undisputed is appellants' 'good faith' in seeking a divorce.

Assuming, as we must on this motion to dismiss the complaint, the truth of the undisputed allegations made by the appellants, it appears that they were unsuccessful in their attempt to bring their divorce actions in the Connecticut courts, simply by reason of their indigency. The clerk of the Superior Court returned their papers 'on the ground that he could not accept them until an entry fee had been paid.' Subsequent efforts to obtain a judicial waiver of the fee requirement and to have the court effect service of process were to no avail.

Appellants thereafter commenced this action in the Federal District Court seeking a judgment declaring that Connecticut's statute and service of process provisions, 'requiring payment of court fees and expenses as a condition precedent to obtaining court relief (are) unconstitutional (as) applied to these indigent (appellants) and all other members of the class which they represent.' As further relief, appellants requested the entry of an injunction ordering the appropriate officials to permit them 'to proceed with their divorce actions without payment of fees and costs.' ***

I

At its core, the right to due process reflects a fundamental value in our American constitutional system. Our understanding of the value is the basis upon which we have resolved this case.

Perhaps no characteristic of an organized and cohesive society is more fundamental than its erection and enforcement of a system of rules defining the various rights and duties of its members, enabling them to govern their affairs and definitively settle their differences in an orderly, predictable manner. Without such a 'legal system,' social organization and cohesion are virtually impossible; with the ability to seek regularized resolution of conflicts individuals are capable of interdependent action that enables them to strive for achievements without the anxieties that would beset them in a disorganized society. Put more succinctly, it is this injection of the rule of law that allows society to reap the benefits of rejecting what political theorists call the 'state of nature.'

American society, of course, bottoms its systematic definition of individual rights and duties, as well as its machinery for dispute settlement, not on custom or the will of strategically placed individuals, but on the common-law model. It is to courts, or other quasi-judicial official bodies, that we ultimately look for the implementation of a regularized, orderly process of dispute settlement. Within this framework, those who wrote our original Constitution, in the Fifth Amendment, and later those who drafted the Fourteenth Amendment recognized the centrality of the concept of due process in the operation of this system. Without this guarantee that one may not be deprived of his rights, neither liberty nor property, without due process of law, the State's monopoly over techniques for binding conflict resolution could hardly be said to be acceptable under our scheme of things. Only by providing that the social enforcement mechanism must function strictly within these bounds can we hope to maintain an ordered society that is also just. It is upon this premise that this Court has through years of adjudication put flesh upon the due process principle.

Such litigation has, however, typically involved rights of defendants — not, as here, persons seeking access to the judicial process in the first instance. This is because our society has been so structured that resort to the courts is not usually the only available, legitimate means of resolving private disputes. Indeed, private structuring of individual relationships and repair of their breach is largely encouraged in American life, subject only to the caveat that the formal judicial process, if resorted to, is paramount. Thus, this Court has seldom been asked to view access to the courts as an element of due process. The legitimacy of the State's monopoly over techniques of final dispute settlement, even where some are denied access to its use, stands unimpaired where recognized, effective alternatives for the adjustment of differences remain. But the successful invocation of this governmental power by plaintiffs has often created serious problems for defendants' rights. For at that point, the judicial proceeding becomes the only effective means of resolving the dispute at hand and denial of a defendant's full access to that process raises grave problems for its legitimacy.

Recognition of this theoretical framework illuminates the precise issue presented in this case. As this Court on more than one occasion has recognized, marriage involves interests of basic importance in our society. It is not surprising, then, that the States have seen fit to oversee many aspects of that institution. Without a prior judicial imprimatur, individuals may freely enter into and rescind commercial contracts, for example, but we are unaware of any jurisdiction where private citizens may covenant for or dissolve marriages without state approval. Even where all substantive requirements are concededly met, we know of no instance where two consenting adults may divorce and mutually liberate themselves from the constraints of legal obligations that go with marriage, and more fundamentally the prohibition against remarriage, without invoking the State's judicial machinery.

Thus, although they assert here due process rights as would-be plaintiffs, we think appellants' plight, because resort to the state courts is the only avenue to dissolution of their marriages, is akin to that of defendants faced with exclusion from the only forum effectively empowered to settle their disputes. Resort to the judicial process by these plaintiffs is no more voluntary in a realistic sense than that of the defendant called upon to defend his interests in court. For both groups this process is not only the paramount dispute-settlement technique, but, in fact, the only available one. In this posture we think that this appeal is properly to be resolved in light of the principles enunciated in our due process decisions that delimit rights of defendants compelled to litigate their differences in the judicial forum.

II

These due process decisions, representing over a hundred years of effort by this Court to give concrete embodiment to this concept, provide, we think, complete vindication for appellants' contentions. In particular, precedent has firmly embedded in our due process jurisprudence two important principles upon whose application we rest our decision in the case before us.

A

Prior cases establish, first, that due process requires, at a minimum, that absent a countervailing state interest of overriding significance, persons forced to settle their claims of right and duty through the judicial process must be given a meaningful opportunity to be heard.... Although '(m)any controversies have raged about the cryptic and abstract words of the Due Process Clause,' as Mr. Justice Jackson wrote for the Court in Mullane v. Central Hanover Bank & Trust Co., 339 U.S. 306, 70 S.Ct. 652, 94 L.Ed. 865 (1950), 'there can be no doubt that at a minimum they require that deprivation of life, liberty or property by adjudication be preceded by notice and opportunity for hearing appropriate to the nature of the case.' Id., at 313, 70 S.Ct. at 656.

Due process does not, of course, require that the defendant in every civil case actually have a hearing on the merits. A State, can, for example, enter a default judgment against a defendant who, after adequate notice, fails to make a timely appearance, or who, without justifiable excuse, violates a procedural rule requiring the production of evidence necessary for orderly adjudication. What the Constitution does require is 'an opportunity * * * granted at a meaningful time and in a meaningful manner,' 'for (a) hearing appropriate to the nature of the case.' The formality and procedural requisites for the hearing can vary, depending upon the importance of the interests involved and the nature of the subsequent proceedings. That the hearing required by due process is subject to waiver, and is not fixed in form does not affect its root requirement that an individual be given an opportunity for a hearing before he is deprived of any significant property interest, except for extraordinary situations where some valid governmental interest is at stake that justifies postponing the hearing until after the event. In short, 'within the limits of practicability,' a State must afford to all individuals a meaningful opportunity to be heard if it is to fulfill the promise of the Due Process Clause.

B

Our cases further establish that a statute or a rule may be held constitutionally invalid as applied when it operates to deprive an individual of a protected right although its general validity as a measure enacted in the legitimate exercise of state power is beyond question. Thus, in cases involving religious freedom, free speech or assembly, this Court has often held that a valid statute was unconstitutionally applied in particular circumstances because it interfered with an individual's exercise of those rights.

No less than these rights, the right to a meaningful opportunity to be heard within the limits of practicality, must be protected against denial by particular laws that operate to jeopardize it for particular individuals.

* * *

Just as a generally valid notice procedure may fail to satisfy due process because of the circumstances of the defendant, so too a cost requirement, valid on its face, may offend due process because it operates to foreclose a particular party's opportunity to be heard. The State's obligations under the Fourteenth Amendment are not simply generalized ones; rather, the State owes to each individual that process which, in light of the values of a free society, can be characterized as due.

III

Drawing upon the principles established by the cases just canvassed, we conclude that the State's refusal to admit these appellants to its courts, the sole means in Connecticut for obtaining a divorce, must be regarded as the equivalent of denying them an opportunity to be heard upon their claimed right to a dissolution of their marriages, and, in the absence of a sufficient countervailing justification for the State's action, a denial of due process.

The arguments for this kind of fee and cost requirement are that the State's interest in the prevention of frivolous litigation is substantial, its use of court fees and process costs to allocate scarce resources is rational, and its balance between the defendant's right to notice and the plaintiff's right to access is reasonable.

In our opinion, none of these considerations is sufficient to override the interest of these plaintiff-appellants in having access to the only avenue open for dissolving their allegedly untenable marriages. Not only is there no necessary connection between a litigant's assets and the seriousness of his motives in bringing suit, but it is here beyond present dispute that appellants bring these actions in good faith. Moreover, other alternatives exist to fees and cost requirements as a means for conserving the time of courts and protecting parties from frivolous litigation, such as penalties for false pleadings or affidavits, and actions for malicious prosecution or abuse of process, to mention only a few. In the same vein we think that reliable alternatives exist to service of process by a state-paid sheriff if the State is unwilling to assume the cost of official service. This is perforce true of service by publication which is the method of notice least calculated to bring to a potential defendant's attention the pendency of judicial proceedings. We think in this case service at defendant's last known address by mail and posted notice is equally effective as publication in a newspaper.

We are thus left to evaluate the State's asserted interest in its fee and cost requirements as a mechanism of resource allocation or cost recoupment. Such a justification was offered and rejected in Griffin v. Illinois, 351 U.S. 12, 76 S.Ct. 585, 100 L.Ed. 891 (1956). In Griffin it was the requirement of a transcript beyond the means of the indigent that blocked access to the judicial process. While in Griffin the transcript could be waived as a convenient but not necessary predicate to court access, here the State invariably imposes the costs as a measure of allocating its judicial resources. Surely, then, the rationale of Griffin covers this case.

IV

In concluding that the Due Process Clause of the Fourteenth Amendment requires that these appellants be afforded an opportunity to go into court to obtain a divorce, we wish to re-emphasize that we go no further than necessary to dispose of the case before us, a case where the bona fides of both appellants' indigency and desire for divorce are here beyond dispute. We do not decide that access for all individuals to the courts is a right that is, in all circumstances, guaranteed by the Due Process Clause of the Fourteenth Amendment so that its exercise may not be placed beyond the reach of any individual, for, as we have already noted, in the case before us this right is the exclusive precondition to the adjustment of a fundamental human relationship. The requirement that these appellants resort to the judicial process is entirely a state-created matter. Thus we hold only that a State may not, consistent with the obligations imposed on it by the Due Process Clause of the Fourteenth Amendment, pre-empt the right to dissolve this legal relationship without affording all citizens access to the means it has prescribed for doing so.

Reversed.

M. L. B. v. S. L. J.

519 U.S. 102 (1996)

By order of a Mississippi Chancery Court, petitioner M. L. B.'s parental rights to her two minor children were forever terminated. M. L. B. sought to appeal from the termination decree, but Mississippi required that she pay in advance record preparation fees estimated at $2,352.36. Because M. L. B. lacked funds to pay the fees, her appeal was dismissed.

Urging that the size of her pocketbook should not be dispositive when "an interest far more precious than any property right" is at stake, M. L. B. tenders this question, which we agreed to hear and decide: May a State, consistent with the Due Process and Equal Protection Clauses of the Fourteenth Amendment, condition appeals from trial court decrees terminating parental rights on the affected parent's ability to pay record preparation fees? We hold that, just as a State may not block an indigent petty offender's access to an appeal afforded others, see *Mayer v. Chicago*, 404 U.S. 189, 195–196, 92 S.Ct. 410, 415–416, 30 L.Ed.2d 372 (1971), so Mississippi may not deny M. L. B., because of her poverty, appellate review of the sufficiency of the evidence on which the trial court found her unfit to remain a parent.

I

Petitioner M. L. B. and respondent S. L. J. are, respectively, the biological mother and father of two children, a boy born in April 1985, and a girl born in February 1987. In June 1992, after a marriage that endured nearly eight years, M. L. B. and S. L. J. were divorced. The children remained in their father's custody, as M. L. B. and S. L. J. had agreed at the time of the divorce.

S. L. J. married respondent J. P. J. in September 1992. In November of the following year, S. L. J. and J. P. J. filed suit in Chancery Court in Mississippi, seeking to terminate the parental rights of M. L. B. and to gain court approval for adoption of the children by their stepmother, J. P. J. The complaint alleged that M. L. B. had not maintained reasonable visitation and was in arrears on child support payments. M. L. B. counterclaimed, seeking primary custody of both children and contending that S. L. J. had not permitted her reasonable visitation, despite a provision in the divorce decree that he do so.

After taking evidence on August 18, November 2, and December 12, 1994, the Chancellor, in a decree filed December 14, 1994, terminated all parental rights of the natural mother, approved the adoption, and ordered that J. P. J., the adopting parent, be shown as the mother of the children on their birth certificates. Twice reciting a segment of the governing Mississippi statute, Miss.Code Ann. § 93-15-103(3)(e) (1994), the Chancellor declared that there had been a "substantial erosion of the relationship between the natural mother, [M. L. B.], and the minor children," which had been caused "at least in part by [M. L. B.'s] serious neglect, abuse, prolonged and unreasonable absence or unreasonable failure to visit or communicate with her minor children."

The Chancellor stated, without elaboration, that the natural father and his second wife had met their burden of proof by "clear and convincing evidence." Nothing in the Chancellor's order describes the evidence, however, or otherwise reveals precisely why M. L. B. was decreed, forevermore, a stranger to her children.

In January 1995, M. L. B. filed a timely appeal and paid the $100 filing fee. The Clerk of the Chancery Court, several days later, estimated the costs for preparing and transmitting the record: $1,900 for the transcript (950 pages at $2 per page);

$438 for other documents in the record (219 pages at $2 per page); $4.36 for binders; and $10 for mailing.

Mississippi grants civil litigants a right to appeal, but conditions that right on pre-payment of costs. Relevant portions of a transcript must be ordered, and its preparation costs advanced by the appellant, if the appellant "intends to urge on appeal," as M. L. B. did, "that a finding or conclusion is unsupported by the evidence or is contrary to the evidence."

Unable to pay $2,352.36, M. L. B. sought leave to appeal *in forma pauperis*. The Supreme Court of Mississippi denied her application in August 1995. Under its precedent, the court said, "[t]he right to proceed in forma pauperis in civil cases exists only at the trial level."

M. L. B. had urged in Chancery Court and in the Supreme Court of Mississippi, and now urges in this Court, that

> "where the State's judicial processes are invoked to secure so severe an alter-ation of a litigant's fundamental rights—the termination of the parental re-lationship with one's natural child—basic notions of fairness [and] of equal protection under the law, ... guaranteed by [the Mississippi and Federal Constitutions], require that a person be afforded the right of appellate review though one is unable to pay the costs of such review in advance."

II

Courts have confronted, in diverse settings, the "age-old problem" of "[p]roviding equal justice for poor and rich, weak and powerful alike." *Griffin v. Illinois*, 351 U.S. 12, 16, 76 S.Ct. 585, 589, 100 L.Ed. 891 (1956). Concerning access to appeal in general, and transcripts needed to pursue appeals in particular, *Griffin* is the foundation case.

* * *

The plurality in *Griffin* recognized "the importance of appellate review to a correct adjudication of guilt or innocence." "[T]o deny adequate review to the poor," the plurality observed, "means that many of them may lose their life, liberty or property because of unjust convictions which appellate courts would set aside." Judging the Illinois rule inconsonant with the Fourteenth Amendment, the *Griffin* plurality drew support from the Due Process and Equal Protection Clauses.

Justice Frankfurter, concurring in the judgment in *Griffin*, emphasized and ex-plained the decision's equal protection underpinning:

> "Of course a State need not equalize economic conditions.... But when a State deems it wise and just that convictions be susceptible to review by an appellate court, it cannot by force of its exactions draw a line which precludes convicted indigent persons, forsooth erroneously convicted, from securing such a review...."

... Summarizing the *Griffin* line of decisions regarding an indigent defendant's access to appellate review of a conviction, we said in *Rinaldi v. Yeager*, 384 U.S. 305, 310, 86 S.Ct. 1497, 1500, 16 L.Ed.2d 577 (1966): "This Court has never held that the States are required to establish avenues of appellate review, but it is now fundamental that, once established, these avenues must be kept free of unreasoned distinctions that can only impede open and equal access to the courts."

Of prime relevance to the question presented by M. L. B.'s petition, *Griffin*'s principle has not been confined to cases in which imprisonment is at stake.... The *Griffin* principle, *Mayer* underscored, "is a flat prohibition," against "making access to appellate processes from even [the State's] most inferior courts depend upon the [convicted] defendant's ability to pay." An impecunious party, the Court ruled, whether found guilty of a felony or conduct only "quasi criminal in nature," *id.*, at 196, 92 S.Ct., at 415, "cannot be denied a record of sufficient completeness to permit proper [appellate] consideration of his claims."

In contrast to the "flat prohibition" of "bolted doors" that the *Griffin* line of cases securely established, the right to counsel at state expense, as delineated in our decisions, is less encompassing. A State must provide trial counsel for an indigent defendant charged with a felony, *Gideon v. Wainwright*, but that right does not extend to nonfelony trials if no term of imprisonment is actually imposed, *Scott v. Illinois*. A State's obligation to provide appellate counsel to poor defendants faced with incarceration applies to appeals of right. *Douglas v. California*. In *Ross v. Moffitt*, however, we held that neither the Due Process Clause nor the Equal Protection Clause requires a State to provide counsel at state expense to an indigent prisoner pursuing a discretionary appeal in the state system or petitioning for review in this Court.

III

We have also recognized a narrow category of civil cases in which the State must provide access to its judicial processes without regard to a party's ability to pay court fees. In *Boddie v. Connecticut*, 401 U.S. 371, 91 S.Ct. 780, 28 L.Ed.2d 113 (1971), we held that the State could not deny a divorce to a married couple based on their inability to pay approximately $60 in court costs. Crucial to our decision in *Boddie* was the fundamental interest at stake. "[G]iven the basic position of the marriage relationship in this society's hierarchy of values and the concomitant state monopolization of the means for legally dissolving this relationship," we said, due process "prohibit[s] a State from denying, solely because of inability to pay, access to its courts to individuals who seek judicial dissolution of their marriages." *Id.*, at 374, 91 S.Ct., at 784; see also *Little v. Streater*, 452 U.S. 1, 13–17, 101 S.Ct. 2202, 2209–2211, 68 L.Ed.2d 627 (1981) (State must pay for blood grouping tests sought by an indigent defendant to enable him to contest a paternity suit).

Soon after *Boddie*, in *Lindsey v. Normet*, 405 U.S. 56, 92 S.Ct. 862, 31 L.Ed.2d 36 (1972), the Court confronted a double-bond requirement imposed by Oregon law only on tenants seeking to appeal adverse decisions in eviction actions. We referred first to precedent recognizing that, "if a full and fair trial on the merits is provided, the Due Process Clause of the Fourteenth Amendment does not require a State to provide appellate review." *Id.*, at 77, 92 S.Ct., at 876. We next stated, however, that "[w]hen an appeal is afforded, ... it cannot be granted to some litigants and capriciously or arbitrarily denied to others without violating the Equal Protection Clause." *Ibid.* Oregon's double-bond requirement failed equal protection measurement, we concluded, because it raised a substantial barrier to appeal for a particular class of litigants—tenants facing eviction—a barrier "faced by no other civil litigant in Oregon." *Id.*, at 79, 92 S.Ct., at 877. The Court pointed out in *Lindsey* that the classification there at issue disadvantaged nonindigent as well as indigent appellants, *ibid.*; the *Lindsey* decision, therefore, does not guide our inquiry here.

* * *

In sum, as *Ortwein* underscored, this Court has not extended *Griffin* to the broad array of civil cases. But tellingly, the Court has consistently set apart from the mine run of cases those involving state controls or intrusions on family relationships. In that domain, to guard against undue official intrusion, the Court has examined closely and contextually the importance of the governmental interest advanced in defense of the intrusion.

IV

Choices about marriage, family life, and the upbringing of children are among associational rights this Court has ranked as "of basic importance in our society," *Boddie*, 401 U.S., at 376, 91 S.Ct., at 785, rights sheltered by the Fourteenth Amendment against the State's unwarranted usurpation, disregard, or disrespect. M. L. B.'s case, involving the State's authority to sever permanently a parent-child bond, demands the close consideration the Court has long required when a family association so undeniably important is at stake. We approach M. L. B.'s petition mindful of the gravity of the sanction imposed on her and in light of two prior decisions most immediately in point: *Lassiter v. Department of Social Servs. of Durham Cty.*, 452 U.S. 18, 101 S.Ct. 2153, 68 L.Ed.2d 640 (1981), and *Santosky v. Kramer*, 455 U.S. 745, 102 S.Ct. 1388, 71 L.Ed.2d 599 (1982).

Lassiter concerned the appointment of counsel for indigent persons seeking to defend against the State's termination of their parental status. The Court held that appointed counsel was not routinely required to assure a fair adjudication; instead, a case-by-case determination of the need for counsel would suffice, an assessment to be made "in the first instance by the trial court, subject ... to appellate review."

For probation-revocation hearings where loss of conditional liberty is at issue, the *Lassiter* Court observed, our precedent is not doctrinaire; due process is provided, we have held, when the decision whether counsel should be appointed is made on a case-by-case basis. See *Gagnon v. Scarpelli*, 411 U.S. 778, 790, 93 S.Ct. 1756, 1763–1764, 36 L.Ed.2d 656 (1973). In criminal prosecutions that do not lead to the defendant's incarceration, however, our precedent recognizes no right to appointed counsel. See *Scott v. Illinois*, 440 U.S., at 373–374, 99 S.Ct., at 1161–1162. Parental termination cases, the *Lassiter* Court concluded, are most appropriately ranked with probation-revocation hearings: While the Court declined to recognize an automatic right to appointed counsel, it said that an appointment would be due when warranted by the character and difficulty of the case. See *Lassiter*, 452 U.S., at 31–32, 101 S.Ct., at 2161–2162.

Significant to the disposition of M. L. B.'s case, the *Lassiter* Court considered it "plain ... that a parent's desire for and right to 'the companionship, care, custody, and management of his or her children' is an important interest," one that "'undeniably warrants deference and, absent a powerful countervailing interest, protection.'" *Id.*, at 27, 101 S.Ct., at 2159. The object of the proceeding is "not simply to infringe upon [the parent's] interest," the Court recognized, "but to end it"; thus, a decision against the parent "work[s] a unique kind of deprivation." *Lassiter,* 452 U.S., at 27, 101 S.Ct., at 2160. For that reason, "[a] parent's interest in the accuracy and justice of the decision ... is ... a commanding one." *Ibid.;* see also *id.,* at 39, 101 S.Ct., at 2165–2166 (Blackmun, J., dissenting) ("A termination of parental rights is both total and irrevocable. Unlike other custody proceedings, it leaves the parent with no right to visit or communicate with the child...." (footnote omitted)).

* * *

V

Guided by this Court's precedent on an indigent's access to judicial processes in criminal and civil cases, and on proceedings to terminate parental status, we turn to the classification question this case presents: Does the Fourteenth Amendment require Mississippi to accord M. L. B. access to an appeal—available but for her inability to advance required costs—before she is forever branded unfit for affiliation with her children? Respondents urge us to classify M. L. B.'s case with the generality of civil cases, in which indigent persons have no constitutional right to proceed *in forma pauperis.* See *supra,* at 562–564. M. L. B., on the other hand, maintains that the accusatory state action she is trying to fend off12 is barely distinguishable from criminal condemnation in view of the magnitude and permanence of the loss she faces. For the purpose at hand, M. L. B. asks us to treat her parental termination appeal as we have treated petty offense appeals; she urges us to adhere to the reasoning in *Mayer v. Chicago,* 404 U.S. 189, 92 S.Ct. 410, 30 L.Ed.2d 372 (1971), see *supra,* at 561, and rule that Mississippi may not withhold the transcript M. L. B. needs to gain review of the order ending her parental status. Guided by *Lassiter* and *Santosky,* and other decisions acknowledging the primacy of the parent-child relationship, *e.g., Stanley v. Illinois,* 405 U.S., at 651, 92 S.Ct., at 1212–1213; *Meyer v. Nebraska,* 262 U.S., at 399, 43 S.Ct., at 626–627, we agree that the *Mayer* decision points to the disposition proper in this case.

We observe first that the Court's decisions concerning access to judicial processes, commencing with *Griffin* and running through *Mayer,* reflect both equal protection and due process concerns. As we said in *Bearden v. Georgia,* 461 U.S. 660, 665, 103 S.Ct. 2064, 2068–2069, 76 L.Ed.2d 221 (1983), in the Court's *Griffin*-line cases, "[d]ue process and equal protection principles converge." The equal protection concern relates to the legitimacy of fencing out would-be appellants based solely on their inability to pay core costs. The due process concern homes in on the essential fairness of the state-ordered proceedings anterior to adverse state action. A "precise rationale" has not been composed because cases of this order "cannot be resolved by resort to easy slogans or pigeonhole analysis," *Bearden,* 461 U.S., at 666, 103 S.Ct., at 2069.

Nevertheless, "[m]ost decisions in this area," we have recognized, "res[t] on an equal protection framework," *id.*, at 665, 103 S.Ct., at 2068, as M. L. B.'s plea heavily does, for, as we earlier observed, see *supra*, at 560, due process does not independently require that the State provide a right to appeal. We place this case within the framework established by our past decisions in this area. In line with those decisions, we inspect the character and intensity of the individual interest at stake, on the one hand, and the State's justification for its exaction, on the other.

We now focus on *Mayer* and the considerations linking that decision to M. L. B.'s case. *Mayer*, described *supra*, at 561, applied *Griffin* to a petty offender, fined a total of $500, who sought to appeal from the trial court's judgment. See *Mayer*, 404 U.S., at 190, 92 S.Ct., at 412–413. An "impecunious medical student," the defendant in *Mayer* could not pay for a transcript. We held that the State must afford him a record complete enough to allow fair appellate consideration of his claims. The defendant in *Mayer* faced no term of confinement, but the conviction, we observed, could affect his professional prospects and, possibly, even bar him from the practice of medicine. The State's pocketbook interest in advance payment for a transcript, we concluded, was unimpressive when measured against the stakes for the defendant.

Similarly here, the stakes for petitioner M. L. B.—forced dissolution of her parental rights—are large, " 'more substantial than mere loss of money.' " In contrast to loss of custody, which does not sever the parent-child bond, parental status termination is "irretrievabl[y] destructi[ve]" of the most fundamental family relationship. And the risk of error, Mississippi's experience shows, is considerable.

Consistent with *Santosky*, Mississippi has, by statute, adopted a "clear and convincing proof" standard for parental status termination cases. Nevertheless, the Chancellor's termination order in this case simply recites statutory language; it describes no evidence, and otherwise details no reasons for finding M. L. B. "clear[ly] and convincing [ly]" unfit to be a parent. Only a transcript can reveal to judicial minds other than the Chancellor's the sufficiency, or insufficiency, of the evidence to support his stern judgment.

The countervailing government interest, as in *Mayer*, is financial. Mississippi urges, as the justification for its appeal cost prepayment requirement, the State's legitimate interest in offsetting the costs of its court system. But in the tightly circumscribed category of parental status termination cases, appeals are few, and not likely to impose an undue burden on the State.

In States providing criminal appeals, as we earlier recounted, an indigent's access to appeal, through a transcript of relevant trial proceedings, is secure under our precedent. That equal access right holds for petty offenses as well as for felonies. But counsel at state expense, we have held, is a constitutional requirement, even in the first instance, only when the defendant faces time in confinement. When deprivation of parental status is at stake, however, counsel is sometimes part of the process that is due. See *Lassiter*, 452 U.S., at 31–32, 101 S.Ct., at 2161–2162. It would be anomalous to recognize a right to a transcript needed to appeal a misdemeanor conviction—

though trial counsel may be flatly denied—but hold, at the same time, that a transcript need not be prepared for M. L. B.—though were her defense sufficiently complex, state-paid counsel, as *Lassiter* instructs, would be designated for her.

In aligning M. L. B.'s case and *Mayer*—parental status termination decrees and criminal convictions that carry no jail time—for appeal access purposes, we do not question the general rule, stated in *Ortwein*, that fee requirements ordinarily are examined only for rationality. See *supra*, at 563. The State's need for revenue to offset costs, in the mine run of cases, satisfies the rationality requirement, States are not forced by the Constitution to adjust all tolls to account for "disparity in material circumstances." *Griffin*, 351 U.S., at 23, 76 S.Ct., at 592 (Frankfurter, J., concurring in judgment).

But our cases solidly establish two exceptions to that general rule. The basic right to participate in political processes as voters and candidates cannot be limited to those who can pay for a license. Nor may access to judicial processes in cases criminal or "quasi criminal in nature," *Mayer*, 404 U.S., at 196, 92 S.Ct., at 415 turn on ability to pay. In accord with the substance and sense of our decisions in *Lassiter* and *Santosky*, we place decrees forever terminating parental rights in the category of cases in which the State may not "bolt the door to equal justice," *Griffin*, 351 U.S., at 24, 76 S.Ct., at 593.

VI

In numerous cases, respondents point out, the Court has held that government "need not provide funds so that people can exercise even fundamental rights." ... To comprehend the difference between the case at hand and cases controlled by *Washington v. Davis*, one need look no further than this Court's opinion in *Williams v. Illinois*, 399 U.S. 235, 90 S.Ct. 2018, 26 L.Ed.2d 586 (1970). *Williams* held unconstitutional an Illinois law under which an indigent offender could be continued in confinement beyond the maximum prison term specified by statute if his indigency prevented him from satisfying the monetary portion of the sentence. The Court described that law as "'nondiscriminatory on its face,'" and recalled that the law found incompatible with the Constitution in *Griffin* had been so characterized. 399 U.S., at 242, 90 S.Ct., at 2022–2023 (quoting *Griffin*, 351 U.S., at 17, n. 11, 76 S.Ct., at 590, n. 11); see *Griffin*, 351 U.S., at 17, n. 11, 76 S.Ct., at 590, n. 11 "[A] law nondiscriminatory on its face may be grossly discriminatory in its operation."). But the *Williams* Court went on to explain that "the Illinois statute in operative effect exposes *only indigents* to the risk of imprisonment beyond the statutory maximum." 399 U.S., at 242, 90 S.Ct., at 2023 (emphasis added). Sanctions of the *Williams* genre, like the Mississippi prescription here at issue, are not merely *disproportionate* in impact. Rather, they are wholly contingent on one's ability to pay, and thus "visi[t] different consequences on two categories of persons," *ibid.*; they apply to all indigents and do not reach anyone outside that class.

In sum, under respondents' reading of *Washington v. Davis*, our overruling of the *Griffin* line of cases would be two decades overdue. It suffices to point out that this

Court has not so conceived the meaning and effect of our 1976 "disproportionate impact" precedent. See *Bearden v. Georgia,* 461 U.S., at 664–665, 103 S.Ct., at 2068–2069 (adhering in 1983 to "*Griffin* 's principle of 'equal justice' ").

Respondents and the dissenters urge that we will open floodgates if we do not rigidly restrict *Griffin* to cases typed "criminal." But we have repeatedly noticed what sets parental status termination decrees apart from mine run civil actions, even from other domestic relations matters such as divorce, paternity, and child custody. To recapitulate, termination decrees "wor[k] a unique kind of deprivation." *Lassiter,* 452 U.S., at 27, 101 S.Ct., at 2160. In contrast to matters modifiable at the parties' will or based on changed circumstances, termination adjudications involve the awesome authority of the State "to destroy permanently all legal recognition of the parental relationship." *Rivera,* 483 U.S., at 580, 107 S.Ct., at 3005. Our *Lassiter* and *Santosky* decisions, recognizing that parental termination decrees are among the most severe forms of state action, *Santosky,* 455 U.S., at 759, 102 S.Ct., at 1397–1398, have not served as precedent in other areas. See *supra,* at 565, n. 11. We are therefore satisfied that the label "civil" should not entice us to leave undisturbed the Mississippi courts' disposition of this case.

* * *

For the reasons stated, we hold that Mississippi may not withhold from M. L. B. "a 'record of sufficient completeness' to permit proper [appellate] consideration of [her] claims." *Mayer,* 404 U.S., at 198, 92 S.Ct., at 416. Accordingly, we reverse the judgment of the Supreme Court of Mississippi and remand the case for further proceedings not inconsistent with this opinion.

Justice THOMAS, with whom Justice SCALIA joins, and with whom THE CHIEF JUSTICE joins except as to Part II, dissenting.

Today the majority holds that the Fourteenth Amendment requires Mississippi to afford petitioner a free transcript because her civil case involves a "fundamental" right. The majority seeks to limit the reach of its holding to the type of case we confront here, one involving the termination of parental rights. I do not think, however, that the new-found constitutional right to free transcripts in civil appeals can be effectively restricted to this case. The inevitable consequence will be greater demands on the States to provide free assistance to would-be appellants in all manner of civil cases involving interests that cannot, based on the test established by the majority, be distinguished from the admittedly important interest at issue here. The cases on which the majority relies, primarily cases requiring appellate assistance for indigent criminal defendants, were questionable when decided, and have, in my view, been undermined since. Even accepting those cases, however, I am of the view that the majority takes them too far. I therefore dissent.

E. Appointed Counsel in
Civil Proceedings

Following *Gideon,* the Court signaled the possible extension of the right to appointed counsel in civil proceedings. In the first case, *In re Gault,* the Court extended the right to juvenile proceedings where the juvenile faces confinement. This outcome intuitively makes sense as the juvenile's liberty is at stake in such proceedings. In *Argersiner v. Hamlin,* the Court relied on the liberty interest concern to extend the right to counsel to any misdemeanor prosecution that involves jail time. Despite the apparent movement toward an extension of the right to counsel to include counsel in civil proceedings, the Court failed to establish such a broad right in the years that following *Gault* and *Argersinger.* Any hope for a right broad enough to include civil proceedings was put to rest with *Turner.*

Turner v. Rogers
564 U.S. 431 (2011)

South Carolina's Family Court enforces its child support orders by threatening with incarceration for civil contempt those who are (1) subject to a child support order, (2) able to comply with that order, but (3) fail to do so. We must decide whether the Fourteenth Amendment's Due Process Clause requires the State to provide counsel (at a civil contempt hearing) to an *indigent* person potentially faced with such incarceration. We conclude that where as here the custodial parent (entitled to receive the support) is unrepresented by counsel, the State need not provide counsel to the non-custodial parent (required to provide the support). But we attach an important caveat, namely, that the State must nonetheless have in place alternative procedures that assure a fundamentally fair determination of the critical incarceration-related question, whether the supporting parent is able to comply with the support order.

I

A

South Carolina family courts enforce their child support orders in part through civil contempt proceedings. Each month the family court clerk reviews outstanding child support orders, identifies those in which the supporting parent has fallen more than five days behind, and sends that parent an order to "show cause" why he should not be held in contempt. S.C. Rule Family Ct. 24 (2011). The "show cause" order and attached affidavit refer to the relevant child support order, identify the amount of the arrearage, and set a date for a court hearing. At the hearing that parent may demonstrate that he is not in contempt, say, by showing that he is not able to make the required payments. If he fails to make the required showing, the court may hold him in civil contempt. And it may require that he be imprisoned unless and until he purges himself of contempt by making the required child support payments (but not for more than one year regardless). See S.C.Code Ann. §63-3-620 (Supp.2010) (imprisonment for up to one year of "adult who wilfully violates" a court order).

B

In June 2003 a South Carolina family court entered an order, which (as amended) required petitioner, Michael Turner, to pay $51.73 per week to respondent, Rebecca Rogers, to help support their child. Over the next three years, Turner repeatedly failed to pay the amount due and was held in contempt on five occasions. The first four times he was sentenced to 90 days' imprisonment, but he ultimately paid the amount due (twice without being jailed, twice after spending two or three days in custody). The fifth time he did not pay but completed a 6-month sentence.

After his release in 2006 Turner remained in arrears. On March 27, 2006, the clerk issued a new "show cause" order. And after an initial postponement due to Turner's failure to appear, Turner's civil contempt hearing took place on January 3, 2008. Turner and Rogers were present, each without representation by counsel.

The hearing was brief. The court clerk said that Turner was $5,728.76 behind in his payments. The judge asked Turner if there was "anything you want to say." Turner replied,

> "Well, when I first got out, I got back on dope. I done meth, smoked pot and everything else, and I paid a little bit here and there. And, when I finally did get to working, I broke my back, back in September. I filed for disability and SSI. And, I didn't get straightened out off the dope until I broke my back and laid up for two months. And, now I'm off the dope and everything. I just hope that you give me a chance. I don't know what else to say. I mean, I know I done wrong, and I should have been paying and helping her, and I'm sorry. I mean, dope had a hold to me." App. to Pet. for Cert. 17a.

The judge then said, "[o]kay," and asked Rogers if she had anything to say. *Ibid.* After a brief discussion of federal benefits, the judge stated,

> "If there's nothing else, this will be the Order of the Court. I find the Defendant in willful contempt. I'm [going to] sentence him to twelve months in the Oconee County Detention Center. He may purge himself of the contempt and avoid the sentence by having a zero balance on or before his release. I've also placed a lien on any SSI or other benefits." *Id.,* at 18a.

The judge added that Turner would not receive good-time or work credits, but "[i]f you've got a job, I'll make you eligible for work release." *Ibid.* When Turner asked why he could not receive good-time or work credits, the judge said, "[b]ecause that's my ruling." *Ibid.*

The court made no express finding concerning Turner's ability to pay his. Nor did the judge ask any followup questions or otherwise address the ability-to-pay issue. After the hearing, the judge filled out a prewritten form titled "Order for Contempt of Court," which included the statement:

> "Defendant (was) (was not) gainfully employed and/or (had) (did not have) the ability to make these support payments when due." *Id.,* at 60a, 61a.

But the judge left this statement as is without indicating whether Turner was able to make support payments.

C

While serving his 12-month sentence, Turner, with the help of *pro bono* counsel, appealed. He claimed that the Federal Constitution entitled him to counsel at his contempt hearing. The South Carolina Supreme Court decided Turner's appeal after he had completed his sentence. And it rejected his "right to counsel" claim. The court pointed out that civil contempt differs significantly from criminal contempt. The former does not require all the "constitutional safeguards" applicable in criminal proceedings. 387 S.C., at 145, 691 S.E.2d, at 472. And the right to government-paid counsel, the Supreme Court held, was one of the "safeguards" not required. *Ibid.*

III

A

We must decide whether the Due Process Clause grants an indigent defendant, such as Turner, a right to state-appointed counsel at a civil contempt proceeding, which may lead to his incarceration. This Court's precedents provide no definitive answer to that question. This Court has long held that the Sixth Amendment grants an indigent defendant the right to state-appointed counsel in a *criminal* case. *Gideon v. Wainwright,* 372 U.S. 335, 83 S.Ct. 792, 9 L.Ed.2d 799 (1963). And we have held that this same rule applies to *criminal contempt* proceedings (other than summary proceedings).

But the Sixth Amendment does not govern civil cases. Civil contempt differs from criminal contempt in that it seeks only to "coerc[e] the defendant to do" what a court had previously ordered him to do. A court may not impose punishment "in a civil contempt proceeding when it is clearly established that the alleged contemnor is unable to comply with the terms of the order." And once a civil contemnor complies with the underlying order, he is purged of the contempt and is free. *Id.,* at 633, 108 S.Ct. 1423 (he "carr[ies] the keys of [his] prison in [his] own pockets" (internal quotation marks omitted)).

Consequently, the Court has made clear (in a case not involving the right to counsel) that, where civil contempt is at issue, the Fourteenth Amendment's Due Process Clause allows a State to provide fewer procedural protections than in a criminal case. *Id.,* at 637–641, 108 S.Ct. 1423 (State may place the burden of proving inability to pay on the defendant).

This Court has decided only a handful of cases that more directly concern a right to counsel in civil matters. And the application of those decisions to the present case is not clear. On the one hand, the Court has held that the Fourteenth Amendment requires the State to pay for representation by counsel in a *civil* "juvenile delinquency" proceeding (which could lead to incarceration). Moreover, in *Vitek v. Jones,* 445 U.S. 480, 496–497, 100 S.Ct. 1254, 63 L.Ed.2d 552 (1980), a plurality of four Members of this Court would have held that the Fourteenth Amendment requires representation by counsel in a proceeding to transfer a prison inmate to a state hospital for the mentally ill. Further, in *Lassiter v. Department of Social Servs. of Durham Cty.,* 452 U.S.

18, 101 S.Ct. 2153, 68 L.Ed.2d 640 (1981), a case that focused upon civil proceedings leading to loss of parental rights, the Court wrote that the "pre-eminent generalization that emerges from this Court's precedents on an indigent's right to appointed counsel is that such a right has been recognized to exist only where the litigant may lose his physical liberty if he loses the litigation." *Id.*, at 25, 101 S.Ct. 2153.

And the Court then drew from these precedents "the presumption that an indigent litigant has a right to appointed counsel only when, if he loses, he may be deprived of his physical liberty." *Id.*, at 26–27, 101 S.Ct. 2153.

On the other hand, the Court has held that a criminal offender facing revocation of probation and imprisonment does *not* ordinarily have a right to counsel at a probation revocation hearing. *Gagnon v. Scarpelli*, 411 U.S. 778, 93 S.Ct. 1756, 36 L.Ed.2d 656 (1973). And, at the same time, *Gault*, *Vitek*, and *Lassiter* are readily distinguishable. The civil juvenile delinquency proceeding at issue in *Gault* was "little different" from, and "comparable in seriousness" to, a criminal prosecution. 387 U.S., at 28, 36, 87 S.Ct. 1428. In *Vitek*, the controlling opinion found *no* right to counsel. 445 U.S., at 499–500, 100 S.Ct. 1254 (Powell, J., concurring in part) (assistance of mental health professionals sufficient). And the Court's statements in *Lassiter* constitute part of its rationale for *denying* a right to counsel in that case. We believe those statements are best read as pointing out that the Court previously had found a right to counsel "*only*" in cases involving incarceration, not that a right to counsel exists in *all* such cases (a position that would have been difficult to reconcile with *Gagnon*).

B

Civil contempt proceedings in child support cases constitute one part of a highly complex system designed to assure a noncustodial parent's regular payment of funds typically necessary for the support of his children. Often the family receives welfare support from a state-administered federal program, and the State then seeks reimbursement from the noncustodial parent. See 42 U.S.C. §§ 608(a)(3) (2006 ed., Supp. III), 656(a)(1) (2006 ed.); S.C.Code Ann. §§ 43-5-65(a)(1), (2) (2010 Cum.Supp.). Other times the custodial parent (often the mother, but sometimes the father, a grandparent, or another person with custody) does not receive government benefits and is entitled to receive the support payments herself.

The Federal Government has created an elaborate procedural mechanism designed to help both the government and custodial parents to secure the payments to which they are entitled. See generally *Blessing v. Freestone*, 520 U.S. 329, 333, 117 S.Ct. 1353, 137 L.Ed.2d 569 (1997) (describing the "interlocking set of cooperative federal-state welfare programs" as they relate to child support enforcement); 45 CFR pt. 303 (2010) (prescribing standards for state child support agencies). These systems often rely upon wage withholding, expedited procedures for modifying and enforcing child support orders, and automated data processing. 42 U.S.C. §§ 666(a), (b), 654(24). But sometimes States will use contempt orders to ensure that the custodial parent receives support payments or the government receives reimbursement. Although some experts have criticized this last-mentioned procedure, and the Federal Government believes that "the routine use of contempt for non-payment of child support is likely to be an ineffective strategy," the Government also tells us that "coercive enforcement remedies, such as contempt, have a role to play."

We here consider an indigent's right to paid counsel at such a contempt proceeding. It is a civil proceeding. And we consequently determine the "specific dictates of due process" by examining the "distinct factors" that this Court has previously found useful in deciding what specific safeguards the Constitution's Due Process Clause requires in order to make a civil proceeding fundamentally fair. *Mathews v. Eldridge*, 424 U.S. 319, 335, 96 S.Ct. 893, 47 L.Ed.2d 18 (1976) (considering fairness of an administrative proceeding). As relevant here those factors include (1) the nature of "the private interest that will be affected," (2) the comparative "risk" of an "erroneous deprivation" of that interest with and without "additional or substitute procedural safeguards," and (3) the nature and magnitude of any countervailing interest in not providing "additional or substitute procedural requirement [s]." *Ibid.* See also *Lassiter*, 452 U.S., at 27–31, 101 S.Ct. 2153 (applying the *Mathews* framework).

The "private interest that will be affected" argues strongly for the right to counsel that Turner advocates. That interest consists of an indigent defendant's loss of personal liberty through imprisonment. The interest in securing that freedom, the freedom "from bodily restraint," lies "at the core of the liberty protected by the Due Process Clause." *Foucha v. Louisiana*, 504 U.S. 71, 80, 112 S.Ct. 1780, 118 L.Ed.2d 437 (1992). And we have made clear that its threatened loss through legal proceedings demands "due process protection." *Addington v. Texas*, 441 U.S. 418, 425, 99 S.Ct. 1804, 60 L.Ed.2d 323 (1979).

Given the importance of the interest at stake, it is obviously important to assure accurate decision making in respect to the key "ability to pay" question. Moreover, the fact that ability to comply marks a dividing line between civil and criminal contempt, *Hicks*, 485 U.S., at 635, n. 7, 108 S.Ct. 1423, reinforces the need for accuracy. That is because an incorrect decision (wrongly classifying the contempt proceeding as civil) can increase the risk of wrongful incarceration by depriving the defendant of the procedural protections (including counsel) that the Constitution would demand in a criminal proceeding. And since 70% of child support arrears nationwide are owed by parents with either no reported income or income of $10,000 per year or less, the issue of ability to pay may arise fairly often.... See also, *e.g.*, *McBride v. McBride*, 334 N.C. 124, 131, n. 4, 431 S.E.2d 14, 19, n. 4 (1993) (surveying North Carolina contempt orders and finding that the "failure of trial courts to make a determination of a contemnor's ability to comply is not altogether infrequent").

On the other hand, the Due Process Clause does not always require the provision of counsel in civil proceedings where incarceration is threatened. And in determining whether the Clause requires a right to counsel here, we must take account of opposing interests, as well as consider the probable value of "additional or substitute procedural safeguards." *Mathews, supra*, at 335, 96 S.Ct. 893.

Doing so, we find three related considerations that, when taken together, argue strongly against the Due Process Clause requiring the State to provide indigents with counsel in every proceeding of the kind before us.

First, the critical question likely at issue in these cases concerns, as we have said, the defendant's ability to pay. That question is often closely related to the question of the defendant's indigence. But when the right procedures are in place, indigence can be a question that in many—but not all—cases is sufficiently straightforward to warrant determination *prior* to providing a defendant with counsel, even in a criminal case. Federal law, for example, requires a criminal defendant to provide information showing that he is indigent, and therefore entitled to state-funded counsel, *before* he can receive that assistance. See 18 U.S.C. §3006A(b).

Second, sometimes, as here, the person opposing the defendant at the hearing is not the government represented by counsel but the custodial parent *un* represented by counsel. The custodial parent, perhaps a woman with custody of one or more children, may be relatively poor, unemployed, and unable to afford counsel. Yet she may have encouraged the court to enforce its order through contempt. She may be able to provide the court with significant information. Cf. *id.*, at 41a–43a (Rogers describes where Turner lived and worked). And the proceeding is ultimately for her benefit.

A requirement that the State provide counsel to the noncustodial parent in these cases could create an asymmetry of representation that would "alter significantly the nature of the proceeding." *Gagnon, supra,* at 787, 93 S.Ct. 1756. Doing so could mean a degree of formality or delay that would unduly slow payment to those immediately in need. And, perhaps more important for present purposes, doing so could make the proceedings *less* fair overall, increasing the risk of a decision that would erroneously deprive a family of the support it is entitled to receive. The needs of such families play an important role in our analysis.

Third, as the Solicitor General points out, there is available a set of "substitute procedural safeguards," *Mathews,* 424 U.S., at 335, 96 S.Ct. 893, which, if employed together, can significantly reduce the risk of an erroneous deprivation of liberty. They can do so, moreover, without incurring some of the drawbacks inherent in recognizing an automatic right to counsel. Those safeguards include (1) notice to the defendant that his "ability to pay" is a critical issue in the contempt proceeding; (2) the use of a form (or the equivalent) to elicit relevant financial information; (3) an opportunity at the hearing for the defendant to respond to statements and questions about his financial status (*e.g.,* those triggered by his responses on the form); and (4) an express finding by the court that the defendant has the ability to pay. In presenting these alternatives, the Government draws upon considerable experience in helping to manage statutorily mandated federal-state efforts to enforce child support orders. It does not claim that they are the only possible alternatives, and this Court's cases suggest, for example, that sometimes assistance other than purely legal assistance (here, say, that of a neutral social worker) can prove constitutionally sufficient. But the Government does claim that these alternatives can assure the "fundamental fairness" of the proceeding even where the State does not pay for counsel for an indigent defendant.

While recognizing the strength of Turner's arguments, we ultimately believe that the three considerations we have just discussed must carry the day. In our view, a categorical right to counsel in proceedings of the kind before us would carry with it disadvantages (in the form of unfairness and delay) that, in terms of ultimate fairness, would deprive it of significant superiority over the alternatives that we have mentioned. We consequently hold that the Due Process Clause does not *automatically* require the provision of counsel at civil contempt proceedings to an indigent individual who is subject to a child support order, even if that individual faces incarceration (for up to a year). In particular, that Clause does not require the provision of counsel where the opposing parent or other custodian (to whom support funds are owed) is not represented by counsel and the State provides alternative procedural safeguards equivalent to those we have mentioned (adequate notice of the importance of ability to pay, fair opportunity to present, and to dispute, relevant information, and court findings).

We do not address civil contempt proceedings where the underlying child support payment is owed to the State, for example, for reimbursement of welfare funds paid to the parent with custody. Those proceedings more closely resemble debt-collection proceedings. The government is likely to have counsel or some other competent representative. And this kind of proceeding is not before us. Neither do we address what due process requires in an unusually complex case where a defendant "can fairly be represented only by a trained advocate." *Gagnon, supra*, at 788, 93 S. Ct. 1756, 36 L. Ed. 2d 656.

IV

The record indicates that Turner received neither counsel nor the benefit of alternative procedures like those we have described. He did not receive clear notice that his ability to pay would constitute the critical question in his civil contempt proceeding. No one provided him with a form (or the equivalent) designed to elicit information about his financial circumstances. The court did not find that Turner was able to pay his arrearage, but instead left the relevant "finding" section of the contempt order blank. The court nonetheless found Turner in contempt and ordered him incarcerated. Under these circumstances Turner's incarceration violated the Due Process Clause.

We vacate the judgment of the South Carolina Supreme Court and remand the case for further proceedings not inconsistent with this opinion.

Lassiter v. Department of Social Services
452 U.S. 18 (1981)

I

In the late spring of 1975, after hearing evidence that the petitioner, Abby Gail Lassiter, had not provided her infant son William with proper medical care, the District Court of Durham County, N. C., adjudicated him a neglected child and transferred him to the custody of the Durham County Department of Social Services, the respondent here. A year later, Ms. Lassiter was charged with first-degree murder, was convicted of second-degree murder, and began a sentence of 25 to 40 years of imprisonment. In 1978 the Department petitioned the court to terminate Ms. Lassiter's parental rights because, the Department alleged, she "has not had any contact with the child since December of 1975" and "has willfully left the child in foster care for more than two consecutive years without showing that substantial progress has been made in correcting the conditions which led to the removal of the child, or without showing a positive response to the diligent efforts of the Department of Social Services to strengthen her relationship to the child, or to make and follow through with constructive planning for the future of the child."

Ms. Lassiter was served with the petition and with notice that a hearing on it would be held. Although her mother had retained counsel for her in connection with an effort to invalidate the murder conviction, Ms. Lassiter never mentioned the forthcoming hearing to him (or, for that matter, to any other person except, she said, to "someone" in the prison). At the behest of the Department of Social Services' attorney, she was brought from prison to the hearing, which was held August 31, 1978. The hearing opened, apparently at the judge's instance, with a discussion of whether Ms. Lassiter should have more time in which to find legal assistance. Since the court concluded that she "has had ample opportunity to seek and obtain counsel prior to the hearing of this matter, and [that] her failure to do so is without just cause," the court did not postpone the proceedings. Ms. Lassiter did not aver that she was indigent, and the court did not appoint counsel for her.

A social worker from the respondent Department was the first witness. She testified that in 1975 the Department "received a complaint from Duke Pediatrics that William had not been followed in the pediatric clinic for medical problems and that they were having difficulty in locating Ms. Lassiter...." She said that in May 1975 a social worker had taken William to the hospital, where doctors asked that he stay "because of breathing difficulties [and] malnutrition and [because] there was a great deal of scarring that indicated that he had a severe infection that had gone untreated." The witness further testified that, except for one "prearranged" visit and a chance meeting on the street, Ms. Lassiter had not seen William after he had come into the State's custody, and that neither Ms. Lassiter nor her mother had "made any contact with the Department of Social Services regarding that child." When asked whether William should be placed in his grandmother's custody, the social worker said he should not, since the grandmother "has indicated to me on a number of occasions that she was not able to take responsibility for the child" and since "I have checked with people in the community and from Ms. Lassiter's church who also feel that this additional responsibility would be more than she can handle." The social worker added that William "has not seen his grandmother since the chance meeting in July of '76 and that was the only time."

After the direct examination of the social worker, the judge said:

"I notice we made extensive findings in June of '75 that you were served with papers and called the social services and told them you weren't coming; and the serious lack of medical treatment. And, as I have said in my findings of the 16th day of June '75, the Court finds that the grandmother, Ms. Lucille Lassiter, mother of Abby Gail Lassiter, filed a complaint on the 8th day of

May, 1975, alleging that the daughter often left the children, Candina, Felicia and William L. with her for days without providing money or food while she was gone."

Ms. Lassiter conducted a cross-examination of the social worker, who firmly reiterated her earlier testimony. The judge explained several times, with varying degrees of clarity, that Ms. Lassiter should only ask questions at this stage; many of her questions were disallowed because they were not really questions, but arguments.

Ms. Lassiter herself then testified, under the judge's questioning, that she had properly cared for William. Under cross-examination, she said that she had seen William more than five or six times after he had been taken from her custody and that, if William could not be with her, she wanted him to be with her mother since "He knows us. Children know they family.... They know they people, they know they family and that child knows us anywhere.... I got four more other children. Three girls and a boy and they know they little brother when they see him."

Ms. Lassiter's mother was then called as a witness. She denied, under the questioning of the judge, that she had filed the complaint against Ms. Lassiter, and on cross-examination she denied both having failed to visit William when he was in the State's custody and having said that she could not care for him.

The court found that Ms. Lassiter "has not contacted the Department of Social Services about her child since December, 1975, has not expressed any concern for his care and welfare, and has made no efforts to plan for his future." Because Ms. Lassiter thus had "willfully failed to maintain concern or responsibility for the welfare of the minor," and because it was "in the best interests of the minor," the court terminated Ms. Lassiter's status as William's parent.2

On appeal, Ms. Lassiter argued only that, because she was indigent, the Due Process Clause of the Fourteenth Amendment entitled her to the assistance of counsel, and that the trial court had therefore erred in not requiring the State to provide counsel for her. The North Carolina Court of Appeals decided that "[w]hile this State action does invade a protected area of individual privacy, the invasion is not so serious or unreasonable as to compel us to hold that appointment of counsel for indigent parents is constitutionally mandated." *In re Lassiter*, 43 N.C.App. 525, 527, 259 S.E.2d 336, 337. The Supreme Court of North Carolina summarily denied Ms. Lassiter's application for discretionary review, and we granted certiorari to consider the petitioner's claim under the Due Process Clause of the Fourteenth Amendment.

II

For all its consequence, "due process" has never been, and perhaps can never be, precisely defined. "[U]nlike some legal rules," this Court has said, due process "is not a technical conception with a fixed content unrelated to time, place and circumstances." *Cafeteria Workers v. McElroy*, 367 U.S. 886, 895, 81 S.Ct. 1743, 1748, 6 L.Ed.2d 1230. Rather, the phrase expresses the requirement of "fundamental fairness," a requirement whose meaning can be as opaque as its importance is lofty. Applying the Due Process Clause is therefore an uncertain enterprise which must discover what "fundamental fairness" consists of in a particular situation by first considering any relevant precedents and then by assessing the several interests that are at stake.

A

The pre-eminent generalization that emerges from this Court's precedents on an indigent's right to appointed counsel is that such a right has been recognized to exist only where the litigant may lose his physical liberty if he loses the litigation. Thus, when the Court overruled the principle of *Betts v. Brady*, 316 U.S. 455, that counsel in criminal trials need be appointed only where the circumstances in a given case demand it, the Court did so in the case of a man sentenced to prison for five years. *Gideon v. Wainwright*, 372 U.S. 335. And thus *Argersinger v. Hamlin*, 407 U.S. 25, established that counsel must be provided before any indigent may be sentenced to prison, even where the crime is petty and the prison term brief.

That it is the defendant's interest in personal freedom, and not simply the special Sixth and Fourteenth Amendments right to counsel in criminal cases, which triggers the right to appointed counsel is demonstrated by the Court's announcement in *In re Gault*, 387 U.S. 1, that "the Due Process Clause of the Fourteenth Amendment requires that in respect of proceedings to determine delinquency *which may result in commitment to an institution in which the juvenile's freedom is curtailed*," the juvenile has a right to appointed counsel even though proceedings may be styled "civil" and not "criminal." *Id.*, at 41, 87 S.Ct., at 1451 (emphasis added). Similarly, four of the five Justices who reached the merits in *Vitek v. Jones*, 445 U.S. 480, 100 S.Ct. 1254, 63 L.Ed.2d 552, concluded that an indigent prisoner is entitled to appointed counsel before being involuntarily transferred for treatment to a state mental hospital. The fifth Justice differed from the other four only in declining to exclude the "possibility that the required assistance may be rendered by competent laymen in some cases."

Significantly, as a litigant's interest in personal liberty diminishes, so does his right to appointed counsel. In *Gagnon v. Scarpelli*, 411 U.S. 778, 93 S.Ct. 1756, 36 L.Ed.2d 656, the Court gauged the due process rights of a previously sentenced probationer at a probation-revocation hearing. In *Morrissey v. Brewer*, 408 U.S. 471, 480, 92 S.Ct. 2593, 2599, 33 L.Ed.2d 484, which involved an analogous hearing to revoke parole, the Court had said: "Revocation deprives an individual, not of the absolute liberty to which every citizen is entitled, but only of the conditional liberty properly dependent on observance of special parole restrictions." Relying on that discussion, the Court in *Scarpelli* declined to hold that indigent probationers have, *per se*, a right to counsel at revocation hearings, and instead left the decision whether counsel should be appointed to be made on a case-by-case basis.

Finally, the Court has refused to extend the right to appointed counsel to include prosecutions which, though criminal, do not result in the defendant's loss of personal liberty. The Court in *Scott v. Illinois*, 440 U.S. 367, 99 S.Ct. 1158, 59 L.Ed.2d 383, for instance, interpreted the "central premise of *Argersinger*" to be "that actual imprisonment is a penalty different in kind from fines or the mere threat of imprisonment," and the Court endorsed that premise as "eminently sound and warrant[ing]

adoption of actual imprisonment as the line defining the constitutional right to appointment of counsel." *Id.*, 440 U.S., at 373, 99 S.Ct., at 1162. The Court thus held
"that the Sixth and Fourteenth Amendments to the United States Constitution require
only that no indigent criminal defendant be sentenced to a term of imprisonment
unless the State has afforded him the right to assistance of appointed counsel in his
defense." *Id.*, at 373–374, 99 S.Ct., at 1162.

In sum, the Court's precedents speak with one voice about what "fundamental
fairness" has meant when the Court has considered the right to appointed counsel,
and we thus draw from them the presumption that an indigent litigant has a right
to appointed counsel only when, if he loses, he may be deprived of his physical liberty.
It is against this presumption that all the other elements in the due process decision
must be measured.

B

The case of *Mathews v. Eldridge*, propounds three elements to be evaluated in deciding what due process requires, viz., the private interests at stake, the government's
interest, and the risk that the procedures used will lead to erroneous decisions. We
must balance these elements against each other, and then set their net weight in the
scales against the presumption that there is a right to appointed counsel only where
the indigent, if he is unsuccessful, may lose his personal freedom.

This Court's decisions have by now made plain beyond the need for multiple citation
that a parent's desire for and right to "the companionship, care, custody and management of his or her children" is an important interest that "undeniably warrants
deference and, absent a powerful countervailing interest, protection." *Stanley v. Illinois*,
405 U.S. 645, 651, 92 S.Ct. 1208, 1212, 31 L.Ed. 551. Here the State has sought not
simply to infringe upon that interest but to end it. If the State prevails, it will have
worked a unique kind of deprivation. A parent's interest in the accuracy and justice
of the decision to terminate his or her parental status is, therefore a commanding one.

Since the State has an urgent interest in the welfare of the child, it shares the
parent's interest in an accurate and just decision. For this reason, the State may share
the indigent parent's interest in the availability of appointed counsel. If, as our adversary system presupposes, accurate and just results are most likely to be obtained
through the equal contest of opposed interests, the State's interest in the child's welfare
may perhaps best be served by a hearing in which both the parent and the State acting
for the child are represented by counsel, without whom the contest of interests may
become unwholesomely unequal. North Carolina itself acknowledges as much by
providing that where a parent files a written answer to a termination petition, the
State must supply a lawyer to represent the child. N.C. Gen.Stat. §7A-289.29
(Supp.1979).

The State's interests, however, clearly diverge from the parent's insofar as the State
wishes the termination decision to be made as economically as possible and thus
wants to avoid both the expense of appointed counsel and the cost of the lengthened
proceedings his presence may cause. But though the State's pecuniary interest is le-

gitimate, it is hardly significant enough to overcome private interests as important as those here, particularly in light of the concession in the respondent's brief that the "potential costs of appointed counsel in termination proceedings ... is [*sic*] admittedly *de minimis* compared to the costs in all criminal actions."

Finally, consideration must be given to the risk that a parent will be erroneously deprived of his or her child because the parent is not represented by counsel. North Carolina law now seeks to assure accurate decisions by establishing the following procedures: A petition to terminate parental rights may be filed only by a parent seeking the termination of the other parent's rights, by a county department of social services or licensed child-placing agency with custody of the child, or by a person with whom the child has lived continuously for the two years preceding the petition. § 7A-289.24. A petition must describe facts sufficient to warrant a finding that one of the grounds for termination exists, § 7A-289.25(6), and the parent must be notified of the petition and given 30 days in which to file a written answer to it, § 7A-289.27. If that answer denies a material allegation, the court must, as has been noted, appoint a lawyer as the child's guardian *ad litem* and must conduct a special hearing to resolve the issues raised by the petition and the answer. § 7A-289.29. If the parent files no answer, "the court shall issue an order terminating all parental and custodial rights ...; provided the court shall order a hearing on the petition and may examine the petitioner or others on the facts alleged in the petition." § 7A-289.28. Findings of fact are made by a court sitting without a jury and must "be based on clear, cogent, and convincing evidence." § 7A-289.30. Any party may appeal who gives notice of appeal within 10 days after the hearing. § 7A-289.34.

The respondent argues that the subject of a termination hearing—the parent's relationship with her child—far from being abstruse, technical, or unfamiliar, is one as to which the parent must be uniquely well informed and to which the parent must have given prolonged thought. The respondent also contends that a termination hearing is not likely to produce difficult points of evidentiary law, or even of substantive law, since the evidentiary problems peculiar to criminal trials are not present and since the standards for termination are not complicated. In fact, the respondent reports, the North Carolina Departments of Social Services are themselves sometimes represented at termination hearings by social workers instead of by lawyers.

Yet the ultimate issues with which a termination hearing deals are not always simple, however commonplace they may be. Expert medical and psychiatric testimony, which few parents are equipped to understand and fewer still to confute, is sometimes presented. The parents are likely to be people with little education, who have had uncommon difficulty in dealing with life, and who are, at the hearing, thrust into a distressing and disorienting situation. That these factors may combine to overwhelm an uncounseled parent is evident from the findings some courts have made. Thus, courts have generally held that the State must appoint counsel for indigent parents at termination proceedings. *State ex rel. Heller v. Miller*, 61 Ohio St.2d 6, 399 N.E.2d 66 (1980). The respondent is able to point to no presently authoritative case, except for the North Carolina judgment now before us, holding that an indigent parent has no due process right to appointed counsel in termination proceedings.

C

The dispositive question, which must now be addressed, is whether the three *Eldridge* factors, when weighed against the presumption that there is no right to appointed counsel in the absence of at least a potential deprivation of physical liberty, suffice to rebut that presumption and thus to lead to the conclusion that the Due Process Clause requires the appointment of counsel when a State seeks to terminate an indigent's parental status. To summarize the above discussion of the *Eldridge* factors: the parent's interest is an extremely important one (and may be supplemented by the dangers of criminal liability inherent in some termination proceedings); the State shares with the parent an interest in a correct decision, has a relatively weak pecuniary interest, and, in some but not all cases, has a possibly stronger interest in informal procedures; and the complexity of the proceeding and the incapacity of the uncounseled parent could be, but would not always be, great enough to make the risk of an erroneous deprivation of the parent's rights insupportably high.

If, in a given case, the parent's interests were at their strongest, the State's interests were at their weakest, and the risks of error were at their peak, it could not be said that the *Eldridge* factors did not overcome the presumption against the right to appointed counsel, and that due process did not therefore require the appointment of counsel. But since the *Eldridge* factors will not always be so distributed, and since "due process is not so rigid as to require that the significant interests in informality, flexibility and economy must always be sacrificed," neither can we say that the Constitution requires the appointment of counsel in every parental termination proceeding. We therefore adopt the standard found appropriate in *Gagnon v. Scarpelli*, and leave the decision whether due process calls for the appointment of counsel for indigent parents in termination proceedings to be answered in the first instance by the trial court, subject, of course, to appellate review.

III

Here, as in *Scarpelli*, "[i]t is neither possible nor prudent to attempt to formulate a precise and detailed set of guidelines to be followed in determining when the providing of counsel is necessary to meet the applicable due process requirements," since here, as in that case, "[t]he facts and circumstances ... are susceptible of almost infinite variation...." 411 U.S., at 790, 93 S.Ct., at 1764. Nevertheless, because child-custody litigation must be concluded as rapidly as is consistent with fairness, we decide today whether the trial judge denied Ms. Lassiter due process of law when he did not appoint counsel for her.

The respondent represents that the petition to terminate Ms. Lassiter's parental rights contained no allegations of neglect or abuse upon which criminal charges could be based, and hence Ms. Lassiter could not well have argued that she required counsel for that reason. The Department of Social Services was represented at the hearing by counsel, but no expert witnesses testified and the case presented no specially troublesome points of law, either procedural or substantive. While hearsay evidence was no doubt admitted, and while Ms. Lassiter no doubt left incomplete her defense that the Department had not adequately assisted her in rekindling her interest in her son, the weight of the evidence that she had few sparks of such interest was sufficiently great that the presence of counsel for Ms. Lassiter could not have made a determinative difference. True, a lawyer might have done more with the argument that William should live with Ms. Lassiter's mother — but that argument was quite explicitly made by both Lassiters, and the evidence that the elder Ms. Lassiter had said she could not handle another child, that the social worker's investigation had led to a similar conclusion, and that the grandmother had displayed scant interest in the child once he had been removed from her daughter's custody was, though controverted, sufficiently substantial that the absence of counsel's guidance on this point did not render the proceedings fundamentally unfair. Finally, a court deciding whether due process requires the appointment of counsel need not ignore a parent's plain demonstration that she is not interested in attending a hearing. Here, the trial court had previously found that Ms. Lassiter had expressly declined to appear at the 1975 child custody hearing, Ms. Lassiter had not even bothered to speak to her retained lawyer after being notified of the termination hearing, and the court specifically found that Ms. Lassiter's failure to make an effort to contest the termination proceeding was without cause. In view of all these circumstances, we hold that the trial court did not err in failing to appoint counsel for Ms. Lassiter.

IV

In its Fourteenth Amendment, our Constitution imposes on the States the standards necessary to ensure that judicial proceedings are fundamentally fair. A wise public policy, however, may require that higher standards be adopted than those minimally tolerable under the Constitution. Informed opinion has clearly come to hold that an indigent parent is entitled to the assistance of appointed counsel not only in parental termination proceedings, but also in dependency and neglect proceedings as well. IJA-ABA Standards for Juvenile Justice, Counsel for Private Parties 2.3(b) (1980). Most significantly, 33 States and the District of Columbia provide statutorily for the appointment of counsel in termination cases. The Court's opinion today in no way implies that the standards increasingly urged by informed public opinion and now widely followed by the States are other than enlightened and wise.

For the reasons stated in this opinion, the judgment is affirmed.

It is so ordered.

Chief Justice BURGER, concurring.

I join the Court's opinion and add only a few words to emphasize a factor I believe is misconceived by the dissenters. The purpose of the termination proceeding at issue here was not "punitive." *Post*, at 2170. On the contrary, its purpose was *protective* of the child's best interests. Given the record in this case, which involves the parental rights of a mother under lengthy sentence for murder who showed little interest in her son, the writ might well have been a "candidate" for dismissal as improvidently granted. See *ante*, at 2162–2163. However, I am content to join the narrow holding of the Court, leaving the appointment of counsel in termination proceedings to be determined by the state courts on a case-by-case basis.

Justice BLACKMUN, with whom Justice BRENNAN and Justice MARSHALL join, dissenting.

The Court today denies an indigent mother the representation of counsel in a judicial proceeding initiated by the State of North Carolina to terminate her parental rights with respect to her youngest child. The Court most appropriately recognizes that the mother's interest is a "commanding one," and it finds no countervailing state interest of even remotely comparable significance. Nonetheless, the Court avoids what seems to me the obvious conclusion that due process requires the presence of counsel for a parent threatened with judicial termination of parental rights, and, instead, revives an ad hoc approach thoroughly discredited nearly 20 years ago in *Gideon v. Wainwright*, 372 U.S. 335, 83 S.Ct. 792, 9 L.Ed.2d 799 (1963). Because I believe that the unique importance of a parent's interest in the care and custody of his or her child cannot constitutionally be extinguished through formal judicial proceedings without the benefit of counsel, I dissent.

A

At stake here is "the interest of a parent in the companionship, care, custody, and management of his or her children." This interest occupies a unique place in our legal culture, given the centrality of family life as the focus for personal meaning and responsibility. "[F]ar more precious ... than property rights," parental rights have been deemed to be among those "essential to the orderly pursuit of happiness by free men," and to be more significant and priceless than " 'liberties which derive merely from shifting economic arrangements.' " Accordingly, although the Constitution is verbally silent on the specific subject of families, freedom of personal choice in matters of family life long has been viewed as a fundamental liberty interest worthy of protection under the Fourteenth Amendment. Within the general ambit of family integrity, the Court has accorded a high degree of constitutional respect to a natural parent's interest both in controlling the details of the child's upbringing, and in retaining the custody and companionship of the child.

In this case, the State's aim is not simply to influence the parent-child relationship but to *extinguish* it. A termination of parental rights is both total and irrevocable.3 Unlike other custody proceedings, it leaves the parent with no right to visit or communicate with the child, to participate in, or even to know about, any important decision affecting the child's religious, educational, emotional, or physical development. It is hardly surprising that this forced dissolution of the parent-child relationship has been recognized as a punitive sanction by courts, Congress, and commentators. The Court candidly notes, as it must, that termination of parental rights by the State is a "unique kind of deprivation."

The magnitude of this deprivation is of critical significance in the due process calculus, for the process to which an individual is entitled is in part determined "by the extent to which he may be 'condemned to suffer grievous loss.'" Surely there can be few losses more grievous than the abrogation of parental rights. Yet the Court today asserts that this deprivation somehow is less serious than threatened losses deemed to require appointed counsel, because in this instance the parent's own "personal liberty" is not at stake.

I do not believe that our cases support the "presumption" asserted, that physical confinement is the only loss of liberty grievous enough to trigger a right to appointed counsel under the Due Process Clause. Indeed, incarceration has been found to be neither a necessary nor a sufficient condition for requiring counsel on behalf of an indigent defendant. The prospect of canceled parole or probation, with its consequent deprivation of personal liberty, has not led the Court to require counsel for a prisoner facing a revocation proceeding. On the other hand, the fact that no new incarceration was threatened by a transfer from prison to a mental hospital did not preclude the Court's recognition of adverse changes in the conditions of confinement and of the stigma that presumably is associated with being labeled mentally ill. For four Members of the Court, these "other deprivations of liberty," coupled with the possibly diminished mental capacity of the prisoner, compelled the provision of counsel for any indigent prisoner facing a transfer hearing.

Moreover, the Court's recourse to a "pre-eminent generalization," misrepresents the importance of our flexible approach to due process. That approach consistently has emphasized attentiveness to the particular context. Once an individual interest is deemed sufficiently substantial or fundamental, determining the constitutional necessity of a requested procedural protection requires that we examine the nature of the proceeding—both the risk of error if the protection is not provided and the burdens created by its imposition.

Rather than opting for the insensitive presumption that incarceration is the only loss of liberty sufficiently onerous to justify a right to appointed counsel, I would abide by the Court's enduring commitment to examine the relationships among the interests on both sides, and the appropriateness of counsel in the specific type of proceeding. The fundamental significance of the liberty interest at stake in a parental termination proceeding is undeniable, and I would find this first portion of the due process balance weighing heavily in favor of refined procedural protections.

In the Interest of T.M.
131 Hawai'i 419 (2014)

We hold that the failure of the Family Court of the Third Circuit (the court) to appoint counsel for Petitioner/Mother-Appellant Jane Doe (Petitioner) until nearly nineteen months after Respondent-Appellee Department of Human Services (DHS) filed a Petition for Temporary Foster Custody over Petitioner's son, T.M. constituted an abuse of discretion under Hawai'i Revised Statutes (HRS) § 587-34 (2006) and § 587A-17 (Supp. 2012) which necessitates vacating the court's April 17, 2012 Order "Terminating [Petitioner's] Parental Rights and Awarding Permanent Custody" to

DHS. We recognize that parents have a substantive liberty interest in the care, custody, and control of their children that is protected by the due process clause of article I, section 5 of the Hawai'i Constitution. *In re Doe*, 99 Hawai'i 522, 533, 57 P.3d 447, 458 (2002). Therefore, we additionally hold that parents have a constitutional right to counsel under article I, section 5 in parental termination proceedings and that from and after the filing date of this opinion, courts must appoint counsel for indigent parents once DHS files a petition to assert foster custody over a child.

I

A

T.M. was born to Petitioner on June 8, 2009, when Petitioner was fifteen years old. In August, 2009, Petitioner was "diagnosed with Psychotic Disorder, Bipolar [Disorder], Panic Disorder, and Adjustment Disorder with Mixed Disturbance Emotions/Conduct." DHS filed two Petitions for Temporary Foster Custody, one over Petitioner and one over T.M., on January 6, 2010.

On January 7, 2010, the court held a hearing on the DHS petition. At the hearing, the court advised both Petitioner's parents and Petitioner herself of the salutary purpose of having a court-appointed attorney:

[The Court]: You all, the parents, have an opportunity to either agree or disagree with the allegations. If you disagree, that's fine. I mean, you know, I'm not holding anything against anyone until the evidence is presented and I have to make a decision. It's always wise, however, when children are in temporary out-of-home placement, that you have the benefit of having an attorney help you.

And if you cannot afford an attorney, then the Court may appoint an attorney to represent you at no cost to you. All I would need is an application to be completed. I'll review it, and if you qualify financially, I will appoint an attorney to represent you. That's always a good idea only because there's a lot of legal things that happen in the courtroom that you may not be aware of or familiar with, and having an attorney by your side is always a great benefit.

You may choose to represent yourself if you wish. That's fine, and I will try my best to help — or let you know what's happening. I cannot give you legal advice, but at least I can kind of give you your options, and you make your decisions on what you want to do. You may, if you wish, hire your own attorney. That's up to you, but that will be at your cost. So there's a couple of options.

(*Emphases added.*) The court stated it would attempt to find one person to act *both* as guardian ad litem and as an attorney for Petitioner but suggested that having separate persons act as a guardian ad litem and as an attorney might be necessary:

Now, [Petitioner], her situation is a little different, and that is because she's a minor under the law, she's entitled to *a guardian ad litem. At the same time she is a mother, a parent, and so she's entitled to an attorney. I'm going to try*

my best to find a person that can act in both responsibilities. There may be,
though, the situation where she will have both an attorney and a guardian ad
litem, two people, because what the guardian ad litem may feel would be in her
best interest may not be what she would like. So that's why she would need an
attorney.

(*Emphasis added.*) The record does not indicate that Petitioner submitted an
application for court-appointed counsel at that point.

Following the hearing, the court approved court-appointed counsel for Petitioner's
mother and T.M.'s father. However, the court did not appoint counsel for Petitioner.
Instead, the court apparently had Stephanie St. John (St. John) act as Petitioner's
guardian ad litem. At the next hearing, on January 14, 2010, the court suggested that
St. John was serving both as Petitioner's guardian ad litem and Petitioner's attorney:

THE COURT: Okay. Very well. *Ms. St. John, you're pretty much playing a*
dual role here.

MS. ST. JOHN: Well, that's my first thing, your Honor, is that at this point
understanding that I haven't spoken with [Petitioner] yet, and *I need to speak*
with her about this stuff because if there's going to be a difference of opinion in
working as a guardian ad litem than working as her attorney, then I would be
suggesting that she have a separate attorney to deal with her as a mother over
[T.M]. But at this point I haven't spoken with her to find out whether or not
there is any conflict between those two positions.

(*Emphases added.*) But, as indicated above, St. John did not confirm that she
was serving as Petitioner's attorney. Instead, St. John told the court that there
might be a conflict in serving in both capacities and she would "speak with
[Petitioner]" to determine if Petitioner desired to have "a separate attorney".

According to finding 7 of the court's May 3, 2013 findings and conclusions,
"[f]amily court jurisdiction over [T.M.] and his parents [including Petitioner]
was established at [the] hearing on February 10, 2010. Foster custody was
awarded to the [DHS]. For purposes of the Child Protective Act, [T.M.'s]
date of entry into foster care was <u>February 10, 2010</u>." (Emphasis in original.)

B

A service plan hearing was held on March 3, 2010. The Family Service Plan established the "initial goal" as "[m]aintain[ing] [T.M.] in placement or in a safe family
home with his mother, [Petitioner]," and the "reunification of [Petitioner] with her
mother, or her father and his fiancé." The "final goal" was to "[m]aintain [Petitioner]
and ... [T.M.] in a safe family home without the need for further DHS intervention."
The family plan stated that the "target date" to "maintain [Petitioner] and her son,
[T.M.] in a safe family home without the need for further DHS intervention" was
February 2011.

The Plan provisions required Petitioner to "continue to participate in services provided by [the Department of Health, Family Guidance Center], including compliance

with any prescribed medication," and "to make efforts to complete [her] education via attendance at school, work on correspondence courses, and participation in the [ ] Grads Program." The Plan was to "remain in effect until August 23, 2010, or further order of the court." The Plan also set forth "consequences," which explained to Petitioner that "your parental and custodial duties and rights concerning ... [T.M.] ... may be terminated by an award of permanent custody unless you are willing and able to provide ... [T.M.] with a safe family home within the reasonable period of time specified in this family service plan."

However, no provision of the Plan specified the "reasonable period of time" in which Petitioner was required to provide T.M. with a safe family home. The Ohana conference report stated that "if the parents are unable to provide the children with a safe family home within a reasonable period of time up to one year, even with a service plan, parental rights may be subject to termination." However, at the time the service plan was filed, although HRS § 587-72 (2006) did allow DHS to file a motion for a permanent plan hearing if the child was outside the family home for twelve consecutive months, parents could prevail at that hearing by demonstrating that it was "reasonably foreseeable" that they would be able to provide the child with a safe family home in "a reasonable period of time which shall not exceed two years from the date upon which the child was first placed under foster custody by the court." HRS § 587-73 (2006) (emphasis added). This two-year requirement is also reflected in present Hawai'i law. HRS § 587A-33(a)(2) (Supp.2012).

Petitioner was apparently found to have possessed marijuana on November 30, 2010. The terms of her probation included the requirement that she "shall not consume or possess any alcoholic beverages, illegal drugs, non-prescribed prescription drugs, or drug paraphernalia."

A combined second periodic review hearing and permanency hearing was held on January 26, 2011. At a permanency hearing, "[t]he court shall review the status of the case to determine whether the child is receiving appropriate services and care, that case plans are being properly implemented, and that activities are directed toward a permanent placement for the child." HRS § 587A-31(b). Under HRS § 587A-31, one of the options at a permanency hearing is for the court to order "the child's continued placement in foster care" if, *inter alia*, "[r]eunification is expected to occur within a time frame that is consistent with the developmental needs of the child." HRS § 587A-31(d).

On January 21, 2011, DHS formulated a revised family service plan. The revised plan added the provision that [Petitioner] "[f]ollow all the requirements of her probation, including additional treatment needs such as substance abuse treatment, etc."

At the January 26, 2011 hearing both DHS and T.M.'s guardian ad litem, Susan M. Kim (Kim), "recommended that [Petitioner] be given more time to reunify with her son." This recommendation was consistent with the goals of the family plan, i.e., to reunify Petitioner with either her mother or father and to reunify T.M. with Petitioner.

At the hearing, St. John noted that she disagreed with Petitioner regarding Petitioner completing a therapeutic home process: "I have to state this because as her guardian ad litem, I have to notify the Court that what I'm going to say is different from what she wants, and I know that she wants to go home to mom. The problem is that my recommendation would be for her to complete her therapeutic home process."

The court informed Petitioner that she needed to accept more responsibility for the care of T.M. The court also approved the revised "family service plan dated January 21st, 2011," and entered an order finding that "[t]he parents of [T.M.] [including Petitioner] have partially complied with the Family Service Plan. They have only made limited progress toward making their respective homes safe for [T.M.]"

The court order concluded that "each party present at the hearing understands that unless the family is willing and able to provide the child(ren) with a safe family home, even with the assistance of a service plan, within a reasonable period of time stated in the service plan, their parental and custodial duties and rights shall be subject to termination." (Emphases added.) The service plan did not define "a reasonable period of time[.]"

A combined third periodic review hearing and permanency hearing was held on May 24, 2011. At the hearing, DHS advised that "given the time that's passed so far," it "would like to go ahead and set a [termination of] parental rights [(TPR)] hearing." However, DHS agreed to wait to set the TPR motion until September. The court then stated that it would set a hearing for September 13, 2011. The court explained that "that's not a trial date."

Instead, the court related that "[t]hat's a date to find out where we're going to go. The state's going to file their motion to terminate parental rights. We'll hear that motion at that time." St. John then asserted that an attorney was needed to represent Petitioner with regard to T.M. because Petitioner had "never been assigned ... an attorney in her case involving [T.M.]":

> MS. ST. JOHN: 8:30 a.m.... *[B]ecause I am only [Petitioner's guardian ad litem]—and I've mentioned this several times in this case. She has never been assigned anybody as her attorney in her case involving her child, [T.M.]. If we are going to permanency at this point and [Petitioner] is going to be turning 18, the suggestion is that she apply for and look at getting her own attorney for that case.*
>
> THE COURT: Okay. Well, maybe perhaps you can assist her in that, I mean filling out the application. Okay?
>
> MS. ST. JOHN: Sure.
>
> (*Emphasis added.*)

On May 25, 2011 DHS filed its Motion to Set TPR Hearing, because "[T.M.] has been in foster care ... for an aggregate of fifteen out of the most recent twenty-two months from the date of entry into foster care." On about August 31, 2011, an application for court-appointed counsel was submitted. The application was signed by Petitioner on August 31, 2011, prior to her eighteenth birthday.

C

At a combined permanency hearing and termination of parental rights hearing on September 13, 2011, Petitioner still was not represented by counsel. The court noted that it had received Petitioner's application for counsel, but wanted to check with the DHS to see if the case would be resolved by mutual agreement before appointing an attorney. DHS informed the court of a possible agreement with Petitioner whereby T.M.'s current foster mother (foster mother) would become his legal guardian, and Petitioner's parental rights would not be terminated. However, DHS explained that before it could commit to that agreement, it was "required to check out relatives who may be interested in guardianship or adoption." DHS also asserted that it believed "it would be best to have an attorney for [Petitioner]," because "this is a pretty important juncture of the case."

The court then asked St. John if there would be a conflict were she appointed attorney for Petitioner. St. John replied that such an appointment would be a conflict of interest:

> MS. ST. JOHN: Your Honor, at this point I believe that it is a conflict. There are a lot of different things that [Petitioner] has basically not followed through with as a mother to her son, and *I don't feel that where my position as to what's in her best interest really coincides with what she needs to be doing as an adult and as a mother and for somebody to advocate for her.*
>
> The other thing too is that when we discussed this at the Ohana conference, I was very concerned that she wasn't really listening to what the attorneys and the social workers were telling her in the hearing that she needed to hear. *I think she really does need to sit down with somebody as an attorney for her ... and get the advice that she needs as a mother dealing with her child,* given her and her struggles through her teenage stuff that she's been doing these past couple of years.
>
> (*Emphases added.*) The court ruled that it "would go ahead and appoint an attorney to represent [Petitioner]." On September 13, 2011, an order was issued appointing Joan Jackson (Jackson) as counsel for Petitioner.

On September 20, 2011, the court again held a combined periodic review hearing and termination of parental rights hearing "for tracking purposes only." Jackson appeared for the first time at the hearing. DHS explained that it was "going to be checking out some relatives to see if they're interested in a long-term caretaker for the child." According to DHS, "if the relatives don't pan out, then we'd be looking at the foster parent as being the guardian for this child, and that would be without terminating parental rights." The court however, wanted to "do the termination of parental rights now" and explained that it "appointed [Jackson] so that she could explain to her client that option."

Jackson, however, related that she had "just met with [Petitioner] this morning," and "didn't discuss with her termination of parental rights because [Jackson] didn't think that [was] the way the case was going." When the court again questioned Jackson regarding Petitioner's willingness to terminate parental rights, Jackson reiterated that she "didn't really discuss it with [Petitioner]," and did not want to "whisper[ ] about it for a moment in court."

The hearing concluded to allow DHS to investigate placement of T.M. with relatives. With regard to the potential guardianship, the court noted that foster mother was the "only ... psychological family" that T.M. knew, and that it might have an impact having the child leave foster mother for a "stranger." DHS stated that "the whole family liked" the option of allowing T.M. to remain with foster mother as a guardian.

On October 4, 2011, DHS reported that there were possible problems with the two relatives they had targeted to potentially adopt T.M. Petitioner's father's sister was not an option because of financial difficulty. Further, T.M.'s paternal aunt and uncle (aunt and uncle) had not returned calls from DHS. The hearing concluded with both Petitioner and DHS stating that they wanted to pursue a guardianship with foster mother.

Following the October 4, 2011 hearing, aunt and uncle apparently stated that they were willing to adopt T.M. At an Ohana Conference, foster mother "decided that she would like to be considered as [an] alternative option, and that the primary option should be [T.M.]'s adoption by [aunt and uncle.]" Because foster mother indicated she would be the second option, DHS made "adoption of [T.M.] by his aunt and uncle the first choice for the Permanent Plan" and no longer pursued placement with foster mother. According to DHS, T.M. would therefore be adopted instead of placed in a guardianship and DHS would seek to terminate Petitioner's parental rights. Petitioner was required to show that she could provide a safe family home for T.M. herself in order for reunification to occur.

On December 13, 2011, a periodic review hearing was held. At the hearing, the court noted that "we're switching now to adoption." Petitioner requested that the TPR hearing be postponed:

> [Jackson]: Now the case is about her son. So [Petitioner] really now does not want to lose her child and does not want to have her parental rights terminated. *And because she's been an adult herself for just a couple of months, we're asking the Court for a little more time so that [Petitioner] can do what she needs to do to provide a home for herself and her son. She is presently going to substance abuse treatment three times a week and will be going into the women's program, the in-patient BISAC program, when a bed becomes available.*
>
> *At this point we'd ask the Court not to set a hearing to terminate parental rights but to give mother a little more time to show everyone in this room and the Court that she is able and willing and ready to be a full-time parent for [T.M.]* because obviously [T.M.] can't wait for anybody else to get their life together. However, the child is very, very happy with the foster mother. He's actually, according to everyone who spoke at the Ohana conference, a very well-adjusted, happy child, who knows who all of his relatives are and feels loved

by all these people. But I think it would be very difficult and sad for [T.M.] to suddenly be moved to a different home and lose contact with his mother. So I'm asking the Court for a little more time so that Petitioner can do what she needs to do to provide a home for herself and her son.

(*Emphases added.*) The court recounted that "we have a deadline to meet according to the statute, two years from the date of entry into foster care." According to the court, "what that means for the parents is that unless you can have the child back in your home within that two-year mark ... the child goes elsewhere permanently." The court stated that, therefore, "February 10, 2012 [was a] deadline here that we need to make or meet." A review hearing, which would also serve as a pretrial conference, was scheduled for February 7, 2012 and the TPR hearing for March 2, 2012.

At the pretrial hearing on February 7, 2012, Petitioner moved for a six-month continuance of the TPR hearing because Petitioner had done "a tremendous turnaround":

[Jackson]: You know, on behalf of [Petitioner], who just turned 18 in September, I would like to say or reiterate a couple of things and ask the Court to consider her age and *to consider the fact that recently, certainly since the last hearing, she's done a tremendous turn-around.*

[Petitioner] feels that she's going to lose contact with [T.M.], that he's going to be in Ocean View, raised by people who probably can provide him a good home, but she's afraid of losing him and of losing contact with him. And as I say, she's very, very young. *She apparently has gotten the message that this child, you know, is her child and that if she wants to be his mother and raise him, she has to do a number of things to be able to provide a home for him, including employment, earning a living, having a home, an actual residence where she can live with him and raise him, an ability to pay the rent and to provide for him in every other way.*

And at this point although we have the hearing scheduled in just a few weeks, *I'm asking the Court to consider delaying that hearing and continuing it for another six months.*

(*Emphases added.*) Petitioner further stated that she wanted to "continue on her path to be independent and to be able to provide a home for her son because that is really what she wants to do." Hence, Petitioner's position at the February 7, 2012 hearing apparently was that she wanted to obtain custody of T.M. in six months.

DHS, however, asked the court to "proceed as scheduled." DHS said that "apparently mother has done really well in the past few weeks," but also felt "it's important that ... pressure continue to be put [sic] in terms of trying to get something done because up to this point ... [Petitioner's] record was really pretty bad in terms of drug use and not doing services and not visiting." Similarly, Kim related that Petitioner had "only been clean for maybe about a month," and "as of December, she was still testing dirty[.]" The court denied Petitioner's motion for a continuance.

IV

In her Application Petitioner asks in pertinent part whether "counsel for an indigent minor parent[,]" such as Petitioner, should have been appointed "to defend her parental rights and advise her while her child remained in foster care for more than nineteen months[.]"

V

We hold that the court's failure to appoint counsel for Petitioner prior to September 13, 2012 constituted an abuse of discretion under HRS § 587-34 and § 587A-17. Because those statutes stated that the court may appoint an attorney to represent a legal parent who is indigent, HRS § 587A-17; *see also* HRS § 587-34, "discretion resided in the court as to whether to do so [.]" *In re Doe,* 108 Hawai'i at 153, 118 P.3d at 63 (holding that a statute that provided that the court "may" appoint a guardian ad litem left the court with discretion to make an appointment). "In reviewing a court's exercise of discretion it must be determined whether the court abused its discretion." *In re Doe,* 108 Hawai'i at 153, 118 P.3d at 63. "An abuse of discretion occurs when the trial court exceeds the bounds of reason or disregards rules of principles of law or practice to the substantial detriment of a party[.]" *Id.*

A

The record demonstrates that the court was aware from the inception of the proceedings that Petitioner required an attorney in her role as mother yet failed to appoint one until September 13, 2011. The nineteen-month delay in the appointment of counsel for Petitioner constituted an abuse of discretion.

As noted, on January 6, 2010, DHS filed a petition to assert temporary custody over both Petitioner and T.M. A hearing on the Petition was held on January 7, 2010, and the court informed all of the parties that they could file an application for a court-appointed attorney. As to Petitioner, the court explained that she was entitled to a guardian ad litem as a child, and to an attorney as a mother. The court stated that it would try to appoint an individual to "act in both responsibilities," but acknowledged that there might be a conflict if the same person was appointed to serve both roles.

After the initial hearing, the court immediately granted the applications for a court-appointed attorney for T.M.'s father and Petitioner's mother. However, the court did not appoint an attorney for Petitioner, even though it recognized the potential conflict of having one person serving both as guardian ad litem and as attorney. Instead, St. John was appointed as Petitioner's guardian ad litem. At the January 14, 2010 hearing the court told St. John that she was "playing a dual role here." However, St. John, rejected the assertion that she was also serving as Petitioner's attorney. The record does not indicate that the court followed through with St. John to determine whether a conflict existed between her "dual role[s]."

Despite the court's recognition at the January 7, 2010 hearing that it was "a good idea" for the parties to be represented by counsel, and that unrepresented parties would have difficulty understanding the legal significance of the proceedings, the court failed to appoint Petitioner an attorney. Thus, Petitioner was the only primary party18 without counsel.

At the May 24, 2011 hearing, St. John brought Petitioner's absence of counsel to the court's attention. St. John stated that she was only serving as Petitioner's guardian ad litem, and reminded the court that Petitioner had never been assigned an attorney. At the same hearing, DHS informed the court that it was going to file a motion to terminate Petitioner's parental rights. St. John then suggested to the court that because the DHS sought to terminate Petitioner's parental rights, counsel should be appointed for Petitioner. However, the court took no action even though it had the discretion to appoint counsel for Petitioner. Instead, the court left it to the guardian ad litem who had taken opposing positions to that of Petitioner to do so.

On September 13, 2011, the court noted that it had received Petitioner's application for counsel but that it had "not appointed anyone yet" because of the "possibility that this matter is going to be resolved by way of [an agreement between the parties regarding] a guardianship." Thus, despite the existence of ongoing negotiations among the parties, Petitioner was left unrepresented. The court's decision to delay the appointment of counsel until after the outcome of the settlement proceedings left Petitioner without a legal advocate for her position in the crucial negotiations among Petitioner, T.M.'s guardian, and DHS.

On September 20, 2011, only five months before the termination hearing, Jackson appeared for the first time. The court at several points asked Jackson if Petitioner was willing to agree to terminate her parental rights, even though Petitioner's counsel had "just met with Petitioner [that] morning." Jackson disclosed that she "didn't think that [the termination of parental rights was] the way the case was going." Thus, it is apparent that at the September 20, 2011 hearing DHS abandoned its original approach of guardianship without parental rights termination, and the court shifted to asking Petitioner to accede to the termination of her parental rights. Consequently, it was crucial that Petitioner was provided counsel at the inception of the proceedings to inform her of the limitations of the guardianship approach and of the possibility that if other options were pursued, her parental rights would be in jeopardy.

Additionally, nothing in the record demonstrates that Petitioner was aware that she had a two-year deadline to provide T.M. with a safe family home under the Child Protective Act.20 The report from the first Ohana Conference incompletely stated that Petitioner had one year to provide a safe family home for T.M. Thus, Petitioner was without counsel to advise her of significant deadlines.

Finally, the events following the appointment of counsel indicate the necessity of appointing counsel for Petitioner at the time T.M. was taken into DHS custody. At the September 13, 2011 hearing, St. John noted that Petitioner "wasn't really listening to what the attorneys and the social workers were telling her in the hearing that she needed to hear." Therefore, St. John believed that Petitioner "really [did] need to sit down with somebody as an attorney for her ... *[to] get the advice that she needs as a mother dealing with her child.*" (Emphases added.) St. John's statement makes it clear that, prior to September 13, 2011, Petitioner was not afforded legal advice on how to maintain her parental rights to T.M.

However, following the court's appointment of an attorney, Petitioner's behavior improved significantly. Petitioner began to pass her drug tests and become more involved in her substance abuse counseling. This was reflected in the court's findings after the termination hearing. The court stated that Petitioner had "made positive progress and matured over the last couple of months." Petitioner made rapid strides following the appointment of counsel.

Additionally, Petitioner had made progress in being able to provide a safe family home for T.M. Petitioner had lived with T.M. for eight months in foster mother's home, and visited once a week after August 15, 2010. Before trial, Petitioner would wake up before 5 a.m. to travel to foster mother's home to spend both Saturday and Sunday with T.M. Therefore, Petitioner had probably developed a connection with T.M. It may be that had counsel been appointed sooner, Petitioner may have been able to comply with the terms of the family plan and provided T.M. with a safe family home at an earlier date.

B

In sum, the court did not appoint counsel for Petitioner until more than nineteen months after T.M. entered foster custody, and only five months prior to the hearing that ultimately terminated Petitioner's parental rights. The failure to immediately appoint counsel for Petitioner even after it became apparent that DHS would seek to terminate Petitioner's parental rights left Petitioner without the necessary assistance to prepare for the March 2, 2012 termination hearing. Petitioner was without legal guidance and did not have an advocate to represent her in negotiations with DHS.

Because for most of the proceedings, Petitioner was the only primary party without counsel, it was unreasonable not to have afforded Petitioner the assistance of counsel while the other primary parties, including DHS, were represented by counsel. Consequently, the court abused its discretion in failing to appoint counsel earlier in the proceedings. Thus, the court's April 17, 2012 Order Terminating Parental Rights and Awarding Permanent Custody to DHS must be vacated, and the case remanded for a new hearing.

VI

The foregoing review of the instant case reveals the inadequacy of an approach that allows the appointment of counsel to be determined on a case-by-case basis once DHS moves to assert foster custody over a child.21 In *Doe,* this court "affirmed, independent of the federal constitution, that parents have a substantive liberty interest in the care, custody, and control of their children protected by the due process clause of article I, section 5 of the Hawai'i Constitution." 99 Hawai'i at 533, 57 P.3d at 459. *Doe* explained that "parental rights guaranteed under the Hawai'i constitution would mean little if parents were deprived the custody of their children a fair hearing." *Id.* "Indeed, '[p]arents have a fundamental liberty interest in the care, custody, and management of their children and the state may not deprive a person of his or her liberty interest without providing a fair procedure for the deprivation.'" *Id.* (quoting *Hollingsworth v. Hill,* 110 F.3d 733, 738–39 (10th Cir.1997)). *Doe* therefore held that the right to a "fair procedure" required the appointment of interpreters "at family court proceedings where [ ] parental rights are substantially affected." 99 Hawai'i at 534, 57 P.3d at 460.

In *In re "A" Children,* the ICA held that the court's failure to timely appoint counsel resulted in the father not receiving notice of hearings. 119 Hawai'i at 58, 193 P.3d at 1258. Judge Watanabe, writing for the ICA, pointed out that this created "a chain of events" that led to the termination of his parental rights and "that could have been broken if Father had had counsel." *Id.* The ICA applied the case-by-case approach adopted by a majority of the Supreme Court in *Lassiter,* where that court balanced the parent's interests, the state's interests, and the risk that a parent will be erroneously deprived of his or her child. *Id.* at 57, 193 P.3d at 1257. The ICA concluded that the dispositive factor was the third factor, and ruled that the "belated appointment of an attorney created an appreciable risk [the father] would be erroneously deprived of his parental rights[.]" *Id.* at 58, 193 P.3d at 1258.

However, the ICA "express[ed] grave concerns … about the case-by-case approach adopted in *Lassiter* for determining the right to counsel." *Id.* at 60, 193 P.3d at 1260. According to the ICA, "as Justice Blackmun observed," under the case-by-case ap-proach, "[a] trial judge will be required to determine in advance what difference legal representation might make." *Id.* The ICA then concluded that "the *Lassiter* dissents present compelling arguments for a bright-line rule regarding the provision of counsel in termination-of-parental rights cases[.]" *Id.*

C

Inherent in the substantive liberty interest that parents have in the care, custody, and control of their children under the Hawai'i Constitution is the right to counsel to prevent erroneous deprivation of their parental interests. As Justice Stevens asserted in *Lassiter,* the State's decision to deprive a parent of his or her child is often "more grievous" than the State's decision to incarcerate a criminal defendant. *Lassiter,* 452 U.S. at 59, 101 S.Ct. 2153 (Stevens, J., dissenting). Hence, "the reasons supporting the conclusion that the Due Process Clause … entitles the defendant in a criminal case to representation by counsel apply with equal force" in cases where the state seeks to terminate parental rights. *Id.* (emphasis added).

This court has held that "[t]he right to counsel is an essential component of a fair trial" in the criminal context. The same considerations suggest that an attorney is necessary for a "fair procedure" in parental termination proceedings.

Furthermore, as Justice Blackmun explained in *Lassiter,* a parent in termination proceedings may struggle with legal issues that are "neither simple nor easily defined," and with a standard that is "imprecise and open to the subjective values of the judge." 452 U.S. at 45, 101 S.Ct. 2153 (Blackmun, J., dissenting). A parent must "be prepared to adduce evidence about his or her personal abilities and lack of fault, as well as proof of progress and foresight as a parent[.]" *Id.* at 46, 101 S.Ct. 2153. They are

faced "with an adversary—the State—that commands great investigative and prosecutorial resources, with standards that involve ill-defined notions of fault and adequate parenting, and with the inevitable tendency of a court to apply subjective values
or to defer to the State's 'expertise.'" *Id.*

In *Matter of K.L.J.*, 813 P.2d 276 (Alaska 1991), the Alaska Supreme Court held
that counsel is necessary in termination proceedings because "'the crucial determination about what will be best for the child can be an exceedingly difficult
one[,] ... it requires a delicate process of balancing many complex and competing
considerations that are unique to every case.'" *Id.* at 282 (quoting *Flores v. Flores*,
598 P.2d 893, 896 (Alaska 1979)). Thus, "a parent cannot possibly succeed" without
"the guiding hand of counsel." Hence, the appointment of an attorney is crucial to
ensure that parents are provided a "fair procedure." *See Doe*, 99 Hawai'i at 533, 57
P.3d at 458.

Doe held that an interpreter was necessary where "parental rights are substantially
affected." 99 Hawai'i at 534, 57 P.3d at 459. In the context of the Child Protective
Act, the filing of a petition to assert custody initiates the termination process. As
stated before, once a child is "is in foster care under the department's responsibility"
for an aggregate of fifteen of twenty two months, DHS must file "a motion to terminate
parental rights." HRS § 587A-33(I). At a termination hearing, parents must establish
that they can provide a safe family home within two years of the child's entry into
foster care. HRS § 587A-33(a)(2). However, before the termination hearing itself,
issues that may be decisive in that proceeding may have been determined subsequent
to DHS attaining custody of the child. Thus, as soon as DHS files a petition asserting
custody over a child, parents' rights are "substantially affected." At that point, an attorney is essential to protect an indigent parent's liberty interest in the care, custody
and control of his or her children.

VII

Mandating the appointment of counsel for indigent parents once DHS moves for
custody would remove the vagaries of a case-by-case approach. As mentioned before,
under the case-by-case approach, "'it will not always be possible for the trial court
to predict accurately, in advance of the proceedings, what facts will be disputed, the
character of cross-examination, or the testimony of various witnesses.'" *Matter of
K.L.J.*, 813 P.2d at 282 n. 6. Hence, in a case-by-case approach, there is a "'possibility
that appointment of counsel will be denied erroneously by the trial court.'" *Matter
of K.L.J.*, 813 P.2d at 282 n. 6.

Similarly, "'the case-by-case approach ... does not lend itself practically to judicial
review.'" *Id.* (quoting Shaughnessy, Note, *A New Interest Balancing Test*, at 282–83).
"'[T]he reviewing court must expand its analysis into a cumbersome and costly,
time-consuming investigation of the entire proceeding.'" *Id.* (quoting Note, *A New
Interest Balancing Test*, at 282–83). Moreover, the harm suffered by parents proceeding
without counsel may not be readily apparent from the record, especially because
without the aid of counsel, it is unlikely that a case is "adequately presented."

Additionally, real human costs are sustained by all of the parties when, as in the instant case, the court's failure to appoint counsel results in a remand for further proceedings. Under such circumstances, the court's ultimate determination regarding a child's placement may be significantly delayed. Both parents and children face continued uncertainty regarding parental status and a child's future. These costs would be mitigated by a rule cognizant of the reality that counsel is essential to ensuring that parents are provided a "fair procedure."

In sum, difficulties stemming from the case-by-case approach can result in the erroneous termination of parental rights. Thus, in light of the constitutionally protected liberty interest at stake in a termination of parental rights proceeding, we hold that indigent parents are guaranteed the right to court-appointed counsel in termination proceedings[26] under the due process clause in article I, section 5 of the Hawai'i Constitution. We direct that upon the filing date of this opinion, trial courts must appoint counsel for indigent parents upon the granting of a petition to DHS for temporary foster custody of their children.

VIII

Based on the foregoing, the court's April 17, 2012 order terminating parental rights, the May 3, 2012 findings and conclusions "re TPR Hearing", and the July 26, 2013 judgment of the ICA filed pursuant to its June 28, 2013 Summary Disposition Order affirming the court's order are vacated, and the case is remanded to the court for a new hearing consistent with this opinion.

F. Legal Aid Funding and Advocacy

Legal aid offices provide legal assistance with civil legal issues to more poor clients than any other resources in the United States. Local and statewide legal services offices are funded in large part by the federal government under the Legal Services Act. As enacted in 1974, the LSA prohibited LSC-funded legal services offices from engaging in political campaigns, criminal proceedings, abortion rights, or school desegregation cases. The 1996 restrictions expanded this list to include:

- Lobbying government offices, agencies, or legislative bodies with *any* funding, except for limited situations.
- Representing people who are not U.S. citizens with limited exceptions, such as lawful permanent residents, H2A agricultural workers, H2B forestry workers, and victims of battering, extreme cruelty, sexual assault, or trafficking.
- Class actions.
- Soliciting clients in-person.
- Abortion-related litigation of any kind.
- Representing prisoners.
- Representing people who are being evicted from public housing because they face criminal charges of selling or distributing illegal drugs.

- Most activities involving welfare reform.
- Redistricting activities.
- Influencing the time or manner of census-taking.

In 2010, Congress removed the 1996 restriction on the ability of LSC-funded legal services offices to claim, collect, or retain attorney's fees. *See* Pub. L. No. 111-117.

LSC funding for legal services has been restricted by Congress since the beginning of the program. This means that a local or statewide legal aid office may not use LSC funding for certain types of cases or to represent clients in certain groups. There are several stated purposes for the LSC's restrictions, including: the desire to ensure that the scarce legal services offered through LSC funding are targeted to eligible recipients and not siphoned off by those who could otherwise afford to hire an attorney (45 C.F.R. § 1609.1); to ensure that LSC resources will be used to provide high-quality legal assistance, and not to engage in political activity (45 C.F.R. § 1608.1) or lobbying, unless requested by the legislative body (45 C.F.R. § 1612.1); to prevent LSC funding from being used in criminal proceedings (45 C.F.R. § 1613.1) including post-conviction relief through habeas corpus proceedings (45 C.F.R. § 1615.1); and to ensure that only citizens of the United States and eligible aliens receive assistance (45 C.F.R. § 1626.1). Legal Services Corporation regulations contain a somewhat arcane procedure when cases involving possible attorney's fees are involved:

45 C.F.R. § 1609.3 Authorized representation in a fee-generating case.

(a) Except as provided in paragraph (b) of this section, a recipient may not use Corporation funds to provide legal assistance in a fee-generating case unless:

(1) The case has been rejected by the local lawyer referral service, or by two private attorneys; or

(2) Neither the referral service nor two private attorneys will consider the case without payment of a consultation fee.

(b) A recipient may provide legal assistance in a fee-generating case without first attempting to refer the case pursuant to paragraph (a) of this section only when:

(1) An eligible client is seeking benefits under Subchapter II of the Social Security Act, 42 U.S.C. 401 *et seq.,* as amended, Federal Old Age, Survivors, and Disability Insurance Benefits; or Subchapter XVI of the Social Security Act, 42 U.S.C. 1381 *et seq.,* as amended, Supplemental Security Income for Aged, Blind, and Disabled;

(2) The recipient, after consultation with appropriate representatives of the private bar, has determined that the type of case is one that private attorneys in the area served by the recipient ordinarily do not accept, or do not accept without prepayment of a fee; or

(3) The director of the recipient, or the director's designee, has determined that referral of the case to the private bar is not possible because:

(i) Documented attempts to refer similar cases in the past generally have been futile;

(ii) Emergency circumstances compel immediate action before referral can be made, but the client is advised that, if appropriate, and consistent with professional responsibility, referral will be attempted at a later time; or

(iii) Recovery of damages is not the principal object of the recipient's client's case and substantial statutory attorneys' fees are not likely to be available.

———————

The framework of restrictions requires a legal aid lawyer to navigate between ethical duties of the profession and limitations required by Congress and applied through the LSC. In the late 1990s the Supreme Court considered this framework in a series of cases brought by legal aid lawyers.

Legal Aid Society of Hawaii v. Legal Services Corporation

145 F.3d 1017 (9th Cir. 1998)

The issue presented in this appeal is whether government restrictions on the activities of organizations who accept funds distributed by the Legal Services Corporation (LSC) are facially unconstitutional. Appellants, a group of organizations and an individual involved in the provision of legal services to indigent persons, contend that the restrictions impose unconstitutional conditions on the exercise of their First Amendment rights and violate equal protection and due process rights protected by the United States Constitution. We affirm the judgment of the district court that the restrictions do not violate the First Amendment.

I. BACKGROUND

This case arises from recent enactments by Congress that place additional limitations on legal service organizations that accept LSC funds. In 1996, as a result of controversy over the activities pursued by some organizations receiving LSC funds, Congress expanded the number of limitations governing recipients of LSC funds. *See* (1996 Budget Act). The 1996 Budget Act prohibited recipients of LSC funds from, among other things: 1) advocating or opposing the alteration of an elective district, § 504(a)(1); 2) influencing the issuance of any regulation by any Federal, State, or local agency, § 504(a)(2); 3) influencing any part of any agency adjudicatory proceeding if the proceeding concerns the formulation or modification of any policy of general applicability, § 504(a)(3); 4) influencing the passage or defeat of any legislation, § 504(a)(4); 5) participating in a class action suit, § 504(a)(7); 6) representing certain aliens, § 504(a)(11); 7) claiming or collecting attorneys' fees pursuant to laws requiring the award of such fees, § 504(a)(13); 8) participating in abortion litigation, § 504(a)(14); 9) participating in litigation on behalf of a prisoner, § 504(a)(15); 10) participating in efforts to reform a welfare system, § 504(a)(16); and 11) defending a person in eviction proceedings if the person is involved in illegal drug activity, § 504(a)(17).

Enactment of these restrictions prompted the LSC to promulgate new regulations to ensure that recipients of LSC funding did not use funds received from the LSC to support prohibited activities. Under LSC regulations existing prior to the enactment of the 1996 Budget Act, funds held by organizations under the "control" of an organization receiving LSC funds were "subject to the same restrictions as if the funds were held by the recipient. The LSC defined "control" as the ability to "[d]etermine the direction of management and policies" or "influence the management or policies" of another organization "to the extent that an arm's length transaction may not be achieved. Under the LSC's initial implementation of the 1996 Budget Act, the restrictions enacted by Congress applied to any organization "interrelated," as determined by application of the "control" test, with a recipient of LSC funds.

On January 9, 1997, appellants filed suit against the LSC in the United States District Court for the District of Hawaii challenging the facial constitutionality of the restrictions and implementing regulations. The plaintiffs consisted of five legal service organizations that receive a portion of their funds from the LSC, a group representing legal services clients, two organizations that fund work by legal services organizations, and two lawyers employed by legal services organizations. They asserted that the restrictions imposed an unconstitutional condition on their First Amendment rights, and violated the equal protection and due process rights of their clients. Appellants requested a preliminary injunction to prevent the LSC from enforcing the restrictions.... The district court enjoined numerous restrictions contained in the Acts.

In response to the district court's ruling, the LSC revised the regulations governing the ability of organizations who receive funds from the LSC, known as "recipients," to maintain relationships with organizations pursuing prohibited activities, organizations we will refer to as "unrestricted organizations." The final rule issued by the LSC "nullified" its prior policy on "interrelated organizations" and adopted "program integrity" regulations modeled on the regulations upheld in *Rust v. Sullivan*. The new regulations mandate that a recipient of LSC funds maintain physical and financial separation from unrestricted organizations. *See* 45 C.F.R. 1610.8. To determine if the organizations are separate, the LSC will examine certain factors, such as the existence of separate personnel and facilities. In addition, the unrestricted organization must be a legally separate entity. 1610.8(a)(1).

After the issuance of the new regulations, the United States intervened in the district court to defend their constitutionality. In ruling on cross-motions for summary judgment filed by the parties, the district court concluded that *Rust* was dispositive on the constitutionality of the LSC requirement that a recipient have separate personnel and facilities from an unrestricted organization. The court upheld the requirement that the unrestricted organization be a "legally separate entity," 45 CFR 1610.8(a)(1), which was not a part of the regulations challenged in *Rust*, because the requirement did not prevent appellants from exercising their constitutional rights, and the additional burden imposed by the separate incorporation requirement was insignificant. 981 F. Supp at 1297. The district court rejected the due process and equal protection arguments presented by appellants. The court granted the summary judgment motions of the LSC and the United States, and denied appellants' motion. The court also dissolved its earlier injunction.

This appeal followed.

III. DISCUSSION

We begin, as the Supreme Court did in *Rust*, by discussing the posture of this case. Appellants bring a *facial* challenge to the restrictions and therefore must satisfy a stringent standard: Petitioners face a heavy burden in seeking to have the regulations invalidated as facially unconstitutional.

"A facial challenge to a legislative Act is, of course, the most difficult challenge to mount successfully, since the challenger must establish that no set of circumstances exists under which the Act would be valid. The fact that [the regulations] might operate unconstitutionally under some conceivable set of circumstances is insufficient to render [them] wholly invalid." *Rust*, 500 U.S. at 183, 111 S. Ct. 1759. It bears emphasizing that, under *Rust*, even if appellants presented a factual situation that suggested the restrictions were unconstitutional in only limited circumstances (and we do not hold that they have presented such circumstances), we would not strike down the restrictions as unconstitutional.

A. The Unconstitutional Conditions Challenge

Appellants' primary argument is that the restrictions imposed on those organizations who choose to receive LSC funds violate the First Amendment by prohibiting recipients from using non-LSC funds to engage in activities protected by the First Amendment, such as the right of legal services organizations and their attorneys to lobby legislators and administrators, *see California Motor Transport Co. v Trucking Unlimited*, 404 U.S. 508, 510 (1972), or express their views on matters of public concern. Appellants claim that the restrictions are unconstitutional because they condition the receipt of a benefit, in this case the grant of federal funds, on the relinquishment of the right to engage in protected activities. They claim this case fits within the Supreme Court's statement in *Perry v. Sinderman*, 408 U.S. 593 (1972), that "even though the government may deny [a] benefit for any number of reasons, there are some reasons upon which the government may not rely. It may not deny a benefit to a person on a basis that infringes his constitutionally protected interests—especially, his interest in freedom of speech." *Id.* at 597.

Appellants' unconstitutional conditions argument is without merit because neither the congressional enactments nor the implementing regulations infringe on First Amendment rights. The regulations promulgated by the LSC to preserve the distinction between restricted and unrestricted organizations are nearly identical to the regulations upheld in *Rust* and there is no basis for distinguishing this case from *Rust*.

The regulations challenged in *Rust* governed implementation of the Title X program, which provided grants to projects offering family planning services. 500 U.S. at 178. However, Congress prohibited the use of Title X funds in any program where abortion was a method of family planning. To implement this restriction, the Secretary of the Department of Health and Human Services promulgated regulations to ensure that organizations offering Title X programs maintained a certain degree of separation between Title X programs and programs offering abortion services.

Three principal conditions were placed on grants awarded under Title X. *Id.* at 179. First, a Title X project could not provide counseling or referrals concerning abortion as a method of family planning. Second, the project could not encourage abortion as a method of family planning, including any lobbying effort or legal action to encourage abortion. Third, under the Secretary's "program integrity" regulations, Title X projects were required to have objective integrity and independence from prohibited activities.

Given the similarity of the regulations, the Court's discussion in *Rust* of why the Secretary's regulations were constitutional controls the disposition of this case.

In *Rust*, the Court rejected petitioners' reliance on an unconstitutional conditions argument because the government was not denying a benefit to anyone, but "instead simply insisting that public funds be spent for the purposes for which they were authorized." 500 U.S. at 196. As in *Rust*, the LSC regulations do not force a recipient to give up prohibited activities; "they merely require that the [recipient] keep such activities separate and distinct from [LSC] activities," *id.* If an organization wishes to engage in prohibited activities, it simply is required to conduct those activities through entities that are separate and independent from the organization that receives LSC funds.

Appellants correctly note that *Rust* distinguished between Title X "grantees," which were normally health-care organizations, and Title X "projects," which received funds under Title X for specific purposes. *Id.; see* Appellants' Opening Br. at 35, 41–42. Under the *Rust* regulations, a "grantee" could continue to engage in prohibited activities if it complied with the Secretary's program integrity regulations. Appellants rely on a difference in terminology between the LSC and Title X regulations to argue that because the LSC regulations apply to "recipients," and not "projects," the regulations are unconstitutional. They find support for their argument in the Court's statement in *Rust* that characterized "unconstitutional conditions" cases as "situations in which the Government has placed a condition on the *recipient* of the subsidy rather than on a particular program or service, thus effectively prohibiting the recipient from engaging in the protected conduct outside the scope of the federally funded program." 500 U.S. at 197.

However, appellants' reliance on the fact that the term "recipients" is employed in the LSC regulations instead of the term "projects" is misplaced. The proper constitutional test does not focus on the particular term used by the government agency, but whether the regulations "effectively prohibit[ ] the recipient from engaging in the protected conduct outside the scope of the federally funded program." *Id.* The LSC regulations pass this test.

First, the *Rust* regulations required that a project supported by Title X funds maintain the same degree of separation from an organization engaging in abortion activities as a recipient of LSC funds must maintain from an unrestricted organization, with the exception that the LSC requires that the unrestricted organization be a "legally separate entity," 45 C.F.R. 1610.8(a)(1). A recipient of LSC funds may engage in conduct protected by the First Amendment outside the scope of the federally funded program if, as in *Rust*, the recipient sets up a separate entity that complies with the program integrity regulations.

Second, the LSC regulations are consistent with the two cases the Court discussed in *Rust* as standing for the proposition that Congress could not entirely prohibit certain constitutionally protected conduct outside the scope of a federally funded program. In *Regan v. Taxation with Representation of Wash.*, 461 U.S. 540 (1983) the Court rejected the argument that a federal statute prohibiting lobbying by organizations who qualified for tax-exempt status under 26 USC 501(c)(3) imposed an unconstitutional condition on the receipt of tax-deductible contributions. The Court noted that the prohibition represented a legislative choice to prevent subsidized lobbying with public funds. Under the statute, petitioners could continue lobbying by forming a nonlobbying organization qualified for the tax benefits of 501(c)(3) and a separate lobbying organization under a less favorable provision of the Internal Revenue Code. However, if the petitioners pursued this option, they "would ... have to ensure that the 501(c)(3) organization did not subsidize" the unrestricted organization. Moreover, the two organizations would have to be "separately incorporated.".

* * *

The LSC regulations are consistent with the decisions in *Regan* and *League of Women Voters*. The regulations simply require that if a recipient wishes to engage in prohibited activities, it must establish an organization separate from the recipient in order to ensure that federal funds are not spent on prohibited activities. Or, as the Court stated in *Rust*:

By requiring that the Title X grantee engage in abortion-related activity separately from activity receiving federal funding, Congress has, consistent with our teachings in *League of Women Voters* and *Regan*, not denied it the right to engage in abortion-related activities. Congress has merely refused to fund such activities out of the public fisc, and the Secretary has simply required a certain degree of separation from the Title X project in order to ensure the integrity of the federally funded program. In sum, there is no force to the argument that the use of term "recipients" in the LSC regulations instead of the term "projects" requires us to find the regulations unconstitutional.

* * *

Presumably, the restrictions make it more difficult for organizations to engage in prohibited activities. However, similar restrictions in *Rust* required that an organization engaging in abortion activities "conduct those activities through programs that are separate and independent from the project that receives Title X funds." The Court did not find it constitutionally significant that the restrictions required the recipient of Title X funds to expend effort to comply with the restrictions. Similarly, the fact that the LSC restrictions may require additional compliance efforts by a recipient if it wishes to engage in prohibited activities furnishes no basis for departing from *Rust*.

Moreover, we do not find it significant that the LSC regulations require that the unrestricted organization be a "legally separate entity." 45 C.F.R. 1610.8(a)(1). *Regan* approved of this specific requirement when it noted that an organization that wanted to engage in prohibited lobbying activities would have to be "separately incorporated" from the organization receiving a more favorable tax subsidy. We agree with the district court that the combination of the separate incorporation requirement approved in *Regan* and the program integrity requirements approved in *Rust* "does not create an unconstitutional burden on [appellants'] exercise of their constitutional rights." As the district court observed, legal services organizations have significant access to legal counsel, and appellants fail to demonstrate how the requirement of filing incorporation papers for an unrestricted organization imposes any significant burden. *See id. Rust* does not suggest that the Title X regulations are the maximum permissible separation requirements that the government can impose and we decline to find that the minor additional requirement present in this case has constitutional significance.

* * *

Finally, appellants claim that the restrictions violate the First Amendment rights of full-time legal services lawyers. In a footnote in their Opening Brief, they suggest that the regulations are unconstitutional because full-time legal services lawyers are barred from engaging in the outside practice of law. Thus, they argue, full-time lawyers may not pursue prohibited activities on their own time, unlike the doctors in *Rust*, who could pursue abortion-related activities when they were not working for the Title X project. Even if we were to assume that it is sufficient to raise an argument by placing it in a footnote on page forty-six of an opening brief, we would reject the argument.

It is true that longstanding LSC regulations generally prohibit the outside practice of law. *See* 45 C.F.R. pt. 1604 (1976). The purpose of this provision, which is common in government agencies, is to ensure that outside demands "do not hinder fulfillment of the attorney's overriding responsibility to serve those eligible for assistance under the Act." 45 C.F.R. 1604.1. According to the LSC, the provision "is essential to insure that a legal services lawyer does not compete with lawyers in private practice, is not burdened by excessive court appointments," and does not accept other commitments that might interfere with rendering quality full-time legal assistance to eligible clients. Like the restrictions on doctors in *Rust*, the restrictions on a LSC-funded attorney are a consequence of that attorney's decision to accept full-time employment with a LSC-funded organization. If an attorney wishes to engage in prohibited activities, the attorney could work part-time at an unrestricted organization in certain circumstances or engage on his own time in restricted activities that do not involve the outside practice of law, such as lobbying. Appellants' unsupported assertion that the restriction on sharing of personnel precludes working part-time at an unrestricted organization is contradicted by the record. *See* Supplemental Excerpts of R. at 34–35 (allowing attorney to convert full-time employment with a LSC recipient to part-time employment and permitting his participation in prohibited activities outside of his work for the LSC recipient). Appellants' argument is without support and we reject it.

B. Equal Protection and Due Process

Appellants argue that the restrictions violate the Fifth Amendment rights of legal services clients "to obtain fair and equal access to the courts." They claim that the restrictions violate the Due Process Clause by interfering with the client's right to retain a lawyer of his or her choice and the client's right to engage in meaningful advocacy. They also raise an equal protection challenge because, according to appellants, the restrictions deny clients "equal access to the courts based on their indigence and the causes they wish to espouse." *Id.* at 53.

Appellees argue that appellants lack standing to assert the rights of clients of legal services organizations, and, in any event, the claims are meritless. The district court held that appellant CSCC had standing, but rejected appellants' claims on the merits.

Prior to the recent decision of the Supreme Court in *Steel Co. v. Citizens for a Better Environment*, 523 U.S. 83 (1998), we may have found it easier to avoid the issue of standing by assuming jurisdiction and proceeding to the merits under the doctrine of "hypothetical jurisdiction." Under this doctrine, a court will assume jurisdiction and decide the merits if the merits are "more readily resolved" and "the prevailing party on the merits would be the same as the prevailing party were jurisdiction denied." The Supreme Court rejected this doctrine "because it carries the courts beyond the bounds of authorized judicial action and thus offends fundamental principles of separation of powers." Thus, we must "spend [our] time and energy puzzling over the correct answer to an intractable jurisdictional matter," even if we think that the substantive merits are easily disposed of by well-settled law.

The "irreducible constitutional minimum of standing" contains three requirements. *Lujan v. Defenders of Wildlife*, 504 U.S. 555, 560 (1992). First, there must be an "injury in fact." The "injury in fact" must be the invasion of a legally protected interest which is "concrete and particularized," *id.*, and "actual or imminent, not 'conjectural' or 'hypothetical.'" Second, there must be causation—"a fairly traceable connection between the plaintiff's injury and the complained-of conduct of the defendant." Third, there must be redressability—"a likelihood that the requested relief will redress the alleged injury."

Appellants asserted below that indigent clients of legal service organizations are parties to this action through the California State Client Council (CSCC). CSCC "is an unincorporated association whose members are indigent clients of legal services programs who also sit on the boards of those programs." Compl. ¶ 40. The purpose of CSCC is to "meet and discuss issues of concern to the community of impoverished legal services organization clients, to develop policies of assistance in alleviating their adverse conditions, to work with legal services programs to ensure that those programs meet the needs of their clients, and to encourage leadership activities" of low-income clients.

The district court found that CSCC had suffered an "injury in fact." The court relied on an affidavit submitted by the Chair of the CSCC stating that CSCC's "own organizational efforts have been adversely affected by LSC restrictions ... [because]

[t]he new LSC restrictions have prevented some legal services programs ... from using non-LSC money to provide assistance" for CSCC's efforts to assist low-income clients. Thus, relying on Havnes Realty Corp. v. Coleman, 455 U.S. 363 (1982), the court concluded that CSCC established an injury and "has standing to challenge the restrictions on behalf of the clients."

The district court erred. The district court conflated the question of whether CSCC has standing to press claims for injury *on its own behalf* with the question of whether CSCC has representative standing to assert claims *on behalf of its members*. CSCC may have standing on its own behalf to assert a claim that the LSC restrictions resulted in a concrete injury to the CSCC. But we need not decide that issue because CSCC does not argue that the restrictions violate the rights of the organization. Instead, CSCC seeks representative standing to press the claim that the restrictions violate the equal protection and due process rights of its members.

The district court erred in basing its conclusion on an affidavit claiming that CSCC *as an organization* suffered an adverse impact from the restrictions. This conclusion was contrary to the requirements for establishing representative standing. "An association has standing to sue or defend in such capacity ... only if its members would have standing in their own right." *Arizonans for Official English v. Arizona*, 520 U.S. 43 (1997). As the United States points out, *see* Br. at 37, and appellants fail to respond to, *see* Reply Br. at 26, "there is nothing in the record to suggest that any individual member of the CSCC has standing." United States Br. at 37.

Instead, appellants argue that "numerous declarations" allege that the restrictions have denied unnamed indigent persons the opportunity to pursue claims. Reply Br. at 26. However, the "injury in fact" test " 'requires that the party seeking review be himself among the injured.' " *Lujan*, 504 U.S. at 563. To survive a summary judgment motion, appellants "had to submit affidavits or other evidence showing, through specific facts, ... that *one or more of [their] members* would [be] 'directly' affected apart from their 'special interest' in th[e] subject," *Lujan*, 504 U.S. at 563. Appellants do not point us to any evidence in the record establishing that these unnamed clients of legal services organizations are members of the CSCC or exactly how these clients satisfy the standing requirements so that we may scrutinize the affidavits of these members. *See Lujan*, 504 U.S. 563–64 (discussing specific allegations contained in affidavits of members of environmental organization to determine if standing exists). Thus, CSCC fails to establish that it has standing to assert the rights of its members.

IV. CONCLUSION

We AFFIRM the district court's judgment that the LSC restrictions do not violate appellants' First Amendment rights. We VACATE the district court's judgment that the LSC restrictions do not violate the due process and equal protection rights of indigent persons and REMAND the case with instructions to dismiss the complaint insofar as it asserts the rights of indigent persons because appellants have no standing to raise these issues.

Legal Services Corporation v. Velazquez
531 U.S. 533 (2001)

This suit requires us to decide whether one of the conditions imposed by Congress on the use of LSC funds violates the First Amendment rights of LSC grantees and their clients. For purposes of our decision, the restriction, to be quoted in further detail, prohibits legal representation funded by recipients of LSC moneys if the representation involves an effort to amend or otherwise challenge existing welfare law. As interpreted by the LSC and by the Government, the restriction prevents an attorney from arguing to a court that a state statute conflicts with a federal statute or that either a state or federal statute by its terms or in its application is violative of the United States Constitution.

Lawyers employed by New York City LSC grantees, together with private LSC contributors, LSC indigent clients, and various state and local public officials whose governments contribute to LSC grantees, brought suit in the United States District Court for the Eastern District of New York to declare the restriction, among other provisions of the Act, invalid. The United States Court of Appeals for the Second Circuit approved an injunction against enforcement of the provision as an impermissible viewpoint-based discrimination in violation of the First Amendment, 164 F. 3D 757 (1999). We granted certiorari, and the parties who commenced the suit in the District Court are here as respondents. The LSC as petitioner is joined by the Government of the United States, which had intervened in the District Court. We agree that the restriction violates the First Amendment, and we affirm the judgment of the Court of Appeals.

I

From the inception of the LSC, Congress has placed restrictions on its use of funds. For instance, the LSC Act prohibits recipients from making available LSC funds, program personnel, or equipment to any political party, to any political campaign, or for use in "advocating or opposing any ballot measures." 42 U.S.C. 2996 e(d)(4). The Act further proscribes use of funds in most criminal proceedings and in litigation involving nontherapeutic abortions, secondary school desegregation, military desertion, or violations of the Selective Service statute. §§ 2996f(b)(8)–(10). Fund recipients are barred from bringing class-action suits unless express approval is obtained from LSC. Sc. 2996e(d)(5)

The restrictions at issue were part of a compromise set of restrictions enacted in the Omnibus Consolidated Rescissions and Appropriations Act of 1996 (1996 Act), § 504, 110 Stat. 1321-53, and continued in each subsequent annual appropriations Act. The relevant portion of § 504(a)(16) prohibits funding of any organization "that initiates legal representation or participates in any other way, in litigation, lobbying, or rulemaking, involving an effort to reform a Federal or State welfare system, except that this paragraph shall not be construed to preclude a recipient from representing an individual eligible client who is seeking specific relief from a welfare agency if such relief does not involve an effort to amend or otherwise challenge existing law in effect on the date of the initiation of the representation."

The prohibitions apply to all of the activities of an LSC grantee, including those paid for by non-LSC funds. §§ 504(d)(1) and (2). We are concerned with the statutory provision which excludes LSC representation in cases which "involve an effort to amend or otherwise challenge existing law in effect on the date of the initiation of the representation."

In 1997, LSC adopted final regulations clarifying § 504(a)(16). 45 CFR pt. 1639 (1999). LSC interpreted the statutory provision to allow indigent clients to challenge welfare agency determinations of benefit ineligibility under interpretations of existing law. For example, an LSC grantee could represent a welfare claimant who argued that an agency made an erroneous factual determination or that an agency misread or misapplied a term contained in an existing welfare statute. According to LSC, a grantee in that position could argue as well that an agency policy violated existing law. § 1639.4. Under LSC's interpretation, however, grantees could not accept representations designed to change welfare laws, much less argue against the constitutionality or statutory validity of those laws. Brief for Petitioner in No. 99-603, p. 7. Even in cases where constitutional or statutory challenges became apparent after representation was well under way, LSC advised that its attorneys must withdraw. *Ibid.*

* * *

II

The United States and LSC rely on Rust v. Sullivan, 500 U.S. 173 (1991), as support for the LSC program restrictions. In Rust, Congress established program clinics to provide subsidies for doctors to advise patients on a variety of family planning topics. Congress did not consider abortion to be within its family planning objectives, however, and it forbade doctors employed by the program from discussing abortion with their patients. Recipients of funds under Title X of the Public Health Service Act, challenged the Act's restriction that provided that none of the Title X funds appropriated for family planning services could "be used in programs where abortion is a method of family planning." The recipients argued that the regulations constituted impermissible viewpoint discrimination favoring an antiabortion position over a proabortion approach in the sphere of family planning. 500 U.S. at 192. They asserted as well that Congress had imposed an unconstitutional condition on recipients of federal funds by requiring them to relinquish their right to engage in abortion advocacy and counseling in exchange for the subsidy.

We upheld the law, reasoning that Congress had not discriminated against viewpoints on abortion, but had "merely chosen to fund one activity to the exclusion of the other." The restrictions were considered necessary "to ensure that the limits of the federal program [were] observed." Title X did not single out a particular idea for suppression because it was dangerous or disfavored; rather, Congress prohibited Title X doctors from counseling that was outside the scope of the project.

* * *

Neither the latitude for government speech nor its rationale applies to subsidies for private speech in every instance, however. As we have pointed out, "[i]t does not follow ... that viewpoint-based restrictions are proper when the [government] does not itself speak or subsidize transmittal of a message it favors but instead expends funds to encourage a diversity of views from private speakers." Rosenberg, at 834, 115 S.Ct. 2510.

Although the LSC program differs from the program at issue in Rosenberger in that its purpose is not to "encourage a diversity of views," the salient point is that, like the program in Rosenberg, the LSC program was designed to facilitate private speech, not to promote a governmental message. Congress funded LSC grantees to provide attorneys to represent the interests of indigent clients. In the specific context of § 504(a)(16) suits for benefits, an LSC-funded attorney speaks on the behalf of the client in a claim against the government for welfare benefits. The lawyer is not the government's speaker. The attorney defending the decision to deny benefits will deliver the government's message in the litigation. The LSC lawyer, however, speaks on the behalf of his or her private, indigent client. Cf. Polk County v. Dodson, 454 U.S. 312 (1981) (holding that a public defender does not act "under color of state law" because he "works under canons of professional responsibility that mandate his exercise of independent judgment on behalf of the client" and because there is an "assumption that counsel will be free of state control").

The Government has designed this program to use the legal profession and the established Judiciary of the States and the Federal Government to accomplish its end of assisting welfare claimants in determination or receipt of their benefits. The advice from the attorney to the client and the advocacy by the attorney to the courts cannot be classified as governmental speech even under a generous understanding of the concept. In this vital respect this suit is distinguishable from Rust.

The private nature of the speech involved here, and the extent of LSC's regulation of private expression, are indicated further by the circumstance that the Government seeks to use an existing medium of expression and to control it, in a class of cases, in ways which distort its usual functioning. Where the government uses or attempts to regulate a particular medium, we have been informed by its accepted usage in determining whether a particular restriction on speech is necessary for the program's purposes and limitations. In FCC v. League of Women Voters of Cal., 468 U.S. 364 (1984), the Court was instructed by its understanding of the dynamics of the broadcast industry in holding that prohibitions against editorializing by public radio networks were an impermissible restriction, even though the Government enacted the restriction to control the use of public funds. The First Amendment forbade the Government from using the forum in an unconventional way to suppress speech inherent in the nature of the medium. In Arkansas Ed. Television Comm'n v. Forbes, 523 U.S. 666 (1988), the dynamics of the broadcasting system gave station programmers the right to use editorial judgment to exclude certain speech so that the broadcast message could be more effective. And in Rosenberger, the fact that student newspapers expressed many different points of view was an important foundation for the Court's decision to invalidate viewpoint-based restrictions.

When the government creates a limited forum for speech, certain restrictions may be necessary to define the limits and purposes of the program. The same is true when the government establishes a subsidy for specified ends. *** Here the program presumes that private, nongovernmental speech is necessary, and a substantial restriction is placed upon that speech. At oral argument and in its briefs the LSC advised us that lawyers funded in the Government program may not undertake representation in suits for benefits if they must advise clients respecting the questionable validity of a statute which defines benefit eligibility and the payment structure. The limitation forecloses advice or legal assistance to question the validity of statutes under the Constitution of the United States. It extends further, it must be noted, so that state statutes inconsistent with federal law under the Supremacy Clause may be neither challenged nor questioned.

By providing subsidies to LSC, the Government seeks to facilitate suits for benefits by using the state and federal courts and the independent bar on which those courts depend for the proper performance of their duties and responsibilities. Restricting LSC attorneys in advising their clients and in presenting arguments and analyses to the courts distorts the legal system by altering the traditional role of the attorneys in much the same way broadcast systems or student publication networks were changed in the limited forum cases we have cited. Just as government in those cases could not elect to use a broadcasting network or a college publication structure in a regime which prohibits speech necessary to the proper functioning of those systems, it may not design a subsidy to effect this serious and fundamental restriction on advocacy of attorneys and the functioning of the judiciary.

LSC has advised us, furthermore, that upon determining a question of statutory validity is present in any anticipated or pending case or controversy, the LSC-funded attorney must cease the representation at once. This is true whether the validity issue becomes apparent during initial attorney-client consultations or in the midst of litigation proceedings. A disturbing example of the restriction was discussed during oral argument before the Court. It is well understood that when there are two reasonable constructions for a statute, yet one raises a constitutional question, the Court should prefer the interpretation which avoids the constitutional issue. Yet, as the LSC advised the Court, if, during litigation, a judge were to ask an LSC attorney whether there was a constitutional concern, the LSC attorney simply could not answer. Tr. of Oral Arg. 8–9.

Interpretation of the law and the Constitution is the primary mission of the judiciary when it acts within the sphere of its authority to resolve a case or controversy. Marbury v. Madison, 1 Cranch 137 (1803). ("It is emphatically the province and the duty of the judicial department to say what the law is"). An informed, independent judiciary presumes an informed, independent bar. Under § 504(a)(16), however, cases would be presented by LSC attorneys who could not advise the courts of serious questions of statutory validity. The disability is inconsistent with the proposition that attorneys should present all the reasonable and well-grounded arguments necessary for proper resolution of the case. By seeking to prohibit the analysis of certain legal issues and to truncate presentation to the courts, the enactment under review prohibits speech and expression upon which courts must depend for the proper exercise of the judicial power. Congress cannot wrest the law from the Constitution which is its source. "Those then who controvert the principle that the constitution is to be considered, in court, as a paramount law, are reduced to the necessity of maintaining that courts must close their eyes on the constitution, and see only the law." Id. at 178.

The restriction imposed by the statute here threatens severe impairment of the judicial function. Section 504(a)(16) sifts out cases presenting constitutional challenges in order to insulate the Government's laws from judicial inquiry. If the restriction on speech and legal advice were to stand, the result would be two tiers of cases. In cases where LSC counsel were attorneys of record, there would be lingering doubt whether the truncated representation had resulted in complete analysis of the case, full advice to the client, and proper presentation to the court. The courts and the public would come to question the adequacy and fairness of professional representations when the attorney, either consciously to comply with this statute or unconsciously to continue the representation despite the statute, avoided all reference to questions of statutory validity and constitutional authority. A scheme so inconsistent with accepted separation-of-powers principles is an insufficient basis to sustain or uphold the restriction on speech.

It is no answer to say the restriction on speech is harmless because, under LSC's interpretation of the Act, its attorneys can withdraw. This misses the point. The statute is an attempt to draw lines around the LSC program to exclude from litigation those arguments and theories Congress finds unacceptable but which by their nature are within the province of the courts to consider.

The restriction on speech is even more problematic because in cases where the attorney withdraws from a representation, the client is unlikely to find other counsel. The explicit premise for providing LSC attorneys is the necessity to make available representation "to persons financially unable to afford legal assistance." There often will be no alternative source for the client to receive vital information respecting constitutional and statutory rights bearing upon claimed benefits. Thus, with respect to the litigation services Congress has funded, there is no alternative channel for expression of the advocacy Congress seeks to restrict. This is in stark contrast to Rust. There, a patient could receive the approved Title X family planning counseling funded by the Government and later could consult an affiliate or independent organization to receive abortion counseling. Unlike indigent clients who seek LSC representation, the patient in Rust was not required to forfeit the Government-funded advice when she also received abortion counseling through alternative channels. Because LSC attorneys must withdraw whenever a question of a welfare statute's validity arises, an individual could not obtain joint representation so that the constitutional challenge would be presented by a non-LSC attorney, and other, permitted, arguments advanced by LSC counsel.

Finally, LSC and the Government maintain that § 504(a)(16) is necessary to define the scope and contours of the federal program, a condition that ensures funds can be spent for those cases most immediate to congressional concern. In support of this contention, they suggest the challenged limitation takes into account the nature of the grantees' activities and provides limited congressional funds for the provision of simple suits for benefits. In petitioners' view, the restriction operates neither to maintain the current welfare system nor insulate it from attack; rather, it helps the current welfare system function in a more efficient and fair manner by removing from the program complex challenges to existing welfare laws.

The effect of the restriction, however, is to prohibit advice or argumentation that existing welfare laws are unconstitutional or unlawful. Congress cannot recast a condition on funding as a mere definition of its program in every case, lest the First Amendment be reduced to a simple semantic exercise. Here, notwithstanding Congress' purpose to confine and limit its program, the restriction operates to insulate current welfare laws from constitutional scrutiny and certain other legal challenges, a condition implicating central First Amendment concerns. In no lawsuit funded by the Government can the LSC attorney, speaking on behalf of a private client, challenge existing welfare laws. As a result, arguments by indigent clients that a welfare statute is unlawful or unconstitutional cannot be expressed in this Government-funded program for petitioning the courts, even though the program was created for litigation involving welfare benefits, and even though the ordinary course of litigation involves the expression of theories and postulates on both, or multiple, sides of an issue.

It is fundamental that the First Amendment " 'was fashioned to assure unfettered interchange of ideas for the bringing about of political and social changes desired by the people.' " New York Times Co, v Sullivan 376 U.S. 254 (1964). There can be little doubt that the LSC Act funds constitutionally protected expression; and in the context of this statute there is no programmatic message of the kind recognized in Rust and which sufficed there to allow the Government to specify the advice deemed necessary for its legitimate objectives. This serves to distinguish § 504(a)(16) from any of the Title X program restrictions upheld in Rust, and to place it beyond any congressional funding condition approved in the past by this Court.

Congress was not required to fund an LSC attorney to represent indigent clients; and when it did so, it was not required to fund the whole range of legal representations or relationships. The LSC and the United States, however, in effect ask us to permit Congress to define the scope of the litigation it funds to exclude certain vital theories and ideas. The attempted restriction is designed to insulate the Government's interpretation of the Constitution from judicial challenge. The Constitution does not permit the Government to confine litigants and their attorneys in this manner. We must be vigilant when Congress imposes rules and conditions which in effect insulate its own laws from legitimate judicial challenge. Where private speech is involved, even Congress' antecedent funding decision cannot be aimed at the suppression of ideas thought inimical to the Government's own interest.

For the reasons we have set forth, the funding condition is invalid. The Court of Appeals considered whether the language restricting LSC attorneys could be severed from the statute so that the remaining portions would remain operative. It reached the reasoned conclusion to invalidate the fragment of § 504(a)(16) found contrary to the First Amendment, leaving the balance of the statute operative and in place. That determination was not discussed in the briefs of either party or otherwise contested here, and in the exercise of our discretion and prudential judgment we decline to address it.

The judgment of the Court of Appeals is *Affirmed.*

Chapter Eleven

Access to Justice in the Criminal Justice System

A. Mass Incarceration

Throughout this text we have examined policies implemented to aid poor families in the United States, many of which also benefit the nonpoor. Mass incarceration is no exception. Beginning with Nixon's War on Drugs through Reagan's "tough on crime" bills, which opened the door to mandatory minimum prison sentences, most notably the racial disparities that distinguished crack and powder cocaine sentences—the prison industrial complex was born. A complex interplay of government and for-profit organizations came together to house, feed, clothe, provide health services, and oversee the growing number of individuals entering the criminal justice system. Incarceration rates continued to rise exponentially through the turn of the century and began to flatten with the Bush administration's efforts to reduce recidivism by putting monies into reentry programs and the Obama administration's policies to reduce racial disparities in sentencing. Today, there are more than 2.3 million people incarcerated in the United States.[1] America has the unenviable distinction of holding more prisoners than any other nation in the world, including China. While efforts are underway to decrease our prison population, the poverty-to-prison pipeline shows no sign of slowing down.

Most of the incarcerated were living in poverty prior to imprisonment and remain in poverty once released. Sawyer and Wagner argue that "poverty is not only a predictor of incarceration; it is also frequently the outcome, as a criminal record and time spent in prison destroys wealth, creates debt, and decimates job opportunities."[2] The following cases explore access to justice and civil rights while either being detained or incarcerated in the United States. Prison overcrowding, police training, and government protections all demonstrate different ways that the criminal justice system impacts the poor specifically. Each case provides a historical yet relevant example of a precedent that has either harmed or helped our ever-growing criminal justice system. The Prison Policy Initiative provides key information on how the prison pipeline op-

---

1. WENDY SAWYER & PETER WAGNER, PRISON POLICY INITIATIVE, MASS INCARCERATION: THE WHOLE PIE 2020, https://www.prisonpolicy.org/reports/pie2020.html (last visited June 7, 2020).
2. *Id.*

erates as well as who is imprisoned. See www.prisonpolicy.org for data and demographics revealing the state of the U.S. incarceration infrastructure.

The following case demonstrates how and why prison conditions have worsened over time, while exploring what "cruel and unusual punishment" means in the prison context.

Rhodes v. Chapman

452 U.S. 337 (1981)

Justice POWELL delivered the opinion of the Court.

The question presented is whether the housing of two inmates in a single cell at the Southern Ohio Correctional Facility is cruel and unusual punishment prohibited by the Eighth and Fourteenth Amendments.

Respondents Kelly Chapman and Richard Jaworski are inmates at the Southern Ohio Correctional Facility (SOCF), a maximum-security state prison in Lucasville, Ohio. They were housed in the same cell when they brought this action in the District Court for the Southern District of Ohio on behalf of themselves and all inmates similarly situated at SOCF. Asserting a cause of action under 42 U.S.C. § 1983, they contended that "double celling" at SOCF violated the Constitution. The gravamen of their complaint was that double celling confined cellmates too closely. It also was blamed for overcrowding at SOCF, said to have overwhelmed the prison's facilities and staff. As relief, respondents sought an injunction barring petitioners, who are Ohio officials responsible for the administration of SOCF, from housing more than one inmate in a cell, except as a temporary measure.

The District Court made extensive findings of fact about SOCF on the basis of evidence presented at trial and the court's own observations during an inspection that it conducted without advance notice. 434 F.Supp. 1007 (1977). These findings describe the physical plant, inmate population, and effects of double celling. Neither party contends that these findings are erroneous.

...

Each cell at SOCF measures approximately 63 square feet. Each contains a bed measuring 36 by 80 inches, a cabinet-type night stand, a wall-mounted sink with hot and cold running water, and a

toilet that the inmate can flush from inside the cell. Cells housing two inmates have a two-tiered bunk bed. Every cell has a heating and air circulation vent near the ceiling, and 960 of the cells have a window that inmates can open and close. All of the cells have a cabinet, shelf, and radio built into one of the walls, and in all of the cells one wall consists of bars through which the inmates can be seen.

The "dayrooms" are located adjacent to the cellblocks and are open to inmates between 6:30 a. m. and 9:30 p. m. According to the District Court, "[t]he day rooms are in a sense part of the cells and they are designed to furnish that type of recreation or occupation which an ordinary citizen would seek in his living room or den." *Id.*, at 1012. Each dayroom contains a wall-mounted television, card tables, and chairs. Inmates can pass between their cells and the dayrooms during a 10-minute period per hour, on the hour, when the doors to the dayrooms and cells are opened.

As to the inmate population, the District Court found that SOCF began receiving inmates in late 1972 and double celling them in 1975 because of an increase in Ohio's statewide prison population. At the time of trial, SOCF housed 2,300 inmates, 67% of whom were serving life or other long-term sentences for first-degree felonies. Approximately 1,400 inmates were double celled. Of these, about 75% had the choice of spending much of their waking hours outside their cells, in the dayrooms, school, workshops, library, visits, meals, or showers. The other double-celled inmates spent more time locked in their cells because of a restrictive classification.

...

We consider here for the first time the limitation that the Eighth Amendment, which is applicable to the States through the Fourteenth Amendment, *Robinson v. California*, 370 U.S. 660, 82 S.Ct. 1417, 8 L.Ed.2d 758 (1962), imposes upon the conditions in which a State may confine those convicted of crimes. It is unquestioned that "[c]onfinement in a prison ... is a form of punishment subject to scrutiny under the Eighth Amendment standards." *Hutto v. Finney*, 437 U.S. 678, 685, 98 S.Ct. 2565, 2570, 57 L.Ed.2d 522 (1978); see *Ingraham v. Wright*, 430 U.S. 651, 669, 97 S.Ct. 1401, 1411, 51 L.Ed.2d 711 (1977); cf. *Bell v. Wolfish*, 441 U.S. 520, 99 S.Ct. 1861, 60 L.Ed.2d 447 (1979). But until this case, we have not considered a disputed contention that the conditions of confinement at a particular prison constituted cruel and unusual punishment. Nor have we had an occasion to consider specifically the principles relevant to assessing claims that conditions of confinement violate the Eighth Amendment. We look, first, to the Eighth Amendment precedents for the general principles that are relevant to a State's authority to impose punishment for criminal conduct.

The Eighth Amendment, in only three words, imposes the constitutional limitation upon punishments: they cannot be "cruel and unusual." The Court has interpreted these words "in a flexible and dynamic manner," *Gregg v. Georgia*, 428 U.S. 153, 171, 96 S.Ct. 2909, 2924, 49 L.Ed.2d 859 (1976) (joint opinion), and has extended the Amendment's reach beyond the barbarous physical punishments at issue in the Court's earliest cases. See *Wilkerson v. Utah*, 99 U.S. 130, 25 L.Ed. 345 (1879); *In re Kemmler*, 136 U.S. 436, 10 S.Ct. 930, 34 L.Ed. 519 (1890). Today the Eighth Amendment prohibits punishments which, although not physically barbarous, "involve the unnecessary and wanton infliction of pain," *Gregg v. Georgia, supra*, at 173, 96 S.Ct., at 2925, or are grossly disproportionate to the severity of the crime, *Coker v. Georgia*, 433 U.S. 584, 592, 97 S.Ct. 2861, 2866, 53 L.Ed.2d 982 (1977) (plurality opinion); *Weems v. United States*, 217 U.S. 349, 30 S.Ct. 544, 54 L.Ed. 793 (1910). Among "unnecessary and wanton" inflictions of pain are those that are "totally without penological justification." *Gregg v. Georgia, supra*, 428 U.S., at 183, 96 S.Ct., at 2929; *Estelle v. Gamble*, 429 U.S. 97, 103, 97 S.Ct. 285, 290, 50 L.Ed.2d 251 (1976).

No static "test" can exist by which courts determine whether conditions of confinement are cruel and unusual, for the Eighth Amendment "must draw its meaning from the evolving standards of decency that mark the progress of a maturing society." *Trop v. Dulles*, 356 U.S. 86, 101, 78 S.Ct. 590, 598, 2 L.Ed.2d 596 (1958) (plurality opinion). The Court has held, however, that "Eighth Amendment judgments should neither be nor appear to be merely the subjective views" of judges. *Rummel v. Estelle*, 445 U.S. 263, 275, 100 S.Ct. 1133, 1139, 63 L.Ed.2d 382 (1980). To be sure, "the Constitution contemplates that in the end [a court's] own judgment will be brought to bear on the question of the acceptability" of a given punishment. *Coker v. Georgia, supra*, 433 U.S., at 597, 97 S.Ct., at 2868 (plurality opinion); *Gregg v. Georgia, supra*, 428 U.S., at 182, 96 S.Ct., at 2929 (joint opinion). But such " 'judgment[s] should be informed by objective factors to the maximum possible extent.' " *Rummel v. Estelle, supra*, 445 U.S., at 274–275, 100 S.Ct., at 1139, quoting *Coker v. Georgia, supra*, at 592, 97 S.Ct., at 2866 (plurality opinion). For example, when the question was whether capital punishment for certain crimes violated contemporary values, the Court looked for "objective indicia" derived from history, the action of state legislatures, and the sentencing by juries. *Gregg v. Georgia, supra*, 428 U.S., at 176–187, 96 S.Ct., at 2926–2931; *Coker v. Georgia, supra*, 433 U.S., at 593–596, 97 S.Ct., at 2868. Our conclusion in *Estelle v. Gamble, supra*, that deliberate indifference to an inmate's medical needs is cruel and unusual punishment rested on the fact, recognized by the common law and state legislatures, that "[a]n inmate must rely on prison authorities to treat his medical needs; if the authorities fail to do so, those needs will not be met." 429 U.S., at 103, 97 S.Ct., at 290.

These principles apply when the conditions of confinement compose the punishment at issue. Conditions must not involve the wanton and unnecessary infliction of pain, nor may they be grossly disproportionate to the severity of the crime warranting imprisonment. In *Estelle v. Gamble, supra*, we held that the denial of medical care is cruel and unusual because, in the worst case, it can result in physical torture, and, even in less serious cases, it can result in pain without any penological purpose. 429 U.S., at 103, 97 S.Ct., at 290. In *Hutto v. Finney, supra*, the conditions of confinement in two Arkansas prisons constituted cruel and unusual punishment because they resulted in unquestioned and serious deprivation of basic human needs. Conditions other than those in *Gamble* and *Hutto*, alone or in combination, may deprive inmates of the minimal civilized measure of life's necessities. Such conditions could be cruel and unusual under the contemporary standard of decency that we recognized in *Gamble, supra*, at 103–104, 97 S.Ct., at 290–291. But conditions that cannot be said to be cruel and unusual under contemporary standards are not unconstitutional. To the extent that such conditions are restrictive and even harsh, they are part of the penalty that criminal offenders pay for their offenses against society.

In view of the District Court's findings of fact, its conclusion that double celling at SOCF constitutes cruel and unusual punishment is insupportable. Virtually every one of the court's findings tends to *refute* respondents' claim. The double celling made necessary by the unanticipated increase in prison population did not lead to deprivations of essential food, medical care, or sanitation. Nor did it increase violence among inmates or create other conditions intolerable for prison confinement. 434 F.Supp., at 1018. Although job and educational opportunities diminished marginally as a result of double celling, limited work hours and delay before receiving education do not inflict pain, much less unnecessary and wanton pain; deprivations of this kind simply are not punishments. We would have to wrench the Eighth Amendment from its language and history to hold that delay of these desirable aids to rehabilitation violates the Constitution.

The five considerations on which the District Court relied also are insufficient to support its constitutional conclusion. The court relied on the long terms of imprisonment served by inmates at SOCF; the fact that SOCF housed 38% more inmates than its "design capacity"; the recommendation of several studies that each inmate have at least 50–55 square feet of living quarters; the suggestion that double-celled inmates spend most of their time in their cells with their cellmates; and the fact that double celling at SOCF was not a temporary condition. *Supra*, at 2397. These general considerations fall far short in themselves or proving cruel and unusual punishment, for there is no evidence that double celling under these circumstances either inflicts unnecessary or wanton pain or is grossly disproportionate to the severity of crimes warranting imprisonment. At most, these considerations amount to a theory that double celling inflicts pain. Perhaps they reflect an aspiration toward an ideal environment for long-term confinement. But the Constitution does not mandate comfortable prisons, and prisons of SOCF's type, which house persons convicted of serious crimes, cannot be free of discomfort. Thus, these considerations properly are weighed by the legislature and prison administration rather than a court. There being no constitutional violation, the District Court had no authority to consider whether double celling in light of these considerations was the best response to the increase in Ohio's statewide prison population.

This Court must proceed cautiously in making an Eighth Amendment judgment because, unless we reverse it, "[a] decision that a given punishment is impermissible under the Eighth Amendment cannot be reversed short of a constitutional amendment," and thus "[r]evisions cannot be made in the light of further experience." *Gregg v. Georgia*, 428 U.S., at 176, 96 S.Ct., at 2926. In assessing claims that conditions of confinement are cruel and unusual, courts must bear in mind that their inquiries "spring from constitutional requirements and that judicial answers to them must reflect that fact rather than a court's idea of how best to operate a detention facility." *Bell v. Wolfish*, 441 U.S., at 539, 99 S.Ct., at 1874.

Courts certainly have a responsibility to scrutinize claims of cruel and unusual confinement, and conditions in a number of prisons, especially older ones, have justly been described as "deplorable" and "sordid." *Bell v. Wolfish, supra*, at 562, 99 S.Ct., at 1886.17 When conditions of confinement amount to cruel and unusual punishment, "federal courts will discharge their duty to protect constitutional rights." *Procunier v. Martinez*, 416 U.S. 396, 405–406, 94 S.Ct. 1800, 1807–1808, 40 L.Ed.2d 224 (1974); see *Cruz v. Beto*, 405 U.S. 319, 321, 92 S.Ct. 1079, 1081, 31 L.Ed.2d 263

(1972) (*per curiam*). In discharging this oversight responsibility, however, courts cannot assume that state legislatures and prison officials are insensitive to the requirements of the Constitution or to the perplexing sociological problems of how best to achieve the goals of the penal function in the criminal justice system: to punish justly, to deter future crime, and to return imprisoned persons to society with an improved change of being useful, law-abiding citizens.

In this case, the question before us is whether the conditions of confinement at SOCF are cruel and unusual. As we find that they are not, the judgment of the Court of Appeals is reversed.

It is so ordered.

Justice BRENNAN, with whom Justice BLACKMUN and Justice STEVENS join, concurring in the judgment.

Today's decision reaffirms that "[c]ourts certainly have a responsibility to scrutinize claims of cruel and unusual confinement." *Ante*, at 2401. With that I agree. I also agree that the District Court's findings in this case do not support a judgment that the practice of double celling in the Southern Ohio Correctional Facility is in violation of the Eighth Amendment. I write separately, however, to emphasize that today's decision should in no way be construed as a retreat from careful judicial scrutiny of prison conditions, and to discuss the factors courts should consider in undertaking such scrutiny.

Although this Court has never before considered what prison conditions constitute "cruel and unusual punishment" within the meaning of the Eighth Amendment, see *ante*, at 2397–2398, such questions have been addressed repeatedly by the lower courts. In fact, individual prisons or entire prison systems in at least 24 States have been declared unconstitutional under the Eighth and Fourteenth Amendments, with litigation underway in many others Thus, the lower courts have learned from repeated investigation and bitter experience that judicial intervention is *indispensable* if constitutional dictates—not to mention considerations of basic humanity—are to be observed in the prisons.

No one familiar with litigation in this area could suggest that the courts have been overeager to usurp the task of running prisons, which, as the Court today properly notes, is entrusted in the first instance to the "legislature and prison administration rather than a court." *Ante*, at 2400. And certainly, no one could suppose that the courts have ordered creation of "comfortable prisons," *ibid.*, on the model of country clubs. To the contrary, "the soul-chilling inhumanity of conditions in American prisons has been thrust upon the judicial conscience." *Inmates of Suffolk County Jail v. Eisenstadt*, 360 F.Supp. 676, 684 (Mass.1973).

Judicial opinions in this area do not make pleasant reading. For example, in *Pugh v. Locke*, 406 F.Supp. 318 (MD Ala.1976), aff'd as modified, 559 F.2d 283 (CA5 1977), rev'd in part on other grounds, 438 U.S. 781, 98 S.Ct. 3057, 57 L.Ed.2d 1114 (1978) (*per curiam*), Chief Judge Frank Johnson described in gruesome detail the conditions then prevailing in the Alabama penal system. The institutions were "horrendously overcrowded,' 406 F.Supp., at 322, to the point where some inmates were forced to sleep on mattresses spread on floors in hallways and next to urinals. *Id.*, at 323. The physical facilities were "dilapidat[ed]" and "filthy," the cells infested with roaches, flies, mosquitoes, and other vermin. *Ibid.* Sanitation facilities were limited and in ill repair, emitting an overpowering odor"; in one instance over 200 men were forced to share one toilet. *Ibid.* Inmates were not provided with toothpaste, toothbrush, shampoo, shaving cream, razors, combs, or other such necessities. *Ibid.* Food was "unappetizing and unwholesome," poorly prepared and often infested with insects, and served without reasonable utensils. *Ibid.* There were no meaningful vocational, educational, recreational, or work programs. *Id.*, at 326. A United States health officer described the prisons as "wholly unfit for human habitation according to virtually every criterion used for evaluation by public health inspectors." *Id.*, at 323–324. Perhaps the worst of all was the "rampant violence" within the prison. *Id.*, at 325. Weaker inmates were "repeatedly victimized" by the stronger; robbery, rape, extortion, theft, and assault were "everyday occurrences among the general inmate population." *Id.*, at 324. Faced with this record, the court—not surprisingly—found that the conditions of confinement constituted cruel and unusual punishment, and issued a comprehensive remedial order affecting virtually every aspect of prison administration

Unfortunately, the Alabama example is neither abberational nor anachronistic. Last year, in *Ramos v. Lamm*, 639 F.2d 559 (1980), cert. denied, 450 U.S. 1041, 101 S.Ct. 1759, 68 L.Ed.2d 239 (1981), for example, the Tenth Circuit declared conditions in the maximum-security unit of the Colorado State Penitentiary at Canon City unconstitutional. The living areas of the prison were "unfit for human habitation," *id.*, at 567; the food unsanitary and "grossly inadequate," *id.*, at 570; the institution "fraught with tension and violence," often leading to injury and death, *id.*, at 572; the health care "blatant[ly] inadequat[e]" and "appalling," *id.*, at 574; and there were various restrictions of prisoners' rights to visitation, mail, and access to courts in violation of basic constitutional rights, *id.*, at 578–585. Similar tales of horror are recounted in dozens of other cases. See, *e. g.*, cases cited in n. 1, *supra*.

Overcrowding and cramped living conditions are particularly pressing problems in many prisons. Out of 82 court orders in effect concerning conditions of confinement in federal and state correctional facilities as of March 31, 1978, 26 involved the issue of overcrowding. 3 American Prisons and Jails 32. Two-thirds of all inmates in federal, state, and local correctional facilities were confined in cells or dormitories providing less than 60 square feet per person—the minimal standard deemed acceptable by the American Public Health Association, the Justice Department, and other authorities.

The problems of administering prisons within constitutional standards are indeed "'complex and intractable,'" *ante*, at 2401, n. 16, quoting *Procunier v. Martinez*, 416 U.S. 396, 404, 94 S.Ct. 1800, 1807, 40 L.Ed.2d 224 (1974), but at their core is a lack of resources allocated to prisons. Confinement of prisoners is unquestionably an expensive proposition: the average direct current expenditure at adult institutions in

1977 was $5,461 per inmate, 3 American Prisons and Jails 115; the average cost of constructing space for an additional prisoner is estimated at $25,000 to $50,000. *Id.*, at 119. Oftentimes, funding for prisons has been dramatically below that required to comply with basic constitutional standards. For example, to bring the Louisiana prison system into compliance required a supplemental appropriation of $18,431,622 for a single year's operating expenditures, and of $105,605,000 for capital outlays. *Williams v. Edwards*, 547 F.2d 1206, 1219–1221 (CA5 1977) (Exhibit A).

Over the last decade, correctional resources, never ample, have lagged behind burgeoning prison populations. In *Ruiz v. Estelle*, 503 F.Supp. 1265 (SD Tex.1980), for example, the court stated that an "unprecedented surge" in the number of inmates has "undercut any realistic expectation" of eliminating double and triple celling, despite construction of a new $43 million unit. *Id.*, at 1280–1281. The number of inmates in federal and state correctional facilities has risen 42% since 1975, and last year grew at its fastest rate in three years. Krajick, The Boom Resumes, 7 Corrections Magazine 16–17 (Apr.1981) (report of annual survey of prison populations).6 A major infusion of money would be required merely to keep pace with prison populations.

Public apathy and the political powerlessness of inmates have contributed to the pervasive neglect of the prisons. Chief Judge Henley observed that the people of Arkansas "knew little or nothing about their penal system" prior to the *Holt* litigation, despite "sporadic and sensational" exposés. *Holt v. Sarver*, 309 F.Supp. 362, 367 (ED Ark.1970). Prison inmates are "voteless, politically unpopular, and socially threatening." Morris, The Snail's Pace of Prison Reform, in Proceedings of the 100th Annual Congress of Correction of the American Correctional Assn. 36, 42 (1970). Thus, the suffering of prisoners, even if known, generally "moves the community in only the most severe and exceptional cases." *Ibid.* As a result even conscientious prison officials are "[c]aught in the middle," as state legislatures refuse "to spend sufficient tax dollars to bring conditions in outdated prisons up to minimally acceptable standards." *Johnson v. Levine*, 450 F.Supp. 648, 654 (Md.), aff'd in part, 588 F.2d 1378 (CA4 1978).7 After extensive exposure to this process, Chief Judge Pettine came to view the "barbaric physical conditions" of Rhode Island's prison system as "the ugly and shocking outward manifestations of a deeper dysfunction, an attitude of cynicism, hopelessness, predatory selfishness, and callous indifference that appears to infect, to one degree or another, almost everyone who comes in contact with the [prison]." *Palmigiano v. Garrahy*, 443 F.Supp. 956, 984 (RI 1977), remanded, 599 F.2d 17 (CA1 1979).

Under these circumstances the courts have emerged as a critical force behind **2406 efforts to ameliorate inhumane conditions. Insulated as they are from political pressures, and charged with the duty of enforcing the Constitution, courts are in the strongest position to insist that unconstitutional conditions be remedied, even at significant financial cost. Justice BLACKMUN, then serving on the Court of Appeals, set the tone in *Jackson v. Bishop*, 404 F.2d 571, 580 (CA8 1968): "Humane considerations and constitutional requirements are not, in this day, to be measured or limited by dollar considerations...."

...

Justice BLACKMUN, concurring in the judgment.

Despite the perhaps technically correct observation, *ante*, at 2397–2398, that the Court is "consider[ing] here for the first time the limitation that the Eighth Amendment ... imposes upon the conditions in which a State may confine those convicted of crimes," it obviously is not writing upon a clean slate. See *Hutto v. Finney*, 437 U.S. 678, 685–688, 98 S.Ct. 2565, 2570–2572, 57 L.Ed.2d 522 (1978); cf. *Bell v. Wolfish*, 441 U.S. 520, 99 S.Ct. 1861, 60 L.Ed.2d 447 (1979). Already, concerns about prison conditions and their constitutional significance have been expressed by the Court.

Jackson v. Bishop, 404 F.2d 571 (CA8 1968), cited by both Justice BRENNAN, and by Justice MARSHALL in dissent here, was, I believe, one of the first cases in which a federal court examined state penitentiary practices and held them to be violative of the Eighth Amendment's proscription of "cruel and unusual punishments." I sat on that appeal, and I was privileged to write the opinion for a unanimous panel of the court. My voting in at least one prison case since then further discloses my concern about the conditions that sometimes are imposed upon confined human beings.

I perceive, as Justice BRENNAN obviously does in view of his separate writing, a possibility that the Court's opinion in this case today might be regarded, because of some of its language, as a signal to prison administrators that the federal courts now are to adopt a policy of general deference to such administrators and to state legislatures, deference not only for the purpose of determining contemporary standards of decency, *ante*, at 2398, but for the purpose of determining whether conditions at a particular prison are cruel and unusual within the meaning of the Eighth Amendment, *ante*, 2400–2402. That perhaps was the old attitude prevalent several decades ago. I join Justice BRENNAN's opinion because I, too, feel that the federal courts must continue to be available to those state inmates who sincerely claim that the conditions to which they are subjected are violative of the Amendment. The Court properly points out in its opinion, *ante*, at 2399, that incarceration necessarily, and constitutionally, entails restrictions, discomforts, and a loss of privileges that complete freedom affords. But incarceration is not an open door for unconstitutional cruelty or neglect. Against that kind of penal condition, the Constitution and the federal courts, it is to be hoped, together remain as an available bastion.

Justice MARSHALL, dissenting.

From reading the Court's opinion in this case, one would surely conclude that the Southern Ohio Correctional Facility (SOCF) is a safe, spacious prison that happens to include many two-inmate cells because the State has determined that that is the best way to run the prison. But the facility described by the majority is not the one involved in this case. SOCF is overcrowded, unhealthful, and dangerous. None of those conditions results from a considered policy judgment on the part of the State. Until the Court's opinion today, absolutely no one—certainly not the "state legislatures" or "prison officials" to whom the majority suggests, see *ante*, at 2401, that we defer in analyzing constitutional questions—had suggested that forcing long-term inmates to share tiny cells designed to hold only one individual might be a good thing. On the contrary, as the District Court noted, "everybody" is in agreement that double celling is undesirable No one argued at trial and no one has contended here that double celling was a legislative policy judgment. No one has asserted that prison officials imposed it as a disciplinary or a security matter. And no one has claimed that the practice has anything whatsoever to do with "punish[ing] justly," "deter[ring] future crime," or "return[ing] imprisoned persons to society with an improved chance of being useful law-abiding citizens." See *ante*, at 2402. The evidence and the District Court's findings clearly demonstrate that the *only* reason double celling was imposed on inmates at SOCF was that more individuals were sent there than the prison was ever designed to hold.

I do not dispute that the state legislature indeed made policy judgments when it built SOCF. It decided that Ohio needed a maximum-security prison that would house some 1,600 inmates. In keeping with prevailing expert opinion, the legislature made the further judgments that each inmate would have his own cell and that each cell would have approximately 63 square feet of floor space. But because of prison overcrowding, hundreds of the cells are shared, or "doubled," which is hardly what the legislature intended.

In a doubled cell, each inmate has only some 30–35 square feet of floor space. Most of the windows in the Supreme Court building are larger than that. The conclusion of every expert who testified at trial and of every serious study of which I am aware is that a long-term inmate must have to himself, at the very least, 50 square feet of floor space—an area smaller than that occupied by a good-sized automobile—in order to avoid serious mental, emotional, and physical deterioration The District Court found that as a fact. Even petitioners, in their brief in this Court, concede that double celling as practiced at SOCF is "less than desirable." Brief for Petitioners 17.

The Eighth Amendment "embodies 'broad and idealistic concepts of dignity, civilized standards, humanity and decency,'" against which conditions of confinement must be judged. *Estelle v. Gamble*, 429 U.S. 97, 102, 97 S.Ct. 285, 290, 50 L.Ed.2d 251 (1976), quoting *Jackson v. Bishop*, 404 F.2d 571, 579 (CA8 1968). Thus the State cannot impose punishment that violates "the evolving standards of decency that mark the progress of a maturing society." *Trop v. Dulles*, 356 U.S. 86, 101, 78 S.Ct. 590, 598, 2 L.Ed.2d 596 (1958) (plurality opinion). For me, the legislative judgment and the consistent conclusions by those who have studied the problem provide considerable evidence that those standards condemn imprisonment in conditions so crowded that serious harm will result. The record amply demonstrates that those conditions are present here. It is surely not disputed that SOCF is severely overcrowded. The prison is operating at 38% above its design capacity.5 It is also significant that some two-thirds of the inmates at SOCF are serving lengthy or life sentences, for, as we have said elsewhere, "the length of confinement cannot be ignored in deciding whether the confinement meets constitutional standards." *Hutto v. Finney*, 437 U.S. 678, 686, 98 S.Ct. 2565, 2571, 57 L.Ed.2d 522 (1978). Nor is double-celling a short-term response to a temporary problem. The trial court found, and it is not contested, that double-celling, if not enjoined, will continue for the foreseeable future. The trial court also found that most of the double-celled inmates spend most of their time in their cells.

It is simply not true, as the majority asserts, that "there is no evidence that double-celling under these circumstances either inflicts unnecessary or wanton pain or is grossly disproportionate to the severity of crimes warranting imprisonment." *Ante,* at 2399. The District Court concluded from the record before it that long exposure to these conditions will "*necessarily*" involve "excess limitation of general movement as well as physical and mental injury...." 434 F.Supp., at 1020 (emphasis added). And of course, of all the judges who have been involved in this case, the trial judge is the only one who has actually visited the prison. That is simply an additional reason to give in this case the deference we have always accorded to the careful conclusions of the finder of fact. There is not a shred of evidence to suggest that anyone who has given the matter serious thought has ever approved, as the majority does today, conditions of confinement such as those present at SOCF. I see no reason to set aside the concurrent conclusions of two courts that the overcrowding and double celling here in issue are sufficiently severe that they will, if left unchecked, cause deterioration in respondents' mental and physical health. These conditions in my view go well beyond contemporary standards of decency and therefore violate the Eighth and Fourteenth Amendments. I would affirm the judgment of the Court of Appeals.

If the majority did no more than state its disagreement with the courts below over the proper reading of the record, I would end my opinion here. But the Court goes further, adding some unfortunate dicta that may be read as a warning to federal courts against interference with a State's operation of its prisons. If taken too literally, the majority's admonitions might eviscerate the federal courts' traditional role of preventing a State from imposing cruel and unusual punishment through its conditions of confinement.

The majority concedes that federal courts "certainly have a responsibility to scrutinize claims of cruel and unusual confinement," *ante,* at 2401, but adds an apparent caveat:

"In discharging this oversight responsibility, however, courts cannot assume that state legislatures and prison officials are insensitive to the requirements of the Constitution or to the perplexing sociological problems of how best to achieve the goals of the penal function in the criminal justice system: to punish justly, to deter future crime, and to return imprisoned persons to society with an improved chance of being useful, law-abiding citizens." *Ibid.*

As I suggested at the outset, none of this has anything to do with this case, because no one contends that the State had those goals in mind when it permitted SOCF to become overcrowded. This dictum, moreover, takes far too limited a view of the proper role of a federal court in an Eighth Amendment proceeding and, I add with some regret, far too sanguine a view of the motivations of state legislators and prison officials. Too often, state governments truly are "insensitive to the requirements of the Eighth Amendment," as is evidenced by the repeated need for federal intervention to protect the rights of inmates. See, *e. g., Hutto v. Finney*, 437 U.S. 678, 98 S.Ct. 2565, 57 L.Ed.2d 522 (1978) (lengthy periods of punitive isolation); *Estelle v. Gamble*, 429 U.S. 97, 97 S.Ct. 285, 50 L.Ed.2d 251 (1976) (failure to treat inmate's medical needs); *Battle v. Anderson*, 564 F.2d 388 (CA10 1977) (severe overcrowding); *Gates v. Collier*, 501 F.2d 1291 (CA5 1974) (overcrowding and poor housing conditions); *Holt v. Sarver*, 442 F.2d 304 (CA8 1971) (unsafe conditions and inmate abuse); *Pugh v. Locke*, 406 F.Supp. 318 (MD Ala.1976) (constant fear of violence and physical harm), aff'd, 559 F.2d 283 (CA5 1977), rev'd in part on other grounds, 438 U.S. 781, 98 S.Ct. 3057, 57 L.Ed.2d 1114 (1978) (*per curiam*). See also *ante*, at 2402–2406 (BRENNAN, J., concurring in judgment).

A society must punish those who transgress its rules. When the offense is severe, the punishment should be of proportionate severity. But the punishment must always be administered within the limitations set down by the Constitution. With the rising crime rates of recent years, there has been an alarming tendency toward a simplistic penological philosophy that if we lock the prison doors and throw away the keys, our streets will somehow be safe. In the current climate, it is unrealistic to expect legislators to care whether the prisons are overcrowded or harmful to inmate health. It is at that point — when conditions are deplorable and the political process offers no redress — that the federal courts are required by the Constitution to play a role. I believe that this vital duty was properly discharged by the District Court and the Court of Appeals in this case. The majority today takes a step toward abandoning that role altogether. I dissent.

B. Police Training

Police tactics and training have been a dominant topic in the news and public discourse in recent history. The prevalence of video records showing brutal actions by police, the impact of systemic racism, and the growing awareness of corruption among individual police forces has resulted in widespread public outcries for criminal justice reform. Even when individual officers have broken the law and harmed or killed innocent people, reform has been avoided. The limits of municipal liability may be one reason why criminal justice reform has been delayed.

Canton v. Harris

489 U.S. 378 (1989)

Opinion

Justice WHITE delivered the opinion of the Court.

In this case, we are asked to determine if a municipality can ever be liable under 42 U.S.C. § 1983 for constitutional violations resulting from its failure to train municipal employees. We hold that, under certain circumstances, such liability is permitted by the statute.

I

In April 1978, respondent Geraldine Harris was arrested by officers of the Canton Police Department. Mrs. Harris was brought to the police station in a patrol wagon.

When she arrived at the station, Mrs. Harris was found sitting on the floor of the wagon. She was asked if she needed medical attention, and responded with an incoherent remark. After she was brought inside the station for processing, Mrs. Harris slumped to the floor on two occasions. Eventually, the police officers left Mrs. Harris lying on the floor to prevent her from falling again. No medical attention was ever summoned for Mrs. Harris. After about an hour, Mrs. Harris was released from custody, and taken by an ambulance (provided by her family) to a nearby hospital. There, Mrs. Harris was diagnosed as suffering from several emotional ailments; she was hospitalized for one week and received subsequent outpatient treatment for an additional year.

Some time later, Mrs. Harris commenced this action alleging many state-law and constitutional claims against the city of Canton and its officials. Among these claims was one seeking to hold the city liable under 42 U.S.C. § 1983 for its violation of Mrs. Harris' right, under the Due Process Clause of the Fourteenth Amendment, to receive necessary medical attention while in police custody.

A jury trial was held on Mrs. Harris' claims. Evidence was presented that indicated that, pursuant to a municipal regulation, shift commanders were authorized to determine, in their sole discretion, whether a detainee required medical care. In addition, testimony also suggested that Canton shift commanders were not provided with any special training (beyond first-aid training) to make a determination as to when to summon medical care for an injured detainee.

At the close of the evidence, the District Court submitted the case to the jury, which rejected all of Mrs. Harris' claims except one: her § 1983 claim against the city resulting from its failure to provide her with medical treatment while in custody. In rejecting the city's subsequent motion for judgment notwithstanding the verdict, the District Court explained the theory of liability as follows:

"The evidence construed in a manner most favorable to Mrs. Harris could be found by a jury to demonstrate that the City of Canton had a custom or policy of vesting complete authority with the police supervisor of when medical treatment would be administered to prisoners. Further, the jury could find from the evidence that the vesting of such *carte blanche* authority with the police supervisor without adequate training to recognize when medical treatment is needed was grossly negligent or so reckless that future police misconduct was almost inevitable or substantially certain to result." *Id.*, at 16a.

On appeal, the Sixth Circuit affirmed this aspect of the District Court's analysis, holding that "a municipality is liable for failure to train its police force, [where] the plaintiff ... prove[s] that the municipality acted recklessly, intentionally, or with gross negligence." *Id.*, at 5a. The Court of Appeals also stated that an additional prerequisite of this theory of liability was that the plaintiff must prove "that the lack of training was so reckless or grossly negligent that deprivations of persons' constitutional rights were substantially certain to result." *Ibid.* Thus, the Court of Appeals found that there had been no error in submitting Mrs. Harris' "failure to train" claim to the jury. However, the Court of Appeals reversed the judgment for respondent, and remanded this case for a new trial, because it found that certain aspects of the District Court's jury instructions might have led the jury to believe that it could find against the city on a mere *respondeat superior* theory. Because the jury's verdict did not state the basis on which it had ruled for Mrs. Harris on her § 1983 claim, a new trial was ordered.

The city petitioned for certiorari, arguing that the Sixth Circuit's holding represented an impermissible broadening of municipal liability under § 1983. We granted the petition. 485 U.S. 933, 108 S.Ct. 1105, 99 L.Ed.2d 267 (1988).

II

We first address respondent's contention that the writ of certiorari should be dismissed as improvidently granted, because "petitioner failed to preserve for review the principal issues it now argues in this Court."

We think it clear enough that petitioner's three "Questions Presented" in its petition for certiorari encompass the critical question before us in this case: Under what circumstances can inadequate training be found to be a "policy" that is actionable under § 1983? See Pet. for Cert. i. The petition itself addressed this issue directly, attacking the Sixth Circuit's "failure to train" theory as inconsistent with this Court's precedents. See *id.,* at 8–12. It is also clear—as respondent conceded at argument, that her brief in opposition to our granting of certiorari did not raise the objection that petitioner had failed to press its claims on the courts below.

As to respondent's contention that the claims made by petitioner here were not made in the same fashion below, that failure, if it occurred, does not affect our jurisdiction; and because respondent did not oppose our grant of review at that time based on her contention that these claims were not pressed below, we will not dismiss the writ as improvidently granted. "[T]he 'decision to grant certiorari represents a commitment of scarce judicial resources with a view to deciding the merits ... of the questions presented in the petition.'" *St. Louis v. Praprotnik,* 485 U.S. 112, 120, 108 S.Ct. 915, 922, 99 L.Ed.2d 107 (1988). As we have expressly admonished litigants in respondent's position: "Nonjurisdictional defects of this sort should be brought to our attention *no later* than in respondent's brief in opposition to the petition for certiorari; if not, we consider it within our discretion to deem the defect waived." *Tuttle, supra,* at 816, 105 S.Ct. at 2432.

It is true that petitioner's litigation posture with respect to the questions presented here has not been consistent; most importantly, petitioner conceded below that "'inadequate training' [is] a means of establishing municipal liability under Section 1983." However, at each stage in the proceedings below, petitioner contested any finding of liability on this ground, with objections of varying specificity. It opposed the District Court's jury instructions on this issue, Tr. 4-369; claimed in its judgment notwithstanding verdict motion that there was "no evidence of a ... policy or practice on the part of the City ... [of] den[ying] medical treatment to prisoners," Motion for Judgment Notwithstanding Verdict in No. C80-18-A (ND Ohio), p. 1; and argued to the Court of Appeals that there was no basis for finding a policy of denying medical treatment to prisoners in this case. See Brief for Appellant in No. 85-3314 (CA6), pp. 26–29. Indeed, petitioner specifically contended that the Sixth Circuit precedents that permitted inadequate training to be a basis for municipal liability on facts similar to these, were in conflict with our decision in *Tuttle*. These various presentations of the issues below might have been so inexact that we would have denied certiorari had this matter been brought to our attention at the appropriate stage in the proceedings. But they were at least adequate to yield a decision by the Sixth Circuit on the questions presented for our review now.

Here the Sixth Circuit held that where a plaintiff proves that a municipality, acting recklessly, intentionally, or with gross negligence, has failed to train its police force—resulting in a deprivation of constitutional rights that was "substantially certain to result"—§ 1983 permits that municipality to be held liable for its actions. Petitioner's petition for certiorari challenged the soundness of that conclusion, and respondent did not inform us prior to the time that review was granted that petitioner had arguably conceded this point below. Consequently, we will not abstain from addressing the question before us.

III

In *Monell v. New York City Dept. of Social Services*, 436 U.S. 658, 98 S.Ct. 2018, 56 L.Ed.2d 611 (1978), we decided that a municipality can be found liable under § 1983 only where the municipality *itself* causes the constitutional violation at issue. *Respondeat superior* or vicarious liability will not attach under § 1983. *Id.*, at 694–695, 98 S.Ct. at 2037–38. "It is only when the 'execution of the government's policy or custom ... inflicts the injury' that the municipality may be held liable under § 1983." *Springfield v. Kibbe*, 480 U.S. 257, 267, 107 S.Ct. 1114, 1119, 94 L.Ed.2d 293 (1987).

Thus, our first inquiry in any case alleging municipal liability under § 1983 is the question whether there is a direct causal link between a municipal policy or custom and the alleged constitutional deprivation. The inquiry is a difficult one; one that has left this Court deeply divided in a series of cases that have followed *Monell;* one that is the principal focus of our decision again today.

A

Based on the difficulty that this Court has had defining the contours of municipal liability in these circumstances, petitioner urges us to adopt the rule that a municipality can be found liable under § 1983 only where "the policy in question [is] itself unconstitutional." Whether such a rule is a valid construction of § 1983 is a question the Court has left unresolved. Under such an approach, the outcome here would be rather clear: we would have to reverse and remand the case with instructions that judgment be entered for petitioner. There can be little doubt that on its face the city's policy regarding medical treatment for detainees is constitutional. The policy states that the city jailer "shall ... have [a person needing medical care] taken to a hospital for medical treatment, with permission of his supervisor...." It is difficult to see what constitutional guarantees are violated by such a policy.

Nor, without more, would a city automatically be liable under § 1983 if one of its employees happened to apply the policy in an unconstitutional manner, for liability would then rest on *respondeat superior.* The claim in this case, however, is that if a concededly valid policy is unconstitutionally applied by a municipal employee, the city is liable if the employee has not been adequately trained and the constitutional wrong has been caused by that failure to train. For reasons explained below, we conclude, as have all the Courts of Appeals that have addressed this issue, that there are limited circumstances in which an allegation of a "failure to train" can be the basis for liability under § 1983. Thus, we reject petitioner's contention that only unconstitutional policies are actionable under the statute.

B

Though we agree with the court below that a city can be liable under § 1983 for inadequate training of its employees, we cannot agree that the District Court's jury instructions on this issue were proper, for we conclude that the Court of Appeals provided an overly broad rule for when a municipality can be held liable under the "failure to train" theory. Unlike the question whether a municipality's failure to train employees can ever be a basis for § 1983 liability—on which the Courts of Appeals have all agreed,—there is substantial division among the lower courts as to what *degree of fault* must be evidenced by the municipality's inaction before liability will be permitted. We hold today that the inadequacy of police training may serve as the basis for § 1983 liability only where the failure to train amounts to deliberate indifference to the rights of persons with whom the police come into contact. This rule is most consistent with our admonition in *Monell,* 436 U.S., at 694, 98 S.Ct., at 2037, and *Polk County v. Dodson,* 454 U.S. 312, 326, 102 S.Ct. 445, 454, 70 L.Ed.2d 509 (1981), that a municipality can be liable under § 1983 only where its policies are the "moving force [behind] the constitutional violation." Only where a municipality's failure to train its employees in a relevant respect evidences a "deliberate indifference" to the rights of its inhabitants can such a shortcoming be properly thought of as a city "policy or custom" that is actionable under § 1983. As Justice BRENNAN's opinion in *Pembaur v. Cincinnati,* 475 U.S. 469, 483–484, 106 S.Ct. 1292, 1300–1301, 89 L.Ed.2d 452 (1986) (plurality) put it: "[M]unicipal liability under § 1983 attaches where—and only where—a deliberate choice to follow a course of action is made from among various alternatives" by city policymakers. Only where a failure to train reflects a "deliberate" or "conscious" choice by a municipality—a "policy" as defined by our prior cases—can a city be liable for such a failure under § 1983.

Monell's rule that a city is not liable under § 1983 unless a municipal policy causes a constitutional deprivation will not be satisfied by merely alleging that the existing training program for a class of employees, such as police officers, represents a policy for which the city is responsible. That much may be true. The issue in a case like this one, however, is whether that training program is adequate; and if it is not, the question becomes whether such inadequate training can justifiably be said to represent "city policy." It may seem contrary to common sense to assert that a municipality will actually have a policy of not taking reasonable steps to train its employees. But it may happen that in light of the duties assigned to specific officers or employees the need for more or different training is so obvious, and the inadequacy so likely to result in the violation of constitutional rights, that the policymakers of the city can reasonably be said to have been deliberately indifferent to the need. In that event, the failure to provide proper training may fairly be said to represent a policy for which the city is responsible, and for which the city may be held liable if it actually causes injury.

In resolving the issue of a city's liability, the focus must be on adequacy of the training program in relation to the tasks the particular officers must perform. That a particular officer may be unsatisfactorily trained will not alone suffice to fasten liability on the city, for the officer's shortcomings may have resulted from factors other than a faulty training program. It may be, for example, that an otherwise sound program has occasionally been negligently administered. Neither will it suffice to prove that an injury or accident could have been avoided if an officer had had better or more training, sufficient to equip him to avoid the particular injury-causing conduct. Such a claim could be made about almost any encounter resulting in injury, yet not condemn the adequacy of the program to enable officers to respond properly to the usual and recurring situations with which they must deal. And plainly, adequately trained officers occasionally make mistakes; the fact that they do says little about the training program or the legal basis for holding the city liable.

Moreover, for liability to attach in this circumstance the identified deficiency in a city's training program must be closely related to the ultimate injury. Thus in the case at hand, respondent must still prove that the deficiency in training actually caused the police officers' indifference to her medical needs.12 Would the injury have been avoided had the employee been trained under a program that was not deficient in the identified respect? Predicting how a hypothetically well-trained officer would have acted under the circumstances may not be an easy task for the factfinder, particularly since matters of judgment may be involved, and since officers who are well trained are not free from error and perhaps might react very much like the untrained officer in similar circumstances. But judge and jury, doing their respective jobs, will be adequate to the task.

To adopt lesser standards of fault and causation would open municipalities to unprecedented liability under § 1983. In virtually every instance where a person has had his or her constitutional rights violated by a city employee, a § 1983 plaintiff will be able to point to something the city "could have done" to prevent the unfortunate incident. Thus, permitting cases against cities for their "failure to train" employees to go forward under § 1983 on a lesser standard of fault would result in *de facto respondeat superior* liability on municipalities—a result we rejected in *Monell*, 436 U.S., at 693– 694, 98 S.Ct., at 2037. It would also engage the federal courts in an endless exercise of second-guessing municipal employee-training programs. This is an exercise we believe the federal courts are ill suited to undertake, as well as one that would implicate serious questions of federalism.

Consequently, while claims such as respondent's—alleging that the city's failure to provide training to municipal employees resulted in the constitutional deprivation she suffered—are cognizable under § 1983, they can only yield liability against a municipality where that city's failure to train reflects deliberate indifference to the constitutional rights of its inhabitants.

IV

The final question here is whether this case should be remanded for a new trial, or whether, as petitioner suggests, we should conclude that there are no possible grounds on which respondent can prevail. It is true that the evidence in the record now does not meet the standard of § 1983 liability we have set forth above. But, the standard of proof the District Court ultimately imposed on respondent (which was consistent with Sixth Circuit precedent) was a lesser one than the one we adopt today. Whether respondent should have an opportunity to prove her case under the "deliberate indifference" rule we have adopted is a matter for the Court of Appeals to deal with on remand.

Consequently, for the reasons given above, we vacate the judgment of the Court of Appeals and remand this case for further proceedings consistent with this opinion.

It is so ordered.

C. Qualified Immunity

The U.S. Constitution secures individual rights that limit governments and protect individuals. These include a right to be free from unreasonable searches (Fourth Amendment) ensure due process (Fifth Amendment), and protect against unduly harsh punishment, use of force, or conditions of confinement (Eighth Amendment). These rights were first articulated as limits on the Federal government and later applied to the state governments following the Civil War through passage of the Fourteenth Amendment in 1870.

As one might imagine, the officers, wardens, and officials who administer the U.S. criminal justice system are often sued in cases alleging violations of a right protected the U.S. Constitution. This can happen when the police arrest someone they think may have been involved in a crime and an injury results from the arrest. Earlier, in Part Two, 42 U.S.C. § 1983 was introduced, along with a description of how the Civil Rights Act can be used to hold government officials responsible for violating an individual's rights. 42 U.S.C. § 1983 also allows an agent of government to be sued for violating a person's right to be free from unlawful search and seizure; to enjoy a life without torture or excessive force, and to be treated equally under the law. At the same time, it would be extremely difficult for police officers to perform their jobs if they lived in constant fear of being sued and held personally responsible for any losses. The doctrine of qualified immunity addresses this issue.

Qualified immunity is a judicially created doctrine that protects officers, wardens, jailers, and others from civil liability. The doctrine of qualified immunity protects "government officials from liability for civil damages insofar as their conduct does not violate clearly established statutory or constitutional rights." *Pearson v. Callahan*, 555 U.S. 223, 229 (2009). There are other immunities, such as those given to judges and the President of the United States, but these are not used as regularly as qualified immunity. One can see the need for a doctrine such as qualified immunity because it balances the need for official accountability with the need to enable officials to perform their duties without fear of being held personally liable as a result. Of course, no one would expect the doctrine to allow officials to get away with any harm they might cause. Indeed, qualified immunity does not protect an official "if the official knew or reasonably should have known that the action he took within his sphere of official responsibility would violate the constitutional rights of the plaintiff." *Harlow v. Fitzgerald*, 457 U.S. 800, 812.

The two cases that follow explore the application of qualified immunity in the criminal justice system.

Mullenix v. Luna

136 S. Ct. 305 (2015)

PER CURIAM.

On the night of March 23, 2010, Sergeant Randy Baker of the Tulia, Texas Police Department followed Israel Leija, Jr., to a drive-in restaurant, with a warrant for his arrest. When Baker approached Leija's car and informed him that he was under arrest, Leija sped off, headed for Interstate 27. Baker gave chase and was quickly joined by Trooper Gabriel Rodriguez of the Texas Department of Public Safety (DPS). 773 F.3d, at 716.

Leija entered the interstate and led the officers on an 18-minute chase at speeds between 85 and 110 miles per hour. *Ibid.* Twice during the chase, Leija called the Tulia Police dispatcher, claiming to have a gun and threatening to shoot at police officers if they did not abandon their pursuit. The dispatcher relayed Leija's threats, together with a report that Leija might be intoxicated, to all concerned officers.

As Baker and Rodriguez maintained their pursuit, other law enforcement officers set up tire spikes at three locations. Officer Troy Ducheneaux of the Canyon Police Department manned the spike strip at the first location Leija was expected to reach, beneath the overpass at Cemetery Road. Ducheneaux and the other officers had received training on the deployment of spike strips, including on how to take a defensive position so as to minimize the risk posed by the passing driver. *Ibid.*

DPS Trooper Chadrin Mullenix also responded. He drove to the Cemetery Road overpass, initially intending to set up a spike strip there. Upon learning of the other spike strip positions, however, Mullenix began to consider another tactic: shooting at Leija's car in order to disable it. Mullenix had not received training in this tactic and had not attempted it before, but he radioed the idea to Rodriguez. Rodriguez responded "10-4," gave Mullenix his position, and said that Leija had slowed to 85 miles per hour. Mullenix then asked the DPS dispatcher to inform his supervisor, Sergeant Byrd, of his plan and ask if Byrd thought it was "worth doing." 773 F.3d, at 716–717. Before receiving Byrd's response, Mullenix exited his vehicle and, armed with his service rifle, took a shooting position on the overpass, 20 feet above I-27. Respondents allege that from this position, Mullenix still could hear Byrd's response to "stand by" and "see if the spikes work first." *Ibid.* *

As Mullenix waited for Leija to arrive, he and another officer, Randall County Sheriff's Deputy Tom Shipman, discussed whether Mullenix's plan would work and how and where to shoot the vehicle to best carry it out. Shipman also informed Mullenix that another officer was located beneath the overpass.

Approximately three minutes after Mullenix took up his shooting position, he spotted Leija's vehicle, with Rodriguez in pursuit. As Leija approached the overpass, Mullenix fired six shots. Leija's car continued forward beneath the overpass, where it engaged the spike strip, hit the median, and rolled two and a half times. It was later determined that Leija had been killed by Mullenix's shots, four of which struck his upper body. There was no evidence that any of Mullenix's shots hit the car's radiator, hood, or engine block.

Respondents sued Mullenix under Rev. Stat. § 1979, 42 U.S.C. § 1983, alleging that he had violated the Fourth Amendment by using excessive force against Leija. Mullenix moved for summary judgment on the ground of qualified immunity, but the District Court denied his motion, finding that "[t]here are genuine issues of fact as to whether Trooper Mullenix acted recklessly, or acted as a reasonable, trained peace officer would have acted in the same or similar circumstances."

Mullenix appealed, and the Court of Appeals for the Fifth Circuit affirmed. The court agreed with the District Court that the "immediacy of the risk posed by Leija is a disputed fact that a reasonable jury could find either in the plaintiffs' favor or in the officer's favor, precluding us from concluding that Mullenix acted objectively reasonably as a matter of law."

Judge King dissented. She described the "'fact issue' referenced by the majority" as "simply a restatement of the objective reasonableness test that applies to Fourth Amendment excessive force claims," which, she noted, the Supreme Court has held "'is a pure question of law.'" (quoting *Scott v. Harris*, 550 U.S. 372, 381, n. 8, 127 S.Ct. 1769, 167 L.Ed.2d 686 (2007)). Turning to that legal question, Judge King concluded that Mullenix's actions were objectively reasonable. When Mullenix fired, she emphasized, he knew not only that Leija had threatened to shoot the officers involved in his pursuit, but also that Leija was seconds away from encountering such an officer beneath the overpass. Judge King also dismissed the notion that Mullenix should have given the spike strips a chance to work. She explained that because spike strips are often ineffective, and because officers operating them are vulnerable to gunfire from passing cars, Mullenix reasonably feared that the officers manning them faced a significant risk of harm.

Mullenix sought rehearing en banc before the Fifth Circuit, but the court denied his petition. Judge Jolly dissented, joined by six other members of the court. Judge King, who joined Judge Jolly's dissent, also filed a separate dissent of her own. 777 F.3d 221 (2014) (*per curiam*). On the same day, however, the two members forming the original panel's majority withdrew their previous opinion and substituted a new one. The revised opinion recognized that objective unreasonableness is a question of law that can be resolved on summary judgment—as Judge King had explained in her dissent—but reaffirmed the denial of qualified immunity. The majority concluded that Mullenix's actions were objectively unreasonable because several of the factors that had justified deadly force in previous cases were absent here: There were no innocent bystanders, Leija's driving was relatively controlled, Mullenix had not first given the spike strips a chance to work, and Mullenix's decision was not a split-second judgment. The court went on to conclude that Mullenix was not entitled to qualified immunity because "the law was clearly established such that a reasonable officer would have known that the use of deadly force, absent a sufficiently substantial and immediate threat, violated the Fourth Amendment."

We address only the qualified immunity question, not whether there was a Fourth Amendment violation in the first place, and now reverse.

The doctrine of qualified immunity shields officials from civil liability so long as their conduct " 'does not violate clearly established statutory or constitutional rights of which a reasonable person would have known.' " *Pearson v. Callahan*, 555 U.S. 223, 231, 129 S.Ct. 808, 172 L.Ed.2d 565 (2009) (quoting *Harlow v. Fitzgerald*, 457 U.S. 800, 818, 102 S.Ct. 2727, 73 L.Ed.2d 396 (1982)). A clearly established right is one that is "sufficiently clear that every reasonable official would have understood that what he is doing violates that right." *Reichle v. Howards*, 566 U.S. ___, ___, 132 S.Ct. 2088, 2093, 182 L.Ed.2d 985 (2012) (internal quotation marks and alteration omitted). "We do not require a case directly on point, but existing precedent must have placed the statutory or constitutional question beyond debate." *Ashcroft v. al-Kidd*, 563 U.S. 731, 741, 131 S.Ct. 2074, 179 L.Ed.2d 1149 (2011). Put simply, qualified immunity protects "all but the plainly incompetent or those who knowingly violate the law." *Malley v. Briggs*, 475 U.S. 335, 341, 106 S.Ct. 1092, 89 L.Ed.2d 271 (1986).

"We have repeatedly told courts ... not to define clearly established law at a high level of generality." *al-Kidd, supra*, at 742, 131 S.Ct. 2074. The dispositive question is "whether the violative nature of *particular* conduct is clearly established." *Ibid.* (emphasis added). This inquiry " 'must be undertaken in light of the specific context of the case, not as a broad general proposition.' " *Brosseau v. Haugen*, 543 U.S. 194, 198, 125 S.Ct. 596, 160 L.Ed.2d 583 (2004) (*per curiam*) (quoting *Saucier v. Katz*, 533 U.S. 194, 201, 121 S.Ct. 2151, 150 L.Ed.2d 272 (2001)). Such specificity is especially important in the Fourth Amendment context, where the Court has recognized that "[i]t is sometimes difficult for an officer to determine how the relevant legal doctrine, here excessive force, will apply to the factual situation the officer confronts." 533 U.S., at 205, 121 S.Ct. 2151.

In this case, the Fifth Circuit held that Mullenix violated the clearly established rule that a police officer may not "'use deadly force against a fleeing felon who does not pose a sufficient threat of harm to the officer or others.'" 773 F.3d, at 725. Yet this Court has previously considered—and rejected—almost that exact formulation of the qualified immunity question in the Fourth Amendment context. In *Brosseau*, which also involved the shooting of a suspect fleeing by car, the Ninth Circuit denied qualified immunity on the ground that the officer had violated the clearly established rule, set forth in *Tennessee v. Garner*, 471 U.S. 1, 105 S.Ct. 1694, 85 L.Ed.2d 1 (1985), that "deadly force is only permissible where the officer has probable cause to believe that the suspect poses a threat of serious physical harm, either to the officer or to others." *Haugen v. Brosseau*, 339 F.3d 857, 873 (C.A.9 2003) (internal quotation marks omitted). This Court summarily reversed, holding that use of *Garner*'s "general" test for excessive force was "mistaken." *Brosseau*, 543 U.S., at 199, 125 S.Ct. 596. The correct inquiry, the Court explained, was whether it was clearly established that the Fourth Amendment prohibited the officer's conduct in the "'situation [she] confronted': whether to shoot a disturbed felon, set on avoiding capture through vehicular flight, when persons in the immediate area are at risk from that flight." *Id.*, at 199–200, 125 S.Ct. 596. The Court considered three court of appeals cases discussed by the parties, noted that "this area is one in which the result depends very much on the facts of each case," and concluded that the officer was entitled to qualified immunity because "[n]one of [the cases] *squarely governs* the case here." *Id.*, at 201, 125 S.Ct. 596 (emphasis added).

Anderson v. Creighton, 483 U.S. 635, 107 S.Ct. 3034, 97 L.Ed.2d 523 (1987), is also instructive on the required degree of specificity. There, the lower court had denied qualified immunity based on the clearly established "right to be free from warrantless searches of one's home unless the searching officers have probable cause and there are exigent circumstances." *Id.*, at 640, 107 S.Ct. 3034. This Court faulted that formulation for failing to address the actual question at issue: whether "the circumstances with which Anderson was confronted ... constitute[d] probable cause and exigent circumstances." *Id.*, at 640–641, 107 S.Ct. 3034. Without answering that question, the Court explained, the conclusion that Anderson's search was objectively unreasonable did not "follow immediately" from—and thus was not clearly established by—the principle that warrantless searches not supported by probable cause and exigent circumstances violate the Fourth Amendment. *Id.*, at 641, 107 S.Ct. 3034.

In this case, Mullenix confronted a reportedly intoxicated fugitive, set on avoiding capture through high-speed vehicular flight, who twice during his flight had threatened to shoot police officers, and who was moments away from encountering an officer at Cemetery Road. The relevant inquiry is whether existing precedent placed the conclusion that Mullenix acted unreasonably in these circumstances "beyond debate." *al-Kidd, supra*, at 741, 131 S.Ct. 2074. The general principle that deadly force requires a sufficient threat hardly settles this matter. See *Pasco v. Knoblauch*, 566 F.3d 572, 580 (C.A.5 2009) ("[I]t would be unreasonable to expect a police officer to make the numerous legal conclusions necessary to apply *Garner* to a high-speed car chase ...").

Far from clarifying the issue, excessive force cases involving car chases reveal the hazy legal backdrop against which Mullenix acted. In *Brosseau* itself, the Court held that an officer did not violate clearly established law when she shot a fleeing suspect out of fear that he endangered "other officers on foot who [she] *believed* were in the immediate area," "the occupied vehicles in [his] path," and "any other citizens who *might* be in the area." 543 U.S., at 197, 125 S.Ct. 596 (first alteration in original; internal quotation marks omitted; emphasis added). The threat Leija posed was at least as immediate as that presented by a suspect who had just begun to drive off and was headed only in the general direction of officers and bystanders. *Id.,* at 196–197, 125 S.Ct. 596. By the time Mullenix fired, Leija had led police on a 25-mile chase at extremely high speeds, was reportedly intoxicated, had twice threatened to shoot officers, and was racing towards an officer's location.

This Court has considered excessive force claims in connection with high-speed chases on only two occasions since *Brosseau*. In *Scott v. Harris,* 550 U.S. 372, 127 S.Ct. 1769, the Court held that an officer did not violate the Fourth Amendment by ramming the car of a fugitive whose reckless driving "posed an actual and imminent threat to the lives of any pedestrians who might have been present, to other civilian motorists, and to the officers involved in the chase." *Id.,* at 384, 127 S.Ct. 1769. And in *Plumhoff v. Rickard,* 572 U.S. ___, 134 S.Ct. 2012, 188 L.Ed.2d 1056 (2014), the Court reaffirmed *Scott* by holding that an officer acted reasonably when he fatally shot a fugitive who was "intent on resuming" a chase that "pose[d] a deadly threat for others on the road." 572 U.S., at ___, 134 S.Ct., at 2022. The Court has thus never found the use of deadly force in connection with a dangerous car chase to violate the Fourth Amendment, let alone to be a basis for denying qualified immunity. Leija in his flight did not pass as many cars as the drivers in *Scott* or *Plumhoff*; traffic was light on I-27. At the same time, the fleeing fugitives in *Scott* and *Plumhoff* had not verbally threatened to kill any officers in their path, nor were they about to come upon such officers. In any event, none of our precedents "squarely governs" the facts here. Given Leija's conduct, we cannot say that only someone "plainly incompetent" or who "knowingly violate[s] the law" would have perceived a sufficient threat and acted as Mullenix did. *Malley,* 475 U.S., at 341, 106 S.Ct. 1092.

The dissent focuses on the availability of spike strips as an alternative means of terminating the chase. It argues that even if Leija posed a threat sufficient to justify deadly force in some circumstances, Mullenix nevertheless contravened clearly established law because he did not wait to see if the spike strips would work before taking action. Spike strips, however, present dangers of their own, not only to drivers who encounter them at speeds between 85 and 110 miles per hour, but also to officers manning them. See, *e.g., Thompson v. Mercer,* 762 F.3d 433, 440 (C.A.5 2014); Brief for National Association of Police Organizations et al. as *Amici Curiae* 15–16. Nor are spike strips always successful in ending the chase. See, *e.g., Cordova v. Aragon,* 569 F.3d 1183, 1186 (C.A.10 2009); Brief for National Association of Police Organizations et al. as *Amici Curiae* 16 (citing examples). The dissent can cite no case from this Court denying qualified immunity because officers entitled to terminate a high-speed chase selected one dangerous alternative over another.

Even so, the dissent argues, there was no governmental interest that justified acting before Leija's car hit the spikes. Mullenix explained, however, that he feared Leija might attempt to shoot at or run over the officers manning the spike strips. Mullenix also feared that even if Leija hit the spike strips, he might still be able to continue driving in the direction of other officers. The dissent ignores these interests by suggesting that there was no "possible marginal gain in shooting at the car over using the spike strips already in place." *Post*, at 315 (opinion of SOTOMAYOR, J.). In fact, Mullenix hoped his actions would stop the car in a manner that avoided the risks to other officers and other drivers that relying on spike strips would entail. The dissent disputes the merits of the options available to Mullenix, *post*, at 314–315, but others with more experience analyze the issues differently. See, *e.g.*, Brief for National Association of Police Organizations et al. as *Amici Curiae* 15–16. Ultimately, whatever can be said of the wisdom of Mullenix's choice, this Court's precedents do not place the conclusion that he acted unreasonably in these circumstances "beyond debate." *al-Kidd*, 563 U.S., at 741, 131 S.Ct. 2074.

More fundamentally, the dissent repeats the Fifth Circuit's error. It defines the qualified immunity inquiry at a high level of generality—whether any governmental interest justified choosing one tactic over another—and then fails to consider that question in "the specific context of the case." *Brosseau v. Haugen*, 543 U.S., at 198, 125 S.Ct. 596 (internal quotation marks omitted). As in *Anderson*, the conclusion that Mullenix's reasons were insufficient to justify his actions simply does not "follow immediately" from the general proposition that force must be justified. 483 U.S., at 641, 107 S.Ct. 3034.

Cases decided by the lower courts since *Brosseau* likewise have not clearly established that deadly force is inappropriate in response to conduct like Leija's. The Fifth Circuit here principally relied on its own decision in *Lytle v. Bexar County*, 560 F.3d 404 (2009), denying qualified immunity to a police officer who had fired at a fleeing car and killed one of its passengers. That holding turned on the court's assumption, for purposes of summary judgment, that the car was moving away from the officer and had already traveled some distance at the moment the officer fired. See *id.*, at 409. The court held that a reasonable jury could conclude that a receding car "did not pose a sufficient threat of harm such that the use of deadly force was reasonable." *Id.*, at 416. But, crucially, the court also recognized that if the facts were as the officer alleged, and he fired as the car was coming towards him, "he would likely be entitled to qualified immunity" based on the "threat of immediate and severe physical harm." *Id.*, at 412. Without implying that *Lytle* was either correct or incorrect, it suffices to say that *Lytle* does not clearly dictate the conclusion that Mullenix was unjustified in perceiving grave danger and responding accordingly, given that Leija was speeding towards a confrontation with officers he had threatened to kill.

Cases that the Fifth Circuit ignored also suggest that Mullenix's assessment of the threat Leija posed was reasonable. In *Long v. Slaton*, 508 F.3d 576 (2007), for example, the Eleventh Circuit held that a sheriff's deputy did not violate the Fourth Amendment by fatally shooting a mentally unstable individual who was attempting to flee in the deputy's car, even though at the time of the shooting the individual had not yet operated the cruiser dangerously. The court explained that "the law does not require officers in a tense and dangerous situation to wait until the moment a suspect uses a deadly weapon to act to stop the suspect" and concluded that the deputy had reason to believe Long was dangerous based on his unstable state of mind, theft of the cruiser, and failure to heed the deputy's warning to stop. *Id.*, at 581–582. The court also rejected the notion that the deputy should have first tried less lethal methods, such as spike strips. "[C]onsidering the unpredictability of Long's behavior and his fleeing in a marked police cruiser," the court held, "we think the police need not have taken that chance and hoped for the best." *Id.*, at 583 (alteration and internal quotation marks omitted). But see *Smith v. Cupp*, 430 F.3d 766, 774–777 (C.A.6 2005) (denying qualified immunity to an officer who shot an intoxicated suspect who had stolen the officer's cruiser where a reasonable jury could have concluded that the suspect's flight did not immediately threaten the officer or any other bystander).

Other cases cited by the Fifth Circuit and respondents are simply too factually distinct to speak clearly to the specific circumstances here. Several involve suspects who may have done little more than flee at relatively low speeds. See, *e.g., Walker v. Davis*, 649 F.3d 502, 503 (C.A.6 2011); *Kirby v. Duva*, 530 F.3d 475, 479–480 (C.A.6 2008); *Adams v. Speers*, 473 F.3d 989, 991 (C.A.9 2007); *Vaughan v. Cox*, 343 F.3d 1323, 1330–1331, and n. 7 (C.A.11 2003). These cases shed little light on whether the far greater danger of a speeding fugitive threatening to kill police officers waiting in his path could warrant deadly force. The court below noted that "no weapon was ever seen," 773 F.3d, at 723, but surely in these circumstances the police were justified in taking Leija at his word when he twice told the dispatcher he had a gun and was prepared to use it.

Finally, respondents argue that the danger Leija represented was less substantial than the threats that courts have found sufficient to justify deadly force. But the mere fact that courts have approved deadly force in more extreme circumstances says little, if anything, about whether such force was reasonable in the circumstances here. The fact is that when Mullenix fired, he reasonably understood Leija to be a fugitive fleeing arrest, at speeds over 100 miles per hour, who was armed and possibly intoxicated, who had threatened to kill any officer he saw if the police did not abandon their pursuit, and who was racing towards Officer Ducheneaux's position. Even accepting that these circumstances fall somewhere between the two sets of cases respondents discuss, qualified immunity protects actions in the "'hazy border between excessive and acceptable force.'" *Brosseau, supra*, at 201, 125 S.Ct. 596.

Because the constitutional rule applied by the Fifth Circuit was not "'beyond debate,'" *Stanton v. Sims*, 571 U.S. ___, ___, 134 S.Ct. 3, 7, 187 L.Ed.2d 341 (2013) (*per curiam*), we grant Mullenix's petition for certiorari and reverse the Fifth Circuit's determination that Mullenix is not entitled to qualified immunity.

It is so ordered.

Richardson v. McKnight

521 U.S. 399 (1997)

The issue before us is whether prison guards who are employees of a private prison management firm are entitled to a qualified immunity from suit by prisoners charging a violation of 42 U.S.C. § 1983. We hold that they are not.

Ronnie Lee McKnight, a prisoner at Tennessee's South Central Correctional Center (SCCC), brought this federal constitutional tort action against two prison guards, Darryl Richardson and John Walker. He says the guards injured him by placing upon him extremely tight physical restraints, thereby unlawfully "subject[ing]" him "to the deprivation of" a right "secured by the Constitution" of the United States. Rev. Stat. § 1979, 42 U.S.C. § 1983. Richardson and Walker asserted a qualified immunity from § 1983 lawsuits, and moved to dismiss the action. The District Court noted that Tennessee had "privatized" the management of a number of its correctional facilities, and that consequently a private firm, not the state government, employed the guards. See Tenn.Code Ann. § 41-24-101 *et seq.* (1990 and Supp.1996). The court held that, because they worked for a private company rather than the government, the law did not grant the guards immunity from suit. It therefore denied the guards' motion to dismiss. The guards appealed to the Sixth Circuit. See *Mitchell v. Forsyth,* 472 U.S. 511, 530, 105 S.Ct. 2806, 2817–2818, 86 L.Ed.2d 411 (1985) (permitting interlocutory appeals of qualified immunity determinations); see also *Johnson v. Jones,* 515 U.S. 304, 115 S.Ct. 2151, 132 L.Ed.2d 238 (1995); *Behrens v. Pelletier,* 516 U.S. 299, 116 S.Ct. 834, 133 L.Ed.2d 773 (1996). That court also ruled against them. *McKnight v. Rees,* 88 F.3d 417, 425 (C.A.6 1996). The Court of Appeals conceded that other courts had reached varying conclusions about whether, or the extent to which, private sector defendants are entitled to immunities of the sort the law provides governmental defendants. See, *e.g., Eagon v. Elk City,* 72 F.3d 1480, 1489–1490 (C.A.10 1996); *Williams v. O'Leary,* 55 F.3d 320, 323–324 (C.A.7), cert. denied, 516 U.S. 993, 116 S.Ct. 527, 133 L.Ed.2d 434 (1995); *Frazier v. Bailey,* 957 F.2d 920, 928–929 (C.A.1 1992). But the court concluded, primarily for reasons of "public policy," that the privately employed prison guards were not entitled to the immunity provided their governmental counterparts. We granted certiorari to review this holding. We now affirm.

We take the Court's recent case, *Wyatt v. Cole,* 504 U.S. 158, 112 S.Ct. 1827, 118 L.Ed.2d 504 (1992), as pertinent authority. The Court there considered whether private defendants, charged with § 1983 liability for "invoking state replevin, garnishment, and attachment statutes" later declared unconstitutional were "entitled to qualified immunity from suit." *Id.,* at 159, 112 S.Ct., at 1827. It held that they were not. *Id.,* at 169, 112 S.Ct., at 1834. We find four aspects of *Wyatt* relevant here.

First, as *Wyatt* noted, § 1983 basically seeks "to deter *state* actors from using the badge of their authority to deprive individuals of their federally guaranteed rights" and to provide related relief. *Id.,* at 161, 112 S.Ct., at 1829–1830 (emphasis added) (citing *Carey v. Piphus,* 435 U.S. 247, 254–257, 98 S.Ct. 1042, 1047–1049, 55 L.Ed.2d 252 (1978)); see also *Owen v. Independence,* 445 U.S. 622, 654, 100 S.Ct. 1398, 1417,

63 L.Ed.2d 673 (1980). It imposes liability only where a person acts "under color" of a state "statute, ordinance, regulation, custom, or usage." 42 U.S.C. § 1983. Nonetheless, *Wyatt* reaffirmed that § 1983 can *sometimes* impose liability upon a private individual. 504 U.S., at 162, 112 S.Ct., at 1830; see also *Lugar v. Edmondson Oil Co.,* 457 U.S. 922, 924, 102 S.Ct. 2744, 2746–2747, 73 L.Ed.2d 482 (1982).

Second, *Wyatt* reiterated that after *Harlow, supra,* and this Court's reformulation of the qualified immunity doctrine, see *Anderson v. Creighton,* 483 U.S. 635, 645, 107 S.Ct. 3034, 3042, 97 L.Ed.2d 523 (1987), a distinction exists between an "immunity from suit" and other kinds of legal defenses. 504 U.S., at 166–167, 112 S.Ct., at 1832–1833; see also *Mitchell, supra,* at 526, 105 S.Ct., at 2815–2816. As the *Wyatt* concurrence pointed out, a legal defense may well involve "the essence of the wrong," while an immunity frees one who enjoys it from a lawsuit whether or not he acted wrongly. 504 U.S., at 171–172, 112 S.Ct., at 18351836 (Kennedy, J., concurring).

Third, *Wyatt* specified the legal source of § 1983 immunities. It pointed out that although § 1983 "creates a species of tort liability that on its face admits of no immunities," *id.,* at 163, 112 S.Ct., at 1831 (quoting *Imbler v. Pachtman,* 424 U.S. 409, 417, 96 S.Ct. 984, 989–990, 47 L.Ed.2d 128 (1976)), this Court has nonetheless accorded immunity where a tradition of immunity was so firmly rooted in the common law and was supported by such strong policy reasons that "Congress would have specifically so provided had it wished to abolish the doctrine." 504 U.S., at 164, 112 S.Ct., at 1831 (quoting *Owen v. Independence, supra,* at 637, 100 S.Ct., at 1408–1409).

Wyatt majority, in deciding whether or not the private defendants enjoyed immunity, looked both to history and to "the special policy concerns involved in suing government officials." 504 U.S., at 167, 112 S.Ct., at 1833; see also *Mitchell, supra,* at 526, 105 S.Ct., at 2815–2816; *Harlow, supra,* at 807, 102 S.Ct., at 2732; *Imbler v. Pachtman, supra,* at 424, 96 S.Ct., at 992. And in this respect—the relevant *sources* of the law—both the *Wyatt* concurrence and the dissent seemed to agree. Compare 504 U.S., at 169–171, 112 S.Ct., at 1834–1835 (KENNEDY, J., concurring) (existence of immunity depends upon "historical origins" and "public policy"), with *id.,* at 175–176, 112 S.Ct., at 1837–1838 (REHNQUIST, C.J., dissenting) ("immunity" recognized where "similarly situated defendant would have enjoyed an immunity at common law" or "when important public policy concerns suggest the need for an immunity").

Fourth, *Wyatt* did not consider its answer to the question before it as one applicable to *all* private individuals—irrespective of the nature of their relation to the government, position, or the kind of liability at issue. Rather, *Wyatt* explicitly limited its holding to what it called a "narrow" question about "private persons ... who conspire with state officials," *id.,* at 168, 112 S.Ct., at 1834, and it answered that question by stating that private defendants "faced with § 1983 liability for invoking a state replevin, garnishment, or attachment statute" are *not* entitled to immunity, *id.,* at 168–169, 112 S.Ct., at 1833–1834.

Wyatt, then, did not answer the legal question before us, whether petitioners—
two employees of a private prison management firm—enjoy a qualified immunity
from suit under § 1983. It does tell us, however, to look both to history and to the
purposes that underlie government employee immunity in order to find the answer.

History does *not* reveal a "firmly rooted" tradition of immunity applicable to privately employed prison guards. Correctional services in the United States have un-
dergone various transformations. See D. Shichor, Punishment for Profit 33, 36 (1995)
(Shichor). *Government*-employed prison guards may have enjoyed a kind of immunity
defense arising out of their status as public employees at common law. See *Procunier
v. Navarette*, 434 U.S. 555, 561–562, 98 S.Ct. 855, 859–860, 55 L.Ed.2d 24 (1978)
(extending qualified immunity to state prison guards). But correctional functions
have never been exclusively public. Shichor 33, 36. Private individuals operated local
jails in the 18th century, G. Bowman, S. Hakim, & P. Seidenstat, Privatizing the
United States Justice System 271, n. 1 (1992), and private contractors were heavily
involved in prison management during the 19th century. Shichor 33, 36.

During that time, some States, including southern States like Tennessee, leased
their entire prison systems to private individuals or companies which frequently took
complete control over prison management, including inmate labor and discipline.
G. Bowman, S. Hakim, & P. Seidenstat, Privatizing Correctional Institutions 42
(1993); see generally B. McKelvey, American Prisons: A Study in American Social
History Prior to 1915, pp. 172–180 (1968) (describing 19th-century American prison
system); see also Shichor 34; G. de Beaumont & A. de Tocqueville, On the Penitentiary
System in the United States and Its Application in France 35 (1833) (describing more
limited prison contracting system in Massachusetts and Pennsylvania). Private prison
lease agreements (like inmate suits) seem to have been more prevalent after § 1983's
enactment, see generally M. Mancini, One Dies, Get Another (1996), but we have
found evidence that the common law provided mistreated prisoners in prison leasing
States with remedies against mistreatment by those private lessors. See, *e.g., Dade
Coal Co. v. Haslett*, 83 Ga. 549, 550–551, 10 S.E. 435, 435–436 (1889) (convict can
recover from contractor for injuries sustained while on lease to private company);
Boswell v. Barnhart, 96 Ga. 521, 522–523, 23 S.E. 414, 415 (1895) (wife can recover
from contractor for chain-gang-related death of husband); *Dalheim v. Lemon*, 45 F.
225, 228–230 (1891) (contractor liable for convict injuries); *Tillar v. Reynolds*, 96
Ark. 358, 360–361, 365–366, 131 S.W. 969, 970, 971–972 (1910) (work farm owner
liable for inmate beating death); *Weigel v. Brown*, 194 F. 652 (C.A.8 1912) (prison
contractor liable for unlawful whipping); see also *Edwards v. Pocahontas*, 47 F. 268
(CC Va. 1891) (inmate can recover from municipal corporation for injuries caused
by poor jail conditions); *Hall v. O'Neil Turpentine Co.*, 56 Fla. 324, 47 So. 609 (1908)
(private prison contractor and subcontractor liable to municipality for escaped prisoner under lease agreement); see generally Mancini, *supra* (discussing abuses of 19th-
century private lease system). Yet, we have found no evidence that the law gave purely
private companies or their employees any special immunity from such suits. Cf. *Al-
mango v. Board of Supervisors of Albany County*, 32 N.Y.Sup.Ct. 551 (1881) (no cause

of action against private contractor where contractor designated state instrumentality by statute). The case on which the dissent rests its argument, *Williams v. Adams*, 85 Mass. 171 (1861) (which could not — without more — prove the existence of such a tradition and does not, moreover, clearly involve a private prison operator) actually supports our point. It suggests that no immunity from suit would exist for the type of intentional conduct at issue in this case. See *ibid.* (were "battery" at issue, the case would be of a different "character" and "the defendant might be responsible"); see *id.*, at 176 (making clear that case only involves claim of ordinary negligence for lack of heat and other items, not "gross negligence," "implied malice," or "intention to do the prisoner any bodily injury"); cf. *Tower v. Glover*, 467 U.S. 914, 921, 104 S.Ct. 2820, 2825, 81 L.Ed.2d 758 (1984) (concluding that state public defenders do not enjoy immunity from suit where conduct intentional and no history of immunity for intentional conduct was established).

Correctional functions in England have been more consistently public, see generally 22 Encyclopedia Brittanica [sic], "Prison" 361–368 (11th ed.1911); S. Webb & B. Webb, English Prisons Under Local Government (1922) (Webb), but historical sources indicate that England relied upon private jailers to manage the detention of prisoners from the Middle Ages until well into the 18th century. Shichor 21; see also Webb 4–5; 1 E. Coke, Institutes 43 (1797). The common law forbade those jailers to subject "'their prisoners to any pain or torment,'" whether through harsh confinement in leg irons, or otherwise. See *In re Birdsong*, 39 F. 599, 601 (S.D.Ga.1889); 1 Coke, *supra*, at 315, 316, 381; 2 C. Addison, A Treatise on the Law of Torts § 1016, pp. 224–225 (1876); see also 4 Geo. IV, ch. 64, § X Twelfth. And it apparently authorized prisoner lawsuits to recover damages. 2 Addison, *supra*, § 1016. Apparently, the law *did* provide a kind of immunity for certain private defendants, such as doctors or lawyers who performed services at the behest of the sovereign. See *Tower, supra*, at 921, 104 S.Ct., at 2825; J. Bishop, Commentaries on Non-Contract Law §§ 704, 710 (1889). But we have found no indication of any more general immunity that might have applied to private individuals working for profit.

Our research, including the sources that the parties have cited, reveals that in the 19th century (and earlier) sometimes private contractors and sometimes government itself carried on prison management activities. And we have found no conclusive evidence of a historical tradition of immunity for private parties carrying out these functions. History therefore does not provide significant support for the immunity claim. Cf. *Briscoe v. LaHue*, 460 U.S. 325, 330–334, 103 S.Ct. 1108, 1112–1115, 75 L.Ed.2d 96 (1983) (immunity for witnesses); *Pierson v. Ray*, 386 U.S. 547, 554–555, 87 S.Ct. 1213, 1217–1218, 18 L.Ed.2d 288 (1967) (immunity for judges and police officers); *Tenney v. Brandhove*, 341 U.S. 367, 372–376, 71 S.Ct. 783, 786–788, 95 L.Ed. 1019 (1951) (immunity for legislators).

Whether the immunity doctrine's *purposes* warrant immunity for private prison guards presents a closer question. *Wyatt*, consistent with earlier precedent, described the doctrine's purposes as protecting "government's ability to perform its traditional functions" by providing immunity where "necessary to preserve" the ability of government officials "to serve the public good or to ensure that talented candidates were not deterred by the threat of damages suits from entering public service." 504 U.S., at 167, 112 S.Ct., at 1833. Earlier precedent described immunity as protecting the public from unwarranted timidity on the part of public officials by, for example, "encouraging the vigorous exercise of official authority," *Butz v. Economou*, 438 U.S. 478, 506, 98 S.Ct. 2894, 2911, 57 L.Ed.2d 895 (1978), by contributing to "'principled and fearless decision-making,'" *Wood v. Strickland*, 420 U.S. 308, 319, 95 S.Ct. 992, 999, 43 L.Ed.2d 214 (1975)(quoting *Pierson, supra*, at 554, 87 S.Ct., at 1217–1218), and by responding to the concern that threatened liability would, in Judge Hand's words, "'dampen the ardour of all but the most resolute, or the most irresponsible,'" public officials, *Harlow*, 457 U.S., at 814, 102 S.Ct., at 2736 (quoting *Gregoire v. Biddle*, 177 F.2d 579, 581 (C.A.2 1949) (L. Hand, J.), cert. denied, 339 U.S. 949, 70 S.Ct. 803, 94 L.Ed. 1363 (1950)); see also *Mitchell*, 472 U.S., at 526, 105 S.Ct., at 2815 (lawsuits may "distrac[t] officials from their governmental duties").

The guards argue that those purposes support immunity whether their employer is private or public. Brief for Petitioners 35–36. Since private prison guards perform the same work as state prison guards, they say, they must require immunity to a similar degree. To say this, however, is to misread this Court's precedents. The Court has sometimes applied a functional approach in immunity cases, but only to decide which type of immunity — absolute or qualified — a public officer should receive. See, *e.g.*, *Buckley v. Fitzsimmons*, 509 U.S. 259, 113 S.Ct. 2606, 125 L.Ed.2d 209 (1993); *Burns v. Reed*, 500 U.S. 478, 111 S.Ct. 1934, 114 L.Ed.2d 547 (1991); *Forrester v. White*, 484 U.S. 219, 108 S.Ct. 538, 98 L.Ed.2d 555 (1988); *Cleavinger v. Saxner*, 474 U.S. 193, 106 S.Ct. 496, 88 L.Ed.2d 507 (1985); *Harlow, supra*. And it never has held that the mere performance of a governmental function could make the difference between unlimited § 1983 liability and qualified immunity, see, *e.g.*, *Tower*, 467 U.S., at 922–923, 104 S.Ct., at 2825–2826, especially for a private person who performs a job without government supervision or direction. Indeed, a purely functional approach bristles with difficulty, particularly since, in many areas, government and private industry may engage in fundamentally similar activities, ranging from electricity production, to waste disposal, to even mail delivery.

Petitioners' argument also overlook certain important differences that, from an immunity perspective, are critical. First, the most important special government immunity-producing concern — unwarranted timidity — is less likely present, or at least is not special, when a private company subject to competitive market pressures operates a prison. Competitive pressures mean not only that a firm whose guards are too aggressive will face damages that raise costs, thereby threatening its replacement, but also that a firm whose guards are too timid will face threats of replacement by other firms with records that demonstrate their ability to do both a safer and a more effective job.

These ordinary marketplace pressures are present here. The private prison guards before us work for a large, multistate private prison management firm. C. Thomas, D. Bolinger, & J. Badalamenti, Private Adult Correctional Facility Census 1 (10th ed.1997) (listing the Corrections Corporation of America as the largest prison management concern in the United States). The firm is systematically organized to perform a major administrative task for profit. Cf. Tenn.Code Ann. § 41-24-104 (Supp.1996) (requiring that firms contracting with the State demonstrate a history of successful operation of correctional facilities). It performs that task independently, with relatively less ongoing direct state supervision. Compare § 41-4-140(c)(5) (exempting private jails from certain monitoring) with § 41-4-116 (requiring inspectors to examine publicly operated county jails once a month or more) and § 41-4-140(a) (requiring Tennessee Correctional Institute to inspect public correctional facilities on an annual basis and to report findings of such inspections). It must buy insurance sufficient to compensate victims of civil rights torts. § 41-24-107. And, since the firm's first contract expires after three years, § 41-24-105(a), its performance is disciplined, not only by state review, see §§ 41-24-105(c)–(f), 41-24-109, but also by pressure from potentially competing firms who can try to take its place. Cf. § 41-24-104(a)(4) (permitting State, upon notice, to cancel contract at any time after first year of operation); see also §§ 41-24-105(c) and (d) (describing standards for renewal of contract).

In other words, marketplace pressures provide the private firm with strong incentives to avoid overly timid, insufficiently vigorous, unduly fearful, or "nonarduous" employee job performance. And the contract's provisions—including those that might permit employee indemnification and avoid many civil-service restrictions—grant this private firm freedom to respond to those market pressures through rewards and penalties that operate directly upon its employees. See § 41-24-111. To this extent, the employees before us resemble those of other private firms and differ from government employees.

This is not to say that government employees, in their efforts to act within constitutional limits, will always, or often, sacrifice the otherwise effective performance of their duties. Rather, it is to say that government employees typically act within a *different* system. They work within a system that is responsible through elected officials to voters who, when they vote, rarely consider the performance of individual sub-departments or civil servants specifically and in detail. And that system is often characterized by multidepartment civil service rules that, while providing employee security, may limit the incentives or the ability of individual departments or supervisors flexibly to reward, or to punish, individual employees. Hence a judicial determination that "effectiveness" concerns warrant special immunity-type protection in respect to this latter (governmental) system does not prove its need in respect to the former. Consequently, we can find no *special* immunity-related need to encourage vigorous performance.

Second, "privatization" helps to meet the immunity-related need "to ensure that talented candidates" are "not deterred by the threat of damages suits from entering public service." *Wyatt*, 504 U.S., at 167, 112 S.Ct., at 1833; see also *Mitchell*, 472 U.S., at 526, 105 S.Ct., at 2815–2816 (citing *Harlow*, 457 U.S., at 816, 102 S.Ct., at 2737). It does so in part because of the comprehensive insurance-coverage requirements just mentioned. The insurance increases the likelihood of employee indemnification and to that extent reduces the employment-discouraging fear of unwarranted liability potential applicants face. Because privatization law also frees the private prison-management firm from many civil service law restraints, Tenn.Code Ann. §41-24-111 (1990), it permits the private firm, unlike a government department, to offset any increased employee liability risk with higher pay or extra benefits. In respect to this second government-immunity-related purpose then, it is difficult to find a *special* need for immunity, for the guards' employer can operate like other private firms; it need not operate like a typical government department.

Third, lawsuits may well "'distrac[t]'" these employees "'from their ... duties,'" *Mitchell, supra,* at 526, 105 S.Ct., at 2815 (quoting *Harlow,* 457 U.S., at 816, 102 S.Ct., at 2737), but the risk of "distraction" alone cannot be sufficient grounds for an immunity. Our qualified immunity cases do not contemplate the complete elimination of lawsuit-based distractions. Cf. *id.,* at 818–819, 102 S.Ct., at 2738–2739 (officials subject to suit for violations of clearly established rights). And it is significant that, here, Tennessee law reserves certain important discretionary tasks—those related to prison discipline, to parole, and to good time—for state officials. Tenn.Code Ann. §41-24-110 (1990). Given a continual and conceded need for deterring constitutional violations and our sense that the firm's tasks are not enormously different in respect to their importance from various other publicly important tasks carried out by private firms, we are not persuaded that the threat of distracting workers from their duties is enough virtually by itself to justify providing an immunity. Moreover, Tennessee, which has itself decided not to extend sovereign immunity to private prison operators (and arguably appreciated that this decision would increase contract prices to some degree), §41-24-107, can be understood to have anticipated a certain amount of distraction.

Our examination of history and purpose thus reveals nothing special enough about the job or about its organizational structure that would warrant providing these private prison guards with a governmental immunity. The job is one that private industry might, or might not, perform; and which history shows private firms did sometimes perform without relevant immunities. The organizational structure is one subject to the ordinary competitive pressures that normally help private firms adjust their behavior in response to the incentives that tort suits provide—pressures not necessarily present in government departments. Since there are no special reasons significantly favoring an extension of governmental immunity, and since *Wyatt* makes clear that private actors are not *automatically* immune (*i.e.,* §1983 immunity does not automatically follow §1983 liability), we must conclude that private prison guards, unlike those who work directly for the government, do not enjoy immunity from suit in a §1983 case.

We close with three caveats. First, we have focused only on questions of §1983 immunity and have not addressed whether the defendants are liable under §1983 even though they are employed by a private firm. Because the Court of Appeals assumed, but did not decide, §1983 liability, it is for the District Court to determine whether, under this Court's decision in *Lugar v. Edmondson Oil Co.,* 457 U.S. 922, 102 S.Ct. 2744, 73 L.Ed.2d 482 (1982), defendants actually acted "under color of state law."

Second, we have answered the immunity question narrowly, in the context in which it arose. That context is one in which a private firm, systematically organized to assume a major lengthy administrative task (managing an institution) with limited direct supervision by the government, undertakes that task for profit and potentially in competition with other firms. The case does not involve a private individual briefly associated with a government body, serving as an adjunct to government in an essential governmental activity, or acting under close official supervision.

Third, *Wyatt* explicitly stated that it did not decide whether or not the private defendants before it might assert, not immunity, but a special "good-faith" defense. The Court said that it "d[id] not foreclose the possibility that private defendants faced with § 1983 liability under *Lugar v. Edmondson Oil Co.*, 457 U.S. 922, 102 S.Ct. 2744, 73 L.Ed.2d 482 (1982), could be entitled to an affirmative defense based on good faith and/or probable cause or that § 1983 suits against private, rather than governmental, parties could require plaintiffs to carry additional burdens." *Wyatt,* 504 U.S., at 169, 112 S.Ct., at 1834.

But because those issues were not fairly before the Court, it left "them for another day." *Ibid.* Similarly, the Court of Appeals in this case limited its holding to the question of immunity. It said specifically that it "may be that the appropriate balance to be struck here is to permit the correctional officers to assert a good faith defense, rather than qualified immunity.... However, that issue is not before this Court in this interlocutory appeal." 88 F.3d, at 425. Like the Court in *Wyatt,* and the Court of Appeals in this case, we do not express a view on this last-mentioned question.

For these reasons the judgment of the Court of Appeals is

Affirmed.

Justice SCALIA, with whom THE CHIEF JUSTICE, Justice KENNEDY, and Justice THOMAS join, dissenting.

In *Procunier v. Navarette,* 434 U.S. 555, 98 S.Ct. 855, 55 L.Ed.2d 24 (1978), we held that state prison officials, including both supervisory and subordinate officers, are entitled to qualified immunity in a suit brought under 42 U.S.C. § 1983. Today the Court declares that this immunity is unavailable to employees of private prison management firms, who perform the same duties as state-employed correctional officials, who exercise the most palpable form of state police power, and who may be sued for acting "under color of state law." This holding is supported neither by common-law tradition nor public policy, and contradicts our settled practice of determining § 1983 immunity on the basis of the public function being performed.

The doctrine of official immunity against damages actions under § 1983 is rooted in the assumption that that statute did not abolish those immunities traditionally available at common law. See *Buckley v. Fitzsimmons,* 509 U.S. 259, 268, 113 S.Ct. 2606, 2612–2613, 125 L.Ed.2d 209 (1993). I agree with the Court, therefore, that we must look to history to resolve this case. I do not agree with the Court, however, that the petitioners' claim to immunity is defeated if they cannot provide an actual case, antedating or contemporaneous with the enactment of § 1983, in which immunity was successfully asserted by a private prison guard. It is only the absence of such a case, and not any explicit rejection of immunity by any common-law court, that the Court relies upon. The opinion observes that private jailers existed in the 19th century, and that they were successfully sued by prisoners. But one could just as easily show that government-employed jailers were successfully sued at common law, often with no mention of possible immunity, see Schellenger, Civil liability of sheriff or other officer charged with keeping jail or prison for death or injury of prisoner, 14 A.L.R.2d 353 (1950) (annotating numerous cases where sheriffs were held liable). Indeed, as far as my research has disclosed, there may be more case-law support for immunity in the private-jailer context than in the government-jailer context. The only pre-§ 1983 jailer-immunity case of any sort that I am aware of is *Williams v. Adams*, 85 Mass. 171 (1861), decided only 10 years before § 1983 became law. And that case, which explicitly acknowledged that the issue of jailer immunity was "novel," *ibid., appears to have conferred immunity upon an independent contractor*

The truth to tell, *Procunier v. Navarette, supra*, which established § 1983 immunity for state prison guards, did not trouble itself with history, as our later § 1983 immunity opinions have done, see, *e.g., Burns v. Reed*, 500 U.S. 478, 489–490, 111 S.Ct. 1934, 1940–1941, 114 L.Ed.2d 547 (1991); *Tower v. Glover*, 467 U.S. 914, 920, 104 S.Ct. 2820, 2824–2825, 81 L.Ed.2d 758 (1984), but simply set forth a policy prescription. At this stage in our jurisprudence it is irrational, and productive of harmful policy consequences, to rely upon lack of case support to create an artificial limitation upon the scope of a doctrine (prison-guard immunity) that was itself not based on case support. I say an artificial limitation, because the historical *principles* on which common-law immunity was based, and which are reflected in our jurisprudence, plainly cover the private prison guard if they cover the nonprivate. Those principles are two: (1) immunity is determined by function, not status, and (2) even more specifically, private status is not disqualifying.

"[O]ur cases clearly indicate that immunity analysis rests on functional categories, not on the status of the defendant." *Briscoe v. LaHue*, 460 U.S. 325, 342, 103 S.Ct. 1108, 1119, 75 L.Ed.2d 96 (1983). Immunity "flows not from rank or title or 'location within the Government,' ... but from the nature of the responsibilities of the individual official." *Cleavinger v. Saxner*, 474 U.S. 193, 201, 106 S.Ct. 496, 501, 88 L.Ed.2d 507 (1985), quoting *Butz v. Economou*, 438 U.S. 478, 98 S.Ct. 2894, 57 L.Ed.2d 895 (1978). "Running through our cases, with fair consistency, is a 'functional' approach to immunity questions.... Under that approach, we examine the nature of the functions with which a particular official or class of officials has been lawfully entrusted, and we seek to evaluate the effect that exposure to particular forms of liability would likely have on the appropriate exercise of those functions." The parties concede that petitioners perform a prototypically governmental function (enforcement of state-imposed deprivation of liberty), and one that gives rise to qualified immunity.

The point that function rather than status governs the immunity determination is demonstrated in a prison-guard case virtually contemporaneous with the enactment of § 1983. *Alamango v. Board of Supervisors of Albany Cty.*, 32 N.Y. Sup.Ct. 551 (1881), held that supervisors charged under state law with maintaining a penitentiary were immune from prisoner lawsuits. Although they were not formally state officers, the court emphasized the irrelevance of this fact:

"The duty of punishing criminals is inherent in the Sovereign power. It may be committed to agencies selected for that purpose, but such agencies, while engaged in that duty, stand so far in the place of the State and exercise its political authority, and do not act in any private capacity." *Id.,* at 552

Private individuals have regularly been accorded immunity when they perform a governmental function that qualifies. We have long recognized the absolute immunity of grand jurors, noting that like prosecutors and judges they must "exercise a discretionary judgment on the basis of evidence presented to them." *Imbler,* 424 U.S., at 423, n. 20, 96 S.Ct., at 991, n. 20. "It is the functional comparability of [grand jurors'] judgments to those of the judge that has resulted in [their] being referred to as 'quasi-judicial' officers, and their immunities being termed 'quasi-judicial' as well." *Ibid.* Likewise, witnesses who testify in court proceedings have enjoyed immunity, regardless of whether they were government employees. "[T]he common law," we have observed, "provided absolute immunity from subsequent damages liability for all persons— *governmental or otherwise*—who were integral parts of the judicial process." *Briscoe, supra,* at 335, 103 S.Ct., at 1115–1116 (emphasis added). I think it highly unlikely that we would deny prosecutorial immunity to those private attorneys increasingly employed by various jurisdictions in this country to conduct high-visibility criminal prosecutions. See, *e.g.,* Kaplan, State Hires Private Lawyer for Bryant Family Trial, Los Angeles Times, Apr. 28, 1993, p. B4, col. 2; Estrich, On Building the Strongest Possible Prosecution Team, Los Angeles Times, July 10, 1994, p. M1, col. 1. There is no more reason for treating private prison guards differently.

Later in its opinion, the Court seeks to establish that there are policy reasons for denying to private prison guards the immunity accorded to public ones. As I have indicated above, I believe that history and not judicially analyzed policy governs this matter—but even on its own terms the Court's attempted policy distinction is unconvincing. The Court suggests two differences between civil-service prison guards and those employed by private prison firms which preclude any "special" need to give the latter immunity. First, the Court says that "unwarranted timidity" on the part of private guards is less likely to be a concern, since their companies are subject to market pressures that encourage them to be effective in the performance of their duties. If a private firm does not maintain a proper level of order, the Court reasons, it will be replaced by another one—so there is no need for qualified immunity to facilitate the maintenance of order.

This is wrong for several reasons. First of all, it is fanciful to speak of the consequences of "market" pressures in a regime where public officials are the only purchaser, and other people's money the medium of payment. Ultimately, one prison-management firm will be selected to replace another prison-management firm only if a decision is made by some *political* official not to renew the contract. See Tenn.Code Ann. §§ 41-24-103 to 105 (Supp.1996). This is a government decision, not a market choice. If state officers turn out to be more strict in reviewing the cost and performance of privately managed prisons than of publicly managed ones, it will only be because they have *chosen* to be so. The process can come to resemble a market choice only to the extent that political actors *will* such resemblance—that is, to the extent that political actors (1) are willing to pay attention to the issue of prison services, among the many issues vying for their attention, and (2) are willing to place considerations of cost and quality of service ahead of such political considerations as personal friendship, political alliances, in-state ownership of the contractor, etc. Secondly and more importantly, however, if one assumes a political regime that *is* bent on emulating the market in its purchase of prison services, it is almost certainly the case that, short of mismanagement so severe as to provoke a prison riot, *price* (not discipline) will be the predominating factor in such a regime's selection of a contractor. A contractor's price must depend upon its costs; lawsuits increase costs3 ; and "fearless" maintenance of discipline increases lawsuits. The incentive to down-play discipline will exist, moreover, even in those States where the politicians' zeal for market emulation and budget cutting has waned, and where prison-management contract renewal is virtually automatic: the more cautious the prison guards, the fewer the lawsuits, the higher the profits. In sum, it seems that "market-competitive" private prison managers have even greater need than civil-service prison managers for immunity as an incentive to discipline.

The Court's second distinction between state and private prisons is that privatization "helps to meet the immunity-related need to ensure that talented candidates are not deterred by the threat of damages suits from entering public service" as prison guards. *Ante,* at 2107 (internal quotation marks omitted). This is so because privatization brings with it (or at least has brought with it in the case before us) (1) a statutory requirement for insurance coverage against civil-rights claims, which assertedly "increases the likelihood of employee indemnification," and (2) a liberation "from many civil service law restraints" which prevent increased employee risk from being "offset … with higher pay or extra benefits," *ibid.* As for the former (civil-rights liability insurance): surely it is the *availability* of that protection, rather than its actual presence in the case at hand, which decreases (if it does decrease, which I doubt) the *need* for immunity protection. (Otherwise, the Court would have to say that a private prison-management firm that is not required to purchase insurance, and does not do so, is more entitled to immunity; and that a government-run prison system that *does* purchase insurance is *less* entitled to immunity.) And of course civil-rights liability insurance is no less *available* to public entities than to private employers. But the second factor — liberation from civil-service limitations — is the more interesting one. First of all, simply as a philosophical matter it is fascinating to learn that one of the prime justifications for § 1983 immunity should be a phenomenon (civil-service laws) that did not even exist when § 1983 was enacted and the immunity created. Also as a philosophical matter, it is poetic justice (or poetic revenge) that the Court should use one of the principal economic benefits of "prison out-sourcing" — namely, the avoidance of civil-service salary and tenure encrustations — as the justification for a legal rule rendering out-sourcing more expensive. Of course the savings attributable to out-sourcing will not be wholly lost as a result of today's holding; they will be transferred in part from the public to prisoner-plaintiffs and to lawyers. It is a result that only the American Bar Association and the American Federation of Government

Employees could love. But apart from philosophical fascination, this second factor is subject to the same objection as the first: governments *need not* have civil-service salary encrustations (or can exempt prisons from them); and hence governments, no more than private prison employers, have any *need* for § 1983 immunity.

There is one more possible rationale for denying immunity to private prison guards worth discussing, albeit briefly. It is a theory so implausible that the Court avoids mentioning it, even though it was the primary reason given in the Court of Appeals decision that the Court affirms. *McKnight v. Rees,* 88 F.3d 417, 424–425 (C.A.6 1996). It is that officers of private prisons are more likely than officers of state prisons to violate prisoners' constitutional rights because they work for a profit motive, and hence an added degree of deterrence is needed to keep these officers in line. The Court of Appeals offered no evidence to support its bald assertion that private prison guards operate with different incentives than state prison guards, and gave no hint as to how prison guards might possibly increase their employers' profits by violating constitutional rights. One would think that private prison managers, whose § 1983 damages come out of their own pockets, as compared with public prison managers, whose § 1983 damages come out of the public purse, would, if anything, be more careful in training their employees to avoid constitutional infractions. And in fact, States having experimented with prison privatization commonly report that the overall caliber of the services provided to prisoners has actually improved in scope and quality. Matters Relating To The Federal Bureau Of Prisons: Hearing before the Subcommittee on Crime of the House Committee on the Judiciary, 104th Cong., 1st Sess., 110 (1995).

* * *

In concluding, I must observe that since there is no apparent *reason*, neither in history nor in policy, for making immunity hinge upon the Court's distinction between public and private guards, the precise *nature* of that distinction must also remain obscure. Is it privity of contract that separates the two categories—so that guards paid directly by the State are "public" prison guards and immune, but those paid by a prison-management company "private" prison guards and not immune? Or is it rather "employee" versus "independent contractor" status—so that even guards whose compensation is paid directly by the State are not immune if they are not also supervised by a state official? Or is perhaps state supervision alone (without direct payment) enough to confer immunity? Or is it (as the Court's characterization of *Alamango,* see n. 2, *supra,* suggests) the formal designation of the guards, or perhaps of the guards' employer, as a "state instrumentality" that makes the difference? Since, as I say, I see no sense in the public-private distinction, neither do I see what precisely it consists of.

Today's decision says that two sets of prison guards who are indistinguishable in the ultimate source of their authority over prisoners, indistinguishable in the powers that they possess over prisoners, and indistinguishable in the duties that they owe toward prisoners, are to be treated quite differently in the matter of their financial liability. The only sure effect of today's decision—and the only purpose, as far as I can tell—is that it will artificially raise the cost of privatizing prisons. Whether this will cause privatization to be prohibitively expensive, or instead simply divert state funds that could have been saved or spent on additional prison services, it is likely that taxpayers and prisoners will suffer as a consequence. Neither our precedent, nor the historical foundations of § 1983, nor the policies underlying § 1983, support this result.

I respectfully dissent.

D. The Right to Appointed Counsel

A right to counsel has been recognized in criminal proceedings, but no right to counsel has been established in civil proceedings except in very limited instances.

Gideon v. Wainwright
372 U.S. 335 (1963)

Petitioner was charged in a Florida state court with having broken and entered a poolroom with intent to commit a misdemeanor. This offense is a felony under Florida law. Appearing in court without funds and without a lawyer, petitioner asked the court to appoint counsel for him, whereupon the following colloquy took place:

'The COURT: Mr. Gideon, I am sorry, but I cannot appoint Counsel to represent you in this case. Under the laws of the State of Florida, the only time the Court can appoint Counsel to represent a Defendant is when that person is charged with a capital offense. I am sorry, but I will have to deny your request to appoint Counsel to defend you in this case.

'The DEFENDANT: The United States Supreme Court says I am entitled to be represented by Counsel.'

Put to trial before a jury, Gideon conducted his defense about as well as could be expected from a layman. He made an opening statement to the jury, cross-examined the State's witnesses, presented witnesses in his own defense, declined to testify himself, and made a short argument 'emphasizing his innocence to the charge contained in the Information filed in this case.' The jury returned a verdict of guilty, and petitioner was sentenced to serve five years in the state prison. Later, petitioner filed in the Florida Supreme Court this habeas corpus petition attacking his conviction and sentence on the ground that the trial court's refusal to appoint counsel for him denied him rights 'guaranteed by the Constitution and the Bill of Rights by the United States Government.' Treating the petition for habeas corpus as properly before it, the State Supreme Court, 'upon consideration thereof' but without an opinion, denied all relief. Since 1942, when Betts v. Brady was decided by a divided Court, the problem of a defendant's federal constitutional right to counsel in a state court has been a continuing source of controversy and litigation in both state and federal courts. To give this problem another review here, we granted certiorari. Since Gideon was proceeding in forma pauperis, we appointed counsel to represent him and requested both sides to discuss in their briefs and oral arguments the following: 'Should this Court's holding in *Betts v. Brady* be reconsidered?'

I

The facts upon which Betts claimed that he had been unconstitutionally denied the right to have counsel appointed to assist him are strikingly like the facts upon which Gideon here bases his federal constitutional claim. Betts was indicted for robbery in a Maryland state court. On arraignment, he told the trial judge of his lack of funds to hire a lawyer and asked the court to appoint one for him. Betts was advised that it was not the practice in that county to appoint counsel for indigent defendants except in murder and rape cases. He then pleaded not guilty, had witnesses summoned, cross-examined the State's witnesses, examined his own, and chose not to testify himself. He was found guilty by the judge, sitting without a jury, and sentenced to eight years in prison. Like Gideon, Betts sought release by habeas corpus, alleging that he had been denied the right to assistance of counsel in violation of the Fourteenth Amendment. Betts was denied any relief, and on review this Court affirmed. It was held that a refusal to appoint counsel for an indigent defendant charged with a felony did not necessarily violate the Due Process Clause of the Fourteenth Amendment, which for reasons given the Court deemed to be the only applicable federal constitutional provision. The Court said:

> "Asserted denial (of due process) is to be tested by an appraisal of the totality of facts in a given case. That which may, in one setting, constitute a denial of fundamental fairness, shocking to the universal sense of justice, may, in other circumstances, and in the light of other considerations, fall short of such denial."

Treating due process as 'a concept less rigid and more fluid than those envisaged in other specific and particular provisions of the Bill of Rights,' the Court held that refusal to appoint counsel under the particular facts and circumstances in the Betts case was not so 'offensive to the common and fundamental ideas of fairness' as to amount to a denial of due process. Since the facts and circumstances of the two cases are so nearly indistinguishable, we think the *Betts v. Brady* holding if left standing would require us to reject Gideon's claim that the Constitution guarantees him the assistance of counsel. Upon full reconsideration we conclude that *Betts v. Brady* should be overruled.

II

The Sixth Amendment provides, "In all criminal prosecutions, the accused shall enjoy the right to have the Assistance of Counsel for his defense." We have construed this to mean that in federal courts counsel must be provided for defendants unable to employ counsel unless the right is competently and intelligently waived. Betts argued that this right is extended to indigent defendants in state courts by the Fourteenth Amendment. In response the Court stated that, while the Sixth Amendment laid down 'no rule for the conduct of the states, the question recurs whether the constraint laid by the amendment upon the national courts expresses a rule so fundamental and essential to a fair trial, and so, to due process of law, that it is made obligatory upon the states by the Fourteenth Amendment.' In order to decide whether the Sixth Amendment's guarantee of counsel is of this fundamental nature, the Court in Betts set out and considered '(r)elevant data on the subject ... afforded by constitutional and statutory provisions subsisting in the colonies and the states prior to the inclusion of the Bill of Rights in the national Constitution, and in the constitutional, legislative, and judicial history of the states to the present date.' On the basis of this historical data the Court concluded that 'appointment of counsel is not a fundamental right, essential to a fair trial.' It was for this reason the Betts Court refused to accept the contention that the Sixth Amendment's guarantee of counsel for indigent federal defendants was extended to or, in the words of that Court, 'made obligatory upon the states by the Fourteenth Amendment.' Plainly, had the Court concluded that appointment of counsel for an indigent criminal defendant was 'a fundamental right, essential to a fair trial,' it would have held that the Fourteenth Amendment requires appointment of counsel in a state court, just as the Sixth Amendment requires in a federal court.

We think the Court in Betts had ample precedent for acknowledging that those guarantees of the Bill of Rights which are fundamental safeguards of liberty immune from federal abridgment are equally protected against state invasion by the Due Process Clause of the Fourteenth Amendment. This same principle was recognized, explained, and applied in *Powell v. Alabama*, 287 U.S. 45, 53 S.Ct. 55, 77 L.Ed. 158 (1932), a case upholding the right of counsel, where the Court held that despite sweeping language to the contrary in *Hurtado v. California*, 110 U.S. 516, 4 S.Ct. 292, 28 L.Ed. 232 (1884), the Fourteenth Amendment 'embraced' those "fundamental principles of liberty and justice which lie at the base of all our civil and political institutions," even though they had been "specifically dealt with in another part of the Federal Constitution." In many cases other than Powell and Betts, this Court has looked to the fundamental nature of original Bill of Rights guarantees to decide whether the Fourteenth Amendment makes them obligatory on the States. Explicitly recognized to be of this "fundamental nature' and therefore made immune from state invasion by the Fourteenth, or some part of it, are the First Amendment's freedoms of speech, press, religion, assembly, association, and petition for redress of grievances. For the same reason, though not always in precisely the same terminology, the Court has made obligatory on the States the Fifth Amendment's command that private property shall not be taken for public use without just compensation, the Fourth Amendment's prohibition of unreasonable searches and seizures, and the Eighth's ban on cruel and unusual punishment. On the other hand, this Court in *Palko v. Connecticut*, 302 U.S. 319, 58 S.Ct. 149, 82 L.Ed. 288 (1937), refused to hold that the Fourteenth Amendment made the double jeopardy provision of the Fifth Amendment obligatory on the States. In so refusing, however, the Court, speaking through Mr. Justice Cardozo, was careful to emphasize that 'immunities that are valid as against the federal government by force of the specific pledges of particular amendments have been found to be implicit in the concept of ordered liberty, and thus, through the Fourteenth Amendment, become valid as against the states' and that guarantees 'in their origin ... effective against the federal government alone' had by prior cases 'been taken over from the earlier articles of the Federal Bill of Rights and brought within the Fourteenth Amendment by a process of absorption."

We accept *Betts v. Brady*'s assumption, based as it was on our prior cases, that a provision of the Bill of Rights which is "fundamental and essential to a fair trial' is made obligatory upon the States by the Fourteenth Amendment. We think the Court in Betts was wrong, however, in concluding that the Sixth Amendment's guarantee of counsel is not one of these fundamental rights. Ten years before *Betts v. Brady*, this Court, after full consideration of all the historical data examined in Betts, had unequivocally declared that 'the right to the aid of counsel is of this fundamental character." *Powell v. Alabama*, 287 U.S. 45, 68, 53 S.Ct. 55, 63, 77 L.Ed. 158 (1932). While the Court at the close of its Powell opinion did by its language, as this Court frequently does, limit its holding to the particular facts and circumstances of that case, its conclusions about the fundamental nature of the right to counsel are unmistakable. Several years later, in 1936, the Court reemphasized what it had said about the fundamental nature of the right to counsel in this language:

> "We concluded that certain fundamental rights, safeguarded by the first eight amendments against federal action, were also safeguarded against state action by the due process of law clause of the Fourteenth Amendment, and among them the fundamental right of the accused to the aid of counsel in a criminal prosecution." *Grosjean v. American Press Co.*, 297 U.S. 233, 243–244, 56 S.Ct. 444, 446, 80 L.Ed. 660 (1936).

And again in 1938 this Court said:

> "(The assistance of counsel) is one of the safeguards of the Sixth Amendment deemed necessary to insure fundamental human rights of life and liberty.... The Sixth Amendment stands as a constant admonition that if the constitutional safeguards it provides be lost, justice will not 'still be done.'"

In light of these and many other prior decisions of this Court, it is not surprising that the Betts Court, when faced with the contention that 'one charged with crime, who is unable to obtain counsel, must be furnished counsel by the state,' conceded that '(e)xpressions in the opinions of this court lend color to the argument * * *' 316 U.S., at 462–463, 62 S.Ct., at 1256, 86 L.Ed. 1595. The fact is that in deciding as it did—that 'appointment of counsel is not a fundamental right, essential to a fair trial'—the Court in *Betts v. Brady* made an abrupt break with its own well-considered precedents. In returning to these old precedents, sounder we believe than the new, we but restore constitutional principles established to achieve a fair system of justice. Not only these precedents but also reason and reflection require us to recognize that in our adversary system of criminal justice, any person haled into court, who is too poor to hire a lawyer, cannot be assured a fair trial unless counsel is provided for him. This seems to us to be an obvious truth. Governments, both state and federal, quite properly spend vast sums of money to establish machinery to try defendants accused of crime. Lawyers to prosecute are everywhere deemed essential to protect the public's interest in an orderly society. Similarly, there are few defendants charged with crime, few indeed, who fail to hire the best lawyers they can get to prepare and present their defenses. That government hires lawyers to prosecute and defendants who have the money hire lawyers to defend are the strongest indications of the widespread belief that lawyers in criminal courts are necessities, not luxuries. The right of one charged with crime to counsel may not be deemed fundamental and essential to fair trials in some countries, but it is in ours. From the very beginning, our state and national constitutions and laws have laid great emphasis on procedural and substantive safeguards designed to assure fair trials before impartial tribunals in which every defendant stands equal before the law. This noble ideal cannot be realized if the poor man charged with crime has to face his accusers without a lawyer to assist him. A defendant's need for a lawyer is nowhere better stated than in the moving words of Mr. Justice Sutherland in *Powell v. Alabama*:

> "The right to be heard would be, in many cases, of little avail if it did not comprehend the right to be heard by counsel. Even the intelligent and educated layman has small and sometimes no skill in the science of law. If charged with crime, he is incapable, generally, of determining for himself whether the indictment is good or bad. He is unfamiliar with the rules of evidence. Left without the aid of counsel he may be put on trial without a proper charge, and convicted upon incompetent evidence, or evidence irrelevant to the issue or otherwise inadmissible. He lacks both the skill and knowledge adequately to prepare his defense, even though he have a perfect one. He requires the guiding hand of counsel at every step in the proceedings against him. Without it, though he be not guilty, he faces the danger of conviction because he does not know how to establish his innocence." 287 U.S., at 68–69, 53 S.Ct., at 64, 77 L.Ed. 158.

The Court in *Betts v. Brady* departed from the sound wisdom upon which the Court's holding in *Powell v. Alabama* rested. Florida, supported by two other States, has asked that *Betts v. Brady* be left intact. Twenty-Two States, as friends of the Court, argue that Betts was 'an anachronism when handed down' and that it should now be overruled. We agree.

The judgment is reversed and the cause is remanded to the Supreme Court of Florida for further action not inconsistent with this opinion.

Reversed.

The Court in *Gideon* was trying to make it so that the fundamental right of counsel was available to all. In response to the case, states had to change their criminal statutes so that none could be outright denied counsel in serious crimes. The right would later be extended to include any charge punishable by imprisonment. *Argersinger v. Hamlin*, 407 U.S. 25, 30 (1972). However, while the right to counsel may apply to all charged with serious crimes, it is not equal. Access to justice functions differently for the poor.

In response to *Gideon v. Wainwright*, Congress passed the Criminal Justice Act (18 U.S.C. §3006A) just a year later. The act requires representation to be furnished to anyone who meets the financial requirements and is charged with one of multiple different types of charges. This act sought to replace the old system of judges merely requesting members of the local bar to take cases. The act set up a system that would require compensation for attorneys appointed, as opposed to the attorneys taking cases *pro bono*. It wasn't until 1970 that the act was amended to authorize districts to create individual federal defender organizations. These organizations and their employees are paid by the government and the head defenders are appointed by the courts. This system is present in some form at the state level as well, though their funding and administrative setup can vary widely.[3]

The purpose of these public defender systems is to make sure that the right to counsel can apply to all, regardless of financial status. The Supreme Court in *Gideon* required that even indigent defendants be assigned counsel, but the mere existence of an attorney is not enough. The attorney must be able to provide "effective" assistance.

United States v. Cronic

466 U.S. 648 (1984)

Respondent and two associates were indicted on mail fraud charges involving the transfer of over $ 9,400,000 in checks between banks in Tampa, Fla., and Norman, Okla., during a 4-month period in 1975. Shortly before the scheduled trial date, respondent's retained counsel withdrew. The court appointed a young lawyer with a real estate practice to represent respondent, but allowed him only 25 days for pretrial preparation, even though it had taken the Government over four and one-half years to investigate the case and it had reviewed thousands of documents during that investigation. The two codefendants agreed to testify for the Government; respondent was convicted on 11 of the 13 counts in the indictment and received a 25-year sentence.

The Court of Appeals reversed the conviction because it concluded that respondent did not "have the Assistance of Counsel for his defense" that is guaranteed by the Sixth Amendment to the Constitution. This conclusion was not supported by a determination that respondent's trial counsel had made any specified errors, that his actual performance had prejudiced the defense, or that he failed to exercise "the skill, judgment, and diligence of a reasonably competent defense attorney"; instead the conclusion rested on the premise that no such showing is necessary "when circumstances hamper a given lawyer's preparation of a defendant's case." The question presented by the Government's petition for certiorari is whether the Court of Appeals has correctly interpreted the Sixth Amendment.

---

3. For example, Louisiana's public defender system is funded primarily through fees from traffic violations, whereas other state public defender systems are merely part of the state's budget.

II

An accused's right to be represented by counsel is a fundamental component of our criminal justice system. Lawyers in criminal cases "are necessities, not luxuries." Their presence is essential because they are the means through which the other rights of the person on trial are secured. Without counsel, the right to a trial itself would be "of little avail," as this Court has recognized repeatedly. "Of all the rights that an accused person has, the right to be represented by counsel is by far the most pervasive for it affects his ability to assert any other rights he may have."

The special value of the right to the assistance of counsel explains why "[it] has long been recognized that the right to counsel is the right to the effective assistance of counsel." *McMann v. Richardson*, 397 U.S. 759, 771, n. 14 (1970). The text of the Sixth Amendment itself suggests as much. The Amendment requires not merely the provision of counsel to the accused, but "Assistance," which is to be "for his defence." Thus, "the core purpose of the counsel guarantee was to assure 'Assistance' at trial, when the accused was confronted with both the intricacies of the law and the advocacy of the public prosecutor." *United States v. Ash*, 413 U.S. 300, 309 (1973). If no actual "Assistance" "for" the accused's "defence" is provided, then the constitutional guarantee has been violated. To hold otherwise "could convert the appointment of counsel into a sham and nothing more than a formal compliance with the Constitution's requirement that an accused be given the assistance of counsel. The Constitution's guarantee of assistance of counsel cannot be satisfied by mere formal appointment." *Avery v. Alabama*, 308 U.S. 444, 446 (1940) (footnote omitted).

Thus, in *McMann* the Court indicated that the accused is entitled to "a reasonably competent attorney," 397 U.S., at 770, whose advice is "within the range of competence demanded of attorneys in criminal cases." Id., at 771. In *Cuyler v. Sullivan*, 446 U.S. 335 (1980), we held that the Constitution guarantees an accused "adequate legal assistance." Id., at 344. And in *Engle v. Isaac*, 456 U.S. 107 (1982), the Court referred to the criminal defendant's constitutional guarantee of "a fair trial and a competent attorney." Id., at 134.

III

Moreover, because we presume that the lawyer is competent to provide the guiding hand that the defendant needs, see *Michel v. Louisiana*, 350 U.S. 91, 100–101 (1955), the burden rests on the accused to demonstrate a constitutional violation. There are, however, circumstances that are so likely to prejudice the accused that the cost of litigating their effect in a particular case is unjustified.

Most obvious, of course, is the complete denial of counsel. The presumption that counsel's assistance is essential requires us to conclude that a trial is unfair if the accused is denied counsel at a critical stage of his trial. Similarly, if counsel entirely fails to subject the prosecution's case to meaningful adversarial testing, then there has been a denial of Sixth Amendment rights that makes the adversary process itself presumptively unreliable. No specific showing of prejudice was required in *Davis v. Alaska*, 415 U.S. 308 (1974), because the petitioner had been "denied the right of effective cross-examination" which " 'would be constitutional error of the first magnitude and no amount of showing of want of prejudice would cure it.' " Id., at 318 (citing *Smith v. Illinois*, 390 U.S. 129, 131 (1968), and *Brookhart v. Janis*, 384 U.S. 1, 3 (1966)). Circumstances of that magnitude may be present on some occasions when although counsel is available to assist the accused during trial, the likelihood that any lawyer, even a fully competent one, could provide effective assistance is so small that a presumption of prejudice is appropriate without inquiry into the actual conduct of the trial.

In *Cronic* the Court upgraded the Sixth Amendment right to be more than the presence of an attorney during a trial. Now an attorney must be present during "critical stages" and perform cross-examination during a trial. However, it did not have much of a tangible effect when it came to providing the right to those too poor to hire counsel. Because nearly 80% of criminal defendants require the aid of indigent defense services, many public defenders are overextended and their offices under-funded.[4] This creates two different realms of criminal justice. A retained attorney can limit the amount of cases she gets, and thus afford herself more time to meet with the client and hire personnel such as investigators and physicians to assist in the res-olution of the case. However, appointed counsel is at the mercy of their caseload, and may only be able to spare brief moments to speak with a client or risk completely neglecting one of their many other clients. In many jurisdictions the amount of time an attorney can spend on their client is measured in minutes instead of hours, effec-tively creating "a mill for processing people into prison."[5] While the Court required "effective assistance of counsel," it did not quantify what exactly that involved in the criminal context, and no legislative or regulatory mandate was established to see that this right was given.

The defendant in *Cronic* ultimately lost his appeal. Despite his loss, however, this case has become increasingly utilized to argue that indigent defense systems are in-adequate and individuals are being denied their constitutional rights. Over the past decade there have been lawsuits throughout the country using the language of *Cronic* and cases holding that their state's indigent defense system is deficient in providing this constitutional right due to insufficient funding.

Hurrell-Harring v. State of New York
930 N.E.2d 217 (N.Y. 2010)

The Sixth Amendment to the United States Constitution guarantees a criminal defendant "the right to ... have the Assistance of Counsel for his defense," and since *Gideon v. Wainwright* (372 US 335, 83 S Ct 792, 9 L Ed 2d 799 [1963]) it has been

---

4. Lorelei Laird, *Starved of Money for Too Long, Public Defender Offices Are Suing—and Starting to Win*, A.B.A.J. (Jan., 2017), http://www.abajournal.com/magazine/article/the_gideon_revolution.
5. Debbie Elliott, *Public Defenders Hard to Come by in Louisiana*, NPR (March 10, 2017), https://www.npr.org/2017/03/10/519211293/public-defenders-hard-to-come-by-in-louisiana.

established that that entitlement may not be effectively denied by the State by reason of a defendant's inability to pay for a lawyer. *Gideon* is not now controversial either as an expression of what the Constitution requires or as an exercise in elemental fair play. Serious questions have, however, arisen in this and other jurisdictions as to whether *Gideon's* mandate is being met in practice (see e.g. *Lavallee v. Justices* in Hampden Superior Ct., 442 Mass 228, 812 NE2d 895 [2004].)

In New York, the Legislature has left the performance of the State's obligation under Gideon to the counties, where it is discharged, for the most part, with county resources and according to local rules and practices (see County Law arts 18-A, 18-B). Plaintiffs in this action, defendants in various criminal prosecutions ongoing at the time of the action's commencement in Washington, Onondaga, Ontario, Schuyler and Suffolk counties, contend that this arrangement, involving what is in essence a costly, largely unfunded and politically unpopular mandate upon local government, has functioned to deprive them and other similarly situated indigent defendants in the aforementioned counties of constitutionally and statutorily guaranteed representational rights. They seek a declaration that their rights and those of the class they seek to represent are being violated and an injunction to avert further abridgment of their right to counsel; they do not seek relief within the criminal cases out of which their claims arise. *** [T]he Supreme Court in Strickland has noted pointedly that HN3 "the purpose of the effective assistance guarantee of the Sixth Amendment is not to improve the quality of legal representation, although that is a goal of considerable importance to the legal system[,] ... [but rather] to ensure that criminal defendants receive a fair trial" (466 US at 689).

According to the complaint, 10 of the 20 plaintiffs — two from Washington, two from Onondaga, two from Ontario and four from Schuyler County — were altogether without representation at the arraignments held in their underlying criminal proceedings. Eight of these unrepresented plaintiffs were jailed after bail had been set in amounts they could not afford. It is alleged that the experience of these plaintiffs is illustrative of what is a fairly common practice in the aforementioned counties of arraigning defendants without counsel and leaving them, particularly when accused of relatively low-level offenses, unrepresented in subsequent proceedings where pleas are taken and other critically important legal transactions take place. One of these plaintiffs remained unrepresented for some five months and it is alleged that the absence of clear and uniform guidelines reasonably related to need has commonly resulted in denials of representation to indigent defendants based on the subjective judgments of individual jurists.

In addition to the foregoing allegations of outright nonrepresentation, the complaint contains allegations to the effect that although lawyers were eventually nominally appointed for plaintiffs, they were unavailable to their clients — that they conferred with them little, if at all, were often completely unresponsive to their urgent inquiries and requests from jail, sometimes for months on end, waived important rights without consulting them, and ultimately appeared to do little more on their behalf than act as conduits for plea offers, some of which purportedly were highly unfavorable. It is repeatedly alleged that counsel missed court appearances, and that when they did appear, they were not prepared to proceed, often because they were entirely new to the case, the matters having previously been handled by other similarly unprepared counsel. There are also allegations that the counsel appointed for at least one of the plaintiffs was seriously conflicted and thus unqualified to undertake the representation.

It is clear that a criminal defendant, regardless of wherewithal, is entitled to "the guiding hand of counsel at every step in the proceedings against him" (*Gideon v. Wainwright*, 372 US at 345, quoting *Powell v. Alabama*, 287 US 45, 69, 53 S Ct 55, 77 L Ed 158 [1932]). The right attaches at arraignment (*see Rothgery v. Gillespie County*, 554 US 191, 128 S Ct 2578, 171 L Ed 2d 366 [2008]) and entails the presence of counsel at each subsequent "critical" stage of the proceedings (*Montejo v. Louisiana*, 556 US 129 S Ct 2079, 173 L Ed 2d 955 [2009]). As is here relevant, arraignment itself must under the circumstances alleged be deemed a critical stage since, even if guilty pleas were not then elicited from the presently named plaintiffs, a circumstance which would undoubtedly require the "critical stage" label (see *Coleman v. Alabama*, 399 US 1, 9, 90 S Ct 1999, 26 L Ed 2d 387 [1970]), it is clear from the complaint that plaintiffs' pretrial liberty interests were on that occasion regularly adjudicated (see also CPL 180.10 [6]) with most serious consequences, both direct and collateral, including the loss of employment and housing, and inability to support and care for particularly needy dependents. There is no question that "a bail hearing is a critical stage of the State's criminal process" (*Higazy v. Templeton*, 505 F3d 161, 172 [2d Cir 2007] [internal quotation marks and citation omitted]).

Recognizing the crucial importance of arraignment and the extent to which a defendant's basic liberty and due process interests may then be affected, CPL 180.10 (3) expressly provides for the "right to the aid of counsel at the arraignment and at every subsequent stage of the action" and forbids a court from going forward with the proceeding without counsel for the defendant, unless the defendant has knowingly agreed to proceed in counsel's absence (CPL 180.10 [5]). Contrary to defendants' suggestion and that of the dissent, nothing in the statute may be read to justify the conclusion that the presence of defense counsel at arraignment is ever dispensable, except at a defendant's informed option, when matters affecting the defendant's pretrial liberty or ability subsequently to defend against the charges are to be decided. Nor is there merit to defendants' suggestion that the Sixth Amendment right to counsel is not yet fully implicated (see *Rothgery*, 554 US at 209).

Also "critical" for Sixth Amendment purposes is the period between arraignment and trial when a case must be factually developed and researched, decisions respecting grand jury testimony made, plea negotiations conducted, and pretrial motions filed. Indeed, it is clear that "to deprive a person of counsel during the period prior to trial may be more damaging than denial of counsel during the trial itself" (*Maine v Moulton*, 474 US 159, 170, 106 S Ct 477, 88 L Ed 2d 481 [1985]).

This complaint contains numerous plain allegations that in specific cases counsel simply was not provided at critical stages of the proceedings. The complaint additionally contains allegations sufficient to justify the inference that these deprivations may be illustrative of significantly more widespread practices; of particular note in this connection are the allegations that in numerous cases representational denials are premised on subjective and highly variable notions of indigency, raising possible due process and equal protection concerns. These allegations state a claim, not for ineffective assistance under *Strickland*, but for basic denial of the right to counsel under *Gideon*.

Similarly, while variously interpretable, the numerous allegations to the effect that counsel, although appointed, were uncommunicative, made virtually no efforts on their nominal clients' behalf during the very critical period subsequent to arraignment, and, indeed, waived important rights without authorization from their clients, may be reasonably understood to allege nonrepresentation rather than ineffective representation. Actual representation assumes a certain basic representational relationship. The allegations here, however, raise serious questions as to whether any such relationship may be really said to have existed between many of the plaintiffs and their putative attorneys and cumulatively may be understood to raise the distinct possibility that merely nominal attorney-client pairings occur in the subject counties with a fair degree of regularity, allegedly because of inadequate funding and staffing of indigent defense providers. It is very basic that

> "[i]f no actual 'Assistance' 'for' the accused's 'defence' is provided, then the constitutional guarantee has been violated. To hold otherwise 'could convert the appointment of counsel into a sham and nothing more than a formal compliance with the Constitution's requirement that an accused be given the assistance of counsel. The Constitution's guarantee of assistance of counsel cannot be satisfied by mere formal appointment.' *Avery v Alabama*, 308 US 444, 446, 60 S Ct 321, 322, 84 L Ed 377 (1940) (footnote omitted)" (*United States v Cronic*, 466 US 648, 654–655, 104 S Ct 2039, 80 L Ed 2d 657 [1984]).

"Of all [of] the rights that an accused person has, the right to be represented by counsel is by far the most pervasive for it affects his ability to assert any other rights he may have" (*United States v Cronic*, 466 US at 654, quoting Schaefer, *Federalism and State Criminal Procedure*, 70 Harv L Rev 1, 8 [1956]). The failure to honor this right, then, cannot but be presumed to impair the reliability of the adversary process through which criminal justice is under our system of government dispensed. This action properly understood, as it has been by distinguished members of the prosecution and defense bars alike, does not threaten but endeavors to preserve our means of criminal adjudication from the inevitably corrosive effects and unjust consequences of an unfair adversary process.

Assuming the allegations of the complaint to be true, there is considerable risk that indigent defendants are, with a fair degree of regularity, being denied constitutionally mandated counsel in the five subject counties. The severe imbalance in the adversary process that such a state of affairs would produce cannot be doubted. Nor can it be doubted that courts would in consequence of such imbalance become breeding grounds for unreliable judgments. Wrongful conviction, the ultimate sign of a criminal justice system's breakdown and failure, has been documented in too many cases. Wrongful convictions, however, are not the only injustices that command our present concern. As plaintiffs rightly point out, the absence of representation at critical stages is capable of causing grave and irreparable injury to persons who will not be convicted. *Gideon*'s guarantee to the assistance of counsel does not turn upon a defendant's guilt or innocence, and neither can the availability of a remedy for its denial.

Accordingly, the order of the Appellate Division should be modified, without costs, by reinstating the complaint in accordance with this opinion, and remitting the case to that court to consider issues raised but not determined on the appeal to that court, and, as so modified, affirmed.

The case never went to trial and was instead settled in 2014 in a settlement that required the state to fully fund defender systems in the five counties involved in the case. In 2016, New York passed legislation extending that settlement statewide, amounting to a request of funds between $450 and 480 million.[6] The unprecedented victory was tempered, however, when the governor of New York vetoed the bill in 2017 and instead opted to give $250 million.[7] *Hurrell-Harring* shows that these systems are in such a state that the poor are not provided their constitutional rights, even in one of the wealthiest states. Politicians are also reluctant to provide funds for these services, as it can be unpopular with many voters who are not poor or do not have to deal with the criminal justice system themselves.

New York is not the only state with a successful lawsuit in this realm. Missouri, a state that shares few similarities to New York, is also plagued by an underfunded public defender system. However, the Missouri case was not brought about by public defenders simply unable to perform their job. It came from their offices refusing to take cases outright.

State ex rel. Mo. Pub. Defender Comm'n v. Waters

370 S.W.3d 592 (Mo. 2012)

The Missouri Public Defender Commission petitions this Court for a writ of prohibition ordering the trial court to withdraw its appointment of the public defender's office to represent Jared Blacksher, alleging that the appointment violated 18 CSR 10-4.010 ("the rule"). That administrative rule, promulgated by the commission pursuant to its rulemaking authority under section 600.017(10), adopts a "caseload protocol" that permits a district defender office to decline additional appointments when

---

6. Lorelei Laird, *Starved of Money for Too Long, Public Defender Offices Are Suing—and Starting to Win*, A.B.A.J. (Jan., 2017), http://www.abajournal.com/magazine/article/the_gideon_revolution.

7. Lorelei Laird, *For the First Time, New York Will Provide Some State Funding for Indigent Defense*, A.B.A.J. (April 14, 2017), http://www.abajournal.com/news/article/for_the_first_time_new_york_will_provide_some_state_funding_for_indigent_de/.

it has been certified as being on limited availability after exceeding its caseload capacity for at least three consecutive calendar months.

[T]he trial court said it believed it "had no choice" but to appoint a public defender, regardless of the public defender's ability to provide competent and effective representation in another case, because to do otherwise would have violated the defendant's Sixth Amendment right to counsel, as the court could identify no other realistic mechanism by which to provide other counsel.

The trial court erred insofar as it believed that the Sixth Amendment requires appointment of counsel without regard to whether counsel would be able to offer competent representation. *State ex rel. Missouri Pub. Defender Comm'n v. Pratte*, 298 S.W.3d 870, 875 (Mo. banc 2009), held, and the Court here reaffirms, that the Sixth Amendment right to counsel is a right to effective and competent counsel, not just a pro forma appointment whereby the defendant has counsel in name only.

The key issue in dispute here and below is whether the duty of public defenders to provide a defense to indigent criminal defendants as set out in section 600.042.4 requires them to accept a judge's appointment to act as counsel no matter the size of their existing caseload and their ability to provide effective representation to their existing or any additional clients and despite the mechanisms contained in 18 CSR 10-4.010. *** The public defender argues that the duty to represent indigent defendants can and must be balanced with the obligation of an attorney to provide competent and effective assistance in order to meet an attorney's ethical and constitutional obligations. This position finds strong support in the fact that, just as regulations must be read in light of the statutes they implement, statutes must be read with the presumption that the General Assembly "did not intend to violate the Constitution." *Becker*, 34 S.W.2d at 29.

Of particular relevance here is the Sixth Amendment. It provides in pertinent part, "In all criminal prosecutions, the accused shall enjoy the right ... to have the Assistance of Counsel for his defence." U.S. Const. amend. VI. Because this right is "fundamental and essential to a fair trial," the constitutional guarantee of counsel is "protected against state invasion by the Due Process Clause of the Fourteenth Amendment." *Gideon v. Wainwright*, 372 U.S. 335, 341, 83 S. Ct. 792, 9 L. Ed. 2d 799 (1963). To that end, Missouri's Constitution similarly provides, "in criminal prosecutions the accused shall have the right to appear and defend, in person and by counsel." Mo. Const. art. I, § 18(a).

As fully amplified, these provisions guarantee that, "absent a knowing and intelligent waiver, no person may be imprisoned for any offense, whether classified as petty, misdemeanor, or felony, unless he was represented by counsel at his trial." *Argersinger v. Hamlin*, 407 U.S. 25, 37, 92 S. Ct. 2006, 32 L. Ed. 2d 530 (1972). "This means, in practical effect, that an indigent accused ... cannot be prosecuted, convicted, and incarcerated in Missouri unless he is furnished counsel." *State v. Green*, 470 S.W.2d 571, 572 (Mo. banc 1971).

To fulfill *Gideon*'s promise that "every defendant stands equal before the law," 372 U.S. at 344, the Missouri General Assembly has enacted an elaborate public defender system to provide legal services to indigent defendants. See §§ 600.011–600.101. Section 600.042.4 provides that the director of the state's public defender system, as well as the defenders within it, "shall provide legal services to an eligible person." Rule 31.02(a) also reflects this principle by stating:

> If any person charged with an offense, the conviction of which would probably result in confinement, shall be without counsel upon his first appearance before a judge, it shall be the duty of the court to advise him of his right to counsel, and of the willingness of the court to appoint counsel to represent him if he is unable to employ counsel.

The rule further specifies that, "[u]pon a showing of indigency, it shall be the duty of the court to appoint counsel to represent" a person charged with an offense likely to result in imprisonment. Rule 31.02(a).

"That a person who happens to be a lawyer is present at trial alongside the accused, however, is not enough to satisfy the constitutional command." *Strickland v. Washington*, 466 U.S. 668, 687, 104 S. Ct. 2052, 80 L. Ed. 2d 674 (1984). Neither judges nor public defenders satisfy "[t]he Constitution's guarantee of assistance to counsel ... by mere formal appointment." *Avery v. Alabama*, 308 U.S. 444, 446, 60 S. Ct. 321, 84 L. Ed. 377 (1940). Rather, "[a]n accused is entitled to be assisted by an attorney, whether retained or appointed, who plays the role necessary to ensure that the trial is fair." *Strickland*, 466 U.S. at 685. "In other words, the right to counsel is the right to effective assistance of counsel." *Kimmelman v. Morrison*, 477 U.S. 365, 377, 106 S. Ct. 2574, 91 L. Ed. 2d 305 (1986) (emphasis added).

This Court has reiterated these principles on numerous occasions. Most recently, in *Pratte*, this Court affirmed that, notwithstanding "that the resources provided for indigent defense are inadequate," a judge nevertheless has the duty to "ensure that the defendant has effective assistance of counsel." 298 S.W.3d at 873, 875 (emphasis in original). ***

Simply put, a judge may not appoint counsel when the judge is aware that, for whatever reason, counsel is unable to provide effective representation to a defendant. Effective, not just pro forma, representation is required by the Missouri and federal constitutions.

No exception exists to the ethics rules for lawyers who represent indigent persons. To the contrary, as the American Bar Association has aptly noted, there is an "implicit premise that governments, which establish and fund providers of public defense, never intended that the lawyers who furnish the representation would be asked to do so if it meant violating their ethical duties pursuant to professional conduct rules." Am. Bar Ass'n, Eight Guidelines of Public Defense Related to Excessive Workloads, August 2009, at 11. For this reason, "public defenders are risking their own professional lives" when appointed to an excessive number of cases. *Pratte*, 298 S.W.3d at 880.

And while the ethical rules do not supplant "a trial judge's obligation to protect [a] defendant's Sixth Amendment rights," they do "run parallel to" that duty and, therefore, can assist both judges and public defenders in ensuring that constitutional rights are protected when appointments are made. State ex rel. *Kinder v. McShane*, 87 S.W.3d 256, 265 (Mo. banc 2002); see also *Frye*, 566 U.S. 132 S. Ct. 1399, 182 L. Ed. 2d 379, WL 932020 * 9 (2012) ("Though the standard for counsel's performance is not determined solely by reference to codified standards of professional practice, these standards can be important guides.").

Therefore, as Pratte noted, section 600.042.4's mandate that "[t]he director and defenders shall provide legal services to an eligible person" must be read to require representation that does satisfy the constitution's guarantee. This means, Pratte held, that appointed counsel must be in a position to provide effective assistance. 298 S.W.3d at 875.

For the reasons set forth above, this Court holds that the trial court exceeded its authority by appointing the public defender's office to represent a defendant in contravention of 18 CSR 10-4.010.…

This Court, therefore, makes clear that trial judges have the responsibility to use their inherent authority to manage their dockets to take an active and productive role in the effort to avoid or limit the need to certify a public defender office as having limited availability.

————————

While this case was a win for the public defender's office, it was a loss for indigent defendants. Because the caseload capacities were reached, poor defendants spent longer in jail waiting for someone to be available for appointment. After this case concluded, a study was conducted. The study, called The Missouri Project,[8] was conducted by an accounting firm to determine the effectiveness of the Missouri public defenders. It compared their recorded hours for a given type of case to what a panel of experts, all criminal attorneys, determined is reasonable to provide effective assistance of counsel. The results were public defenders spending tens of hours less on average than what was determined to be a reasonable amount of time on a case. For some case types, the average time spent was one-fourth or one-fifth of what should be spent to provide effect assistance of counsel.[9]

As a result of this case and the subsequent study in 2014, the Missouri legislature voted to increase the office's budget by $3.5 million in 2014. Missouri Governor Jay Nixon vetoed the budget increase. Even when overruled by the legislature, he only released $500,000. In 2015, the indigent defense budget was cut by $3.47 million. The legislature tried again in 2016, voting for $4.5 million budget increase. Governor Nixon only released $1 million.[10]

————————

8. Rubin Brown, *The Missouri Project: A Study of the Missouri Public Defender System and Attorney Workload Standards*, AM. BAR. ASS'N (June 2014), https://www.americanbar.org/content/dam/aba/events/legal_aid_indigent_defendants/2014/ls_sclaid_5c_the_missouri_project_report.authcheckdam.pdf.

9. *Id.* at 21.

10. Lorelei Laird, *Starved of Money for Too Long, Public Defender Offices Are Suing—and Starting to Win*, A.B.A.J. (Jan. 2017), http://www.abajournal.com/magazine/article/the_gideon_revolution.

The need for effective representation for the poor is met with concerns over budgets. While the right to counsel is "fundamental" in criminal cases involving imprisonment, it is often ineffective in its application. The poor are often provided an attorney, but only see the attorney for a few hours or even minutes before they are sentenced to months or years in prison.

E. The Bail Bond System

Representation is not the only way that access to justice is different for the poor. The money bail system that courts use in the United States has a highly detrimental impact on the poor. Like a lack of effective counsel, pretrial detention negatively affects the outcome of a case for a defendant. Those who are not released pretrial are, on average, sentenced to jail or prison more often and for longer.[11] They have less ability to find and work with counsel. For individuals in poverty this can also affect them in ways not pertaining to their case. If they are not able to get released, they may lose their job or their housing. If someone is unable to pay bail, they will likely be more inclined to take a less favorable plea deal than a defendant who was able to pay their bail and walk free.

The way most judges assign bail is not based on risk or assets. Often there are "bail schedules" in a jurisdiction that set a standardized amount of bail for a given charge. Sometimes these schedules are not mandatory, but many judges still do not take individualized factors into account when setting bail. Even if done without any malice, this practice has a disparate impact on the poor. In counties around the country, lawsuits are arising to challenge these systems.

Odonnell v. Harris County

882 F.3d 528 (5th Cir. 2018)

Maranda ODonnell and other plaintiffs (collectively, "ODonnell") brought a class action suit against Harris County, Texas, and a number of its officials—including County Judges, Hearing Officers, and the Sheriff (collectively, the "County")—under 42 U.S.C. § 1983. ODonnell alleged the County's system of setting bail for indigent misdemeanor arrestees violated Texas statutory and constitutional law, as well as the equal protection and due process clauses of the Fourteenth Amendment. ODonnell moved for a preliminary injunction, and the County moved for summary judgment. After eight days of hearings, at which the parties presented numerous fact and expert witnesses and voluminous written evidence, the district court denied the County's summary judgment motion and granted ODonnell's motion for a preliminary injunction. The County then applied to this court for a stay of the injunction pending appeal, but the motion was denied, and the injunction went into effect. Before this

---

11. Justice Pol'y Inst., Bail Fail: Why the U.S. Should End the Practice of Using Money for Bail (Sept. 2012), http://www.justicepolicy.org/uploads/justicepolicy/documents/bailfail_executive_summary.pdf.

court now is the County's appeal, seeking vacatur of the injunction and raising numerous legal challenges.

For the reasons set forth, we affirm most of the district court's rulings, including its conclusion that ODonnell established a likelihood of success on the merits of its claims that the County's policies violate procedural due process and equal protection. We disagree, however, with the district court's analysis in three respects: First, its definition of ODonnell's liberty interest under due process was too broad, and the procedures it required to protect that interest were too onerous. Second, it erred by concluding that the County Sheriff can be sued under § 1983. Finally, the district court's injunction was overbroad. As a result, we will dismiss the Sheriff from the suit, vacate the injunction, and order the district court to modify its terms in a manner consistent with this opinion.

Bail in Texas is either secured or unsecured. Secured bail requires the arrestee to post bond either out of the arrestee's pocket or from a third-party surety (often bail bondsmen, who generally require a 10% non-refundable premium in exchange for posting bond). Unsecured bail, by contrast, allows the arrestee to be released without posting bond, but if he fails to attend his court date and/or comply with any nonfinancial bail conditions, he becomes liable to the County for the bail amount. Both secured and unsecured bail may also include nonfinancial conditions to assure the detainee's attendance at future hearings.

The Hearing Officers and County Judges are legally proscribed from mechanically applying the bail schedule to a given arrestee. Instead, the Texas Code requires officials to conduct an individualized review based on five enumerated factors, which include the defendant's ability to pay, the charge, and community safety. Tex. Code of Crim. Proc. art. 17.15. The Local Rules explicitly state the schedule is not mandatory. They also authorize a similar, individualized assessment using factors which partially overlap with those listed in the Code. Local Rule 4.2.4. Hearing Officers and County Judges sometimes receive assessments by Pretrial Services, which interviews the detainees prior to hearings, calculates the detainees flight and safety risk based on a point system, and then makes specific recommendations regarding bail.

Despite these formal requirements, the district court found that, in practice, County procedures were dictated by an unwritten custom and practice that was marred by gross inefficiencies, did not achieve any individualized assessment in setting bail, and was incompetent to do so. The district court noted that the statutorily mandated probable cause hearing (where bail is usually set) frequently does not occur within 24 hours of arrest. The hearings often last seconds, and rarely more than a few minutes. Arrestees are instructed not to speak, and are not offered any opportunity to submit evidence of relative ability to post bond at the scheduled amount.

The court found that the results of this flawed procedural framework demonstrate the lack of individualized assessments when officials set bail. County officials "impose the scheduled bail amounts on a secured basis about 90 percent of the time. When [they] do change the bail amount, it is often to conform the amount to what is in the bail schedule." The court further found that, when Pretrial Services recommends release on personal bond, Hearing Officers reject the suggestion 66% of the time. Because less than 10% of misdemeanor arrestees are assigned an unsecured personal bond, some amount of upfront payment is required for release in the vast majority of cases.

The court also found that the "Next Business Day" hearing before a County Judge fails to provide a meaningful review of the Hearing Officer's bail determinations. Arrestees routinely must wait days for their hearings. County Judges adjust bail amounts or grant unsecured bonds in less than 1% of cases. Furthermore, prosecutors routinely offer time-served plea bargains at the hearing, and arrestees are under immense pressure to accept the plea deals or else remain incarcerated for days or weeks until they are appointed a lawyer.

The district court further noted the various ways in which the imposition of secured bail specifically targets poor arrestees. For example, under the County's risk-assessment point system used by Pretrial Services, poverty indicators (such as not owning a car) receive the same point value as prior criminal violations or prior failures to appear in court. Thus, an arrestee's impoverishment increased the likelihood he or she would need to pay to be released.

The court also observed that Hearing Officers imposed secured bails upon arrestees after having been made aware of an arrestee's indigence by the risk-assessment reports or by the arrestee's own statements. And further, after extensive review of numerous bail hearings, the court concluded Hearing Officers were aware that, by imposing a secured bail on indigent arrestees, they were ensuring that those arrestees would remain detained.

The court rejected the argument that imposing secured bonds served the County's interest in ensuring the arrestee appeared at the future court date and committed no further crime. The court's review of reams of empirical data suggested the opposite: that "release on secured financial conditions does not assure better rates of appearance or of law-abiding conduct before trial compared to release on unsecured bonds or nonfinancial conditions of supervision." Instead, the County's true purpose was "to achieve pretrial detention of misdemeanor defendants who are too poor to pay, when those defendants would promptly be released if they could pay." In short, "secured money bail function[ed] as a pretrial detention order" against the indigent misdemeanor arrestees.

The district court also reviewed voluminous empirical data and academic literature to evaluate the impact of pretrial detention on an arrestee. The court found that the expected outcomes for an arrestee who cannot afford to post bond are significantly worse than for those arrestees who can. In general, indigent arrestees who remain incarcerated because they cannot make bail are significantly more likely to plead guilty and to be sentenced to imprisonment. They also receive sentences that are on average twice as long as their bonded counterparts. Furthermore, the district court found that pretrial detention can lead to loss of job, family stress, and even an increase in likeliness to commit crime.

The County contends that ODonnell's complaint "is an Eighth Amendment case wearing a Fourteenth Amendment costume." The Eighth Amendment states in relevant part that "[e]xcessive bail shall not be required." U.S. CONST. amend. VIII. It is certainly true that, when a constitutional provision specifically addresses a given claim for relief under 42 U.S.C. § 1983, a party should seek to apply that provision directly. See *Graham v. Connor*, 490 U.S. 386, 394, 109 S. Ct. 1865, 104 L. Ed. 2d 443 (1989); cf. *Manuel v. City of Joliet*, 137 S. Ct. 911, 917, 197 L. Ed. 2d 312 (2017). But we have already concluded that "[t]he incarceration of those who cannot [pay money bail], without meaningful consideration of other possible alternatives, infringes on both due process and equal protection requirements." *Pugh v. Rainwater*, 572 F.2d 1053, 1057 (5th Cir. 1978) (en banc). ODonnell's present claims do not run afoul of Graham.

On the one hand, bail is meant "to secure the presence of the defendant in court at his trial." Ex parte Vance, 608 S.W.2d 681, 683 (Tex. Crim. App. 1980). Accordingly, "ability to make bail is a factor to be considered, [but] ability alone, even indigency, does not control the amount of bail." Ex parte Charlesworth, 600 S.W.2d 316, 317 (Tex. Crim. App. 1980). On the other hand, Texas courts have repeatedly emphasized the importance of bail as a means of protecting an accused detainee's constitutional right "in remaining free before trial," which allows for the "unhampered preparation of a defense, and ... prevent[s] the infliction of punishment prior to conviction." *Ex parte Anderer*, 61 S.W.3d 398, 404–05 (Tex. Crim. App. 2001) (en banc). Accordingly, the courts have sought to limit the imposition of "preventive [pretrial] detention" as "abhorrent to the American system of justice." *Ex parte Davis*, 574 S.W.2d 166, 169 (Tex. Crim. App. 1978). Notably, state courts have recognized that "the power to ... require bail," not simply the denial of bail, can be an "instrument of [such] oppression." *Taylor v. State*, 667 S.W.2d 149, 151 (Tex. Crim. App. 1984).

The Constitution creates a right to bail on "sufficient sureties," which includes both a concern for the arrestee's interest in pretrial freedom and the court's interest in assurance. Since bail is not purely defined by what the detainee can afford, see *Charlesworth*, 600 S.W.2d at 317, the constitutional provision forbidding denial of release on bail for misdemeanor arrestees does not create an automatic right to pretrial release. Instead, Texas state law creates a right to bail that appropriately weighs the detainees' interest in pretrial release and the court's interest in securing the detainee's attendance. Yet, as noted, state law forbids the setting of bail as an "instrument of oppression." Thus, magistrates may not impose a secured bail solely for the purpose of detaining the accused. And, when the accused is indigent, setting a secured bail will, in most cases, have the same effect as a detention order.

The court's factual findings (which are not clearly erroneous) demonstrate that secured bail orders are imposed almost automatically on indigent arrestees. Far from demonstrating sensitivity to the indigent misdemeanor defendants' ability to pay, Hearing Officers and County Judges almost always set a bail amount that detains the indigent. In other words, the current procedure does not sufficiently protect detainees from magistrates imposing bail as an "instrument of oppression." ... The district court's definition of ODonnell's liberty interests is too broad, and the procedural protections it required are too strict. Nevertheless, even under our more forgiving framework, we agree that the County procedures violate ODonnell's due process rights.

The district court held that the County's bail-setting procedures violated the equal protection clause of the Fourteenth Amendment because they treat otherwise similarly-situated misdemeanor arrestees differently based solely on their relative wealth. The County makes three separate arguments against this holding. It argues: (1) ODonnell's disparate impact theory is not cognizable under the equal protection clause, see Johnson v. Rodriguez, 110 F.3d 299, 306 (5th Cir. 1997); (2) rational basis review applies and is satisfied; (3) even if heightened scrutiny applies, it is satisfied. We disagree.

First, the district court did not conclude that the County policies and procedures violated the equal protection clause solely on the basis of their disparate impact. Instead, it found the County's custom and practice purposefully "detain[ed] misdemeanor defendants before trial who are otherwise eligible for release, but whose indigence makes them unable to pay secured financial conditions of release." The conclusion of a discriminatory purpose was evidenced by numerous, sufficiently supported factual findings, including direct evidence from bail hearings. This custom and practice resulted in detainment solely due to a person's indigency because the financial conditions for release are based on predetermined amounts beyond a person's ability to pay and without any "meaningful consideration of other possible alternatives." *Rainwater*, 572 F.2d at 1057. Under this circuit's binding precedent, the district court was therefore correct to conclude that this discriminatory action was unconstitutional. *Id.* at 1056–57 (noting that pre-trial "imprisonment solely because of indigent status is invidious discrimination and not constitutionally permissible" under both "due process and equal protection requirements"); see also *Griffin v. Illinois*, 351 U.S. 12, 18, 76 S. Ct. 585, 100 L. Ed. 891 (1956) (noting that the indigent are protected by equal protection "at all stages of [criminal] proceedings"). Because this conclusion is sufficient to decide this case, we need not determine whether the equal protection clause requires a categorical bar on secured money bail for indigent misdemeanor arrestees who cannot pay it.

Second, the district court's application of intermediate scrutiny was not in error. It is true that, ordinarily, "[n]either prisoners nor indigents constitute a suspect class." *Carson v. Johnson*, 112 F.3d 818, 821–22 (5th Cir. 1997). But the Supreme Court has found that heightened scrutiny is required when criminal laws detain poor defendants because of their indigence. See, e.g., *Tate v. Short*, 401 U.S. 395, 397–99, 91 S. Ct. 668, 28 L. Ed. 2d 130 (1971) (invalidating a facially neutral statute that authorized imprisonment for failure to pay fines because it violated the equal protection rights of indigents); *Williams v. Illinois*, 399 U.S. 235, 241–42, 90 S. Ct. 2018, 26 L. Ed. 2d 586 (1970) (invalidating a facially neutral statute that required convicted defendants to remain in jail beyond the maximum sentence if they could not pay other fines associated with their sentences because it violated the equal protection rights of indigents). Reviewing this case law, the Supreme Court later noted that indigents receive a heightened scrutiny where two conditions are met: (1) "because of their impecunity they were completely unable to pay for some desired benefit," and (2) "as a consequence, they sustained an absolute deprivation of a meaningful opportunity to enjoy that benefit." *San Antonio Indep. Sch. Dist. v. Rodriguez*, 411 U.S. 1, 20, 93 S. Ct. 1278, 36 L. Ed. 2d 16 (1973).

We conclude that this case falls into the exception created by the Court. Both aspects of the Rodriguez analysis apply here: indigent misdemeanor arrestees are unable to pay secured bail, and, as a result, sustain an absolute deprivation of their most basic liberty interests — freedom from incarceration. Moreover, this case presents the same basic injustice: poor arrestees in Harris County are incarcerated where similarly situated wealthy arrestees are not, solely because the indigent cannot afford to pay a secured bond. Heightened scrutiny of the County's policy is appropriate. ***
Additionally, the court considered a comprehensive study of the impact of Harris County's bail system on the behavior of misdemeanor detainees between 2008 and 2013. The study found that the imposition of secured bail might increase the likelihood of unlawful behavior. See Paul Heaton et al., *The Downstream Consequences of Misdemeanor Pretrial Detention*, 69 STAN. L. REV. 711, 786–87 (2017) (estimating that the release on personal bond of the lowest-risk detainees would have resulted in 1,600 fewer felonies and 2,400 fewer misdemeanors within the following eighteen months). These findings mirrored those of various empirical studies from other jurisdictions.

In sum, the essence of the district court's equal protection analysis can be boiled down to the following: take two misdemeanor arrestees who are identical in every way — same charge, same criminal backgrounds, same circumstances, etc. — except that one is wealthy and one is indigent. Applying the County's current custom and practice, with their lack of individualized assessment and mechanical application of the secured bail schedule, both arrestees would almost certainly receive identical secured bail amounts. One arrestee is able to post bond, and the other is not. As a result, the wealthy arrestee is less likely to plead guilty, more likely to receive a shorter sentence or be acquitted, and less likely to bear the social costs of incarceration. The poor arrestee, by contrast, must bear the brunt of all of these, simply because he has less money than his wealthy counterpart. The district court held that this state of affairs violates the equal protection clause, and we agree.

Odonnell is not just changing things in Harris County. As a result of this case, legislation is in the works in Texas for statewide reform. Some cities and counties in Texas are reforming their bail systems of their own accord.[12] The success of this case

---

12. Jolie McCullough, *How Harris County's Federal Bail Lawsuit Spreads Beyond Houston*, TEX. TRIB. (Oct. 2, 2017), https://www.texastribune.org/2017/10/02/how-harris-countys-bail-lawsuit-spreads-beyond-houston/.

spurred other suits. For example, Glynn County, Georgia, was sued by the ACLU in March 2018, less than one month after *Odonnell* was decided, over their money bail system. The county follows a money bail schedule requiring fixed-rate bail amounts based on the charge, with no consideration of ability to pay. In addition, the county of more than 80,000 has one public defender for all misdemeanor cases.[13] This combination of ineffective assistance of counsel and a fixed bail schedule creates a system of railroading the poor to guilty pleas.

---

13. Andrea Woods, Ga ACLU, No Money to Make Bail or Pay for a Lawyer? Too Bad, Say Officials in Glynn County (Mar. 12, 2018), https://www.aclu.org/blog/mass-incarceration/smart-justice/no-money-make-bail-or-pay-lawyer-too-bad-say-officials-glynn.

Chapter Twelve

Community Development

Poverty occurs within social and economic systems and includes the physical communities where poor people live. Consequently, anti-poverty responses often require community-wide approaches. "Community development" may be seen as a particular strategy that encompasses efforts to create economic opportunity through broadbased community efforts focused on job creation and infrastructure improvement. Community development strategies were a key element of the Great Society programs launched by the Johnson Administration during the 1960s, but they too often ignored the voice of the poor. Community-based strategies have continued in more recent programs, such as HOPE VI.

Despite the impact of such efforts on communities and the people who live and work in them, community development is often a "top-down" strategy that is directed by centralized government. The materials in this section consider the process of community development when directed by public agencies, as well as private efforts led by nonprofit organizations. Common questions run through these efforts, including the potential such efforts have to address areas of concentrated poverty and the place of the community in both the decision-making process and the ultimate outcome.

A. Linking Community Development to Economic Growth

Community development emerged as a problem-solving strategy in the United States in the late nineteenth century. At the time, the country's booming industrial growth was burdened by crowded areas of low-wage workers living in unsanitary and unsustainable "slums."[1] Over the course of the next several years, as social reformers (often referred to as "Progressives") drew attention to these areas, new strategies emerged to improve the quality of life for these low-income citizens.[2] Many of these efforts were targeted toward improving housing conditions for these citizens.

---

1. Alexander von Hoffman, *The Past, Present, and Future of Community Development in the United States, in* INVESTING IN WHAT WORKS FOR AMERICA'S COMMUNITIES (Dec. 2012), http://www.jchs. harvard.edu/sites/jchs.harvard.edu/files/w12-6_von_hoffman.pdf.

2. *Id.*

The Progressive movement saw its first national contribution toward community development with Franklin D. Roosevelt's implementation of the New Deal. Although well-intentioned, the programs associated with the New Deal reflected a "top-down" structure — that is, resources were not injected directly into the needy communities, but instead trickled down from the top levels of government according to the top-level assessment of where, how, and what need was to be addressed.[3] This approach was further cemented with the adoption of the Housing Act of 1949 and remained pervasive up through President Lyndon Johnson's declared "War on Poverty."[4]

Today, the U.S. Department of Housing and Urban Development describes community development as follows:

Community development activities build stronger and more resilient communities through an ongoing process of identifying and addressing needs, assets, and priority investments. Community development activities may support infrastructure, economic development projects, installation of public facilities, community centers, housing rehabilitation, public services, clearance/acquisition, microenterprise assistance, code enforcement, homeowner assistance and many other identified needs. Federal support for community development encourages systematic and sustained action by State, and local governments.[5]

HUD has historically hosted a number of programs, initiatives, and assistance programs to achieve these goals, such as the Community Development Block Grant program, loan guarantee programs, disaster recovery programs, and neighborhood stabilization programs.[6]

Although a broad and elusive concept, a well-executed community development initiative can have a significant impact on the targeted communities and can lead to substantial economic growth within that community. From a global perspective, community development initiatives are useful for adapting rural areas to become more self-sufficient systems. In the United States in particular, successful community development initiatives can increase employment and income as well as expand opportunities for residents.

B. Community Development Block Grant Program

Identifying the problem and proposing solutions are only the first two steps of the battle. In order to implement meaningful changes and beneficial programs, there is a significant roadblock: funding. For the last 40 years, a popular source of funding

---

3. *Id.*
4. *Id.*
5. U.S. Dep't of Housing and Urban Development, *Community Development*, https://www.hud.gov/program_offices/comm_planning/communitydevelopment (last visited May 4, 2018).
6. *Id.*

for various community development programs has been the application for and allotment of funds from the Community Development Block Grant program.

The Housing and Community Development Act of 1974 ("HCDA") was signed into law by President Gerald Ford and took effect in 1975.[7] The HCDA was hailed as one of the most important pieces of community development legislation. The HCDA created the Community Development Block Grant ("CDBG") as well as Section 8 housing, among other programs.[8] The purpose of the CDBG was to "ensure decent affordable housing, to provide services to the most vulnerable in our communities, and to create jobs through the expansion and retention of businesses."[9] This was done through a series of funding distributions to local communities and development activities, which was a change from the previous federal approach to community development. In Ford's own words, in fact, the CDBG was intended to "redistribute influence from the federal bureaucracies to local governments."[10]

In its first fiscal year (1975), the CDBG program received $2.5 billion in block grants with another $8.4 billion authorized for distribution over the course of the following three years.[11] To be eligible for distribution, the grantee needs to be either a principal city of Metropolitan Statistical Areas, another metropolitan city with populations of at least 50,000, or a qualified urban county with a population of at least 200,000 (excluding the population of entitled cities).[12] To be in compliance with the grant, the activity for which a grant was requested needs to meet one of a number of national objectives including benefiting low- and moderate-income people, preventing or eliminating slums or blight, or other community development activities addressing an urgent threat to health or safety.[13] Additionally, 70% or more of the CDBG funds allocated to a project need to benefit low- and moderate-income people over a set period—either one, two, or three years, as selected by the grantee.[14] Finally, CDBG fund grantees are required to develop and follow plans providing for and encouraging citizen participation by arranging and giving adequate notice of local meetings and public hearings, providing timely written answers to citizen complaints,

---

7. National Low Income Housing Coalition, 40 Years Ago: August 22, President Ford Signs Housing and Community Development Act of 1974 (2014), http://nlihc.org/article/40-years-ago-august-22-president-ford-signs-housing-and-community-development-act-1974 (last visited May 4, 2018).

8. *Id.*

9. U.S. Dep't of Housing and Urban Development, *Community Development Block Grant Program — CDBG*, https://www.hud.gov/program_offices/comm_planning/communitydevelopment/programs (last visited May 4, 2018).

10. William Frej & Harry Specht, *The Housing and Community Development Act of 1974: Implications for Policy and Planning*, 50 Soc. Serv. Rev. 275–292 (1976), http://www.jstor.org.go.libproxy.wakehealth.edu/stable/pdf/30015353.pdf?refreqid=excelsior:0c87932ea667a158aff9c6f109f7b790.

11. *Id.*

12. *Id.*

13. *CDBG Entitlement Program Eligibility Requirements*, HUD Exchange, https://www.hud exchange.info/programs/cdbg-entitlement/cdbg-entitlement-program-eligibility-requirements/ (last visited May 5, 2018).

14. *Id.*

and identifying how they would identify the needs of non-English-speaking individuals at public hearings.[15]

Generally speaking, eligible activities for which CDBG funds are authorized include acquisition of real property, rehabilitation of structures, construction of public facilities, public services, or assistance to profit-motivated businesses committed to carrying out economic development and job creation or retention activities.[16] Some specific examples of successful CDBG programs include a new library and senior center in Mellen, Wisconsin, and necessary road reconstruction in Sauk Rapids, Minnesota.[17]

In early 2018, President Donald Trump proposed a budget for the 2019 fiscal year that completely eradicated the CDBG program.[18] The proposal also reduced the overall HUD budget by 18.3 percent, or $8.8 billion, from 2017 spending levels.[19] The Trump Administration made a similar proposal in 2017 for the 2018 fiscal year budget with the CDBG program alone seeing a cut of over $3 billion,[20] although that proposal never made it to Congress for a vote.[21] The CDBG program has seen a cut of more than $1 billion since its 2010 fiscal year levels.[22]

This battle has continued on in light of 2019 fiscal year budget proposals. Components of the Trump Administration's original 2019 fiscal year budget proposal included imposing work requirements on citizens receiving public housing subsidies, as well as the aforementioned $8.8 billion cut to HUD funding.[23] A subsequent addendum to the proposal added a $2 billion allotment to HUD, nevertheless leaving it well below prior years' budgets.[24] A senior policy analyst at the Center on Budget and Policy Priorities calls the proposal "harsh" for housing programs intended to help low-income citizens and families "keep a roof over their head."[25]

---

15. *Id.*

16. *Id.*

17. Mike Larson & Nate Day, *16 Inspiring Examples of Communities Capitalizing on CDBG Funding*, SEH INC. (2018), http://www.sehinc.com/news/16-inspiring-examples-communities-capitalizing-cdbg-funding (last visited May 4, 2018).

18. Steven Malanga, *Anti-Poverty Community Development Block Grants Are A Total Failure—So Why Don't We Kill This Program?*, INVESTOR'S BUS. DAILY (last visited May 4, 2018).

19. NATIONAL LOW INCOME HOUSING COALITION, PRESIDENT TRUMP CALLS FOR DRASTIC CUTS TO AFFORDABLE HOUSING, February 12, 2018 (2018), http://nlihc.org/article/president-trump-calls-drastic-cuts-affordable-housing-february-12-2018 (last visited May 4, 2018).

20. *$6,822,500,000: Trump FY 18 HUD Budget Cut to Impact 1,319,000 Families*, AFFORDABLE HOUSING ONLINE (2017), https://affordablehousingonline.com/FY18-HUD-Budget-Cuts (last visited May 4, 2018).

21. *Id.*

22. DARIA DANIEL, NATIONAL ASSOCIATION OF COUNTIES, SUPPORT LOCAL DEVELOPMENT AND INFRASTRUCTURE PROJECTS: THE COMMUNITY DEVELOPMENT BLOCK GRANT (CDBG) PROGRAM (Feb. 15, 2018), http://www.naco.org/resources/support-local-development-and-infrastructure-projects-community-development-block-grant-1 (last visited May 4, 2018).

23. Brakkton Booker, *White House Budget Calls For Deep Cuts To HUD*, NPR (Feb. 13, 2018), https://www.npr.org/2018/02/13/585255697/white-house-budget-calls-for-deep-cuts-to-hud (last visited May 5, 2018).

24. *Id.*

25. *Id.*

Naturally, the Trump Administration's proposal has sparked feedback and commentary. For example, former presidential candidate and head of the Department of Housing and Urban Development, Ben Carson, tweeted that the proposal is "focused on moving more people toward self-sufficiency."[26] Another commentator remarks that the CDBGs are a "total failure" and better off left unfunded.[27] Yet another draws attention to a 2016 audit of Riverside County, California, that the Office of Inspector General of the U.S. Department of Housing and Urban Development presented as evidence of a failing program.[28] Specifically, the audit concluded that Riverside County often failed to obtain proper documentation to show that the program's eligibility requirements were being met before expending program funds on various community improvements.[29]

On the other hand, the proposal's critics are calling the proposal "devastating" and warn of all the "local initiatives [that] would die if Trump got his way."[30] United States Senator Tammy Baldwin, a member of the Senate Appropriations Committee, is one such opponent.[31] When the Trump Administration's proposal for the 2017 fiscal year was released, Senator Baldwin, feeling particularly moved by firsthand examples of how Community Development Block Grants have helped people across Wisconsin, led the fight in getting full federal funding restored for the 2018 fiscal year.[32]

The city of Philadelphia, Pennsylvania, has a legion of opponents to the Trump Administration's proposal, and for good reason. Philadelphia is notoriously one of the most impoverished cities in the country. As of 2017, it suffers from a 25.7% poverty rate — the highest among the 10 largest U.S. cities.[33] This reflects an increase of nearly 10.3 percentage points between 1970 and 2016, despite a generally stable national average.[34] Accordingly, it suffers from crippling homelessness, blight, a lack of access to community resources, and all of the other tell-tale indicators of an impoverished community. Since the inception of the CDBG program 40 years ago, Philadelphia has relied on these funds to provide affordable housing, basic repairs, and commercial development.[35]

---

26. *Id.*

27. Malanga, *supra* note 18.

28. Scott Shackford, *The Community Development Block Grant Program Is Awful and Should Be Cut*, REASON.COM (Mar. 16, 2017), https://reason.com/blog/2017/03/16/the-community-development-block-grant-pr (last visited May 5, 2018).

29. Tanya E. Schulze, U.S. Dep't of Housing and Urban Development, Office of the Inspector General, *Audit Report Number: 2016-LA-1002* (Feb. 18, 2016), https://www.hudoig.gov/sites/default/files/documents/2016-LA-1002.pdf.

30. Malanga, *supra* note 18.

31. Press Release, U.S. Sen. Tammy Baldwin (Jul. 28, 2017), https://www.baldwin.senate.gov/press-releases/reverses-cuts-to-cdbg (last visited May 4, 2018).

32. *Id.*

33. THE PEW CHARITABLE TRUSTS, PHILADELPHIA'S POOR (Nov. 15, 2017), http://www.pewtrusts.org/en/research-and-analysis/reports/2017/11/philadelphias-poor (last visited May 4, 2018).

34. *Id.*

35. PHILA.GOV, COMMUNITY DEVELOPMENT BLOCK GRANT (CDBG-R), http://www.phila.gov/recovery/ED_CDBG.html (last visited May 4, 2018).

In the 1996 fiscal year, Philadelphia was allocated more than $126.5 million in CDBG funds (adjusted for inflation).[36] In 2001, it received approximately $97.8 million (adjusted for inflation).[37] In 2017, this number dropped to a mere $39 million.[38] From that, $10.9 million went to assisting low-income homeowners pay for repairs on their homes and $5.1 million went to housing counseling and foreclosure prevention, a program responsible for keeping thousands of families in their homes since 2008.[39]

The proposed changes to the 2019 HUD budget would have a devastating effect on these programs. Specifically, the proposal would mean the complete elimination of CDBG funding, the HOME Investment Partnerships program, and many other housing and community development programs relied on by the city of Philadelphia and other cities nationwide.[40] Brendan F. Boyle, a Pennsylvania Congressman and member of the House Committee on the Budget, calls the 2019 budget proposal an "all-out assault on the middle class."[41] Congressman Dwight Evans added that "At a time when our cities are already pressed for resources and funding we should be in the business of 'doing no harm' and it is more than evident that the president and his administration seek to do just the opposite." Boyle and Evans are joined by Congressman Bob Brady, Philadelphia Mayor Jim Kenney, and many other local officials in vocal opposition to the budget proposal and its decimation of community development programs.[42]

C. Blight and Gentrification

Gentrification occurs when "original working-class occupiers are displaced" by higher-income residents.[43] Some see benefits in gentrification,[44] including higher

---

36. Pamela Bridgeforth & Rick Sauer, Phila. Ass'n Community Dev. Corp., Make No Little Plans: Ending Philly's Housing Crisis (2016), http://pacdc.org/2017/wp-content/uploads/2017/06/PACDC2016_.pdf.

37. Jake Blumgart, PlanPhilly, What's at Stake if Toomey and Trump Cut Funding to Philly? (Dec. 2, 2016), http://planphilly.com/articles/2016/12/02/what-s-at-stake-if-toomey-and-trump-cut-funding-to-philly (last visited May 4, 2018).

38. Community Leg. Serv. of Phila., Proposed Cuts to HUD Would Be Devastating to Philadelphia (Mar. 9, 2017), https://clsphila.org/news/proposed-cuts-hud-would-be-devastating-philadelphia (last visited May 5, 2018).

39. Blumgart, *supra* note 37.

40. News Release, Rep. Dwight Evans (Apr. 9, 2018), https://evans.house.gov/media-center/press-releases/philly-congressional-delegation-philly-mayor-and-city-councilmembers.

41. *Id.*

42. *Id.*

43. *See* Ruth Glass, London: Aspects of Change (1964).

44. *Contra* Jacob Vigdor, *Does Gentrification Harm the Poor?* Brookings-Wharton Papers on Urban Affairs 133 (2002) (reasoning displacement not necessary in gentrification analysis), *with* Lance Freeman, *Displacement or Succession? Residential Mobility in Gentrifying Neighborhoods,* 40 Urb. Aff. Rev. 4 (2005) (presenting more complex analysis of gentrification, including displacement of lower-income households).

property values with attendant tax revenues, yet it is widely agreed that the consequences for displaced residents is particularly burdensome on individuals with little political voice.[45] Moreover, gentrification reflects racial dynamics as areas that experience gentrification generally have larger minority populations.[46] Although racial components are found in the process of gentrification, its core elements are economic in nature. Gentrification reflects "the process by which people of higher incomes move into lower income urban areas and seek to change its physical and social fabric to better meet their needs and preferences."[47] The economic processes of gentrification are expressed in ways other than displacement, including situations where areas have "convert[ed] industrial lofts to residences and shops, causing only minimal displacement" as well as those where "low-income residents who remain in a gentrifying neighborhood with a low vacancy rate may be harmed by paying a higher percentage of their income for rent."[48]

Whether desired or not, the process of gentrification "results in the displacement of low-income individuals, families, and people of color, thereby changing the character of the neighborhood, whereas revitalization invests in and enhances the physical, social, and commercial components of the neighborhoods."[49] As an economic force, gentrification plays out along expected lines of wealth and power. Residents of communities with higher poverty rates may not experience displacement, yet midmarket cities may displace the poor to nearby suburbs, and wealthy cities may displace the poor "from the city and even the surrounding region"[50] altogether, resulting in "the replacement of a less affluent group by a wealthier social group — a definition which relates gentrification to class."[51]

Multiple forces propel gentrification, involving an "interweaving of State influence, private development, a consumerist middle class, and a vulnerable low-income population ..."[52] As the process proceeds, its beneficiaries see "progress." Gentrification addresses "unemployment, poverty, or broken homes," not by solving these issues, but rather by displacing the problems elsewhere, which has the result of "geographically marginalizing the urban poor and ensuring their economic location and political irrelevance."[53]

---

45. *See* Justin Feldman, *Gentrification, Urban Displacement and Affordable Housing: Overview and Research Roundup*, JOURNALIST'S RESOURCE, http://journalistsresource.org/studies/economics/real-estate/gentrification-urban-displacement-affordable-housing-overview-research-roundup (last updated Aug. 15, 2014).

46. *See generally* Jackelyn Hwang, Robert Sampson, *Divergent Pathways of Gentrification: Racial Inequality and the Social Order of Renewal in Chicago Neighborhoods*, 79 AM. SOC. REV. 726 (2014).

47. J. Peter Byrne, *Two Cheers for Gentrification*, 46 HOW. L.J. 405, 406 (Spring 2003).

48. *Id.* at 406, 407.

49. Bethany Y. Li, *Now Is the Time!: Challenging Resegregation and Displacement in the Age of Hypergentrification*, 85 FORDHAM L. REV. 1189 (December 2016).

50. *Id.*

51. Emily Ponder, *Gentrification and the Right to Housing: How HIP Becomes a Human Rights Violation*, 22 SW. J. INT'L L. 359, 362 (2016).

52. *Id.*

53. *Id.* at 363.

State and local governments often fuel the process of gentrification through the use of targeted incentives, strategic planning, public services, and rezoning,[54] often with a desire to attract wealthy professional class. As neighborhoods gentrify, they become "the affluent professional's 'discovery' of the city has not been by accident or merely created by twenty-first-century consumption tastes," but rather "coincides quite evenly with a decades-old policy of cities trying to attract the upper-middle class to the city."[55] Just as local government incentivizes business relocation, targeted incentives and general policies aimed at creating amenities draw the professional class.[56] The theory, and explanation, for gentrification is that creating a safer, revitalized[57] neighborhood in areas of more concentrated poverty will decrease crime and increase property taxes. These impacts include increased property tax bases, greater tourism revenue, reduced crime rates and drug use, more economic activity, and integrated neighborhoods. Businesses will even claim that "gentrification may benefit the poor."[58]

Gentrification then applies to "the affluent class-based nature of restructuring," with restructuring more narrowly defined as "a deliberate, as well as structural, dimension to the changes taking place in the city."[59] Gentrification can either be "induced or spontaneous"—inducement being the result of specific government planning while spontaneous is "driven not by planners but individuals discovering the excellent urban qualities of the place."[60]

Economic forces lead to movements of people with wealth into areas of poverty, with the result being a cultural change to that community. Intentional displacement may not be necessary for the processes of gentrification to occur in this dynamic—some level of "indirect displacement" occurs due to rising housing costs regardless of intent.[61]

A working definition of gentrification for present purposes would be:

---

54. *Id.* at 364.

55. Audrey G. McFarlane, *The New Inner City: Class Transformation, Concentrated Affluence and the Obligations of the Police Power*, 8 U. PA. J. CONST. L. 1 (January 2006).

56. *Id.* at 6.

57. Revitalization is distinct from gentrification. Revitalization generally refers to process where money is funneled into certain areas, through building more shops, bringing in businesses, etc. in order to create economic stimulus in a targeted neighborhood.

58. *See* Patrick Gillespie, *How Gentrification May Benefit the Poor*, CNN (Nov. 12, 2015), http://money.cnn.com/2015/11/12/news/economy/gentrification-may-help-poor-people/. The article cites studies explaining that benefits for low-income residents include new job opportunities, rising property values, decline in crime, and increased credit scores for poor residents. However, even these studies concede that if lower-income residents move, they will move to even poorer neighborhoods, and have difficulty maintaining residence in a gentrified neighborhood. *See also Gentrification Is Good for the Poor*, BUS. INSIDER (Feb. 21, 2015), http://www.businessinsider.com/gentrification-is-good-for-the-poor-2015-2 (defending gentrification).

59. *Id.* at 26.

60. *Id.*

61. Byrne at 412.

(1) the movement of those with wealth into historical areas of poverty,

(2) resulting in cultural changes to that community,

(3) encouraged by general government development policies, and

(4) results in the displacement of people through rising housing costs or other circumstances.

This definition does not consider race. Racial dynamics of gentrification are implied although not stated in each of these factors, as the neighborhoods most affected by gentrification are communities of color.[62]

Efforts to redevelop prior industrial or commercial areas into entrepreneurship districts reflect such gentrification processes.

1. Gentrification's Process of Displacement

Inevitable in the process, gentrification brings displacement.[63] The process of displacement is directly linked to the increased desirability of real estate. When neighborhoods gentrify, landlords increase rent as higher-income residents move in. As property values increase with new affluent tenants, taxes increase. As jobs are created that pay more, new residents who earn more push out existing residents. While economic in nature, gentrification's impacts are far more widespread.[64] Displacement causes emotional harm to the low-income residents who are forced to leave their communities.[65] As low-income residents are forced to move to more suburban or depressed areas that have greater affordable living options, they often find fewer job opportunities and increased travel. Public transportation becomes a problem as low-income residents move farther away from cities. The social networks, established over lifetimes and generations, are left behind out of necessity.

2. Origins and Causes of Gentrification

While gentrification is driven by economic forces, its origins are multidimensional. In the residential housing context, historical redlining practices continue to shape neighborhoods in ways that enable gentrification. Redlining was a highly prevalent, lawful method to segregate cities until the second half of the twentieth century. The

---

62. An irony underlies this process. The pre-gentrification state of urban areas itself often resulted from "white flight" to the suburbs, which is now being reversed by wealthy whites returning to these communities, which have low prices and supposed "character."

63. It is the extent and harms of such displacement that are disputed.

64. *See generally* GARY ORFIELD, CIVIL RIGHTS PROJECT HARVARD UNIV., SCHOOLS MORE SEPARATE: CONSEQUENCES OF A DECADE OF RESEGREGATION (2001); GARY ORFIELD & JOHN T. YUN, CIVIL RIGHTS PROJECT HARVARD UNIV., RESEGREGATION IN AMERICAN SCHOOLS (1999).

65. *See generally* MINDY THOMPSON FULLILOVE, ROOT SHOCK: HOW TEARING UP CITY NEIGH-BORHOODS HURTS AMERICA, AND WHAT WE CAN DO ABOUT IT 11 (2005).

practice of redlining began in the 1930s.[66] The federal housing administration and bank board drew lines in 239 cities to determine which neighborhoods were deemed "risky" for mortgage support.[67] These neighborhoods were primarily low-income, African American, and economically depressed.[68] As a result of these redlining reports, banks would refuse to issue mortgages to families seeking to buy homes in these areas, essentially exposing any resident in the neighborhood to rent abuse through landlords who would buy property without a mortgage and charge exorbitant rates. Redlining is plainly unlawful,[69] yet the expansive impacts of redlining remain.

Redlining resulted in artificially suppressed land values in cities throughout the United States. Gentrification, however, may be seen as a correction to this process. Through gentrification the market is able to set accurate values for housing, commercial, and industrial land. State and local governments generally support gentrification for its broad policy benefits. Local governments will incentivize investment in areas targeted for development.[70] Cities will have adverse zoning plans in gentrified areas and give tax breaks to landlords and building management companies to engage in gentrification efforts. In the belief that doing so helps increase attractiveness to outside investors.[71] Accordingly, gentrification may be seen by some as a positive development.

Kelo v. City of New London

545 U.S. 469 (2005)

In 2000, the city of New London approved a development plan that, in the words of the Supreme Court of Connecticut, was "projected to create in excess of 1,000 jobs, to increase tax and other revenues, and to revitalize an economically distressed city, including its downtown and waterfront areas." 268 Conn. 1, 5, 843 A.2d 500, 507 (2004). In assembling the land needed for this project, the city's development agent has purchased property from willing sellers and proposes to use the power of eminent domain to acquire the remainder of the property from unwilling owners in exchange for just compensation. The question presented is whether the city's proposed disposition of this property qualifies as a "public use" within the meaning of the Takings Clause of the Fifth Amendment to the Constitution.

---

66. Amy Hillier, *Redlining and the Homeowners' Loan Corporation*, 29 Urban, Community, and Regional Planning Commons 4, 394 (2003).

67. *Id.*

68. *Id.*

69. Federal Reserve, *Federal Fair Lending Regulations and Statutes* (2006) https://www.federalreserve.gov/boarddocs/supmanual/cch/fair_lend_fhact.pdf. *See also* Nationwide Mut. Ins. v. Cisneros, 52 F.3d 1351, 1358 (6th Cir. 1995); NAACP v. Am. Family Mut. Ins., 978 F.2d 287, 290 (7th Cir. 1992).

70. *See* Peter Marcuse, *Gentrification, Abandonment, and Displacement: Connections, Causes, and Policy Responses in New York City*, 28 Wash. U. J. Urb. & Contemp. L. 195, 228 (1985).

71. Different studies contest the actual declination in crime rates and drug usage as a result of gentrification.

I

The city of New London (hereinafter City) sits at the junction of the Thames River and the Long Island Sound in southeastern Connecticut. Decades of economic decline led a state agency in 1990 to designate the City a "distressed municipality." In 1996, the Federal Government closed the Naval Undersea Warfare Center, which had been located in the Fort Trumbull area of the City and had employed over 1,500 people. In 1998, the City's unemployment rate was nearly double that of the State, and its population of just under 24,000 residents was at its lowest since 1920.

These conditions prompted state and local officials to target New London, and particularly its Fort Trumbull area, for economic revitalization. To this end, respondent New London Development Corporation (NLDC), a private nonprofit entity established some years earlier to assist the City in planning economic development, was reactivated. In January 1998, the State authorized a $5.35 million bond issue to support the NLDC's planning activities and a $10 million bond issue toward the creation of a Fort Trumbull State Park. In February, the pharmaceutical company Pfizer Inc. announced that it would build a $300 million research facility on a site immediately adjacent to Fort Trumbull; local planners hoped that Pfizer would draw new business to the area, thereby serving as a catalyst to the area's rejuvenation. After receiving initial approval from the city council, the NLDC continued its planning activities and held a series of neighborhood meetings to educate the public about the process. In May, the city council authorized the NLDC to formally submit its plans to the relevant state agencies for review. Upon obtaining state-level approval, the NLDC finalized an integrated development plan focused on 90 acres of the Fort Trumbull area.

The Fort Trumbull area is situated on a peninsula that juts into the Thames River. The area comprises approximately 115 privately owned properties, as well as the 32 acres of land formerly occupied by the naval facility (Trumbull State Park now occupies 18 of those 32 acres). The development plan encompasses seven parcels. Parcel 1 is designated for a waterfront conference hotel at the center of a "small urban village" that will include restaurants and shopping. This parcel will also have marinas for both recreational and commercial uses. A pedestrian "riverwalk" will originate here and continue down the coast, connecting the waterfront areas of the development. Parcel 2 will be the site of approximately 80 new residences organized into an urban neighborhood and linked by public walkway to the remainder of the development, including the state park. This parcel also includes space reserved for a new U.S. Coast Guard Museum. Parcel 3, which is located immediately north of the Pfizer facility, will contain at least 90,000 square feet of research and development office space. Parcel 4A is a 2.4-acre site that will be used either to support the adjacent state park, by providing parking or retail services for visitors, or to support the nearby marina. Parcel 4B will include a renovated marina, as well as the final stretch of the riverwalk. Parcels 5, 6, and 7 will provide land for office and retail space, parking, and water-dependent commercial uses. App. 109–113.

The NLDC intended the development plan to capitalize on the arrival of the Pfizer facility and the new commerce it was expected to attract. In addition to creating jobs, generating tax revenue, and helping to "build momentum for the revitalization of downtown New London," *id.*, at 92, the plan was also designed to make the City more attractive and to create leisure and recreational opportunities on the waterfront and in the park.

The city council approved the plan in January 2000, and designated the NLDC as its development agent in charge of implementation. The city council also authorized the NLDC to purchase property or to acquire property by exercising eminent domain in the City's name. § 8-193. The NLDC successfully negotiated the purchase of most of the real estate in the 90-acre area, but its negotiations with petitioners failed. As a consequence, in November 2000, the NLDC initiated the condemnation proceedings that gave rise to this case.

II

Petitioner Susette Kelo has lived in the Fort Trumbull area since 1997. She has made extensive improvements to her house, which she prizes for its water view. Petitioner Wilhelmina Dery was born in her Fort Trumbull house in 1918 and has lived there her entire life. Her husband Charles (also a petitioner) has lived in the house since they married some 60 years ago. In all, the nine petitioners own 15 properties in Fort Trumbull—4 in parcel 3 of the development plan and 11 in parcel 4A. Ten of the parcels are occupied by the owner or a family member; the other five are held as investment properties. There is no allegation that any of these properties is blighted or otherwise in poor condition; rather, they were condemned only because they happen to be located in the development area.

In December 2000, petitioners brought this action in the New London Superior Court. They claimed, among other things, that the taking of their properties would violate the "public use" restriction in the Fifth Amendment. After a 7-day bench trial, the Superior Court granted a permanent restraining order prohibiting the taking of the properties located in parcel 4A (park or marina support). It, however, denied petitioners relief as to the properties located in parcel 3 (office space).

After the Superior Court ruled, both sides took appeals to the Supreme Court of Connecticut. That court held, over a dissent, that all of the City's proposed takings were valid. It began by upholding the lower court's determination that the takings were authorized by chapter 132, the State's municipal development statute. That statute expresses a legislative determination that the taking of land, even developed land, as part of an economic development project is a "public use" and in the "public interest." 268 Conn., at 18–28, 843 A.2d, at 515–521. Next, the court held that such economic development qualified as a valid public use under both the Federal and State Constitutions. 268 Conn., at 40, 843 A.2d, at 527.

Finally, adhering to its precedents, the court went on to determine, first, whether the takings of the particular properties at issue were "reasonably necessary" to achieving the City's intended public use, and, second, whether the takings were for "reasonably foreseeable needs". The court upheld the trial court's factual findings as to parcel 3, but reversed the trial court as to parcel 4A, agreeing with the City that the intended use of this land was sufficiently definite and had been given "reasonable attention" during the planning process.

The three dissenting justices would have imposed a "heightened" standard of judicial review for takings justified by economic development. Although they agreed that the plan was intended to serve a valid public use, they would have found all the takings unconstitutional because the City had failed to adduce "clear and convincing evidence" that the economic benefits of the plan would in fact come to pass

We granted certiorari to determine whether a city's decision to take property for the purpose of economic development satisfies the "public use" requirement of the Fifth Amendment.

III

Two polar propositions are perfectly clear. On the one hand, it has long been accepted that the sovereign may not take the property of A for the sole purpose of transferring it to another private party B, even though A is paid just compensation. On the other hand, it is equally clear that a State may transfer property from one private party to another if future "use by the public" is the purpose of the taking; the condemnation of land for a railroad with common-carrier duties is a familiar example. Neither of these propositions, however, determines the disposition of this case.

As for the first proposition, the City would no doubt be forbidden from taking petitioners' land for the purpose of conferring a private benefit on a particular private party. Nor would the City be allowed to take property under the mere pretext of a public purpose, when its actual purpose was to bestow a private benefit. The takings before us, however, would be executed pursuant to a "carefully considered" development plan. The trial judge and all the members of the Supreme Court of Connecticut agreed that there was no evidence of an illegitimate purpose in this case. Therefore, as was true of the statute challenged in *Midkiff*, 467 U.S., at 245, 104 S.Ct. 2321, the City's development plan was not adopted "to benefit a particular class of identifiable individuals."

On the other hand, this is not a case in which the City is planning to open the condemned land—at least not in its entirety—to use by the general public. Nor will the private lessees of the land in any sense be required to operate like common carriers, making their services available to all comers. But although such a projected use would be sufficient to satisfy the public use requirement, this "Court long ago rejected any literal requirement that condemned property be put into use for the general public." Indeed, while many state courts in the mid-19th century endorsed "use by the public" as the proper definition of public use, that narrow view steadily eroded over time. Not only was the "use by the public" test difficult to administer (*e.g.*, what proportion of the public need have access to the property? at what price?), but it proved to be impractical given the diverse and always evolving needs of society. Accordingly, when this Court began applying the Fifth Amendment to the States at the close of the 19th century, it embraced the broader and more natural interpretation of public use as "public purpose." Thus, in a case upholding a mining company's use of an aerial bucket line to transport ore over property it did not own, Justice Holmes' opinion for the Court stressed "the inadequacy of use by the general public as a universal test." We have repeatedly and consistently rejected that narrow test ever since.

The disposition of this case therefore turns on the question whether the City's development plan serves a "public purpose." Without exception, our cases have defined that concept broadly, reflecting our longstanding policy of deference to legislative judgments in this field.

In *Berman v. Parker*, 348 U.S. 26, 75 S.Ct. 98, 99 L.Ed. 27 (1954), this Court upheld a redevelopment plan targeting a blighted area of Washington, D. C., in which most of the housing for the area's 5,000 inhabitants was beyond repair. Under the plan, the area would be condemned and part of it utilized for the construction of streets, schools, and other public facilities. The remainder of the land would be leased or sold to private parties for the purpose of redevelopment, including the construction of low-cost housing.

The owner of a department store located in the area challenged the condemnation, pointing out that his store was not itself blighted and arguing that the creation of a "better balanced, more attractive community" was not a valid public use. Writing for a unanimous Court, Justice Douglas refused to evaluate this claim in isolation, deferring instead to the legislative and agency judgment that the area "must be planned as a whole" for the plan to be successful. The Court explained that "community redevelopment programs need not, by force of the Constitution, be on a piecemeal basis—lot by lot, building by building." The public use underlying the taking was unequivocally affirmed:

> "We do not sit to determine whether a particular housing project is or is not desirable. The concept of the public welfare is broad and inclusive.... The values it represents are spiritual as well as physical, aesthetic as well as monetary. It is within the power of the legislature to determine that the community should be beautiful as well as healthy, spacious as well as clean, well-balanced as well as carefully patrolled. In the present case, the Congress and its authorized agencies have made determinations that take into account a wide variety of values. It is not for us to reappraise them. If those who govern the District of Columbia decide that the Nation's Capital should be beautiful as well as sanitary, there is nothing in the Fifth Amendment that stands in the way." *Id.,* at 33, 75 S.Ct. 98.

* * *

Viewed as a whole, our jurisprudence has recognized that the needs of society have varied between different parts of the Nation, just as they have evolved over time in response to changed circumstances. Our earliest cases in particular embodied a strong theme of federalism, emphasizing the "great respect" that we owe to state legislatures and state courts in discerning local public needs. For more than a century, our public use jurisprudence has wisely eschewed rigid formulas and intrusive scrutiny in favor of affording legislatures broad latitude in determining what public needs justify the use of the takings power.

IV

Those who govern the City were not confronted with the need to remove blight in the Fort Trumbull area, but their determination that the area was sufficiently distressed to justify a program of economic rejuvenation is entitled to our deference. The City has carefully formulated an economic development plan that it believes will provide appreciable benefits to the community, including—but by no means limited to—new jobs and increased tax revenue. As with other exercises in urban planning and development,12 the City is endeavoring to coordinate a variety of commercial, residential, and recreational uses of land, with the hope that they will form a whole greater than the sum of its parts. To effectuate this plan, the City has invoked a state statute that specifically authorizes the use of eminent domain to promote economic development. Given the comprehensive character of the plan, the thorough deliberation that preceded its adoption, and the limited scope of our review, it is appropriate for us, as it was in *Berman*, to resolve the challenges of the individual owners, not on a piecemeal basis, but rather in light of the entire plan. Because that plan unquestionably serves a public purpose, the takings challenged here satisfy the public use requirement of the Fifth Amendment.

To avoid this result, petitioners urge us to adopt a new bright-line rule that economic development does not qualify as a public use. Putting aside the unpersuasive suggestion that the City's plan will provide only purely economic benefits, neither precedent nor logic supports petitioners' proposal. Promoting economic development is a traditional and long-accepted function of government. There is, moreover, no principled way of distinguishing economic development from the other public purposes that we have recognized. In our cases upholding takings that facilitated agriculture and mining, for example, we emphasized the importance of those industries to the welfare of the States in question, *see, e.g., Strickley*, 200 U.S. 527, 26 S.Ct. 301; in *Berman*, we endorsed the purpose of transforming a blighted area into a "well-balanced" community through redevelopment, 348 U.S., at 33, 75 S.Ct. 98; in *Midkiff*, we upheld the interest in breaking up a land oligopoly that "created artificial deterrents to the normal functioning of the State's residential land market,"; and in *Monsanto*, we accepted Congress' purpose of eliminating a "significant barrier to entry in the pesticide market." It would be incongruous to hold that the City's interest in the economic benefits to be derived from the development of the Fort Trumbull area has less of a public character than any of those other interests. Clearly, there is no basis for exempting economic development from our traditionally broad understanding of public purpose.

Petitioners contend that using eminent domain for economic development impermissibly blurs the boundary between public and private takings. Again, our cases foreclose this objection. Quite simply, the government's pursuit of a public purpose will often benefit individual private parties. For example, in *Midkiff*, the forced transfer of property conferred a direct and significant benefit on those lessees who were previously unable to purchase their homes. In *Monsanto,* we recognized that the "most direct beneficiaries" of the data-sharing provisions were the subsequent pesticide applicants, but benefiting them in this way was necessary to promoting competition in the pesticide market. The owner of the department store in *Berman* objected to "taking from one businessman for the benefit of another businessman," 348 U.S., at 33, 75 S.Ct. 98, referring to the fact that under the redevelopment plan land would be leased or sold to private developers for redevelopment. Our rejection of that contention has particular relevance to the instant case: "The public end may be as well or better served through an agency of private enterprise than through a department of government—or so the Congress might conclude. We cannot say that public ownership is the sole method of promoting the public purposes of community redevelopment projects."

It is further argued that without a bright-line rule nothing would stop a city from transferring citizen *A*'s property to citizen *B* for the sole reason that citizen *B* will put the property to a more productive use and thus pay more taxes. Such a one-to-one transfer of property, executed outside the confines of an integrated development plan, is not presented in this case. While such an unusual exercise of government power would certainly raise a suspicion that a private purpose was afoot, the hypothetical cases posited by petitioners can be confronted if and when they arise. They do not warrant the crafting of an artificial restriction on the concept of public use.

Alternatively, petitioners maintain that for takings of this kind we should require a "reasonable certainty" that the expected public benefits will actually accrue. Such a rule, however, would represent an even greater departure from our precedent. "When the legislature's purpose is legitimate and its means are not irrational, our cases make clear that empirical debates over the wisdom of takings—no less than debates over the wisdom of other kinds of socioeconomic legislation—are not to be carried out in the federal courts." Indeed, earlier this Term we explained why similar practical concerns (among others) undermined the use of the "substantially advances" formula in our regulatory takings doctrine. The disadvantages of a heightened form of review are especially pronounced in this type of case. Orderly implementation of a comprehensive redevelopment plan obviously requires that the legal rights of all interested parties be established before new construction can be commenced. A constitutional rule that required postponement of the judicial approval of every condemnation until the likelihood of success of the plan had been assured would unquestionably impose a significant impediment to the successful consummation of many such plans.

Just as we decline to second-guess the City's considered judgments about the efficacy of its development plan, we also decline to second-guess the City's determinations as to what lands it needs to acquire in order to effectuate the project. "It is not for the courts to oversee the choice of the boundary line nor to sit in review on the size of a particular project area. Once the question of the public purpose has been decided, the amount and character of land to be taken for the project and the need for a particular tract to complete the integrated plan rests in the discretion of the legislative branch." *Berman,* 348 U.S., at 35–36, 75 S.Ct. 98.

In affirming the City's authority to take petitioners' properties, we do not minimize the hardship that condemnations may entail, notwithstanding the payment of just compensation. We emphasize that nothing in our opinion precludes any State from placing further restrictions on its exercise of the takings power. Indeed, many States already impose "public use" requirements that are stricter than the federal baseline. Some of these requirements have been established as a matter of state constitutional law, while others are expressed in state eminent domain statutes that carefully limit the grounds upon which takings may be exercised. As the submissions of the parties and their *amici* make clear, the necessity and wisdom of using eminent domain to promote economic development are certainly matters of legitimate public debate. This Court's authority, however, extends only to determining whether the City's proposed condemnations are for a "public use" within the meaning of the Fifth Amendment to the Federal Constitution. Because over a century of our case law interpreting that provision dictates an affirmative answer to that question, we may not grant petitioners the relief that they seek.

The judgment of the Supreme Court of Connecticut is affirmed.

Kelo was a very controversial decision. Most of the controversy focused on the process sanctioned by the Court that allowed the State of Connecticut to take private property and forcibly transfer that property to another private party under claims of public benefit. The dynamic is clear. The powerful may take the property of the less powerful and use the machinery of the courts and government to accomplish this goal. A sense of class may underlie *Kelo* that supports the Court's decision.

A recurring theme in the Court's discussion and decision of *Kelo* was the idea of "blighted" property. Also known as "urban decay," "blight" is a multifaceted and complex term that refers generally to a decrepit or deteriorated community.[72] Specific showings of blight in a community include substandard housing, abandoned buildings, and vacant lots.[73] Blighted communities are often the result of years of neglect, lack of economic support, community discord, crime, or unemployment, and its effects are far-reaching and complicated.[74]

Blight is a serious problem not only because of the eyesore inherent to a blighted community, but also because it is a reflection of much more deep-seated issues within the community. A 2017 joint research report between Columbia University and the Urban Institute explores the direct connection between the quality of our homes and communities and our health. For example, mold, rodent infestations, poor air quality, and other deficiencies are the culprits behind many health issues including asthma,

---

72. Patricia Hureston Lee, *Shattering "Blight" and the Hidden Narratives that Condemn,* 42 Seton Hall Legis. J. 29 (2017).

73. *Id.*

74. *Id.*

respiratory illnesses, learning and behavioral problems, and more.[75] It is a logical step, then, to associate blighted communities with greater instances of these health issues.

The *Kelo* Court's discussion of blight in the context of the Takings Clause has invited a multitude of commentary. A recent article published in the *Seton Hall Law Legislative Journal*, for example, calls blight takings such as that allowed in *Kelo* a "systemic failure."[76] The article's use of poetic quotes and literary comparisons to Don Quixote's battles illustrate the "predicament of property owners" in blighted communities. These property owners become susceptible to governmental takings and a number of resulting horrors, including displacement and a lack of just compensation. The cause, it explains, is from a culmination of economic disasters, including the 2007 mortgage crisis, outsourcing of jobs, and predatory lending.

There is little argument that blight is not a problem—however, the question remains the best way to combat it. Governmental takings of blighted property began as a method for controlling urban development. Specifically, urban planners and civic leaders—having health, safety, and welfare concerns in these communities—set out to eradicate blight by simply removing and redeveloping them.[77] Today, the government, through cases such as *Kelo*, takes the position that blighted properties should be taken out of the legal possession and control of their inhabitants and redistributed or redesigned in the name of "community development." Unfortunately, however, these decisions are made without the interest of the property owners in mind, and the property owners are thus faced with an impossible decision: voluntarily surrender their homes or properties to the government for little (and often unfair) compensation, or be subjected to lengthy and costly eminent domain actions only to be left with the same ultimate outcome—no property and no resources.[78] The problem with this approach, of course, is that without proper compensation, the displaced owners of blighted properties are in no better a position to support themselves or their communities than prior to the governmental taking. Therein lies the vicious cycle associated with taking property from "the most vulnerable communities."[79] Thus, while they may be used as a bandage, governmental takings do not appear to be solutions to the underlying problems contributing to blight in the first place.

In response, the article calls for directly addressing the framework for condemnation decisions and proceedings used in blighted communities. This can be done through legislative reforms, finding and encouraging alternatives to implementing the public takings doctrine, or making definitional changes to what constitutes

75. Erwin de Leon & Joseph Schilling, Urban Institute, Urban Blight and Public Health: Addressing the Impact of Substandard Housing, Abandoned Buildings, and Vacant Lots (Apr. 2017), https://www.urban.org/sites/default/files/publication/89491/2017.04.03_urban_blight_and_public_health_vprn_report_finalized.pdf.

76. *Id.*

77. *Id.*

78. *Id.*

79. *Id.*

"blight," "public use," et cetera. For example, pursuant to *Kelo*, a city government can take private property and redevelop it for any "public use," broadly construed. Instead, any one of several modifications to this broad doctrine would reduce the amount of properties vulnerable under the *Kelo* decision. These modifications range from a complete discontinuation of private property takings for public use—which is not an approach taken by any jurisdiction or court—to simply tightening the definition of "public use."[80]

Another possibility this article explores is for the government to exercise better timing in responding to distressed communities. Instead of being reactionary, as condemning property and exercising blight takings is, the government should practice "in-time" responses. Adopting more policies consistent with appropriately timed intervention instead of reactionary redevelopment will go a long way toward shattering blight.

A final note here on *Kelo*: interestingly, the former site of Susette Kelo's home remained vacant for years following the Supreme Court's decision. In 2015, the major of New London, Connecticut, authorized a plan to construct a memorial park honoring "all those adversely effected by the city's use of eminent domain."[81] May this decision serve as an example to other governments as they consider the most fair and effective method for combating blight.

3. Gentrification Winners and Losers

Kelo raises another important question: who are these policies actually intended to protect, and what are the most efficient ways to do that? As illustrated in *Kelo*, to simply declare a property as "blighted" does nothing to improve the quality of the property or the property owners' access to necessary resources. The city of New London claimed to be acting in the interest of public benefit, but at what cost to the individual property owners and to the lower-class citizens of the community?

A similar question is raised with respect to gentrification. The mention of "gentrification" evokes a range of sentiments. Definitionally, gentrification refers to "the buying and renovation of houses and stores in deteriorated urban neighborhoods by upper- or middle-income families or individuals, raising property values but often displacing low-income families and small businesses."[82]

---

80. *Id.*

81. Ilya Somin, *New London May Build a "Memorial Park" Honoring Victims of Eminent Domain on the Former Site of the Kelo House*, WASH. POST (Apr. 1, 2015), https://www.washingtonpost.com/news/volokh-conspiracy/wp/2015/04/01/new-london-may-build-a-memorial-park-on-former-site-of-the-kelo-house/?utm_term=.6b667bb43337 (last visited May 4, 2018).

82. *Gentrification*, Dictionary.com, http://dictionary.reference.com/browse/gentrification (last visited May 4, 2018).

Who is gentrification *actually* intended to benefit? Gentrification is advocated for from a policy standpoint as being the means to achieving "more socially mixed, less segregated, more livable communities."[83] In its execution, however, does gentrification improve the lives of the people living in the areas targeted for gentrification? Or does most of the benefit go to the middle-class population who then move into these previously uninhabitable areas?

D. The Role of Community Benefit Agreements

Community and economic development efforts, if effective, lead to increased property values or other benefits flowing to private parties. Oftentimes, these parties are not members of the community that is targeted for development. How do residents of low-wealth communities and the poor ensure that economic development projects benefit them? Eradicating blight through governmental takings and funding gentrification may improve the physical structure of urban and impoverished communities, but these efforts seemingly fall short of effecting change and improvement to the lives of the people who dwell in those communities. What, then, can be done to both improve the physical manifestation of poverty as well as provide for the people it affects?

One approach is for these residents to advocate for the use of Community Benefit Agreements ("CBAs") in conjunction with community development efforts. In a 2007 article for the American Bar Association's *Journal of Affordable Housing*, Julian Gross describes "Community Benefit Agreement" as an elusive and inconsistently used term. Noting the need for a cohesive term in order to effectively apply its associated principles and benefits, however, he proposes the following definition:

> A CBA is a legally binding contract (or set of related contracts), setting forth a range of community benefits regarding a development project, and resulting from substantial community involvement.[84]

Gross also adds three elements to this definition: inclusiveness, democracy, and accountability. Only the agreements that satisfy the above definition can successfully promote these core values. Put more simply, a CBA is a contract that may be contemplated before a community undertakes a significant development project. When the success of the project or development depends on widespread community support, the developers may enter into a contract with the nearby community to guarantee

---

83. Loretta Lees, *Gentrification and Social Mixing: Towards an Inclusive Urban Renaissance?*, 45 URBAN STUDIES 2449–2470 (Nov. 2008), http://journals.sagepub.com/doi/pdf/10.1177/004209800 8097099 (last visited May 4, 2018).

84. Julian Gross, *Community Benefits Agreements: Definitions, Values, and Legal Enforceability*, 17 J. AFFORDABLE HOUSING 1–2 (2007).

certain opportunities or engagements for the community members contingent upon the needs and concerns of the community. It is, in essence, a *quid pro quo* resulting in fewer societal roadblocks to the project for the developer and guaranteed opportunities and benefits for community members. One noteworthy example of the CBA approach includes the Los Angeles Staples Center, where the LA Lakers play, which was built in 2001. Under the Staples Center CBA, the City of Los Angeles and the LA Lakers agreed to provide first-hire opportunities to residents of the adjoining community, along with preferential contract sourcing during the construction phase. In exchange, the residents agreed not to oppose the development.[85]

1. Community Reinvestment Act

The execution of Community Building Agreements is one method for increasing opportunity, participation, and representation for impoverished communities. This approach, however, depends on the undertaking and execution of development efforts within the community. For a more individual, human-focused (rather than business or building-focused) approach, the Community Reinvestment Act proves immensely useful. The Community Reinvestment Act was a product of the Housing and Community Development Act of 1977.[86] The Community Reinvestment Act ("CRA") addresses the needs of low- and moderate-income financial borrowers and is specifically targeted toward banks, savings associations, and credit unions.[87] It is an integral part of the larger discussion of access to capital.

The passage of the CRA was a direct response to concerns about the urban decay occurring in lower-income and minority neighborhoods.[88] Prior to the inception of the CRA, credit opportunities in low- and moderate-income neighborhoods were substantially limited. Few banks were willing to lend to low- and moderate-income earners due to a culmination of social, economic, and regulatory factors.[89] From a social perspective, racial discrimination was a deeply rooted barrier to access to various financial resources. A practice known as "redlining" (see above) emerged around 1935 and remained a barrier to low-income borrowers. "Redlining" refers to routine

---

85. Patricia E. Salkin & Amy Lavine, *Understanding Community Benefit Agreements: Equitable Development, Social Justice and Other Considerations for Developers, Municipalities and Community Organizations*, 26 UCLA J. ENVTL L. & POL'Y 291 (2008).

86. Eugene A. Ludwig et al., *The Community Reinvestment Act: Past Successes and Future Opportunities*, REVISITING THE CRA: PERSPECTIVES ON THE FUTURE OF THE COMMUNITY REINVESTMENT ACT, https://www.frbsf.org/community-development/files/cra_past_successes_future_opportunities1.pdf (last visited May 4, 2018).

87. *Id.*

88. BEN S. BERNANKE, BOARD OF GOVERNORS OF THE FEDERAL RESERVE SYSTEM, THE COMMUNITY REINVESTMENT ACT: ITS EVOLUTION AND NEW CHALLENGES (Mar. 30, 2007), https://www.federalreserve.gov/newsevents/speech/Bernanke20070330a.htm (last visited May 4, 2018).

89. Ludwig, *supra* note 86.

denial of credit to low-income borrowers solely because of their socioeconomic status.[90] The practice seemingly began in 1935 when the Home Owners' Loan Corporation created color-coded "residential security maps" in 239 cities to indicate the risk levels associated with long-term real estate investment within certain areas in those cities.[91] These maps were rediscovered in the late 1970s and classified as a medium for redlining.[92]

Credit opportunities were also limited in lower-income areas for economic reasons. Lower-income neighborhoods, for example, are apt to have fewer home sales, and the homes within these areas are likely to suffer from conditions making accurate appraisals difficult.[93] Low-income borrowers are also more likely to have poor credit histories.[94] Finally, banking regulations prior to enactment of the CRA also limited credit access. Bank branching and acquisition was heavily restricted, thereby reducing the ability of lenders to diversify geographic risk.[95] Additionally, interest rates were prohibitive to many borrowers.[96] These social, economic, and regulatory factors together justified discriminatory lending practices and highlighted the need for a protective act such as the CRA.

At its outset, the CRA "set minimal compliance requirements for depository institutions."[97] The CRA has since seen three substantial amendments—one in 1989, another in 1995, and most recently in 2005. In 1989, Congress adopted the Financial Institution Recovery and Reform Act of 1989 ("FIRREA") as an amendment to the original CRA. The FIRREA implemented an additional obligation on institutions to disclose their ratings and performance evaluations based on a four-tiered system: banks' compliance with the CRA was rated as either Outstanding, Satisfactory, Needs to Improve, or Substantial Noncompliance.[98] Additionally, the 1989 revisions expanded data collection and reporting procedures.[99] This was a defining addition to the CRA insofar as a greater access to information led to more sophisticated data analyses on the attempts and successes of banks in meeting the credit needs of their communities.[100]

The CRA underwent massive regulatory reforms again in 1995 in an attempt to "emphasize performance rather than process, to promote consistency in evaluations,

---

90. Amy E. Hillier, *Residential Security Maps and Neighborhood Appraisals: The Home Owners Loan Corporation and the Case of Philadelphia*, 29 Soc. Sci. Hist. 207–233 (2005), http://www.jstor.org.go.libproxy.wakehealth.edu/stable/pdf/40267873.pdf?refreqid=excelsior:8059330c8d0a27aff666fc62f123976e.

91. *Id.*

92. *Id.*

93. Bernanke, *supra* note 88.

94. *Id.*

95. *Id.*

96. *Id.*

97. Bernanke, *supra* note 88.

98. Darryl E. Getter, *The Effectiveness of the Community Reinvestment Act*, Cong. Res. Serv. (Jan. 7, 2015), https://www.newyorkfed.org/medialibrary/media/outreach-and-education/cra/reports/CRS-The-Effectiveness-of-the-Community-Reinvestment-Act.pdf.

99. Bernanke, *supra* note 88.

100. *Id.*

and to eliminate unnecessary burden."[101] Specifically, the amendment addressed pervasive concerns that the methods used to assess CRA compliance were subjective, inconsistent, and favored the institutions' plans for low- and moderate-income lending rather than their actual performance in these areas.[102] In response to these concerns, President Bill Clinton motivated a shift in the regulatory scheme of the CRA to become more objective and representative. Following the 1995 regulatory reforms, paperwork burdens declined, the number of CRA-compliant bank loan commitments increased, and CRA performance evaluation methods became "tougher" and more objective.[103] Additionally, it expanded CRA examination to account for different bank sizes and models.

The CRA was reformed in 2005 to address various definitional concerns; specifically, it expanded the definition of "community development" and revised bank size definitions as well as indexing them to the Consumer Price Index.[104] In its current incarnation, the CRA provides that any banking institution is subject to evaluation by its "appropriate Federal financial supervisory agency" in determining "the institution's record of meeting the credit needs of its entire community, including low-income and moderate-income neighborhoods, consistent with the safe and sound operation of such institution."[105] The supervisory agencies are then required by the Act to "take such record into account" in their evaluations of any facility applications by the institution.[106]

Studies overwhelmingly show that the CRA has been successful in increasing access to credit in low- and moderate-income neighborhoods and eliminating the discriminatory act of redlining.[107] CRA credits are applied for investment in special-purpose community development entities, providing support to minority-owned financial institutions, providing low-cost educational loans to low-income borrowers, among other massive benefits.[108] In this regard, the CRA effectively combats poverty from the bottom up, rather than the top down.

E. Community Economic Development

Community Economic Development refers to a method of economic development that is a blend among the private sector, public agencies, and the nonprofit sector. CED is seen by some as a powerful response to the limitations of litigation strategies

---

101. 60 F.R. 22156.
102. Ludwig, *supra* note 86.
103. *Id.*
104. Getter, *supra* note 98.
105. 12 U.S.C.S. § 2903.
106. *Id.*
107. Ludwig, *supra* note 86.
108. Getter, *supra* note 98.

as well as the need for community voice and equity in development initiatives. Efforts that are described as part of the CED movement reflect a few common themes:

1. Market based—meaning that the employed strategies focus on creating economic exchanges between people.

2. Led by private, nonprofit organizations—usually, development efforts in this space are organized by nonprofit community development corporations.

3. Accountable to the community they serve—the leadership is accountable to the community either directly or through the nonprofit organizations whose members are drawn from the community.

4. Integrate professional skills and advice—CED efforts tend to involve complex housing or business development transactions that draw on legal, accounting, and business consulting services.

CED strategies are pursued in urban and rural communities across the United States, with much of this work driven by law school clinics focused on small business development and nonprofit organizations.

CED relies heavily on local, regional, and national support systems. These supports include organizations that provide technical assistance, government agencies, private funders, and grassroots organizations. The relationship between CED strategies and these organizations is reminiscent of relationships within both Redevelopment and Community Action policies.[109] Redevelopment involved significant investments by the federal and state governments, along with intentional efforts to build local businesses driven by external agencies. Redevelopment operated as a joint state-federal partnership where the federal government provided grant and loan funds to states that developed and implemented redevelopment plans under the National Housing Act of 1949. Redevelopment efforts were often used to restructure cities through displacing minority communities while erecting permanent barriers, often arterial highways, between ethnic groups. Thus, Redevelopment effectively reinforced poverty and marginalization in many cities across the United States. While there may be similar dynamics across CED and Redevelopment, any similarities are superficial. Redevelopment policies failed to reflect local concerns or values, and oftentimes Redevelopment plans implemented goals that were directly opposed to or contrary to the interests of the affected community. In contract, Community Action, with its emphasis on maximum feasible participation among the communities to be served by government initiatives, provides a better analogy for CED's approach and goals.

---

109. *See* William H. Simon, *The Community Economic Development Movement*, 2002 Wis. L. Rev. 377 (available at: https://scholarship.law.columbia.edu/faculty_scholarship/872), discussing the historical context of the CED movement within earlier Redevelopment and Community Action programs during from the early 1950s to the mid-1960s.

Community Action was a centerpiece of the Economic Opportunity Act of 1964, which included many War on Poverty initiatives. The Community Action Program served to deliver a range of services to poor communities through decentralized, non-profit organizations. Services included job training, housing repair, education, community organizing, and community economic development. Governmental and private nonprofit organizations could apply to the Department of Health and Human Services to be certified as a "community action program," and thereby become eligible to receive funding from the federal government once certified. All community action programs were obligated to assure "maximum feasible participation" from communities to be served. The result was locally operated, federally funded agencies that were engaged in community and economic development while remaining accountable to the communities being served. Decision making and policy directives were decentralized in the Community Action Program model, and ultimately served to better voice the concerns of the communities that were being served. By the early 1970s, the Community Action Program had ended, a result of limited engagement from community members as well as political opposition occasioned by the lobbying and policy activism within some Community Action Programs. Nevertheless, two significant advances that resulted from these efforts remain. First, the Equal Opportunity Act first provided for targeted grants to Community Development Corporations. The CDC is now the most common form for CED efforts in cities and rural communities across the United States. Second, the idea of community participation in setting local development goals and plans was carried forward into the Community Development Block Grant program. The CDBG program integrates community input into grant and planning processes from a very early stage and requires local CDBG recipients to create and sustain community development boards as part of the CDBG development process.

F. Taxes, Capital, and Banking

1. Access to Banking

Even with the wide range of alternatives to traditional banks, consumers need a relationship with a bank. Having a bank account is required for nearly all aspects of daily life — paying bills, savings money, buying things on short-term credit, or buying a home. Despite the centrality of a banking relationship to daily life, many people lack access to a bank or financial services. Approximately eight percent of families in the United States lack access to a bank account.[110] Families whose income falls below the median income in the United States, $63,688 in 2019, are five times more likely not to have a bank account than the population overall.[111] Geography also plays a role as banks are less prevalent in rural communities, as well as non-rural communities

---

110. www.fdic.gov.
111. *Id.*

with higher-than-average poverty rates.[112] A larger percentage of Latino and African American families also lack access to banking or to the financial services they need.

Since 2009, the Federal Deposit Insurance Corporation has been required to conduct a national household survey on banking access. The results of this survey have been published biannually. Key findings of the 2017 FDIC Survey of Unbanked and Underbanked Households report are:

- In 2017, 6.5 percent of U.S. households were unbanked. Approximately 8.4 million U.S. households, made up of 14.1 million adults and 6.4 million children, were unbanked in 2017.

- 18.7 percent of U.S. households were underbanked in 2017, meaning that the household had an account at an insured institution, but also obtained financial products or services outside of the banking system. Approximately 24.2 million U.S. households, composed of 48.9 million adults and 15.4 million children, were underbanked in 2017.

- The unbanked rate in 2017 declined to the lowest level since the survey began in 2009. Since the survey was last administered in 2015, the unbanked rate has fallen by 0.5 percentage points.

  ○ The decline from 2015 to 2017 can be explained almost entirely by changes in household characteristics across survey years, particularly improvements in the socioeconomic circumstances of U.S. households.

- Use of mobile banking to access a bank account continued to increase sharply, while use of bank tellers declined somewhat.

  ○ The proportion of banked households that used mobile banking to access their accounts increased from 23.2 percent in 2013 to 31.9 percent in 2015 and 40.4 percent in 2017.

  ○ Use of bank tellers remained quite prevalent: 73.6 percent of banked households used bank tellers to access their accounts in 2017.

  ○ Use of bank tellers as the primary means of account access also remained prevalent among certain segments of the population, including lower-income households, less-educated households, older households, and households in rural areas.

- In 2017, 86.0 percent of banked households visited a bank branch in the past 12 months. 30.8 percent of banked households visited a branch one to four times, 18.2 percent visited five to nine times, and 35.4 percent visited 10 or more times.

  ○ Branch visits were prevalent even among banked households that used online or mobile banking as their primary method of account access. For example,

---

112. BOARD OF GOVERNORS OF THE FEDERAL RESERVE SYSTEM, PERSPECTIVES FROM MAIN STREET: BANK BRANCH ACCESS IN RURAL COMMUNITIES (November 2019), https://www.federalreserve.gov/publications/files/bank-branch-access-in-rural-communities.pdf.

81.0 percent of banked households that used mobile banking as their primary method visited a branch in the past 12 months, and 23.0 percent visited 10 or more times.

- The proportion of households that used prepaid cards decreased from 9.8 percent in 2015 to 9.2 percent in 2017, but it remained higher than in 2013 (7.9 percent). Consistent with previous survey results, use of prepaid cards was most prevalent among unbanked households.

- AFS use continued to be much higher among unbanked households than banked households.

  ○ The proportion of unbanked households that used AFS decreased substantially in recent years and is attributable to declines in the use of both transaction and credit AFS over this period.

  ○ Use of AFS among banked households also decreased in recent years and is attributable almost entirely to the decline in the use of transaction AFS over this period.

- In 2017, 57.8 percent of households saved for unexpected expenses or emergencies in the past 12 months, which increased from 56.3 percent in 2015. Consistent with previous survey results, unbanked households saved at a much lower rate than underbanked and fully banked households.

- Credit cards were the most common type of mainstream credit in 2017 (68.7 percent of households had a credit card from Visa, MasterCard, American Express, or Discover, and 41.6 percent had a store credit card), followed by mortgages, home equity loans, or home equity lines of credit (HELOCs); and auto loans.

  ○ In 2017, 19.7 percent of households had no mainstream credit in the past 12 months and likely did not have a credit score.

  ○ Lower-income households, less-educated households, black and Hispanic households, working-age disabled households, and foreign-born, noncitizen households were more likely to have had no mainstream credit. These differences persist even after accounting for other socioeconomic and demographic characteristics (such as income, education, and age) and bank account ownership.

- As in 2015, unbanked households in 2017 primarily went outside of the banking system to pay bills and receive income in a typical month. Underbanked households, on the other hand, used banks extensively to handle their financial transactions, but they also used other methods to pay bills.

  ○ Approximately two-thirds of unbanked households paid bills using cash in 2017, the most prevalent method. The most prevalent way unbanked households received income was paper check or money order, followed by cash and direct deposit onto a prepaid card.

  ○ About two-thirds of underbanked households paid bills using an electronic payment from a bank account. Approximately one in four underbanked households used cash to pay bills in a typical month, and a similar share used non-bank money orders. Direct deposit into a bank account was by far the most prevalent method of receiving income for underbanked households.[113]

Lack of access to simple banking services or means to save increases the costs of being poor. A worker without a checking account, for example, may be forced to use a pay check casher twice a month. Such services can cost three to five percent of the value of the check. If a family does not have a checking account, it is difficult to pay utility or other bills, leading them to buy money orders for several dollars each, compared to a few cents for a personal check. Such transaction costs associated with fringe banking services can add several percent to the costs of any purchase, depleting resources for the poor, and over a lifetime cost low-income families thousands of dollars.

Conclusion

There is no one reason for poverty to exist or for a family to be poor. Poverty is a multicausal reality, consequently a multifaceted approach offers better hopes for impact. Advocacy may include litigation as well as expanding access to banking or business development services. Such a rich environment can energize advocates who see the opportunity to apply themselves in creative ways, but it can be challenging to learn new areas of law and practice and move initiatives in innovative directions. Despite more than 50 years of legal advocacy, poverty remains prevalent in the United States. Perhaps the goal of advocacy in such an environment should not be the end of poverty, but instead to maintain a continued response.

---

113. FDIC, 2017 National Survey of Unbanked and Underbanked Households.

Index